A. Nasmyth pinx.t   J. Beugo sculp.t

ROBERT BURNS

ROBERT CRAWFORD

THE BARD

Robert Burns,
A Biography

Princeton University Press
Princeton and Oxford

Copyright © Robert Crawford 2009

Requests for permission to reproduce material from this work should
be sent to Permissions, Princeton University Press

Published in the United States and the Philippine Islands by
Princeton University Press, 41 William Street, Princeton, New Jersey 08540

Frontispiece courtesy of the University of St. Andrews Library

Library of Congress Control Number 2008937561
ISBN 978-0-691-14171-8

This book has been composed in Sabon

Printed on acid-free paper.

press.princeton.edu

Printed and bound in the United States of America

2 4 6 8 10 9 7 5 3 1

for Alice, Lewis, and Blyth
with love

and for Kenneth Dunn,
a staunch friend

Contents

Acknowledgements

When I was a little boy my Uncle John pointed out an old man walking with the aid of a stick beside the grass verge on the main road through the Stirlingshire village of Balfron in central Scotland, and explained to me that the hunched figure was a descendant of Robert Burns. That memory came back to me late in the making of this book, and I realise now that I have written *The Bard* partly to show how, even in the twenty-first century, a remarkable number of people may still feel an excited sense of close connection to a poet who was born in rural Ayrshire in 1759. Writing a biography of Burns incurs many substantial debts, not all of them easy to define. If I owe a loving indebtedness to members of my own family over the last fifty years, then I also owe enormous gratitude to generations of scholars, some of whom are named in my introduction, text and endnotes. Here, before making some remarks about further reading and web resources, I mention some special debts not elsewhere explicitly acknowledged.

Dr Alice Crawford and Mr David Hopes first alerted me to St Andrews University Library's Macdonald papers. Alice's role in this book, like that of our patient children, is further acknowledged in the dedication, but I should say here that her suggestions about digital searching and her other gifts made *The Bard* possible to write. David Hopes's astute helpfulness has continued in his current role as Project Curator for the National Trust for Scotland at the Robert Burns Birthplace and Museum, Alloway – guardian of the hoard.

At a critical moment Kenneth Dunn of the National Library of Scotland gave me a copy of James Kinsley's three-volume edition of Burns; he could have given me no more generous or practical a

piece of counsel. Skilled advice and support were supplied by my hard-hitting agent, David Godwin, and by my outstanding editor at Jonathan Cape, Robin Robertson: would that all editors were such remarkable poet-publishers. The typescript was shrewdly copy-edited by Beth Humphries.

I hope at some moments the fact I write poetry has helped this biography; sometimes it has certainly hindered it. Exigencies of time have only increased my debt to the National Burns Collection and its cataloguers; to many other providers of digital and paper resources; and specifically to Mr Peter Westwood whose *Definitive Illustrated Companion to Robert Burns* (2004) makes accessible many far-flung, treasured items from British and American Libraries, and is one of the greatest of Mr Westwood's many services to Burns and Burnsians. Though I cannot go so far as the outspoken yet shy poet Edwin Muir, who boasted he knew of 'Burns Nights only through hearsay ... for I have never attended one,' I confess to being wary of many self-professed Burnsians, if only because they tend to know far more than I do about obscure and not so obscure Burns lore.[1] However, I owe a great debt to the Burns Federation (now the Robert Burns World Federation Ltd) for making available through their annual *Burns Chronicle* and in other ways information about Burns and his circle, and for providing a worldwide physical and virtual forum for Burns enthusiasts. The Federation's and local Burns Clubs' work in education – not least at school level – is admirable. I am grateful also to Greenock Burns Club. Some of my distant relatives were Burnsians in Greenock and Paisley. I had heard about them through the late John Murray of Greenock, and when Greenock Burns Club invited me to speak to them about Robert Fergusson some years ago, I jumped at the chance. The substantially female committee showed me how even the oldest of Burns Clubs might be vital, alert and inclusive in the twenty-first century; if only Burns Clubs generally were in closer touch with contemporary poetry and poets. A kind invitation from Colin Macallister, George McIntosh, and the officers of the St Andrews Burns Club to deliver their Immortal Memory in 2006 came at just the right time and place.

Dr Brian Lang, then Principal of the University of St Andrews, allowed me to negotiate with him the research leave that let me

---

[1] Edwin Muir, '[Robert Burns:] The Poetry', *Scottish Field*, January 1959, 30.

write *The Bard*: I hope he does not regret his bargain. To long-suffering friends, colleagues and students in the School of English at St Andrews, thank you again. In particular, thanks to my then Head of School at St Andrews, Professor Nicholas Roe, who read a draft of the last chapter, and to my colleagues, Dr Tom Jones (scrutineer of chapter 2) and Dr Christopher MacLachlan who read a draft of the lot with his experienced editorial eye. Far from St Andrews, Professor David Simpson of the University of California at Davis also generously agreed to look over a draft of the whole typescript. In Dumfries Dr Valentina Bold of Glasgow University's Crichton Campus gave me the benefit of her local knowledge, introduced me to people, and proved to me the Globe Inn is the best place for an atmospheric Burns lunch. Other specific questions were generously answered by Dr Rhona Brown, Dr Gerard Carruthers, Professor Nigel Leask, Dr Kirsteen McCue, and Professor Murray Pittock of my *alma mater*, the University of Glasgow, as well as by Dr Lorn Macintyre, Professor Donald Meek and Dr Karina Williamson. All mistakes, though, are my own. I just wish that both my old schoolteacher, Arthur E. Meikle, a committed Burnsian, and my kindly doctoral supervisor, the astonishing biographer Richard Ellmann, were still around with their meticulous nibs.

Thanks are due to the librarians, curators and staff of the Robert Burns Birthplace and Museum, Alloway; Edinburgh City Library; Edinburgh University Library; Ellisland Farm Trust; the Ewart Library, Dumfries, and Dumfries Museums; Glasgow University Library; the Mitchell Library, Glasgow (whose 1996 publication of their splendid *Robert Burns Collection Catalogue* is, like the librarians, hugely helpful under pressure); the National Burns Collection and its many Scottish contributing institutions; the National Library of Scotland (where examining Clarinda's letters while being filmed in their stacks was a cramped delight); the National Trust for Scotland (especially at Alloway, Culzean, Kirkoswald, Mauchline and Tarbolton); St Andrews University Library; the Library of the University of California at Berkeley (with special thanks to Professor Ian Duncan of the Department of English whose characteristic generosity not only led to my talking about Burns at his wonderful 2006 conference on 'Scottish Romanticism in World Literatures' but also made it easy for me to roam the Berkeley library stacks); and the Woodruff Memorial Library at Emory University, Atlanta (where Dr Steve

Enniss let me see one of the few Burns poetry manuscripts to escape Peter Westwood's attention).

For guidance in matters of portraiture I am happy to thank Professor Duncan Macmillan; and Dr James Holloway, Director of the Scottish National Portrait Gallery, who, eyeball to eyeball with one of his great Scottish gallery's greatest treasures, patiently listened to my interpretation of Nasmyth's 1787 portrait of Burns, then generously alerted me to important Nasmyth scholarship.

The most important further reading – Burns's verse – is dealt with in the separate note on 'Reading Burns's Poems' which follows these Acknowledgements. The best extensive scholarly editions of Burns's poetry and letters – those published by Oxford University Press under the distinguished editorship of J. De Lancey Ferguson, James Kinsley and G. Ross Roy – are fully and respectfully detailed in the Introduction, which also mentions work by leading critics of Burns's poetry. Readers who want a fuller sense of Scottish literary history may wish to consult my *Scotland's Books: The Penguin History of Scottish Literature* (2007) as well as the anthology which Mick Imlah and I edited and which entered the Penguin Classics series in 2006 as *The Penguin Book of Scottish Verse*. Editing *Robert Burns and Cultural Authority* for Edinburgh University Press in 1997 I learned a lot from poring over the essays of all my contributors. I am arrogant enough to recommend that book as one of the two best collections of modern essays on Burns; the other is Carol McGuirk's selection of *Critical Essays on Robert Burns*, published by G. K. Hall in 1998.

Work on *The Bard* has been helped hugely by digital resources garnered by Ms Jean Young of St Andrews University Library, especially the Eighteenth-Century Collections Online (ECCO) database. However, aware that ECCO is an expensive, password-protected and subscriber-only database, wherever possible I have referred to printed books that are more likely to be available free of charge to interested readers.

On the web, the most authoritative and freely available guide to poetry in the English-speaking world has an expert's selection of Burns sites as one of the 'poetry rooms' in the virtual Poetry House at www.thepoetryhouse.org

The advantage of the virtual Poetry House is that it is edited by an international team of reputable specialist authorities. There is too much information about Burns, not too little, on the Internet,

Acknowledgements

and some of it is of variable quality. For those interested in making virtual visits to Burns sites and learning about Burns-related objects, the best website is that of Scotland's National Burns Collection at www.burnsscotland.com

If you would like to know more about the work of the Robert Burns World Federation Ltd, go to www.worldburnsclub.com

Such is Burns's remarkable international popularity that if you simply Google 'Robert Burns' and start going through all the entries, you will never come out alive.

R.C.
Castle House / The Poetry House
University of St Andrews
2007

Reading Burns's Poems

Where appropriate in this biography line-by-line glosses have been supplied for Scots expressions in Burns's poems, but I hope that reading *The Bard* will encourage people to seek out and enjoy more of this remarkable poet's work. Surprisingly, it is not as easy as it might seem for modern readers to find a good, accessible selection of Burns's writings. Bargain-basement editions often reprint unglossed, untrustworthy nineteenth-century texts, and even textually reliable modern editions lack on-page, line-by-line glossing of Scots words and phrases. Though the most comprehensive scholarly edition of Burns's verse remains the three-volume one which James Kinsley edited for Oxford University Press in 1968, this has long been out of print, and in any case it runs to over 1,600 pages. The formidable textual scholarship of Kinsley's edition, and its inclusion of almost all of Burns's poems and songs makes it the standard scholarly reference point in this biography and among Burns experts. However, most readers need something more manageable in size, style and layout. Anyone seeking a single-volume selection of Burns's poems is advised to choose *The Best Laid Schemes*, edited and annotated by Robert Crawford and Christopher MacLachlan. Published in Edinburgh by Polygon in 2009, *The Best Laid Schemes* contains most of the poems quoted in *The Bard* plus a selection of the best of Burns's other verse along with a substantial biographical and critical introduction. Aimed at general readers, it is the only twenty-first-century Burns volume to contain not just a generous gathering of his poetry but also selections from his autobiographical prose and writing notebooks. It also contains the full texts of several rediscovered Burns poems which are available in no other edition.

Introduction

No writer is more charismatic than Robert Burns. Passionate, intelligent, and a consummate wordsmith, he is the world's most popular love poet. He sought to become, and became, the archetypal national bard. Though it was dangerous to be so in his age and place, he also made himself through tone and temperament the master poet of democracy. All this makes Burns one of the most important authors of modernity, but also one of the hardest to write about. He will not be pigeonholed. His life and work resist the imposition of grandeur.

In that lies at least part of his dignity and international appeal. Loved today from New Zealand to New York and from Beijing to Berlin, Burns achieved his successes not with transcendental illumination but with daftness, deftness, warmth, humour, and a sometimes painful sense of his own vulnerability. No poet has been at once so brilliant and so down-to-earth. A celebrity who could mock his public status, Burns was ambitious and sometimes exploitative but almost never pompous. As soon as he had established himself as 'bard', he began making fun of the title; but the term 'bard' also denoted his commitment to his poetic vocation and his sense of a vital poetic relationship with his community – matters strengthened, not diminished, by his instinct for fun and self-mockery. Shakespeare never called himself a bard, and hardly ever used the word in his work; he came to be called 'bard' partly as a result of an anxious English response to Burns and Scots' pride in finding a great national poet.[1] Burns, an admirer of Shakespeare and English literature as well as a patriotic lover of Scotland and Scottish literature, delighted in being hailed as Scotland's bard.

In writing this biography I have tried wherever possible to give readers direct contact with Burns's own words – in poems, letters

3

and conversations – as well as with the comments of his contem-
poraries. In that way, through quotation as well as through narration
people can sense just how *reachable* this poet remains. His fun,
intelligence, radicalism, seductive allure and suffering can still be
ours, for all that he lived in the now distant eighteenth century.

Born into obscurity, Burns became the first poet in the English-
speaking world to be treated in his lifetime as a national celebrity.
At times his life is about celebrity and how to cope with it. He lived
that life with a performative intensity which is also part of his poetry.
Burns's performances – poetic, political, sexual, religious – are
searches for individual liberty, but a liberty to be achieved without
sacrificing the bond of community.

Sex, class, gender and politics offered him virulent excitement at
the same time as threatening to trap him in narrow roles he didn't
want. His life and poetry confront such threats with irony, vigour and
protean guile. His poetry is frequently bound up with his biography,
but his deep-rooted Scottish song-making is also so universally
beguiling that songs like 'Auld Lang Syne' are not just relished but
used in cultures very different from his own. As the first modern
writer to be hailed as a national bard, he was soon an internation-
ally recognised icon. Though he sometimes self-protectively concealed
it, the modernity of his democratic radicalism did not compromise
his artistic gift; today it presses the case that contemporary egalitarian
societies around the world should regard him as both ancestral and
familiar – should recognise him as 'the bard'.

Few poets' biographies are more striking or more heartbreakingly
remarkable. Burns's often sly resistance to authority enlivens all his
negotiations with it. Peasant and dandy, he fused in his work popular
and high culture, loving both throughout his short, packed, un-
repeatably intense existence. If at the bicentenary of Burns's birth
his countryman Hugh MacDiarmid maintained that thanks to the
'Industrial Revolution . . . Everything in Scotland has changed out
of all recognition since his time', then our own anxieties about global
environmental damage and a demeaning separation of people from
other creatures and their habitats makes Burns more vitally import-
ant than he may have seemed fifty years ago.[2] In his articulation
of how human domination has destroyed the ecology of 'Nature's
social union', or in his uneasy engagement with his society's darkest
secret – slavery – and with other issues of inequality, his attitudes
and expression are more disturbingly urgent than ever.[3] Yet when I

was first considering writing this biography, the gifted Scottish poet Don Paterson, whose brilliantly written 2001 essay on Burns is the most insightful and provocative of all short overviews of the poet's work, suggested to me there were so many existing accounts that a new biography of Burns would be 'the world's least necessary book'.[4]

Astonished by a 'furious shapeshifting' which makes Burns the energetic precursor of his admirer Keats's 'chameleon poet', Paterson argues that 'Burns was born in a lean time for verse. He was unfortunate not to have been born twenty years later, when, with far more stimulating company and better drugs, he would have made a fine Romantic.'[5] Yet, for all he was clearly nourished by that fountainhead of modernity, the Scottish Enlightenment, Burns *was* in several ways the first of the English-speaking world's great Romantic poets. Paterson, whose essay even gets the year of Burns's death wrong, is not to be trusted on dates: it was his 1770s and subsequent experience of the era of the American and French Revolutions which set Burns in the vanguard of Romanticism in the English-speaking world where Romantic tonalities had earlier been essayed by his countrymen James Thomson and James 'Ossian' Macpherson. Presenting a doctrinaire purist's selection of Burns's verse that omits not only 'Auld Lang Syne' and 'O my Luve's like a red, red rose' but also the famous songs beginning 'Scots, wha hae' and 'Is there for honest poverty', Paterson has effectively attempted to neuter Burns's political, and even some of his erotic, power. This biography presents those fascinating aspects of Burns in full, and shows how they fuelled some of his finest and best-known poetry.

If, for a moment, I may slip into the tones of a professor of literary history, let me point out that the admiration for democratic, revolutionary America in Burns's subversive earliest political poetry predates that of William Blake, as does Burns's admiration for the English republican poet John Milton's arch-rebel, Satan. It was the erotically intense Burns who showed the schoolboy Wordsworth what it might mean to write in a selection of the language really used by men, but, writing in standard English, Wordsworth cast off Burns's vital synthesis of tangy vernacular, his potent humour, and most of his eroticism. The spectator Wordsworth's ultimate love was grand scenery. Burns's was lovingly, flytingly, and democratically engaging with his fellow creatures. This is as evident in the Scottish poet's life as in his writing. If Burns's poetry's democratic tone

alienated the Oxonian Matthew Arnold, it was treasured elsewhere, and attracted the great poets of democratic America from Whitman, Poe, Dickinson and Longfellow to Whittier and Robert Frost. There are more statues of Burns in the United States than there are of any American poet, and his present-day US admirers range from Maya Angelou to several ex-presidents.[6] Growing up mute, poor and black in the American South, Angelou developed a lifelong and deep conviction that 'Robert Burns belonged to me'.[7] For all the unfamiliarity of some of his Scots language many readers and listeners in very different societies have come to feel this. I remember similar sentiments being voiced by Yuan Kejia of the People's Republic of China when he proudly signed himself 'the translator of Burns' in a copy of his *Poems of Robert Burns* in 1986, and I have even seen Burns drawn in Chinese costume by the artist Chiang Yee, who felt so strongly a connection between Burns's songs and traditional Chinese lyrics that he suggested the bard was 'perhaps . . . brought back as a baby from China by some Scottish missionary named Burns'.[8]

A warm sense of vitality, engrafted by remarkable skill into his best work, comes from what was most vital in Burns's life, so that some knowledge of his biography and situation are particularly, enjoyably important. As the Scottish poet Norman MacCaig noted, 'What is surprising is that the man who emerges from the poems and the man who emerges from the documents are one and the same person. We find nothing in the life that contradicts the poetry and nothing in the poetry that is not parelleled [*sic*] in the life.'[9] Burns's life has many clearly dramatic elements – struggle against 'obscurity', mental illness, political persecution and ruin, in addition to the upheavals of many love affairs, marriage and adultery. His personality, mixing warmth with humour and shrewdness, but also an attraction to excess and self-recrimination, compelled and still compels worldwide attention.

Burns's spectacular career and intense love affairs make him the ideal biographical subject. Still, some of the most important experiences for any poet are moments of reading and listening. It is hard to combine convincingly an account of a writer's subtle internal acoustic and intellectual education with tales of more obviously dramatic external events, and Burns's biographers have often failed in this regard. In the eighteenth century the first of them, Robert Heron, hastily produced a piece of hack-work, ignoring the nature

of the poet's linguistic gifts and censuring him for 'the evils of drunkenness and licentious love'.[10] Thereafter, Burns's first, now often maligned, nineteenth-century biographer and editor, James Currie, was concerned to sanitise those and other aspects of the poet while generously making available private information all later scholars have quarried. Though Currie has been the subject of recent academic interest, Burns's most generally influential biographer in the nineteenth century was Walter Scott's ambitious Tory lawyer son-in-law John Gibson Lockhart whose 1828 *Life of Robert Burns* was 'for a century and more the standard account of the poet and his work'.[11] For much of the twentieth century Lockhart's *Life* was reprinted in Everyman's Library, confirming its long-lasting 'classic' status. In the last two centuries probably Lockhart's has been read by more people than any other Burns biography.

This is unfortunate. For all his literary style, Lockhart furthered the 'gentlemanly' agenda which so conditioned biography throughout the Victorian era and shaped misleading nineteenth-century presentations of Burns, making him safe for many an imperialists' dinner or parlour ornament. Thomas Carlyle, who discussed Burns with men who had known him well, saw the poet as 'the most gifted British soul' of the eighteenth century, and made him a heroic 'Man of Letters' in his 1841 lectures *On Heroes and Hero-Worship*.[12] Later the Victorian Robert Chambers, born less of a gentleman than Lockhart but grown more of a scholar, wrote more fairly and carefully about Burns, who was worshipped by then internationally as a hero. Like that of Currie, Chambers's work combined biographical material with an edition of the poems. It was expertly updated in 1896, by which time it ran to over two thousand pages – impossibly long for anyone wanting a manageable biography. In the twentieth century, when Lytton Strachey stylishly debunked the Victorians' eminent, amplitudinously written-up heroes, and when D. H. Lawrence considered Burns as the protagonist for a projected novel of sexual liberation, Lawrence's friend the Scottish novelist Catherine Carswell authored a highly controversial, novelistic biography. Carswell inventively debunked aspects of Burns's reputation, introducing a much-needed note of feminist critique. For this she famously received a bullet in the post, and was asked to shoot herself, leaving 'the world a better and cleaner place'.[13]

If other twentieth-century biographies, most notably that of the sympathetic American scholar Franklyn Bliss Snyder, manoeuvred

more successfully between hero-worship and brass tacks, they also veered way off course: Snyder in 1932 condemned Burns's supposed part in capturing a smugglers' ship as a mere 'picturesque legend' fit for 'Gilbert and Sullivan'.[14] Today we can be sure this incident happened. For a biographer there are not only many problems in ascertaining details of Burns's life and milieu; there is also the way Burns presents an extreme example of the tensions between the 'laundering process' of hero-worship and the less elevated recording of sometimes awkward facts, blemishes, gossip, censored opinions – tensions in the art-form of biography that go back at least as far as Plutarch. Still fascinating critics, historians and professors of biography, such torsions are probably as old as the biographical form itself.[15]

Sadly, though revealingly, by the late twentieth century, for all his continuing international popularity, Burns was generally out of favour with the academic world's critics, professors and historians. This tells us more about conformist pedagogy than it tells us about the nimble-witted bard. Insightful literary critics from the magisterial David Daiches and Thomas Crawford to the shrewd Raymond Bentman and the subtly astute Carol McGuirk published and re-published monographs on him, but the steady trajectory of Burns's decline in the research culture of modern academia has been expertly traced by Murray Pittock.[16] Most recent books on Burns, including biographies, have emanated from outside the universities.

Burns may be relished by readers, leaders, singers and listeners from Moscow in Ayrshire to Moscow in Russia, but globally classroom taste for his work is limited. The problem lies with institutional academia, rather than with the poet who gleefully cocked a snook at 'Colledge-classes!'[17] Even in Scotland, traditional headquarters of an impressively active worldwide federation of popular Burns Clubs, and where the poet's work is studied in schools and universities, it has fallen as much to writers as to scholars to say just why Robert Burns matters. In 1996, speaking in the Scottish capital two hundred years after Burns's death, Seamus Heaney mounted a spirited, loving defence of Burns's 'art speech', while in St Andrews Douglas Dunn examined Burns's metrical craftsmanship and A. L. Kennedy spoke incisively about the creative impulses that warred within this poet of love, and sometimes also affected his spouse whose 'passivity' (Kennedy reflected memorably, if harshly) 'seems occasionally to border on the cataleptic'.[18]

The twenty-first-century Burns biographer requires an instinct for self-defence, and, ideally, a Kevlar vest. Yet there is an evident need for a fresh, lucid, sensibly proportioned biography of Robert Burns. Though I tracked down several mid-twentieth-century biographies in my local learned library, in bookshops in 2006 when I started writing this book I could find no biographies of Scotland's most dearly loved poet. Eventually I was able to buy an Ayrshire reprint of a translation of Hans Hecht's clear and short account, first published in German in 1919 and considerably dated in its scholarship.

The 1990s, though, had seen two fresh full-scale biographies. Ian McIntyre's 1995 account of the poet was eminently readable, but added nothing to the sum of human knowledge. James Mackay's prizewinning 750-page Burns tome of 1992 was clogged with facts and stodgily scripted. Accusations of plagiarism levelled against Mackay's prodigious biographical output by Niall Ferguson (now Laurence A. Tisch Professor of History at Harvard University), Catherine Lockerbie (now Director of the Edinburgh International Book Festival) and other sceptics, combined with his 'outing' for an earlier criminal indiscretion, had cast a shadow over his work.[19] In the case of Mackay's Burns biography, to an extent this was unfair; though his quotations could be inaccurate and (as modern Burns biographers must) he relied on earlier writings, his genealogical investigations in particular, some drawing on the work of the Mormon Church and conducted while he edited the *Burns Chronicle*, were thorough and sometimes pioneeringly productive. Those charges of plagiarism, however, had severely damaged his reputation as a biographer before his death in 2007. Professor Carol McGuirk called Mackay's work 'indispensable'; also 'unreadable'.[20] In *The Bard* I have not sought to match Mackay's vast, formidable amassing of information.

Question marks surrounding Mackay's scholarship were nothing compared with those overshadowing the 1997 study by Patrick Scott Hogg. Going far beyond the shrewd 1960s speculations of Lucyle Werkmeister, Hogg claimed to have discovered a host of 'lost poems' by Burns.[21] Many of these were soon republished in the now notorious *Canongate Burns* edition which Hogg edited in 2001 with academic Dr Andrew Noble. The furore over the 'radical' Noble–Hogg edition, which was riddled with textual errors (I counted ten in just a few stanzas of a single poem), inaccuracies and splenetic

outbursts, became a *cause célèbre* of modern Scottish publishing. It made working on Burns confusing and sometimes perilous.

Sadly this row and its aftermath have obscured perceptive essays on Burns and politics by Marilyn Butler and by W. J. Murray, as well as N. R. Paton's populist book *Song o' Liberty: The Politics of Robert Burns* (1994) and Liam McIlvanney's more scholarly *Burns the Radical: Poetry and Politics in Late Eighteenth-Century Scotland* (2002).[22] If Hogg and Noble's hearts were in the right place, their heads were most definitely not. The impact of their questionable scholarship and its turbulent reception has threatened to ruin efforts to build a nuanced case for Burns's radicalism which rescues him from those many monarchists, imperialists, staunch British Unionist supperers, and others who over the centuries have controlled – and sometimes still seek to control – his posthumous reputation.

Today Burns's supposed authorship of all those Canongate 'lost poems' has been disproved or so convincingly contested that none can safely be called his. The most dogged scholarly attacks on the 'appalling' *Canongate Burns* as a 'hugely unreliable product' which is 'a demonstrably inept and shoddy performance, frequent, wilful and purblind in its flaws' and filled with 'a shocking level of inadequate, unlikely and even falsified argumentation' have been mounted by the distinguished Burns textual scholar Dr Gerry Carruthers. Though I have described the *Canongate Burns* elsewhere in terms perhaps more generous than those used by Carruthers, in writing the present biography I have deliberately avoided arguments that depend on its discredited scholarship.[23]

This means *The Bard* returns for most of its textual information to the great three-volume edition of *The Poems and Songs of Robert Burns* edited for the Clarendon Press, Oxford, in 1968 by the Nottingham-based Scottish literary scholar James Kinsley. At times I have supplemented reference to Kinsley's edition with the publication from manuscript of 'new' poetry by Burns rediscovered during the research for this biography. These fresh attributions are discussed at more length in *The Best Laid Schemes*, the selection of Burns's work which I have edited for the general reader with Dr Christopher MacLachlan. Though the Reverend Professor Kinsley has rightly been regarded as conservative with a small (and perhaps a capital) *c*, his vast edition remains invaluable for its sure-footedness and sheer erudition. Even though his three volumes may be too extended for most people, it is one of the tragedies of Burns scholarship that

Kinsley's edition, unsurpassed for four decades, has long been out of print in its full form. Its references keyed to Kinsley's text of the poems, and to the standard edition of Burns's *Letters* edited by the American scholar J. De Lancey Ferguson, then updated by his fellow countryman and distinguished Burnsian G. Ross Roy, *The Bard* acknowledges the most thorough and trustworthy textual work, so I hope that my arguments about Burns's texts may avoid some of the pitfalls that have afflicted several recent writers on Burns.

My aim has been to pay close attention to the poems and letters and to avoid most of the 'Burns lore' which, while it is a legitimate subject for sociological research, often clutters accounts of Burns's life, so that, as even James Mackay (who amassed an almost endless amount of it) admitted, 'it is difficult at this remove in time to distinguish between hard fact and the myths and legends'.[24] In his second commonplace book Burns once quoted the English poet Thomas Gray on how 'half a word fixed upon or near the spot, is worth a cart-load of recollection'.[25] I agree. This biography almost always relies on accounts given by people who met Burns during his lifetime; it also quotes extensively, though not uncritically, from Burns's own, sometimes self-dramatising writings. In his late teens Burns's son James Glencairn Burns, who admired writing that displayed 'a superior manner', liked his father's 'letters better than his Poetry'.[26] Few today would concur, but at times, for all their polished 'superior manner', the letters give an energetic sense of what Burns's conversation and anecdotes, which impressed so many who met him but are now largely buried under a tonnage of 'lore', must have been like. This is not a book of Burns lore; I would not be qualified to write one.

Published two hundred and fifty years after his birth, *The Bard* is the first twenty-first-century biography of Robert Burns. Addressed to an international audience, it does not assume detailed knowledge of his work or circumstances. It aims simply to offer a clear, manageable account of his life which gives some indication of what made him a great poet. In doing this, I have tried to avoid over-aestheticising Burns, aiming instead to show his political as well as his lyric imagination. He was constantly in dialogue with his community and with other voices beyond; his craftsmanship, his literary learning, are as important as any other parts of his experience. At times, I quote some of his poems, both great and minor, hoping to shed light on their value for readers who may or may not be familiar

with the complicated mixtures of vernacular and formal language, English and Scots, which Burns so loved and which give energy to the busy, sculpted interchange that is his verse. There is no point in writing a biography of the bard without outlining what the bard wrote. I want to show why his poetry still matters.

'The Bard' is also the title of a 1757 poem by Thomas Gray about a Welsh poet who commits suicide rather than submitting to English imperialism. Gray's poem helped spur an enthusiasm for bards and for that 'medievalism' which has been the subject of recent renewed scholarly interest.[27] Burns was familiar with and hugely admired the Scottish bardic work of Ossian which, I've argued in *The Modern Poet*, helped create a conception of poets as at once primitive and sophisticated, domestic and wild.[28] These assumptions about poets continue to this day, and surely fit Robert Burns. Still, having written elsewhere about Burns in several books of literary criticism and literary history, having edited a selection of his work and a collection of essays about him, and having discussed the way the words 'the bard' came to be applied to both Burns and Shakespeare, I am happy to refer readers to these separately published arguments.[29] This biography is not about fitting Burns into some extended critical thesis or literary history. It is about painting a credible portrait.

Apparently straightforward matters of Burns portraiture have long been a difficult area. When a late-eighteenth-century portrait miniature of a man with tied hair, inscribed on the back of the frame 'Robert Burns', and with a provenence traceable to the poet's brother, came up for auction at Bonhams in London on 23 May 2007, even as bids were placed scholars were disagreeing on whether or not it was an authentic likeness of the bard.[30] Each portrait of a human being, however vouched for, is only a partial likeness, a person seen at best in a revealing slant of light. That is the most I can hope for *The Bard*.

A quarter of a millennium after Robert Burns's birth, it is time for a biography that tries to bridge the gulf between too familiar touristic conceptions of Burns as a brand-name Scottish national icon and those now embattled defences of Burns as a poet whose resilient international popularity seems inversely related to his unfashionable status in academia. *The Bard* depends on new research as well as on the work of earlier generations of investigators. It is the first biography to draw on the Macdonald manuscript, which not only provides unpublished late-eighteenth-century accounts of

places Burns knew, but also affords the last extended account of Burns's conversation written down in his lifetime and an important insight into his republican Scottish political thought. *The Bard* is, too, the first biography to make use of published materials from the journals of Stebbing Shaw to sermons by William Dalrymple, David Trail and others to show in new ways how Burns was both formed by and shaped the culture around him. As well as drawing on some rediscovered Burns poems and newly located newspaper materials such as the interview with Highland Mary's mother, I have paid a good amount of attention to Burns's reading. I show how this nourished his imagination, and, identifying for the first time, for instance, the book of letters which he pored over in his youth, I suggest how this affected his lifelong desire to assemble around him a group of literary wits.

In writing about Burns's hothouse love affair with Agnes McLehose, I have used familiar letters, and much less familiar correspondence which has lain unpublished since the 1920s and has been ignored by previous editors and biographers. Elsewhere in this book I put forward new interpretations of well-known works such as Alexander Nasmyth's 1787 portrait of Burns or Burns's own 'Tam o' Shanter' – that poem surely connected to his excited awareness of his adultery. No previous biographer has made such detailed use of materials relating to Burns's infant knowledge of song, his youthful aware-ness of the American War, or his community's 1790s alertness to European political affairs as reflected in the *Dumfries Weekly Journal*. If some of the new material in this book may be controversial, it may also aid future readers. Most of all, I hope *The Bard* offers twenty-first-century audiences a picture of a great poet that is free from excessive bardolatry or verbiage. While drawing on the most admirable scholarship – such as that of Chambers and Wallace in the nineteenth century and Kinsley in the twentieth – I have tried to add some new and worthwhile stones to the big cairn of Burns biography.

My purpose in writing, though, is not primarily to make a memorial, a contribution to cultural tourism, or a treatise, but to present to an international audience a credible, engaging and nuanced likeness of a uniquely talented individual. In so doing I pay propor-tionately more attention than previous biographers to Burns's formative childhood and youth, to the years when he made his greatest breakthroughs as a poet, and to his political attitudes in

I

First an' Foremost

Robert Burns was born in wartime. Wars shaped his consciousness, community and country. In his early infancy, muskets, shot and gunpowder were being sent to his local West of Scotland port of Ayr and volunteers trained to ward off threatened French attacks. In his teens he lived through and was fascinated by the American Revolution. His late twenties saw the run-up to the French Revolution, its ideals dangerously important to his work. In his thirties Burns was in uniform, marching to defend the British Crown against another threatened French invasion, while harbouring his own republican sympathies: 'But while we sing, GOD SAVE THE KING,/ We'll ne'er forget THE PEOPLE!'[1]

Love, not war, would be Burns's greatest passion. Conflicts and imperial conquests, however, linked Ayrshire to the wider world. Traders and troops were familiar sights. Shortly before Burns's birth Ayr had a provost who had travelled throughout Russia and China. Ayr had a long history of trading with European ports from the Baltic to the Mediterranean, then extensively with America and the Caribbean. Local people had family links to America, India and continental Europe. Founded as a burgh in 1205, Ayrshire's county town was proud of its history and connections. Sixteenth-century historian George Buchanan singled out Ayr's 'brave men' in his history of Scotland, and a Latin poem of that era calls Ayr a small but big-hearted city, second to none for the nobleness of its menfolk.[2] 'Auld Ayr, wham ne'er a town surpasses,/ For honest men and bonny lasses' would be Burns's version of this.[3] He noticed Ayr's womenfolk too.

One eighteenth-century visitor noted that Ayr, 'built on a gentle eminence & surrounded by an extensive plain, looks exceedingly well from a distance'.[4] A 1780s English tourist admired the 'good

harbour' of this town 'charmingly situated in a sandy plain, on the mouth of the river Ayr'.[5] The sandy soil on which Ayr was built made its seaside environs ideal for 'walking, ... [horse] racing, golfing, &c. Every one has easy access to the turf, covered at all seasons with a beautiful verdure, and in Spring and Summer adorned with wild daisies and other flowers.'[6] Since the Middle Ages Ayr had hosted fairs, attracting travelling traders as well as local people. During Scotland's medieval Wars of Independence William Wallace reputedly mustered troops at nearby Mauchline, and burned the Barns of Ayr with their English garrison. King Robert the Bruce defeated the English at Ayrshire's Loudoun Hill. The loved, 'badly constructed' Wallace Tower (later rebuilt) dominated the low houses of Ayr High Street in Burns's boyhood.[7] Over four centuries earlier, Wallace was said to have been held prisoner there. Robert the Bruce, victor over the English at Bannockburn, was Earl of Carrick in Ayrshire. He met with the Scottish Parliament in 1315 at Ayr's ancient St John's Church – in Burns's day, as today, an eye-catching ruin. By the sixteenth-century European Reformation preachers like John Knox and George Wishart came to preach the Protestant gospel. Witch-burning, smuggling and bitter religious conflict – some of it anti-monarchical and seditiously democratic in matters of church government – were also part of local history. A geography book used in Burns's household lists Ayrshire's principal districts – 'Kyle, Carrick, and Cunningham' – and the chief towns, including the seaports of Ayr and Irvine. These were spirited, historic places. After Scotland lost its political independence in 1707, Ayr's trade declined substantially, but grew again after several decades. Published in London, Burns's eighteenth-century geography book views Scotland as in some ways unsophisticated. It highlights the sometimes 'dangerous powers over the laity' which had in the past been exercised by the governing bodies or 'kirk sessions' of local Church of Scotland congregations. This included the policing of sexuality. 'Fornicators of both sexes' were made 'to sit upon what they call a repenting-stool, in the church, and in full view of the congregation'. The author thought this practice was beginning to cease under the influence of 'very moderate' clergy.[8] Burns would put that to the test.

He was born into a working family on 25 January 1759 in Alloway. Just inland from Ayr, and once an ancient barony, today a prosperous suburb, Alloway was then a riverside hamlet with a cloth-mill.

Burns's mother, Agnes Broun, had been baptised on 26 March 1732 in another small Ayrshire settlement, Kirkoswald, by the Reverend William Cupples. Years afterwards Burns would live in Kirkoswald for a time, in close contact with his mother's relatives. Cupples's son Tam would be mentioned in Burns's poem 'Halloween'. Many of his poems suggest how strong were traditional Ayrshire family links, beliefs, songs and gosssip.

Agnes Broun's own mother, Agnes Rainie, had given birth to six children but had died when Agnes, her eldest, was ten. Young Agnes remembered her mother's spirit of pious resignation, but also her practicality. Visited by her sister, the dying Agnes Rainie rightly maintained her husband would soon get another wife.[9] Though young Agnes helped raise her siblings for a couple of years, her father, son of an Ayrshire tenant farmer, took little interest in her after he remarried. Agnes's formal schooling ended with her mother's death. She seems to have been taught to read a little – the Bible and the Catechism – by an old village weaver. She was brought up by her maternal grandmother, who was remembered as having given shelter to the persecuted, anti-government Presbyterian Covenanters when they were threatened by the army.[10] Robert Burns would come to be proud of the fact that his ancestors had sided with persecuted rebels – both Covenanters on his mother's side, and Jacobites on his father's. Though Burns's mother was not taught to write, she learned to spin and keep house; she had a good memory for Scots ballads (which she sang to her grandmother), Scots songs, and the Psalms in English metrical paraphrase central to traditions of Scottish Protestant worship. Sharing her love of the Psalms, Burns later made psalm paraphrases of his own. He remembered his red-haired mother singing in his childhood. She was his first source and teacher of song; he was her greatest pupil. She is said to have kept his portrait on her wall, a memorial of the famous son whom she outlived by twenty-four years.

Poets learn through their ears. Burns grew up in a family and community which quickened what he called 'my early attachment to ballads'.[11] Oral culture shaped his imagination, even when he went against its wisdom: 'advice which my grandmother, rest her soul! often gave me, and I as often neglected – "Leuk twice or ye loup ance!" [Look twice before you leap once]'.[12] This kind of proverbial wisdom was not just commonplace. It could have a proudly radical edge.

Among the many wise adages which have been treasured up by our Scotish Ancestors, this is one of the best – 'Better be the head o' the Commonality, as the tail o' the Gentry.'[13]

Burns relished his mother's sayings and phrases, but she taught him more than old adages. He picked up songs and tunes from her, including one with a Gaelic refrain which modern scholars think may have been originally 'Leig Air Mo Chois' (Let me get up) – perhaps a lullaby sung by a mother lying beside a restless infant who craves attention and who will not settle to sleep.[14] Burns recalled this song as

> the old Highland one, Leiger m' chose – the only fragment remaining of the old words, is the chorus, still a favorite lullaby of my old mother, from whom I learned it –

> > Leiger m' chose, my bonie wee lass,
> >   An leiger m' chose, my dearie;
> > A' the lee-lang winter night,
> >   Leiger m' chose, my dearie. –

This long-remembered fragment of Gaelic is the earliest indication of a sympathy for the language of Highland culture which would be lifelong in the Lowlander Burns. Towards the end of his life he wrote new words for this tune, which he recognised as a reel played at country weddings under the name 'Liggeram cosh', a Lowland corruption of the original Gaelic, and he altered its first stanza, giving it a sexual energy as he addressed 'Nancy', one of the loves of his life,

> > Thine I am, my faithful Fair,
> >   Well thou may'st discover;
> > Every pulse along my veins
> >   Tells the ardent Lover. –[15]

It may seem odd Burns should link his mother's lullaby with ardently sexual verses, but he portrayed her as singing openly erotic songs rather than simply childish or churchy ones. In a household where parents and children shared one living-room-cum-bedroom, and where byre and house were one small building, sex was hardly a secret. In a 1786 account of a flirtation Burns juxtaposes his misquotation of

St Paul – 'Brethren, salute one another with a holy kiss' – with a more frankly sexual verse,

> 'Kissin is the key o' love,
> 'An' clappin is the lock,
> 'An' making o's the best thing
> 'That ere a young thing got' –

This, he explains, is 'An auld Sang o' my Mither's'.[16] If Burns later reflected gleefully on his mother's song repertoire, he delighted that her side of his family was well versed in Scots oral tradition. At the end of his twenties he wrote to a friend,

> ... I would transcribe you a stanza of an old Scots Ballad, called, 'The life & age of Man;['] beginning thus –
>
> > "Twas in the sixteenth hunder year
> > Of God & fifty three
> > Frae Christ was born that bought us dear,
> > As Writings testifie' –
>
> I had an old Grand uncle with whom my Mother lived a while in her girlish years; the good old man, for such he was, was long blind ere he died, during which time, his most voluptuous enjoyment was to sit down & cry while my Mother would sing the simple old song of, The Life & Age of Man. –[17]

Burns seldom recorded anecdotes about his mother, but in each of these just quoted she is singing; he remembers exactly what she sang. Her repertoire included lullabies, love songs, and ballads, all in the Scots tongue. She passsed on a sung heritage savoured in her rural Ayrshire family; specifically she educated her eldest son, Robert, in vernacular song and ballad culture. Beginning from that loving education, he would do more than anyone else for Scots song and vernacular poetry. In Ayrshire in 1786 Dugald Stewart became the first leading Scottish Enlightenment intellectual to meet Burns. He was struck that

> His memory was uncommonly retentive, at least for poetry, of which he recited to me frequently long compositions with the most minute accuracy. They were chiefly ballads, and other pieces in our Scottish

19

dialect; great part of them (he told me) he had learned in his child-
hood, from his mother, who delighted in such recitations, and whose
poetical taste, rude as it probably was, gave, it is presumable, the
first direction to her son's genius . . .[18]

By the time he met Stewart, Burns was not generally so forthcoming
about how much he owed to his mother, but Stewart's observations
are perceptive. On other occasions, usually in passing, Burns con-
sistently attributes songs and quotations to various older female
relatives: 'I remember a grand Aunt of mine used to sing [a reel],
by the name of "Liggeram cosh, my bonie wee lass".'[19] Burns later
wrote two sets of words for this tune which he had known since
infancy; as a man he discussed it with musicologists and a Gaelic
expert.[20]

Folk-tales were transmitted through Burns's family mainly by
women. The boy loved this: 'the Devil . . . , my grannie (an old
woman *indeed*!) often told me, rode on Will-o'-wisp, or, in her more
classic phrase, SPUNKIE'.[21] As an adult Burns treasured such child-
hood memories. He liked to describe his own personality as that of
a will-o'-the-wisp, and signed at least one letter 'yours – SPUNKIE'.[22]
His poem 'Halloween' is a remarkable anthology of folk-beliefs
about love. It presents a 'Graunie' (granny) telling tales about life
half a century earlier. The stories of the 'rev'rend *Graunie*' of 'Address
to the Deil' enrich that poem with its 'moss-traversing *Spunkies*'.[23]
Speculating about what in his 'infant and boyish days' had 'culti-
vated the latent seeds of Poesy', he recalled with pride the widow
of his mother's cousin, who had frequently helped in the running of
his childhood home. Betty Davidson

> had, I suppose, the largest collection in the county of tales and songs
> concerning devils, ghosts, fairies, brownies, witches, warlocks,
> spunkies, kelpies, elf-candles, dead-lights, wraiths, apparitions,
> cantraips, giants, inchanted towers, dragons and other trumpery.[24]

'Trumpery' sounds dismissive, but Burns loved this oral culture.
Later, when he read modern philosophers like John Locke, one part
of his mind belonged to the Enlightenment; another part, though,
remained from childhood 'naturally of a superstitious cast'.[25] 'Early
impressions', he said, had given him a 'horror of Spectres'.[26] In his
poetry and elsewhere Burns loved recalling old stories and anecdotes

that mixed horror with a note of daftness: 'In the words of the Highlandman when he saw the Deil [Devil] on Shanter-hill in the shape of five swine – "My hair stood and my p—— stood, and I swat & trembled."'[27] If, like Betty Davidson, he enjoyed the childhood *frisson* created by tales of brownies (domestic spirits that do house-work), bogles (spectres), kelpies (horse-shaped water demons) and apparitions, then as a mature man he liked to launch into all this with oratorical indulgence:

> O, thou Spirit! whatever thou art, or wherever thou makest thyself visible! Be thou a Bogle by the eerie side of an old thorn, in the dreary glen through which the herd-callan maun bicker in his gloamin route frae the fauld! – Be thou a BROWNIE, set, at dead of night, to thy task by the blazing ingle, or in the solitary barn where the repercussions of thy iron flail half affright thyself, as thou performest the work of twenty of the sons of men, ere the cock-crowing summon thee to thy ample cog of substantial BROSE! – Be thou a KELPIE, haunting the ford, or ferry, in the starless night, mixing thy laughing yell with the howling of the storm & the roaring of the flood, as thou viewest the perils & miseries of Man on the foundering horse, or in the tumbling boat! – Or, lastly, be thou a GHOST, paying thy nocturnal visits to the hoary ruins of decayed Grandeur; or performing thy mystic rites in the shadow of the time-worn Church while the Moon looks, without a cloud, on the silent, ghastly dwellings of the dead around thee . . .[28]

Just as supernatural horrors – part entertainment, part folk belief and wisdom – had been laid on thick to captivate, excite and spook him as a child, so Burns as an adult liked to cultivate a relish for these things in his audience – whether in his great nocturnal gathering of old wives' tales in 'Address to the Deil', or in the hellish legion's night-ride of 'Tam o' Shanter'. As a poet he was certainly aware of the charnel-house verse moralistically set forth in formal English by solemn and wordy eighteenth-century poets like Edward Young in 'Night Thoughts' or Robert Blair in 'The Grave', but Burns's appetite for teasing pacy horrors owes more to his earliest Scots vernacular upbringing: one full of stories of magical creatures, ballads of hanged men, songs of love and ruin.

One of his main published sources of geographical knowledge, William Guthrie's *New Geographical, Historical, and Commercial Grammar; and Present State of the Several Kingdoms of the World*

(a book Burns later recommended), contends that 'The inhabitants of those parts of Scotland, who live chiefly by pasture, have a natural vein for poetry; and the beautiful simplicity of the Scotch tunes is relished by all true judges of nature.' The same book argues 'The Scotch commonalty ... affect a fondness for the memory and language of their forefathers beyond, perhaps, any people in the world.'[29] Burns grew up with access not only to rich, maternal sources of song and oral tradition, but also in a culture where published authorities were beginning to value these. His own work would further that treasuring, transmitting some of the performative energy of oral culture through the very different medium of print.

He had a remarkable memory. 'The earliest Song I remember to have got by heart. – When a child, an old woman sung it to me, & I pickt it up, every word, at first hearing.' Burns's pride in remembering Scots songs is palpable here, but the precise wording of this first song he learned is also significant. 'The Blathrie o't' celebrates song itself, as well as love and proud independence from authority. Love is more important than money or social status:

> I wad rather hae my lassie, tho' she cam in her smock,
> Than a Princess wi' the gear & the blathrie o't.
>
> *wealth and trumpery of it*

In this song poor people's pride and way of life are prized by a singer who asserts potentially disrespectful independence from monarchy and organised religion. As the last stanza puts it,

> I'll not meddle wi' th' affairs o' the Kirk or the Queen,
> They're nae matters for a sang, let them sink, let them swim.
> On your Kirk I'll ne'er encroach, but I'll hold it still remote,
> Sae tak this for the gear & the blathrie o't.[30]

Burns did not just make songs; songs made Burns. This process began in early childhood, and the poet's oral memory meant he was shaped by words like these, which nurtured in him a creative disrespect for political and other kinds of authority even as he was schooled in the ways of Kirk and community. In adult life, however much he knew it 'may possibly be a contemptible performance in the scientific eyes of the literati', he would relish 'the honest effusion of a poetic, though rustic heart ... the composition of an

illiterate Millwright, about thirty or forty years ago, somewhere in Ayr-shire'.[31]

A rebellious ballad Burns remembered 'from oral tradition in Ayrshire, where, when I was a boy, it was a popular song', is 'Hughie Graham'. The determined Hughie is hunted down by 'lords' for stealing a bishop's mare. Despite the pleas of 'brave Whitefoord' and his lady fair (Burns's version has Ayrshire people's names in it), Hughie is hanged in Stirling; going to his death he denounces his wife as horse-thief and 'bishop's whore'. His last words are a violently anti-clerical incitement:

> And ye may tell my kith and kin,
>   I never did disgrace their blood;
> And when they meet the bishop's cloak,
>   To mak it shorter by the hood. —[32]

Burns's boyhood was spent in a Protestant community with little time for bishops, but these sentiments are hardly pious in anyone's terms. Their vernacular kick can be heard in some of Burns's own compositions. When as an adult he presents himself as an itinerant balladeer, signing a letter 'Johnny Faa', he invokes a ballad of gypsies and upper-class domestic violence viewed from the standpoint of the people. The ballad is set in terrain where he had grown up and where his mother first met his father.[33] He loved such ballad lore, writing of 'Johnny Faa' that

> The people in Ayrshire began this song –
>   The gypsies cam to my lord Cassilis yet.   *gate*
> They have a great many more stanzas in this song than I ever saw
> in any printed copy. – The castle is still remaining at Maybole where
> his Lordship shut up his wayward Spouse & kept her for life.[34]

Burns grew up with folk-tales linked to local places: Cassilis (pronounced 'Castles') was not just a ballad site, it was also a haunted zone where fairies danced at Halloween on 'certain little, romantic, rocky, green hills, in the neighbourhood of the ancient seat of the Earls of Cassilis'.[35] The places associated with his parents, childhood and youth were real but also story-places, song-places, poem-places. He grew up in an Ayrshire of peasant imagination as well as in a world of eighteenth-century wars, politics and ecclesiastical scuffles.

Agnes Broun, Burns's mother, had been born near Culzean before that name designated the more modern 'noble Castle' designed by Robert Adam. Culzean Castle was being developed throughout Burns's lifetime so local gentry might view from its palatial splendour the Isle of Arran's 'magnificence over the water'.[36] His mother's Culzean, Burns knew, was rich in folk-life. In his 'Halloween' supernatural creatures dance there 'Beneath the moon's pale beams'. There was, Burns wrote, 'A noted cavern near Colean-house, called the Cove of Colean; which . . . is famed, in country story, for being a favourite haunt of Fairies'.[37] Still visible today, this cave was a notorious smugglers' hiding place. Agnes Broun appears to have had relatives who were smugglers; an associate of one may have been the James Young who witnessed the baptism of her first child, Robert, into the Church of Scotland on 26 January 1759.[38] Another relative kept a tea shop in Ayr. As in her singing, so in her Ayrshire connections, Agnes combined godly, polite respectability with wilder aspects of local life. When she married her husband, William Burnes, in late 1757, she was eleven years his junior. Having ended her earlier relationship with a farmhand when she discovered he was cheating on her, she had met William at a fair in Maybole in 1756. 'Thin' and 'sinewy', he was about five-foot-nine.[39] Fifteen months later they married and went to live in their first home – a substantial thatched cottage William had constructed at Alloway.

It was a robust marriage. Agnes was capable. When part of the gable wall of the Alloway cottage subsided in a storm just ten days after their first child was born, she moved with the baby Robert to a neighbour's while William looked after repairs. In an age when many children died young and medical science was hardly reliable, Agnes, with help from her extended family, brought up all seven children born to her in the course of a dozen years, while William strove to get them education. Agnes was remembered by one of her daughters as 'about the ordinary height: a well-made sonsy [buxom] figure, with . . . red hair, dark eyes and eyebrows, with a fine square forehead; with all her good qualities – and they were many – her temper at times was irascible'.[40] William was seen as the leading, patriarchal partner, while Agnes, following the conventional gender roles of the age, took charge of household tasks for her busy, growing family. At Alloway were born Robert and, on 28 September 1760, his brother Gilbert, to whom he was always close; the sisters Agnes (born 30 September 1762) and Annabella (known in the family as

Nannie and born on 14 November 1764) also came to occupy the Alloway cottage before the family sought larger premises at nearby Mount Oliphant in 1765. Three further children were born to the couple – William (b. 30 July 1767), John (b. 10 July 1769), and Isobel or Isabella (b. 27 July 1771). Robert was not the only member of the family to develop a taste for song and poetry; to the end of her life Isobel recalled her eldest sister repeating poetry while milking a cow, and Isobel herself delighted in singing and reciting verse, including work by her famous brother.[41] Bringing up all these young-sters, the Burnes parents remained strong, attached to each other and to their children. A male observer who knew Agnes and William well, and who had lodged with the family, recalled how

> At all times, and in all companies, she listened to him with a more marked attention than to any body else. When under the necessity of being absent while he was speaking, she seemed to regret as a real loss, that she had missed what the good man had said. This worthy woman, Agnes Brown, had the most thorough esteem for her husband of any woman I ever knew ... He was an excellent husband, if I may judge from his assiduous attention to the ease and comfort of his worthy partner and from her affectionate behaviour to him, as well as her unwearied attention to the duties of a mother.[42]

Robert's first surviving familial letter formally but sincerely sends his mother his 'dutiful respects'; his last letter to his oldest brother ends simply '– Remember me to my Mother. –'[43] She is glimpsed sending a present of cheese from the family's stock (which she seems to have made), and later as an 'aged parent' about whom her eldest child worries, but who was well enough to visit and occasionally help with a grandchild. In the man's world of Burns's letters and most of his biographers, she features much less than her husband. But as the source of Burns's love of song she was more influential than they knew.

Unlike Agnes, William Burnes was an incomer to Ayrshire. His spelling of his surname was true to his north-east Scottish heritage, though his most famous son would prefer the spelling 'Burns'. For at least a century before Robert Burns's birth generations of the Burnes family had farmed among the hills less than ten miles inland from the port of Stonehaven, south of Aberdeen. Never settling far from ancestors and kin, these Burneses worked the land close to territory later made famous in one of Scotland's most celebrated

twentieth-century novels, *Sunset Song* by Lewis Grassic Gibbon. Gibbon, who wrote with lyricism and grit of life on the land in north-east Scotland, is buried at the heart of the area he wrote about, Arbuthnott, just a few miles south of Glenbervie, where the graves of some of Burns's ancestors can still be seen.

According to family traditions cited by the poet, the paternal grandfather after whom he was named was an able, intelligent, relatively prosperous man who had married into the Keith family and worked as a gardener for the Jacobite Earl Marischal Keith at Inverugie Castle in Aberdeenshire. The Keiths and their employees suffered after the failure of the 1715 Jacobite rebellion. Just over seventy years later Burns wrote, 'My Fathers rented land of the noble Kieths [sic] of Marshal, and had the honor to share their fate.'[44] Whether or not this was historically accurate, Burns associated his paternal ancestors with Jacobitism and noble ruin. Cherished 'Fathers', they had

> left their humble cottages only to add so many units more to the unnoted croud that followed their Leaders; yet, what they could they did, and what they had they lost: with unshaken firmness and unconcealed Political Attachments, they shook hands with Ruin for what they esteemed the cause of their King and their Country. –[45]

This story is rooted in tales his own father told. The poet in Burns liked this version of family history: 'the Scotish Muses were all Jacobites'.[46] Jacobites were generally opposed to the 1707 political Union between Scotland and England. However exaggerated in later accounts, by the time of the Jacobite rebellion of 1745 and the ensuing 1746 massacre at Culloden, financial collapse threatened the Burnes family. Robert Burnes had to give up one farm and borrow money to move to another nearby; he could not repay his loan, and the venture failed. All his sons moved south.

The eldest, James, the poet's uncle, became a canny businessman in Montrose, a port north of Dundee. James had little contact with the poet's father. Both Robert Burnes's other surviving sons, Robert and William, followed one of their father's vocations, becoming gardeners. Not mentioning his grandfather's financial failure, the poet in 1787 linked the family's earlier troubles to their supposed Jacobitism. Burns grew up with a sense of Jacobite 'Ruin' which 'threw my father on the world at large; where after many

years' wanderings and sojournings, he pickt up a pretty large quantity of Observation and Experience, to which I am indebted for most of my little pretensions to wisdo'.[47] 'Many years' wanderings and sojournings' make William sound like Moses, or Ulysses, father of Telemachus. Certainly there were treasured family stories about William's exodus from the north-east. Gilbert Burns recalled how

> I have often heard my father . . . describe the anguish of mind he felt when they [he and his elder brother Robert] parted on the top of a hill, on the confines of their native place, each going off his several way in search of new adventures, and scarcely knowing whither he went. My father undertook to act as a gardener and shaped his course to Edinburgh, where he wrought hard when he could get work, passing through a variety of difficulties . . .[48]

Where the poet wrote of his father's family's 'Ruin', his younger brother recalls a tale of 'anguish of mind'. On his father's side ancestral memories could have a bleak cast, though they also indicate a pride in working through difficulties.

William Burnes had arrived in Scotland's capital around 1748, with a testimonial saying he was 'a very well inclind lad'.[49] He helped with the landscaping of Edinburgh's Hope Park – today called the Meadows. Created from the drained South Loch, Hope Park was one of the early stages in Edinburgh's neoclassical town planning that led to major 'improvements'. The man behind Hope Park was Thomas Hope of Rankeillor, chairman of the new Society of Improvers in the Knowledge of Agriculture in Scotland, and someone eager to show how land might be upgraded. In 1752 proposals for Edinburgh public works heralded the building of the New Town and led to the draining of the North Loch to create what is now Princes Street Gardens. In the years just after the 1745 Jacobite rebellion had thrown Edinburgh into turmoil, plans for 'improvement' were everywhere. An intelligent man who wrote in a confident, clear hand, the gardener William Burnes was in town while Adam Smith was giving improving public lectures on 'Rhetoric and Belles Lettres' and the Scottish Enlightenment was burgeoning. Though we might think landscaping and 'belles-lettres', agriculture and culture are very different, in eighteenth-century Scotland the author of a book on ploughing might go on to be a professor of literature. St Andrews

professor William Barron, like Edinburgh judge Lord Kames – farmer and literary critic – argued there was a universal need for improved and refined ways of working.

William Burnes was on the side of the improvers. He was soon hired by West of Scotland 'improving' landowner Alexander Fairlie, who wintered in Edinburgh and lived on his Ayrshire estate during spring and summer. Having gardened for Fairlie and won the good opinion of local church authorities, William then worked as gardener for John Crawford at Doonside House near Alloway. In 1756 he took a perpetual lease on just over seven acres of local land, hoping to establish a market garden. The traditional story (recounted by William's son Gilbert) is that William began building his cottage at Alloway. The lower part of the walls of the surviving structure may have been constructed using rubble or stones cleared from fields as part of agricultural improvement. Though modern roughcast or, in Scots, 'harling' makes detailed internal examin-ation of the walls impossible, recent architectural investigations suggest that rather than building the whole cottage from scratch, William may have substantially extended and 'improved' an earlier structure. Instead of using old-fashioned turf infill, the upper walls of William's house were built from 'a mud and straw mixture', then coated in limewash. The house had some glazed windows and separate entrances to the living quarters and byre. Today's visitors to 'Burns Cottage' may find it primitive, but, for a working man's first home, it was modern, 'improved' in its day, particu-larly after its gable end was repaired using 'rubble masonry with lime mortar rather than clay' in 1759, and a byre added 'with rubble stonewalls and lime mortar ... in a more expensive construction method'.[50]

William Burnes was a valued member of the local community. In November 1754 the minister of Maybole wrote on a kirk certificate that William had throughout the preceding two years behaved (as the official phrasing has it) 'honestly soberly and without offence or ground of publick Censure'.[51] Alloway was a small settlement on the long, winding River Doon, situated over a mile from where the Doon flows through Ayr to the sea. In the early fourteenth century, Robert the Bruce had confirmed the royal burgh of Ayr's tenure of the barony of Alloway, though Ayr had sold Alloway's lands in 1754. The second stanza of Burns's 'Halloween' opens with 'countra folks' gathering

Amang the bonie, winding banks,
   Where *Doon* rins, wimplin, clear,   *meandering*
Where BRUCE ance rul'd the martial ranks,
   An' shook his *Carrick* spear . . .[52]

This terrain was, and is, historic. Alloway's old cobbled bridge, close to which William Burnes set up house, was perhaps erected in the early fifteenth century and was associated with Bishop James Kennedy, Chancellor of the University of St Andrews. You can still walk over the high, single-span Brig o' Doon and admire the river, its grassy, tree-lined banks flecked with wild flowers, a path on either side. Near the stone bridge is sixteenth-century Kirk Alloway, which had fallen into disrepair when Alloway became part of Ayr parish. The old kirk was used for baptisms until the mid-1750s, and William got together some Alloway villagers to tend its neglected churchyard, but his interests lay more with modern improvements than with restoration or antiquarianism; the church remained a ruin. As well as beginning his market-garden plans William also assisted Provost Fergusson of Doonholm in redesigning and improving his estate. Robert inherited something of his father's taste for improvement; as a farmer he would write in 1788 of having 'improvements to tend'.[53] Both he and his brother learned from their father a need to prize, if possible, some sense of self-worth and independence, even in what was essentially a position of social dependency. Gilbert was conscious his father had been 'servant' to a local landowner, but also that he had carried some degree of authority as 'Gardener and Overseer'.[54]

William Guthrie wrote of the Scottish climate as 'agreeable and healthy . . . moist and temperate', arguing 'Late experience has proved, that industry, and skilful agriculture, can render the soil of Scotland as fruitful as that of England.' He noted, however, that 'the inequality of the soil of Scotland is surprising'.[55] Commentators recognised farming was chancy. In another book Burns recalled from his boyhood, *The British Gardener's New Director*, the Scot Sir James Justice remarked, '*Our Situation not being so well adapted as other's to the Purposes of Vegetation, requires the Hand of Industry and Experience to forward its Improvements.*' William Burnes worked hard, but was all too aware of what Justice called '*the quick Transition of our Seasons, and the abrupt Manner in which they visit us*' in 'Scotland, *where the Seasons are sharp,*

attended with great Moistures, turbulent Winds, and chilling Blasts, from its Vicinity to the Western *and* Atlantic Oceans'.[56] Some of William's closest friends also worked the land, trying to improve it in the face of those *'chilling Blasts'*.

John Tennant of Glenconner, a man of William's generation, was recalled by Robert as 'a worthy, intelligent farmer, my father's friend and my own'; the Burnses knew this family well. Tennant combined farming with acting as factor for the Ochiltree estate owned by Elizabeth, Countess of Glencairn, mother of Burns's future patron Lord Glencairn.[57] William Burnes's connections were less aristocratic, but he too tried to balance working his land with toiling for the better-off. Though his 'New Gardens' did not prosper, and he reduced the extent of his feued ground, he was kept busy with landscape improvements for Provost Fergusson's expanding Doonholm estate. At home his young wife Agnes looked after what was left of the Gardens, now largely given over to a few cows and poultry.

Today owned by the National Trust for Scotland, the long, low Alloway house William built is deservedly the nation's most visited small home. The earliest picture of it dates from the early nineteenth century. In the gable wall of its living quarters, and halfway along the roof at the wall between them and the byre, chimneys protrude above the roofline. Refurbished several times, having long served as an inn, it curves along the line of an old road. William's single-storey structure has two rooms for people under its thatched roof – a living-room (sometimes called a parlour or 'spence') and a kitchen – with a door between them. A further door leads to barn and byre. The family spent most time in the kitchen area, warmed by the fire; opposite it, in a substantial recessed 'concealed bed', Agnes gave birth to Robert.[58] The family bed was soon full to capacity. The local midwife who attended Robert's birth was married to Alloway's blacksmith. It was probably he who formally witnessed the birth along with another local man.

The parish register also records Robert Burns's baptism by the Reverend William Dalrymple. Religion was crucially important in Burns's family. Recalling his father as 'a sober man who had read some and reflected much', Gilbert stressed William's 'plain good sense'.[59] Often the information we have about his family comes ultimately from Church of Scotland parish records. These indicate not just that William was of good character but also that he was 'admitted to partake of the Lord's Supper', meaning he took Christian

communion, ritually eating the bread and drinking the wine which symbolise the body and blood of Christ. William Burnes was a sincere believer eager to bring up his children in the Christian faith. Having his eldest son baptised by the parish minister was part of that.

This Kirk minister was one of the most important authority figures in Burns's young life. William Dalrymple was no bigot or fanatic but a well-educated man of liberal sympathies. Born in nearby Kilmarnock and educated at Glasgow University, he had ministered in Ayr for thirteen years before baptising Robert Burns. Later Dalrymple was awarded an honorary degree by the University of St Andrews and elected Moderator (leader) of the Church of Scotland. When Burns was eight Dalrymple preached a sermon on 'Christian Unity', arguing against small-minded, quarrelsome sectarianism and asking 'When shall the narrow, separating hedges of each party-contrivance be set aside, by the pure, healing spirit of Christian moderation . . . ?' Moderation was a word loved by the liberal Kirk ministers who played a crucial part in the Scottish Enlightenment.[60] Defending 'pure, disinterested goodness', and contending that the example of the early Church 'ought to teach Christians, to live together, as in the closest possible union of judgment and affection', Dalrymple pointed out how damaging were recent 'variances, emulations, strifes, heresies, in the church'. He urged 'great simplicity of language, and freedom from wrath' among believers, not least ministers themselves. 'It is the affixing of names to people, with a design to stigmatize, and render them suspected, that has sadly molested the peace of the church.' Emphasising 'the great law of love', Dalrymple maintained staunchly,

> there is no one thing in religion which can pretend to more evidence, or of which the Holy Ghost hath spoken with so great earnestness as that of charity or love; so every thing that seems to oppose, or counteract its influence, ought with the utmost care to be avoided.

He went on to say of religious zealots, 'if their zeal be without love, every thing else is gross delusion or hypocrisy, and hypocrisy extremely prejudicial to our common Christianity'.[61]

Strong aversion to hypocritical zealotry came from Burns's earliest Christian upbringing: from within, not outside, his Kirk. Gilbert remembered how the Burneses attended Sunday services at

Dalrymple's church in Ayr, today one of that town's most impressive historic riverside buildings. Sometimes after the service they would visit the family of a Latin-teacher friend, William Paterson, and borrow works like 'the *Spectator*' from his 'library'.[62] This is one of many indications that William Burnes was a man of intellectual ability, able to appreciate the company and conversation of formally educated men like Paterson, Dalrymple, and the precentor of Dalrymple's church, writing-teacher William Robinson. John Ramsay of Ochtertyre, with whom Burns discussed Dalrymple's influence, recorded that Burns's father 'was so pleased with [Dalrymple's] strain of preaching and benevolent conduct, that he embraced his religious opinions. But, his son added, that for all that he continued a Calvinist in practice.'[63] William was less liberal than his minister.

Dalrymple continued to matter to the adult Burns as an example of ideal Christian purity. He features in what Robert called 'The first of my poetic offspring that saw the light' ('The Holy Tulzie', a poem about a zealous religious quarrel) and in several other works including the later 'The Kirk of Scotland's Garland' where the voice of a zealot urges 'Calvin's sons' to 'seize your spiritual guns' and go after all and sundry:

> D'rymple mild, D'rymple mild, tho' your heart's like a child,
>   And your life's like the new-driven snaw;
> Yet that winna save ye, auld Satan maun have ye,
>   For preaching that three's ane and twa, &c.[64]

Burns the satirist was not mild, but showed long-lasting signs of admiration and support for Dalrymple's position. This minister, so influential on the Burns household that even Calvinistic William Burnes admired him, was concerned the poor should not be ignored in an age of 'improvement'. He liked to write plainly for 'parents, and teachers of youth in schools', presenting the Christian gospel 'for the use of the unlearned', and dedicating his *History of Christ* 'to the inhabitants of the town and parish of Ayr'. Dalrymple's *History* quotes an epigraph from his admired Dr Newcome: 'In the Gospels, we see God as it were face to face; we seem to converse with him as a man with his friend.'[65] Such idealising of friendly conversation would be important in Burns's poetry. Dalrymple had a particular interest in 'young minds' and liked to sustain 'wise, affectionate, Christian parents', maintaining that 'Our children

should be accustomed to repeat short scripture histories, as well as proverbs, and portions of sacred poetry.'[66] He was eager to promote the better-off to engage in 'short easy reading, on *Lord's Day Evenings*, to aid their *Household Servants*'. Burns's father seems to have done something like this, and a practice like it is celebrated in Burns's poem 'The Cotter's Saturday Night'. In Burns's childhood, and long after, Dalrymple argued,

> The holy Scripture was not given to men, especially Christians, that out of it they might confute and condemn one another in endless disputations. The design of it is, to promote *peace*; and from beginning to end breathes and inculcates mutual love, and forbearance.

A minister who got on well with local gentry, yet also visited '*from house to house*' in his parish over half a century, Dalrymple saw '*gospel truth*' as 'quite conducive to *human happiness*', and cited the Scottish Enlightenment philosopher Thomas Reid on Common Sense philosophy. Dalrymple maintained 'Christ Teacheth Self-Knowledge', pointing out that Christ's apostles, men of 'honest industry', were 'wisely chosen from low outward estate'. They were 'Men of *low rank*, with nothing to support them, but rather opposed by all'. Burns's imagination repeatedly gravitated towards such people, finding among them his closest Ayrshire friends. Dalrymple's Christ was 'an example of friendship'.[67]

Presenting to William Burnes and his young family an educated, liberal but committed moderate Presbyterianism which warned against hypocritical zealotry, championed love and friendship and was sympathetic to 'low rank', Dalrymple, as the most obvious figure of moral authority in Burns's local community, played a significant part in shaping Burns's views of conduct and religion. Throughout his poetry Burns would ridicule zealotry and hypocrisy among the 'unco guid and rigidly righteous'. He attributed anti-religious words to some speakers in his poetry; but he defended religious moderates and went through phases of intense, even disturbed immersion in theological argument, maintaining a sense of a God, however unknowable. More wild than mild, Burns recognised in Dalrymple purity of heart combined with straightforward human warmth: qualities he always valued. Dalrymple knew at first hand the sufferings his eighteenth-century parishioners routinely endured. He and his wife Susannah Hunter had lost two daughters in infancy. His

sister Sarah was the mother of Ayr lawyer Robert Aiken who became one of Burns's principal encouragers, and to whom Burns dedicated his poem of often heartfelt piety, 'The Cotter's Saturday Night'. In the Ayrshire community such close networks of relationship and patronage were not unusual; Dalrymple's influence on Burns, direct and indirect, was lifelong.

Burns's later defence of Dalrymple's moderate Ayr colleague, the Reverend William McGill, for what Burns mockingly called 'the blasphemous heresies of squaring Religion by the rules of Common Sense, and attempting to give a decent character to Almighty God and a rational account of his proceedings with the Sons of Men', was entirely in keeping with Dalrymple's theology.[68] McGill, whose later *Practical Essay on the Death of Jesus Christ* (1786) is dedicated to his 'dear colleague' Dalrymple, argued Christ's death was bound up with 'the plan of Divine wisdom and goodness for promoting the true happiness of man'. McGill sought to use 'the best principles of natural reason' alongside 'divine revelation' and saw humanity as created ultimately 'for happiness – happiness without end'. His God would punish 'the obstinately wicked', overlooking 'smaller blemishes'.[69] In a sermon preached when Burns was nine years old McGill stressed the importance of Christian unity, urging his congregation to 'bend their chief attention to the things in which they all agree, and which they themselves must allow to be of greatest importance, rather than to those in which they happen to differ'. He urged people to avoid 'affecting to distinguish themselves by insolent pretensions to orthodoxy of opinion (which is only paying a compliment to themselves at the expence of their brethren)'. They needed to show 'love to one another', not petty hostilities.[70] Like Dalrymple's, McGill's teaching formed the climate in which Burns developed. Dalrymple has a substantial memorial tablet on the outside wall of Ayr's Auld Kirk, beside a memorial to McGill, but when I visited in 2007 the inscription memorialising the man who baptised Burns was badly eroded, some of it no longer legible.

It is hard to exaggerate the extent to which religion was bound up with Burns's education. His early biographer, James Currie, wrote that Burns 'suffered by deviating from the precepts of his excellent father', though Currie admitted Burns never 'got quit of his religion'.[71] William Burnes was keen to have his children – particularly his sons – educated. Burns experienced boyhood 'enthusiastic, idiot piety. – I say idiot piety, because I was then but a child.'[72] This piety came

not just from authority figures around him, but also from books. Fisher's *English Grammar* regularly included scriptural histories, psalms, and other devotional works like Alexander Pope's 'The Universal Prayer', beginning,

> FATHER of all! in every Age,
> In ev'ry Clime ador'd,
> By Saint, by Savage, and by Sage,
> JEHOVAH, JOVE, or LORD!
>
> Thou great first Cause, least understood,
> Who all my Sense confin'd
> To know but this, that thou art good,
> And that myself am blind . . .

This same prayer was reprinted in another of Burns's influential schoolbooks, Arthur Masson's *A Collection of English Prose and Verse*. Mixing religious and secular work, such texts helped shape Burns's understanding of the world. His greatest editor, James Kinsley, indicates that a poem of Burns's copied out neatly in 1784, but perhaps written some years earlier, clearly follows in form and content Pope's 'Universal Prayer':

> O Thou unknown, Almighty Cause
> Of all my hope and fear!
> In whose dread Presence, ere an hour,
> Perhaps I must appear!

If Burns as a youth was guided by a poem from his very earliest reading, then the same poem by English Catholic Alexander Pope was consonant with the teaching of those Scottish Presbyterians Dalrymple and McGill in that it urged readers not to 'deal Damnation round the Land/ On each I judge thy Foe', but instead to show sympathy and mercy, treating all creation as existing to praise God.[73] As a mature poet Burns would cling to the image of a benign Creator, having little time for those who 'deal Damnation round the Land'.

The sentiments of the Ayr ministers' teaching and Pope's 'Universal Prayer' accord with much of what William Burnes, though a sterner Calvinist, wished to teach his children. Burns loved his father, but recalled him as combining deep knowledge of humanity with

'stubborn, ungainly Integrity, and headlong, ungovernable Irrasci-
billity'.[74] After William's death, Robert sometimes thought of him
with conflicting emotions. Usually, though, Burns remembered
friendly paternalism. William spoke to his sons a lot and during
Burns's boyhood went so far as to develop a manual of religious
belief in the form of a father-and-son dialogue. If this work sounds
to us formal or stilted, it may be worth remembering it was initiated
by a Scots-speaker who had learned to express himself in alien English
and who is conscious, even as 'Father' and 'Son' express clear affec-
tion for each other, that education is a serious matter:

> S. Dear father, you have often told me, while you were initiating
> me into the Christian religion, that you stood bound for me, to
> give me a Christian education, and recommend a religious life to
> me: I would therefore, if you please, ask you a few questions, that
> may tend to confirm my faith, and clear its evidences to me.
> F. My Dear child, with gladness I will resolve to you, (so far as I
> am able,) any question you shall ask; only with this caution, that
> you will beleive my answers, if they are founded in the word of
> God.
> Q. How shall I evidence to myself that there is a God?
> A. By the works of Creation; for nothing can make itself and this
> fabrick of nature demonstrates its creator to be possessed of all
> possible perfection, and for that cause we owe all that we have to
> him.[75]

Burns's father emphasised the power of Christ's message, including
its appeal to the scorned poor, and 'the wonderful progress of His
religion, in spite of all the power of the Roman Empire – and that
by means of his disciples, a few poor illiterate fishermen'.[76] This
instruction manual moves from being a dialogue to taking the form
of the sort of 'catechism' or question-and-answer book used by
Protestant churches in the eighteenth century and earlier. It accords
with theology Burns went on to read, like that of William Derham,
who argued that the world and the heavens were testimony to
their own divine creation, evidence for the existence of a benign
God.

Education, though, was not always benign. Gilbert recalled his
father occasionally using the rod; Robert remembered 'some thrash-
ings' at school.[77] Usually through friendly instruction, his father, his
minister and the community around him all encouraged the young

Burns to acquire a thorough knowledge of biblical stories, theo-
logical arguments and Christian knowledge. His poetry and letters
are full of evidence he did so to a remarkable degree. In adulthood
he quotes the Bible repeatedly, in addition to passages from poetry
at the heart of Protestant literary tradition: paraphrases of the Psalms.
When, for instance, Burns quotes from a 1720s psalm paraphrase
by Richard Daniel, Dean of Armagh, it is likely he is recalling
resolutely independent lines first encountered as a child:

> Tho' hungry Ruin has me in the Wind,
> Tho' *Saul*, avenging *Saul* should stalk behind,
> My fiercest Foes undaunted I'll abide,
> Thy Arm my Shield, thy Providence my Guide.[78]

This is the sort of material Burns's father approved of. But the person
who did most to educate the boy not just in reading sacred texts
and paraphrases, but also in his more general education was the
young man in whose clear hand William Burnes's manual of religious
belief survives in manuscript, Burns's outstanding early schoolteacher,
John Murdoch.

By the age of six Robert was enrolled in a local school at Alloway
Mill taught by William Campbell. Campbell, however, left after a
few weeks to become Master of Ayr's large Workhouse. With deter-
mination and support from local teacher friends, William Burnes
went to Ayr Grammar School in March 1765. There he approached
Murdoch who was 'improving in writing'. Murdoch was asked if
he might be engaged by Burnes and four neighbours to teach at
Alloway and board by turns with the pupils' five families. Just turned
eighteen, Murdoch had been educated in Ayr and Edinburgh. Inter-
viewing him at a local inn, William 'examined' his writing – another
signal the improving gardener was unflustered in matters of educa-
tion. Murdoch got the job, and found in Burns's father attributes
people would later detect in Robert: 'He always treated superiors
with a becoming respect, but he never gave the smallest encour-
agement to aristocratical arrogance ... He spoke the English
language with more propriety (both with respect to diction and
pronunciation) than any man I ever knew, with no greater advan-
tages. This had a very good effect on the boys, who began to talk
and reason like men much sooner than their neighbours.'[79]
Suddenly Murdoch, an ambitious teenager, was in charge of a

school. Over twenty years later, writing to Burns from London, he recalled details brought back through his reading of Burns's poetry.[80] The youthful teacher began teaching the boys at Alloway in May 1765, probably around the time he penned the fair copy of William Burnes's short manual of religious instruction. Murdoch seems to have encouraged memory development through repetition. Gilbert recalled he would make his pupils copy out advice such as *custom makes things familiar and easy*.[81] Murdoch regarded Robert and Gilbert as his best Alloway pupils and his teaching confirmed Robert as a lifelong voracious reader.[82] Later Murdoch explained his teaching methods, indicating he worked closely with William and that the Old and New Testaments were used alongside texts like Masson's *Collection of English Prose and Verse* and Fisher's *English Grammar*.

> They committed to memory the hymns and other poems of that collection with uncommon facility. This facility was partly owing to the method pursued by their father and me in instructing them, which was, to make them thoroughly acquainted with the meaning of every word in each sentence that was to be committed to memory. By the bye, this may be easier done and at an earlier period, than is generally thought. As soon as they were capable of it, I taught them to turn verse into its natural prose order, sometimes to substitute synonimous expressions for poetical words and to supply all the ellipses. These, you know, are the means of knowing that the pupil understands his author. These are excellent helps to the arrangement of words in sentences, as well as to a variety of expression.[83]

These are ambitious ways to teach boys of seven or eight, but William Burnes was an ambitious father, Murdoch an ambitious teacher. His methods were designed to promote deep learning and thorough understanding as well as conveying a body of knowledge and developing memory. Robert recalled being a tenacious child with a 'retentive memory'.[84] He remembered passages of prose and verse from Masson's *Collection* for the rest of his life, sometimes quoting them in letters. Gilbert went with his older brother to be taught by Murdoch how to read and write English, rather than the Scots the boys would have spoken informally:

> I was too young to profit much from his lessons in grammar, but Robert made some proficiency in it, a circumstance of considerable

weight in the unfolding of his genius and character; as he soon became remarkable for the fluency and correctness of his expression, and read the few books that came in his way with much pleasure and improvement; for even then he was a reader when he could get a book.[85]

Burns, then, from an early age was an eager reader with a flair for language, and was able to express himself in English as well as Scots. This bi-cultural upbringing gave him access equally to the vernacular heritage of song and folk-tale strong in his mother's family, and to that world of 'improvement' of which his father was part and whose language was formal English. For Murdoch 'Pronunciation' was 'the first thing to be attended to in teaching a living language'; he taught Burns to speak English with a 'correctness' that surprised others.[86] Murdoch had a sense of humour and a good ear for verse. His system of teaching also encouraged Burns to understand how poetry and prose were constructed, and to think about differences between them in structure and vocabulary, even if Murdoch seems to imply an idea of poetry as characterised by un-idiomatic word order, 'on account of the verse'.[87] Like Burns's father, he saw education and morality as bound together:

> ... in proportion as METHOD is attended to in the education of youth, they not only make progress in learning, but also in virtuous habits. If the love of REGULARITY, ORDER or METHOD, and the love of VIRTUE, be not quite synonimous terms, it must at least be allowed that they are nearly allied, and that the transition from the one to the other is easy. There are but few methodical men, comparatively speaking, who are either very foolish or very vicious: whereas, those who are unmethodical, and indifferent about ORDER and REGULARITY are, in general, the pests of human society.[88]

From this demanding teacher who thought, when it came to 'church-music', Robert's 'ear ... was remarkably dull, and his voice untunable', Burns learned a lot.[89]

The young Robert's first experiments with rhyme took place in his early schooldays. None survives; they may never have been written down. Burns called them 'crambo-jingle' – a distinctively jokey Scots term for rhyme. He implies his first interest in rhyme had a clearly Scots accent, even though it occurred when he was being taught by Murdoch to relish the beauties of English. This was no mere gesture of linguistic rebellion; Burns loved and learned from English-language

poetry, and went on to write it. But his crambo-jingling confirms his bi-culturalism, and signals independent-mindedness. Spelling written language in correct English, he crooned to himself in Scots. He remembered this years later in a verse letter of April 1785 to a self-taught poet friend:

> But first an' foremost, I should tell,
> Amaist as soon as I could spell,
> I to the *crambo-jingle* fell,
>   Tho' rude an' rough,
> Yet crooning to a body's sel,
>   Does weel eneugh.[90]

This notion of private 'crooning', of a tune as bound up with the origins of a poem, links verse to song, indicating that in early child-hood Burns developed what later became 'invariably my way' of composing a Scots song:

> . . . untill I am compleat master of a tune, in my own singing, (such as it is) I can never compose for it. – My way is: I consider the poetic Sentiment, correspondent to my idea of the musical expression; then chuse my theme; begin one Stanza; when that is composed, which is generally the most difficult part of the business, I walk out, sit down now & then, look out for objects in Nature around me that are in unison or harmony with the cogitations of my fancy & workings of my bosom; humming every now & then the air with the verses I have framed: when I feel my Muse beginning to jade, I retire to the solitary fireside of my study, & there commit my effusions to paper; swinging, at intervals, on the hind-legs of my elbow-chair, by way of calling forth my own critical strictures, as my pen goes on. –[91]

This account of song composition describes Burns's adult practice – the boy poet had neither a study nor his own elbow chair – but confirms what accounts by Gilbert and others suggest: Burns composed orally and in his head before putting words on paper. His boyhood private crooning of 'rude an' rough' rhymes preceded by some years the making of his first extant song.

Oral culture, then, was vital to Burns from his beginnings as a poet, but books mattered too. When it came to imaginative writing, the young Burns was excited by what he read:

The earliest thing of Composition that I recollect taking pleasure in was, The vision of Mirza and a hymn of Addison's beginning – 'How are Thy servants blest, O Lord!' I particularly remember one half-stanza which was music to my boyish ear –

> 'For though in dreadful whirls we hung,
> 'High on the broken wave' –

I met with these pieces in Mas[s]on's English Collection, one of my school-books.[92]

These pieces which Burns recalled twenty years or so later were accompanied in Masson's book by a variety of psalm paraphrases, religious accounts of 'ancient bards', paeans to 'liberty', wartime Addisonian denunciations of 'haughty *Gaul*' (a phrase Burns would recycle decades afterwards) and of 'Nations of slaves, with tyranny debas'd'. Here ballads mixed with an old man's poem called 'The Horn-book', Shakespearian speeches with extracts from Milton's *Paradise Lost* about 'The spirit of love, and amorous delight' and other matters.[93] Masson included almost no Scottish authors other than the James Thomson of *The Seasons* and the John Home of a recently published Highland drama, *Douglas*. Both became favourites with Burns. *Douglas* was 'the first tragedy I ever saw performed', and there are many quotations from *The Seasons* in his letters. Thomson in Masson hymned the natural world, created by the 'Great Shepherd', as well as idealising a country girl like 'Lavinia' – a name Gilbert Burns would bestow on an early girlfriend; in Masson's book Thomson's Lavinia lives 'in a cottage, far retir'd/ Among the windings of a woody vale'; a young countryman falls in love with her at harvest.[94] However idealised, such poetry contained scenes recognisable to Burns and his brother growing up in rural Ayrshire. By the year of his death one of Burns's own poems was included in a 'new and much enlarged edition' of Masson's *Collection*, published by local printers J. and P. Wilson in Ayr.

While Masson presented nothing in the Scots tongue, his book provided in capsule form an introduction to English authors and a celebration of the power of poetry. Both Addison passages Burns singled out deal with religious anxiety. In the prose 'Vision of Mirza', set in ancient Baghdad, the speaker visualises life as a thronged bridge between clouds. Murdoch probably made his pupils memorise parts of Masson's book: over twenty years after reading this passage at

school, Burns could quote its opening almost verbatim; it is also contained in a Burnes family volume of the *Spectator*.[95] From Addison's Baghdad bridge people vanish into an abyss below, plunging through trapdoors that open up under their feet. Years afterwards, Burns recalled this disturbing image, exclaiming, 'What hidden trap-doors of disaster . . . waylay, & beset our paths of life!'[96] Vertiginous imaginings gripped him as a boy. In Addison's hymn, 'How are thy servants blest, O Lord!' the saving power of God is celebrated but the 'affrighted' speaker dwells with imaginative excitement on the horrors of life imaged as 'waves on waves, and gulphs on gulphs' of a tempestuous sea:

> For tho' in dreadful whirls we hung
> High on the broken wave,
> I knew thou wert not slow to hear,
> Nor impotent to save.[97]

Both these passages which so struck the young Burns are about the fear of absolute loss. Their impression on a child in an Ayrshire where, for all the expressions of 'moderate' theology, Calvinists argued that God had preordained many to eternal damnation, may foreshadow Burns's later depressive episodes, not to mention his religious crisis and breakdown.

If some passages in Masson's school text were excitingly scary, others reinforced a sense of self-worth. Burns seems to have attended Murdoch's school six days a week, so there was plenty of time for reading. Masson's was a Whiggish book, presenting fables where kings might be elected and 'first places' in society 'bestowed where there is most merit'. It showed episodes from history where Roman emperors were got rid of, and where King Canute came to reflect that on earth 'none truly deserved the name of king' except God: 'earthly royalty [is] nothing else than poor contemptible vanity'.[98] In Masson's anthology a king longs 'to know what a rural life is', and when a shepherd eventually rises to a position as a courtier he values nothing so much as his former life. Christ's apostles, we are reminded in one of several abridged Bible stories, 'invited all sorts of people without distinction', while Shakespeare's Cardinal Wolsey is quoted reflecting on 'ruin' and on 'how wretched/ Is that poor man, that hangs on princes favours!'[99] The noble speech of a Roman Consul argues,

'My poverty does not lessen the weight and influence of my counsels in the senate', continuing,

> What value then can I put upon your gold and silver? What king can add any thing to my fortune? always attentive to discharge the duties incumbent on me: I have a mind free from SELF-REPROACH, and I have an HONEST FAME.[100]

Such praise of honest poverty underpins Burns's subsequent work. In Masson's selected extracts from the *Spectator* magazine, he read how sometimes people might aspire to positions for which they were not fitted; many a man might struggle to be a minister 'who might have done his country excellent service at a plough tail'. Burns also read about the value of education and how 'The philosopher, the saint, or the hero, the wise, the good, or great man, very often lie hid and concealed in a plebeian, which a proper education might have disinterred and brought to light.' Encouraged by his father and Murdoch, Burns strove to bring to light his better self through intensive reading. He may also have been affected by the floridly emotional letters 'Moral and Entertaining' by Mrs Rowe which Masson anthologised. Supposedly penned by correspondents like 'Diana' and 'Rosalinda', these rejoice in rhetorically supercharged emotionalism:

> It is impossible for me to express the present disposition of my soul, the vast uncertainty I am struggling with: no words can paint the force and vivacity of my apprehensions; every doubt wears the face of horror, and would perfectly overwhelm me, but for some faint gleams of hope, which dart across the tremendous gloom. What tongue can utter the anguish of a soul suspended between the extremes of infinite joy or eternal misery? I am throwing my last stake for eternity, and tremble and shudder for the important event.

This was volatile stuff for a little boy. With its tempestuously lingering parting scenes ('For ever now I turn my eyes from you'), Mrs Rowe's rhetoric can seem to prefigure later excitedly amorous and despairingly self-dramatising moments in Burns's correspondence.[101]

Another passage from Masson which impressed him was from Mark Akenside's recent poem *The Pleasures of Imagination* where Akenside writes how God

43

tells the heart,
He meant, he made us to behold and love
What he beholds and loves, the general orb
Of life and being; to be great like him,
Beneficent and active.

Akenside's beneficent God, milder than Calvin's, gives man his sense
of artistic taste 'when first his active hand/ Imprints the secret bias of
the soul'.[102] Burns would quote that passage from memory in a letter
two decades later, and Akenside's phrasing undergirds part of the last
stanza of Burns's 'Address to the Unco Guid, or the Rigidly Right-
eous' when he writes of God's relationship with man's innermost being,

Who made the heart, 'tis *He* alone
Decidedly can try us,
He knows each chord its various tone,
Each spring its various bias . . .[103]

Here in the 1780s Burns went on to express man's relationship with
God in terms of what Dryden, in another poem in Masson's anthology,
calls 'The Power of Music'. Burns had heard singing since earliest
infancy; its hold on him strengthened, even if Murdoch didn't notice.

Learning to read gave Burns access not only to schoolbooks, but
also to private reading for pleasure. Gilbert recalled that Murdoch
from his own small library lent his brother '*The Life of Hannibal*,
which was the first book he read, (the school books excepted) and
almost the only one he had an opportunity of reading while he was
at school'.[104] By this Gilbert seems to mean Burns read the book
privately during the period of education at Alloway which ended
when Robert was nearly ten. By then the family was living at Mount
Oliphant, two miles south-east of Alloway, on a seventy-acre farm
William Burnes had leased from his employer Provost Fergusson in
late 1765. Moving to this farm in 1766 gave the Burneses a larger
house and avoided William's being obliged to hire out Robert as an
agricultural labourer. However, after dwelling at Alloway on his
own land, William was now (as he would for the rest of his life)
living as someone else's tenant. Mount Oliphant needed much
improving. Burns's father was unable to offload the cottage and
ground at Alloway, which caused financial anxieties.

Unsignposted, Mount Oliphant's farm buildings still survive.
Considerably modified since Burns's time, they are on a single-track

road surrounded by green fields and birdsong. The view east towards the sea is expansively beautiful. In Burns's day the 138-foot-high spire of Ayr's Tolbooth, St John's Tower, and the Wallace Tower would have been striking landmarks. South-east towards the Heads of Ayr lay gentle hills and small farms. Even now the elevated situation of Mount Oliphant is far enough beyond major roads for you to imagine Burns growing up there, walking down through the farms to Alloway, or further inland over the hill to nearby Purclewan Mill. In winter, though, Mount Oliphant's farm buildings look scrummed down against the elements. Built round three sides of a square, they back on to winds from the west. The farmhouse was only slightly bigger than the Alloway cottage. Downstairs was a main room and kitchen; above these, under what was probably a slate roof, Burns shared the windowless attic with his three brothers. On the several occasions Murdoch visited the family between 1766 and 1768 he too slept up there. Privacy was hard to come by, but Burns sought it out, especially when he wanted to read.

He recalled the Hannibal biography with glee as one of 'The two first books I ever read in private, and which gave me more pleasure than any two books I ever read again'. 'Translated from the French of Mr Dacier', *The Life of Hannibal* was in keeping with Murdoch's interest in French literature, but for Burns it had more immediate excitements. A story of 'oppressions and tyranny', it begins with nine-year-old Hannibal swearing an oath to his father to 'be an implacable enemy to the *Romans*' as the Carthaginians fight imperial domination. A heroic fighter who experiences an inspiring vision, fights for 'freedom' and urges his men to '*conquer or die*', Hannibal comes from a distinctive speech community: 'the *Carthaginians* pronounced the *Latin* words but ill'. Though ultimately a figure of 'ruin' who commits suicide after '*great reverse of fortune*' when 'all his affairs were on the decline', Hannibal, cleaving to his implacable hatred of Rome, is also an exciting soldier, leading troops and elephants across the Alps to attack his imperial enemies.[105]

Burns would later have Robert the Bruce rousingly urge his troops to 'DO – or DIE!!!' for Scottish freedom in their war for independence.[106] More mockingly he would warn one of William Dalrymple's ecclesiastical opponents (in the context of a dispute over parish boundaries), 'Hannibal's just at your gates'.[107] In boyhood *The Life of Hannibal* was exciting because, more than just a book to read, it was a story to play at: 'Hannibal gave my young ideas such a

turn that I used to strut in raptures up and down after the recruiting drum and bagpipe, and wish myself tall enough to be a soldier'.[108] Burns would have seen recruiters in Ayr when he went there with his father, crossing the Auld Brig, still today a sizeable stone foot-bridge, to enter the town near the High Street. The notion of joining the British army even as his imagination was excited by the figure of a great rebel would recur to Burns in later years; mention of 'recruiting drum and bagpipe' signals that even when the country was not actually at war in Burns's childhood, it was actively seeking Ayrshire examples of Scottish martial valour for its regiments.

Gilbert maintained his brother read about William Wallace 'some years afterwards'. Robert, though, linked reading about Hannibal to reading about the heroic, doomed Scottish freedom fighter, recalling Wallace's life as the other of those first two books read in private. 'The story of Wallace poured a Scottish prejudice in my veins which will boil along there till the flood-gates of life shut in eternal rest.'[109] 'Scots, wha hae wi' Wallace bled' begins one of Burns's most famous songs. His admiration for Wallace was lifelong. In 1787 he 'kneel'd at the tomb of Sir John the Graham, the gallant friend of the immortal WALLACE', but this genuflection continued earlier devotions dating back to childhood.[110] He recalled to an Ayrshire descendant of the Wallace family how

The first books I met with in my early years, which I perused with pleasure, were, the lives of Hannibal, and Sir William Wallace. – For several of my earlier years, I had few other Authors; and many a solitary hour have I stole out, after the laborious vocations of the day, to shed a tear over their glorious, but unfortunate Story. – In those boyish days, I remember in particular, being much struck with that part of Wallace' [sic] history where these lines occur –

'Syne to the Leglen wood when it was late
'To make a silent and a safe retreat' –

I chose a fine summer Sunday, the only day of the week in my power, and walked half a dozen miles to pay my respects to the 'Leglen wood,' with as much devout enthusiasm as ever Pilgrim did to Loretto; and as I explored every den and dell where I could suppose my heroic Countryman to have sheltered, I recollect (for even then I was a Rhymer) that my heart glowed with a wish to make a Song on him equal to his merits. –[111]

This pilgrimage is one of many signs of the impact his early reading made on Burns. Gilbert recalled Robert borrowing William Hamilton of Gilbertfield's 1722 updating of Blind Hary's late medieval epic *Wallace* from 'the blacksmith who shod our horses', Henry McCandlish. Henry's bright son James was, Robert said, 'the earliest friend except my only brother that I have on earth'.[112] The same age as Robert, James lived at Purclewan, a hamlet about a mile beyond Mount Oliphant. The two boys used to play together, probably mischievously, given Burns's later biblical phrasing when, aged twenty-eight, he wrote to his 'ever dear old acquaintance' (then completing medical studies at Glasgow University), assuring him, 'I am still, in the apostle Paul's phrase, "The old man with his deeds" as when we were sporting about the Lady thorn.'[113] 'The old man with his deeds' is the unregenerate self which, St Paul writes, the reborn Christian must outgrow. Renowned for having 'a stubborn, sturdy something in my disposition', Burns as a child had a naughty side. Murdoch, however, thought it was 'Gilbert's face said "Mirth, with thee I mean to live," and certainly, if any person who knew the two boys had been asked which of them was the most likely to court the muses, he would surely never have guessed that Robert had a propensity of that kind.'[114]

Murdoch knew the young Burns well, but when, years later in London, he read Robert's poems, he wrote to his former pupil that at first 'I was not absolutely certain that you were the author'.[115] Probably Robert, like most boys, showed different aspects of himself to his schoolfriends and to his teacher. An apparently serious-minded little boy borrowed *The Life of Hannibal* from Murdoch; a more playful, excited lad strutted up and down after the recruiting drum and bagpipe, or went sporting in the fields with his best pal, James.

Whether Burns read Hamilton's *Life and Heroick Actions of the Renoun'd Sir William Wallace, General and Governour of Scotland* at the same time as he read about Hannibal or a little later, in his memory and imagination the two were connected. Hamilton's verse account, written, like many of Burns's later poems, in English inflected with Scots words, tells how 'our ancestors, brave true ancient Scots' fought for their freedom against 'the Southron' – the English who try to defeat and rule Scotland. Where Hannibal urged his men to 'conquer or die', Hamilton's Wallace fought to 'win or die'. Here was a Hannibal from Burns's own nation, even from his

own backyard. William Hamilton was an Ayrshireman; his *Wallace* is full of mentions of places local to Burns – not just 'the pleasant ancient town of Ayr' (featured repeatedly and scene of several Wallace exploits), but also Craigie, Irvine Water, Laigland wood, Ochter house, Loudon Hill, Richardtoun (Riccarton), Mauchline muir, Kyle, Cunningham, Carrick, Auchinleck, Arran, Cumnock, Dalswintoun, Dumfries.[116]

Wallace to Burns was a local as well as national hero. Burns was a boy in Wallace territory. His father worked with a man called William Wallace; Ayrshire families claimed descent from the hero. In Burns's boyhood a new area of Ayr, Wallacetown, was being laid out; Burns mentions Ayr's Wallace Tower clock in his poetry. A 'Wallace's Stone' stands not far from Alloway. Reintroduced to poetry by William Hamilton, Wallace in the eighteenth as in other centuries was a Scottish cultural icon. Not a royal figure, he was seen as a popular leader striving for his people's right to self-government. Hamilton's *Wallace* was enormously popular because it loudly and confidently asserted Scottish distinctiveness and independence. Guthrie's *Geographical, Historical, and Commercial Grammar*, alert to 'the disputed point, how far Scotland was benefited by its union with England', mentioned 'brave William Wallace, the truest hero of his age', before contending that after 1707's Union of Parliaments 'the history of Scotland becomes the same with that of England'.[117] Hamilton of Gilbertfield, however, implied that Wallace's heroic past might inspire present-day Scots. This poem, little known today, but read across the eighteenth-century Scottish nation, was the *Braveheart* of Burns's boyhood. It schooled him as a Scottish and an Ayrshire patriot, showing how his own locality could be made classic ground in verse.

Hamilton's Wallace sees a vision in which 'Quickly to him descended there a queen,/ All shining bright, and with majestic mien'. She draws a saltire on Wallace's face. In a scene parodying old legends of Coilus, King of Kyle, Wallace is mockingly called 'king of Kyle'. Burns in his own mid-1780s poem 'The Vision' encounters Coila, spirit of Kyle, who wears a mantle on which the local terrain is depicted.[118] This is the landscape of the rivers Doon, Irvine and Ayr, and especially of the 'ancient BOROUGH' of Ayr whose race of heroes is presented in conflict with 'Their Suthron foes'. At the head of this race stands 'His COUNTRY'S SAVIOUR', identified by Burns in a note: 'William Wallace'.[119] No doubt, writing to

correspondents who claimed Wallace descent, Burns later played up his devotion to Wallace's memory, but the hero of Hamilton's poem mattered to him. He points out that in the concluding stanza of 'Scots, wha hae' he has

borrowed the last stanza from the common Stall edition of Wallace –

> 'A false usurper sinks in every foe,
> And liberty returns with every blow' –

These lines from Hamilton's *Wallace* become in Burns's poem

> Lay the proud Usurpers low!
> Tyrants fall in every foe!
> LIBERTY's in every blow!
> Forward! Let us DO, or DIE!!![120]

This is an important indicator of the continuing presence of Hamilton's poem in Burns's imagination decades after he first read it. A subtler, more diffused effect of the *Wallace* was that it showed Burns how names of local places and local landscape might become part of printed poetry with a popular impact, poetry mixing English and Scots words. He was too young to learn this lesson immediately, but his youthful pilgrimage shows how strongly he linked the Ayrshire poet's *Wallace* to his local landscape.

The move to Mount Oliphant in spring 1766 meant Robert and Gilbert walked two miles downhill to school in Alloway six days a week, and two miles back, uphill. This was hardly arduous by eighteenth-century standards, but Mount Oliphant was further from Ayr than Alloway, and felt more isolated than their previous home. Gilbert recalled 'we rarely saw any body but the members of our own family. There were no boys of our own age, or near it, in the neighbourhood.' This may have served to intensify Robert's reading habits, but the farm was also a struggle. In bad weather its hillside location was rainswept, windswept, bleak. Gilbert, later a seasoned professional farmer, called the ground 'almost the very poorest soil I know of in a state of cultivation'.[121] His father had taken out a lease lasting until 1777 and was probably paying over the odds for it. He had also had to borrow £100 from Provost Fergusson to attempt essential improvements; for William this was a substantial sum. It began to look unlikely that he could repay it.

So when in early 1768 John Murdoch obtained a position as a teacher in Dumfries, Burnes's sons ceased to attend Alloway school and started work on the farm. Robert was nine. He did light work only at this stage; his father did the heavy stuff, not having enough money to hire outside labour. William Burnes worked hard. In April 1767 he got permission from Provost Fergusson to carry away stones from Mount Oliphant farm 'to repair your houses at Alloway' – more improvements.[122] William needed his sons' help, but did not wish their schooling to be abandoned. He taught Robert, Gilbert, Agnes and Annabella 'arithmetic in the winter evenings, by candle-light, and in this way', Gilbert wrote in the late 1790s, 'my two elder sisters got all the education they received'.[123] William also did his best for his sons. Often he spoke to them as if they were adults, treating them as what Burns later called their 'Parental FRIEND'.[124] The brothers had to grow up quickly. Their intellectual maturity was quickened by William's attitude, as Gilbert sensed:

> My father was for some time almost the only companion we had. He conversed familiarly on all subjects with us as if we had been men, and was at great pains while we accompanied him in the labours of the farm, to lead the conversation to such subjects as might tend to encrease our knowledge, or confirm us in virtuous habits.[125]

Robert later recalled William as a man 'advanced in life when he married' who, 'worn out by early hardship' grew 'unfit for labour'. William needed his children's help, but was not the sort of person to do anything to discourage his bookish eldest son from reading. Robert recalled of his own childhood that 'against the years of ten or eleven, I was absolutely a Critic in substantives, verbs and particles'.[126] This was Murdoch's doing. Before the schoolteacher left for Dumfries in 1768 he visited the Burnes household, bringing two presents: 'a small compendium of English Grammar, and the tragedy of *Titus Andronicus*'. This horrifically violent play was an odd gift for small boys. Perhaps Murdoch thought its gore would appeal. He began to read it aloud to the assembled family, but they all began to cry. When he reached the part in the second act where one of the characters has her hands cut off and her tongue cut out, the family asked him to stop. Murdoch suggested he might leave the play with them. Robert threatened to burn it if it remained at Mount Oliphant. This anecdote suggests Robert was then rather like his

father, 'the sport of strong passions'.[127] Remembering Robert's behaviour on this occasion, Gilbert recalled, 'My father was going to chide him for this ungrateful return to his tutor's kindness; but Murdoch interfered, declaring that he liked to see so much sensibility; and he left *The School for Love,* a comedy (translated I think from the French) in its place.'[128]

Clearly Murdoch expected these boys to cope with adult reading matter. This episode shows how emotionally Burns reacted to imaginative works in an age when sensibility could be valued as highly as sense; his weeping and outburst at *Titus Andronicus* is of a piece with his shedding tears over Hamilton's *Wallace,* or with his later recorded emotional reactions to books and works of art. The play Murdoch left instead of *Titus Andronicus* indicates the tutor's taste for French literature, and for drama. Based on a French original by Bernard de Fontenelle, *The School for Lovers* was a 1762 comedy, recently performed in Drury Lane. Its title page proclaimed it 'By William Whitehead, Esq; POET LAUREAT'. Verse prologues prefacing this prose play refer laughingly to *'our Bard'*, a joke Burns would later repeat. The comedy's 'Men of the Town', Modely and Belmour, subscribe to a code of honour different from that of William Burnes. If this play gave precocious hints to nine-year-old Robert how to 'act the lover', with its 'agreeable rascal', 'deceiver', and comedy of 'pretended marriage' and 'Sympathetic feelings', it also introduced him to the flirtatious repartee of contemporary theatre where a character might justify himself by claiming

> A heart like mine its *own* distress contrives,
> And feels *most* sensibly the pain it gives;
> Then even its frailties candidly approve,
> For, if it errs, it errs from too much love.[129]

As an adult, Robert Burns, sometimes behaving like a transplanted Man of the Town, might often seem to err from too much love. Affording such early access to '*the* LOVER'S SCHOOL' of contemporary London theatricals, Mount Oliphant was not quite as isolated as has sometimes been assumed.

Though for the time being they lost their teacher, William Burnes was keen to give his sons reading matter more suitable for home-schooling. Still, the boys felt deprived of educational possibilities that went with a community of schoolfriends. Writing an account

of his life at the age of twenty-five, Gilbert allows momentary expression to his sense of lost opportunities: 'Thus were we early excluded from the benefits of a public school which is allowed on all hands to give an early knowledge of the world and consequently make one act there [*sic*] part with more freedom at their first entrance.'[130] Though his boyhood friend James McCandlish (later Candlish) went on to study at Glasgow University, this never seems to have been a possibility for Burns. His surviving remarks indicate at times resentful suspicion of 'college classes'. Quite possibly, university would have ruined him, pressuring him away from his Scots vernacular background, encouraging him to purify his language. In any case, the fledgling poet was not without books, and Gilbert maintained his father 'had the best method of educating children I think of any man I ever knew'.[131] William had friends with good libraries, while William Dalrymple, schoolteacher David Tennant, and other men William befriended belonged to 'Air Library Society', founded in 1762. Probably he had access to its books. Gilbert recorded,

> He borrowed *Salmon's Geographical Grammar* for us, and endeavoured to make us acquainted with the situation and history of the different countries in the world; while from a book-society in Ayr, he procured for us the reading of *Derham's Phisico and Astro-theology*, and *Ray's Wisdom of God in the Creation*, to give us some idea of astronomy and natural history. Robert read all these books with an avidity and industry scarcely to be equalled. My father had been a subscriber to *Stackhouse's History of the Bible*, then lately published by James Meuros in Kilmarnock; from this Robert collected a competent knowledge of ancient history; for no book was so voluminous as to slacken his industry, or so antiquated as to damp his researches.[132]

Throughout boyhood and youth Burns read constantly, often piously. In Thomas Stackhouse's *New History of the Holy Bible, from the Beginning of the World, to the Establishment of Christianity* he would have learned how 'When Natural Religion . . . prov'd ineffectual to make Men truly religious' in ancient times, God, like a nurse changing a patient's diet, 'instituted the *Christian*'.[133] Burns read many religious works, but their contents went beyond what we might now think of as theology. The whole natural world, William Derham informed him, was a '*Physico-Theology*' providing '*a Demonstration of the Being and Attributes of God*'. Not just the starry heavens but even 'field mice . . . hiding their food before-hand

against winter' might demonstrate 'the great Creator's providence', so that as John Ray, Fellow of the Royal Society, put it in *The Wisdom of God Manifested in the Works of the Creation*, 'provision ... is made for the preservation and security of weak and timorous creatures'.[134] Burns would go on to write of his own wee, sleekit, timorous creature. Reading writers like Ray taught him to find moral lessons among even the unlikeliest beasties:

> ... I cannot but look upon the strange instinct of this noisome and troublesome creature a louse, of searching out foul and nasty cloathes to harbour and breed in, as an effect of divine providence, designed to deter men and women from sluttishness and sordidness, and to provoke them to cleanliness and neatness. God himself hateth uncleanliness, and turns away from it, as appears by Deut. xxiii. 12, 13, 14. But if God requires and is pleased with bodily cleanliness, much more is he so with the pureness of the mind, *Blessed are the pure in heart, for they shall see God*, Mat. v. 10.[135]

Later in 'To a Louse' Burns's moral would be a little different, but he too would link his louse to Divine Power, preaching a memorable sermon on it. Gilbert remembered that their father knew some 'Natural Philosophy, Astronomy' and 'Geography', and 'encouraged us to read on these subjects and make our observations to which he shewed so much defference and treated us so much like his equals and like men that we became very fond of his company and whatever study he recommended was pursued with eagerness.'[136] William was not always an easy man. In 1771 he seems to have been involved in legal wrangles with 'Robert Kennedy and William Campbell'.[137] Nevertheless, he set aside every Sunday evening to speak with his sons about religion. His tastes had moulded Burns's early non-fiction reading. This and his father's theological conversation must have encouraged a view of the natural creation as providing proof of the Creator's wisdom. Burns's religious reading increased in his later teens until it became obsessive. Later he was very wary of 'the wild-goose heights of Calvinistic Theology' but, for all his scepticism and doubts, he went on believing in God.[138] Looking back on boyhood, youth and 'a few vices of manhood' in his mid-thirties, 'still', he wrote, 'I congratulate myself on having had in early days religion strongly impressed on my mind.'[139]

Though at this time most of their education was supplied through

William Burnes, the boys picked up a little additional schooling. In the summer of 1772 or '73, as Gilbert recalled, their father, worried about the way they wrote, sent them to the parish school in the village of Dalrymple in alternate summer weeks. It seems during his few weeks at this school Robert befriended James McCandlish. On the banks of the Doon, further upstream than Alloway, Dalrymple was less than a couple of miles' walk from Mount Oliphant, which lies a little north of it. Cassilis, known to Burns from balladry and local folklore, is near Dalrymple Wood, again beside the Doon. Not far off are the ancient ruined Abbey of Crossraguel and several abandoned castles. It was beautiful, historic countryside to grow up in, and Burns got to know it well.

These few weeks at school may have improved their writing and introduced them to friends, but the two older Burns boys learned more from their father and his circle. A local gardener, probably another of William Burnes's 'improving' friends, lent them an English history book concentrating on the reigns of James I and Charles I. A 'bookish acquaintance of my father's', wrote Gilbert, 'procured us a reading of two volumes of Richardson's *Pamela*, which was the first novel we read'.[140] With its subtitle, *Virtue Rewarded*, Richardson's novel was in a sense suitable reading for William Burnes's household. Still, the Kirk was often suspicious of fiction, and modern readers may wonder just what Robert made of Richardson's account of the attempted seduction and rape of a fifteen-year-old girl, Pamela, by 'Mr B.' Presented entirely through letters and journals, *Pamela* has at times a hothouse sexuality. Eventually Pamela marries her would-be rapist and all ends happily, but the novel is powered by extreme emotionalism, sexual deceit and protestations of love: a striking introduction to prose fiction for young boys, one at least of whom would grow into a master of seduction.

Pamela too was part of Burns's school for lovers. Though he later lost something of his enthusiasm for Richardson, Burns stated that this English novelist's characters might 'captivate the unexperienced, romantic fancy of a boy'.[141] Another work he sampled around this time was Tobias Smollett's *Adventures of Ferdinand Count Fathom*. Smollett's novel presents an energetically drawn portrait of a roguish seducer whose repeated triumphs over female virtue are celebrated with authorial gusto until, eventually, the Count 'has recourse to the matrimonial noose'.[142] That Burns was unable to get hold of all Smollett's tale suggests it was not a work

his father had recommended for educational purposes. As he grew up, though, Burns became a fan of this Scottish novelist's work. He later ordered Smollett's fiction for his own library. His literary tastes were forming at the start of his teens.

In 1772 John Murdoch moved back into the neighbourhood as English teacher at Ayr's burgh school. He was now more mature. Authoritative modern print and digital scholarship presents him as the John Murdoch who had published the previous year a translation of Turin Professor of Eloquence and Belles Lettres Carlo Denina's *Essay on the Revolutions of Literature*.[143] This short history of European writing was especially treasured in Scotland for its chapter on Scottish literature: 'of late, the principal adornments of the BRITISH literature have received their birth and education in SCOTLAND'. Many of these Scots, Denina pointed out in the Murdoch translation, 'came from villages whose only pretensions to fame were that they had produced men of such eminence.' For a small-town schoolteacher or a village boy, Denina's demonstration that a great writer such as Virgil or Boccaccio came from 'an obscure village' was encouraging. Murdoch's Denina took it for granted correct metropolitan English was the proper language for Scottish authors, arguing it was '*possible for those to write elegantly, who were neither born nor educated where the language is spoken in its purity*'.[144]

All this sounds appropriate to the Ayrshire Murdoch and his most famous pupil. However, apparently authoritative modern scholarship is probably mistaken. A footnote to a much older essay mentions another contemporary John Murdoch who shared several interests with Burns's tutor.[145] The Murdoch translation of Denina's Scottish-published *Essay* is a good indication of contemporary taste, especially in the West of Scotland where Denina's essay was republished, but not a book with indisputable links to Burns or his tutor.[146] Denina praised Alexander Pope as 'undoubtedly the most judicious and elegant, perhaps the most nervous and sublime, poet that EVER England produced.' In particular Denina (in Murdoch's translation) contended, 'no poet ever treated a subject so profound as that of the ESSAY ON MAN with a sublimity equal to Pope'.[147]

Returned to Ayr, Burns's Murdoch did all he could to encourage Robert and Gilbert at Mount Oliphant. He sent them Pope's poems. Robert had already read some Pope in Masson's schoolbook. He had also been reading, Gilbert recalled, '*The Edinburgh Magazine* for 1772'.[148] Gilbert's memory seems inaccurate here. It is impossible to

tell whether he means William Creech's *Edinburgh Magazine* which began in 1773, or a volume of Walter Ruddiman's *Weekly Magazine, or Edinburgh Amusement*, which had been known as the *Edinburgh Magazine* in an earlier incarnation. Either way, however, the presence of this periodical in his household is an indication that Burns in his early teens already had some sense of Edinburgh cultural life, even if he had never left Ayrshire. Thanks to Murdoch's gift, Pope's poetry now became a lifelong enthusiasm. Pope is the poet Burns quotes most frequently in early letters. Witty, measured, shrewd, Pope's verse showed Burns what could be accomplished in modern English. At once contemporary and wise, it could encapsulate recent philosophical thought within what was still a Christian framework, as in the 'Essay on Man' which Burns especially relished. From *The Dunciad* to 'Eloisa to Abelard' Pope epitomised a voice that could be both satirical and tender. His work had been admired by earlier Scottish vernacular poets such as Allan Ramsay (to whose works Pope had subscribed), and became familiar to Burns from schooldays onwards. Murdoch's gift was a treasured one.

The schoolteacher's companionship was also enlivening, so much so that in summer 1773 William sent Robert to lodge in Murdoch's two-storey house in Ayr's Sandgate to revise his English grammar. After just a week, Robert had to return to Mount Oliphant to help with the harvest, but once his labour at home was done, he returned to stay two more weeks with Murdoch in Ayr. Pupil and teacher spent all their time together. Murdoch started teaching Robert some French and Burns was surely guided by his tutor's tastes. In 1773 a Francophile John Murdoch published *The Tears of Sensibility*, a collection of four novellas by 'M. D'Arnaud', then one of France's most admired writers.[149] These novellas have subtitles such as *The Man of Benevolence and the Man of Gratitude*. They are very much part of the then new European movement of 'Sensibility' and the 'Sentimental' which promoted warm, sympathetic understanding and often tearful emotionalism; one of Sentimentalism's most successful English-language adherents was the Scot Henry Mackenzie whose 1771 *The Man of Feeling* would soon be Burns's favourite novel. Remembered by Gilbert as remarking that 'he liked to see so much sensibility', Robert's Francophile tutor was surely aware of such literature, even if he was not the Murdoch of *The Tears of Sensibility*. Burns developed more than a taste for his tutor's admired Pope. He loved sentimental literature.

The Ayrshireman Murdoch's memory of Burns indicates the boy was also a keen reader of newspapers. With his talk of 'attacking the French', the Francophile Murdoch signals an awareness that for much of Burns's life, not least in the mid-1770s, France was an enemy country. Murdoch recalled,

> At the end of one week I told him that, as he was now pretty much master of the parts of speech, &c., I should like to teach him something of French pronunciation, that when he should meet with the name of a French town, ship, officer, or the like, in the newspapers, he might be able to pronounce it something like a French word. Robert was glad to hear this proposal, and immediately we attacked the French with great courage.
>
> Now there was little to be heard but the declension of nouns, the conjugation of verbs, &c. When walking together, and even at meals, I was constantly telling him the names of different objects, as they presented themselves, in French, so that he was hourly laying in a stock of words and sometimes little phrases. In short, he took such pleasure in learning, and I in teaching, that it was difficult to say which of the two was most zealous in the business, and about the end of our second week of the study of the French we began to read a little of the *Adventures of Telemachus*, in Fénélon's own words.[150]

Winter began to approach, though, and it was time for Burns to go back to the farm. He went with a French dictionary and a copy of Fénelon's *Télémaque*, a 1699 prose romance set in the ancient Greek world and presenting the adventures of Odysseus's son, Telemachus. This work was very popular, and a model for fictions like Fénelon's secretary Ayr-born Jacobite Andrew Ramsay's *Travels of Cyrus*.[151] With his dictionary and *Télémaque*, Burns taught himself French to the extent that, according to Gilbert,

> he had acquired such a knowledge of the language, as to read and understand any French author in prose. This was considered as a sort of prodigy, and through the medium of Murdoch, procured him the acquaintance of several lads in Ayr, who were at that time gabbling French, and the notice of some families, particularly that of Dr Malcolm, where a knowledge of French was a recommendation.
>
> Observing the facility with which he had acquired the French language, Mr Robinson, the established writing-master in Ayr, and Mr Murdoch's particular friend, having himself acquired a considerable

57

knowledge of the Latin language by his own industry, without ever having learnt it at school, advised Robert to make the same attempt, promising him every assistance in his power. Agreeably to this advice, he purchased [the Scottish Jacobite Latinist Thomas Ruddiman's] *The Rudiments of the Latin Tongue*, but finding this study dry and uninteresting, it was quickly laid aside.[152]

Long afterwards, Burns would occasionally return to attempting Latin. Each time he gave up after a few days. Disappointed in love, he would announce to Gilbert, *'So I'll to my Latin again'*, with the result that this became a private joke and Burns wrote several (now lost) stanzas on the topic. If a Classical education distinguished an eighteenth-century gentleman, Burns never attained that distinction; sometimes he felt the lack of it. He later complained wryly to a Classically educated correspondent of being 'forced to pick up my fragments of knowledge as the hog picks up his husks, at the plough-tail'.[153] However, in knowing Murdoch, Burns enjoyed fruitful contact with an Ayrshire teacher alert to developments in European as well as English-language literature.

Teaching in Ayr, Murdoch often visited the Burnes household on Saturday afternoons. He dropped in at other times too, sometimes reading with the boys so that 'by his assistance and conversation with that of some others men of taste and letters about Ayr we gathered a taste for reading poetry and writings of sentiment, of wit, and humour in all which we were tolerable lucky in getting books'.[154] Gilbert's mention here of 'sentiment' is yet another hint that Murdoch shaped his protégés' taste. Mention of 'wit and humour' implies Murdoch had a side to him that was lighter than the demeanour of William Burnes, who laid such emphasis on piety, frugality, improvement and other solemn virtues. Probably the Murdoch who had given the Burneses *The School for Lovers* also had a hand in alerting Robert to writers like Richardson and Smollett. Murdoch may also have had a more *louche* side. In 1776, after being 'overtaken in liquor' he called Ayr's Reverend Dalrymple 'a Lyar or a damned lyar' and was dismissed from his teaching position.[155] 'In Ayr,' Gilbert remarked, 'he might as well have spoken blasphemy.'[156] Murdoch headed south, spent considerable time in France, then settled in London where he published books on French and taught English to foreigners, including the French revolutionary statesman Talleyrand. Occasionally corresponding with Burns,

Murdoch later fell on hard times, dying in 1824. Outside Burns's immediate family, he influenced the young poet more than anyone else.

Burns's time with Murdoch involved intensive learning, but was also a holiday from physically demanding farm-work. He recalled how at the start of his teens at Mount Oliphant 'We lived very poorly', combining 'the chearless gloom of a hermit with the unceasing moil of a galley-slave'.[157] Jobs he and Gilbert had to do included threshing corn, ploughing the poor-quality soil with a team of horses, harvesting and general farm-work. Since William could not afford a labourer, Robert took on that role. Repeatedly stressing the need to be frugal, his father was showing signs of exhaustion. His eldest son did all he could to help. Utensils were patched up rather than replaced. Peter Westwood has identified the words 'to a hoe mended' written by the young Robert in a surviving fragment of his father's accounts.[158] Gilbert recalled years of 'hard labour' and 'rigid economy' in his teens. 'For several years butcher's meat was a stranger in the house.'[159]

Still, few things beat farm-work for exercise, and Burns was proud to be growing up physically strong: 'At the plough, scythe or reap-hook I feared no competitor.'[160] As the eldest brother, he took the lead, but sometimes, later, he recalled bitterly the sheer slog. Gilbert worried that this told on Robert in his teens both physically and psychologically.

> My brother at the age of thirteen assisted in threshing the crop of corn, and at fifteen was the principal labourer on the farm, for we had no hired servant, male or female. The anguish of mind we felt at our tender years, under these straits and difficulties, was very great. To think of our father growing old (for he was now above fifty) broken down with the long continued fatigues of his life, with a wife and five other children, and in a declining state of circumstances, these reflections produced in my brother's mind and mine sensations of the deepest distress.[161]

In such circumstances, where the toughest farm-work seemed only to stave off impending financial crisis, reading and imagination offered Burns the solace of escape. Gilbert, though, remembered Robert in his teens 'almost constantly afflicted in the evenings with a dull headache', and related this to other symptoms which became

worse in later life, when headaches were exchanged for 'a palpita-
tion of the heart and a threatening of fainting and suffocation in
his bed, in the night-time'. Growing up beside his brother, Gilbert
knew him better than anyone. He detected not only physical but
also psychological problems which seemed to originate in Burns's
teens. 'I doubt not but the hard labour and sorrow of this period
of his life, was in a great measure the cause of that depression of
spirits with which Robert was so often afflicted through his whole
life afterwards.'[162]

Medical terminology has changed greatly since the eighteenth
century. Still, what Gilbert terms 'depression of spirits' seems akin
to what we now call depressive illness – which often has its onset
during the teenage years. This condition would climax in Burns's
breakdown around the age of twenty-one. Meanwhile, at Mount
Oliphant, it was a problem the teenager struggled with in the rela-
tively small amounts of privacy he had. If reading, conversation,
poetry and song were escapes from the demands of work on the
farm, they were also antidotes to painful 'depression of spirits'.

Song entranced Burns. From boyhood he knew Scots songs could
not only be sung, but printed. Detailing the earliest poetry he and
his brother came across around 1772, Gilbert mentions in passing
'*those excellent new songs* that are hawked about the country in
baskets, or exposed on stalls in the streets'.[163] Robert remembered
how what he came to regard as 'one of the most beautiful songs in
the Scots, or any other language ... about the year 1771, or 72 ...
came first on the streets as a Ballad'. In this song about the return
of the man of the house he loved the lines

> And will I see his face again!
> And will I hear him speak!

and the proverbial wisdom about uncertainty,

> The present moment is our ain,
> The neist we never saw.[164]   *next*

Song, like religion, articulated and set in order people's hopes and
fears. It would be hard to exaggerate how closely Burns remem-
bered passages of the Bible, poetry and Scots songs. They would be
a frequent source and resource for his lifelong work. At least some

boyhood friends such as James McCandlish knew of and shared this love of song. When young, Burns began to memorise songs, but did not write them down. In his twenties he sent an Edinburgh author samples of 'old pieces that are still to be found among our Peasantry in the West', remarking that 'I once had a great many of these fragments and some of these here entire; but as I had no idea then that any body cared for them, I have forgot them.'[165] This is probably rather disingenuous. Even in boyhood Burns was aware songs might be collected, written down, brought to book.

Pious, singing psalms with his family, the young Burns continued crooning other songs too; his crooning was reinforced, challenged and quickened by reading. Though the exact chronology of his youthful experiences is often impossible to establish, he recalled another book from this early period as particularly important to him. This 'select Collection of English songs' was 'my vade mecum. – I pored over them, driving my cart or walking to labor, song by song, verse by verse; carefully noting the true tender or sublime from affectation and fustian. – I am convinced I owe much to this for my critic-craft such as it is. –'[166] There was an eighteenth-century *Select Collection of English Songs*, edited by Joseph Ritson, but it did not appear until 1783. We cannot be certain which song-book the teenage Burns pored over. The London-published *The Goldfinch* (1748) carried the prominent subtitle *a Select Collection of the most celebrated English Songs*. Burns's German biographer Hans Hecht argued that *The Lark*, republished in Edinburgh in 1765, was Burns's 'select Collection'.[167] It does carry such a subtitle, and contains not just English but Scots songs too. Some of these are written to tunes to which Burns (who late in life adopted the lark as his heraldic emblem) would set his own words. Another similar collection, *The Masque*, describes itself as *a New and Select Collection of the best English, Scotch, and Irish Songs, Catches, Duets, and Cantatas.*

In such collections swains long to gaze 'Upon *Clarinda*'s panting breast' and nymphs like 'chaste *Clarinda*' strive to maintain their honour. Clarinda was a common name in eighteenth-century pastoral love songs where Burns would have found a fair bit of 'affectation and fustian'. There were also heartier numbers – 'Let's be jovial, fill our Glasses.'[168] Works like *The Masque* stressed national traditions in song. They allowed their Scottish songs a distinctive accent, in keeping with that encouraged by earlier eighteenth-century song

collectors such as Allan Ramsay, David Herd and others. Sometimes even improper songs might be admitted to books:

> John Anderson, my jo, John,
>   When first you did begin,
> You had as good a tail tree
>   As ony ither man –
> But now 'tis waxen weak, John,
>   And wriggles to and fro;
> I gi'e twa gae ups for ane gae down,
>   John Anderson, my jo.[169]

Later in life Burns collected a similar version of 'John Anderson, my Jo' for his bawdy anthology *The Merry Muses of Caledonia*. His other, better known and more popular version turns this song into a paean to married love. Whether or not such songs formed part of the 'select Collection' he pored over in adolescence, he knew them from oral tradition. The songbook showed him how lyrics he had grown up with might be collected in a book, closely examined, and subjected to the sort of 'critic-craft' which sometimes benefits young writers.

Revealingly, when Burns lists aspects of the songs which he 'noted carefully', the 'true tender' comes first. From the very beginning he would aim for that in many of his finest lyrics. 'I have paid more attention to every description of Scots Songs,' he wrote a few years before his death, 'than perhaps any body living has done.'[170] This was true, and had been so ever since childhood when he listened to his mother's singing, learned songs from those around him, and carried a songbook as his 'vade mecum'.

Unsurprisingly, the first serious written composition he chose to preserve was a song. 'For my own part, I never had the least thought, or inclination, of turning Poet, till I got once heartily in love; & then Rhyme & Song were, in a manner the spontaneous language of my heart.'[171] Like all accounts of his childhood, this one is retrospective, and a little mannered. Quite possibly, just as today's boys may imagine aspects of their lives in terms of films, so Burns cast himself in a role when he had his first love affair and formally made a song of it. The role was one that also appealed to his younger brother when he set down the account of his own affair with 'Lavinia'. Though Robert and Gilbert fell for different girls, the

circumstances of each relationship can be linked to the passage from Thomson's 'Autumn' in Masson's schoolbook. What Masson calls the 'Story of Lavinia' is set on a hard-working farm in harvest season:

> Before the ripen'd field the reapers stand,
> In fair array; each by the lass he loves,
> To bear the rougher part, and mitigate
> By nameless gentle offices her toil.
> At once they stoop and swell the lusty sheaves,
> While thro' their chearful band, the rural talk,
> The rural scandal, and the rural jest
> Fly harmless, to deceive the tedious time ...

Here 'The pride of swains', Palemon, a representative of 'the rural life in all its joy' and '*Arcadian* song', falls in love with Lavinia.[172] For someone so impressed by poetry as Burns, this must have been a suggestive scenario. It is not hard to relate it to the long, wittily phrased, self-conscious 1787 account he gave Dr John Moore of his first love and first song in the not quite so Arcadian, thistly fields of Ayrshire where Burns presents himself as first committing 'the sin of RHYME'.

You know our country custom of coupling a man and woman together as Partners in the labors of Harvest. – In my fifteenth autumn, my Partner was a bewitching creature who just counted an autumn less. – My scarcity of English denies me the power of doing her justice in that language; but you know the Scotch idiom, She was a bonie, sweet, sonsie lass. – In short, she altogether unwittingly to herself, initiated me in a certain delicious Passion, which in spite of acid Disappointment, gin-horse Prudence and bookworm Philosophy, I hold to be the first of human joys, our dearest pleasure here below. – How she caught the contagion I can't say; you medical folks talk much of infection by breathing the same air, the touch, &c. but I never expressly told her that I loved her. – Indeed I did not well know myself, why I liked so much to loiter behind with her, when returning in the evening from our labors; why the tones of her voice made my heartstrings thrill like an Eolian harp; and particularly, why my pulse beat such a furious ratann when I looked and fingered over her hand, to pick out the nettle-stings and thistles. – Among her other love-inspiring qualifications, she sung sweetly; and 'twas her favorite reel to which I attempted giving an embodied vehicle in rhyme. – I was

not so presumptive as to imagine that I could make verses like printed ones, composed by men who had Latin and Greek; but my girl sung a song which was said to be composed by a small country laird's son, on one of his father's maids, with whom he was in love; and I saw no reason why I might not rhyme as well as he, for excepting smearing sheep and casting peats, his father living in the moors, he had no more Scholarcraft than I had.[173]

Here is Burns in the situation of Thomson's reapers, but also aware of more earthy matters like 'smearing sheep'. Writing this account as an adult, he flourishes polite culture – 'an Eolian harp' – alongside 'Scotch idiom'. Conscious of his lack of Classical education, and with a note of what we now call class consciousness, he knows himself as good as any laird's son. He communicates physical sexual excitement – 'my pulse beat such a furious ratann when I looked and fingered over her hand' – but also the allure of a voice. This girl, like his mother and the woman he would eventually marry, sings sweetly, and sings Scots song. The way Burns here describes his early composing style – words shaped around a pre-existing tune to make 'an embodied vehicle in rhyme' – accords with his 'crambo-jingle' and accounts of how he made songs later.

Yet, witty and tender, erotically excited but also minutely attentive, this passage presents a poet who has moved beyond 'crambo-jingle' into purposeful lyrical composition. The song was no masterpiece. Burns later picked it to pieces. It begins,

> O once I lov'd a bonnie lass,
>   An' aye I love her still,
> An' whilst that virtue warms my breast
>   I'll love my handsome Nell.[174]

Burns afterwards decided lines one and two were 'quite too much in the flimsy strain of our ordinary street ballads', while lines three and four were 'too much in the other extreme. The expression is a little akward, and the sentiment too serious.' Writing these comments he confirms that stylistically this early attempt at song drew both on demotic verses he heard around him and on the more formal English songs in his 'vade mecum'. Later his poetry would splice these two strains more successfully, but whenever he called to mind the final stanza of this early song he remembered composing it 'in a wild enthusiasm of passion, and to this hour I never recollect it,

but my heart melts, and my blood sallies at the remembrance'.[175]
Burns writes about these lines in terms of pulses beating and blood
sallying because the song, not least in its conclusion, even as it sings
of 'innocence and modesty', is about one of his great themes, the
uncontrollable energy of love:

> 'Tis this in Nelly pleases me,
>   'Tis this enchants my soul;
> For absolutely in my breast
>   She reigns without controul.[176]

Excitedly, a little awkwardly, the teenage Burns had announced
himself as lover, singer and poet. In many ways his boyhood on the
farm was ordinary; but the way his hunger for reading and listening
was nourished by people around him was not. An ability to fuse his
everyday Scots working-lad's ordinariness with the extraordinariness
of his schooled imagination and instincts was about to make him
impressively and unstoppably a bard.

II

Wits

Like many people, Burns was educated as much by accident as design. Subject to no secondary-school or university curriculum, he had to live off his wits. One day in his mid-teens he came across a book that would affect him for the rest of his life. Gilbert recalled how

> A brother of my mother who had lived with us some time, and had learnt some arithmetic by our winter evening's candle, went into a bookseller's shop in Ayr, to purchase *The Ready Reckoner*, or *Tradesman's sure Guide*, and a book to teach him to write letters. Luckily, in place of *The Complete Letter-Writer*, he got by mistake a small collection of letters by the most eminent writers, with a few sensible directions for attaining an easy epistolary stile. This book was to Robert of the greatest consequence. It inspired him with a strong desire to excel in letter-writing, while it furnished him with models by some of the first writers in our language.[1]

Linking it to the development of his skills as a writer, Robert remembered spending many hours with this volume. Now, for the first time, it can be identified. John Newbery's small-format *Letters on the Most Common, as well as Important Occasions in Life* anthologises 'writers of distinguished merit'. With introductory 'Instructions for Epistolary Writing', it has at its core letters by wits of the era of Queen Anne. The collection includes one letter Burns twice quotes from memory in correspondence, and another about dying he would quote in his own most famous epistolary love affair.[2]

Burns 'pored over' Newbery's *Letters* and followed the book's advice.[3] It explained: 'the method by which a proficiency in this art may be best obtained' is 'by imitating very frequently, and with due attention, the letters of those who have been most celebrated and

distinguished for this species of writing'. These writers were often poets. The volume showcases the warmth, wit and friendship of Alexander Pope and his circle. Letters were to seem like the 'conversation . . . of the learned and polite', not the chatter of 'the ploughman'. Throughout his life, in his own way Burns tried to gather round him groups of like-minded literary wits. Newbery, like Murdoch and Arthur Masson, emphasised the study of correct English models:

> Those who keep polite company acquire, as it were naturally, an air of politeness. They speak correctly, and with a becoming boldness, ease and freedom: and so it is in writing; those who constantly read polite, correct, and elegant authors, will acquire not only their manner of expression, but, in some measure, their manner of thinking; and notwithstanding the numerous tracts that have been written on *style*, there is in reality no acquiring a good one, by any rules whatever, nor is it to be obtained in any other manner, than by conversing with polite company, who speak correctly, and by frequently reading the best authors. Read, therefore, Mr *Addison* again and again . . .[4]

Burns took such advice to heart. 'My knowledge of modern manners, and of literature and criticism, I got from the Spectator,' he wrote, citing Addison's famous periodical, and indicating an early interest in English-language politeness that, for good and ill, shaped his often mannered epistolary style, not least in matters amatory.[5] He would have found other things in the *Spectator* too. A volume belonging to William Burnes details how Sappho's 'soul seems to have been made up of love and poetry. She felt the passion in all its warmth, and described it in all its symptoms.'[6] Burns later likened the 'melting soul' of his inamorata Agnes McLehose to Sappho, matching Gilbert's contention that his brother's 'symptoms of . . . passion' were sometimes almost as strong as Sappho's.[7] It is unlikely this is what *Spectator*-reading William Burnes wished to teach his sons, but the same periodical also contained matter of more immediate social relevance. Newbery included a long *Spectator* passage which would have spoken particularly to the Burns who must have found it hard to find throngs of elegant English-speaking polite companions in the rainy fields of Mount Oliphant:

> I am always very well pleased with a country *Sunday*, and think, if keeping holy the seventh day were only a human institution, it would be the best method that could have been thought of for the polishing

and civilizing of mankind. It is certain, the country people would soon degenerate into a kind of savages and barbarians, were there not such frequent returns of a stated time, in which the whole village meet together with their best faces and in their cleanliest habits, to converse with one another, upon different subjects, hear their duties explained to them, and join together in adoration of the Supreme Being. *Sunday* clears away the rust of the whole week, not only as it refreshes in their minds the notions of religion, but as it puts both sexes upon appearing in their most agreeable forms, and exerting all such qualities as are apt to give them a figure in the eye of the village. A country fellow distinguishes himself as much in the *church-yard*, as a citizen does upon the *Exchange*, the whole parish-politics being generally discussed in that place, either after sermon, or before the bell rings.[8]

The young Burns seems to have taken such advice to heart. Sometimes participating in theological debate, sometimes just testing his rhetorical skills, he was 'ambitious of shining in conversation parties on sundays between sermons, funerals, &c.' Proximity to Ayr, with its sometimes cultivated clergy, teachers, schools and scholars 'was of great advantage to me'.[9] In conversation and argument as well as in correspondence he honed his skill with language. He noticed that disparities in society around him were intensified when seen in God's house:

> I remember, & 'tis almost the earliest thing I do remember, when I was quite a boy, one day at church, being enraged at seeing a young creature, one of the maids of his house, rise from the mouth of the pew to give way to a bloated son of Wealth & Dullness, who waddled surlily past her. – Indeed the girl was very pretty; & he was an ugly, stupid, purse-proud, money-loving old monster, as you can imagine.[10]

As a boy, Burns found it hard to accept how pious respectability and social class might mask true worth,

> . . . your children of Sanctity move among their fellow-creatures with a nostril snuffing putrescence, & a foot spurning filth, in short, with that conceited dignity which your titled Douglases, Hamiltons, Gordons, or any other of your Scots Lordlings of seven centuries standing, display when they accidentally mix among the many-aproned Sons of Mechanical life. – I remember, in my Plough-boy days, I could not conceive it possible that a noble Lord could be a Fool, or that a godly Man could be a Knave. – How ignorant are Plough-boys![11]

Burns's father saw his son as more than a ploughboy. William wanted to ensure Robert added practical intellectual skills to his gift for voracious reading. So, aged sixteen, Burns spent much of summer and early autumn 1775 at the 'noted school' of self-taught Hugh Rodger at Kirkoswald, about fifteen miles south-west of Mount Oliphant. With Rodger, Burns became a 'pretty good' student of 'Mensuration, Surveying, Dialling, &c.'[12] Mensuration involved rules for calculating lengths of lines, extent of surface areas and volumes of solids. 'Dialling' meant using kinds of sundial and, perhaps, a compass for surveying. Opposite Kirkoswald's old parish kirkyard where Burns's maternal grandmother was buried, on ground sloping up from the back of Rodger's school towards what is now a wood the scholars practised their lessons. Having him study surveying, gardener and tenant farmer William Burnes may have hoped his eldest son would be well equipped for an age of agricultural 'improvement'. Burns's arrival in Kirkoswald meant both a journey into his maternal past of songs and smuggling, and an education in the 'improving' mentality his father was keen to promote.

It was also Robert's first extended stay away from his parents. Fifteen miles may seem short by modern standards, but Burns recalled Kirkoswald as 'a good distance from home'. He lodged with or very near his mother's brother Samuel Brown who lived with his wife and daughter at Ballochneil, a mile outside Kirkoswald, close to Culzean where Burns's mother had grown up. The atmosphere was different from Mount Oliphant. In Kirkoswald 'the contraband trade was at that time very successful'.[13] From the beach, over what is now the manicured turf of Turnberry golf course, locals transported liquor and luxury goods, some smuggled from the Isle of Man. Burns recalled the area as boozy; as a teenager he 'learned to look unconcernedly on a large tavern-bill, and mix without fear in a drunken squabble'.[14] There is a note of swagger here, but Burns's behaviour was probably no wilder than that of other eighteenth-century youths away from home. At Rodger's school his friends included the future banker and improver William Niven from nearby Maybole. Niven was temperamentally different – much keener than Burns to get ahead in business – but they kept in touch. Later, in the 1790s, living in a handsome house in Maybole, Niven denounced '*Vagabond Irish Weavers*' whose radicalism threatened the status quo.[15] Another Kirkoswald classmate was

Thomas Orr who in future years helped out with harvesting on William Burnes's farm, then went to sea, but drowned in 1785. Orr's family had links to smugglers. Some said his grandmother was a witch. For all the smuggling and drinking that went on in Kirkoswald, neither Orr nor Niven was a villain.

If one teenage thrill in Kirkoswald was going to the pub, another was discovering sex. Alluding to Eve in *Paradise Lost* as Satan approaches her, Burns's account of this is written twelve years later in his polished epistolary style – surely encouraged by reading and re-reading letters in Newbery's anthology:

> ... I went on with a high hand in my Geometry; till the sun entered Virgo, a month which is always a carnival in my bosom, a charming Fillette who lived next door to the school overset my Trigonomertry [*sic*], and set me off in a tangent from the sphere of my studies. – I struggled on with my Sines and Co-sines for a few days more; but stepping out to the garden one charming noon, to take the sun's altitude, I met with my Angel,

> > – 'Like Proserpine gathering flowers,
> > 'Herself a fairer flower' –

> It was vain to think of doing any more good at school. – The remaining week I staid, I did nothing but craze the faculties of my soul about her, or steal out to meet with her; and the two last nights of my stay in the country, had sleep been a mortal sin, I was innocent. –[16]

Familiarly known as Peggy, Margaret Thomson, Burns's 'Fillette', was just thirteen in August 1775. 'PEGGY dear, the ev'ning's clear' urges an early 'Song, composed in August': 'Come let us stray our gladsome way,/ And view the charms o' Nature.'[17] The charms of Nature around Kirkoswald were not hard to find. A stream flowed close to the village, which still lies among undulating fields and small farms, some with views to Arran and Ailsa Craig; about two miles away is the ruined medieval Crossraguel Abbey. Parts of modern Kirkoswald are run-down, but the old churchyard remains at the village's heart; nearby, in Souter Johnie's Cottage, the preserved eighteenth-century house of shoemaker John Davidson, visitors can still climb a ladder to the bare, atmospheric attic and touch through the rafters the rough underside of the thatch.

Beginning with imagery of 'slaught'ring guns' and wild birds shot

for sport, Burns's 'Song, composed in August' seeks to attune singer, beloved and song to a landscape of 'Autumn's pleasant weather' among the 'waving grain' of farms where 'ev'ry kind their pleasure find,/ The savage and the tender'. If there may be a hint that courting a girl is like hunting a game-bird, the prevailing note is one of tenderness. Noting the 'social' as well as the 'solitary', Burns speaks of 'Tyrannic man's dominion' over nature. He had been reading the landscape poetry of James Thomson whose 'Autumn' in *The Seasons* delights in the 'social' in the life of 'animal creation', and sets this against the 'thoughtless insolence of power' of the 'tyrant, man'. A decade or so later the mature Burns would make in one of his best-known poems a statement with an especially disturbing resonance for twenty-first-century readers:

> I'm truly sorry Man's dominion
> Has broken Nature's social union . . .

Emerging from the discourse of earlier eighteenth-century poets like Thomson and Pope, such darker thoughts are hinted at in the poem to Peggy, but this very early song looks less to disaster than to the pleasures of teenage romance:

> We'll gently walk, and sweetly talk,
>   While the silent moon shines clearly;
> I'll clasp thy waist, and fondly prest,
>   Swear how I lo'e thee dearly:
> Not vernal show'rs to budding flow'rs,
>   Not Autumn to the Farmer,
> So dear can be, as thou to me,
>   My fair, my lovely Charmer![18]

The relationship between Robert and Peggy seems to have continued later. Thomas Orr recalled taking messages between them in 1782–3. In 1784 Peggy in her early twenties married a man from just outside Kirkoswald, William Neilson. Burns knew him – 'my old acquaintance and a most worthy fellow'. By then Robert was involved in another 'affair of gallantry'.[19] Yet the verses he addressed to his 'old Sweetheart' when he presented her with a copy of his first book, two years after her marriage, suggest their relationship went on mattering to both of them, perhaps even more than it should have done:

Once fondly lov'd, and still rememb'red dear,
Sweet early Object of my youthful vows,
Accept this mark of friendship, warm, sincere,
Friendship – 'tis all cold duty now allows.[20]

Kirkoswald helped mature Burns, and gave him materials for poetry. The name of nearby Shanter farm would feature in the title of his most famous long poem. Much less certain is whether farmer Douglas Graham and his wife Helen McTaggart really provided models for the drunken voyeur and scolding wife in 'Tam o' Shanter'. Long afterwards William Niven, trying to make the most of his Burns connections, maintained they did, and tourists can peer at their graves in Kirkoswald churchyard. Shoemaker John Davidson, whose wife Ann Gillespie had links to Burns's mother's family, came to be identified with Tam's drinking crony, Johnnie, a shoemaker or souter. Davidson's surviving cottage was not built until 1785, a decade after Burns's Kirkoswald schooling, but communicates a strong sense of eighteenth-century village life. Behind it is a restored village alehouse of the sort where Burns, as he put it recalling his time in Kirkoswald, was keen to encounter 'scenes of swaggering riot and roaring dissipation'.[21]

Poetry, he knew, could be part of such scenes. Folk culture showed how wild pub behaviour, the sort of thing he saw and participated in for the first time when away from home in Kirkoswald, could also be bound up with popular art that questioned even as it reproduced the solemn rites of society. Later he recalled an old rhyme said to have saved a Covenanting clergyman 'hunted by the merciless soldiery'; belying 'the gloomy strictness of his sect', the minister sang a wild song and the soldiers, sure he could not be a dour Covenanter, let him go. In Burns's day this song had become 'a favourite kind of dramatic interlude at country weddings in the south west' and involved a young man 'dressed up like an old beggar' who is

brought into the wedding house, frequently to the astonishment of strangers who are not in the secret & begins to sing

O I am a silly auld man
My name it is auld Glenae &c. &c. &c.

He is asked to drink, & by & by to dance, which after some uncouth excuses he is prevailed on to do, the fiddle playing the tune, which here is commonly called Auld Glenae: in short, he is all the time so

plied with liquor that he is understood to get intoxicated & with all the ridiculous gesticulations of an old drunken beggar, he dances & staggers untill he falls on the floor yet still in all his riot nay in his rolling & tumbling on the floor with some or other drunken motion of his body, he beats time to the music, till at last he is supposed to be carried out dead drunk.[22]

Though Burns wrote this note much later, and after he had written his own 'cantata', 'The Jolly Beggars', it indicates how he was encouraged not just by inclination but also by popular culture around him to take the sort of wildness he first tasted at Kirkoswald and to incorporate it into sometimes subversive art.

Yet the teenage Burns was no lout. At Kirkoswald he immersed himself in James Thomson's poetry, and that of refined English pastoralist William Shenstone who praised (as Burns would) 'simplicity', 'social mirth' and 'the warmest heart' as best for the 'bard'.[23] Thomson and Shenstone furnish many quotations in his letters and help underpin the pastoral tones of his verse. If he wrote with a polysyllabic flourish that a few of his schoolfellows had 'joined . . . the *hallachores*' (the lowest of the low), he was not one of those; he simply knew there was good imaginative material among them.[24] Drinking in rough smugglers' pubs at the same time as reading Shenstone's polite, sentimental pastoral poetry, Burns would grow into a poet able to range easily from the refined to the bawdy, and even, on occasion, to fuse them.

Traditions about Burns grew up around Kirkoswald: he began 'Tam o' Shanter' when at school there (it seems to have been composed a decade and a half later); he took his teacher to the pub; he heard the local minister preach against the Union between Scotland and England; he and fellow pupils held sophisticated debates during lunch-breaks. This last tradition sounds credible, and is in keeping with Burns's recollections of wanting to maintain an intellectual community. Leaving Kirkoswald, he stated,

I engaged several of my schoolfellows to keep up a literary correspondence with me. – This last helped me much on in composition. – I had met with a collection of letters by the Wits of Queen Ann's reign, and I pored over them most devoutly. – I kept copies of any of my own letters that pleased me, and a comparison between them and the composition of most of my correspondents flattered my vanity. – I carried this whim so far that though I had not three

farthings worth of business in the world, yet every post brought me as many letters as if I had been a broad, plodding son of Day-book & Ledger. –[25]

What Burns seems to have liked best in Newbery's *Letters* is the witty correspondence of writers anthologised there – men like Wycherley, Dryden, Pope, Swift and Bolingbroke. These grand figures must have seemed far removed from rough Kirkoswald – but occasionally their correspondence brings them surprisingly close to Burns's experience. Pope, wittiest of English poets, writes to Swift from a farm where his friend Bolingbroke is reading 'between two haycocks' close to haymakers and a cart.[26] Years afterwards, Burns would quote from Newbery's book in his own correspondence. A favourite was the letter from Bolingbroke to Swift where, having praised friendship, Bolingbroke signs off, 'Adieu, dear *Swift*, with all thy faults I love thee intirely; make an effort, and love me on with all mine.' Burns quoted that from memory to male and female correspondents.[27] Newbery's *Letters* offered him attractive examples of warm, witty male friendship, with philosophy and lighter matters discussed in a literature-loving community. 'No vows so solemn as those of friendship,' wrote Bolingbroke to Swift in a letter Burns later quoted.[28] Rich in maxims – 'without generosity, it is impossible to be a great man' – Newbery's book also offered an aspiring writer specific counsel about imaginative writing. Dryden stressed that 'genius alone is a greater virtue (if I may so call it) than all other qualifications put together', while Granville, writing of the witty dramatist Wycherley, argued that 'a diamond is not less a diamond for not being polished'.[29] Lacking the formal polish of a university Classical education, Burns sought to develop his own writing style. Such sentiments offered encouragement.

The anthology was not a creative writer's manual, but did contain writerly advice, whether Dryden advocating comic writing and odes (Burns would attempt both), or Walsh writing to Pope about pastoral poems and emphasising that following 'nature' and the 'true spirit' of poetry was more important than critics' 'mechanical rules'.[30] These older, generally neoclassical writers presented in their letters seeds which would germinate in Burns's work. Pope particularly appealed, offering Burns the figure of a poet linking poetry to idleness, and who, in the midst of all the world's biz, seems 'a fellow ... who all his life does nothing'. Though he was really quite interested in

business affairs, Pope called into question the efforts of the plod-
ding sons of Day-book and Ledger:

> but perhaps you'll say, the whole world has something to do, some-
> thing to talk of, something to wish for, something to be employed
> about; but pray, Sir, cast up the account, put all these somethings
> together, and what is the sum total but just nothing?[31]

Surrounded by students of surveying, mensuration and dialling,
Burns seems to have felt the attraction of this. At least as import-
ant may have been the way Newbery's book included letter after
witty letter about friendship. 'In an heavy oppressive atmosphere,
when the spirits sink too low,' wrote Shenstone in a passage Burns
would refer to, 'the best cordial is to read over all the letters of
one's friends.'[32] Burns wanted to develop writing and friendship
together. Newbery's book showed what was possible.

Repeatedly, after that Kirkoswald period when he read Newbery's
Letters, Burns would try to assemble groups of male friends for
witty and philosophical engagement. Sometimes their meeting was
face-to-face, sometimes through correspondence – in verse, prose,
or both. Though he never quite gathered around him the wits of
Queen Anne's reign, the anthology of writers' letters he 'pored over'
in youth strengthened not just his own writerly ambitions but also
his sense that a community of sympathetic friends might be linked
to the life of a poet.

Back home, though, there were pressing practical concerns. The
family's landlord, William Fergusson, died in 1776. Burns's father
signed an 'instrument of seisin', a legal document to assist Fergusson's
daughters to come into their inheritance, but a local factor involved
in Fergusson's legal estate demanded rent owed by an exhausted
William Burnes.[33] Burns remembered angrily how 'the scoundrel
tyrant's insolent, threatening epistles . . . used to set us all in tears'.[34]
The fledgling poet liked to read – and wished to write – the epistles
of a philosophically inclined wit, but he lived in a poor household.
Economic necessity demanded hard manual labour. He ploughed;
he threshed; 'we lived very poorly'. The lease had two years to run
before William Burnes could get out of it, and the whole family
fought to keep the farm going until they could be released from its
terms. 'Toils your sinews brace,' wrote Shenstone, conscious 'how
great a Misfortune it is for a Man of small Estate to have much

'Taste'. Though an educated English gentleman, Shenstone had known his own money troubles. He thought the poet was fated to resent a 'rich churl' and to have to 'war with ruin'.[35] No wonder Burns quoted Shenstone.

Economically, for the Burnes family and others times were dreadful. 'Ruinous' is the word Burns used about the rent of the farm. He later remarked that the factor who harried his father 'sat for the picture I have drawn of one in my Tale of two dogs'.[36] In this poem of 'racked rents', written almost a decade later, 'tenant-bodies, scant o' cash' have to endure a factor whose custom is to 'stamp an' threaten, curse an' swear,/ He'll *apprehend* them, *poind* their gear [impound and sell their belongings]'. The poem contrasts the life of the land-owning class with that of '*poor bodies*' living lives of '*wretches*', digging ditches or building a wall with 'dirty stanes', then meeting with 'loss o' health, or want o' masters'. Though not quite such '*wretches*', the Burnes family knew these things at close hand. The wonder is that Burns's poem is not more bitter. Cleverly, ironically and obliquely looking at divisions of human society from the standpoint of dogs, it has its poor man's dog speak up for 'Love', 'Wit' and (in Shenstone's phrase) 'social Mirth'.[37]

Burns sought these too, but ruin threatened. The Scottish economy was uneasy in the 1770s. In Edinburgh David Hume wrote in 1772 of 'a very melancholy situation: continual bankruptcies, universal loss of credit and endless suspicions'.[38] More locally, the Ayrshire economy had been rocked by the spectacular collapse of Douglas, Heron and Company, the Ayr Bank, which had lent substantially to companies involved in Irish, American and West Indian trade, particularly in the slavery-related businesses of tobacco and sugar. A seven-storey Sugar House was erected at Ayr harbour in 1772, anticipating boom times, but soon abandoned. Having run up huge debts, the ruined Ayr Bank closed its doors the following year. 'Scots gentry Heron's bank may curse,' wrote one local poet, associating its owners with the 'greatest cheats'.[39] By the time Burns returned from Kirkoswald in 1775 it seemed over half the bank's more than 200 proprietors (who included many local gentry and merchants) were bankrupt or nearly so. A decade after the Ayr Bank closed, Burns was still lamenting the 'miserable job of a Douglas, Heron, & Co.'s Bank' which had left 'the major part of our Knights & squires . . . all insolvent'. About three-quarters of a million pounds' worth of lands changed hands as a result of the bank's collapse.

Local people known to the Burneses, such as their future landlord David McClure and Ayr minister William McGill, were directly affected. Knock-on effects were felt at all levels.⁴⁰ The bank had funded improving landowners. For well over a decade after its failure Ayrshire estates were being sold to cover debts. Litigation over the Ayr Bank's collapse lasted half a century. Adam Smith wrote about it in *The Wealth of Nations*. The Burnes family were among many indirect victims of this financial disaster.

At the same time the mid-1770s brought a new outbreak of international war directly affecting Ayr and Ayrshire. The American War of Independence propelled to prominence in Burns's teens arguments about taxation, representation and democracy. Not Scotland, but 'America', is the first nation named in his poetry. It features 'Boston-ha'', 'Philadelphia' and 'New-York' long before getting round to mentioning Edinburgh.⁴¹ Many Ayrshire families had American links. Local people had achieved success in New York and Virginia, where Ayr Hill was founded by a scion of Ayr's prominent Hunter family.⁴²

Burns was the first great Romantic poet to write about America. His verse about the revolutionary war reveals detailed knowledge of its campaigns. He hints jokily he might have joined up and fought in it. Enlisting would have solved concerns about what to do for a living. His attitude towards the American War will be discussed later, but there can be little doubt that war compounded local worries. The conflict decidedly interrupted some of Ayr's most successful business ventures associated with tobacco. The sugar trade was seriously affected too. Times were bad.

In May 1777 William Burnes extricated himself from the Mount Oliphant lease. He moved his family a little further inland to a 130-acre farm at Lochlea in the Ayrshire parish of Tarbolton. Roughly five miles south of Kilmarnock, Lochlea is relatively isolated, bleak and wet in winter. Today surrounding farms with names like Boghead and Mossbog hint that the land, though about 400 feet in elevation, is hard to drain. Some of it remains prone to flooding. In Burns's era the farm lay beside a marshy loch. Tarbolton village was just over two miles south-west, the larger settlement of Mauchline three miles south-east. William tried hard to improve Lochlea. At first his family appears to have been happy there. Their new landlord, David McClure, was an enthusiast for improvement, but had been a shareholder in the Ayr Bank, and war had adversely affected his other businesses. A self-made man in his mid-forties, this Ayr town

councillor had settled at Shawwood in Tarbolton parish, gradually increasing his land-holdings. With interests in shipping, he may have done a bit of smuggling with Douglas Graham of Shanter in Kirkoswald. In a close-knit community full of networks of family, kirk, business and other relationships, McClure was well connected. Burns recalled that for the first few years at Lochlea things went 'comfortably'.[43] Gradually, though, as war dragged on and repercussions of the Ayr Bank collapse spread, relations between William Burnes and their new landlord worsened.

With the instinct for melodrama inherent in many a teenager, Burns seems to have sensed potential for disaster. In his head he began to compose a tragedy – 'I never wrote down anything; so, except a speech or two, the whole has escaped my memory.' A surviving fragment, which he remembered composing around 1777 when he was aged about eighteen, emphasises 'wretchedness', 'the helpless children of Distress' and 'th' Oppressor,/ Rejoicing in the honest man's destruction'. The keynote throughout is 'Ruin'.[44]

Ruin was in the air, but there were ways to evade it, at least temporarily. Around this time, Burns wrote, 'to give my manners a brush, I went to a country dancing school'. An early 1779 letter from James Candlish referred to this. Gilbert thought his elder brother 'distractedly fond' of dancing in his youth. Robert attended classes with some of the younger members of his family, but recalled that this set him at odds with William:

> My father had an unaccountable antipathy against these meetings; and my going was, what to this hour I repent, in absolute defiance of his commands. – My father . . . was the sport of strong passions: from that instance of rebellion he took a kind of dislike to me, which, I believe was one cause of that dissipation which marked my future years. – I only say, Dissipation, comparative with the strictness and sobriety of Presbyterean [sic] country life; for though the will-o'-wisp meteors of thoughtless Whim were almost the sole lights of my path, yet early ingrained Piety and Virtue never failed to point me out the line of Innocence. – The great misfortune of my life was, never to have AN AIM. – I had felt some early stirrings of Ambition, but they were the blind gropins [sic] of Homer's Cyclops round the walls of his cave: I saw my father's situation entailed on me perpetual labor.[45]

Though Gilbert remembered the dancing-school incident rather differently, he too saw Robert's attendance as an act of rebellion:

William Burnes 'about this time began to see the dangerous impetu-osity of my brother's passions, as well as his not being amenable to counsel, which often irritated my father; and which he would naturally think a dancing school was not likely to correct'.[46]

We cannot read them as direct autobiography, but poems and fragments by Burns that survive from this time suggest restlessness, eagerness for sexual experience, and awareness of class divisions. Taking the tune of the bawdy song, 'John Anderson, my jo', a speaker wanders at night where 'Auld Aire ran by before me,/ And bicker'd to the seas;' another night-song has its singer with a girl-friend: 'Wi' sma' persuasion she agreed,/ To see me thro' the barley'.[47] Burns's name has been linked with the names of girls from various nearby farms. The provenance of such stories is dubious. What is clear is that, though he later wrote of 'the cold, obsequious, dancing-school bow of politeness', his passion for dancing was bound up with asserting an identity different from that of his father.[48] Occa-sionally his new identity might let Burns escape from the relentless slog of farm-work. It might even give him a dashing attractiveness.

Like most youths, Burns took time to acquire this manner. Gilbert, closest to him throughout adolescence, stated that 'when young' Robert was 'bashful and awkward' in relationships with women. If reading and imagination fuelled this awkwardness, they also inten-sified an eager sentimental and erotic excitement as Burns approached his later teens. 'His attachment to . . . [women's] society became very strong, and he was constantly the victim of some fair enslaver.' In an autobiographical narrative Gilbert presents his own unhappy affair in terms of Thomson's *Seasons*. As a writer, Gilbert was no more an untutored peasant than his brother. To see one's own life through poetry or fiction was then as easy as it is for us to view our lives in terms of what we see on screen. Even Gilbert, who understood this kind of imaginative identification, was struck by the vehemence of it in his brother. He hints that Burns's passions were moulded at least as much by literature as by life:

The symptoms of his passion were often such as nearly to equal those of the celebrated Sappho. I never indeed knew that he, *fainted, sunk, and died away*, but the agitations of his mind and body, exceeded any thing of the kind I ever knew in real life. He had always a partic-ular jealousy of people who were richer than himself, or who had more consequence in life. His love therefore rarely settled on persons

of this description. When he selected any one out of the sovereignty of his good pleasure to whom he should pay his particular attention, she was instantly invested with a sufficient stock of charms, out of the plentiful stores of his own imagination, and there was often a great dissimilitude between his fair captivator, as she appeared to others, and as she seemed when invested with the attributes he gave her. One generally reigned paramount in his affections, but as Yorick's affections flowed out towards Madame de L—— at the remise door, while the eternal vows of Eliza were upon him, so Robert was frequently encountering other attractions, which formed so many underplots in the drama of his love.[49]

The literature Gilbert alludes to here includes Sappho (associated by Burns in his letters with the height of erotic rapture), Laurence Sterne (whose wildly imaginative sentimental eighteenth-century novel *Tristram Shandy* was a favourite of the teenage Robert), and probably the sort of contemporary drama exemplified by Murdoch's gift, *The School for Lovers*. In Sterne's *A Sentimental Journey* in chapters entitled 'The Remise Door, Calais' and 'The Remise, Calais', the male protagonist, Yorick, enjoys an episode of sentimental erotics with a Lady, while remaining attached to his sweetheart Eliza back home. Writing in 1787 about his youth and early manhood, Burns recalled 'Sterne and Mckenzie. – Tristram Shandy and the Man of Feeling were my bosom favorites.'[50] Nowadays Sterne is still admired, but Mackenzie's soft-centred novel *The Man of Feeling* (1771) – almost a new book when Burns read it – is less fondly remembered. Self-conscious in narrative method, this episodic novel savours what it calls 'romantic melancholy'; it is witty, but its hero Harley can seem disconcertingly over-sensitive in his readiness to burst into tears at others' suffering; the opposite of a businesslike 'man of the world' (title of another Mackenzie novel), Harley struck some readers even in Burns's day as weepily over-emotional. Yet Burns would describe this sentimental novel as 'a book I prize next to the Bible'.[51]

When the teenage Walter Scott met the adult Burns in 1786 he remembered as 'remarkable' the way Burns 'actually shed tears' when he saw on the wall of a grand house a sentimental print of a dead soldier lying in the snow, 'his dog sitting in misery on one side, – on the other, his widow, with a child in her arms'.[52] The Harley-like, emotionally volatile side of Burns was one the poet cultivated at least from his teens. No doubt he built on that tendency to be 'the sport of strong passions' which Burns observed in his father

and probably inherited.⁵³ Reviewing his life at the age of twenty-three, Burns described himself to Murdoch in London as a very unbusinesslike person of 'an extremely delicate constitution'. His 'favorite authors' were 'of the sentim[enta]l kind'. *The Man of Feeling* topped his list of sentimental reading. He went on to name 'Sterne, especially his Sentimental journey, Mcpherson's Ossian, &c. these are the glorious models after which I endeavour to form my conduct'.⁵⁴

Here, explicitly, Burns presents himself as doing what his brother had hinted at: forming his character on books he read. This same Burns routinely engaged in heavy farm-work, but can sound almost like one of his admired bookish wits of Queen Anne's reign. One Lochlea visitor remembered Burns always carrying a book: it was 'his custom to read at table'. Once, sitting in front of a supper of boiled oats, 'he was so intent reading, I think Tristram Shandy, that his spoon falling out of his hand, made him exclaim, in a tone scarcely imitable, "Alas, poor Yorick!"'⁵⁵ Such behaviour became a lifelong habit when Burns was at home. Perhaps endearing to his family, it was also on occasion annoying. His rather affected remarks to Murdoch (that Francophile and sophisticate) show Burns relishing a self-image that sets him apart – a sensitive, imaginative soul among the working-folk of Ayrshire:

> ... these are the glorious models after which I endeavour to form my conduct, and 'tis incongruous, 'tis absurd to suppose that the man whose mind glows with sentiments lighted up at their sacred flame – the man whose heart distends with benevolence to all the human race – he 'who can soar above this little scene of things' – can he descend to mind the paulty conccerns [*sic*] about which the terrae-filial race fret, and fume, and vex themselves? O how the glorious triumph swells my heart!⁵⁶

Shenstone had written of the poet as someone who 'Steals soft, on tip-toe, thro' the croud'.⁵⁷ In this letter, throwing off quotations from Shenstone's favourite poets Thomson and Pope, and self-dramatising in an iambic pentameter which might have come from the tragedy he had composed in his head ('O how the glorious triumph swells my heart!'), Burns is writing a few years after the time of his first amours. He may be scripting himself in 'Wits-of-Queen-Anne' mode, but his self-description matches what Gilbert

observed in him. The high-strung emotionality, the sense at times of being a poor devil, the feeling of specialness: all developed in Burns's teens, nurtured by reading, and noted sometimes with concern by his immediate family, especially his father. 'Let others toil to gain the sordid ore,/ The charms of independence let us sing,' wrote Shenstone, hymning economic freedom from the need to labour.[58] Burns worked hard, but wanted to assert his own kinds of independence. He did so not just through obsessive reading but also through his sexuality.

It is impossible to identify with certainty Burns's early girlfriends. Nineteenth-century stories from the Tarbolton area offer many candidates. Recalling one Tarbolton farmer's daughter, Agnes Fleming, who would have been about fourteen when Burns was twenty, Gilbert mentioned to an inquirer decades later that 'her charms were indeed mediocre, but what she had were sexual, which was the characteristic of the greater part of the poet's mistresses; for he was no Platonic lover, however he might otherwise pretend, or suppose of himself'.[59] This has a resentful ring of truth about it. As for the specific reference to Agnes Fleming, there is little to suggest that Burns in his late teens was having sex with this girl six years younger. Burns recalled 'My Nanie, O' as a song 'done at a very early period of life', but Agnes and its short-form Nanie were common names in the area, and standard names for lasses in songs.

Even as he sang of love, Burns was as influenced by song itself and by reading. There is a characteristic mixture of book-generated sentiment and real feeling when, aged twenty-five, he writes a note about this song made several years earlier:

Shenstone observes finely that love-verses writ without any real passion are the most nauseous of all conceits; and I have often thought that no man can be a proper critic of Love composition, except he himself, in one, or more instances, have been a warm votary of this passion. – As I have been all along, a miserable dupe to Love, and have been led into a thousand weaknesses and follies by it, for that reason I put the more confidence in my critical skill in distinguishing foppery and conceit, from real passion and nature. – Whether to say the following song will stand the test, I will not pretend to say, because it is my own; only I can say it was, at the time, real.[60]

The seasoned Burns of twenty-five might look back over his 'thousand ... follies'. Burns the teenager had not quite racked up the

full thousand, but was eager to try. In keeping with Gilbert's memory of his brother, Robert's early songs record both a fascination with and a resentment towards girls who look down their noses. There is evident eagerness for sexual experience:

> There lives a lass beside yon park
> I'd rather hae her in her sark
> Than you wi' a' your thousand mark
> That gars you look sae high –[61]

Yet these sentiments from a song Burns remembered composing 'about the age of seventeen' are in part generated by literature. Some phrases come from Shakespeare and Pope. The verse just quoted is powered in part by Burns's early favourite song 'The Blathrie o't', which sings how 'I wad rather hae my lassie, tho' she cam in her smock,/ Than a princess wi' the gear and the blathrie o't'.[62] Song and reading – not just girls he saw around him – made an evident impact.

Burns and his family knew people from surrounding farms. The Steen or Steven family of Littlehill were their neighbours to the west. Burns's wee sister thought her brother in his teens had been sweet on her namesake, Isabella Steven. Another story links Robert's name with that of a female farm servant from Coldcothill, a few hundred yards north of Lochlea. Burns's eye for girls on local farms may not have endeared him to all the farmers. He made scornful verses on James Grieve, 'Laird of Boghead', just west of Lochlea.[63] In Tarbolton itself, a village of over four hundred people, it was easier to meet girls away from family and immediate neighbours.

Tarbolton had known better times, but kept a strong sense of local community. It had alehouses, churches, and a market where the Burns family could sell farm produce. There were several associations for mutual support – the Weavers' Guild, the local farmers' society, two Masonic lodges. Tarbolton was and still is a small place with a long sense of history. The vernacular architecture of single-storey cottages near the centre indicates what the village once looked like. You can still see a medieval motte and bailey, a grassed-over mound known in Burns's day as '*Hood's Hill*' and on which traditionally at the midsummer time of the June Fair, a bonfire was kindled. Four miles inland from the coastal town of Prestwick, its climate 'moist, and subject to frequent rains', Burns's Tarbolton lay

in an Ayrshire dairy-farming area, 'the cows ... famous for the abundance of their milk'. Farms in the area customarily gave over one-third of their arable ground to corn, and two-thirds to 'sown grasses'. The parish minister in the late eighteenth century thought the locals 'in general, a stout, healthy, cleanly, good-looking people, not ill educated, and still impressed with a great and serious respect for the ordinances of religion'.[64]

Tarbolton was classic Kirk ground. Glasgow-University-educated 'prophet' Alexander Peden had worked as a local schoolteacher in the mid-seventeenth century prior to his persecution and imprisonment as a radical Covenanting preacher. Peden was said to have gone into hiding in a cave on the River Lugar. That river is mentioned in some of Burns's earliest work and Peden's Cave is still visible, downstream from Wallace's Cave. Part of that Ayrshire Covenanting heritage dear to Burns's mother's family, Peden was an ordained minister, a radical, an outsider; the cloth mask and wig he is said to have worn to conceal his identity from government troops can still be seen in Edinburgh's Museum of Scotland. In the eighteenth century, as today, the weavers' village of Tarbolton, for all the power of landlords and gentry, could boast of a strong radical heritage.

It had a lively oral culture, not just of song and chat but also of verse-making. This is most clearly represented at the time of Burns's arrival by the local tailor, Alexander, or 'Saunders', Tait. Then in his fifties, Tait had settled in the village a few years earlier. A celebrated local versifier, he even attracted some patronage from gentry. In 1777 he had been active in building Tarbolton's Burgher or Secession Church. Pursuing a stricter, grimmer theology, the Burghers had seceded from the Kirk of Scotland. The Burns family attended the established Kirk with its more liberal minister. Scorning McGill's theology and dismissing Dalrymple as a lightweight – 'a feather' – Tait mocked the ministers Burns admired. For Tait moderate 'New Light' theology was linked with abominations like theatrical performance, dancing and uninhibited sex. Improbably, he imagined 'Newlight priests ... Dancing wi' hizzies [hussies] naked'. Rather attracted to these sorts of abominations, the young Burns too began to make poems on local people, places and events. Little love was lost between him and Tait, some of whose *Poems and Songs* (published in Paisley in 1790) give a good flavour of life in the village whose bard Tait wished to become.

TARBOLTON Village where I dwell,
My tongue maun be thy warning bell,
We've fine commodities to sell,
    They are not scant;
I'll mark them down, ye'll may be tell
    Just what ye want.

        . . .

We've pots, and pans, and dying leads;
We've leeks and plants, and garden seeds,
Sheers, knittings, garters, knives and beads,
    Corn, pease and hay;
We've ruffs, pluffs, muffs, and maiden-heads,
    White, black, or grey.

Cataloguing what's available in Tarbolton, Tait pictures a bustling community of farmers, gardeners, housewives, drinkers, ministers, blacksmiths, wheelwrights and others concerned about horses, clothes, homes, and routinely troubled with fleas. It is a place where, despite the vigilance of the righteous, lewdness is not always under control: there are 'Bra[w] hizzies too, to bob in beds/ Until ye tire'.[65]

This community was the centre of the teenage Burns's social life. The only contemporary observer who gave a detailed description of his appearance then was another of Tarbolton's aspiring poets, farmer's son David Sillar. A year younger than Burns, Sillar had grown up at Spittalside farm, almost in Tarbolton itself. 'Denied', as he put it, 'the advantage of a liberal education', Sillar later maintained that 'however necessary a learned education may be in Divinity, Philosophy, or the Sciences, it is a fact, that some of the best Poetical Performances amongst us have been composed by illiterate men. Natural genius alone is sufficient to constitute a Poet.' Or, as he put it in verse which aligns him closely with Burns,

        I ne'er depended for my knowledge,
        On School, Academy, nor College.
        I gat my learnin' at the flail,
        An' some I catch'd at the plough tail.
        Amang the brutes I own I'm bred,
        Since herding is my native trade.[66]

Sillar's interests ranged from football to farming, but poetry and song were his passions. His published work shows how hard he tried to succeed: 'I've rhym'd at wark, I've rhym'd at rest,/ I've rhym'd till sleep has me opprest:/ In love I've rhym'd up with the best.'[67] Sillar and Burns had much in common. Burns, though, became 'the best', and, at one level, Sillar, with mixed jealousy, pride and gratitude, knew it.

Sillar read English and Scots enthusiastically. His later poetry has an eye for 'The Fair Sex'.[68] When he and Burns met around 1780 Sillar was trying to make a living as a Tarbolton schoolteacher. In 1783 he moved to Irvine to set up as a grocer. Burns at Lochlea found him a real kindred spirit. They shared an 'anxious wish' that through poetry 'fame in life my name would bless', as Sillar put it; a lively farmer's son with a sense of wide cultural horizons, he was another wit.[69]

Written mainly in the 1780s, Sillar's poems show a taste for authors like Robert Blair whose sepulchral *The Grave* Burns too admired. Sillar relished Pope, Shenstone, Milton, Dryden, and Ovid in translation, not to mention earlier eighteenth-century Scots poets like Allan Ramsay and Robert Fergusson. Burns's new friend also refers to John Locke's *Essay Concerning Human Understanding*, another text Robert read as a young man. Like Burns, Sillar knew 'melancholy' and a fear of living 'on Poortith's [poverty's] brink', but could also see himself as a 'hairum scairum head,/ Mair stuff'd wi nonsense than wi' greed'.[70] He could savour 'satire's keenest style'.[71] He was in many ways the perfect local companion, and his verse reads frequently like a smudgy carbon-copy of Burns's. Burns went on to call Sillar '*Ace o' Hearts*' – best pal.[72] Sillar liked that, and quoted it back.[73]

A fiddler with a liking for Scots songs, Sillar composed music and wrote words to accompany tunes like 'My Nanie O' and 'Corn Rigs are Bonie'. The young Burns set songs to the same airs. Consciously or not, these friends vied with each other. Burns, aware of being an almost unknown country lad, asserts that love matters more than wealth:

> My riches a's my penny-fee,
> An' I maun guide it cannie, O;
> But warl's gear ne'er troubles me,
> My thoughts are a', my Nanie, O.[74]

Sillar brings similar sentiments to the same tune in his mischievous song about a shepherd tricked by an old man into marrying a bride without a dowry; but Sillar's expression is more awkward:

> 'If I hae gotten a' ye had,
> 'Tae grudge wad be but folly O;
> 'I'll never mak a worse a bad,
> 'But live content wi' Nelly O.'[75]

Burns's youngest sister recalled how, following Sillar's example, Burns at Lochlea bought himself a fiddle, but wasn't very good at it. Within a decade Burns and Sillar would publish collections of poetry with the same Kilmarnock printer. Burns's would be a runaway success; Sillar's, for all its 'respectable and numerous Subscribers', a failure.[76] Burns's first book contains his warm 'Epistle to Davie, a Brother Poet' (or, as one manuscript has it, 'a brother Poet, Lover, Ploughman and Fiddler') with a sly personal allusion to Davie's taste for 'Foot Ball'.[77] Burns's poem also celebrates walks the two youths had shared in Ayrshire countryside, their friendship strengthened by love of making Scots songs:

> What tho', like Commoners of air,
> We wander out, we know not where,
>   But either house or hal'?
> Yet *Nature*'s charms, the hills and woods,
> The sweeping vales, and foaming floods,
>   Are free alike to all.
> In days when Daisies deck the ground,
>   And Blackbirds whistle clear,
> With honest joy, our hearts will bound,
>   To see the *coming* year:
>   On braes when we please then,
>   We'll sit and *sowth* a tune;
>   Syne *rhyme* till't, we'll time till't,
>   And sing't when we hae done.[78]

Later, reprinting this poem for an Edinburgh audience, Burns explained the Scots word 'sowth' meant 'to try over a tune with a low whistle'.[79] Given that Burns and Sillar went on to publish songs with identical tunes, this 'Epistle to Davie' surely offers an account of the compositional technique they shared. Sillar had a real interest

in how poems were made, and how to become a poet. Like several other works, his 'A Receipt to Make a Poet', published in 1789, may well have had Burns in mind. It explains that the poet, as well as possessing 'tender sympathy' must

> ... have a stock of self-esteem and pride:
> Must know the right; but by his passions strong
> Must be compell'd to do that which is wrong;
> Who, when 'tis done, repentance keen must gnaw
> His very self, for breaking virtue's law:
> Must copy Nature ...[80]

Replying to Burns's 'Epistle to Davie', Sillar's first book has an 'Epistle to R. Burns ... auld Frien' an' Neebor'.[81] Friendship is Sillar's repeated theme. In print he makes much of his links to Burns; in poetry mostly written when he was a grocer in Irvine, Sillar is occasionally resentful of Burns's celebrity. The two men kept in touch in later years; Burns helped Davie get subscribers for his *Poems*; but they were never as close as during and just after Burns's time at Lochlea. Once, writing about the way poetry happens, Sillar exclaimed, 'L——d man! I've laugh'd, an' danc'd, an' sung an' fiddl'd,/ Till joy, like death, my very blood has cruddl'd.'[82] Such sentiments could have been those of the young Burns, eager to attend dancing school, witty, musical, hungry for happiness and song.

Sillar's sympathetic closeness to Burns at Lochlea makes his later, sharply remembered description of his friend about the age of twenty worth quoting at length. After Burns's death Sillar became a founder of Irvine Burns Club and gave this account to Ayr lawyer Robert Aiken:

> Mr ROBERT BURNS was some time in the parish of Tarbolton prior to my acquaintance with him. What he was, and what education he received in the neighbourhood of Ayr, you have in your own place the most genuine sources of information. His social disposition easily procured him acquaintance; but a certain satirical seasoning, with which he and all poetical geniuses are in some degree influenced, while it set the rustic circle in a roar, was not unaccompanied by its kindred attendant – suspicious fear. He wore the only tied hair in the parish; and in the church, he, [*sic*] his plaid, which was of a particular colour, I think fillemot, he wrapped in a particular manner round his shoulders. These surmises, and his exterior, had such a magnetical

influence on my curiosity, as made me particularly solicitous of his acquaintance. Whether my acquaintance with Gilbert was casual or premeditated, I am not now certain. By him I was introduced, not only to his brother, but to the whole of that family, where, in a short time, I became a frequent, and I believe, not unwelcome visitant. After the commencement of my acquaintance with the bard, we frequently met upon Sundays at church, when, between sermons, instead of going with our friends or lasses to the inn, we often took a walk in the fields. In these walks, I have frequently been struck by his facility in addressing the fair sex; and many times, when I have been bashfully anxious how to express myself, he would have entered into conversation with them with the greatest ease and freedom; and it was generally a death-blow to our conversation, however agreeable, to meet a female acquaintance. Some of the few opportunities of a noontide walk that a country-life allows her laborious sons, he spent on the banks of the river, or in the woods, in the neighbourhood of Stair, a situation peculiarly adapted to the genius of a rural bard. Some book (generally one of those mentioned in his letter . . . to Mr John Murdoch) he always carried and read, when not otherwise employed. It was likewise his custom to read at table . . . His, like the genius of many others, was in a great measure directed by adventitious circumstances. Education, associates, and rank in society, are the principal. We know some, and have read of many, born in humbler situations, whose genius has enabled them to surmount astonishing difficulties, and who are filling, and have filled with reputation, the most respectable offices in society, we have also seen the reverse. Our bard's genius or mental power was undoubtedly great; and having such parents to guide, and such a companion as his brother in his juvenile studies, were to him fortunate circumstances. He had in his youth paid considerable attention to the arguments for and against the doctrine of original sin, then making considerable noise in your neighbourhood; and having perused Dr Taylor's work on that subject, and 'Letters on Religion essential to Man,' when he came to Tarbolton, his opinions were of consequence favourable to what you Ayr people call the moderate side. The religion of the people of Tarbolton at that time was purely the religion of their fathers, founded on the Westminster Confession, and taught by one generation to another, uncontaminated by reading, reflection, and conversation, and though divided into different sectaries, the Shorter Catechism was the line which bounded all their controversies. The slightest insinuation of Taylor's opinions made his neighbours suspect, and some even avoid him, as an heretical and dangerous companion.[83]

Here, presenting the somewhat dandyish young Burns whose satir-
ical wit and ease with women annoyed Saunders Tait, Sillar also
mentions riverbank and woodland walks at nearby Stair. This fits
in with the poetic strolls by 'hills and woods . . . and foaming floods'
celebrated in the 'Epistle to Davie', but the exact location is signif-
icant. At Stair House Sillar's future wife Margaret Orr worked as
a servant; Burns is said to have helped Sillar court her, which accords
with Sillar's sense of bashfulness beside his friend's winning fluency,
and with Burns's later remark that he enjoyed 'being in the secret
of half the amours of the parish':

> A country lad rarely carries on an amour without an assisting confi-
> dent. – I possessed a curiosity, zeal and intrepid dexterity in these
> matters which recommended me a proper Second in duels of that
> kind . . .[84]

Burns loved this sort of friendly erotic game-playing. He was
known for it; on the whole it seems to have made him popular.
The wooded, winding banks of the River Ayr around Stair were,
Burns wrote, 'Fit haunts for Friendship or for Love,/ In musing
mood'.[85] Still beautiful, they are rich in birdlife and sites of former
grand houses. Burns celebrates this terrain more through naming
local places and notable families than through extended descrip-
tion. An older woman, Catherine Gordon, wife of Alexander
Stewart of Stair, became in time one of his earliest genteel patrons:
'the first person of her sex & rank . . . that patronised his . . .
humble lays'.[86]

Just west, close to the river, was Coilsfield House. Even bitter
Tait admired the 'pretty plants', elegant trees and teeming birdlife
of its grounds.[87] Burns in 1784 recorded that the supposed 'burial
place' of 'Coilus King of the Picts, from whom the district of Kyle
is said to take its name . . . is still shown' nearby. Coilsfield was
home to 'Sodger Hugh', as the poet called him.[88] The soldier Hugh
Montgomerie fought in the Seven Years War; later, in 1796, he
became twelfth Earl of Eglinton on the death of his cousin Archibald,
governor of Edinburgh Castle and a veteran of combat with
Cherokees in America. The Ayr's banks where Burns walked
boasted several great men's houses. Just over a mile east of Coils-
field was Barskimming, where Burns found 'many a wild, romantic
grove' and 'many a hermit-fancy'd cove'.[89] From boyhood he

had known Thomas Parnell's 'The Hermit', a poem in Masson's *Collection* which features walkers in woodland who pass a mansion:

> Far in a wild unknown to public view,
> From youth to age a rev'rend *Hermit* grew;
> The moss his bed, the cave his humble cell,
> His food the fruits, his drink the crystal well . . .[90]

'Parnell I read when I was young,/ And thought his Muse was silly,' confessed Sillar, admitting, "Tis true I did his Hermit prize.'[91] This was yet another taste Sillar shared with Burns, who, just before mentioning a '*Hermit*' in a 1786 poem about 'meand'ring' by an 'unfrequented stream' would remake the opening of Parnell's most famous poem:

> How blest the Solitary's lot,
> Who, all-forgetting, all-forgot,
>   Within his humble cell,
> The cavern wild with tangling roots,
> Sits o'er his newly-gather'd fruits,
>   Beside his crystal well![92]

Whether his walk was a solitary one, or he accompanied Sillar at Barskimming, Burns knew he was passing the houses of powerful folk. His poetry identifies the '*aged Judge*' of Barskimming as 'the Lord Justice Clerk'.[93] Sir Thomas Miller, Lord President of the Court of Session, was well known to Edinburgh's literati. Hume remarked that this laird of Barskimming 'retained through life the highest relish of the beauties of Nature, and every year spent a considerable part of the recess of business in the enjoyment and improvement of the romantic scenes at his seat 'by the Ayr.[94] This house, now demolished, was approached by a 'noble bridge of one arch ninety feet wide, and one hundred high . . . resting on the perpendicular sides of a rock . . . beneath which the river rolls its blackest streams'. Barskimming's 'romantic beauties' attracted tourists, including, in the 1780s, a young Cambridge graduate who noted that although 'The house itself is nothing remarkable . . . our approach for several miles afforded a charming anticipation; natural woods hanging on the rocky banks of the slowly winding Ayr, and extensive plantations that every where surround the delightful

premises.'⁹⁵ This was the sort of landscape loved by devotees of the picturesque. On a visit to Barskimming the Reverend Dr Hugh Blair, Professor of Rhetoric and Belles Lettres at Edinburgh University, would be astounded by the quality of one of Burns's poems.⁹⁶ Two miles upriver lived 'The learned *Sire* and *Son*' – 'the late doctor, and present Professor Stewart'.⁹⁷ Edinburgh philosophy professor Dugald Stewart, laird of Catrine, would invite Burns to dine there in 1786, discussing with him everything from surveying to poetry; Burns wept 'tears of admiration and rapture' when Stewart quoted poems new to him.⁹⁸

When Burns as a youth and young man at Lochlea strolled beside the River Ayr, all this lay in the future. Yet if he was anything like as ambitious as Sillar, he would have known his walks took him past homes of taste and renown, not just romantic coves. 'The Vision', his 1784–5 paean to poetry and Ayrshire, is in part a walking poem retracing earlier riverbank rambles: it moves up the Ayr, passing Stair, Coilsfield, Barskimming and Catrine; then one version of the poem goes inland along the River Lugar towards Cumnock, past the 'Mansion fine,/ The seat of many a Muse divine' at Auchinleck, home of James Boswell's family.⁹⁹ Burns's youthful route, enriched by poems he had read, was not just a stroll in nature. It also marked the direction of his literary ambitions.

As yet, though, to many in Tarbolton Burns was more notable for potentially 'heretical' views than literary eminence. Tarbolton's religious climate around 1780 may strike us as alien; to Sillar, Burns's relationship to it was important. Sillar had limited patience with those he called 'The Heresy Hunters'. His other friends would include an Ayrshireman studying Divinity at Edinburgh University whom Sillar asks,

> Will ye appear i' the *New Light*,
> Which pits sae mony in a fright;
> Or come an' *Orthodoxian Wight*,
>   Inspir'd an' proud,
> An' roarin' H-ll wi' a your might,
>   Tae please the crowd?¹⁰⁰

Tarbolton Seceders were a crowd eager for such enthusiastic hell-fire preaching. Sillar and Burns felt differently. Careful reading of Sillar's memories of Burns in Lochlea shows it was not unusual for

Robert to attend the local Church of Scotland with his family, listening to more than one sermon at Sunday services. It was an accepted thing for men to go with 'friends or lasses to the inn' between sermons. Sometimes Burns did just that. Though Ayrshire Presbyterian attitudes to religion could be strictly theocratic, among many members of the congregation expectations were more relaxed. Burns's Tarbolton minister during the Lochlea years was Patrick Wodrow, son of a learned chronicler of Covenanters whose lengthy *History of the Sufferings of the Church of Scotland from the Restoration to the Revolution* was well known. Patrick Wodrow, like Burns's childhood minister, 'mild' Dalrymple, belonged to the Kirk's moderate New Light wing; again like Dalrymple, Wodrow was awarded an honorary doctorate by the University of St Andrews.[101] In such a climate more liberal theological views developed.

Sillar suggests several of Burns's neighbours thought him a 'dangerous companion'. Robert at Lochlea showed a strong commitment to the theology of Dr John Taylor of Norwich who argued in his work that in reading the Bible 'we ought not to admit anything contradictory to the common sense and understanding of mankind'.[102] This was central to New Light theology. An attraction to Taylor's work, though, was unlikely to have alienated Burns from Wodrow; there is every indication the poet was a churchgoing member of that minister's congregation. Sillar also recalled Burns reading a translation from the French of Marie Huber's *Letters Concerning the Religion Essential to Man*. Published in Glasgow in 1761, this work addressed 'Moderate and Unprejudiced READERS'. It argued that God 'will never require' mankind to renounce 'intelligence and liberty'.[103] Some saw Huber as deistic in tendency; certainly the book was theologically liberal.

A sign of the Tarbolton Kirk minister's liberalism was that he was an active Freemason. Even today Masonic emblems are not hard to spot in Scottish towns and villages, including Tarbolton. Often associated with deism and sometimes with radicalism, Freemasonry was an important part of social life. Meeting in their regalia with secret rituals and ceremonies, the all-male Masons helped each other and their community. Nowadays Tarbolton Masons run a social club offering bingo evenings and football on satellite television. They also have a splendid website with its own virtual museum, on-line tours of Tarbolton Kilwinning St James No. 135 Masonic Lodge, and a detailed history of the local organisation. Eighteenth-century

Tarbolton Freemasonry brought together working-men and gentry in an organisation at once hierarchical and comparatively classless: a band of initiated 'brothers' who drank together, paid for glasses they smashed, processed on occasion to the parish kirk to hear Brother Wodrow preach, and enjoyed manly fellowship. In an Ayrshire notorious for banking failure, they also lent each other money.

Tracing its provenance to ancient Egypt, Freemasonry was an international brotherhood. Mozart was a Mason; George Washington warmly received the Masonic Constitutions of his American brethren; the Grand Lodge in Prussia was instituted under a constitution from Scotland. As eighteenth-century Masons were proud to testify, their activities extended not just across Europe but also to 'India and America'. Writing in the ninth edition of *Illustrations of Masonry* in 1796, William Preston, 'Past Master of the Lodge of Antiquity acting by immemorial constitution', emphasised that 'the proceedings of the Brethren of Scotland particularly claim attention'.[104] Masonic networks flourished across Burns's native land, not least in Ayrshire.

Masons believed nature offered proof of a deity:

WHOEVER attentively observes the objects which surround him, will find abundant reason to admire the works of Nature, and to adore the Being who directs such astonishing operations: he will be convinced, that infinite wisdom could alone design, and infinite power finish, such amazing works.[105]

These views accord with the theology Burns admired. Masonic emphasis on '*advantages resulting from friendship*', presented as 'the source of universal benevolence', must also have appealed. Even in conflict, 'Conscious integrity supports' the Mason 'against the arm of power; and should he bleed by tyrant-hands, he gloriously dies a martyr in the cause of liberty.' 'Confined to no particular country', but covering 'the whole terrestrial globe', Masonry offered 'an universal language'. Loyalty to immediate connections such as local community or country took precedence, but 'the true mason is a citizen of the world, and his philanthropy extends to all the human race'.[106] Masonry allowed room for individual conscience in belief. Its deistic inclination countered theological fanaticism in Burns's Ayrshire:

The spirit of the fulminating priest will be tamed; and a moral brother, though of a different persuasion, engage his esteem: for mutual toleration in religious opinions is one of the most distinguishing and most valuable characteristics of the Craft. As all religions teach morality, if a brother is found to act the part of a truly honest man, his private speculative opinions are left to God and himself.[107]

Sometimes these ideals faltered in practice: Saunders Tait, zealous attacker of liberal theologians, was a Tarbolton Mason. Still, the Masonic vision of universal brotherhood and liberty of conscience in belief, strong in the Tarbolton area, moulded the young Burns. Masons also liked poetry, having their own songs, odes and anthems. By the time Preston's 1796 edition of *Illustrations of Masonry* was published, these included a song by Burns, addressing his 'Dear brothers of the mystic tie'.[108] Burns did not become a Tarbolton Mason until summer 1781, but may have been attracted by Masonic ideals even before he formally joined.

The Reverend Wodrow had offered prayers at the foundation of the Tarbolton Kilwinning Lodge in 1771. Participants included local landowners like the Montgomeries of Coilsfield and Sir Thomas Wallace Dunlop of Craigie (son of Burns's future friend and patron, Mrs Dunlop) as well as local farmers and tradesmen; several names are familiar from Burns's writings. By 1780 nearly three hundred Masons had been initiated locally, though not all attended regular meetings. There was friction in Tarbolton's Masonic community. Two rival lodges had united uneasily in 1781 with another Wodrow, Robert, as their secretary. Accusation and counter-accusation throughout the early 1780s saw Robert Wodrow threatened with prosecution. As kinsman of the Kirk minister he had a position in local society; yet in the Masonic world of fraternal equality, that counted for less and he might readily be challenged. In a community where authority was simultaneously accepted, contested, and even sometimes disregarded, Burns matured as an exceptional resident, but was still shaped by Tarbolton's complex nexus of values.

Masonic goings-on give some indication of the conduct of men in the parish; indications of female society in a place where many young women were domestic servants are harder to come by. One account was written by Gilbert Burns in 1785 when he was twenty-five. Coloured by his recent romantic disappointment, it may also be affected by awareness that his elder brother was more successful

with women. Still, it shows how the teenager closest to Burns felt about the girls of Tarbolton parish, and communicates too something of Gilbert's character and literary style as influenced by William Burnes:

> I was about sixteen when we removed from Mount-Oliphant to Lochlee a pretty large farm in the parish of Tarbolton: there a new scene of action opens, I saw myself in a place where no one knew much of me where I was at liberty to assume any character I thought proper and as I was among my peers in point of station I vainly imagined my superior education would enable me to act a distinguished part: nothing less therefore would serve my turn than to be a man of vivacity and gallantry, accomplished in every thing useful and agreable. I stept briskly into all companys and was introduced to some of the most distinguished of the young females on whom I danced attendance in the manner of the place; but though they caused a palpitation in my heart unknown before I soon found they had not that tenderness, that delicacy of sentiment, or that truth which I expected among the sex; I found that those notions and sentiments I had gathered from Philosophers and Poets were of no use to me among illiterate country people, and my youth and ignorance of the world betrayed me into a thousand absurditys which my quick sensibility rendered exceeding painful to me. I therefore quitted these pursuits with a mixture of shame and disgust . . .

At Lochlea Gilbert found among the locals 'low and ungenerous minds' and 'base malignant passion' which made him retreat from society at times, feeling 'misanthropic'. He wrote of the period of late teens and young manhood that 'too much care cannot be taken about this time of life to guard against the incroachments of impure desire'. Remarking that he never allowed himself 'to look on it [impure desire] as some do', he inserts in his manuscript the words 'as an innocent gratification'.[109] He may have had his older brother in mind. It would be incredible if the young Gilbert had not from time to time measured himself against Robert. Writing in his twenties, Gilbert can sound prudish about his 'own virtue', the need to 'banish every impure thought' and avoid 'all obscene conversation and all company who indulge themselves in it'.[110]

Commentators, though, sometimes remarked on similarities between the two oldest Burns boys. At Lochlea Robert, like Gilbert, took an opportunity to reinvent himself. Off to his dancing class,

renowned for wit, and for ease with girls, Burns tried to exhibit vivacity and gallantry. Gilbert's identification with his own reading made it hard for him to come to terms with Tarbolton folk in the flesh. Robert, however, matured by adventures at Kirkoswald, used reading to power his enjoyment of life. He could call not just on bookish 'philosophers and poets' but also on folk traditions of song – and now on his own experience – to make the most of life around him.

Evidence for this lies less in dubious efforts to identify Burns's girlfriends than in the tenor of his writings. 'If any thing on earth,' he wrote at the age of twenty-four, 'deserves the name of rapture or transport it is the feelings of green eighteen in the company of the mistress of his heart when she repays him with an equal return of affection.'[111] An early song written, like one of Sillar's, to the tune 'Corn Rigs are Bonie', refers to 'merry drinking' while 'blythe wi' Comrades dear', as well as to the pleasure of 'happy thinking'. Its heart, though, lies elsewhere:

> I lock'd her in my fond embrace;
>   Her heart was beating rarely:
> My blessings on that happy place,
>   Amang the rigs o barley![112]

Another early song, never published by Burns but accepted as his, was collected by English engraver Robert Cromek for his 1808 *Reliques of Burns* 'from the oral communication of a lady residing at Glasgow, whom the Bard in early life affectionately admired'.[113] The song shows the musical, flirtatious, sexy and intellectual way Burns in English with just a tincture of Scots linked his book-reading to the stuff of Tarbolton parish; the Cessnock Water flows a couple of miles north of Lochlea:

> Her voice is like the ev'ning thrush
>   That sings on Cessnock banks unseen,
> While his mate sits nestling in the bush;
>   An' she has twa sparkling, rogueish een.
>
> But it's not her air, her form, her face,
>   Though matching beauty's fabled Queen;
> 'Tis the mind that shines in ev'ry grace,
>   An' chiefly in her rogueish een.[114]

Probably dating from the start of Burns's twenties, this song hints at how engaging he could be with women. For all his sentimental reading, he liked nothing better than roguish eyes.

'Friendly and entertaining' is how his friend Candlish characterised a letter Burns wrote to him just after turning twenty. That letter is lost, but Candlish's reply shows how much he valued Robert's friendship. Written from Glasgow where twenty-year-old Candlish was studying medicine, it indicates too that Burns was enclosing poems with correspondence. More 'delighted' than he can say with Burns's 'verses', Candlish asks his friend to 'now and then favour me with such stanzas, as you may think fit'. At Glasgow University Candlish feels 'the college is not favourable for cultivating an acquaintance with the muses'. Being told that must have confirmed in Burns a sense that his own reading, practice and observation in Ayrshire could develop his poetry better than formal education. By this time he was reading not just for general enjoyment but specifically to nourish his writing. He discussed poetry with Candlish, mentioning he was enjoying Pope's epistles and using Pope as an 'assistant' to his own development. 'I believe you could not have got one more excellent than him in the poetical way,' Candlish replied, encouraging Burns to follow his own sure taste in literature to guide his 'study'.

This 'study' to which Candlish referred in 1779 was not mensuration, surveying or dialling. It was (as Candlish's damaged, occasionally indecipherable letter indicates) something else Burns had clearly been writing about:

> I am happy to [see] you are engaged in such a useful and agreeable a study this winter as you tell me. It is a study productive of the most rational pleasure and I think it most admirably calculated to your present situation, as being of all studies, one of the most proper to enable men to regulate their conduct right. And, besides, it requires not such a [*words indecipherable*], and expensive train of assistants, as many others. A steady reflection on what passes in oneself, and an attentive observation to what passes among men in the world in general, is the most effectual means one can use for studying human nature to advantage.[115]

The 'study' Burns told his friend he was pursuing is surely that recommended in Pope's 'Epistles to H. St John L. Bolingbroke', commonly known as *An Essay on Man*:

Know then thyself, presume not God to scan;
The proper study of Mankind is Man.[116]

Replying to Burns, Candlish explained that Pope 'adopted most of his philosophical notions from Bollingbrock, his great friend'. Taking exception to 'that part where' Pope 'reduces all the principles of inner action to reason, and self-love', Candlish is referring to the same part of *An Essay on Man*, where Pope contends, 'Two Principles in human nature reign;/ Self-love, to urge, and Reason, to restrain.'[117]

Pope's *Essay on Man* is the first poem from which Burns quotes in his surviving correspondence. It impressed him profoundly. In another poem from which Burns later quoted to Candlish, Pope is the 'Bard unequal'd'; verses commonly prefacing *An Essay on Man* in eighteenth-century editions called Pope a 'heav'nly-taught . . . bard divine'.[118] Pope's *Essay* is not just witty. It has what he calls a 'design . . . (to use my Lord Bacon's expression) [to] *come home to Men's Business and Bosoms*' so as to provide a '*general Map* of MAN'. Writing of his 'science of Human Nature' – what David Hume went on to term the science of man – Pope wanted to steer 'between the extremes of doctrines seemingly opposite'. A poet, he thought the memorable conciseness of verse made it best for mapping mankind.

The young Candlish and Burns were steeped in the Pope of these epistles. Later, Burns wrote many verse letters. For now he contented himself with enclosing verses in his prose correspondence. Pope was a fellow Freemason. Pope's poems accorded with Burns's moderate theology, theological reading, and the Masonic assumptions prevalent in his community. The Creator's hand was visible in the order of creation, so Pope did not seek to argue about God's precise form. Taught by 'Great Nature' – 'Learn of the mole to plow, the worm to weave' – man had advanced to his present-day self: that ploughing, weaving self familiar enough in Tarbolton.[119] 'Happiness' was 'our being's end and aim'. It lay, contended Pope, 'not in the good of one, but all'.[120] Pope's poem scorns mere avarice for gold: 'Is yellow dirt the passion of thy life?'[121] In a song surely written in that winter of 1779–80 Burns upbraids a girl, 'Tibby', for looking down her nose at a youth lacking 'yellow dirt'.[122]

Pope praises not businessmen but those who study man. They understand human nature and the place of the human in nature. The student of man is a 'Slave to no sect, who takes no private

road,/ But looks thro' Nature, up to Nature's God'.[123] Beginning
with love of individual self, Pope's student progresses from part to
whole: to love of other people and the created universe. The student
shows

> erring Pride, WHATEVER IS, IS RIGHT;
> That REASON, PASSION, answer one great aim;
> That true SELF-LOVE and SOCIAL are the same;
> That VIRTUE only makes our Bliss below;
> And all our Knowledge is, OURSELVES TO KNOW.[124]

Cautioning Burns against Pope's wholehearted emphasis on reason
and self-love, Candlish finds it 'almost impossible I think to see in
what sense he takes reason and self-love'. Candlish urges Burns 'to
judge as well as admire' Pope.[125] Burns admired Pope hugely. The
English poet's satirically witty, yet also philosophically benevolent
poetry gave him an aesthetic, even a moral compass.

Consciously assisted by Pope, Burns set himself to study what he
calls in his earliest surviving letter, addressed in July 1780 to William
Niven, 'the soul of man' and 'the human mind'.[126] Conducted outside
academia, Burns's 'analizing' project was thoroughly at one with
the ideals of the Scottish Enlightenment science of man, which owed
its own debts to Pope and Locke. Where Pope takes what sounds
like a vice – 'Self-Love' – and argues it has a good side, Burns in
this letter does the same with 'Pride' which, he contends, is

> [neither go]od nor bad in itself; but, [when] joined [with other man]ly
> dispositions it is part of the noblest vi[rtu]es; or, when mixed with
> corrupted & disingenuous inclinations, it enters largely into the
> composition of many vices. I do not think I can convey my notion
> of it to you better, than by analizing some of the virtues in which it
> is most conspicuous.[127]

Burns here uses 'pride' to mean what is now called self-esteem, but
also admits pride can be negative. At his best he developed a con-
fident sense of self-worth, though at times it imploded into a dark
certainty of abnegation. His earliest letter shows him valuing
character traits such as being 'generous, frank, open', having 'a
delicate taste' and 'uncommonly clear penetration'. Yet sometimes
he likes 'some characters that may be said to be without pride in a
great measure'. Among these in particular, rather like the Pope who

wrote in *An Essay on Man* about 'the sage's indolence', Burns has 'a great esteem' for the man who displays 'Indolence of temper: a man of this sort unless very much harrassed is always easy & calm'.[128]

Here, again in a gesture reminiscent of what Pope does with 'Self-Love', Burns takes what seems a vice – 'Indolence' – and uses it in a positive sense. Philosophically mischievous, this shows how Burns likes upsetting conventional assumptions. It also hints at his wish to defend his apparently indolent inclination to observe mankind, instead of going out and getting a job away from his family. Regarding himself as 'a Physiognomist', he loved observing other people.[129] He was still linking this to his commitment to Pope and 'the proper study of mankind' three years after he and Candlish discussed his Popeian 'study'. In September 1782 he writes to another Kirkoswald friend, Thomas Orr, again making a virtue out of what might be described as indolence. Burns is trying to sound relaxed, telling his correspondent he is

> studying men, their manners, & their ways, as well as I can. Believe me Tom, it is the only study in this world will yield solid satisfaction. To be rich & to be great are the grand concerns of this world's men ... Avoid this sordid turn of mind if you would be happy. Observe mankind around you; endeavour by studying the wisdom & Prudence of some and the folly & madness of others, to make yourself wiser & better.[130]

Burns's wording here – 'studying men, their manners, & their ways' – adapts his admired Pope, who writes in 'January and May', a witty version of Chaucer's Merchant's Tale, about a courtier who has 'study'd Men, their Manners, and their Ways'.[131] In 1783, Burns tells his old teacher, Murdoch,

> In short, the joy of my heart is to 'Study men, their manners, and their ways;' and for this darling subject, I chearfully sacrifice every other consideration: I am quite indolent about those great concerns that set the bustling, busy Sons of Care agog ...[132]

Later in this same letter Burns quotes from Pope's *Essay on Man*. He is going to fairs and markets, 'reading a page or two of mankind, and "catching the manners living as they rise," whilst the men of business jostle me on every side, as an idle encumbrance in their way'.[133] In the mid-1780s Pope would supply epigraphs for 'Holy

Willie's Prayer' and 'The Holy Tulzie', while his work underpins passages in other poems like 'To a Mouse'. Pope's presence can be tracked throughout Burns's career. Having studied Pope's poetry with Murdoch at school, Burns also read it at home, and from at least the end of Burns's teens Pope formed his philosophy and cast of mind. No other poet was then more important to his intellectual development; he saw Ayrshire life through Pope's eyes, and Pope from the standpoint of Tarbolton.

This may sound ridiculous, but it worked. The elegant, witty eighteenth-century English Catholic poet was of fundamental importance to the Presbyterian Burns on his windswept Scottish farm. Both men shared a love of poetry, close observation of human behaviour, and sometimes stinging wit.

If Burns developed a fondness for sex and alcohol, he also grew subtly complicated. 'I love drinking now & then,' he once scribbled, but his scribble takes the form of an annotation on a 1779 copy of Laurence Sterne's now little-read 'Characterium, atque Callimachorum', an outline of Sterne's own character and manners.[134] The fact that Burns scribbled this remark in such a place typifies his character. Constantly he brought together physical and intellectual appetites. Supporting Burns's attending a dancing class in 1779, Candlish enthusiastically invoked both mind and body. Dancing was like poetry itself: physical – felt on the pulse and in the voice as music and movement – fusing the mental and somatic. Burns knew this, and so did his admired Pope: 'True Ease in Writing comes from Art, not Chance/ As those move easiest who have learn'd to dance.'[135] Burns relished bodiliness and bawdiness; this should not blind us to his intellectual sophistication. His liking for Sterne's sentimental, witty prose, like his appetite for drinking now and then or his love of Pope's verse, was one of many predilections formed in his teens then maintained in later life. Burns's literary taste shaped his maturing every bit as much as his attending Kirk services, his theological reading, his enjoyment of alehouse or Masonic culture, and the pleasures of female company. All went together. He thrived on their rich combination.

In 1780, though, he looked as if he was wasting his future. 'When all my school-fellows and youthful compeers ... were striking off with eager hope and earnest intent on some one or other of the many paths of busy life, I was "standing idle in the marketplace," or only left the chace of the butterfly from flower to flower, to hunt

fancy from whim to whim.'¹³⁶ Quoting scripture to his purpose, Burns invokes Christ's parable of the labourers in the vineyard, all of whom were equally rewarded, though some had spent much of their time 'standing idle in the marketplace'.¹³⁷ Poets quite often like to make out that they are idle; sometimes it is necessary simply to live, to read, and to cultivate an openness. If a poet is in the right state of receptiveness, materials arrive from unexpected directions and fuse into an achieved poem. This happens when Burns combines an old Scots song tune with a local place name and a phrase from Pope, the whole undergirded by his maturing experience of love. Sillar, Niven, Candlish and his own family must have had a sense of his poetic aspirations but Robert was not given special treatment. That too benefited his art. He had space in which to develop, but was kept in touch with the life of his community. For all his pose of standing idle, he had to work hard on the farm.

Remembering his brother humming songs as he scythed, Gilbert recalled 'in mowing, the exercise that tires all the muscles most severely, Robert was the only man that, at the end of a summer's day,' out-mowed him.¹³⁸ Farm-work was demanding. 'Such is our hurry that a pleasure ja[u]nt is what I dare not ask,' Robert wrote from Lochlea to Niven in late July 1780. Later that year he was describing autumn as a 'hurried season'. He had a sense of life at times as 'one continued up-hill gallop from the cradle to the grave'. Burns could present himself as drifting idly, but also as industrious. He was growing 'three acres of pretty good flax' that summer, planning to take it to market.¹³⁹ Before substantial nineteenth-century imports of American cotton, flax (sometimes called 'lint') was used widely in clothing, and a common crop around Tarbolton. Praising God, Saunders Tait celebrates 'He wha made Lint-seed for to grow/ ... That Lint might be refin'd from tow [fibre],/ Wi heckles [sharp combs'] care'.¹⁴⁰ Gilbert recalled he and his brother had 'for several years' been granted the use of land by their father to cultivate this crop 'on our own account'.¹⁴¹ On the edge of manhood, the two boys needed to be able to conduct business for themselves, supplementing their struggling father's income.

Flax, Tait makes clear in 'Lint-Seed, A Poem', is a crop requiring 'waters for to overflow'.¹⁴² Moisture was in no short supply at Lochlea, especially on the wet ground round the loch. After harvesting, the flax was processed in places like the nearby coastal town of Irvine. Seeds were removed from the plant's fibres and treated by

'flax-dressers'. Linseed could be made into oil or cattle-food. The treated fibrous materials were ready for spinning into yarn on hand-looms and making into linen. For his 1781 flax crop the government-supported Commissioners and Trustees for Fisheries, Manufactures and Improvements in Scotland eventually granted Burns £3 'for Lintseed saved for sowing'.[143] Robert's surviving early letters say virtually nothing about farm-work, but we know that usually six days a week he slogged on the muddy, not always productive land. At Lochlea in addition to the plough-horses the Burnses kept some cattle; income came from their crops and perhaps the cheese-making of Burns's mother. Work was never in short supply. Lime, 'the staple manure of this county', had to be brought from nearby Cairnhill quarry to improve the soil. Farm walls needed building, buildings required maintenance. Later Burns's talents as a farmer would be praised by William Fullarton in his 1793 *General View of the Agriculture of the County of Ayr*. The way the Burneses ran Lochlea accorded with several of Fullarton's 'observations on . . . improvement'.[144] In a song from the early 1780s whose long lines clearly contain autobiographical references, Burns writes of a farmer's demanding life,

> So I must toil, and sweat and moil, and labor to sustain me, O
> To plough and sow, to reap and mow, my father bred me early, O
> For one, he said, to labor bred, was a match for fortune fairly, O[145]

Though he resented keenly the privileges of idle gentry, and liked to flaunt an apparently unbusinesslike side, Burns knew he was 'to labor bred'. He laboured. At harvest, when they could afford to, the Burneses brought in helpers like Thomas Orr; mainly they relied on their own family. It was an often arduous life, but farm-work did not consume all Burns's imaginative attention: 'I never cared farther for my labors than while I was in actual exercise, I spent the evening in the way after my own heart.'[146]

Sometimes this involved other people's hearts too. He took as much pleasure in knowing about local love affairs 'as ever did Premier at knowing the intrigues of half the courts of Europe'.[147] Writerly panache and facility with women made him useful to men whose wooing skills lagged behind. An undated letter to a woman whose name begins with 'A' was probably written by Burns for someone else's use. It protests that the sender is 'a stranger' in matters of the heart and 'ignorant of the flattering

arts of courtship'.[148] No local person would have believed this of Burns, as Sillar's pen-portrait makes clear. Quite possibly the first pieces of writing where Burns assumed the voice of another person were not poems but letters written on friends' behalf in a community where many people lacked written eloquence. Unlike many Burns love letters, this one attempts nothing witty or psychologically complex in protesting sincerity. It reads as if scripted for another voice.

If the 'A' of this early letter is unidentifiable, there persisted in the nineteenth century a story that Burns had felt the 'strongest attachment' to 'one Alison B*****, servant or housekeeper to Captain W******, of C****h***, for whom his attachment was not only ardent but also respectful'.[149] Some commentators maintained this was Alison Begbie at Cairnhill (now called Carnell) near the River Cessnock, though Alison was not a local name in the 1780s, and some of the sources of this story may be unreliable. It seems impossible now to verify or totally disprove this assertion, though painstaking researches by James Mackay in the 1990s demonstrated from parish registers that the 'E' of other early Burns love letters is most likely Eliza Gebbie. Daughter of a tenant at Pearsland near Galston, about four miles north-east of Lochlea, Eliza was three years younger than the poet. She married a stocking-maker in 1781 before apparently moving to Glasgow.[150] She is probably the Glasgow woman whom Burns 'in early life affectionately admired' and who later supplied Cromek by 'oral communication' with the words of Burns's love song mentioning 'Cessnock banks'. Cessnock Castle is on the outskirts of Galston; the Cessnock Water flows into the River Irvine a mile and a half west of the village. 'Oral communication' indicates that Eliza in her mid-forties sang the song to Robert Cromek. Burns was attracted to women with good voices. Eventually, he married one.

To 'E' Burns wrote with wit, a sophistication that pays tribute to her intellect, and no attempt to disguise his bookishness. He quotes from Pope's hothouse erotic poem of *unfortunate passion* to show his own hopes and ideals:

'O happy state! when souls each other draw,
'When love is liberty, and nature law.'

Later Burns would have his own poetic take on 'Love and Liberty'. For the moment, quoting to Eliza from Pope's 'Eloisa to Abelard'

about lovers the English poet called 'two of the most distinguish'd persons of their age in learning and beauty', Burns implies a tribute not just to his beloved's beauty but also to her wits. He tells Eliza,

> I know, were I to speak in such a style to many a girl, who thinks herself possessed of no small share of sense, she would think it ridiculous – but the language of the heart is, my dear E., the only courtship I shall ever use to you.[151]

Characteristically fusing the self-consciously literary with elegantly sustained emotion, Burns makes Pope the language of his heart. His several extant letters to 'E' probably date from 1781; apparently the relationship began earlier: in the first communication we have, Burns refers to 'all my letters to you'. This first surviving letter hints that while Robert may be in love with Eliza, he is also in love with his own developing writerliness:

> I don't know how it is, my dear; for though, except your company, there is nothing on earth gives me so much pleasure as writing to you, yet it never gives me those giddy raptures so much talked of among lovers. I have often thought that if a well grounded affection be not really a part of virtue, 'tis something extremely akin to it.

To 'E' Burns writes playfully, with fun as well as feeling. He is concerned, in what may be a glance at Tarbolton neighbours, not to sound like 'some zealous bigot, who conversed with his mistress as he would converse with his minister'.[152] Evidently he wanted to enter into what he calls 'the married state' with this woman whose character we can deduce only from his intelligent, teasingly ardent letters. He saw in her not just 'tender feminine softness' and 'endearing sweetness of disposition, with all the charming offspring of a warm feeling heart', but also 'superior good sense'. She had 'an education much beyond any thing I have ever met in any woman I ever dared to approach'.[153]

Repeatedly in later life, Burns would bed uneducated women of his own class, but long for and be excited by elegant, educated women whose higher social position made them sexually inaccessible. On at least one later occasion he came close to being accused by his social 'betters' of attempted rape. Failure to secure Eliza as 'partner . . . companion' and 'bosom friend through life' clearly stung

him.[154] In their actual and epistolary relationship, he recognised, his 'imagination had fondly flattered itself with a wish'.[155]

He seems never again to have come so close to finding a potential wife who combined common sense, beauty and educated intelligence, though his later proposal to Margaret Chalmers and his relationship with the married Agnes McLehose show he continued to be attracted by this combination of qualities. Only a few of Eliza's words to him survive. He quoted them back at her from a letter in which she hinted she would soon be moving away. She had told Burns she could not make him what she called 'a return'. She wished him 'all kind of happiness'.[156] Whatever she had seen in Burns, and perhaps she had seen too much, Eliza Gebbie opted to wed a man seven years Burns's senior and already well established in a trade.[157]

Before this blow, Burns was having fun. Though not yet a Mason, he had founded with friends in Tarbolton a 'Bachelors' Club'. In some ways this resembled a Masonic assembly. Its brethren underwent an initiation ritual; sworn to secrecy about club affairs, they had to abide by an elaborate constitution. The rules, surviving in a version handwritten by David Sillar, read very much as if Burns (elected chairman at the club's first meeting on 11 November 1780) was their principal if not sole author. The club's minute-book carried a less nimble epigraph,

> Of birth or blood we do not boast,
>   Nor gentry does our club afford;
> But ploughmen and mechanics we
>   In Nature's simple dress record.[158]

The ideas behind such a club were not, however, limited to ploughmen and mechanics. Addison had written approvingly in the *Spectator* of 10 March 1711 about 'little nocturnal assemblies, which are commonly known by the name of clubs'. Hans Hecht calls attention to Addison's assertion that 'When men are thus combined for their own improvement, or for the good of others, or at least to relax themselves from the business of the day, by an innocent and cheerful conversation, there may be something very useful in these little institutions and establishments.'[159] Chaired by the Burns whose 'knowledge of modern manners' was 'got from the Spectator', the Bachelors' Club can be seen as Masonic and Addisonian, but was also in some ways like the Scottish Enlightenment student debating

clubs Burns's friend Candlish would have had access to at university.[160] Its constitution reflects something of each of these aspects of eighteenth-century life. Whilst the Bachelors enjoyed a good drink and an annual dance to which each 'brother' invited a female partner, their club was also part of that discourse of 'improvement' Burns's father had instilled into him and which so thoroughly permeated Scottish society.

There were originally seven Bachelors, including Robert and Gilbert. David Sillar joined about six months later. The club never numbered more than about a dozen. Its members were young working men, several from farms; at least one shared an interest with Burns in flax-growing. They met every fourth Monday night in a large upstairs room at John Richard's alehouse in the Sandgate, Tarbolton. The small two-storey building is still there, maintained by the National Trust for Scotland. To stand in the uncarpeted upper room with its relatively low ceiling, several windows, and fireplace at either end is to come as close as is now possible to the society of Burns's day. No other interior is as redolent of his youthful ideals. The room holds up to thirty people, though it must have been a bit cramped for the dances held in it. Apart from the kirk it was the largest public meeting-room in eighteenth-century Tarbolton.

Bachelors' Club meetings centred round a formal debate on a set topic. The first topic – perhaps proposed by Burns as chairman – was,

Suppose a young man, bred a farmer, but without any fortune, has it in his power to marry either of two women, the one a girl of large fortune, but neither handsome in person, nor agreeable in conversation, but who can manage the household affairs of a farm well enough; the other of them a girl every way agreeable in person, conversation, and behaviour, but without any fortune: which of them shall he choose?[161]

Burns seems to have spoken from notes – 'detached memoranda'.[162] In this opening debate he argued for the woman 'agreeable in person, conversation and behaviour'. What he said is not recorded, but he writes spiritedly on a very similar topic in a letter to Eliza Gebbie. His debating style was probably at least as trenchant:

The sordid earth-worm may profess love to a woman's person, whilst in reality his affection is centered in her pocket: and the slavish drudge may go a wooing as he goes to the horse-market, to chuse one who

is stout and firm, and as we may say of an old horse, one who will be a good drudge and draw kindly. I disdain their dirty, puny ideas. I would be heartily out of humour with myself, if I thought I were capable of having so poor a notion of the sex, which were destined to crown the pleasures of society. Poor devils! I don't envy them their happiness who have such notions. For my part I propose quite other pleasures with my dear partner.[163]

The club's topics for debate are in line with Scottish Enlightenment preoccupations. The question '*Whether is the savage man or the peasant of a civilized country in the most happy condition*' was also discussed in universities. Other questions may have been more urgent for working men who occasionally compared themselves to students: '*Whether is a young man of the lower ranks of life likeliest to be happy, who has got a good education and his mind well informed, or he who has just the education and information of those around him?*'[164] Some topics were universal, but no less important to Burns: '*Whether do we derive more happiness from love or friendship?*'

If these questions make the Bachelors' Club sound earnest, its rules encouraged fun. With its 'one or more', the most often quoted is regulation ten:

Every man proper for a member of this Society, must have a frank, honest, open heart; above any thing dirty or mean; and must be a professed lover of one or more of the female sex. No haughty, self-conceited person, who looks upon himself as superior to the rest of the club, and especially no mean-spirited worldly mortal, whose only will is to heap up money, shall upon any pretence whatever be admitted. In short, the proper person for this Society is, a cheerful, honest-hearted lad; who, if he has a friend that is true, and a mistress that is kind, and as much wealth as genteely to make both ends meet – is just as happy as this world can make him.[165]

Members were forbidden to swear or utter profanities during meetings, and had to avoid 'disputed points of religion'. At the end of each gathering they drank 'a general toast to the mistresses of the club'.[166] Drinking, debating, joking and 'improving', Burns had formed around him if not quite a circle of Popeian wits, then certainly an intelligent, lively group of men. The club went on meeting after the Burnes family left the district, but was never the same without Robert.

Soon after the founding of the Bachelors' Club, as was surely inevitable in this community, Burns was invited to become a Freemason. His Scotland had over a hundred Masonic lodges. The 1761 *Freemason's Pocket Companion* explained that Masonry had been brought to Scotland by the Romans, and was well established by the Middle Ages, as evidenced by the building of the Roslin Chapel by the Masonic leader William St Clair. The barons of Roslin were said to have 'held their head court (or in Mason style) assembled their *Grand* Lodge at KILWINNING in the [Ayrshire] West-Country, where it is presumed Masons first began in *Scotland* to hold regular and stated Lodges'.[167] Ayrshire, then, had long been a Masonic heartland. Saunders Tait, Burns's would-be rival, celebrated in his stumbling 'Song on Masonrie' not just the Masonic craft's ancient links with 'Solomon' and 'The great queen o' Sheba, that grand Indian bird', but also how 'it was handed from hand to hand' until 'At last in Scotland I'm sure it did land,/ In St James's lodge, Tarbolton'.[168] Entered an apprentice in the united Tarbolton Lodge on 4 July 1781, Burns progressed to be 'passed and raised' as an initiated Mason on 1 October that year.[169] Among the Masons then present was lodge secretary, Robert Wodrow. Though members of the British royal family and nobility were Masons, and Masonry can be seen in terms of masculine exclusivity, there was nonetheless an egalitarian impulse in the movement, manifest in the way all Masons were addressed as 'brother'. Masonry let a little-known farmer's son meet the local gentry. In this regard, it may seem to us 'democratic', contrasting with the surrounding society. When it came to electing members of the London Parliament, Ayrshire had 205 voters out of a population of 65,000; neither Burns's county nor his country was a democracy in the modern sense.

Yet for men at least, though class awareness persisted, the shared ideals of Masonic lodges let aristocrats and peasants bond. As Burns wrote to local Mason and landowner Sir John Whitefoord around 1782, the lodge also 'let us . . . who are of the lower orders . . . have a fund in view on which we may with certainty depend to be kept from want should we be in circumstances of distress or old age'. Yet at that time, for all Burns's high ideals, his lodge's finances were, he told Sir John, 'in a wretched situation . . . & many of our members never mind their yearly dues or any thing else belonging to the lodge'.[170]

Trying to sort out this financial mess, Burns asked a local nobleman

and brother Mason for help, in line with Masonic ideals. Today Tarbolton Lodge's website proudly displays regalia referred to in Burns's work, even the apron he is reputed to have worn. The website argues that elements of Masonic sentimental deism and liberal benevolence appealed to the independent-minded, sometimes radically inclined weavers and small farmers of the eighteenth-century parish. Clearly there is truth in this. One of Burns's songs from the early 1780s (to which he added '*A Stanza . . . in a Mason Lodge*') expresses such sentiments directly:

> The Peer I don't envy, I give him his bow;
> I scorn not the Peasant, tho' ever so low;
> But a club of good fellows, like those that are here,
> And a bottle like this, are my glory and care.[171]

Burns the Mason with a 'big-bellied bottle' might be caricatured as just a lad out for a good time; yet Gilbert stated he never saw Burns drunk in early manhood. This sounds surprising, but the poet, for all his celebration of Masonic and other drinking, knew there was more to the craft than that. 'Brother Burns' was a committed Mason who would use Masonic networks to further his literary ambitions. However, as with the Bachelors' Club, Freemasonry seems to have had an appeal bound up with his own idealism in an age of improvement. It matched his developing intellectual commitments and love of clubbable male friendship, not just his self-interest. He became Deputy Master of the reformed St James Lodge, Tarbolton, between 1784 and 1788, occasionally chairing meetings. He attended Masonic gatherings not just in Tarbolton but also in nearby places like Sorn and Mauchline. When he went to Edinburgh, Masons were among his most important early contacts.

Sometimes Tarbolton Masons smashed their drinking glasses. Burns in the mid-1780s, when the lodge enjoyed sustenance from John Manson's Tarbolton inn, celebrated the summer 'grand Procession' of the 'Master and the Brotherhood' but also their appetite for 'a swatch o' Manson's barrels'.[172] In 1786, Burns's first book would have a clearly Masonic accent, boasting a poem (written when he was considering emigrating) addressed to his 'Dear brothers' of the Masonic craft, the 'brethren of St James's Lodge, Tarbolton'. He looks back over the good times he had enjoyed from 1781 onwards with these un-Calvinistic elect or, as he called them, 'Ye favour'd,

ye enlighten'd Few,/ Companions of my social joy!' He rejoiced in
their rituals, regalia, and sheer good fellowship:

> Oft have I met your social Band,
>   And spent the chearful, festive night;
> Oft, honor'd with supreme command,
>   Presided o'er the *Sons of light*;
> And by that *Hieroglyphic* bright,
>   Which none but *Craftsmen* ever saw!
> Strong Mem'ry on my heart shall write
>   Those happy scenes when far awa'!
>
> May Freedom, Harmony and Love
>   Unite you in the *grand Design*,
> Beneath th' Omniscient Eye above,
>   The glorious ARCHITECT Divine!
> That you may keep th' *unerring line*,
>   Still rising by the *plummet's law*,
> Till *Order* bright, completely shine,
>   Shall be my Pray'r when far awa'.[173]

This sort of Masonic celebration was no doubt good for the sales
of his work in Ayrshire and beyond. More profoundly the Masonic
ideals of 'Freedom, Harmony and Love' strong in the Tarbolton
community also played their part in shaping Burns: the word 'brother'
in his work is propelled into a position of importance by these
Masonic ideals of his young manhood. Certainly he was excited by
the *fraternité* of the French Revolution in 1789, but long before that
he had been stirred in Tarbolton by the ideal of an enlightened,
worldwide brotherhood. When eventually he writes of how

> Its comin yet for a' that,
> That Man to Man the world o'er,
> Shall brothers be for a' that. —[174]

his expression is not only politically radical. It is also Masonic.

Masonry and the Kirk gave Burns ideals. Yet he was also aware
in both institutions of schism and quarrelsomeness. Late 1781 saw
the row in Burns's lodge that centred round Robert Wodrow, a
kinsman of Burns's minister, the Reverend Patrick Wodrow. Accused
of removing papers from the lodge's charter chest, Robert Wodrow

was prosecuted by members who encouraged the Sheriff of Ayr to arrest him. Long and rancorous, the case ran on for six years. Attempts were made to involve the Court of Session in Edinburgh. Among those embroiled were Brother David Cathcart, a Mason and advocate from Alloway who later became Lord Alloway, a Lord of the Court of Session. In the life of the Masons as in the life of the Kirk, with its bitter wrangling between stricter 'Auld Licht' and more liberal 'New Licht' factions, Burns saw how brotherly and high-minded ideals could become at times mere lip-service. This was grist to his poetic mill. Though his earliest surviving poems about local rows and hypocrisies date from a little later, by the end of the 1770s he was sending friends verses, and sometimes – as from Niven in 1780 – receiving material relished as 'keenly satirical'.[175]

Local Masonic feuding and kirk quarrels could have their amusing aspects. At home Burns faced a grim truth. Though with their four sons and three daughters William and Agnes did their best to keep Lochlea going, William's health was failing and the farm in trouble. When eventually this became unignorable there were not many people to provide assistance. The Lochlea Burneses seem to have had relatively little contact with William's brother and his children John, William and Fanny Burnes, the poet's cousins, who lived only about fifteen miles away at Stewarton near Kilmarnock. In a rare surviving letter, William Burnes described them in April 1781 as in 'very indifferent' circumstances.[176] The same letter hints at pride in having his own family around him, 'virtuously inclined'. Enjoying his Bachelors' Club and about to be initiated as a Mason, Robert, attentive perhaps to his own virtue, wrote to Niven on 12 June 1781,

> I know you will hardly believe me when I tell you, that by a strange conjuncture of circumstances, I am intirely got rid of all connections with the tender sex, I mean in the way of courtship: it is, however absolutely certain that I am so; though how long I shall continue so, Heaven only knows; but be that as it may, I shall never be involved as I was again. –[177]

Written about five months before her marriage, this surely refers to the conclusion of Burns's relationship with Eliza Gebbie. To her he had presented himself as a would-be 'husband'.[178] His June letter to Niven mentions attending 'Our communion' at Wodrow's church. Disappointed in love, he continued faithful in religion.

William Burnes encouraged Robert and Gilbert to grow their flax. Informed opinion in the 1778 *Present State of Husbandry in Scotland* argued that flax let farmers extend their income. 'In a northern country like Scotland, where day-light is very short during winter, the women spin by candle-light, but the men do nothing.' Burns liked reading and relaxing in his evenings, but the great and good had better ideas: Lord Kames, gentleman farmer, had 'a plan for remedying the defect of light' in winter by encouraging the growing of flax in summer, with the farmers 'dressing the flax themselves during the dark hours of winter'.[179] Robert's experience of selling flax prompted the thought that he might set up as a flax dresser. Gilbert remembered his brother thinking a career in flax-dressing would be 'suitable to his grand view of settling in life'.[180] This suggests Robert had larger ambitions, but, whatever they were, the flax-dressing scheme went spectacularly wrong at the beginning of 1782. Gilbert recalled his brother worked at it for six months, which means Robert began in summer 1781, leaving Lochlea then to go to Irvine.

Linked to Wallace, Bruce and the struggles of the Reformation, Irvine had a strong sense of its own history. A royal burgh since medieval times, it boasted several castles. Around the mid-eighteenth century it was Scotland's third most substantial seaport. Most trade was with Ireland, but, even though its harbour was silting up by Burns's day, the presence of sailors who had conducted business from the Baltic to the West Indies, France to America, made Irvine more internationally minded than Tarbolton. Irvine had a Sailors' Society, in addition to its seven traditional trades guilds – hammermen, weavers (in Scots 'wobsters' or 'wabsters'), tailors, cordwainers, skinners, wrights and coopers. Nearby, coal mining was developing. Whether from its linen company or from the persistent activity of smuggling, Irvine was a busy place where money could be made and soon spent – at the racecourse, in more than thirty pubs, or at agricultural markets. Like Ayr, Irvine in 1781 was at once local and cosmopolitan. With a population of over four thousand, it was Ayrshire's largest settlement. In Irvine, Burns reminisced six years later, 'I learned something of a town-life'.[181]

Irvine was also disputatious. Throughout the Renaissance two families, the fighting Montgomeries and the feisty Cunninghams, had maintained a blood feud of legendary proportions. Public riots, whether over such matters as the right to use common land or (as

in 1777) distribution of food, were not uncommon. If there was money in the area, there were also needy paupers. A thousand beggars were said to have attended the Earl of Eglinton's funeral in 1729, knowing money would be distributed. Anxieties about begging and poverty persisted. The 1780s saw the establishment of Irvine's Friendly Society to try to alleviate social problems. Burns must have seen those at first hand.

The local Kirk had money and high ideals. In 1770 it planned a new parish church, with 1,770 seats. Completed in 1773, the building had a 150-foot-high steeple added in 1778; individuals and groups rented pews, securing good seats for Sundays, though the poor got free admission. In 1775 the Irvine Carters Society had to swear to 'behave themselves decently' in their pews.[182] As at Tarbolton, unruliness and godliness were near neighbours. Irvine's strong religious sectarianism meant that in 1779 the Town Council 'formally protested at the parliamentary repeal of penal laws against Roman Catholics'.[183] For all his churchgoing Presbyterianism, the young Burns had been taught by relatively liberal ministers like Dalrymple and McGill; schooled by the Masons (who opened a new lodge in Irvine in 1780) to respect other religious beliefs, he is unlikely to have shared such prejudice against the religion of his favourite poet, Pope. Irvine attracted religious enthusiasts, though. Evangelical Methodist missionary George Whitefield had pulled a crowd of five thousand when he preached on the town's Golf-fields in 1742. Moravians were active locally at the start of the 1770s. Anxious to choose their own minister, religious dissidents from the Kirk met on the Golf-fields and decided to build their own Relief Kirk.

In 1782 that Relief Kirk called as its minister Hugh White. He had been in America during the years of the Shaker leader Ann Lee, an advocate of free love who presented herself as a divine prophetess. To Irvine White came with his own prophetess, Elspeth Buchan, presented in his *Divine Dictionary* as 'God's only light on earth in this generation'. They gathered around them a group of enthusiasts, who, though White denounced 'adulterous persons, full of lust and lechery', apparently practised free love. Certainly the sect believed knowledge of God had to be obtained 'by the external organs of sense', and they disputed the need for conventional 'matrimony'.[184] Though he thought their beliefs 'folly', Burns was, he wrote in 1784, 'personally acquainted with most' of these Buchanites.[185] Some he had probably met when he first moved to Irvine. In this town of

sailors, weavers, smugglers and beggars he saw grandeur, wealth and authority, but also harsh poverty. It was a place susceptible to wild religious enthusiasm, and where authority might readily be challenged.

He certainly enjoyed aspects of the place. Local bookseller William Templeton later subscribed to Burns's first book, and helped him sell it. He recalled the young poet coming into his shop looking for ballads, sometimes reading one aloud. The parish minister remembered Burns in his grand, new church. Another local spoke of arguing about Calvinism on Sunday evenings, Robert taking the side of orthodoxy. Gathered at the start of the twentieth century, these accounts tend to lack precise documentation.[186] Much more accurate is Burns's account of his closest Irvine friend.

> He was the son of a plain mechanic; but a great Man in the neighbour-hood taking him under his patronage gave him a genteel education with a view to bettering his situation in life. – The Patron dieing just as he was ready to launch forth into the world, the poor fellow in despair went to sea . . .
>
> This gentleman's mind was fraught with courage, independance, Magnanimity, and every noble, manly virtue. – I loved him, I admired him to a degree of enthusiasm; and I strove to imitate him. – In some measure I succeeded: I had the pride before, but he taught it to flow in proper channels. – His knowledge of the world was vastly superi-our to mine, and I was all attention to learn. – He was the only man I ever saw who was a greater fool than myself when WOMAN was the presiding star; but he spoke of a certain fashionable failing with levity, which hitherto I had regarded with horror . . .[187]

In this Richard Brown – a working man's son, yet also a person of 'genteel education' – Burns, away from home for his first really extended period, found a steadfast companion. The two went walking together in woods on the outskirts of Irvine near Eglinton Castle, then a crenellated four-storey tower-house. Its outbuildings were surrounded by elegantly laid-out parkland – a landscape of 'improve-ment' clear on a 1775 map.[188] One Sunday in the Eglinton woods Burns recited some of his poetry to Brown. His friend was surprised Burns 'could resist the temptation of sending verses of such merit to a magazine'. In a 1787 letter to Brown, Burns said it was this suggestion that let him think of his own poetry as material that might one day be published.[189]

Burns then portrayed himself to Brown as 'just the same will-o'-wisp being I used to be'.[190] Yet he saw himself as matured by their friendship. Filled with 'enthusiasm', at twenty-one the poet found in this well-travelled, experienced sailor six years his senior something of a surrogate father-figure. Brown's views were very different from William Burnes's. The poet hints, for instance, that Brown took lightly 'a certain fashionable failing' – probably the use of prostitutes. This does not imply Burns spent his time in Irvine whoring. It does show him being exposed to attitudes conducive to excitement and guilt.

Exactly when Burns met Brown is unclear. Certainly their friendship persisted through difficult times. Burns experienced what we would now call the onset of mental illness. This suffering and its aftermath would be one of his most formative experiences. 'My twenty third year' was 'to me an important era'.[191] This is an understatement. At the ages of twenty-two and twenty-three he went through intense personal suffering which marked him for the rest of his life.

At first, though, his problems were simpler. Lodging in a street called Glasgow Vennel (vennel is Scots for an alley), he was in partnership with a man he disliked. This person's surname seems to have been Peacock. Burns described him as 'a scoundrel of the first water who made money by the mystery of thieving'. This may suggest that Peacock was involved with smuggling; certainly it indicates the young Burns was naïve, or at least deficient in business nous, when he entered into partnership with this 'flax-dresser . . . , to learn his trade and carry on the business of manufacturing and retailing flax'.[192] Burns worked in a confined space called a heckling shop or heckling shed. Such sheds, Lord Kames had pointed out, needed to be 'carefully cleaned out every evening, so as to prevent any hazard of fire'.[193] Men traditionally known as hecklers used 'heckling combs' – wooden boards studded with sharp nails – to comb impurities out of the flax fibres. Modern 'hecklers' interrogate politicians and public speakers, separating truth from rubbish; these eighteenth-century flax hecklers engaged in hard physical labour. Judging from surviving heckling sheds (one is now a museum in Irvine's reconstituted Glasgow Vennel), the atmosphere was badly ventilated, full of dry flax dust. Burns was a healthy man when he came to Irvine, but flax-dressing was not a healthy occupation.

Exactly what happened to Burns in Irvine no one knows, but he suffered a severe breakdown in addition to a business disaster. The breakdown was the expression of a strand of anxiety and fear of ruin already perceptible in some of his early writings and which would dog him till he died. Writing to Dr Moore about his Irvine period, Burns presents first of all the business disaster: 'while we were given [sic] a welcoming carousal to the New Year, our shop, by the drunken carelessness of my Partner's wife, took fire and was burnt to ashes; and left me like a true Poet, not worth sixpence. – I was obliged to give up business . . .' As Lord Kames and others knew, heckling-shed fires were not uncommon. To Moore Burns then lists his other problems: jilting by 'a belle-fille [Eliza Gebbie] whom I adored and who had pledged her soul to meet me in the field of matrimony'; his father's troubles on the farm; lastly, his own breakdown.[194]

The breakdown does not seem to have occurred immediately after he was jilted, and it preceded the heckling-shed fire. In 1787 Burns recalled his illness in Irvine in terms of 'evil' and 'infernal' events. Modern medical diagnoses and terminology are so different from their eighteenth-century predecessors that it is difficult to be sure exactly what Burns means by his 'hypochondriac complaint'.[195] What he does not mean is what we now casually call 'hypochondria'; he indicates something more serious. In late eighteenth-century medicine 'hypochondriasis, or low spirits' was often associated with 'dyspepsy' and 'flying gout' (with which Burns was later diagnosed) – all diseases which 'appear more generally among men of learning, genius, and property, whose minds are frequently upon the rack of thought'; most at risk were 'those who are possessed of fine sensibility, and irritability, of great vivacity, spirits, and ready wit'.[196] James Currie, the Scottish doctor who wrote the first full-length biography of Burns, was author of a 1779 'Essay on Hypochondriasis' which identified the disease as involving 'a train of imaginative ideas connected with grief and fear'.[197] In 'hypochondriasis . . . derangement of the nervous functions' was accompanied by loss of 'natural tone and energy' in 'the stomach and intestines' so that often, doctors argued, 'it becomes necessary to administer vomits and purges'.[198]

This is how Burns was treated. Having gone to Tarbolton on 1 October 1781 to be passed and raised as a Freemason, by November in Irvine he fell seriously ill. He was visited by Charles

Fleeming, a local doctor with some reputation further afield. Now the property of Irvine Burns Club, Fleeming's day-book was discovered in the 1950s. In 1992 James Mackay published entries showing Fleeming visited Burns five times in the eight days beginning 14 November.[199] Fleeming prescribed ipecacuanha (a strong emetic), followed by an anodyne (perhaps opium) and then large quantities of powdered cinchona. Sometimes called 'Peruvian Bark', cinchona is listed under 'stomachics' in Sir John Elliot's late eighteenth-century *Medical Pocket-book*.[200] It was thought useful in 'strengthening the tone of the stomach'; some argued that with cold-water bathing it promoted recovery from hypochondriasis.[201] The 1771 *Encyclopaedia Britannica* has a substantial entry for cinchona, 'a most effectual remedy in intermittent fevers of almost every kind'. Since it strengthens 'the whole nervous system, and proves useful in weakness of the stomach', cinchona was often applied successfully 'to the cure of periodic head-achs, hysteric and hypochondriac fits, and other disorders, which have regular intermissions'.[202]

Himself depressive, Dr Currie, who later met Burns and discussed him with Gilbert, wrote that the poet was 'endowed by nature with great sensitivity of nerves'. Currie went into details which correspond with accounts given by both Gilbert and Robert:

> He was liable, from a very early period of life, to that interruption in the process of digestion, which arises from deep and anxious thought, and which is sometimes the effect, and sometimes the cause of depression of spirits. Connected with this disorder of the stomach, there was a disposition to headache, affecting more especially the temples and eye-balls, and frequently accompanied by violent and irregular movements of the heart.[203]

Diagnosing Burns's illnesses is a perilous business. Even in the eighteenth century there was dispute about the precise nature of hypochondriasis. The famous Scottish physician William Cullen saw it as subtly different from 'dyspepsia' and '*melancholia*', though sharing properties with them; for Cullen hypochondriasis involved stomach problems and 'generally the gloomy and rivetted apprehension of evil'.[204] Writing in the 1780s, Burns recalls experiencing in Irvine symptoms of eighteenth-century hypochondriasis which we now associate with severe depression:

The finishing evil that brought up the rear of this infernal file was my hypochondriac complaint being irritated to such a degree, that for three months I was in diseased state of body and mind, scarcely to be envied by the hopeless wretches who have just got their mittimus, 'Depart from me, ye Cursed.' –[205]

Burns's quotation here is from a vision of the Last Judgment in St Matthew's Gospel when the souls of those who have ignored Christ are told, 'Depart from me, ye cursed, into everlasting fire, prepared for the devil and his angels.' They are sent to 'everlasting punishment'.[206] Though he later recounted his sufferings to Dr Moore with stylish wit, a sense of hellish disturbance underlies this comment on his three months' illness in Irvine.

At the time, Burns wrote of it in terms of exhausted longing for death. His father visited him in Irvine in late 1781, probably in November when Burns was already ill. In his only surviving letter to his father, Robert writes from Irvine on 27 December in a confused state. He complains of hard work; of almost being out of meal; of having to abandon a plan to visit Lochlea; of hopes and fears, gratitude and respect to his parents; but at the heart of his letter is a sense of being seriously disturbed:

My health is much about what it was when you were here only my sleep is rather sounder and on the whole I am rather better than otherwise tho it is but by very slow degrees. – The weakness of my nerves has so debilitated my mind that I dare not, either review past events, or look forward into futurity; for the least anxiety, or perturbation in my breast, produces most unhappy effects on my whole frame. – Sometimes, indeed, when for an hour or two, as is sometimes the case, my spirits are a little lightened, I glimmer a little into futurity; but my principal, and indeed my only pleasurable employment is looking backwards & forwards in a moral & religious way – I am quite transported at the thought that ere long, perhaps very soon, I shall bid an eternal adieu to all the pains, & uneasiness & disquietudes of this weary life; for I assure you I am heartily tired of it, and, if I do not very much much [sic] deceive myself I could contentedly & gladly resign it. –

The Soul uneasy & confin'd from home,
Rests and expatiates in a life to come.
Pope.[207]

'Confin'd from home', Burns demonstrates to his farmer dad that he can quote Pope; the passage from *An Essay on Man* is about awaiting 'the great teacher Death'.[208] But this letter is not just literary showing-off. It is the sort of evidence that leads the modern professor of psychiatry Kay Redfield Jamison to discuss Burns in her work on manic depression.[209] Even if the Burns who wept in public and veered between enthusiasm and despair was not bipolar there is strong evidence (of which this Irvine letter is part) that his 'hypo-chondria' was the mental illness now known as depression. Sometimes he suffered acutely.

It may not always have been politically correct to admit that Scotland's national poet suffered from mental illness, but he did. In Irvine he thought he was going to die. Just as much as some of the Buchanites he grew fixated on verses from the Book of Revelation. He pored over the comforts of heaven for those who will go there after death.

Poems he wrote at this time have titles like 'To Ruin', 'A Prayer, in the Prospect of Death', and 'A Prayer, Under the Pressure of violent Anguish'. Ruin is an 'inexorable lord'; the speaker senses its storm 'thick'ning, and black'ning,/ Round my devoted head' as he prays to resign 'Life's *joyless* day'. God has given him 'Passions wild and strong'; he prays for help 'These headlong, furious passions to confine'. There is a sense of being very close to the Final Judgment of God, 'In whose dread Presence, ere an hour,/ Perhaps I must appear!'[210] Just over two years later, Burns called this period 'dreadful'. He had expected his 'Misfortunes' to 'undo me alto-gether', and carried a darkness inside him: 'though the weather has brightened up a little with me, yet there has always been since, a "tempest brewing round me in the grim sky" of futurity which I pretty plainly see will some time or other, perhaps ere long, over-whelm me'.[211]

In the mid-nineteenth century it was argued that Burns had made many paraphrases of biblical psalms during this time, and a facsimile of a manuscript was published to illustrate this assertion.[212] Though the evidence for this is quite unconvincing, versions of the first psalm and part of the ninetieth psalm which Burns published in 1787 prob-ably date from his Irvine period, and several other poems written then have markedly anguished religious aspects.[213] His note on 'A Prayer, in the Prospect of Death' again suggests the affliction he suffered in winter 1781–2 was a malady he feared thereafter. He

described the poem as 'A prayer, when fainting fits, and other alarming symptoms of a Pleurisy or some other dangerous disorder, which indeed still threatens me, first put Nature on the alarm'.[214] This is the one place where Burns suggests it was a straightforwardly physical disease that made him ill. Elsewhere he repeatedly hints it was a mental affliction with physical symptoms. Recollections of March 1784 link the Irvine collapse to the familial financial troubles he encountered when he returned to Lochlea, but the depressive episode in Irvine takes precedence over these:

> There was a certain period of my life that my spirit was broke by repeated losses & disasters, which threatened, & indeed effected the utter ruin of my fortune. My body too was attacked by that most dreadful distemper, a Hypochondria, or confirmed Melancholy: in this wretched state, the recollection of which makes me yet shudder, I hung my harp on the willow trees, except in some lucid intervals . . .[215]

Three months in this condition gave Burns a psychological wound. It returned to torment him on several later occasions. He had larked around in Kirkoswald. Through letter-writing, conversation and clever organisation he had set himself at the centre of several circles of young male wits. In Irvine, though, he was almost fatally at his own wits' end. Though he stayed on for some time after the burning down of the heckling shed, early in 1782 he returned to Lochlea. Physically recovered, he had failed at his chosen career. Around him he felt the increasing worries of a family whose farm was nearing financial collapse.

It was a dark time, but Burns wrote himself out of it. Many of his finest poems take their speakers or protagonists very close to extinction. If death and ruin continued to be among his muses, there was also a sometimes desperate resolution to discover in poetry and song a purgative or antidote even stronger than ipecacuanha or cinchona. The youth who failed in preparing flax for spinning by local weavers was also the poet who composed a new 'wild Rhapsody' to the old, quick tune 'The Weaver and his shuttle O'. Glancingly autobiographical, it is jaunty to the point of daftness. Its wild bounce manifests the speaker's determination, even if 'all obscure, unknown, and poor, thro' life I'm doom'd to wander', still to be 'chearful' and to resist depression. Like many of Burns's poems, this

one has a witty lightness about it. He took a 'particular pleasure in conning it over', and knew well the hurt underlying it.

> When sometimes by my labor I earn a little money, O
> Some unforseen misfortune comes generally upon me; O
> Mischance, mistake, or by neglect, or my good-natur'd folly; O
> But come what will I've sworn it still, I'll ne'er be melancholy, O.[216]

III

Belles

Burns came home in a hard year. Across Ayrshire farmers were suffering. On the moors near Muirkirk, about a dozen miles east of Lochlea, a local poet complained of 'This April Eighty-two' that 'It's cold doth make *frail sheep* to shrink:/ It stops the growth' . . .[1] Burns and his family were not sheep-farmers, but shared with their neighbours months of unusually bad weather. Summer remained cold and stormy. In Ayrshire it snowed before harvest time. Many crops were ruined. Across Scotland rural people fell into poverty. 'Dreadful famine' threatened. 'All ranks felt nothing but gloomy despondence.'[2]

Home after his breakdown in Irvine, Burns tried at times to sound almost laid-back, assuring his old Kirkoswald schoolfellow Thomas Orr in early September that 'I am going on in my old way – taking as light a burden as I can, of the cares of the world'. He mentions the 'backwardness of our harvest' that November, but only in passing. More revealing are references to differences between rich and poor. Burns sees 'the man whose only wish is to become great & rich' as 'a miserable wretch', and tries to sound unconcerned about money-grubbing. Maintaining such a pose was hard when his livelihood was threatened. The strain shows in the assertive detachment Burns recommends to Orr:

> I love to see a man who has a mind superior to the world & the world's men – a man who, conscious of his own integrity, & at peace with himself, despises the censures & opinions of the unthinking rabble of mankind.[3]

Burns developed a lifelong ideal he later called 'The man of inde-pendant mind' who, confronted by trappings of power and riches,

'looks and laughs at a' that'. Though on occasion Burns could sympathise with slaves and even (in 'Scots, wha hae') urge uprising against 'Chains and Slaverie', sometimes his impulse towards independent-mindedness involved scorning people who could not or would not stand up for their own dignity – 'The coward-slave, we pass him by.'[4] Rather than simple democratic confidence, Burns's dismissal of 'the unthinking rabble of mankind' in his letter to Orr suggests almost Nietzschean scorn. His 1782 formulation of 'integrity' may build on his earlier, 1780 thinking about how 'Pride' plays a part in 'possessing one's mind calmly in ruffling circumstances of life'.

Now, though, Burns had endured physical and mental breakdown. To be 'at peace with himself' required assertive resolution; envisaging a struggle against 'censures & opinions', he can sound at times arrogantly detached. His emergent democratic voice is not always comfortable; asserting the rights of the poor, it can contain pride as well as generosity. Like Alexander Pope, the well-off sophisticate whose work he admired, Burns would use satire and epigram, as well as epistle, moral essay and religious verse to articulate his vision. To find space and permission to do so required sometimes resisting, sometimes learning from, his family's – and society's – expectations.

Most immediately, he learned from his struggles in Irvine and his father's at Lochlea. William's situation quickened his eldest son's combativeness. Some 'wretches' wanted to 'grasp at riches', treating the poor as if 'Poverty were but another word for Damnation'.[5] In 1782 William faced demands for unpaid rent. He claimed his landlord, Ayr businessman David McClure, had not stuck to the terms of an agreement which should have seen McClure contribute to agricultural improvements. Tough farming conditions made things worse. Legal arbitration between the two parties dragged on throughout harvest, then continued into 1783. William Burnes's health suffered under the strain, but he fought on. His youngest daughter, then aged ten, remembered her father 'somewhat bent with toil; his haffet-locks [the hair growing on his temples] thin and bare'.[6] Claiming they owed arrears of rent and other compensation totalling £775, McClure tried to have the farm sequestered; the Burneses might lose everything. They could not, and would not, pay.

Conscious of having lost his investment in the Irvine flax-dressing partnership and of being a potential burden at home, Robert

considered enlisting in the army. Once he had paraded behind recruiters and read lives of Hannibal and Wallace; now he scribbled in a farm notebook,

> O why the deuce should I repine,
> And be an ill foreboder;
> I'm twenty-three, and five feet nine,
> I'll go and be a sodger.[7]

Soldiering may have been a passing fancy, but several later references to enlisting suggest he seriously entertained the possibility. Instead, he tried his best on the farm. 'O why the deuce should I repine' suggests spirited resistance to the threat of dejection; other verses about 'raging Fortune's withering blast' hint he knew that threat was real.[8]

Embittered by his father's sufferings, in a poem about 'damnation' Burns lashed out against a neighbouring farmer who (according to Saunders Tait) took McClure's side in the law case.[9] Years afterwards, Robert was still calling his father's creditors 'rapacious hellhounds', and remembering (though he avoided details) how William spent 'three years tossing and whirling in the vortex of Litigation'.[10] Tait imaged Burns 'in Lochly' poverty-stricken: 'on your back was scarce a sark [shirt],/ The dogs did at your buttocks bark'. By early summer 1783 Tarbolton's town crier had proclaimed the Burnes family's goods were under sequestration. Tait, who 'heard the yell', loved that moment: 'He sent the drum Tarbolton through,/ That no man was to buy frae you . . .'[11]

In the 1930s researchers unearthed the complex legal proceedings according to which the Burnes family's assets were listed while William Burnes and David McClure fought each other through the courts.[12] After the long arbitration process failed, in August 1783 a local 'oversman' judged Burnes owed over £230 plus interest. However, McClure's own financial affairs were so spectacularly rocky after the Ayr Bank collapse that his creditors claimed any money owed to him. Seen as in debt to McClure's multiple creditors, William was sucked into a case of 'multiplepoinding'. This was heard before the Court of Session. With legal backing, William fought tenaciously, but the strain told on his health.

By June 1783 Robert was writing at William's request to James Burnes, the poet's first cousin, a lawyer in Montrose. William had

re-established contact with the Montrose Burneses two years earlier. Robert tells James in the overcast summer of 1783, 'My father … has been for some months very poorly in health, & is in his own opinion, & indeed in almost ev'ry body's else, in a dying condition.'[13] After struggling so hard to get his children educated and bring them up well, William now faced the threat of his family being left destitute. Though Robert's letter says little else about family matters, fear of desolation is strong when he outlines to his cousin general financial worries and 'the present wretched state of this country':

Our m[arkets] are exceedingly high; oatmeal 17 & 18d pr peck, & [not to] be got even at that price. We have indeed been [pr]etty well supplied with quantities of white pease from England & elsewhere, but that resource is likely to fail us; & what will become of us then, particularly the very poorest sort, Heaven only knows. – This country, till of late was flourishing incredibly in the Manufactures of Silk, Lawn & Carpet Weaving, and we are still carrying on a good deal in that way but much reduced from what it was; we had also a fine trade in the Shoe w[ay], but now entirely ruined & hundreds driven to a starving condition on account of it. – Farming is also at a very low ebb with us. Our lands, generally speaking, are mountainous & barren; and our Landowners, full of ideas of farming gathered from the English, and the Lothians and other rich soils in Scotland; make no allowance for the odds of the quality of land, and consequently stretch us much beyond what, in the event, we will be found able to pay.

Burns explains that for several years 'this country has been, & still is decaying very fast'.

Even in higher life, a couple of our Ayr shire Noblemen, and the major part of our Knights & squires, are all insolvent. A miserable job of a Douglas, Heron, & Co.'s Bank, which no doubt you have heard of, has undone numbers of them; and imitating English, and French, [and] other foreign luxuries & fopperies, has ruined as many more. –[14]

This same letter mentions Gilbert has written to another of the Burnes's Montrose relatives, detailing 'news of our fam[ily]'. Possibly these two letters were part of an appeal for financial, legal or other support. In any event, Burns clearly sees his family's sufferings and

the plight of Ayrshire as intensifying each other. Living in the same house as his father, Robert was bound to be affected by William's struggles. An unnamed correspondent supplied early nineteenth-century Burns scholar Josiah Walker with an account of William's manner at this period:

> To a stranger, at first sight, by this gentleman's description, he had a chill, austere, and backward reserve, which appeared to proceed less from habitual manner, than from natural obtuseness and vacuity of intellect. But when he found a companion to his taste, with whom he could make a fair exchange of mind, he seemed to grow into a different being, or into one suddenly restored to its native element. His conversation became animated and impressive, and discovered an extent of observation, and a shrewdness and sagacity of remark, which occasioned the more gratification the less it had been expected; while the pleasing discovery made his associate eager to repair the injustice of his first impression, by imputing the repulsive manner of his reception to that series of troubles which had dulled the vivacity, and given a suspicious caution to this upright and intelligent rustic. I speak of him as he appeared at Lochlea, when misfortunes were clustering around him.[15]

Dearly loved by his family, William cannot have been easy to live with. Burns sought several means of escape. Masonic meetings were one consolation. So were local alehouses, though no one remembers Burns drunk there. Intellectual and other bravado fill a letter sent to John Murdoch shortly before Burns's twenty-fourth birthday in January 1783. Affectionately respectful towards his father, Robert says nothing about immediate family troubles. However, mentioning that William 'has figured pretty well as un homme des affaires', he emphasises that he, Robert, is the 'reverse' of the 'pushing, active fellow' the world might expect. Sometimes subtle, sometimes not, this distancing of himself from his father was part of Burns's maturing. It implied no lessening of love, but an assertion, even in the midst of financial dependency, of independence.

As his father's miseries intensified, and in the wake of his own breakdown, Burns sought ways to be happy. He liked to think he could face the worst. Yet, for all he makes no mention of his own father's financial problems, there is clear discomfort when he alludes to matters of debt:

Even the last, worst shift of the unfortunate and the wretched, does not much terrify me: I know that even then, my talent for what country folks call 'a sensible crack,' when once it is sanctified by a hoary head, would procure me so much esteem, that even then – I would learn to be happy. However, I am under no apprehensions about that, for though indolent, yet so far as an extremely delicate constitution permits, I am not lazy; and in many things, especially in tavern matters, I am a strict eo-conomist; not, indeed, for the sake of the money; but one of the principal parts in my composition is a kind of pride of stomach; and I scorn to fear the face of any man living: above every thing, I abhor as hell, the idea of sneaking into a corner to avoid a dun – possibly some pitiful, sordid wretch, who in my heart I despise and detest.[16]

A 'dun' is an obdurate creditor. The Burnes family had increasingly painful knowledge of those. His pride hurt, Robert refused to toady to people he despised over money. Still announcing his 'extremely delicate constitution', he uses the phrase 'pride of stomach', indicating spirit, obduracy, even irritation. Having no sooner distanced himself from his father, he begins to sound rather like him. Burns's 'pride of stomach' goes with his ideal of a man 'conscious of his own integrity' despite lack of wealth or position. As he put it in a poem on Tarbolton affairs probably written in 1784,

> For though I be poor, unnoticed, obscure,
> My stomach's as proud as them a', man.[17]

To Murdoch in early 1783 Burns enthused about literature, telling his former teacher he modelled his conduct on the sentimental fictions of Sterne, Mackenzie's *The Man of Feeling*, and other books. Robert knew there was something ironically 'incongruous' or 'absurd' in the disparity between his lofty self-image – a 'man whose mind glows with sentiments lighted up at their sacred flame' and 'whose heart distends with benevolence to all the human race' – and the mundane shenanigans of Ayrshire fairs and markets.[18] Proud of stomach, he could scorn and detest with gusto, but clung all the more to the rather otherworldly ideals of books like *The Man of Feeling*.

At home came a crisis. Burns called in a doctor from nearby Mauchline to see what could be done for his father. Dr John Mackenzie, Ayr-born and trained at Edinburgh University, was a

cultivated fellow Mason, soon a friend of the poet. Later, working as a surgeon at Irvine, Mackenzie remembered well his early visits to the Burnes household, and wrote about them in April 1810:

> When I first saw William Burns he was in very ill health, and his mind suffering from the embarrassed state of his affairs. His appearance certainly made me think him inferior, both in manners and intelligence, to the generality of those in his situation; but before leaving him, I found that I had been led to form a very false conclusion of his mental powers. After giving a short, but distinct account of his indisposition, he entered upon a detail of the various causes that had gradually led to the embarrassment of his affairs; and these he detailed in such earnest language, and in so simple, candid, and pathetic a manner, as to excite both my astonishment and sympathy. His wife spoke little, but struck me as being a very sagacious woman, without any appearance of forwardness, or any of that awkwardness in her manner which many of these people shew in the presence of a stranger. Upon further acquaintance with Mrs Burns I had my first opinion of her character fully confirmed. Gilbert and Robert Burns were certainly very different in their appearance and manner, though they both possessed great abilities, and uncommon information. Gilbert partook more of the manner and appearance of the father, and Robert of the mother. Gilbert, in the first interview I had with him at Lochlea, was frank, modest, well informed and communicative. The poet seemed distant, suspicious, and without any wish to interest or please. He kept himself very silent, in a dark corner of the room: And before he took any part in the conversation, I frequently detected him scrutinising me during my conversation with his father and brother.[19]

Here Gilbert plays the part of the elder brother, talking with the doctor about their father's condition. Robert maintains a wary distance, observing 'men, their manners, and their ways'. Sitting in the shadows while others take the initiative, this Burns sounds more like a young man recovering from a depressive episode than the proud, high-minded sentimental soul he presented to Murdoch. Burns could be both. Like most folk he showed different sides of his personality to a range of people on various occasions. Later Mackenzie found his conversation 'rich in well chosen figures, animated, and energetic', thinking Burns a shrewd judge of character.[20] Yet revealingly he first saw Robert as silent, distant, suspicious. The caricature of Burns tends to be that of jovial companion. He could be

fun, but his nature and painful experiences of early manhood taught him the need to be more complicated, sometimes more scratchily difficult, than simply one of the lads.

As their father neared death, Robert and Gilbert, perhaps without William's knowledge, made plans to save the family from ruin. Later, Saunders Tait claimed Burns had deviously 'play'd wi McL[u]re'; certainly Robert boxed clever.[21] He seems to have got to know several local lawyers. One was Robert Aiken, the Ayr solicitor Burns called his 'lov'd . . . honor'd much respected friend'; to Aiken he later dedicated his celebration of William Burnes's home life, 'The Cotter's Saturday Night'.[22] Another local solicitor friend was Gavin Hamilton, a prominent Mauchline man eight years Burns's senior.

Though he had contacts in Edinburgh's legal fraternity, Hamilton had grown up locally. With a sense of his own style, he had bought medieval Mauchline Castle, a small tower-house, and built his modern villa alongside it. For years here in the heart of the village he wrangled with Mauchline parish kirk over collections for the poor which he was accused of misappropriating. Like Robert, Hamilton had local enemies as well as friends; like William Burnes, he was doggedly involved in a lengthy financial dispute. Well connected, Hamilton had a wild stubbornness in him. He and Robert took to each other; in 1786 this Mauchline lawyer would be the dedicatee of Burns's first book.

Three years earlier they were just becoming acquainted, but in October 1783 Burns confided in Hamilton about a 'private bargain' to buy cows and dairy utensils.[23] Robert and Gilbert knew their father's death would terminate the lease of Lochlea. William's eldest children were making arrangements for the family to move to another farm, Mossgiel, about a mile outside Mauchline; Hamilton would be their new landlord. Gilbert, in charge of keeping the family's accounts, may have taken the lead, but both brothers were clearly involved.

When my father's affairs drew near a crisis, Robert and I took the farm of Mossgiel, consisting of 118 acres, at the rent of £90 per annum, (the farm on which I live at present) from Mr Gavin Hamilton, as an asylum for the family in case of the worst. It was stocked by the property and individual savings of the whole family, and was a joint concern among us. Every member of the family was allowed ordinary wages for the labour he performed on the farm. My brother's allowance and mine was seven pounds per annum each.[24]

Though he may have wished to maintain an onlooker's detachment, Robert was forced to act for his family's good. It was now, rather than at Kirkoswald or Irvine, he really came to maturity. While his father struggled with illness, Burns grew more committed to writing. In April 1783 he started keeping a commonplace book. Into this forty-four-page notebook sewn together with thread he copied extracts from favourite writers. He also recorded his reflections in sometimes mannered prose. When he copied some of his poems into the book these have so few crossings-out they appear fair copies of work composed earlier. Twelve and a half by seven and three-quarter inches, this slim volume was less a portable memo-pad than an album to treasure at home.

On its first page Burns inscribed an elaborate title and self-description. Underneath were two epigraphs from Shenstone: from the rural 'Elegy I . . . in praise of simplicity' and from prose thoughts 'On Writing and Books'. Shenstone's work apparently helped stimulate the whole exercise, while strengthening in Burns love of 'independency' and 'simplicity'.[25] The way Burns presents himself shows interest in his own image, but also renewed vitality – as if the pendulum which had swung into depression was now swinging back towards *joie de vivre*. Robert refers to himself in both the third and the first person, but seems most interested in trying to stand outside his immediate situation, observing himself at twenty-four like an older man looking back at a younger.

In his twenties he penned several reviews of his own character – in this commonplace book, in letters to Murdoch, Moore, and others. Calvinism can encourage self-examination as an individual searches his or her soul for 'signs of grace'; but both sentimental writings like *The Man of Feeling* and some Scottish Enlightenment philosophical texts urged people to contemplate themselves as if from the perspective of another person. Burns's commonplace book reveals he has been reading Adam Smith's 1759 *Theory of Moral Sentiments*. Smith emphasises sympathetic imagination as a way of understanding other people and ourselves. In their mid-twenties both Robert and Gilbert tried to take stock of themselves, speculating how others, including posterity, might view them. In such a spirit, Burns began in his finest penmanship,

Observations, Hints, Songs, Scraps of Poetry &c. by Robt Burness; a man who had little art in making money, and still less in keeping

it; but was, however, a man of some sense, a great deal of honesty, and unbounded good-will to every creature rational or irrational. – As he was but little indebted to scholastic education, and bred at a plough-tail, his performances must be strongly tinctured with his unpolished, rustic way of life; but as I believe, they are really his own, it may be some entertainment to a curious observer of human-nature to see how a plough-man thinks, and feels, under the pressure of Love, Ambition, Anxiety, Grief with the like cares and passions, which, however diversified by the Modes, and Manners of life, operate pretty much alike I believe, in all the Species.————

'There are numbers in the world, who do not want sense, to make a figure; so much as an opinion of their own abilities, to put them upon recording their observations, and allowing them the same importance which they do to those which appear in print.'

Shenstone—

'Pleasing when youth is long expir'd to trace,
'The forms our pencil, or our pen design'd!
'Such was our youthful air and shape and face!
'Such the soft image of our youthful mind—'
Ibidem——[26]

Whatever else he is doing here, Burns is trying to sound like a book. By 1783 he conceived of himself not simply as a 'plough-man' but as an author. Writing of his 'performances' that 'they are really his own', he evidently realises his work is developing its particular signature. Yes, he identifies with 'all the Species', but he also wishes to develop further a sense of himself as his own man.

Writing bookishly, Burns takes on something of an upper- or at least middle-class voice. Just as Ayrshireman Dr Mackenzie sounded removed from the Burneses when he described them as 'these people' and saw Burns skulking in the corner, so Burns here adopts a 'refined', external perspective on his 'unpolished, rustic way of life'. Writing his commonplace book and marking out his specialnesss risked separating him from his own community. At the same time, full of 'good-will to every creature', he identifies with 'all the Species'. Continuing the commonplace book over the next couple of years, an ambitious Burns would try to resolve issues signalled on its first page: how to be at once a local ploughman and to follow Shenstone's hint that his ideas might be as good as 'those which appear in print'.

He had made poems before; he had peppered his letters with favourite quotations and essayistic reflections; he had pored over the anthology of letters and other books. Now, gathering these activities, his commonplace book nourished his imaginative life. If all this sounds impossibly high-toned, then the first entry, dated 'April —83', for all its formal dress, makes no secret of an enthusiasm for the local lasses. Robert tries to sound like a grown-up twenty-four-year-old approving the conduct of the less experienced:

> Notwithstanding all that has been said against Love respecting the folly & weakness it leads a young unexperienced mind into; still I think it, in a great measure, deserves the highest encomiums that have been passed upon it.[27]

After his enthusings about the erotic 'rapture' of eighteen-year-olds Burns wrote nothing more in the commonplace book for several months. Then in August 1783 he copied out an early love song, commenting that 'For my own part I never had the least thought or inclination of turning Poet till I got once heartily in Love, and then Rhyme & Song were, in a manner, the spontaneous language of my heart.'[28] If clarification were needed, this remark confirms that Burns now thought of himself as a poet. After quoting his lines, 'O once I lov'd a bonny lass', he added two-thirds of a page of 'Criticism on the foregoing Song'. His favourite stanza is the second, which, though he does not say so, has the most markedly Scots accent:

> As bonny lasses I hae seen,
>   And mony full as braw;
> But for a modest gracefu' mien,
>   The like I never saw.

On this stanza Burns comments he is 'well pleased': 'I think it conveys a fine idea of that amiable part of the Sex – the agreables; or what in our Scotch dialect we call a sweet sonsy Lass.' Strikingly, the Scots phrase Burns gravitates towards here is not one he gets into his poem; there seems some tension between the Scots language in his mind and formal English moments in the verses. Burns the critic senses this – 'The expression is a little akward.'[29] The serious attention he gives his work here, however, speaks for itself.

Burns's commonplace book began fitfully. In 1783 he made only three entries, the last dated September; in it he praises 'that judicious Philosopher Mr Smith in his excellent Theory of Moral Sentiments', agreeing with him that 'remorse is the most painful sentiment that can embitter the human bosom'. As his father's apparently tubercular illness worsened, Burns may have felt remorseful about his own conduct, amorous or otherwise. His sub-Shakespearian lines about trying to 'force . . . jarring thoughts to peace' are bombastic. Later he wrote they were intended for a tragedy – perhaps another indication he was keen to do substantial literary things, but not yet capable of accomplishing them.[30] Few people today have read a work of philosophy published in the year of their birth. Burns's knowledge of Adam Smith's major work on moral sentiments shows that by 1783 he had done so. While this makes him all the more remarkable, it would be 1784 before he applied himself regularly to his commonplace book. Doing so, he grew confident that as a poet he could really move from handwritten samples to a substantial book of published verse.

Before that, most likely one day in spring 1783, Burns made a breakthrough. Gilbert recalled how his elder brother,

> partly by way of frolic, bought a ewe and two lambs from a neighbour, and she was tethered in a field adjoining the house at Lochlie . . . He and I were going out with our teams, and our two younger brothers to drive for us, at mid-day, when Hugh Wilson, a curious-looking, awkward boy, clad in plaiding, came to us with much anxiety in his face, with the information that the ewe had entangled herself in the tether, and was lying in the ditch. Robert was much tickled with *Huoc*'s appearance and posture on that occasion. Poor Mailie was set to rights, and when we returned from the plough in the evening, he repeated to me her *Death and dying Words* pretty much in the way they now stand.[31]

Though the sheep was rescued, Burns imagined her dead. This let him follow models like William Hamilton of Gilbertfield's 'The Last Dying Words of Bonnie Heck, A Famous Greyhound in the Shire of Fife' and other Scots poems filled with sometimes absurd last words. His own title lays it on thick: 'The Death and Dying Words of Poor Mailie, The Author's only Pet Yowe, An Unco [very] Mournfu' Tale'. If not a masterpiece, this is one of his very first extended Scots poems, and in several ways anticipates his best work.

Farmhand '*Hughoc*' stands by, uselessly statuesque, unable to speak; the sheep is articulate, asking him to 'My *dying words* attentive hear.' Burns endows the farm animal with his own liking for high-flown rhetoric, and a lengthy message for the farmer,

> Tell him, he was a Master kin',
> An' ay was guid to me an' mine;
> An' now my *dying* charge I gie him,
> My helpless *lambs*, I trust them wi' him.

Oratorically, the dying creature expresses hopes for her offspring's future, devoting most attention to the '*toop-lamb*', her young ram,

> My poor *toop-lamb*, my son an' heir,
> O, bid him breed him up wi' care!
> An' if he live to be a beast,
> To pit some havins in his breast!   *manners*
> An' warn him, what I winna name,
> To stay content wi' *yowes* at hame . . .[32]

This poem is entertaining in a Scots tradition of talking-animal verse dating back at least to the Middle Ages and ultimately to Aesop's *Fables*. Isobel Burns remembered Robert telling her an extended animal fable when she was a little girl.[33] In the context of Burns's family around 1783 this ewe's speech takes the figure of a dying parent anxious about farm, future, and children. Presenting these elements as art makes them not just bearable but enjoyable.

The eldest child, and his own father's son and heir, Burns was acquiring a reputation for seeking female companionship away from home. This poem – much of it apparently composed during the day as Robert walked behind the horse-drawn plough, then recited to Gilbert in the evening – must have provided a measure of consoling entertainment in difficult times. It takes the 'Unco Mournfu'' and, through daft but nicely judged language, makes it almost jaunty. It is fun, but underpinned at points by Burns's awareness of being close to a loved parent who was dying. Its Scots is aware of the sort of high-toned sentiment Burns relished in literary English. In consciously, confidently deploying 'our Scotch dialect' and in making the dark and terrible into something light and even life-affirming, Burns set a course some of his finest work would follow.

Several poems he wrote around this time dance with death. 'John

Barleycorn. A Ballad' takes 'the plan of an old song', constructing from it a celebration of the cutting-down of the barley crop and its resurrection as strong drink. The barley, before being scythed, grows 'wan and pale'. John Barleycorn's 'bending joints and drooping head/ Show'd he began to fail'.[34] He dies, but men raise a toast to him so that 'his great posterity' may 'Ne'er fail in old Scotland'. Made from an 'old song' of which Burns was 'very fond', this too is a poem about death and legacy. Ostensibly unconnected with his own father, it is one among a clutch of poems – mock epitaphs, an elegy, a dying speech, a 'Song. – In the character of a ruined Farmer' – all surely drawing on what Burns was experiencing. Watching his father approach death, Robert went on writing. He also contributed to practical arrangements so the family would preserve something of the parental legacy.

Two years later Gilbert described William Burnes's 'lingering disorder' as exacerbated 'in Autumn 1783' by 'a deep concerted scheme of villainy' which made it look as if lawyers acting for McClure would secure ultimate victory.[35] Aged sixty-two, William seemed to be going downhill rapidly. James Burnes sent a message of goodwill in December as Burns's family awaited the Court of Session's judgment. In January Lord Braxfield (later famous for his harsh treatment of political radicals) found in favour of William Burnes. He had won. There was little chance to enjoy his victory. Worn out, he died just weeks later.

Robert and his family had watched William die from what Burns later called 'phthisical consumption'. Remembering him, Burns linked his father to the long-suffering Old Testament figure of Job.[36] Dr Mackenzie had done his best, but the family did not have their troubles to seek. If legal victory at the beginning of 1784 delighted their friends, it also incensed local opponents. Saunders Tait attributed Burns's later 'rise' to 'McLure's downfall', thinking it despicable Burns had plotted McClure's 'destruction and his harm' after the landlord had 'put you in a farm,/ And cost you coals your arse to warm'.[37] Hostility towards Burns's family could extend beyond verbal abuse. Gilbert remembered 'Robert had had a dog, which he called *Luath,* that was a great favourite. The dog had been killed by the wanton cruelty of some person' on the night of 12 February 1784.[38] Isobel (then a girl of twelve) remembered being at her father's bedside next morning with Robert and starting to cry. Her father had trouble speaking, but told her she must 'walk in virtue's paths, and shun

every vice'. If this sounds to us stiffly formal, we should remember deathbed conventions were different for eighteenth-century Christians; setting an example of 'holy dying' was an ideal. As throughout his life so in his own last words William tried to do the best for his children. Isobel remembered him hesitating, then twice suggesting there was a member of the family about whose future conduct he was fearful. Robert approached: 'Oh, father, is it me you mean?' William said it was. Robert wept.[39]

William Burnes died shortly afterwards. His body was taken on a farmer's last journey, his coffin suspended from two poles inserted into the stirrups of two sturdy horses which walked side by side from Lochlea to Alloway. His family are said to have processed behind on the eight-mile journey. Alloway was where William and Agnes had set up their first home and started their family. William had tried to maintain its kirkyard's grounds. It was a special place. A simple memorial stone was erected, but later eroded by weather and souvenir hunters. The present-day stone memorialises both Burns's parents, and differs in wording from that of the original as recorded in 1805:

THIS STONE WAS ERECTED TO THE MEMORY OF

WILLIAM BURNESS,

LATE FARMER IN LOCHLEE PARISH, OF TARBOLTON,

Who died Feb. 13, 1784, aged 63 years; and was buried here.[40]

This was a public memorial, but each of the family had their private memories. The youngest remembered how, when she tended cattle out in the fields, her father used to come and sit beside her to teach her 'the names of the various grasses and wild-flowers'.[41] Scared of thunderstorms, Isobel missed the way William, knowing this, used to comfort her. A few years later Robert quoted with enthusiasm to Dugald Stewart lines from James Beattie's poem about the growth of a poet, *The Minstrel*, assuring Stewart its picture of a father who teaches belief in 'heaven's immortal spirit' was, with regard to his own father, 'a literal statement of fact'.[42] If Burns constructed his self-image from his reading, he found there images of his father also. Thinking of 'pains' caused by 'deceased merit', in April he copied neatly into his commonplace book the epitaph he had written for 'my ever honored Father':

O ye! who sympathise with Virtue's pains!
    Draw near with pious rev'rence & attend;
Here lye the loving HUSBAND'S dear remains,
    The tender FATHER, and the generous FRIEND. –

The pitying heart, that felt for human woe;
    The dauntless heart, that fear'd no human pride;
The friend of man, to vice alone a foe;
    For 'even his failings lean'd to virtue's side.'

Underneath Burns penned 'Finis', and drew a line.[43]

His relationship with his father was one of the most important of Burns's life. The qualities he ascribes to William – 'loving . . . tender . . . generous' – are ones Robert treasured, and responded to in sentimental literature. In the phrase 'Virtue's pains' he sums up his father's rectitude, but also the legal battles which contributed to his death. The words 'friend' and 'heart' each occur twice in the epitaph, emphasising its warmth. Manifest is William's stubborn sense of his own dignity, an ultimately democratic instinct his eldest son inherited – a 'dauntless heart, that fear'd no human pride'. In the substantially autobiographical song from this period that sings of being brought up by a 'father' who is a 'farmer upon the Carrick border', Burns maintains, 'I am as well as a Monarch in a palace'. Aware of how his 'father bred' him, this poem's speaker confidently links his sense of egalitarian worth to his paternal upbringing.[44]

Most moving in the formal epitaph for his father is Burns's acknowledgement that William could be difficult. Having the word 'failings' in the last line may seem odd in a poem of honour and affection; so may concluding with a quotation from a book. Yet in the same breath as he suggests criticism of his father, Burns also acknowledges the man's humanity and turns criticism to compliment. Even his quotation is repayment of a kind, a token of that book-learning his father so struggled to procure for him.

Burns's quotation comes from a relatively recent, protestingly elegiac poem by Oliver Goldsmith. 'The Deserted Village', first published in 1770, championed a 'bold peasantry' in a time when 'Ill fares the land, to hastening ills a prey,/ Where wealth accumulates and men decay'. Its sentiments and narrator's wish to link 'my book-learned skill' with being 'at home' in a peasant community appealed to Burns. The specific line which he applies to his father is used by Goldsmith to describe a generous-spirited village preacher:

> Thus to relieve the wretched was his pride,
> And even his failings leaned to virtue's side;
> But in his duty prompt at every call,
> He watched and wept, he prayed and felt, for all.
> And, as a bird each fond endearment tries
> To tempt its new-fledged offspring to the skies,
> He tried each art, reproved each dull delay,
> Allured to brighter worlds and led the way.[45]

Burns's drawing on this Goldsmith quotation emphasises his sense of William Burnes not just as a dear father, but also as a pastor-like spiritual guide. He described his father in a 1784 letter as 'the best of friends and the ablest of instructors'; William's teachings had been at least as much religious as scholastic.[46] Now Burns was about to pass beyond the immediate presence of such paternal spiritual guidance; that thought seems both to have saddened and excited him. His melding of his father's character with that of a figure in literature was entirely at one with how Burns shaped his own persona from reading as well as experience.

The Burnses were not left penniless. Having won their lawsuit, they paid their debts and moved to Mossgiel as Gilbert and Robert had planned. In 1785, not long after Robert began applying himself seriously to his commonplace book, Gilbert wrote a substantial autobiographical account, recording the previous year's move:

> We had entered to the farm of Mossgiel the Martinmass preceeding [i.e. 11 November 1783] whether [sic] the family now retired and by the savings of the individuals of the family and what we saved privately from the wreck of my fathers fortunes we formed a little common-wealth (in which my brother and I acted as dictator) on a tolerable respectable independant footing. It may not be improper to give some short account of the rest of the family. My Mother my elder brother Robert my two grown sisters Agnes and Annabella younger than I, and my sister Isabel the youngest of the family about the age of twelve came to reside at Mossgiel, my younger brother William was bound at Martinmass apprentice to the Saddler business, as was my youngest brother John to that of a weaver . . .[47]

The elder brothers did their best for the family, but encountered problems. Situated about 600 feet above sea level, Mossgiel was higher, more exposed than Lochlea. Still a working farm in private

hands, it has been much modified over the centuries, but no one who visits it on a fine day can fail to be struck by its commanding position. It has panoramic views of the surrounding landscape, from moors in the east to 'the Peaks of Arran' westwards 'above sea-clouds', as Wordsworth later noted in a sonnet.[48] None of this mattered much to Gilbert: 'very high, and mostly on a cold wet bottom' is how he summed up the location. Mossgiel had drainage problems caused by clay underlying the soil. 'The first four years that we were on the farm were very frosty, and the spring was very late. Our crops in consequence were very unprofitable.'[49] Robert tried hard, but may have contributed to Mossgiel's problems.

> I entered on this farm with a full resolution, 'Come, go to, I will be wise!' – I read farming books; I calculated crops; I attended markets; and in short, in spite of 'The devil, the world and the flesh,' I believe I would have been a wise man; but the first year from unfortunately buying in bad seed, the second from a late harvest, we lost half of both our crops: this overset all my wisdom, and I returned 'Like the dog to his vomit, and the sow that was washed to her wallowing in the mire.'[50]

Trying to unite book-learning and daily slog, Burns made real efforts. 1784 is the publication date on his copy of James Small's *Treatise on Ploughs and Wheel Carriages*. Published in Edinburgh by William Creech, it carries an endorsement from Lord Kames's 1776 *The Gentleman Farmer*.[51] Burns lacked the wherewithal to be a gentleman farmer, but, applying himself seriously to farming books, was conscious of being part of a world where literature and agriculture were often linked. Small's *Treatise* belonged to a lineage of Scottish volumes on improvement and ploughing whose authors included literary critics like Kames and that St Andrews University teacher of literary criticism William Barron whose 1774 *Essay on the Mechanical Principles of the Plough* argued that new sorts of plough were needed for increasingly cultivated Scottish soils. The Burns who complained in 1783 with regard to 'improvements of farming' that 'necessity compels us to leave our old schemes; & few of us have opportunities of being well informed in new ones' is the same Burns who fused – more successfully – the older, supposedly less cultivated language of Scots with the cultivated English language of improvement.[52] To be a literate ploughman and a Scottish poet were both activities requiring negotiation with degrees of cultivation. Each involved the

rugged as well as the refined. Burns was an ambitious poet. In 1784 he was also an ambitious ploughman.

Yet, trying hard to take his father's place as responsible male head of the household, after William's death, his own breakdown, and the family's other problems, understandably he went a bit wild. The phrase he used of his determination to farm – 'I said, I will be wise' – recalls a passage from the biblical Book of Ecclesiastes which continues, 'but it *was* far from me'.[53] In his autobiographical letter to Dr Moore Burns's other biblical quotation about dogs' vomit and a sow wallowing in the mire is even clearer: it concerns 'cursed children' who 'walk after the flesh in the lust of uncleanness'. Here are the verses – often used by the Kirk when reproaching fornicators – on which Burns draws,

> . . . after they have escaped the pollutions of the world through the knowledge of the Lord and Saviour Jesus Christ, they are again entangled therein, and overcome, the latter end is worse with them than the beginning.
>
> 21 For it had been better for them not to have known the way of righteousnesss, than, after they have known *it*, to turn from the holy commandment delivered unto them.
>
> 22 But it is happened unto them according to the true proverb, The dog *is* turned to his own vomit again; and the sow that was washed to her wallowing in the mire.[54]

Burns's nearest mire was Mauchline, which the hostile Saunders Tait, for one, associated with 'deep debauches'.[55] On one level Burns was seized with remorse after the death of a father who feared his eldest son might stray from virtue's path. The month after William died, Burns transcribed into his commonplace book a bombastic 'penitential thought, in the hour of Remorse' indignant at 'the Oppressor/ Rejoicing in the honest man's destruction/ Whose unsubmitting heart was all his crime'. Though this is not a directly autobiographical poem, it surely relates to William Burnes's struggles – and Robert's fears of going to the bad:

> Ye, poor, despis'd, abandon'd vagabonds
> Whom Vice, as usual, has turn'd o'er to ruin.
> O but for kind, though ill requited friends
> I had been driven forth like you forlorn
> The most detested, worthless wretch among ye!

> O! injur'd God! thy goodness has endow'd me
> With talents passing most of my compeers,
> Which I in just proportion have abus'd,
> As far surpassing other common villains
> As Thou in nat'ral parts hast given me more.[56]

Burns associated these lines with an unfinished tragedy he had begun to compose in his head during his teens before a 'cloud of family Misfortunes' overcame him. His supposed speaker was 'a great character – great in occasional instance[s] of generosity, and daring at times in villainies'. Robert wrote out the lines in March 1784. That same month he connected some of their sentiments with himself:

> I have often coveted the acquaintance of that part of mankind commonly known by the ordinary phrase of Blackguards, sometimes farther than was consistent with the safety of my character; those who by thoughtless Prodigality, or headstrong Passions have been driven to ruin: – though disgraced by follies, nay sometimes 'Stain'd with guilt, and crimson'd o'er with crimes;' I have yet found among them, in not a few instances, some of the noblest Virtues, Magnanimity Generosity, disinterested friendship and even modesty, in the highest perfection.[57]

This is hardly the sort of companionship Burns's father encouraged him to seek, but shows insight which would later result in poems like the low-life cantata 'Love and Liberty'. Saunders Tait associated David Sillar, Burns and other local youngsters with 'nasty wild Blackguards'.[58]

His father dead, Burns turned to his local community in a different way. As well as writing William Burnes's epitaph, he looked at friends and neighbours, summing up how they might be viewed when dead. James Humphrey was a local mason who would outlive the poet by almost half a century. As an old man, he loved 'to talk of Burns and of the warm debates beteen them on Effectual Calling and Free Grace'. Long before that, Robert got his retaliation in early: 'O Death, it's my opinion,/ Thou ne'er took such a bleth'ran b-tch,/ Into thy dark dominion!'[59] Another epitaph, on the same page as that for his father in Burns's commonplace book, points to the tight-fistedness of William Hood, 'Celebrated Ruling Elder' in Tarbolton Kirk; for Burns hell is Hood's destination.[60] Not everyone

is so summarily dismissed. Close allies of the Burnes family, William Muir and his wife lived at Tarbolton mill. Muir is presented as honest, knowledgeable, a virtuous warm-hearted friend. Burns's epitaph on him is also absolutely open about the poet's own religious uncertainties:

> If there's another world, he lives in bliss;
> If there is none, he made the best of this. –[61]

His father gone, a wilder, more sceptical, more rakish Burns emerges. Discovery of new kinds of freedom sometimes conflicts with a sense of solemn duty. There were, Burns wrote in April 1784, 'two grand Classes' of young men: 'the Grave, and the Merry'. The grave were interested in money and making 'a figure in the world'. The merry

> are the men of Pleasure, of all denominations; the jovial lads who have too much fire & spirit to have any settled rule of action; but without much deliberation, follow the strong impulses of nature: the thoughtless, the careless, the indolent; and in particular He, who, with a happy sweetness of natural temper, and a cheerful vacancy of thought, steals through life, generally indeed, in poverty & obscurity; but poverty & obscurity are only evils to him, who can sit gravely down, and make a repining comparison between his own situation and that of others; and lastly to grace the quorum, such are, generally, the men whose heads are capable of all the towerings of Genius, and whose hearts are warmed with the delicacy of Feeling. –[62]

Burns's poems of this period frequently praise warm-heartedness and friendship. For some time he had nurtured an image of himself as 'indolent', with a 'heart' that 'distends with benevolence', as he had put it to Murdoch the previous year. His commonplace-book musings further cultivated the image he wished to project. In spring and summer 1784 this persona would emerge full-throatedly delighting (as Burns the Mason was already doing) in 'Social-life and Glee', reinforcing the sexually exciting, sexually excited 'Rob Mossgiel' with his dangerously 'rakish art'.[63]

This emergent full-blooded, energetic self would be accompanied by a poetic discovery of performative energy in the Scots vernacular. Burns had not encountered earlier eighteenth-century Scots poets as part of his Anglocentric formal schooling. Now they would show him how the wit he loved in Pope's work could be fed into the

language of that song culture which had educated his ear outside the classroom and which was so strong in his mother's family. Yet there is also evidence of something more secret, harder to track: the development in Burns not just of a new freedom in life and writing, but also of a sometimes surprising political imagination.

It is impossible to date precisely the composition of his first political poem, but none of its many detailed political and military references alludes to events after spring 1784, so it probably originated around then.[64] This work, the circumstances behind it, and the way Burns went on to make it public are so revealing that they are worth considering here, even though the poem was not published until 1787. A substantial fragment of extended song, it begins, 'When *Guilford* good our Pilot stood'. Its context lets us understand how subtle and striking is Burns's positioning himself on the side of democracy.

For most of Burns's fellow subjects in eighteenth-century Britain 'Democracy' was a dirty word. In his 1796 *Sketch of Democracy* Burns's exact Scottish contemporary Robert Bisset would publish a warning against the 'direful effects' of *'universal suffrage'*. Bisset, a British government loyalist, detested the French Revolution: democracy was a 'curse to mankind'.[65] His views were not new among politically minded Scots. Inveighing in 1786 against 'the dangerous turbulence of Democracy', Historiographer-Royal for Scotland John Gillies merely echoed David Hume's 1752 cautionary words on the 'tumultuous government' of Periclean democracy in ancient Athens.[66] Scotland's kirkmen may have enjoyed a striking amount of democratic freedom in church government, but in Scotland and Britain democracy was frequently seen as dangerous. Subjects, not citizens, most people had no vote. Neither Burns's county nor his country was democratic in the ancient, the modern, or the Revolutionary American sense. During his adolescence widely reported government actions incited, through taxation-without-representation policies, a spirit of democratic revolt among the King's American colonial subjects. The Irish-born MP Edmund Burke, whom Burns calls 'Paddy Burke' in his first political poem, attacked the British government's American policy in the 1770s – as Burns appears to have known. Yet Burke's support for the parliamentary grouping called the Rockingham Whigs helped quell British constitutional reform. English politician William Pitt's attempts to have an inquiry into the system of parliamentary representation were swept aside in 1782 when Burns

was twenty-three. Nowhere in his verse does Burns use the word 'democracy'. Strikingly, though, in 'When *Guilford* good' he becomes the first great Romantic poet to write about America.

Something must have spurred this intense interest. Yet in his surviving correspondence and poetry it is scarcely apparent that throughout his childhood and youth Burns's country was at war, or that one of the conflicts was fought over democratic ideals emerging in America. Stray references show he had access to newspapers, but not what he read there. We do know, however, that a Scot such as Adam Smith's associate the Glasgow University Professor John Millar who advocated 'a much more general diffusion of political power' and supported the cause of the American rebels 'was constantly attacked in the newspapers'.[67] Closer to home Burns's community and even one of his closest friends were victims of the rebel colonies.

The Burns who wrote about America around 1784 had grown up in an Ayrshire and a West of Scotland economically damaged by the American War. The damage could be – sometimes was – exaggerated, but war brought a sudden end to the lucrative Scottish–American tobacco trade, and caused particular alarm in coastal areas. Having spent his boyhood beside one significant trading port, Ayr, Burns had recently mixed with far-travelled sailors in another – Irvine. He would have heard all about the American threat. In 1785 one commentator maintained the war had '"almost annihilated" the shipping stock of the Clyde'.[68] Though modern historians qualify this assessment, fear was generated along the Clyde coast, surrounding areas, and around all Scotland by the threat of American privateers under the command of captains like Scottish-born John Paul Jones. At the end of Burns's teens these were widely reported in the press, so that as an anonymous versifier put it in 1779,

> You've heard what amazement has fill'd all the coast,
> Since the tidings of Jones by the last Wednesday's post,
> When the Mercury, Courant and Ruddiman's Gazette,
> Made the bravest to tremble, and the leanest to sweat . . .[69]

The previous year at Ayr 'a guard of thirteen men had been appointed to raise the alarm' if Jones or other American privateers threatened. 'The local gentry took the precaution of moving their furniture inland.'[70] While amusing, this was also life-threatening and livelihood-threatening. John Paul Jones chased a small cutter into the lower

Firth of Clyde as far as Ailsa Craig off the Ayrshire coast. Sailings from Ayr and Irvine were banned for a time as too dangerous. Shipping from Saltcoats, just north of Irvine, was captured by an American privateer. A naval engagement was fought off Ailsa Craig. The Press Gang operated along the Clyde coast. By 1778 shipping activity at Scottish ports had slumped by half; merchant tonnage operating in and out of Ayr soon contracted even further. Burns was aware of depredations. Writing about his Irvine friend Richard Brown, the poet describes him in 1781–2 as 'a hapless son of misfortune' who 'a little before I was acquainted with him . . . had been set ashore by an American Privateer on the wild coast of Connaught, stript of every thing'.[71] People close to Burns were damaged by this conflict. When he wrote about Ayrshire in 1783 to his lawyer cousin, Burns maintained everything locally had been going downhill rapidly 'since the unfortunate beginning of this American war, & its as unfortunate conclusion'.[72]

Growing up in an area familiar with transatlantic trade, and where 'my young friends and benefactors . . . dropped off for the east or west Indies', Burns was used to being surrounded not just by people threatened by the American War, but also by loyal British participants – of both sexes.[73] John Galt, a sea captain's son born in Irvine in 1779, drew on family memories in his locally set novel, *The Provost*, with its 'tinkler Jean, a randy [vagrant] that had been with the army at the siege of Gibraltar, and, for aught I ken, in the Americas . . . swearing like a trooper'.[74] These are the sort of folk whose company was relished by the Mossgiel farmer who wrote in spring 1784 about his taste for 'Blackguards'. Soon 'Love and Liberty' would feature a soldierly 'Son of Mars' who has seen action in 'many wars' from North America to Cuba and Gibraltar.[75] Dating from 1784 or '85, 'Love and Liberty' includes soldiery back in Ayrshire after fighting abroad, and mentions the 1783 Versailles 'Peace' accord which had brought a formal end to the American struggle. War had impacted not just on men but on women too, as a prostitute in Burns's 'Cantata' sings:

> Full soon I grew sick of my sanctified *Sot*,
> The Regiment AT LARGE for a HUSBAND I got;
> From the gilded SPONTOON to the FIFE I was ready;
> I asked no more but a SODGER LADDIE.

> But the PEACE it reduc'd me to beg in despair,
> Till I met my old boy in a CUNNINGHAM fair;
> His RAGS REGIMENTAL they flutter'd so gaudy,
> My heart it rejoic'd at a SODGER LADDIE.[76]

Ayrshire was familiar with soldiers home from Britain's American and other wars. Struggling with his new farm in atrocious weather, Burns joked things might have gone better if he too had enlisted 'an' sair't [served] the king,/ At Bunker's hill' – an engagement which had taken place when he was sixteen.[77] This reads like a throwaway remark, but, combined with his song about being 'twenty-three' and thinking he might 'go and be a sodger', hints that sailing to soldier against rebels in America may have been something he considered more than once.

That idea is strengthened by a song fragment entitled in the Alloway manuscript 'On the great Recruiting in the year 17——during the American war'. This is written to the tune 'Killiecrankie' that also underpins Burns's more substantial published American War fragment, 'When *Guilford* good'. His lines on recruiting during the American War may well have been written later, but ostensibly their title refers to that period in the early 1780s when he was eager to be seen among the 'merry', having his rakish way with the young women of Mauchline and Tarbolton:

> I MURDER hate by field or flood,
>   Tho' glory's name may screen us;
> In wars at home I'll spend my blood,
>   Life-giving wars of Venus:
> The deities that I adore
>   Are social Peace and Plenty;
> I'm better pleased *to make one more*
>   Than be the death of twenty. —[78]

Urging, in effect, 'Make love not war', these lines strengthen the idea that Burns considered but rejected becoming a British army recruit. He chose not to serve the King at Bunker Hill or elsewhere against democratic revolutionaries; in his verse of the mid-1780s he even hints at revolutionary sympathies. It might sound finely loyal and patriotic to mention the British victory at 'Bunker Hill', but so high were British troop losses that the battle led to eventual rebel triumph. From a 1784 Ayrshire perspective, Bunker Hill must have

seemed a Pyrrhic victory for Britain. There is surely a wink in Burns's mention of it. The adverse effect of the American War on Ayrshire, and Burns's explicit acknowledgement of that, makes such hints all the more significant, setting his early political beliefs at odds with those of his government.

A similar sense of apparently loyal, if jocular, protestation suffuses his first political poem. This fragment on the American War and its aftermath begins by alluding to the efforts of the son of the first Earl of Guilford to guide British policy, taking the helm of Britain's government in the wake of the Boston Tea Party and the establishment of a democratic revolutionary American Congress:

> WHEN *Guilford* good our Pilot stood,
>   An' did our hellim thraw, man,   *helm; turn*
> Ae night, at tea, began a plea,
>   Within *America*, man:
> Then up they gat the maskin-pat,   *got the tea-pot*
>   And in the sea did jaw, man;   *pour*
> An' did nae less, in full Congress,
>   Than quite refuse our law, man.[79]

Using the word 'our' places the singer on the side of loyal Brits. Yet the tune of the verse in its sheer jauntiness undercuts any solemn upholding of 'our law'. The poem is a song. When it first appeared in print in the 1787 edition of Burns's *Poems, Chiefly in the Scottish Dialect*, Burns specified the tune 'Gilliecrankie'. His choice is clever. That tune comes from a traditional song celebrating the 1689 Scottish victory of an irregular Jacobite rebel army led by Viscount Dundee against Dutch and English pro-Hanoverian forces. Setting his poem to this tune lets Burns link his own Jacobite inclinations to rebel American victory against the Hanoverian monarchy. Celebrating what in Burns's day would have been perceived by loyalists as a rebel triumph, use of the Killiecrankie tune suggests sympathy with the poem's 'Buckskins' or American democratic revolutionary troops, those rebels against 'our law'.

Burns names British and American generals and battle sites, revealing how closely he must have followed the war's progress in his teens and after. His poem's most heroic figure is one of General Washington's commanders, Irishman Richard Montgomery, who had

served as a British soldier but defected to the side of the rebel revolutionaries and met his death in the American War.

> Then thro' the lakes *Montgomery* takes,
>   I wat he was na slaw, man;   *know; not slow*
> Down *Lowrie's burn* he took a turn,   *the St Lawrence River*
>   And *C-rl-t-n* did ca', man: [*Britain's*] *General Carleton; hammer*
> But yet, whatreck, he, at *Quebec*,   *nevertheless*
>   Montgomery-like did fa', man,   *fall*
> Wi' sword in hand, before his band,
>   Amang his en'mies a', man.[80]

Burns's use of the approving term 'Montgomery-like' is probably a salute to local Ayrshire Montgomeries like those at Coilsfield to whose house he had walked with David Sillar. Yet while nodding towards such an ancient aristocratic Scottish family the poem celebrates in this stanza an Irish American rebel. 'When *Guilford* good' shows in detail the chaotic political repercussions of the American War as the British political elite 'begin to fear a fa'' when the conflict goes against them. Burns's poem matters not just as evidence of how closely he followed politics, but also because at the very outset of his political verse it deploys a strategy that will repeatedly characterise his later writings: his first political poem *seems* to side with 'our law' while actually manifesting sympathy with rebellion. In Burns's subsequent life and work apparent protestations of loyalty go side by side with a deeper commitment to subversive inclinations. This 'forked-tongued' encoding was part of his political poetry right from its markedly American start.

Burns's political instincts developed out of a sense of social inequality. His lower-class status meant he was linked for ever with 'these people', as Dr Mackenzie called them, the peasant lower orders. Quickened by what he had seen happen to his own father, by aspects of Masonic brotherliness and by the relatively democratic traditions of kirk government he grew up with, Burns's political instincts came not just from proud vulnerability, resentment, and a relishing of comic potential, but also from a familial sense of being linked to groups – Covenanters *and* Jacobites – whose campaigning had sometimes had to be covert and could be viewed as rebellious. He still cherished his early heroes, Hannibal and Wallace, freedom-loving rebels against imperial aspiration. Later he aligned Washington

with Wallace, implying, dangerously and rather inaccurately, that rebellious ideals of American democracy might parallel Wallace's much older Scottish stance. Though he saw damage done to his locality by the American War, Burns was independent-minded enough to side with its ideals in verse written at Mossgiel. He was the first major European poet influenced by those ideals. They shaped the way he would develop into the bard not just of Scotland but of democracy itself.

The democratic ideal in Burns was quickened by attention to politics, but also by new excitements found in vernacular poetry. Apparently around the time of his father's death he discovered the work of Allan Ramsay and Robert Fergusson. Reading this brought a step-change in his own verse. In particular Fergusson incited in him an imitative, even competitive instinct after a period when, following the Irvine breakdown, he had felt his own poetry blocked:

> Rhyme, except some religious pieces which are in print, I had given up; but meeting with Fergusson's Scotch Poems, I strung anew my wildly-sounding, rustic lyre with emulating vigour. –[81]

Like Burns, indigent, witty Fergusson had a strong depressive streak; he had died a decade earlier, in Edinburgh's madhouse, aged twenty-four. Burns copied his own 'Prayer, Under the Pressure of Violent Anguish' into his commonplace book in March 1784, then also into his copy of the 1782 edition of Fergusson's *Poems*.[82] Fergusson had written English-language odes 'to Horror' and 'to Disappointment'. Throughout the rest of his life Burns repeatedly identified with the earlier Robert whom he would call in the Preface to his own first book 'the poor, unfortunate Ferguson'.[83]

Shenstone had written, 'It happens a little unluckily, that the persons who have the most intimate contempt of money, are the same that have the strongest appetites for the pleasures it procures.' Fergusson was a classic example of Shenstone's 'Ill-fated bard'.[84] Burns would hail Fergusson as 'my elder brother in Misfortune,/ By far my elder Brother in the muse', and ask, with Fergusson in mind, 'Why is the Bard unfitted for the world,/ Yet has so keen a relish of its Pleasures?'[85] Burns identified with darkness and poverty in Fergusson. More than that, he knew many of Fergusson's sophisticated, wide-ranging works – particularly the 'Scotch Poems' he singled out – have a counterbalancing jauntiness. Fergusson

celebrates Scottish eating – from fresh oysters to 'a haggis fat' – and Scots drink: whisky is 'the poet's flame'.[86] Fergusson's poems of rural folk festivities like 'Hallow-Fair' complement celebrations of Scots peasant life in works like 'The Farmer's Ingle', while in 'Auld Reikie' and elsewhere he establishes himself as laureate of Edinburgh. Writing Scots dialogues, addresses, epistles, he ranges from pastoral to satire, his subjects as diverse as Masonic artefacts and bed-bugs. Having learned from his predecessor Ramsay, Fergusson became not only Burns's favourite Scottish poet, but also one he emulated in many of his finest works. The two men never met. Burns was fifteen when Fergusson died, but he later knew some of Fergusson's friends, and encouraged a perception of himself as potential successor to the style and tradition which Fergusson represented.

In background, the two poets were quite different. Fergusson had been educated at Dundee High School, then at St Andrews University; quoting Latin readily, he had a St Andrews professor as one of his earliest poet friends. Fergusson was at ease with life in Edinburgh in a way Burns would never be. Yet in poetic tone, Burns had found a soul-mate.[87] Fergusson was a master of mixing Scots demotic with English terminology, learned with colloquial language. In an age when academics taught their students to purify written language of Scotticisms, Fergusson rebelled. He exulted in the language of the people without ever renouncing the discourse of education. A remarkable early poem is his sometimes affectionate, sometimes mocking 'Elegy, on the Death of Mr David Gregory, Late Professor of Mathematics in the University of St Andrews'. It discusses 'surd roots' and Euclidean geometry in Scots, beginning,

> Now mourn, ye college masters a'!
> And frae your een a tear lat fa,   *from your eyes*
> Fam'd Gregory death has taen awa
>   Without remeid;
> The skaith ye've met wi's nae that sma,   *harm*
>   Sin Gregory's deid.[88]

Fergusson here uses the Standard Habbie stanza form, named after an older Scots poem which elegises a bagpiper, Habbie Simson. This same form had been used by Ramsay and Hamilton of Gilbertfield

in verse epistles they exchanged. But a particular rhyme in Fergusson's poem ('remeid . . . deid') suggests it is the specific model for Burns's first attempt at Standard Habbie. This was an elegy supplementing his earlier verses spoken by the pet ewe, Mailie. 'Poor Mailie's Elegy' begins with a stanza placing 'remeid' and 'deid' exactly where they occur in Fergusson's poem. In an early draft Burns also places his proper names in identical positions to Fergusson's:

Lament in rhyme, a' ye wha dow,	*dare*
Your elbuck rub an' claw your pow,	*elbow; head*
Poor Robin's ruin'd stick an' stow	*completely*
Past a' remead;	
His only, darlin, AIN PET YOWE,	
Poor Mailie's dead![89]	

Traditionally used in Scotland for mock-elegy, this stanza form originates in court poetry and the love hymns of the troubadours.[90] Two unusually short lines counterpoint the longer ones, which themselves often have an implied pause at their centre. Standard Habbie became central to Burns's work. It can tilt towards mockery, the short lines subversively skipping and dancing; or towards more measured consideration, the short lines crisply conclusive. Like ballad stanzas, Standard Habbies are always complete sense-units in themselves. The end of each stanza marks the end of a sentence, making for extra punch.

Standard Habbie is often called the 'Burns Stanza'. Burns's adoption of it and the simultaneous strengthening of his attachment to Scots vernacular are the two most important acoustic events in his life – at least after his hearing Scots songs and ballads as a child. If Pope proved wit and poise could be central to poetry, Standard Habbie showed Burns how those qualities could energise verse using Scots. His turn to Standard Habbie and the vernacular language of Lowland Scotland was as crucial for his ear as the discovery of long lines and a 'barbaric yawp' would be for Walt Whitman in the following century. A poet's listening abilities and how he or she learns to make sounds work are the most vital faculties any poet has. In Burns these matured in 1784, stimulated by reading Fergusson.

In 1784–5 Burns noticeably worked at the soundscape of his poetry. There is a quickening in his use of popular speech. The first stanza

of 'Poor Mailie's Elegy' is revised to heighten a play-off between grief and absurdity. In an earlier draft internally repeated 'aw' sounds ('a' ... wha ... claw ... Robin ... a'') head towards the lamenting Gaelic 'Ochon' which opens the second stanza. After revision, sharper 'a' sounds ('Lament ... lament ... *Bardie*'s ... at a ... Past ... last, sad') match sometimes faster syntax. In the final version, contrary to what we might expect, the longer lines go fast, the shorter slowly toll. Burns's revised words are closer to standard English, but the intonation is markedly Scots: 'your' in the second line works much better if pronounced 'yir', while 'remead' and 'dead' demand to be 'remeid' and 'deid'. Burns has already mastered the form:

> LAMENT in rhyme, lament in prose,
> Wi' saut tears trickling down your nose;
> Our *Bardie*'s fate is at a close,
>   Past a' remead!
> The last, sad cape-stane of his woes;
>   *Poor Mailie*'s dead!

In 1784 and 1785 he made many poems in this stanza form, including some of his best, and best-known. Beginning to write in Standard Habbie helped make him Robert Burns.

He took, too, a particular word from Fergusson, and started calling himself a 'bardie'. 'Bardie' is an affectionate diminutive of 'bard', a term familiar to Burns from many sources, but most redolent of his enthusiasm for the poems of Ossian. That supposedly third-century Scottish Gaelic bard made poems later 'translated' into English by Highlander James Macpherson during the 1760s. Across the world readers from Jefferson to Goethe and Napoleon thought Ossian's bardic work 'sublime'. In Edinburgh Professor Hugh Blair compared the Scottish bard with Homer. Ossian, singing the heritage of his people, was a bard who behaved like a bard.

Through 'translation', a concept applied more loosely then than it is today, Macpherson's Ossian reached non-Gaelic-speaking audiences in the wake of the 1746 Battle of Culloden. Culloden had marked the crushing of Jacobitism and the suppression of many elements of Scotland's old Highland clan system. Burns's assumed Jacobite heritage also attracted him to the words of this ancient bard whose poems (presented by Macpherson in English prose) are

characterised by dying falls, lamenting cadences, as they tell of the deeds of heroes like Fingal in ancient Celtic battles:

> ... as the last peal of the thunder of heaven, such is the noise of battle! Though Cormac's hundred bards were there to give the war to song; feeble were the voices of a hundred bards to send the deaths to future times. For many were the falls of heroes; and wide poured the blood of the valiant.[91]

Scotophobes like Dr Samuel Johnson declared the Ossianic poems modern forgeries. They are wordy English-language elaborations of scanty Gaelic materials. Ossian, though, made the idea of a national poet central to literary concerns, and Scots poets like Fergusson (writing shortly after the Ossianic poems appeared) enjoyed calling themselves, with a degree of pride and self-deprecation, 'bardies' – wee bards. Burns took over this word and rejoiced in it, just as he would soon relish being called straightforwardly a bard.

Though he came to poke fun at himself in this role, he also took it seriously: he wanted to sing his land and people. The young man who had named his favourite dog Luath – a name from Ossian – lent friends Ossian's poems. He would refer to those in his first book, and call Ossian 'prince of Poets'.[92] Yet in calling himself 'Bardie' Burns also made a Scots pun. The noun 'bardie' in Fergusson's Scots could mean 'minor poet' or 'little bard'; the same word was a Scots adjective meaning 'bold, impudent of speech ... forward, quarrelsome'. Hamilton of Gilbertfield's 'famous greyhound' Bonnie Heck boasts in Standard Habbie, 'I was a bardy tyke, and bauld.'[93] No doubt Burns's Ossianically named dog was 'bardie' in both senses. Being bardie meant being bolshie; in the months after his father's death, that was what Burns wanted to be. Hinting at support for American rebels, mocking himself and his surroundings, playing at times the part of local rake, Robert was both bardie and a bardie.

One thing he wanted was sex. By September 1784 he was transcribing into his commonplace book a song to the tune, 'Black Joke'. This traditional air was known across Britain. The 'worthless and unhonour'd crowd' yell for it in a London poem by Pope; Ayrshire's aspiring rake from Auchinleck, James Boswell, delighted in it.[94] 'Black joke' meant the female genitalia. Burns's song beginning 'My girl she's airy, she's buxom and gay', which he was still

quoting to a male friend three years later, makes no mistake about that:

> Her eyes are the lightenings of joy and delight:
> Her slender neck, her handsome waist,
> Her hair well buckl'd, her stays well lac'd,
> Her taper white leg with an et and a, c,
> For her a, b, e, d, and her c, u, n, t . . .[95]

Confirming his place among the merry rather than the grave, these bawdy lines are a rare surviving example of Burns's early taste for sex-talk. Other lines in poems written around the same time hint lasciviously: 'Beware a tongue that's smoothly hung.'[96]

Already, it would seem, a veteran of other romantic liaisons, the author of such lines was enjoying sex with Elizabeth Paton. Isobel Burnes many years later recalled that this local girl had 'an exceedingly handsome figure'. Minimally educated, she had worked briefly as a servant for the Burneses at Lochlea during William's last illness. Agnes Burnes was very fond of her. Isobel thought her 'honest and independent'.[97] By late summer 1784 she no longer worked for the Burneses, but was fascinated by Robert and pregnant with his child.

Burns, however, was cultivating the image of a man with many strings to his bow. One song he wrote then boasts how 'Where e'er I gaed, where e'er I rade,/ A Mistress still I had ay'.[98] He catalogued in verse eye-catching young women of Mauchline and Tarbolton. Tarbolton had Peggy ('bonie'), Sophy ('Wha canna win her in a night/ Has little art in courtin'), Mysie ('dour'), Jenny (Mysie's sister, 'bonnie'), and Bessy ('bonnie' again).[99] Burns's song indulges less in conquest than in teasing:

> There's few sae bonny, nane sae guid
> In a' King George' dominion;
> If ye should doubt the truth o' this –
> It's Bessy's ain opinion.

This is performative verse – designed to provoke a scandalised laugh, and quite possibly to be delivered in front of (or at least get back to) Bessy and friends. Work like this got Burns known as a rakishly flirtatious seducer. He prized that reputation. While it may have fascinated some in the locality, it enraged menfolk like Saunders

Tait who sought to blacken Burns's name but came up with verses more notable for their inept bile. 'Yon Bardie's the fox,' girned Tait, warning 'Mauchline wretches' their 'hens' (young women) were not safe when Burns and his pals were about: 'Moll and Meg,/ Jean, Sue, and Lizzey . . ./ There's sax [six] wi' egg.'[100] However fertile or resented, Burns was emerging as ready to engage with and provoke his immediate local community; also as a bard with a reputation for lovemaking. John Blane, a distant relative of Burns's mother, helped on the farm at Mossgiel and lived there from 1783 to 1786, when he 'slept almost constantly in the same room' as Burns. Though years later some disputed Blane's accuracy, he maintained 'That Robert Burns always fixed his fancy on the bold, showy, forward *lasses*, and slighted the reserved or prudent behaved girls.'[101]

Certainly Robert liked making verse assessments of young women he met. Eyeing two local beauties, Jean and Anna Ronald, whose father was 'laird' of local farm the Bennals, Burns hymns Jean for her 'conduct' but Anna for being 'Sae sonsy and sweet' she is 'boast of our bachelors a''. He pays, though, more detailed attention to himself: a bit of a dandy, or at least strikingly better dressed than the average ploughman or peasant farmer. Poet Burns may present himself as poor, but is proud not to be in debt. Outlining his glad rags, he positively swaggers.

> My coat and my vest, they are Scotch o' the best,
> O' pairs o' guid breeks I hae twa, man: *trousers*
> And stockings and pumps to put on my stumps,   *strong, low-heeled*
>   *shoes*
> And ne'er a wrang steek in them a', man.   *wrong stitch*
>
> My sarks they are few, but five o' them new,   *shirts*
> Twal'-hundred, as white as the snaw, man,   *Very finely woven*
>   *linen*
> A ten-shillings hat, a Holland cravat;
> There are no mony poets sae braw, man.[102]

Shenstone counselled that 'men of merit should be allowed to dress in proportion to it'.[103] Cravatted, hatted, proud of his five new shirts woven of fine linen with twelve hundred divisions to the reel, Burns was self-consciously, winkingly, charismatically dressed to kill.

If Tarbolton's young women were listed as 'lasses', in Mauchline Burns found 'proper young Belles'. He suggested a stranger would

think their 'carriage and dress' came from 'Lon'on or Paris'; he wrote a song where each but one is given the title 'Miss'; in another song he pronounced 'novels' like the French 'nouvelles'.[104] Simultaneously he presents these 'belles' as sophisticated consumers, titillating themselves with modern fiction such as Henry Fielding's *Tom Jones* or Samuel Richardson's *Sir Charles Grandison*, and as excitingly endangered females whom Burns, the predatory local Casanova, was all too ready to consume:

> O LEAVE novels, ye Mauchline belles,
>   Ye're safer at your spinning wheel;
> Such witching books, are baited hooks
>   For rakish rooks like Rob Mossgiel.
> Your fine Tom Jones and Grandisons
>   They make your youthful fancies reel;
> They heat your brains, and fire your veins,
>   And then you're prey for Rob Mossgiel.
>
> Beware a tongue that's smoothly hung;
>   A heart that warmly seems to feel;
> That feelin heart but acks a part,
>   'Tis rakish art in Rob Mossgiel.
> The frank address, the soft caress,
>   Are worse than poisoned darts of steel,
> The frank address, and politesse,
>   Are all finesse in Rob Mossgiel.[105]

Chanting his own name and address, Burns here celebrates acting the part as much as he celebrates sex, but the sheer excitement of sex had a lyrical beauty for him. In September 1784 he copied into his commonplace book one of his best-known songs, written to what he later called a 'merry old tune', enrolling himself as one of the merry, rather than one of the grave:

> In the mean time I shall set down the following fragment which, as it is the genuine language of my heart, will enable any body to determine which of the Classes I belong to ——
>
> > Green grow the rashes – O
> > Green grow the rashes – O
> > The sweetest hours that e'er I spend
> > Are spent among the lasses – O

> There's nought but care on ev'ry hand
>   In ev'ry hour that passes – O
> What signifies the life o' man
>   An' 'twere na for the lasses – O
>   Green grow &c.[106]

Here sex is a natural force, at one with the sap and growth of nature. 'The force that through the green fuse drives the flower/ Drives my green age' wrote Dylan Thomas in a later century, but Burns is all the better for being simpler, clearer than Thomas.[107] Burns's is a song by a young man brought up under the strict eye of a father whose Kirk rigorously policed sexuality, frequently criminalising it. 'Green grow the rashes – O' champions the sexual instinct as utterly central to being. Sex, the song goes on, matters more than monetary 'riches'. With 'My arms about my dearie' worldly cares and worldly men 'May a' goe tapsalteerie – O' – may be thrown head over heels.

This song of overthrow challenges what Burns's admirer Thomas Carlyle later called the 'cash nexus', celebrating instead what might be thought 'not worth a rush'. The 'rashes' (rushes) of the chorus were a commonplace, ever-fertile feature of Burns's world. Singing sex, he does not deny affection: the word 'dearie' is hard to sing unaffectionately. Yet implicitly he challenges those who, even if kind, maintain only the values of narrow prudence and sobriety. In his commonplace book Burns's last verse alludes to the proverbially wise Solomon to whom is attributed 'The Song of Solomon', the Bible's celebration of sex. Burns links sexual energy to God's word, challenging the grimmer echelons of the Kirk:

> For you that's douse an' sneers at this
>   Ye're nought but senseless asses – O
> The wisest man the warl' saw
>   He dearly lov'd the Lasses – O
>   Green grow &c.[108]

Immediately after this song in his commonplace book, Burns wrote a piece of prose. Here 'intercourse' carries the eighteenth-century sense of 'communication' or 'communion', yet also plays its part in establishing that the man who enjoys sex, music, poetry, and the sort of reading Burns relished may be accepted as not the worst among God's creatures. Burns's prose relates to 'Green grow the

rashes – O', but also responds to the kirk *Shorter Catechism* question familiar to him from earliest childhood and his father's religious instruction: 'What is the chief end of man?'[109]

> As the grand end of human life is to cultivate an intercourse with that Being, to whom we owe life, with ev'ry enjoyment that renders life delightful; and to maintain an integritive conduct towards our fellow creatures: that so by forming Piety & Virtue into habit, we may be fit members for that society of the Pious, and the Good, which reason and revelation teach us to expect beyond the grave – I do not see that the turn of mind, and pursuits of such a one as the above verses describe – one who spends the hours & thoughts which the vocations of the day can spare with Ossian, Shakespeare, Thomson, Shenstone, Sterne &c. or as the maggot takes him, a gun, a fiddle, or a Song to make, or mend; and at all times some hearts-dear bony lass in view – I say I do not see that the turn of mind & pursuits of such a one are in the least more inimical to the sacred interests of Piety & Virtue, than the, even lawful, bustling, & straining after the worlds riches & honors: and I do not see but he may gain Heaven as well, which by the bye, is no mean consideration, who steals thro the Vale of Life, amusing himself with every little flower that fortune throws in his way; as he, who straining strait forward, & perhaps spattering all about him, gain[s] some of Life's little eminences, where, after all, he can only see & be seen a little more conspicuously, than, what in the pride of his heart, he is apt to term, the poor, indolent, devil he has left behind him. –[110]

What Burns was trying to do in summer 1784, in his commonplace books and elsewhere, was justify his conduct to himself and, to some extent, to his late father. He champions his way of life and sex as natural: a gift from the Creator. Even as he draws on the language of piety, he rejects his father's grave strictness, cultivating instead a merry, even libertine persona.

Acting the part of rakish seducer, enjoying his liaison with Elizabeth Paton, working on the farm and writing with increased skill, Burns in August 1784 was not untroubled. Recalling his illness at Irvine, he mentioned feeling 'still' a sense of being threatened by a 'dangerous disorder'. He copied out several of his prayers and lines on 'DESPONDENCY'.[111] That same month he wrote excitedly to his Montrose cousin about the self-proclaimed holy woman Elspeth Buchan and the Irvine Buchanites, recently expelled from the town,

– Their tenets are a strange jumble of enthusiastic jargon, among others, she pretends to give them the Holy Ghost by breathing on them, which she does with postures & practices that are scandalously indecent; they have likewise disposed of all their effects & hold a community of goods, & live nearly an idle life, carrying on a great farce of pretended devotion in barns, & woods, where they lodge & lye all together, & hold likewise a community of women, as it is another of their tenets that they can commit no moral sin. – I am personally acquainted with most of them, & I can assure you the above mentioned are facts. –[112]

Burns claims the Buchanites illustrate 'the wildest fanaticism' and 'the folly in leaving the guidance of sound reason, & common sense in matters of Religion'. Yet he is fascinated by these people he knew. With their American-trained minister, 'idle life' of apparently unbusinesslike communism, and doctrines of what seemed free love, the Buchanites, like Burns, were rebels against Kirk and community. They tried to celebrate sexuality while maintaining 'an intercourse with that Being to whom we owe life'.

If the Buchanites deviated spectacularly from social assumptions around them, Burns did so less. But he was certainly in conflict with the policemen of the Kirk. In March 1784, the month after his father's death, he had written not only of his own attraction towards 'Blackguards', but also of having 'often observed in the course of my experience of human life that every man even the worst, have something good about them'.[113] He thought most 'virtuous' people seemed so only because they lacked opportunity, or because their sins were well hidden.

Let any of the strictest character for regularity of conduct among us, examine impartially how many of his virtues are owing to constitution & education; how many vices he has never been guilty of, not from any care or vigilance, but from want of opportunity, or some accidental circumstance intervening; how many of the weakness's of mankind he has escaped because he was out of the line of such temptation; and, what often, if not always, weighs more than all the rest; how much he is indebted to the World's good opinion, because the World does not know all; I say any man who can thus think, will scan the failings, nay the faults & crimes of mankind around him, with a brother's eye.[114]

Burns soon versified such sentiments in Standard Habbie and in
other verse forms. He made perhaps his most spirited version of a
biblical text – one he attributes to Solomon – as the epigraph to his
'Address to the Unco Guid, or the Rigidly Righteous'. He presents
a verse of Ecclesiastes – 'Be not righteous over much; neither
make thyself over wise: why shouldest thou destroy thyself?' – as
if spoken by a Scots farmer father to his flirtatious son. So Solomon,
that 'wisest Man the warl' saw' of 'Green grow the rashes', now
champions Burns's standpoint against that of the showily pious:

> My Son, *these maxims make a rule,*
> *And lump them ay thegither;*
> The Rigid Righteous *is a fool,*
> The Rigid Wise *anither:*
> *The cleanest corn that e'er was dight* winnowed
> *May hae some pyles o' caff in;* bits of chaff
> *So ne'er a fellow-creature slight*
> *For random fits o' daffin.* flirtation

SOLOMON – Eccles. ch. vii. vers. 16.[115]

Burns links himself to a paternal and biblical verse to attack those
he considers pharisees. 'O ye' – his poem's opening words – are
again biblical in resonance, most familiar perhaps in Christ's warning
his disciples to beware 'the leaven of the Pharisees': 'O ye of little
faith'.[116] Burns, though, addresses and attacks not people of little,
but of over-self-righteous faith:

> O YE wha are sae guid yoursel,
> Sae pious and sae holy,
> Ye've nought to do but mark and tell
> Your Neebours' fauts and folly!

This poem is all the cleverer in not identifying its targets by name;
to assume the main targets are Kirk elders narrows and oversim-
plifies what Burns is doing. His addressees are at least as much
women as men, for instance. His approach teases, scandalises:

> Ye high, exalted, virtuous Dames,
> Ty'd up in godly laces,
> Before ye gie poor *Frailty* names,
> Suppose a change o' cases;

A dear-lov'd lad, convenience snug,
   A treacherous inclination –
But, let me whisper i' your lug,   *ear*
   Ye're aiblins nae temptation.   *maybe no*

Burns manages the apparently impossible, being both rakish and pious. In lines that draw on some of his early reading, he concludes by presenting theology through imagery of music and attunement, advising his audience not to leap to judgements on fellow humans:

Who made the heart, 'tis *He* alone,
   Decidedly can try us,
He knows each chord its various tone,
   Each spring its various bias:
Then at the balance let's be mute,
   We never can adjust it;
What's *done* we partly may compute,
   But know not what's *resisted*.[117]

Burns knew he could not resist. He wasn't sure he should always be expected to. Many of his poems at this time contain clearly autobiographical elements. The origins of others are more obscure, perhaps most indebted to his ear and imagination.

His beautiful 'Mary Morison', for instance, weaves into a love song the name of a Mauchline soldier's daughter then at the start of her teens. Never earthy, Burns's song assumes she will not return the singer's love; she remains distant, at a window, or dreamed of at a dance. Perhaps this Mary (later to die of tuberculosis at twenty) was a Beatrice figure to Burns. Yet it may be simply that the sound and syllables of her name accidentally fitted the traditional tune he used, called 'Duncan Davison'. Mary Morison is a tuneful appellation: the start of the last name recalls, yet metamorphoses, the sound of the first. Burns's play with sound in the line, 'Ye are na Mary Morison', works subtle variations on vowels and consonants, recapitulating but altering them. That line may owe something to words of Henry Mackenzie ('the reflection that she was not Harriet Wilkins'), but close listening reveals pattern after poetic pattern: the 'Ye are' softened and reversed in the conclusion of the word 'Mary'; the 'na' answered by the softer 'on' at the end of the surname; the rolled *r* connecting and driving the line with a Scots intonation.[118] Sung, these effects become subliminal. Their acoustic presence,

though, is a sign that Burns had become a master of sound and song, able to take a local name and, twining Scots and English, shape it into universal grace. Making his song, Burns may have been acting a part, but the accuracy of his ear, his sense of balanced sounds, and his quickening experience of love all combined to produce breathtaking verbal music.

'My heart was compleatly tinder, and was eternally lighted up by some Goddess or other; and like every warfare in this world, I was sometimes crowned with success, and sometimes mortified with defeat,' he wrote of his young manhood.[119] In mid-1784 he was healthy and elated one moment, low and ill the next. Late June saw him elected Depute Master of his Masonic lodge in Tarbolton; he was with the Masons again in early September. Soon, though, he fell sick – perhaps a recurrence of the depressive collapse recalled in his commonplace book. He was remembered suffering from 'fainting fits' and irregular heart movements, ill 'to a somewhat serious extent'.[120]

Burns's uncertain state of health is evident from a letter of 13 September to his friend John Tennant. Living about five miles away at Ochiltree, Tennant was a miller four years older than Burns, and son of one of Burns's father's friends. 'My dear Sir,' writes the poet,

> My unlucky illness on friday last did not do me a greater disservice than in depriving me of the pleasure I had promised myself in spending an hour with you. – I got so much better on saturday as to be able to ride home, but I am still in a kind of slow fever, and I trouble you with this small letter rather to relieve a little the langor of my spirits than any thing particular I have to tell you. –[121]

Burns gossips about local amours – 'He tells me you used all the powers of your eloquence, first on my friend Miss R—— and next on Miss C——.' Robert was one of a group of male pals, some with literary tastes, showing at times 'the raptures of a Lover in Romance' or 'the rant of a dramatic Hero'. Dancing, Freemasonry, conversation and song were among their preoccupations. Several had interests in the same young women.[122]

The 'belles' had their own gossip. Unfortunately, it has not survived. We know these lasses through men's descriptions. Involved in 1784 in a high-minded dalliance of his own, Gilbert wrote the following year that

In the town of Machline when I came first to Mossgiel there resided several young women of a turn and manner entirely different from any of the sex I had before been acquainted with [;] they agreed in a great measure with Milton's description of the daughters of men who display'd such powers of enchantment so early in the world . . .

Liking smart clothes, dancing, suggestive behaviour and rolling their eyes, this coterie of young women led Burns's younger brother to reflect,

A young woman well drest and with a specious air of gentility has a powerfull effect on the fancy of one used only to the society of plain country girls, yet while [Gilbert's own beloved] Lavinia continued to occupy my attention the Belles of Machline made but little impression on me but when that was fairly over I surveyed their charms with a little more complaisance [;] the reign of mere flippant coquettery however is soon over with a person of any seriousness or gravity if unsuported by some more valuable accomplishments and a little familiarity entirely dissolves the charm.[123]

Despite the grave, somewhat jaded Gilbert, Burns and his merry friends were openly keen on these young women. Several lads close to Burns sought to partner a 'Belle'. Some even enjoyed good marriages.

Among the 'proper young Belles' of Mauchline Burns grouped together in a jaunty song to the tune 'Bonie Dundee', Helen Miller (rated 'fine') would be for a time in summer 1785 'Tenant of my heart'. Soon, though, she dumped Burns – 'huffed my Bardship', as he put it.[124] She later married John Mackenzie, the doctor who had attended his father and became, like Burns, a Tarbolton Freemason in 1784. Another Mauchline Belle was Helen's sister Elizabeth ('Miss Betty is braw'). A third, Jean Markland ('divine'), married a friend of Burns's from Tarbolton, James Findlay. Burns's song of the Belles also praised the 'wit' of Jean Smith. Eventually marrying Burns's clever boyhood friend James Candlish, Jean was sister to another of his pals, Mauchline merchant's son James Smith, four years the poet's junior, but 'a trusty Trojan' and 'old . . . much-valued friend'.[125] Christina Morton, another of this group, went on to marry Burns's crony, Mauchline's Robert Paterson.

When Paterson liked a young woman, he called her 'a grand

cracker'. Burns complained that this local draper could not really appreciate a clever, 'honest-hearted' woman. Seemingly more interested in money than love or sex, Paterson was annoying Burns in September 1784. Yet his annoyance reveals Burns's frustrations. Just a few years earlier he had argued at the Tarbolton Bachelors' Club that it was better for a young farmer to marry a lovely girl without a fortune than a well-off unattractive woman who could handle a farm. Now he found it hard to balance competing demands: the need to make a living on a farm where things were not going well and his mother and siblings depended on financial success; but also the urges of his own body. He was impatient with life in a community which policed sexual 'sin' more vigilantly than smuggling. All this comes out when Burns censures Paterson's failure to appreciate a girl with a 'sweet, sonsy [attractive] face' whose 'good sense and education' are 'superior to his own'. Paterson, he writes, is entangled 'in a thousand difficulties',

> ... but, like a true Merchant he has stated it in the Ledgers of his fancy thus:
>> Stock, Dr to cash, by Mrs Paterson's portion} 300£. –
> We talk of air & manner, of beauty & wit, and lord knows what unmeaning nonsense; but – there – is solid charms for you – Who would not be in raptures with a woman that will make him 300£ richer – And then to have a woman to lye with when one pleases, without running any risk of the cursed expence of bastards and all the other concomitants of that species of Smuggling – These are solid views of matrimony –[126]

After rejection by Eliza Gebbie, Burns was in no rush to marry. He wanted, though, to 'lye with' a woman. Dallying with the comparatively cultured Belles of Mauchline, he relished sex with less-educated Elizabeth Paton, now pregnant by him. Early that August the Burneses' Tarbolton minister, Patrick Wodrow, had mentioned Burns as one of his 'Communicants', formally declaring he and the rest of his family had behaved 'soberly and honestly, free of public scandal; or ground of Church Censure known to the Members of this Kirk Session'.[127] This certification let Burns join neighbouring Mauchline congregation in time for their annual service of holy communion. He knew if it was found he had fathered an illegitimate child, there would be trouble in his new parish.

Burns was not alone in his frustration with the Kirk's strict regime. Before Mauchline's August communion Gavin Hamilton was formally cited by the Kirk Session. Prominent among its elders was local farmer William Fisher. Eventually the lawyer Hamilton successfully appealed against Mauchline Session, who were overruled by the more moderate Ayr Presbytery. Hamilton's case was another annoyance to Burns. Why should he and Hamilton be dictated to by these local pharisees? Trying hard to reconcile his love of sex, flirting, gossip, pubs and joking with his intensifying poetic ambitions and a persisting sense, evident in his commonplace book, that a right relationship with God was essential, Burns did not want his vitality policed by Mauchline Session. Veering between low spirits and satirical glee, his solution was to play the part of the bardie, making poetry out of his predicament.

Burns knew that Robert Fergusson and an admirer had exchanged verse letters in Standard Habbie, full of talk about 'gude black print', 'lasses', 'couthie cracks' (friendly gossip), eating and drinking.[128] Ramsay and Hamilton of Gilbertfield had done likewise, achieving for Scots what Pope's epistles (written in a very different verse form) had accomplished for refined English. Now Burns brought together praise of 'fun an' drinkin'' with biblical allusion and attacks on supposed local 'Saunts' (Saints) of the Kirk Session in a verse epistle sent with a bunch of poems to a 'rough, rude, ready-witted' farmer, John Rankine.

Rankine lived near Tarbolton. A founding member of its local Masonic lodge, he liked a good drink: Saunders Tait claimed Rankine's 'Bible' was whisky, his 'Psalm-book Rum'.[129] Talk of a 'humorous *dream*' Rankine had had was, as Burns put it, 'making a noise in the country-side'.[130] This dream may well have offended the Kirk Session. A later account says it was about going to Hell then finding it full of friends of Lord Kames. Likening Rankine to the Old Testament's Korah, a rebel against religious authority who was swallowed up by the earth 'alive into the pit' and 'perished from among the congregation', Burns saw in Rankine an ally in the face of orthodoxy.[131] 'Unregenerate Heathen', he and Rankine are not among the self-righteous Calvinist select souls God has chosen as his elect. Burns delights that when Rankine gets them drunk those rigidly righteous reveal themselves as examples of 'Hypocrisy'. Rankine's conduct may be conventionally 'wicked': Burns finds it good both in itself and for what it brings out:

Ye hae sae monie cracks an' cants,   *stories and scandalous tales*
And in your wicked, druken rants,
Ye mak a devil o' the *Saunts*,
    An' fill them fou;   *drunk / full*
And then their failings, flaws an' wants,
    Are a' seen thro'.[132]

Burns responds to Rankine the maker-up of scandalous tales by telling him a story of his own: he has gone out hunting and brought down, then stroked, a lovely young female partridge. Word of this – Burns's liaison with Elizabeth Paton – has got out. Now 'The hale affair' has been brought to the attention of 'the *Poacher-Court*', the Kirk Session. Burns has had to pay a fine, 'the *fee*'. Nonetheless, exulting in his own sexuality and that of his '*hen*', his verse letter proclaims he is ready for a lot more 'sportin' of the same kind, even if he has to go into exile in America as a result.[133]

Burns was determined to uphold 'The blissful joys of Lovers'.[134] Flirting with several young women was fun, but hard to manage. On 11 November 1784 he penned a hurried note to his Kirkoswald friend Thomas Orr, glad to have one lass 'off my hands' because now awkwardly involved with another: 'I do'n't chuse to enter into particulars in writing but never was a poor rakish rascal in a more pitiful taking –.'[135] Elizabeth Paton's pregnancy was becoming public knowledge: 'now a rumour's like to rise,/ A whaup's i' the nest.'[136] The 'whaup' or curlew (a bird with a plaintive cry) would be born in May 1785: Burns's first child, Elizabeth. As the pregnancy grew more apparent the Burnes family debated what Robert should do. His mother wanted him to marry; Gilbert and Burns's sisters Agnes and Annabella thought Elizabeth Paton's character 'would soon have disgusted' him.[137] She doted on him.

In the end Robert seems to have been summoned back to Tarbolton, Elizabeth's home parish, ordered by its Kirk Session to do public penance for fornication. Usually this meant appearing in church three successive Sundays, occupying the notorious seat of repentance, the 'cutty stool'. Male fornicators had to attend along with their female accomplices to be upbraided by the minister. Burns did as he was told. He did not, however, marry Elizabeth Paton. Surviving her ignominy, three years later she wed local widower John Andrew. With this farmhand she had four children before dying in the mid-1790s.[138] Schooled in Mauchline, Burns's daughter would

be brought up largely by his own mother. The bard underwent his public humiliation. He paid a fine, but made clear he thought it ridiculous the Kirk should make him pay for having sex. In verse he celebrated his fornication, not as a sin but something to be lingeringly proud of:

> Before the Congregation wide
>   I pass'd the muster fairly,
> My handsome Betsey by my side,
>   We gat our ditty rarely;
> But my downcast eye by chance did spy
>   What made my lips to water,
> Those limbs so clean where I, between,
>   Commenc'd a Fornicator.
>
> With rueful face and signs of grace
>   I pay'd the buttock-hire,
> The night was dark and thro' the park
>   I could not but convoy her;
> A parting kiss, what could I less,
>   My vows began to scatter,
> My Betsey fell – lal de dal lal lal,
>   I am a Fornicator.

Burns never published this poem, but it circulated. He swore to Paton 'That while I own a single crown,/ She's welcome for to share it'.[139] He did not mean to abandon her; he simply was not going to marry her, or deny his pleasure in their having had sex. She, in turn, Burns's sister recalled, 'acknowledged he had broken no promise to her'.[140] Today the position would not be unusual; probably it was common in eighteenth-century Ayrshire where Andrew Noble, Session Clerk of Mauchline, could record in his minute-book with apparent satisfaction, 'only 24 fornicators in the parish since last sacrament'.[141]

Sick of his sex life being criminalised, Burns decided to make sly public mockery of sectarian 'tulzies' (quarrels) within the Kirk. 'The Holy Tulzie', his first poem to do this, was, he recalled, 'The first of my poetical productions that saw the light. – I gave a Copy of it to a particular friend of mine who was very fond of these things, and told him – "I did not know who was the Author, but that I had got a Copy of it by accident."' With its epigraph from Pope

about 'barbarous civil war', Burns's poem did not attack the Kirk as an institution. However, it mercilessly sent up its most rigid representatives: two fundamentalist Old Light ministers revile each other as 'Villain' and 'Hypocrite'. Drinking at 'Calvin's fountain-head', they curse moderation in the Kirk. Their congregations are 'maingie sheep'. They rail against 'Common Sense' philosophy and ministers like Burns's own childhood pastor Dalrymple as well as the moderate Tarbolton minister Patrick Wodrow.[142] The Church of Scotland is exposed as at war with itself. Burns's sympathies for the moderates are clear. A hit 'with a certain side of both clergy and laity', 'The Holy Tulzie' seems to have endeared him to them, rather than alienating him from the Kirk as a whole. Moderates greeted it, he remembered, 'with a roar of applause'.[143]

Attacking 'Orthodoxy', this poem's allusions show how well Burns knew his Bible, and how attentively he listened to sermons. He clearly approves of the 'close nervous excellence' of farmer's son William McGill, minister of Ayr's Auld Kirk. Then working on his *Practical Essay on the Death of Jesus Christ* (1786), McGill was awarded a Doctorate of Divinity by Glasgow University in 1785.[144] Well liked by his congregation, who responded to his commonsensical side, he enraged fundamentalist opponents. Burns admired McGill's preaching and, it would seem, the psychological insights in his writings. Burns's own sense of psychological complexity was magnificently displayed in his next broadside against the rigidly righteous. 'Holy Willie's Prayer' combines his attack on Old Light Kirk fundamentalism with his delight in the power of sex. Writing it Burns made himself as 'bardie' as he possibly could.

His target was one of his friends' persecutors. William Fisher (1737–1809) lived less than two miles from Burns: Montgarswood farm is just west of Mauchline. Though theologically far apart, Fisher and Burns must have met in church and elsewhere. Delighting in local gossip, and friendly with Gavin Hamilton, Burns had plenty of opportunities to hear about Fisher's doings, and observe their course. During their long-running feud, Mauchline Kirk Session grew sick of Hamilton's name. In mid-January 1784, perhaps as part of a deliberate provocation, Hamilton's servant Robert Bryan presented his baby to Mauchline's minister, asking him to christen the wee boy 'Gavin Hamilton Bryan'. The minister, William Auld, could not refuse; the baptism duly took place in Mauchline Kirk. Its Session

fulminated against Hamilton in its minute-book, and the unsaintly lawyer in November accused the elders of acting out of 'pique and ill nature'.

Piqued, they hit back, eventually branding Hamilton a person who 'habitually if not totally neglects the worship of God in his family'. Hamilton appeared before the Session at the end of January 1785 and admitted several failings, but also produced a judgment from Ayr Presbytery, won for him by his friend and fellow lawyer Robert Aiken. This ordered Mauchline Session to remove from their minutes earlier censures against Hamilton. James Mackay, who scrutinised several sets of local Kirk minutes, shows that Mauchline's 'Saunts' appealed against the 'cruel injustice' of this 'despotic' judgment.[145] While the Synod of Glasgow and Ayr considered this lengthy appeal, tempers rose in Mauchline. By March Hamilton was complaining about the Session's 'disgraceful manner'. The Session refused to budge. Petty and vindictive, the dispute ran on for years. It even took in Hamilton's having his servant Bryan dig potatoes on Sundays. Long-running, bitter feuds over trivia are not unknown in organisations, including churches. Fed up with the '*Poacher-Court*' of kirkmen pursuing him for his 'fornication' with Elizabeth Paton, Burns observed Hamilton's case as attentively as he had followed the American War. Later, he recalled the writing of one of his most famous poems in distinctly military terms, dating its production to just after 'The Holy Tulzie',

> – Holy Willie's Prayer next made its appearance, and alarmed the kirk-Session so much that they held three several meetings to look over their holy artillery, if any of it was pointed against profane Rhymers. – Unluckily for me, my idle wanderings led me, on another side, point blank within the reach of their heaviest metal. –[146]

Bombarding Burns for fornication, righteous kirkmen were rightly alarmed by 'Holy Willie's Prayer'. It takes one person – Fisher, who probably played a minor part in the proceedings against Hamilton – making him a caricature of all Burns saw as worst in fundamentalist Scottish Calvinism. 'Were hypocrites to pretend to no uncommon sanctity,' argued Shenstone, 'their want of merit would be less discoverable.' The same poet states, 'A small blemish also presents a clue, which very often conducts us through the most intricate mazes, and dark recesses of their character ... Perhaps

there is not a more effectual key to the discovery of hypocrisy, than a censorious temper.'[147] 'Holy Willie's Prayer' seems written with that in mind.

Never printed in Burns's lifetime, but existing in several manuscript copies in the poet's hand, it certainly circulated among his friends. At some point he added a prose headnote presenting Fisher as aged and single. This is either a false memory, or, more likely, an imaginative recasting of the married farmer who, despite having been a kirk elder for almost a quarter of a century, was under fifty when Burns wrote his 'Prayer'. Probably Burns composed this headnote years later: there would have been no need to explain to the original local audience that Fisher was an 'Elder in the parish of Mauchline'. A small amount of evidence suggests that at some stage in later life Fisher was found drunk; Burns lays it on thick that the man was 'much and justly famed for that polemical chattering which ends in tippling Orthodoxy, and for that Spiritualized Bawdry which refines to Liquorish Devotion'. Burns also celebrates 'the oratorical powers of Mr Robt. Aiken, Mr Hamilton's Counsel', and pays fulsome, perhaps not entirely accurate, tribute to Hamilton as 'one of the most irreproachable and truly respectable characters in the country'.[148] None of the historical inaccuracy matters when we encounter the poem's satiric bite.

Holy Willie glorifies himself as one of God's elect, a 'chosen sample' set aside for salvation through Divine Grace irrespective of conduct on earth. He makes it clear most of his neighbours will certainly be damned. His brilliantly constructed voice prays to God in Standard Habbie with totally self-interested piety,

> O THOU that in the heavens does dwell!
> Wha, as it pleases best thysel,
> Sends ane to heaven and ten to h-ll,
>   A' for thy glory!
> And no for ony gude or ill
>   They've done before thee. –
>
> I bless and praise thy matchless might,
> When thousands thou has left in night,
> That I am here before thy sight,
>   For gifts and grace,
> A burning and a shining light
>   To a' this place. –[149]

'Holy Willie's Prayer' is a dramatic monologue – a speech whose speaker is overheard unintentionally giving away aspects of his personality. Outside the drama, this poem is the greatest such monologue in any variety of English poetry before Robert Browning, who may have learned from Burns's vernacular skill. Burns probably took hints from poems like Ramsay's Standard Habbie 'Last Speech of a Wretched Miser'. However, the Habbie verse form was already being used locally to engage in religious controversy by a poet whose work Burns came to admire at this time: John Lapraik. Lapraik's first wife was sister to Burns's merry Masonic friend Rankine. In a 1782 poem about local affairs of 'Moor Farmers', Lapraik reproached '*charity* and *mercy* haters', and speculated that the elect or '*sanctifi'd*' would welcome rather than reject God's punishments,

> For ev'ry *son* that GOD doth love,
> With chastisements he will him prove;
> If *sanctifi'd*, it will him move
>   To thank his GOD,
> Who did reclaim him, in his *love*,
>   By such a rod.[150]

Burns's Holy Willie makes it clear that he has a certain fondness not so much for 'chastisements' of 'a rod', as for the prodigious 'thorn' with which God has chosen to 'buffet' him. I have found no clear eighteenth-century evidence of the word 'willie' being used (as in modern Scotland) to mean 'penis', but Holy Willie is unmistakably a phallic caricature. Burns fuses Calvinist theology with boastful sexual energy as his speaker, bragging of being 'a shining light', goes on to reveal himself as a less than perfect sexual example. Burns's deployment of Willie's excited voice within the stanza form produces work whose timing and slyness give it a performative gusto, a phallic stand-up comedy,

> But yet – O L——d – confess I must –
> At times I'm fash'd wi' fleshly lust;
> And sometimes too, in warldly trust
>   Vile Self gets in;
> But thou remembers we are dust,
>   Defil'd wi' sin. –

O L——d – yestreen – thou kens – wi' Meg –
Thy pardon I sincerely beg!
O may't ne'er be a living plague,
  To my dishonor!
And I'll ne'er lift a lawless leg
  Again upon her. –

Besides, I farther maun avow,
Wi' Leezie's lass, three times – I trow –
But L——d, that friday I was fou
  When I cam near her;
Or else, thou kens, thy servant true
  Wad never steer her. –

Maybe thou lets this fleshly thorn
Buffet thy servant e'en and morn,
Lest he o'er proud and high should turn,
  That he's sae gifted;
If sae, thy hand maun e'en be borne
  Untill thou lift it. –[151]

The exposure of the speaker's hypocrisy as he wavers between confession and triumphalism is devastating. On to Holy Willie Burns displaced some of his own anxieties about how to reconcile loyalty to the Kirk legacy left him by his father with his own excited pursuit of sexual pleasure. Holy Willie exemplifies how not to do this. He acquires near-manic vituperative energy from opposition to those seductive 'taking arts' he attributes to Gavin Hamilton. Several such arts the seducer 'Rob Mossgiel' (he of 'rakish art') surely shared.

Willie is all the more riled that Hamilton has 'set the warld in a roar/ O' laughin at us'. Pleased 'The Holy Tulzie' had been greeted with 'a roar of applause', Burns is closely allied to the Hamilton of 'Holy Willie's Prayer', just as Willie is in some ways Burns's mirror image. Out of a drama raging in his own psyche and in the community around him Burns projected this great character of Holy Willie, gleefully calling down damnation on Hamilton and his friend 'glib-tongu'd Aiken', yet damning himself out of his own mouth:

L——d, in thy day o' vengeance try him!
L——d visit him that did employ him!
And pass not in thy mercy by them,
    Nor hear their prayer;
But for thy people's sake destroy them,
    And dinna spare!

But L——d, remember me and mine
Wi' mercies temporal and divine!
That I for grace and gear may shine,
    Excell'd by nane!
And a' the glory shall be thine!
    AMEN! AMEN![152]

Structured like a conventional prayer, this poem ends with a gesture towards the Lord's Prayer. It presents a scandalous interpretation of the Calvinist belief that because God had preordained eternal life for some and eternal damnation for others, those chosen to be saved could do anything they liked. Burns's poem was Scots dynamite, an excoriating, brilliantly modulated satire on hypocrisy. It strikes a nerve in Scottish Presbyterian culture which would be probed again in the following century by James Hogg's novel of fundamentalist terrorism, *The Private Memoirs and Confessions of a Justified Sinner*. Robert Louis Stevenson's *The Strange Case of Dr Jekyll and Mr Hyde* and Muriel Spark's *The Pride of Miss Jean Brodie* owe much to this tradition. But like all these works, the private memoirs and confessions of Holy Willie, addressed to God but overheard by readers, have a universal resonance. A poem about hypocrisy, authority, sex and man's relationship with God, 'Holy Willie's Prayer' deals in the deftest, daftest way imaginable with essential human issues. Its vernacular energy, earthed in a world of 'Kail and potatoes', makes it utterly and uniquely convincing. William Fisher, farmer of Montgarswood, Ayrshire, never knew what hit him.

Burns was in the mood to deliver knock-outs. He followed up with an 'Epitaph on Holy Willie', dismissing his adversary as a 'coof' (idiot).[153] Still, his satire on other locals was a little gentler. Gilbert remembered him writing 'Death and Doctor Hornbook. A True Story' in 'early . . . 1785'; Burns dated its events to 'seed-time' that year.[154] A hornbook was what children started with at school: wooden-backed, covered in a thin protective sheet of

transparent horn, it was a paper with the alphabet, the Lord's Prayer, some numbers and basic spelling on it – hardly the sort of thing associated with a qualified doctor. In Tarbolton teacher John Wilson, Burns found a self-important character ripe for sending up. Gilbert recalled,

> The Schoolmaster of Tarbolton parish, to eke out the scanty subsistence allowed to that useful class of men, had set up a shop of grocery goods. Having accidentally fallen in with some medical books, and become most hobby-horsically attached to the study of medicine, he had added the sale of a few medicines to his little trade. He had got a shop-bill printed, at the bottom of which, overlooking his own incapacity, he had advertised, that 'Advice would be given in common disorders at the shop gratis'.[155]

Burns, who knew Wilson as a fellow Tarbolton Freemason, met him at a Masons' gathering in April. Robert thought the poem he composed immediately afterwards 'too trifling and prolix'.[156] Its handling of a slightly drunken night journey when 'The rising Moon began to glowr/ The distant *Cumnock* hills out-owre' and 'ghaists an' witches' might be sensed clearly draws on stories he had loved in his childhood, and in some ways anticipates 'Tam o' Shanter'.[157] Out at night, Death complains he is deprived of work since Dr Hornbook, using medicines like 'Urinus Spiritus of capons' and 'Midge-tail clippings', is killing off all the local people. Burns, familiar (like the good Doctor H) with Edinburgh medico William Buchan's bestselling *Domestic Medicine*, has great fun making up 'uncommon weapons' for his quack-physician's armoury of 'shavings, filings, scrapings'.[158]

As in the humour of 'Holy Willie's Prayer', there is also a darker side. The Burns who had recently thought himself at death's door recorded that when he wrote 'Death and Doctor Hornbook' 'An epidemical fever was then raging in that country.'[159] We know Burns's younger brother John, apprenticed to a weaver around the time of his father's death, was ill. Gilbert wrote in 1785 that John had been 'soon oblidged to quit' his weaving 'on account of a disorder in which he is now languishing and which must probably soon put and [sic] end to his life'.[160] Sick for years, John eventually died that November, aged sixteen. No one knows exactly what killed him, but his slow death at Mossgiel so soon after William Burnes's

demise must have made life there all the harder. When Burns wrote his ridiculous vision of death and doctoring in 1785, just as when he composed his absurd vision of sex addiction and religious fervour in 'Holy Willie's Prayer', he was not escaping from the world around him, but reshaping it into a humorous apotheosis; remaking its darkness as bardie, intelligent, slyly energetic art. His verse was in touch with the Mauchline community, certainly, but for all its vernacular dance and frolic it was also powered by darker private preoccupations.

Probably around the time he wrote 'Death and Doctor Hornbook' Burns first met the woman who was for him 'the jewel' of the Mauchline Belles. In the course of a long, sometimes hurtful relationship she eventually became his wife. Jean Armour remembered the moment clearly.

> The first time ever Mrs B. saw the Bard was in Mauchline ... Mrs B., then about seventeen, was spreading clothes in a bleach-green along with some other girls, when Burns passed in his way to call on Mr Hamilton. He had a little dog which ran on the clothes. Mrs B. scolded, and threw something at the animal. Burns said, 'Lassie, if ye thought ocht o' me, ye wadna hurt my dog!' Mrs B. thought to herself 'I wadna think much o' you at ony rate.' – Saw him afterwards at a dancing room, and got acquainted.[161]

Spirited on both sides, this moment is emblematic: a dirty dog messes up the bleached clean washing. In the course of their relationship Burns would subject Jean to a good deal of physical and psychological disturbance. When they first met he was involved with another woman, probably Mauchline Belle Helen Miller. Burns would become entangled emotionally and sexually with many other people throughout the rest of his lifelong connection with Armour. In spring 1785 Elizabeth Paton, whom he now hardly saw, was about to have his child. But flirting, then dancing with Jean soon impressed Robert. By August, secretly revising one of his earliest poems, he copied a stanza on to the middle of page thirty-seven in his commonplace book. Its third-last line ends with the rhyme-word 'Farmer', before it concludes,

> An' the Moon shines bright when I rove at night
> To muse on

IV

Bard

Jean Armour was remarkable. Burns knew it. Soon after they met he called her the 'jewel' among the Mauchline Belles. Her recollections of their meeting suggest a confident woman of spirited humour. Her surviving letters (written in later life) reinforce an impression of capable intelligence. Armour's relationship with Burns required much resilience. By turns rakish, bookish and blokish, Robert, however charismatic and sensitive, was not easy to live with. Jean coped. In the course of their eleven-year relationship, she would bear him nine children, six of whom died young. Burns worked hard, composed poems intensively, philandered, experienced highs and lows of spirits, cherishing the self-image of a will-o'-the-wisp, a sometimes unstable personality. Yet to say Jean Armour simply coped underestimates her part in their relationship. Journalist John McDiarmid who knew and interviewed her called her 'well-balanced . . . a clever woman' who 'possessed great shrewdness, discriminated character admirably, and frequently made very pithy remarks'. McDiarmid also spoke to people who had known Armour when she was younger. He recorded that during Burns's lifetime and 'up to middle life her jet-black eyes were clear and sparkling, her carriage easy, and her step light'. She was good looking – as McDiarmid put it, 'Her limbs were cast in the finest mould'. Surviving portraits show her in age, alert, settled, even well off, managing to deal with her status as a curiosity, a 'relict', the widow of the bard.[1]

Born in 1765, she was six years younger than Burns. Growing up in Mauchline the second of eleven children, Jean saw several siblings die in infancy. Her mother, Mary Smith, was married to James Armour, local master mason and fundamentalist Calvinist. Mr Armour rented for his family a good pew in the parish kirk; in a large country village of about a thousand people, he enjoyed a certain

social standing. The Armours had a good house at the heart of Mauchline, backing on to a lane behind the respectable Whitefoord Arms inn, roughly opposite the kirk. In an age when many women were illiterate Jean could read and write; her surviving letters show a confident hand, nice phrasing. She had a good Scots tongue in her head, and valued the same in Burns: 'He never spoke English,' she asserted, 'but spoke very correct Scotch.'[2]

In youth and young womanhood, Robert maintained, Jean had read very little other than the Bible and the Psalms. He was pleased she came to read his published poems 'very devoutly'.[3] His fullest (1788) description says she has 'the handsomest figure, the sweetest temper, the soundest constitution, and the kindest heart in the country'. Clearly he liked and desired her but their courtship and marriage were tempestuous, uneasy, disrupted. What we know of Jean's taste can make her sound conventional. Artefacts associated with her – a faded flower painting, a teapot decorated with fruit, plants and flowers – confirm she liked fine domestic things. 'Music, pictures and flowers' were her enjoyments.[4] Later passers-by were impressed by flowers arranged in the windows of her house. When young she was a good dancer: dancing was part of her courtship.

Something else also attracted Burns to her. She knew, he said, 'all the ballads in the country' and had a beautiful voice, 'the finest "wood note wild" I ever heard'.[5] Singing Scots songs in 'a brilliant treble' that 'rose without effort as high as B natural', she was considered a performer of professional standard.[6] Her memory, especially for ballads, was excellent. Like Burns, she could quote at length. One fragment of a September 1788 letter to her (the earliest extant piece of their correspondence) shows he took it for granted he might 'talk of Poetry' and music with her.[7] A contemporary who knew her as a girl remembered her 'always either singing or dancing'.[8] Though no letter from her to him survives, McDiarmid wrote of her singing voice, balladry, memory, and 'aptitude' for Scots verse that 'Of these powers the bard was so well aware that he read to her almost every piece he composed, and was not ashamed to own that he had profited by her judgment.'[9]

This woman with whom Burns fell in love was, he came to realise, astute as well as beautiful. Her love, patience, and ability to manage would be tested to the limit. Burns in 1784–5 was delighting in appearing sexy, bardie, and dangerously distinguished. If Armour, like other local women, found this combination attractive, she also

had sense to see that beyond it was something more. In meeting her, Robert was lucky; luckier, indeed, than he knew.

At Mossgiel he read and wrote a lot. William Patrick, herd-boy at the farm, sometimes ran errands for him. Patrick remembered the poet having a 'lairge leebrary' and 'aye readin''. From Patrick's reminiscences, we know Burns regularly received 'paipers' – newspapers – though it is not clear which he read.[10] This habit, encouraged by Murdoch in Burns's boyhood, kept him in touch with national and international politics, but the dynamics of the village were more central to his art. Mauchline has been called the 'Mecca and Medina of every Burns pilgrim'; its importance lies not in its grandeur but in its still perceptible layout.[11] Mauchline and Mossgiel are where Burns became the bard. This chapter concentrates on the best evidence we have for the workings of his mind in the period when he achieved maturity as a poet: his own writings. To focus on these involves stripping away later accretions of mythology, but to understand Burns it is necessary also to understand aspects of Mauchline, the place that allowed, even encouraged, vital elements in his imagination to combine and ignite.

Mauchline was a village community of much gossip and very few secrets – a social, sexual, theological and linguistic crossroads. Mauchline parish took in around twenty-five square miles, nearly 1,800 people, between five and ten per cent of them farmers. Its countryside was and still is beautiful. From beyond Mauchline to Ayr, wrote one late eighteenth-century traveller, 'the river Ayr winds delightfully the whole way . . . its Banks being steep, bold & highly picturesque'.[12] Mauchline itself, though, was no tourist destination, but a place travellers passed through. Two turnpike roads intersected there, one running from Ayr to Edinburgh, the other from Kilmarnock to Dumfries: national as well as local news was easy to come by. Linguistically, the village was also at an intersection: 'The Scots dialect is the language spoken, but is gradually improving, and approaching nearer to the English,' the local minister opined in 1791.[13] For a poet interested in access to both Scots and English, such a situation was ideal, encouraging Burns to use the full linguistic spectrum.

Mauchline folk were interested in improvements, including agricultural ones. Older manners were giving way to new: tea-drinking, for instance, becoming common. In the mid-eighteenth century 'good two-penny, strong-ale, and home-spirits were in vogue', but as the

century neared its close 'even people in the middling and lower stations of life, deal much in foreign spirits, rum-punch and wine'.[14] Burns's work mentions brandy but tends more towards enthusiastic praise of drinks associated with the older, traditional Scotland. In poetry he wants to register both inherited mores and newer developments, whether in architecture, language, or belief; some of his poems are themselves meeting-points, liveliest where social groups or their spokespeople converse.

At the centre of Mauchline village (or 'town' as its minister called it) was the Cross. This crossroads was near Mauchline Kirk and the old Mauchline Castle. Attached to this twelfth-century castle (then a ruin) was Gavin Hamilton's much more modern house: this odd combination of old and new is in some ways the architectural equivalent of Burns's poetry. Then as now several pubs were very close to Mauchline Kirk. These included not just the Whitefoord Arms but also disreputable Poosie Nancie's lodging-house, attracting prostitutes and the homeless poor. Like Mauchline itself, the poetry Burns made there brought together the settled and the unhoused, the bawdy and the sacred, Scots and English, traditional and 'improved'. Sometimes, as in the village, these different elements would congregate together in his writing; at other times they would be examined individually. The map of the centre of this late eighteenth-century village is a map of Robert Burns's mind.

Ironically, while Alloway has grown rich from the Burns who left as a young child, and so has changed almost out of all recognition, Mauchline, much more crucial to the poetry that made Burns's name, seems nowadays down on its luck. Close to its beautifully remodelled Burns House (now a National Trust for Scotland property), the remains of the medieval castle decay; walkways are strewn with broken glass. The people are warm, friendly, proud of their town's place in a history which takes in more than simply Burns. Mauchline is a place where social problems and prosperous patches are awkwardly cheek by jowl. In that too it remains connected to much of Burns's most celebrated poetry.

William Patrick, aged about nine at the time, remembered the poet as smartly dressed, generally well liked, but upsetting some local people: his 'reputed wildness' contrasted with Gilbert's 'douce, sensible' manner. Burns wrote a lot of letters; his herd-boy had to take some into Mauchline to post. Attractive to 'the lasses', Burns flirted 'in a fresh, open, cheerful manner with smart daffin and

banter'.[15] This accords with Jean Armour's recollection of first meeting him. It chimes too with David Sillar's memories, and with the tone of poems from 1784–5 like 'O leave novels, ye Mauchline belles'. The Mauchline Belles typified changing tastes in the village: 'silk caps and silk cloaks' became desirable so, as the kirk minister noted, 'women, in a middling station, are as fine as ladies of quality were formerly'.[16] Men too became more fashion-conscious, but to a lesser degree. Flirtatious and stylishly got-up, Burns stood out just as he wanted to.

Championing the cause of sex, he also committed himself to the art of poetry. In both he sought several partners. After his affair with Elizabeth Paton cooled, a, perhaps *the*, 'Tenant' of his 'heart' was Elizabeth Miller. She jilted him, according to Burns, when in July 1785 her brother married an heiress rich from 'Jamaica siller [silver]'. In his head Burns began to make a poem to 'burlesque the whole business'. As his imagination presented the 'bony Birdies' preparing for the wedding he apparently got over any pain of being jilted. His description of young women drawing up their stockings and putting on garters signals flirtatious desire more than lingering resentment. By the time he had composed these stanzas to his satisfaction 'Miss Bess & I were once more in Unison'.[17] This may mean they were again an item, or simply that they were not at daggers drawn.

However, if we follow Burns's manuscript dating of his 'Epistle to Davie', then by 'Jan:—1785' he already had strong 'tender feelings' for 'my darling JEAN'.[18] Fourteen years after the event, Gilbert recalled Robert reciting much of that poem in, Gilbert thought, summer 1784 while they were 'weeding in the garden'; even as he put in a day's farm-work Burns developed verse in his head and entertained his brother. Specific mention of Jean may have been added before the writing out of two manuscripts dated January 1785.[19]

Burns's relationship with Jean was developing alongside Elizabeth Paton's pregnancy, and, a little later, while Burns was interested in Elizabeth Miller. By autumn 1785 he had transferred his affections, for the time at least, to Jean Armour, but in the preceding year she does not appear to have been his only lover. James Mackay argues that Burns and Armour probably met in April 1785, but fails to explain why he was already writing of her as 'my JEAN' that January.[20] Though she became more important in his life than anyone

else, when they first knew each other Armour was only one of several women in whom Burns was sexually interested.

His erotic attention was restlessly mobile, not deliberately malign. As early as April 1784 he had a self-image as 'all along, a miserable dupe to Love', someone 'led into a thousand weaknesses & follies by it'. He believed this strengthened him as a poet: as 'Shenstone observes finely . . . love-verses writ without any real passion are the most nauseous of all conceits'. Burns 'put the more confidence in my critical skill in distinguishing foppery & conceit, from real passion & nature', he wrote in his commonplace book. A few months afterwards he copied out an early song, recalling another relationship with a servant at Coilsfield to whom he had felt impelled to 'lay siege' out of 'a vanity of showing my parts in Courtship, particularly my abilities at a Billet doux, which I always piqu'd myself upon'.[21]

Being writer and lover were inextricably entangled for Burns. If he got used to thinking of love affairs as good for his art, then in an age when contraceptives were crude or non-existent there were unavoidable repercussions. While his family dealt with the consequences of his getting Elizabeth Paton pregnant he was in relationships with both Jean Armour and Elizabeth Miller; while he was writing about the latter's underwear he was dancing with the former. His complicated love life must have been apparent to his family and local community, not just to the women most immediately involved. In some poems, and in public penance demanded by the Kirk, his exploits became a kind of public spectacle. This was the Burns whom Alexander Tait would call 'Plotcock' – a name used by Allan Ramsay of a muddy peasant, but probably having additional phallic connotations for the Tait who went on to link Burns with 'brother' David Sillar – 'Fornicator Poet'.[22] There seems to have been substantial correspondence, now lost or destroyed but reputedly strong on 'piety', between Burns and a well-off local farmer's daughter, 'bonie . . . braw' Jean Ronald whose 'sense and guid taste' he praised.[23] His relationships with women were multiple and complex, but seldom restricted to piety.

In 1785 he was not the only family member with a difficult love life. Around the time Robert was feeling some initial 'heat of . . . resentment' over splitting up with Elizabeth Miller, the generally more responsible Gilbert had a letter from the 'Lavinia' he had been courting since before his father's death. Meeting her 'accidentally at the neighbouring village', he had walked her home and asked her

to marry him. But 'bred up and instructed in all the most rigid doctrines of the Kirk', she took issue in early 1785 with something Gilbert had said 'rather contrary to some of these doctrines'. Their relationship went on, uneasily. Then, at the start of August she wrote him a letter full of 'polemical arguments', making it clear 'such a difference of opinion in such an important thing as religion behoved to be an invincible barr against any intimate friendship or connection'.²⁴ Gilbert grew deeply depressed.

None of this could have lessened Robert's resentment against his strict Kirk's interference in sexual relationships. Like Gilbert he knew what it was to sense depression, as well as trouble in love. Where Gilbert turned to writing private autobiographical prose as a way of giving his life shape and order, Burns not infrequently used autobiographical materials to power his poetry. As he had done for years, he used literature to shape his life.

Often this was deliberate and celebratory. January 1785's 'Epistle to Davie, a Brother Poet' reveals resentment against the inequality of 'how things are shar'd' between wealthy and poor. Portraying a wintry season of 'driving snaw' and 'frosty winds', Burns expresses sourness at 'How *best o' chiels* [the best lads] are whiles in want,/ While *Coofs* [Fools] on countless thousands rant'; his poem looks directly at the homeless who have to sleep rough. It is a clear early example of his sympathy with those beggars, homeless people, the supposed dregs of society, some of whom he would have seen hanging around central Mauchline near Poosie Nancie's.

Aspects of this 'Epistle' relate to that sympathy with 'Blackguards' expressed in March 1784.²⁵ Yet, turning away from resentment, the poem seeks even among people who sleep rough a sense of what Burns calls '*content*' – perhaps just a realisation 'Nae *farther* we can *fa*''. He goes on to celebrate apparent aimlessness, a free wandering through a landscape where he and Davie will make verse, will 'rhyme,/ In hamely, *westlin* [West of Scotland] jingle', song-makers together. Discounting 'titles', 'rank', 'wealth' and book-learning as sources of true content, Burns contends instead 'The *heart* ay's the part ay,/ That makes us right or wrang', and, bonding love and poetry, links 'the *Pleasures o' the Heart*' to the pleasures of verse.²⁶

Addressed to David Sillar, his 'brother' not just as 'Poet' but also as 'Lover, Ploughman and Fiddler', the epistle testifies to the warmth of Burns's continuing friendship in 1784–5 with this sharer of all

his most powerful enthusiasms. It also celebrates being in love, specifically Sillar's relationship with Margaret Orr and Burns's with 'darling JEAN' – imaged as his most important source of poetic energy: 'O, how that *name* inspires my style!'[27]

Yet at least as much as celebrating Jean the poem sings Burns's confident wish to be a poet in a distinctly Scottish idiom. His 'Epistle' is patterned on 'The Cherry and the Slae', a Renaissance Scottish poem by Alexander Montgomerie reprinted by several patriotic Scottish literary anthologists, including Allan Ramsay, who had modelled on it his ode 'The Poet's Wish'. Revealingly, Burns quotes a line of Ramsay's poem. As Christopher MacLachlan insightfully pointed out in 2006, Ramsay's ode describes 'a poet's approach to the oracle of the god Apollo to ask, not for riches, but for health and good spirits enough to live a long but simple life'.[28] Ramsay's poem is about the poetic vocation. So is Burns's. For Burns that calling seems more bound up with love; where Ramsay's 'Poet's Wish' is a little pious, Burns wishes to see his poetry, thanks to Jean's inspiration, run 'as fine,/ As *Phoebus* and the famous *Nine*' Classical Muses.[29] Displaying energetic, self-mocking comedy as well as clear ambition, his poem is a declaration of his love for Jean Armour, his friendship with David Sillar, and his serious intention to devote himself to poetry. That poetry will be alert to social inequality, but by no means limited to one theme.

This epistle's Scots idiom and quotation from Ramsay make clear Burns wants his 'hamely, *westlin*' but also ambitious work to be rooted in a particular tradition. On occasion he would deliberately write 'in imitation' of older Scots poetry.[30] As art his poem selects imaginatively from his complicated private life. It turns particular details into material suitable for a formal yet familiar epistle. According to Gilbert, this poem marked 'the first idea of Robert's becoming an author'.[31] It is something of a manifesto. Beginning with 'Davie', Burns was realising he might correspond with other local writers, articulating his own sense of the sort of poet he already was, and just who he wished to become.

'A true, genuine, Scotish Bard' was how he described another Ayrshire poet some of whose work he came to admire in early 1785.[32] When the farmhouse at Mossgiel was filled with 'twelve or fifteen young people' spinning and singing at a party on the evening of Shrove Tuesday, Burns was enjoying the gossip when a song

caught his ear; he thought it heartfelt, and later learned that it was.³³ Maybe he liked it all the more because its praise of married love emblematised something more straightforward than his own tangled affairs:

> When I upon thy bosom lean,
> Enraptur'd, I do call thee mine;
> I glory in those *sacred ties*,
> That made us *one*, who once were *twain*.³⁴

Though written for the Scots tune, '*Johnny's Grey Breeks*', John Lapraik's song was entirely in decorous English and based on magazine verses.³⁵ Burns's addressing its author as 'An Old Scotch Bard' (Lapraik was nearly sixty) suggests he had found out more about Lapraik's work, which often used Standard Habbie and Scots locutions.

The verse letter Burns sent Lapraik on 1 April 1785 praised the 'correct' English of the older man's song by likening it to the work of English-language writers Burns admired, like Pope, Steele, or Aberdeen's Professor James Beattie. Still, Burns soon glides away from this to discussing his own background in '*crambo-jingle*'. He sets treasured vernacular language (of which Lapraik is also a local representative) against the supposed correctness of university students whose polish seems emasculation. Burns, who had never seen the inside of a university classroom, wishes to ally himself with a different, 'natural' tradition. This lets him turn an apparent lack of high culture into a strategic advantage:

> A set o' dull, conceited Hashes,
> Confuse their brains in *Colledge-classes!*
> They *gang in* Stirks, and *come out* Asses,   *go in young bullocks*
>   Plain truth to speak;
> An' syne they think to climb Parnassus   *then*
>   By dint o' Greek!
>
> Gie me ae spark o' Nature's fire,   *one*
> That's a' the learning I desire;
> Then tho' I drudge thro' dub an' mire   *pond*
>   At pleugh or cart,   *plough*
> My Muse, tho' hamely in attire,
>   May touch the heart.

O for a spunk o' ALLAN's glee,   *spark of Allan Ramsay's*
Or FERGUSON's, the bauld an' slee,   *bold and sly*
Or bright L******K's, my friend to be,
   If I can hit it!
That would be *lear* eneugh for me,   *learning*
   If I could get it.[36]

Having just dropped the names of Pope, Steele and Beattie, Burns cannot expect attentive readers to accept unthinkingly his persona of uneducated, muddy ploughman: demonstrating to Lapraik and others he knows his Eng Lit, he is setting up what sounds like a counter-canon of Scots writing. Eager to draw sustenance from that, he links it to 'Nature's fire'.

As often, Burns is being slyly sophisticated. Even in asking for 'Nature's fire' he recalls a request to Apollo in Laurence Sterne's novel *Tristram Shandy*: 'give me ... a single spark of thy own fire'.[37] Burns allies himself with Rousseauesque eighteenth-century assumptions about natural genius, while mapping himself on to a wittily literary lineage. This strategy of the epistle to Lapraik, at once rhetorically clever and warmly endearing, was one Burns would deploy often: in love, in his first book, and in subsequent dealings with Edinburgh's literati. It let him be muddy-booted *and* sophisticated. In literature, love and, sometimes, in politics he could have his cake and eat it.

If this makes the Lapraik epistle sound cynical, Burns's tone emphasises fun and friendship. Bold, sly, having learned from that university-trained vernacular live wire Robert Fergusson, his is a poem of 'friends' and 'brothers' likely to appeal to the farmer Lapraik. Like Burns's other verse of the time, it sees contentment as a virtue, but still makes clear in tone and subject-matter that social inequalities are unjust. Upholding the right of ordinary people to possess learning outside of educational institutions, its implied democratic politics is all the more effective for being couched in warm, unthreatening language. Its humour achieves a political purpose hard to gainsay, but does so in a letter to a particular correspondent, not some generalised manifesto. Companionable tone, rather than revolutionary politics, achieves a result whose implications, recognised alike by the young William Wordsworth and subsequent generations, are powerfully revolutionary.

Very soon Lapraik replied. Burns sent him a further verse epistle

on 21 April. A victim of the Ayr Bank collapse, Lapraik had had to sell his farm. In 1785 financial troubles led to his imprisonment in Ayr for debt. Burns responded to Lapraik as a poet whose '*moorlan harp*' resounded even 'Tho' Fortune use you hard an' sharp'. This appealed to Burns's own sense of having endured misfortune – something that also undergirds his January epistle to Davie. Robert presents himself as having been 'persecuted', yet, despite all local gossip, having come through: '*I, Rob, am here.*' Linking himself with Lapraik gives him heightened confidence.

Lapraik like Sillar was a lesser poet, but an ally in a world that paid too much heed to money and rank, too little to poetry. Burns began imagining what it might mean to communicate his own sentiments 'Thro' Scotland wide', hymning 'The social, friendly, honest man', not '*city-gent*' or 'feudal *Thane*'. He also envisaged an ideal when he and fellow followers of the nine Muses might matter more than mere moneymakers.

> The followers o' the ragged Nine,
> Poor, thoughtless devils! yet may shine
>   In glorious light,
> While sordid sons o' Mammon's line
>   Are dark as night![38]

This was a utopia to excite poets. Lapraik would bring out his own work with Burns's Kilmarnock publisher three years later, and would correspond with Burns's friend John Richmond about subscribers for 'the book'.[39] After Burns's death Wordsworth was heard to recite most of this utopian poem.[40]

The Mossgiel farmer was clearly winning a reputation among educated local contemporaries. In spring 1785 the schoolmaster at nearby Ochiltree village, William Simson, who had studied Divinity at Glasgow University and was just a year younger than Burns, wrote him a letter praising his verse. Simson appears to have linked Burns to earlier Scots poets like Ramsay, Hamilton of Gilbertfield, and Fergusson. Burns replied eagerly in Standard Habbie, cursing the 'whunstane [whinstone] hearts' of those Edinburgh gentry he saw as having let Fergusson starve. He presents himself to Simson as one of several Ayrshire '*Bardies*' praising the local countryside, proud of its woods, wildlife, and associations with Wallace. Simson, like Davie, is a 'rhyme-composing brither', working in broad vernacular.

'We, *Bardies*,' writes Burns, clearly wanting to feel part of a group with a common purpose and common enemies among the tittle-tattling rigidly righteous.[41] Where previously he had been excited by Pope's letters and circle of wits, now, writing poetical epistles of his own, he was convening a group of Ayrshire poet-wits while developing his distinctive poetic signature.

He wrote in the midst of personal tumult. In the month of the epistle to Simson, Elizabeth Paton gave birth. Robert penned a poem called in one manuscript 'A Welcome to a bastart wean' and elsewhere 'A Poet's Welcome to his love-begotten Daughter; the first instance that entitled him to the venerable appellation of Father'. Though he never printed it, his welcome to a 'bonie, sweet, wee Dochter' arrived 'a wee unsought for' is affectionate. Its young father kisses and fondles his child, but resents local gossip and the attitude of 'the Priests'. Having enjoyed the lovemaking which led to the birth, he hopes to be 'a loving Father'.[42]

By the standards of the day, Burns did well by his child, going on to make legal provision for her.[43] Her mother initialled a document witnessed by James Smith and Gavin Hamilton, acknowledging that Burns had made a 'liberale allowance' and that after the girl reached the age of ten her father would be free from paying for 'Board wages, cloathing and Education'.[44] Brought up by his family, the child got at least some education and financial inheritance. Probably around the time of her birth Burns and Elizabeth Paton had to do public penance in Tarbolton kirk for fornication; the kirk records for that period do not seem to have survived. The poet's warmth towards his child, accompanied by a certain 'defensive swagger' as James Kinsley puts it, gets the better of his resentment at being styled in public 'Fornicator'.[45] In his poem 'The Fornicator' he tries to make that a badge of pride.

In reading and corresponding with local Scots poets, Burns was on the lookout for models from which he could learn. Sometimes he practised deliberate imitation. In the work of east-coast Scottish schoolmaster-poet Alexander Ross he was attracted to the vernacular muse figure 'Scota' who told the poet to 'Speak my ain leed [language]'.[46] Ross had died in 1784. A village poet, he used 'broad Scotch dialect' for songs and longer poems like *Helenore, or the Fortunate Shepherdess*. Sometimes linked to the work of Allan Ramsay, *Helenore* featured 'Scota'. Burns called *Helenore* 'a

beautiful Scots poem', a 'precious treasure', and owned a copy. The fact that Burns had lived at Lochlea in Ayrshire while Ross, he knew, had been 'late Schoolmaster at Lochlee' in Angus must have heightened a sense of brotherhood.[47] Another old Scots bard, Ross too might be an ally in Burns's development.

Drawing on Ramsay, Fergusson, Ross and others, Burns was positioning himself as bard of his locality. In August 1785 he wrote self-consciously in his commonplace book,

> However I am pleased with the works of our Scotch Poets, particularly the excellent Ramsay, and the still more excellent Ferguson, yet I am hurt to see other places of Scotland, their towns, rivers, woods, haughs, &c. immortalized in such celebrated performances, whilst my dear native country, the ancient Bailieries of Carrick, Kyle, & Cunningham, famous both in ancient & modern times for a gallant, and warlike race of inhabitants; a country where civil, & particularly religious Liberty have ever found their first support, & their last asylum; a country, the birth place of many famous Philosophers, Soldiers, & Statesmen, and the scene of many important events recorded in Scottish History, particularly a great many of the actions of the GLORIOUS WALLACE, the SAVIOUR of his Country; Yet, we have never had one Scotch Poet of any eminence, to make the fertile banks of Irvine, the romantic woodlands & sequestered scenes on Aire, and the heathy, mountainous source, & winding sweep of Doon emulate Tay, Forth, Ettrick, Tweed, &c. this is a complaint I would gladly remedy, but Alas! I am far unequal to the task, both in native genius & education. – Obscure I am, & obscure I must be, though no young Poet, nor young Soldier's heart ever beat more fondly for fame than mine –[48]

Ambitiously identifying a gap in the poetic market while idealistically asserting his hopes to be classed with 'our Scotch Poets', Burns here rather programatically outlines 'The Vision', a 'digressive Poem' he was working on around this time.[49] In it a young poet is conscious of having apparently 'done nae-thing' in life other than making rhymes for fools to sing. This poet is visited by a tartan-clad 'SCOTTISH MUSE', her elegant legs matched only by those of 'my bonie JEAN'. On the muse's cloak the poet sees detailed depictions of Ayrshire rivers and landscapes. In the second part of 'The Vision' this cloaked figure, Coila, muse of the district, confers on the poet the title and status of Bard:

'All hail! *my own* inspired Bard!
'In me thy native Muse regard!
'Nor longer mourn thy fate is hard,
    'Thus poorly low!
'I come to give thee such *reward,*
    'As *we* bestow.'

Coila and her fellow muses have come to 'teach the *Bard*, a darling
care,/ The tuneful Art'.⁵⁰ In 'The Vision' Burns confirms his bardic
status and enunciates what it might mean. Written in Standard
Habbie, this poem uses Scots vernacular for its poet's own speech,
has a high-toned muse who speaks in English, and is divided into
two Gaelic-sounding 'Duans'. A 'Duan' was a term 'of Ossian's for
the different divisions of a digressive Poem', Burns explains in one
of several footnotes to his 1786 published version. So his poem mixes
Scots form and language, English diction, and a gesture towards
Gaelic poetry.

In so doing 'The Vision' signals bardic ambition to speak not just
for Ayrshire but for Scotland. It mentions 'sweet harmonious
BEATTIE' and *The Minstrel*, Beattie's poem about the poetic vocation
which, drawing on Beattie's own career, sees the poet move even-
tually from rural life into academia. Looking also towards Pope and
Shenstone, 'The Vision' is often elevated in its literary register where
Burns's Standard Habbie verse epistles are more familiar in address.
Burns worked then reworked this piece, adding and deleting stanzas.
Its composition may have had a trajectory like that described by
Gilbert, discussing the first 'Epistle to Davie',

> Robert often composed without any regular plan. When anything
> made a strong impression on his mind, so as to rouse it to any poetic
> exertion, he would give way to the impulse, and embody the thought
> in rhyme. If he hit on two or three stanzas to please him, he would
> then think of proper introductory, connecting, and concluding stanzas;
> hence the middle of a poem was often first produced.⁵¹

Burns's August 1785 entry in his commonplace book corresponds
with the middle of 'The Vision'. Linking himself to Beattie's Minstrel;
bonding his poem to the work of Ossian; having his muse hail him
as 'Bard': all these gestures signal his ambition to be known as a
bard or minstrel singing for his people. Yet most of the folk mentioned
in the poem are famous. Inserted later, references to living eminences

such as 'Professor Stewart' and 'the Lord Justice Clerk' make it hard not to think this *'rustic Bard'* is looking for a possible patron.[52] Burns included explicit mention of 'a Patroness's aid'.[53] New father, struggling farmer, ambitious bard, Burns is confirming his identity as a poet. He is also looking for supporters of more than one kind.

He manifestly resented aspects of a world where it seemed, in words his mother sang, 'man is made to moan'.[54] Recasting this as 'Man was Made to Mourn', Burns saw how 'hundreds labour to support/ A haughty lordling's pride'.[55] Still, he did not simply reproach everyone in society's higher echelons. The Lord Justice Clerk was about to become President of that Court of Session which had found in favour of Burns's father; Professor Dugald Stewart was sympathetic to some in radical politics, and would soon encourage Burns, while Gavin Hamilton would name a son Dugald Stewart Hamilton. The poet was seeking ideological allies who might further his quest for bardic 'fame'.

He sought that fame, but worried he would not find it. He feared being ground down by circumstances on the farm. Sometimes brooding on gloomy topics, he took from the eighteenth-century poet Young's sepulchral *Night Thoughts* with its talk of 'Man's ... endless inhumanities on Man' the basis for his own pithier wording about 'Man's inhumanity to Man' in his 'Dirge', 'Man was Made to Mourn'.[56]

Yet sometimes what stung Burns most was man's inhumanity to animals. Still in his mind was the killing of his dog Luath the night before his father died. To wantonly kill a creature epitomised society at its worst. Though he did not finish it until the end of the year, he was at work on a substantial poem with the mischievous title 'The Twa Dogs. A Tale'. For all its humour, this Ayrshire dialogue ponders social inequalities. Luath, 'a *ploughman's collie*', belongs to 'A rhyming, ranting, raving billie' who has named him after 'Cuchullin's dog in Ossian's Fingal'. Creating a fictional situation in which aspects of his own personality are involved, Burns explores society's workings. Luath talks to 'his Honor's' dog, Caesar, the manuscript (mis-)spellings of whose name – 'Cesar' and 'Ceasar' – associate him with those who seize. Yet neither dog is a mere caricature. It is *'gentleman* an' *scholar'* Caesar who contrasts 'racked rents' of oppressed 'Poor *tenant-bodies*' with the wasteful, lazy life of 'Our *Laird*'. Outlining as the lot of the poor some experiences Burns's father knew – building walls, suffering 'loss o' health' –

Luath emphasises how 'Love . . . Wit . . . an' social Mirth' let poor folk forget their troubles. In the end Caesar shows how the rich with their ennui and boredom can behave 'like ony *unhang'd black-guard*'.[57] In some ways socially conservative, this poem does not preach revolution; the poor are able to put up with their lot. But the poem's lingering impact removes any justification for manifest inequality.

Burns wanted a sense of financial and social independence. His father had sought that for him, but the farm in 1785 seemed unlikely to provide it. Desire for independence is articulated early in his work,

> If I'm design'd yon lordling's slave,
>   By Nature's law design'd,
> Why was an independent wish
>   E'er planted in my mind?[58]

These lines imply that what social authorities present as natural is simply cultural, open to change. In the mid-1780s and after, Burns's poems repeatedly challenge cultural authority by finding vital energy in what the bosses of society suppress.[59] Though sometimes dark, these poems are frequently funny. Tellingly accurate in their language, democratic in implications, but composed in an undemocratic society, they remain politically 'bardie'.

One of the most uproarious is 'The Holy Fair', said in one manuscript to have been 'composed in Autumn 1785', but clearly revised before publication the following year.[60] Holy fairs were a long-established feature of local life: huge communion services where groups of kirk ministers, often working outdoors, would take communion with great gatherings of believers. In his book *Holy Fairs* Eric Schmidt points out that 'at one turbulent communion at Mauchline in 1648 eight ministers and two thousand people were said to be on hand'.[61] In Mauchline as elsewhere in Burns's Scotland it was customary to hold a service of communion – 'a sacramental occasion' – just once a year. In 1785 it fell on the second Sunday in August. This highlight of the church year attracted many people; other events like preliminary preaching meetings accrued round it.

By the 1780s so many folk – over a thousand – came to take communion in Mauchline each year that they thronged the streets of the village. Some slept rough nearby; alehouses opposite the kirk

filled up; preaching, praying, fondling, drinking and wrangling went on cheek-by-jowl. In terms of layout, Mauchline might have been built around such an event. The heart of the gathering was a community-wide religious rite, the dispensing of the bread and wine representing the body and blood of Christ in an act of sacred communion; yet around this celebration developed a crowded semi-riotous public holiday producing, as one mid-eighteenth-century commentator wrote, 'an odd mixture of religion, sleep, drinking, courtship, and a confusion of sexes, ages, and characters'.[62] Burns loved it. In some ways it embodied the competing energies – sexual, religious, solemn and rebellious – which formed his own psychology and on which he fed. Burns wrote 'The Holy Fair', the holy fair wrote Burns. Gilbert recalled the 'farcical' nature of the scenes in Mauchline around communion time as 'a favourite field of his [Robert's] observation, and most of the incidents he mentioned had actually passed before his eyes'.[63]

A medieval, carnivalesque tradition of Scottish poems of folk festivity had been revived by Ramsay and Fergusson. Burns patterns 'The Holy Fair' on works like Fergusson's 'Hallow Fair' and 'Leith Races', presenting a swirl of well-dressed farmers, barefoot country lasses, whores, and weaver lads from Kilmarnock out 'Blackguarding . . . For *fun*'. Recognisable to his Ayrshire audience, his caricatures and vignettes remain vibrant. Preaching in Scots inside a tent, a local Old Light minister is 'stampan, an' . . . jumpan', getting 'wild in wrath'. The crowd, enjoying fiery oratory, drift away from his New Light rival's cooler 'English style' discourses 'Of *moral pow'rs* an' *reason*', heading instead for the pub.[64] Where older poets had detailed physical brawls, Burns features a contest among rival preachers. Locally the Kirk was full of rows. Tarbolton's minister, Wodrow, was at loggerheads with Mauchline's Reverend Auld, himself in dispute with Gavin Hamilton. Among competing preachers in 'The Holy Fair', the one that impresses the crowd most is Kilmarnock's John Russel. In the mid-1780s the historical Russel was attacking Ayrshire moderates like Burns's admired William McGill, warning about 'the inconceivably dreadful distress' of being called to encounter 'divine wrath'.[65] In Burns's poem Russel's words about Hell's 'raging flame, an' scorching heat' cut to the quick all who are still awake.

Decorously avoiding mention of communion sacraments, Burns noticeably enthuses about everyday alcoholic 'Drink! it gies us mair/

Than either School or Colledge'. 'The Holy Fair' ends with a celebration mixing religion and licence – *'faith* an' *hope,* an' *love* an' *drink'*. It mentions *'love divine'* in its last, carnivalesque stanza, but by far the most striking rhyme comes near the end when *'brandy'* rhymes with that *'Houghmagandie'* (fornication) Burns sees as one of the Fair's lasting consequences.[66] Old Light hellfire preaching may be exciting; thankfully sexual energy is stronger.

August 1785 was the first Mauchline communion since Burns's public humiliation as 'fornicator'. Among other things 'The Holy Fair', like 'Holy Willie's Prayer', points out that 'holy' customs of the Kirk are far more bound up with *'Houghmagandie'* than might seem appropriate. To make the hypocrisy absolutely clear, Burns added to 'The Holy Fair' an epigraph which he presents as taken from a play called *Hypocrisy a-la-Mode*. Still, celebrating sex and drink, his poems usually attack religious double-dealing, not religion itself. The poet was keen to find supporters within those sections of the Kirk to which he felt allegiance.

With that in mind, during the month of Mauchline's Holy Fair he wrote a Standard Habbie epistle 'to John Goldie in Kilmarnock, Author of, The Gospel recovered'. A town of about five thousand people a few miles north-west of Mossgiel, Kilmarnock was not only the base of Russel the hellfire Old Light preacher. That August it was also shaken by arguments over hard-line evangelical James Mackinlay. Moderates in Kilmarnock's Laigh Kirk did not wish Mackinlay ordained as their minister. Burns would return to this row a few months later. Meantime he saw Goldie as an intellectual ally in resisting 'Sour Bigotry'.[67] He linked Goldie as New Light liberal with Dr Taylor of Norwich whose common-sense theology Burns had read and admired. An Ayrshire miller's son, Goldie was a polymath. Arguing against always taking scripture literally, he defended figurative readings. Suspicious of Holy-Willie-style interpretations of predestination and Original Sin, in 1784 he had published his six-volume *The Gospel Recovered . . . and Restored to its Original Purity*. Next, in 1785 appeared a second edition of *Essays on various Important Subjects Moral and Divine*. Goldie had worked among other things as a Kilmarnock wine merchant. Burns's epistle praises enjoyment of a good drink as well as liberal theology. Again, Burns was addressing and recruiting a sympathetic, substantial supporter and potential patron. The following year Goldie acted as a guarantor in the publication of Burns's poems.

Ayrshireman John McMath, the young assistant minister at Tarbolton, was someone else Burns sought as an ally. The poet wrote McMath a Standard Habbie epistle on 17 September, 'Inclosing a copy of *Holy Willie's Prayer*, which he had requested'. Burns's epistle defends Gavin Hamilton against the accusations of the 'priest/ Wha sae abus't him'. 'An honest man may like a glass,/ An honest man may like a lass', maintains the poet, wishing for Pope's satirical power to give 'worthless skellums' what they deserved. Burns also praises the 'lib'ral band' of Christian 'public teachers' in Ayr with whom McMath was associated, and who sided with Hamilton.[68] In July Lapraik had written to Burns, censuring him for 'ill nature' towards Old Light ministers. Burns, during that windy September's harvest time, urged Lapraik to turn instead to 'muse-inspirin' aqua-vitae' and make the most of their friendship.[69]

Like Lapraik, Burns studied printed songs as well as making his own. In September 1785 he was reflecting on Robert Bremner's first book of *Thirty Scots Songs adapted for a Voice and Harpsichord*. This collection contained genteel versions of songs he had known from infancy, such as 'The Blathrie o'it', but, for all it attributed the lyrics to 'Allen Ramsey', its English words were awkwardly formal. Burns found some of them 'flat & spiritless' and 'trite' in comparison with the lively 'irregularity' of 'the old Scotch Songs'. He and his friend Sillar composed words for several of the tunes in Bremner, Burns admiring particularly the 'degree of wild irregularity in many of the compositions & Fragments which are daily sung to them by my compeers, the common people – a certain happy arrangement of old Scotch syllables'. For Burns it was not the printed songbook but the songs he had heard around him which carried true authority. Even in writing about them, quoting from Robert Blair's 1743 English-language poem *The Grave* while alluding to Smithian 'sympathy' and perhaps to Gaelic Ossianic 'Fragments' of ancient poetry, he shows how easily he was able to mix a knowledge of formal published verse with a love of the Scots songs he associated with the figure of the bard:

There is a noble Sublimity, a heart-melting tenderness in some of these ancient fragments, which show them to be the work of a masterly hand; and it has often given me many a heart ake to reflect that such glorious old Bards – Bards, who, very probably, owed all their talents to native genius, yet have described the exploits of Heroes, the pangs

of Disappointment, and the meltings of Love with such fine strokes of Nature, and, O mortifying to a Bard's vanity, their very names are 'buried 'mongst the wreck of things which were.' –

O ye illustrious Names unknown! who could feel so strongly and describe so well! the last, the meanest of the Muses train – one who, though far inferiour to your flights, yet eyes your path, and with trembling wing would sometimes soar after you – a poor, rustic Bard unknown, pays this sympathetic pang to your memory![70]

This is one articulation of Burns's bardic manifesto. He goes on to bond 'POESY AND LOVE!', portraying himself as something of a man of feeling, but also makes it absolutely clear his ambition is a bardic one and that, with all his book-learning, he hopes to follow the example of the poets from his Scots community.[71] That Scots community was one that included the mischievous Mauchline living as well as the anonymous bardic dead.

Burns liked being part of Gavin Hamilton's circle. Hamilton's clerk, John Richmond, was probably still a teenager when he became the poet's good friend. Richmond introduced Burns to James Smith, soon another close companion. Before he left for work in Edinburgh in November 1785, Richmond, like Burns, had to do public penance for what the Church saw as sexual sin; eventually, in 1791, Richmond married his local lover, Jenny Surgeoner, mother of his child. Richmond was also a friend of Jean Armour. It was a lively, close-knit, sometimes uproarious community.

James Smith was a Mauchline draper aged about twenty, brought up by his strict, pious stepfather. Smith shared with Burns and Richmond a liking for pretty girls, pub society, slyness and wild fun. Burns told Smith he must have worn out twenty pairs of shoes visiting him in Mauchline. Relishing the company of these younger lads and engaged in sexual relationships with several lasses of his own class, Burns was not averse to eyeing up better-connected local young women. In October he sent a flattering English poem about 'the sweet connubial flame' to Gavin Hamilton's nineteen-year-old sister-in-law. He laid it on thick in an accompanying note, telling this teenager in his grandest letter-writing mode that her beauty approached 'Perfection'. Drafting his note on the back of a sheet (not sent to the young lady) on which he had written 'Brose and Butter', a bawdy poem about the sensations of lovemaking, Burns assured her,

Poets, Madam, of all Mankind, feel most forcibly the powers of BEAUTY; as, if they are really Poets of Nature's making, their feelings must be finer, and their taste more delicate than most of the world. – In The Chearflul [*sic*] bloom of Spring, or the pensive mildness of Autumn; the Grandeur of Summer, or the hoary majesty of Winter; the Poet feels a charm unknown to the rest of his Species: even the sight of a fine flower, or the company of a fine Woman, (by far the finest part of God's works below) has sensations for the Poetic heart that the HERD of Man are strangers to. –[72]

Margaret Kennedy sent him a card of thanks.

Signing himself 'RAB THE RANTER', Burns was frolicking the previous month not just as vernacular poet but also as the musician of famous seventeenth-century Scots verses about another Margaret, 'Maggie Lauder'. This work too had bawdy overtones:

> For I'm a piper to my trade;
>   My name is Rob the Ranter:
> The lasses loup as they were daft,   *leap*
>   When I blaw up my chanter.[73]   *pipe*

Burns's fun-loving, freewheeling side but also his taste for blackguards took him, apparently in autumn 1785, to Agnes Gibson's Mauchline drinking den frequented, as he put it, 'by the lowest orders of Travellers and Pilgrims'.[74] Richmond's nephew recorded that his uncle accompanied Burns to that tavern. Burns may have written his poem some time after, but its Mauchline references place it in this period. Serving her regulars 'a peculiar sort of Whiskie', Agnes Gibson (nicknamed 'Poosie Nansie') had a reputation for drunkenness.[75] The lodging-house of which her tavern formed part was at the corner of Mauchline's Loudoun Street and Cowgate, just opposite the kirkyard. Across the road was the Whitefoord Arms, backing on to Jean Armour's house. At Poosie (in English, 'Pussy') Nancie's Burns set *Love and Liberty – A Cantata*, sometimes called 'The Jolly Beggars'.

Unlike his verse epistles, this celebration of lowlife free-love, drink, popular poetry and rebellion is a piece for several voices, none ostensibly Burns's own. He patterned it to some extent on poems anthologised by Ramsay, 'The Happy Beggars' and 'Merry Beggars'. Featuring a range of characters, these include, as James Kinsley points out, celebrations of 'drink, promiscuity, and liberty'.[76] In *The*

Beggar's Opera (1728) English poet John Gay had helped popularise dramatic depictions of down-and-outs. Burns crowds together a disabled soldier, his lover (who boasts marriage to 'The Regiment AT LARGE'), a Highlander's widow, a fiddler, a tinker, a wandering 'BARD of no regard' and others. This gathering generates a wild yet focused energy as Burns links individuals' songs with a narrative 'Recitativo', ending with a challenging 'Chorus –'

> Life is all a VARIORUM,
>   We regard not how it goes;
> Let them cant about DECORUM,
>   Who have character to lose.
>   A fig for those by law protected!
>   LIBERTY's a glorious feast!
>   Courts for Cowards were erected,
>   Churches built to please the PRIEST.[77]

These are hard-hitting lines: 'as grimly defiant a note as may be found in the literature of Revolutionary Europe,' contended Burns's 1932 biographer F. B. Snyder.[78] Burns wants to sound an extreme, radical note; but to hear it simply as his credo ignores the fact that it is sung by a chorus of invented characters. In poems of late 1785 and after, he gave rein to several aspects of his personality, pushing things to the limit. Rather than producing one psychologically well balanced persona, he explored many – as poets and dramatists have always done.

There definitely *is* a radical ideology detectable in early works like his song of the American Revolution, 'When *Guilford* good'. This poetic ideology becomes more pronounced around the time of the French Revolution. However, Burns is an artist, not a sloganeer, so we also find in his work a series of explorations of points of view and moods. Keats, lover of 'Bards of Passion and of Mirth' and one of Burns's greatest English admirers, argued that poets were like chameleons.[79] Burns was not quite a chameleon, but knew the urge to explore a variety of attitudes and possibilities. He backed the respectable Reverend McGill, but also sought energy and value in anarchic 'blackguard' voices. If at times this risked instabilities in his psyche and values, it unleashed energetic, sometimes angry imaginative adventuring, giving voice to *Love and Liberty*.

There was no shortage of instability in Burns's life while he wrote

intensively in late 1785. His friend Richmond was leaving for Edinburgh. In love with Jean Armour, Burns was sleeping with her – which might result in further children; at home trouble with crops made farming chancy. Worst of all, it had been evident since at least late summer that his brother John was dying. Less than two years earlier Burns had seen his father expire in the midst of a bitter law case when the family faced losing their home. Now he watched as his brother's life ended at sixteen. John was buried on the first of November. Shortly afterwards Robert wrote almost his only poem to have as part of its main title a precise month and year: 'To a Mouse, On turning her up in her Nest, with the Plough, November, 1785'.

Shenstone had written of a 'timourous hare', but Burns's vernacular mouse is much more charged with feeling.[80] On to this 'Wee, sleeket, cowran, tim'rous *beastie*' he projected some of his own anxieties, including the fear of potential homelessness his family had felt at Lochlea, his sense of mortality and of plans that might not work out – complete uncertainty about the future. Nigel Leask points out that the poem may also reflect something of the worries of old-style cotters (tenants or sub-tenants on a farm) made redundant by improving tenant-farmers like the poet himself.[81] Technically Burns's mouse may be in the wrong – a thief – but it is so obviously vulnerable in its struggles to live that it wins immediate sympathy. The words 'Thee' or 'thou' or 'thy' are used so often (fourteen times in forty-eight lines) that they compel intimate solidarity with the tiny creature. Perhaps with a glance at Shenstone's 'deep-laid schemes', but moving with warmly observant humour from power and unintended destructiveness at the start to existential anxiety at the end, the poem's speaker is so obviously conscious 'The best laid schemes o' *Mice* an' *Men,*/ Gang aft agley,' that his position is immediately universal.[82]

'To a Mouse' may involve self-dramatising self-pity, but such close attention is paid to the mouse and its situation that this is purposefully shaped and shared before being released at the end. The poem stands on its own feet. Implicitly a political poem, it invites sympathy for dispossessed people, as well as for the natural world. Yet, in terms of Burns's biography, it is not hard to sense some specific psychological pressures behind it, particularly in those last lines,

> But Och! I *backward* cast my e'e,
>   On prospects drear!
> An' *forward*, tho' I canna *see*,
>   I *guess* an' *fear*![83]

Issues of looking back and looking fearfully forward undergird a number of poems written in late 1785 and early 1786. Family events brought a sense of what the Burneses had been, were now, and might become. Halloween 1785 cannot have been a happy time.[84] On 1 November John Burnes was laid to rest in his unmarked grave in Mauchline kirkyard. Yet when Burns, following the example of his Scottish poet-contemporary John Mayne, made his poem 'Halloween', he focused on old customs familiar to his mother's generation, mentioning places with special meanings for the family, and detailing examples of 'prying into Futurity' which are mostly associated with the search for marriage partners. Set not in Mauchline but notionally on the banks of the Doon where most recently they had buried William Burnes among scenes he had loved, the poem is warm and happy – 'blythe' is Burns's word – if at times obscure to modern readers. It takes its epigraph from Goldsmith's 'The Deserted Village', on which Burns had drawn for his father's epitaph, and chooses lines describing the 'simple blessings' poor people enjoy before they are 'No more'.[85] Though including Burnes family names such as 'Rob' and 'John', it gives these to ideal, generic characters. Enjoying sex with Jean Armour, Burns may have wondered who his own marriage partner might be, but 'Halloween' with its 'Fairies' rather than witches or ghosts is deliberately untroubled. It presents a lively folk idyll, a consoling escape where to guess is not to fear.[86]

Whilst some poems Burns made at Mossgiel express libertarian anger, several sound notes of idyllic nostalgia. One of the earliest manuscripts of 'The Cotter's Saturday Night' was written on paper similar to that used for 'The Holy Fair'.[87] Burns was intensely productive between November 1785 and February 1786. He wrote to Richmond in February, saying he had 'been very busy with the muses'. Asking for a copy of Fergusson's poems, he mentioned 'the Cotter's saturday night' as among recently composed works. Telling him Gavin Hamilton's friend and champion, Ayr lawyer and surveyor of taxes Robert Aiken is 'My chief Patron now', no doubt Burns sought to impress Richmond, the lawyer's clerk. 'Orator Bob' Aiken had a reputation for public speaking. When Aiken read Burns's

poems aloud, the bard realised how impressive his own poetry might sound. Aiken 'is pleased to express great approbation of my works'.[88]

The full title of 'The Cotter's Saturday Night' includes the words 'Inscribed to R. A****, Esq.' Burns presents himself to Aiken as 'No mercenary Bard', and seems keen to secure the lawyer's 'esteem and praise' as a friend, in addition to his more general support. Closely based on Fergusson's 'The Farmer's Ingle', Burns's poem more sentimentally idealises cottage life, while drawing on his own upbringing. Sometimes uneasily he tries nostalgically to fuse the older-fashioned life of a cotter with his own better-off experience in an improving tenant-farmer's family. As in 'The Twa Dogs' he shows that poor people can be happy. Young 'happy love' is watched over by careful parents. Scottish patriotism is invoked – 'From Scenes like these, old SCOTIA's grandeur springs' – and Christian family worship is seen as more genuine than 'Religion's pride' expressed through 'pompous strain' and 'sacerdotal stole'. While aspects of it might question some respectable assumptions, this generally unchallenging poem became for over a century one of Burns's most admired works – a Scottish equivalent of Goldsmith's 'Deserted Village' or Gray's 'Elegy', from which Burns takes his epigraph about *'The short and simple annals of the Poor'*.[89]

Burns once called 'The Cotter's Saturday Night' 'my favorite Poem'; Gilbert was 'electrified' when he heard his brother recite it.[90] With its cheese-making mother and 'priest-like Father' who conducts family worship, it pays tribute to the upbringing the Burnes parents provided. Robert had often remarked to Gilbert 'there was something peculiarly venerable in the phrase, "Let us worship God," used by a decent sober head of a family introducing family worship', and Gilbert, hearing in the poem lines like '"*And let us worship GOD!*" he says with solemn air', recognised its familial roots.[91] If 'The Holy Fair' and 'Holy Willie's Prayer' mock hypocritical piety, 'The Cotter's Saturday Night' seeks to exalt the genuine article. For some readers it awkwardly exhibits the life of the poor to its lawyer addressee. However, along with its pious sentimentalism the poem carries at times a radical charge as it asks,

> What is a lordling's pomp? a cumbrous load,
> Disguising oft the *wretch* of human kind,
> Studied in arts of Hell, in wickedness refin'd!

Whatever else it does, this work presents its poet in no uncertain terms as sharing a heaven-sent *'patriotic tide'* with the 'WALLACE' who struggled to 'stem tyrannic pride'. It announces Burns as a guardian and ornament to his nation, a fully fledged *'Patriot-bard'*.[92]

He was telling his readership and his patron he wished to be seen not just as a local but as a national poet. Developed over time, this self-image grew as he began to contemplate publishing a book: 'about the latter end of 1785 . . . I was meditating to publish my Poems'.[93] In verses beginning, 'HAIL, Poesie!' he ranges through great authors, presenting Ramsay with his 'sweet Caledonian lines' as the one Scot who can be set beside Theocritus as pastoral poet.[94] Burns was as ambitious as Ramsay. Quoting lines on *'Friendship'* from another favourite, Robert Blair's *The Grave*, he wrote a verse letter to his pal James Smith about this time, boasting of being in the midst of a 'fit o' rhyme' and intending 'To try my fate in guid, black *prent'*.[95] Burns winks when he deploys that phrase in his epistle 'To J. S****', for it had also been used by Robert Fergusson when writing to a fan of his work with the identical 'J. S.' initials.[96] Even as Burns protests he cannot match earlier achievements, he maps himself on to a poet he regards as exemplary.

Burns's verse letter to Smith is uncertain about the future. Still, its poet is on the side of *'fun'*, determined to side not with the *'grave'* – 'douse folk, that live by rule' – but with the merry, 'The hairum-scairum, ram-stam boys'.[97] That declaration counterbalances 'The Cotter's Saturday Night'; or at least, having pushed his talent in one direction in that pious poem, Burns now took a different aim. Titles like 'Scotch Drink' and 'The Author's Earnest Cry and Prayer, to the Right Honorable and Honorable, the Scotch Representatives in the House of Commons' show him as *'Patriot-bard'* attempting to speak for Scotland. He even comes close to equating his own pre-dicament with his nation's: *'Scotland* and *me*'s in great affliction', he jokes, pleading Scotch whisky should get relief from punitive excise duties. Signing off, 'Your humble Bardie', Burns shows typically astute knowledge of political characters and national as well as local events. As readily as he addresses a mouse he confidently addresses lords, lawyers, and MPs.[98] Here is the patriot-bard they need: 'Ye Scots wha wish auld Scotland well,/ Ye chief, to you my tale I tell' . . .[99] Speaking for Scotland, he also speaks to 'SCOTLAND, my auld, respected Mither!', asserting loudly, 'FREEDOM and WHISKY gang thegither [go together]'.[100] As 1785 closed and he

arrived at his twenty-seventh birthday on 25 January 1786 Burns was confidently assuming the voice of a national bard.

He remained, though, very uncertain about his future. As early as December 1785 he was corresponding with a contact in Jamaica about 'the planting line', that is, sugar plantations.[101] In an age of empire and slavery many Scots, not least from the West of Scotland, had West Indian contacts. Some made their fortunes on the plantations. It is estimated that around the time of the American Revolution about a third of the white population of Jamaica was Scottish; among themselves these colonists prized 'an independent spirit', yet to their slaves they were ruthlessly authoritarian – figures of what has been called 'egalitarian tyranny'.[102] When 1786 developed into the most hectic year of Burns's life to date, emigration to a Jamaican plantation became a tempting escape route from challenges at home. He missed John Richmond, now away in Edinburgh working as a lawyer's clerk; the two shared a liking for the poetry of Fergusson, who had made his mark on Edinburgh literary circles while doing legal clerking. In Ayrshire, Burns was writing energetically, striving to raise his literary profile, but he felt Richmond's 'silence and neglect'. A bit fed up with Mauchline ('they are just going on in the old way'), he was keen to tell his friend about new poems.[103] These included a Standard Habbie 'Address to the Deil' for which Burns took an epigraph from *Paradise Lost*, a work reprinted in Kilmarnock by local printer John Wilson in 1785. Burns's speaker familiarly hails Satan in Scots vernacular, detailing local superstitions at some length before bidding 'auld *Cloots*' (old Cloven-Hoof) adieu. At different stages of its composition this poem included mention of himself and Jean Armour; to some extent it trades on his developing reputation for wickedness in the eyes of the 'unco guid'. It soon became popular. Several poets, including John Lapraik, penned Standard Habbie replies spoken by the devil. Yet for all its playful wish to scandalise as it entertains, Burns's poem presents its speaker as less devilish than might be assumed:

> An' now, auld *Cloots*, I ken ye're thinkan,
> A certain *Bardie's* rantin, drinkin,
> Some luckless hour will send him linkan,   *skipping*
> To your black pit;
> But faith! he'll turn a corner jinkan,   *dodging*
> An' cheat you yet.[104]

Burns knew he would need to manoeuvre niftily. He told Richmond in February, 'I have some very important news with respect to myself'.[105] Jean was pregnant. Her father, upstanding kirkman, detested Burns: 'hated him, and would raither hae seen the Deil himsel comin to the hoose to coort his dochter than him!'[106] Gilbert recalled that, told of Burns's involvement and his daughter's situation, Mr Armour simply 'fainted away'.[107]

It was not long since Burns's last public penance for fornication. Even if his immediate family did not see him as satanic crony of 'auld *Cloots*', they were hardly delighted he was in trouble again. Burns felt that James Smith was 'all the friend I have NOW in Machlin'. One thing he liked about Smith was that he too had sly, wicked charisma – 'Ye surely hae some warlock-breef [warlock-charter]/ Owre human hearts.'[108] Maintaining that his poetry had a strongly hedonistic impulse – 'I rhyme for *fun*' – Burns often sought to embody in life and work a pleasure principle sternly repressed by Calvinist authority-figures around him. Themes in his poetry and pleasures in his life – sex, drinking, joking, radical political argument – countered the repressive hellfire preachers he mocked. Presenting himself chatting to the devil, or as 'Rob ... The rantin dog' – 'Daddie' of an illegitimate child – he outraged some in his community. Others, though, were delighted, hearing in his voice a defence of natural human instincts, the desires and aspirations so many folk felt but were endlessly discouraged from expressing.[109] Burns could be a poet of society's official aims; more often he sang gleefully its vital unofficial longings. Expressing *both* pieties and repressed desires, he became more completely the bard.

For all her efforts to look chic in a 'fine *Lunardi*' bonnet (named after a contemporary balloonist), the young '*Miss*' in one of the most famous poems Burns wrote around this time cannot escape sniggers and winks. 'To a Louse, On Seeing one on a Lady's Bonnet at Church' begins with the most unchurchy of exclamations – 'Ha!' – as the poet spots the beastie. Ending with a sermonising moral, this poem seems to question the young woman's religious sincerity. It brings together Burns's interest in hypocrisy with his love of apparently small, insignificant representatives of nature. The louse, 'Detested, shunn'd, by saunt [saint] an' sinner', and more usually associated with beggars or imperial slave-owning 'plantations', appears like a return of the repressed. It allows the wicked poet, fascinated by its 'right bauld' [bold] bravado, to

preach a counter-sermon of his own in this churchy, unchurchy poem,

> O wad some Pow'r the giftie gie us
> *To see oursels as others see us!*
> It wad frae monie a blunder free us
>   An' foolish notion:
> What airs in dress an' gait wad lea'e us,
>   And ev'n Devotion![110]

Burns here takes his text from his admired Adam Smith who had written in *The Theory of Moral Sentiments* about the deity as an 'Infinite Power' and how 'If we saw ourselves in the light in which others see us, or in which they would see us if they knew all, a reformation would generally be unavoidable. We could not otherwise endure the sight.'[111] In addressing the louse, Burns enjoyed his own intelligence as well as siding with the sort of modern philosophy liked by those moderates whom the Old Lights associated with 'Curst Common-sense, that imp o' h—ll'.[112] Daringly, his poem moves from speaking to the louse to addressing the young woman, then concludes by praying to God. Such a convincing movement from the microscopic to the all-embracing is emblematic of Burns's mature imagination; it is also typical that he is more fascinated by the tiny than the loftily grand, and that the former trumps the latter.

In another poem, written around the beginning of 1786, Burns satirised conservative Kilmarnock evangelicals. 'The Ordination' seems sympathetic towards 'the wicked town of A[yr]', with its moderate clergy.[113] A visitor to both towns, Burns was savouring his reputation for wickedness, even trying to use it as part of an attempt to cultivate moderate kirkmen. This was a hard circle to square, but he did his best. Often he rode into Kilmarnock on one of the farm's four plough-horses to pick up gossip in the pubs. An inland Ayrshire town less scenic than Ayr, Kilmarnock, one Renfrewshire traveller noted a few years later, was 'a pretty large borough . . . known by its carpet & shoe manufactures . . . The streets are narrow & crooked, the houses are low & mean.'[114] Burns liked some of the people, though, growing friendly with Robert Muir, a Kilmarnock wine merchant a year or so his senior. He sent Muir his celebration of 'Scotch Drink'.

Evidently familiar with affairs in Kilmarnock, Burns was also cultivating his Ayr encourager, Gavin Hamilton's tax-collecting lawyer friend Aiken. On 22 February 1786, as part of a joke about

domestic taxes, Burns sent Aiken his verse inventory of 'riding horses, wives, children, &c.' Though reporting 'nae wife', he hinted at one or more 'misses', expressing concern lest sexual misdemeanours caused him to fall into the clutches of 'kirk folks'. Legal terminology in this poem and its teasing tone may have been occasioned by Aiken's involvement in legal work for Burns. Certainly the two were getting on well. Burns gave a relaxed account of farm life. His light-hearted verse summary of his position reveals the Burns family employed three wickedly boisterous farmboys (*'de'ils'*).[115] One helped with ploughing, one with threshing, and the adopted orphan Wee Davock (David) Hutcheson (whose father had been a ploughman at Lochlea) assisted with the cattle. As his own father had done, each Sunday evening Burns drilled these boys in the basics of Christian faith. Liking to pose as a devil, and with wee devils on the farm, he still wanted to bring them up as Christians.

On 3 March 1786 he sent 'The Cotter's Saturday Night' to John Kennedy, one of Gavin Hamilton's relations who had asked to see it. Burns needed it back quickly. Another friend also wanted to read the poem, and he had no spare copy. Not just his riskier verses but also more respectable ones were earning him a local reputation. John Kennedy was factor to the Earl of Dumfries at Dumfries House, which still stands in its restored Adam-designed grandeur at nearby Cumnock. Built in Burns's infancy and furnished with some of Thomas Chippendale's finest commissions, the house conveyed on those associated with it the status of local notables. Writing to the Earl's factor, Burns enclosed a short verse epistle inviting him for a drink at John Dove's (Johnnie Dow's) inn, Mauchline's Whitefoord Arms. Mauchline might attract the successful and well-connected, not just the homeless and wild.

Presenting himself to Kennedy as a man who drank moderately to stimulate friendship and conversation, Burns remarked on the attractivenesss of some of the lasses in the centre of Mauchline, and on the dubious, even dangerous nature of others 'down the gate' (along the street). In early March Jean Armour's brother Adam was involved in a violent assault on a local prostitute working at Poosie Nancie's.[116] Fifteen-year-old Adam was one of several lads who subjected Agnes Wilson to a 'stanging' – a form of mob justice which made a fornicator ride through the streets astride a 'stang' or rough wooden stake. Mauchline Kirk Session minutes of 6 March recorded this 'late disturbance', mentioning Wilson's 'bad reputation'

for 'lewd and immoral practices'.[117] The violent assault seems to have injured her genitalia; young Armour and his fellow attackers had to go into hiding. Burns wrote 'Adam Armour's Prayer' in which the boy requests God's pity, but evidently sees the whole affair as a joke. Adam calls down damnation on protesters against the stanging. Burns, who has the teenager proclaim himself 'hunted as was William Wallace', shows no sympathy for the 'w[hor]e' who was victim of this 'bloody' attack.[118] Though he never printed this poem, and had just execrated 'The flinty heart that canna feel', Burns treats the boys' assault on this woman as a boisterous romp.[119]

He was in trouble himself, but now determined to build on his growing local reputation by publishing a book with the Ayrshire printer John Wilson in Kilmarnock. He had discussed the idea with Aiken, and no doubt with other supporters like Hamilton. Encouraged by Gilbert and by Richard Brown to send verse to magazines, he does not seem to have done so. A book, though, would confirm his standing as 'the bard'. John Wilson was the same age as Burns, with a clear commitment to Ayrshire. He printed local ministers' sermons, and had shown some interest in poetry, if he thought it would sell. Still, publishing *Paradise Lost* in a community where Protestant theology was constantly argued over and the Bible widely read was a safe bet. Publishing a young poet from a Mauchline farm was more risky. Burns certainly had local champions, but he had outspoken enemies too.

Raising advance subscriptions would ensure any book did not become a financial disaster. Burns and Wilson opted for this recognised publishing practice. Among admirers of Burns's work were lawyers and ministers; he had an excellent network of Masonic contacts; he was attracting attention from 'refined' local ladies with literary tastes.[120] The poet must have consulted potential sponsors, including Ayr merchant and banker, John Ballantine, sixteen years his senior. Ayr's Dean of Guild in 1786, Ballantine was active in town improvements, specifically plans for a fine new bridge; the next year he became Ayr's Provost. Now in his own way as ambitious as Ballantine, Burns discussed with this influential ally what might go into the planned collection of poems. In late March along with Hamilton, Burns attended a meeting of the Masonic lodge at Newmilns whose members included several friends or potential supporters. Among these were John Rankine and John Arnot of Dalquhatswood, to whom Burns soon wrote about subscribing to his book.

While all this was going on, Burns realised he was in a personal

mess. What he and Jean Amour had privately known about for some time – her pregnancy – had become evident to Jean's family. They had arranged she should leave the parish for Paisley, near Glasgow, to stay with relatives, but not before word had got out. Mauchline Kirk Session, less than a month after the disturbance involving Adam Armour, recorded in their minutes of 2 April that they had been informed Jean was with child and had left the parish. 'Holy Willie' Fisher, unlikely to have been among Burns's most fervent Mauchline admirers, was one of two senior elders appointed to contact Jean's parents. Her mother denied the pregnancy, telling Fisher's fellow elder James Lamie (strict stepfather of Burns's draper friend Smith) that Jean had gone to visit friends. James Armour with his fine pew in the kirk must have been furious that for the second time in a month his children's actions were attracting hostile Kirk Session scrutiny. Even worse was the prospect that his own flesh and blood would end up linked to the libertine waster Burns. Both recently involved in a wrangle with Burns's lawyer friend Hamilton, Fisher and Lamie knew Robert as a reprobate. Armour wanted nothing to do with him.

Burns had given Jean a written document which, though it has not survived, seems to have acknowledged his love for her and at least hinted at marriage. Wanting to stop that, Armour needed legal advice. He could hardly go to the local lawyer, Hamilton, whose house Burns frequented. But he did contact Aiken in Ayr and somehow 'prevailed with him to mutilate that unlucky paper' Burns had given Jean.[121] Probably from Aiken word got back to Burns that 'the names were all cut out of the paper'. Having excised the identities of the parties most intimately involved, Armour posssibly thought he had scotched any potential marital alliance between his daughter and Burns.

Legally, though, Armour had no leg to stand on. It is unclear why (as Burns understood matters) a professional lawyer apparently colluded with Jean's father. Aiken remained a supporter of the poet; perhaps he was just trying to pacify Armour. At any rate, Burns was horrified. Stunned, he wrote to his 'Benefactor', Hamilton, on 15 April. The poet had just got the printed proposal forms, inviting subscriptions for his book. Should he send one to his *quondam* [former] friend' Aiken? Burns seems to have been trying to convince Aiken he was not a 'rascal' but an 'honest man'. Written just a day after the mutilation of the paper Armour had got from Jean, Burns's

letter to Hamilton shows anger that Jean had allowed her father to get hold of the document. Burns was indignant at being treated as a villain. Though he still felt something for Jean, he seemed to think their relationship had been terminated:

> – Would you believe it? tho' I had not a hope, nor even a wish, to make her mine after her [damnable (*deleted*)] conduct; yet when he [Aiken] told me, the names were all cut out of the paper, my heart died within me, and he cut my very veins with the news. – Perdition seize her falsehood, and perjurious perfidy! but God bless her and forgive my poor, once-dear, misguided girl. – She is ill-advised. – Do not despise me, Sir: I am indeed a fool, but a *knave* is an infinitely worse character than any body, I hope, will dare to give
> the unfortunate ROBT BURNS[122]

In this letter Burns asks Hamilton about the subscription forms for his book before proceeding to the painful matter of relations with Jean. He went on writing as 'the Bard' to Ballantine about the selection of poems for inclusion. Yet, sending forms to the Ayr lawyer David McWhinnie in mid-April, he also describes himself, with a certain flourish, as 'a poor Poet' fearing 'eternal disgrace' and 'humbled, afflicted, tormented'.[123]

At once ambitiously businesslike and emotionally overwrought, Burns gives the impression of teetering on the edge of another breakdown. The forms he sent out read simply,

APRIL 14th, 1786:

PROPOSALS,

FOR PUBLISHING BY SUBSCRIPTION,

SCOTCH POEMS,

BY ROBERT BURNS

The Work to be elegantly Printed in One Volume, Octavo.
Price Stitched *Three Shillings*.

As the Author has not the most distant *Mercenary* view in Publishing, as soon as so many Subscribers appear as will defray the *necessary* Expence, the Work will be sent to the Press.

211

Set out the brunt side o' your shin,
For pride in *Poets* is nae sin;
Glory's the Prize for which *they* rin,
    And *Fame's* their jo;
And wha blaws best the Horn shall win:
    And wharefore no?

                RAMSAY.

We, under Subscribers, engage to take the above mentioned Work on the Conditions Specified.[124]

No doubt the quotation was chosen to encourage people to associate Burns with the man he called in a letter of 3 April (which quotes from the same stanza) 'the famous Ramsay'.[125] Yet just when Burns hoped to find fame as a proud poet, his life was falling apart. Public embarrassment threatened in Mauchline. Late April brought the local horse races, a time of festivity, but in correspondence Burns presented himself as possessing a heart which, 'as the elegantly melting Gray says, "Melancholy has marked for her own"'.[126] In 'To a Mountain-Daisy, On turning one down, with the Plough, in April – 1786' he linked the crushed daisy both to an 'artless Maid ... By Love's simplicity betray'd' and to a 'simple Bard' who found it hard to be '*prudent*' and so seems 'ruin'd'.[127]

In some ways a more indulgent re-run of 'To a Mouse', this poem had a clearly autobiographical subtext for those who knew Burns's predicament. He was, he told John Kennedy, 'a good deal pleas'd with some sentiments in it myself'.[128] As before, he was tending to view himself almost as a hero from the literature he admired. Quoting from John Home's rhetorical Scottish tragedy *Douglas* – '*how oft does ... sweet* Affection *prove the spring of Woe!*' – he produced an overblown poem about wailing and weeping over a lost love who seems to have betrayed her '*plighted husband*' through '*faithless woman's broken vow*'. Burns presented this as a 'Lament. Occasioned by the Unfortunate Issue of a Friend's Amour', but told Dr Moore the following year it was autobiographical, dealing with 'a shocking affair, which I cannot yet bear to recollect; and [which] had very nearly given [me] one or two of the principal qualifications for a place among those who have lost the chart and mistake the reckoning of Rationality'.[129]

Later he wrote he 'had actually made up some sort of Wedlock'

between himself and Jean, but the wording of his 'unlucky paper' remains unknown.[130] Burns suggested to fellow Mason John Arnot that only the hope of succeeding with poetry stopped him killing himself over the affair with Jean. Writing to Arnot, he works himself into a manic – but also a literary and mannered – state as he alludes to the Bible and quotes *Paradise Lost*,

– I have lost, Sir, that dearest earthly treasure, that greatest blessing here below, that last, best gift which compleated Adam's happiness in the garden of bliss, I have lost – I have lost – my trembling hand refuses its office, the frighted ink recoils up the quill – Tell it not in Gath – I have lost – a – a – A WIFE!

> Fairest of God's creation, last & best!
> *How art thou lost* –[131]

Shooting off into riffs of energetic detail, complaining that 'A damned Star has always kept my zenith', and that he is now 'made a Sunday's laughing stock, & abused like a pick-pocket', Burns goes over his excited pleasure in the soldierly sexual conquest of this lost wife 'vigourously pressing on the siege . . . I had found means to slip a choice detachment into the very citadel'. He then describes in luridly coloured prose the abject sense of loss he felt when she was gone. Presenting his unbalanced state, he relishes writing it up. Around the same time, he versified a passage of the Old Testament Book of Jeremiah beginning 'Ah, woe is me', and inked it into a copy of Fergusson's *Poems*; before he died insane in Edinburgh's Bedlam, Fergusson had paraphrased part of the Book of Job, beginning 'Perish the fatal day when I was born'.[132] Again Burns was mapping himself on to his reading. This too was a way of being a bard.

– There is a pretty large portion of bedlam in the composition of a Poet at any time; but on this occasion, I was nine parts & nine tenths, out of ten, stark staring mad. – At first, I was fixed in stuporific insensibility, silent, sullen, staring, like Lot's wife besaltified in the plains of Gomorha [*sic*]. – But my second paroxysm chiefly beggars description. – The rifted northern ocean, when returning suns dissolve the chains of winter, & loosening precipices of long accumulated ice tempest with hideous crash the foamy Deep – images like these may give some faint shadow of [an idea of (*deleted*)] what was the situation of my bosom. – My chained faculties broke loose; my maddening

passions, roused to tenfold fury, bore over their banks with impetuous, resistless force, carrying every check & principle before them. – Counsel, was an unheeded call to the passing hurricane; Reason, a screaming elk in the [whirling (*deleted*)] vortex of Moskoe strom [*sic*]; & Religion, a feebly-struggling beaver down the roarings of Niagara. –[133]

Burns may have come close to another breakdown. His self-image as 'a Poet' about to publish a book sustained him. So did throwing himself into the search for what he called 'another wife'.[134] He penned 'Despondency, an Ode', bewailing a 'hope-abandon'd' life without 'an *aim*'.[135] He signed himself 'Misery's most humble serv[an]t'.[136] Trying 'to forget' Jean he threw himself into 'all kinds of dissipation and riot, Mason-meetings, drinking matches, and other mischief, to drive her out of my head'.[137] Yet he went on finalising the contents of his book. He pursued another woman. He nourished the emerging aim of just clearing out and going to Jamaica.

The other 'wife' was a young woman surnamed Campbell, but remembered as 'Highland Mary'. According to the poet's youngest sister and others questioned by Robert Chambers more than half a century later, Burns met this new love while she was working as a nursemaid for Gavin Hamilton, though she moved to become 'dairy-maid at Coilsfield'.[138] A fellow servant of Gavin Hamilton's recalled her as 'an unca [very] bonnie bit lass, wi' twa fine black een [eyes], but gae an' Heelan' [very Highland] spoken'.[139] Isobel Burns thought her brother was already acquainted with Campbell, but she felt Burns's passion for this young servant took some time to flare up. However, Burns may have been seeing Campbell at the same time as pursuing Jean Armour. The antiquary Joseph Train, who wrote about the free-loving Buchanites and collected local gossip about Burns's love life, emphasised Mary's 'infidelity' and recorded that the young Highland lass's character 'was loose in the extreme'.[140] Victorian scholars, encouraged by Burns's songs about 'Highland Mary', regarded her as saintly. In 1992 James Mackay concluded her name was Margaret Campbell and that she was born at Dunoon on the Clyde's north bank in 1766 before her family moved to Campbeltown on the Kintyre peninsula.[141]

From scant and scattered surviving evidence, it appears that while Jean Armour was in Paisley, Burns in April and May had an intense relationship with 'Highland Mary'. He was still planning to emigrate

to Jamaica and probably wanted to take her with him, leaving behind all his troubles with Jean, the farm, and the Kirk Session who were after him for fornication. As he wrote to Arnot that spring, after mentioning in passing his idea of 'another wife',

> – Already the holy beagles, the houghmagandie [fornication] pack, begin to snuff the scent; & I expect every moment to see them cast off, & hear them after me in full cry: but as I am an old fox, I shall give them dodging & doubling for it; & by & bye, I intend to earth among the mountains of Jamaica. –[142]

Burns's song 'Highland Lassie O –' is thought to date from around this time. It sings how 'I maun [must] cross the raging sea' to 'Indian wealth', but protests lifelong love for 'my Highland Lassie, O'. She 'has my heart, she has my hand,/ By secret Truth and Honor's band'.[143] The same material features in a song sent to a correspondent in 1792, 'Will ye go to the Indies, my Mary'. Burns described that in terms of his 'earlier love-songs' as a 'farewell of a dear girl' made 'when I was thinking of going to the West Indies'; it was based on 'the breathings' of his own 'ardent Passion'.[144]

Later, Burns's family were tight-lipped about this relationship; if he mentioned it at all, Burns avoided full details. Robert Cromek, eager early nineteenth-century collector of Burnsiana, claimed to have transcribed from among the many song annotations in Burns's 'Glenriddell manuscripts' a page (later lost) on which the poet had written later notes on *The Highland Lassie, O*. This page has now been rediscovered, and is even available digitally.

> My Highland lassie was a warm-hearted, charming young creature as ever blesst a man with generous love. – After a pretty long tract of the most ardent reciprocal attachment, We met by appointment, on the second Sunday of May, in a sequestered spot by the banks of Ayr, where we spent the day in taking a farewel, before she should embark for the West Highlands, to arrange matters among her friends for our projected change of life.[145]

If Burns, apparently dumped by Jean and her family, was enjoying an 'ardent reciprocal attachment' with his 'Highland lassie' by May 1786, this helps explain the jauntiness of a poem sent to Gavin Hamilton from Mossgiel on 3 May, signed 'your LAUREAT ... MINSTREL BURNS'.[146] Playing the part of Beattie's Minstrel rather

than that of insane, despondent Fergusson indicates a change of mood, but swings of mood were hardly alien to Burns. Assuming he took leave of his Highland lover on the second Sunday in May (14 May 1786), then next day, according to a date in his manuscripts, he was sending pious verses of advice to his 'youthfu' friend' Andrew Hunter Aiken, son of Robert Aiken in Ayr. Burns advises the 'lad' to 'keep something to yoursel/ Ye scarcely tell to ony'. He goes on to urge the youth to 'indulge' the sacred flame 'o' weel-plac'd love', but never 'tempt th' *illicit rove*'.[147]

One something Burns was keeping to himself was that he had given his Highland lassie a two-volume bible. These volumes, printed at Edinburgh in 1782, remained in the family of 'Highland Mary's' sister, and are now at Alloway where they have been examined by generations of Burns scholars. Both volumes carry Burns's Masonic mark and the words 'Robert Burns Mossgavill' [an old form of the name Mossgiel], though an attempt appears to have been made to erase these signatures. At the front of each volume in Burns's handwriting is part of a biblical verse. On volume one, 'And ye shall not swear by My Name falsely – I am the Lord. – Levit. 19th Chap: 12th Verse –'; on the second volume '– Thou shalt not forswear thyself but shalt perform unto the Lord thine Oath – Matth: 5 Ch 33d Verse'.[148]

Burns slightly changed the wording of each scriptural text. The Old Testament Book of Leviticus sets down ancient rules of conduct given by God to Moses. In chapter 19, verse 12 Moses is told 'And ye shall not swear by my name falsely, neither shalt thou profane the name of thy God: I *am* the LORD.' By omitting the words about profanity, Burns shifts the focus of the verse away from 'swearing' in the modern colloquial sense of cursing and towards swearing in the sense of making a promise. The context and alterations of his second quotation are even more revealing. In the Sermon on the Mount in chapter five of St Matthew's Gospel Christ moves from discussing the circumstances in which a man may divorce a wife, and 'fornication', to how properly to make a promise:

31 It hath been said, Whosoever shall put away his wife, let him give her a writing of divorcement:
32 But I say unto you, That whosoever shall put away his wife, saving for the cause of fornication, causeth her to commit adultery: and whosoever shall marry her that is divorced committeth adultery.

33 Again, ye have heard that it hath been said by them of old time, Thou shalt not forswear thyself, but shalt perform unto the Lord thine oaths:

34 But I say unto you, Swear not at all; neither by heaven; for it is God's throne:

35 Nor by the earth; for it is his footstool: neither by Jerusalem; for it is the city of the great King.

Both the Old and New Testament passages are about making a promise in God's name. Yet the New Testament one also discourages such oath-taking. Presenting himself in spring 1786 as having just 'lost . . . a wife' and had his written promise to Jean annulled by her family, Burns knew he was about to be summoned to confess 'fornication'. His choice to inscribe this passage from Matthew's Gospel in the bible he gave his new partner is psychologically complex. He would have known well the context about not making a public oath, about fornication, and about separation from a 'wife'. In one sense, that spring Burns seems to have felt a kind of widower – Jean was dead to him – but the verse he chooses here comes from a passage about 'fornication' and difficult separation. Even as, on the rebound, he apparently made an 'Oath' to his 'Highland lassie', his commitment was hardly straightforward.

'Her fingers I lovingly squeezed,/ And kissed her and promised her – naething –' Burns wrote in an 'Extempore – to Mr Gavin Hamilton' around this time. The woman here is probably Jean Armour. Gleefully presenting 'A Poet' about to embark on a dangerous 'voyage' who at once makes and does not make a promise, Burns reveals his general sense of instability in love.[149] His feelings were intense, but he strove to avoid monogamous commitment. From little poems like 'Epitaph on a Henpecked Country Squire' to later, longer depictions of Kate and Tam in 'Tam o' Shanter', he resents the idea of any man whom 'a woman rul'd'.[150] Men needed freedom, needed to be in charge. Their promises were not always what they seemed.

If Margaret or 'Mary' Campbell left for the West Highlands in mid-May 1786, by then Burns was 'much hurried', finalising the contents of his book and gathering subscriptions. 'In about three or four weeks I shall probably set the Press agoing,' he wrote on 16 May.[151] He imagined how his departure for Jamaica might be viewed by fellow rhymers, drinkers and 'bonie lasses', not least in his native Kyle, having

been 'her *Laureat* monie a year'. 'On a Scotch Bard Gone to the West Indies' is one of several poems where Burns tries to anticipate how his work and emigration may be received by a community on 'native soil' where he thought people had been ungenerous towards him. Writing of himself in the third person, he cannot resist a remark directed at the woman he saw as having jilted him. Jean's name is not mentioned, but Burns clearly has her in mind when he writes of his 'Scotch Bard',

> He saw Misfortune's cauld *Nor-west*
> Lang-mustering up a bitter blast;
> A Jillet brak his heart at last,   *jilt*
>   Ill may she be!
> So, took a birth afore the mast,
>   An' owre the Sea.[152]

Conscious the 'holy beagles' of the Kirk Session were on his trail and ready to summon him to penance for fornication, Burns embarked on a pre-emptive strike. Bearing in surviving manuscripts alternative lines which date it either to 12 May or 4 June 1786, his verse 'Libel Summons' presents before its own 'congregated ... brethren' a group of 'Fornicators by profession'. Taking into their 'protection' the pregnant 'quondam maiden', they champion 'the Fornicator's honor'. This jokey poem has a 'COURT OF EQUITY' with 'POET B[urn]s' in 'the chair'. Court officers include Burns's draper friend Smith and 'trusty CLERK' John Richmond. Shoemaker William Hunter is 'MESSENGER AT ARMS'. Together they try named local people for 'HOUGHMAGANDIE'.[153] Doling out daft reproaches, compliments and punishments, they order several accused to appear in the Whitefoord Arms on 5 July. Not written for inclusion in his forthcoming book, this mock-trial poem was for the private amusement of friends like the lawyer's clerk Richmond in Edinburgh. Writing it, Burns prepared himself psychologically for what was coming.

Increasingly convinced his book's appearance would preface his vanishing from the scene, he became more politically outspoken. Dated in one manuscript to 1 June 1786, his poem known as '[Address of Beelzebub]' shows clear support for the leaders of the American Revolution. 'Dunghill sons of dirt an' mire' who 'to PATRICIAN RIGHTS ASPIRE' are among its heroes. Burns has the devil, writing

from Hell, urge a Scottish lord and his officials to crush attempts by Highlanders who are, the poem's headnote explains, 'so audacious as to attempt an escape from theire lawful lords and masters whose property they are emigrating from ... to the wilds of CANADA, in search of that fantastic thing – LIBERTY –'[154] These Highlanders' plight was reported in the *Edinburgh Advertizer* of 30 May. Burns refers to a London meeting about them held a week later. Though he did not publish '[Address of Beelzebub]', its anti-aristocratic politics accord well with the sentiments of the dedicatory poem he was composing for his book around this time. Pointedly, this praises Gavin Hamilton not because he is 'sirnam'd like *His Grace,*' the Duke of Hamilton, but because he is 'my FRIEND and BROTHER'.[155]

Soon after writing about Highlanders who wanted to emigrate, the would-be emigrant Burns read 'in the public papers, the Laureate's Ode' where royal Poet Laureate Thomas Warton celebrated King George III's forty-eighth birthday. Burns – 'My Bardship' – responded with a verse dream. After implying the Laureate's poem sent him to sleep, Burns taunts the King with, among other things, loss of the American colonies. 'Alluding to the Newspaper account of a certain royal Sailor's Amour', the poet, no enthusiast for these royals, calls Prince William 'Young, royal TARRY-BREEKS'. Despite objections, he kept 'A Dream' in successive editions of his work. He had taken care to incorporate an epigraph apparently designed to forestall legal action: '*Thoughts, words and deeds, the Statute blames with reason;/ But surely* Dreams *were n'er indicted Treason.*'[156] Accounts of Burns's political conversation at home or in Mauchline pubs where, he states in his *Poems*, 'he sometimes studies Politics over a glass of guid auld *Scotch Drink*', have not survived, but he continued to take a keen interest in newspaper reports and in contemporary philosophical and political arguments.[157] There are strong hints his sympathies lay with the emergent energies of republican democracy in America and elsewhere. In an April 1786 letter he juxtaposes the defeat of England's King 'Edward at Bannockburn' by the Scottish King Robert the Bruce with the 1777 American revolutionaries' rout of the British loyalist General 'Burgoyne at Saratoga'.[158]

On Friday, 9 June Jean Armour came home. Now without his 'Highland Mary', Burns told a Mauchline friend the following Monday he was feeling 'compleatly miserable' about 'Poor, ill-advised,

ungrateful Armour'. He knew she was back, but not yet how she was feeling about him. Evidently disturbed by her proximity, he felt all his earlier excitement about her flood back:

> Never man lov'd, or rather ador'd, a woman more than I did her; and [, to] confess [a] truth between you and m[e, I] do still love her to distraction after all, tho' I won't tell her so, tho I see her, which I don't want to do. – My poor, dear, unfortunate Jean! how happy have I been in her arms! –[159]

He could not get her out of his head, however hard he tried. Stung that her family had 'made so much noise, and showed so much grief, at the thought of her being *my wife*', he worried they might let her marry someone less suitable. His feelings for her remained strong, but a 'grand cure' was approaching, he wrote, since 'the Ship is on her way home that is to take me out to Jamaica, and then, farewel dear old Scotland, and farewel dear, ungrateful Jean, for never, never will I see you more!'[160]

Towards the end of this letter Burns mentions that his poems are to go to press next day. By this stage he must have finalised the book's title (different from that on his subscription flyer) and decided the contents' running order. On Wednesday, 14 June he sent a verse note to his surgeon friend John Mackenzie, looking forward to seeing him at Friday's Tarbolton Masonic meeting. Presumably Burns took along his new song 'The Farewell. To the Brethren of St James's Lodge, Tarbolton'. Sung to the tune of what was then the traditional Scots song of parting ('Goodnight and joy be wi' you a''), his verses bid 'heart-warm, fond adieu' to his Masonic brothers. He hymned their customs and mysteries. Praising their 'noble Name,/ To MASONRY and SCOTIA dear!' he hoped that they would remember their poet who was off to Jamaica, and propose an annual toast to him. He even supplied the wording,

> A last request, permit me here,
> When yearly ye assemble a',
> One *round*, I ask it with a *tear*,
> To him, *the Bard, that's far awa'*.[161]

Here, as in the Preface to his book, Burns wanted to shape how audiences would regard him. He wished the Masons to toast him not simply as 'Brother Burns' but as '*the Bard*'. He wanted to present

himself to readers of his book as 'a Rhymer from his earliest years' who, though encouraged by his friends to publish, was still 'an obscure, nameless Bard'. Seeking a name for himself, conscious he 'was possest of some poetic abilities', this Bard feared being regarded as 'An impertinent blockhead'. His Preface exhibits nervousness, but also confidence, guiding the reader towards Ramsay and Fergusson, 'two justly admired Scotch Poets he has often had in his eye in the following pieces . . . rather with a view to kindle at their flame, than for servile imitation'. Protesting 'he has not the most distant pretensions' to 'the genius of a Ramsay, or the glorious dawnings of the poor, unfortunate Ferguson', the new Bard makes sure that he has outlined the background against which his work should be read. To subscribers, having already mentioned five authors in his Preface, Burns offers 'Not the mercenary bow over a counter, but the heart-throbbing gratitude of the Bard . . .'[162]

On 13 June 1786, the day when Burns's poems went to press, Jean Armour wrote to the Reverend Auld acknowledging she was pregnant, and Robert Burns the father. She said she was sorry to cause the Kirk Session trouble on her account; they recorded this formally in their minutes. Next Sunday (18 June) during the church service Auld formally asked Jean to step in front of the congregation to be upbraided. She was not there, having sent her letter instead. A week later Burns appeared before the Session, acknowledged his part in the affair, and was told to make three public demonstrations of penitence at church services. He wrote to John Richmond on the morning of Sunday 9 July saying he was about to put on sackcloth and ashes, but explaining he was being treated relatively lightly by the 'Inquisition'. Instead of having to do penance in front of the congregation he was being 'indulged so far as to appear in my own seat'.[163] He also told Richmond his book would be ready in two weeks, and asked his friend in Edinburgh to send any subscriptions he had gathered.

Awaiting his book and anticipating leaving Mauchline for Jamaica, Burns was putting a brave, ironic face on being exhibited once more before the godly as a fornicator. After his exhibition, he was granted a certificate pronouncing him a single, not a married, man. Auld had promised this to Burns if he behaved as the Kirk demanded. More perturbed about how things stood between himself and Jean, Robert had been trying to see her, but her mother had banned him from the house. Expecting Jean would have shown remorse for going

along with her parents' efforts to annul all connection between them, Burns was taken aback when she seemed not to. She and her friends did want her to stand beside Burns in the kirk, but Auld forbade it; Burns, unjustly he felt, got the blame for this. Still, he pronounced himself on 17 July 'well pleased ... not to have her company'.[164] His pride was hurt. He planned to sail to the West Indies in October.

Then another row blew up. James Armour realised that the Burns who had always seemed such a waster might have some money after all – from subscriptions for his poems, if nothing else. Craving damages for what the poet had done to his daughter, Armour wanted that cash. He set about getting a warrant requiring Burns to hand over a large sum of money or face jail with his assets confiscated. Just in time, 'by a channel they little dream of', Burns found out what Armour and his allies were planning.[165] Immediately, and presumably with Hamilton's aid, he arranged to have a deed of assignment drawn up at Mossgiel on Saturday, 22 July. Robert made over all he owned to Gilbert, including the copyright of his *Poems* and any money they might make. Gilbert was to use this to 'aliment clothe and educate' Burns's daughter Elizabeth until she was fifteen.[166] Lodged with the Sheriff-Clerk's office in Ayr, this document meant Burns had nothing for the Armour family. He saw them as having destroyed his happiness with Jean. Still determined to have Burns arrested for damages, James Armour obtained a writ against the bard whom he accused of planning to flee.

Burns did flee. Invoking the Christ of Matthew's Gospel who, though 'The foxes have holes, and the birds of the air *have* nests ... hath not where to lay *his* head', he wrote to Richmond on 30 July explaining, 'I am wandering from one friend's house to another, and like a true son of the Gospel "have no where to lay my head".'[167] That day he was with his maternal aunt and uncle, just outside Kilmarnock.

Cursing her mother, who he felt had undue influence over Jean's affairs, Burns was keeping in touch with John Wilson in Kilmarnock. As the *Poems* went through the press, the poet prepared for his voyage to Jamaica. Through a family with strong Ayrshire connections he had obtained a position on a sugar plantation managed by a Scot, Charles Douglas, who had written on 19 June to his brother Dr Patrick Douglas of Garallan in Ayrshire, asking him to send out a 'young fellow ... that can write & Read so as to be able to answer a Letter I might write to him while I am abroad, a Poor Boy

or any Hind Lad, I suppose you may get enough for 10 or 12 Pound a year or less.'[168] However, the work would involve more than light secretarial duties. Gilbert recalled his brother was to have worked 'as an assistant overseer, or as I believe it is called, a book-keeper'.[169] An overseer was the 'premier minister', sometimes 'tyrant', in charge of slaves; as assistant overseer Burns would have been at the heart of slave management during a period when arguments about the inhumanity of slavery rose to a crescendo.[170] As an early twentieth-century Jamaican scholar pointed out, 'The "bookie" had control of the gangs of negroes in the field, in the boiling house, and in the still-house . . . In addition to a liberality of whip-cord the Jamaican slave-laws of the period admitted of such attentions for misde-meanours as branding, dismemberment, and other mutilations, and with such cases the book-keepers were more or less directly asso-ciated.'[171] The modern historian of Jamaican slavery J. R. Ward points out that 'The overseer and bookkeepers were supposed to ensure that the drivers extracted a reasonable work rate from the field gangs, sit in the boiling house during crop, count out lumber for the carpenters, follow the wain-loads of sugar to the wharf, and watch the livestock being fed.'[172] Living not with the plantation manager but usually in a barracks at the heart of the sugar plantation, book-keepers worked very long hours, and most died young. Situated near the fortified settlement of Port Antonio, north-east of Kingston, the Jamaican sugar plantations at 'Ayr Mount and Nightingale Grove . . . along the basin of the Rio Grande' owned by Ayrshireman Dr Douglas, were very much part of Enlightenment Scotland's close involvement with slavery.[173] Since Burns lacked ready money to pay, Dr Douglas was to 'procure a passage for him' aboard a Jamaica-bound ship.[174] On arrival Burns's salary was to be a modest £30 per annum. His knowledge of the West Indies was not exten-sive, but he knew about the slave trade. His readiness to become involved in slave management may have been a sign of personal desperation; it is still shocking, and contradicts the ideology implicit and explicit in much of his poetry. That Scotland's bard should have been so ready to become part of the system of slavery is one of the most striking indications of how complicit Scotland was in the slave trade.

Burns spoke to people who had been to the West Indies. He had grown up with books offering overviews of Jamaican conditions. Guthrie's *Geographical, Historical and Commercial Grammar*, a

book Burns mentions, detailed the 'hurricanes, earthquakes, and bad seasons' of the Caribbean, giving some account of how slaves 'are subsisted' there; 'the whites are kept in constant terror of insurrections and plots'. Of Jamaica in particular Guthrie recorded the air was often 'excessive hot and unfavourable to European constitutions'. Mentioning 'most terrible' diseases and flesh-eating insects, he catalogued tropical fruits but emphasised that 'The misery and hardships of the negroes is truly moving . . . They look on death as a blessing . . .'[175] So, though Burns might fantasise about 'the lime and the orange/ And the apple on the pine', he knew there was more to Jamaica than pineapples.[176] Emigration might be an escape from Ayrshire troubles; it could also be fatal. Hoping the *Jamaica bodies* would 'use him weel [well]', he surely felt trepidation.[177]

He might go to meet his 'Highland lassie'; perhaps he would eventually return to her from the Caribbean. But he could not get Jean out of his mind. He wrote to Smith in Mauchline, speechifying in verse like a stage hero; the first line here is patterned on one in a play by Addison:

O Jeany, thou hast stolen away my soul!
In vain I strive against the lov'd idea:
Thy tender image sallies on my thoughts,
My firm resolves become an easy prey![178]

Yet his firm resolve about Jeany persisted. Determined to leave home, after the way the Armours had treated him, Burns was 'Against . . . owning her conjugally'. 'Witless wild, and wicked', he waited impatiently for his book and emigration.[179]

For all his hectic emotions, he remained resolutely and ambitiously focused. Published on 31 July 1786, *Poems, Chiefly in the Scottish Dialect* contained very few typographical errors in its 240 pages. Printing each page involved fitting together hundreds of individual pieces of metal type, so continuous proof-reading was painstaking. With no experience of the job, Burns proof-read intently, visiting Wilson's premises on several occasions. One error which slipped through, 'Theocrites' for 'Theocritus', may just conceivably have been deliberate, emphasising that these are not poems by an author 'with all the advantages of learned art'. Nevertheless, Burns inserted footnotes indicating allusions to Ossian, Milton, Shakespeare, Edward Young, Goldsmith, Taylor of Norwich, and several local

customs. These indicate he sought a polite, educated audience. There was also a full, double-columned glossary of Scots words, making the book more accessible to genteel readers. The proofs demanded, and got, Burns's very careful attention.

Whatever his state of hostilities with the Armours, he appeared in Mauchline kirk for the third of his public reproaches on Sunday 6 August. After that, certified bachelor and published author, he was all set for Jamaica, but busy helping distribute his book. Out of a print run of 612 copies, over half were for subscribers. Prominent among them his Kilmarnock friend Muir had collected seventy subscriptions. His loyal brother Gilbert, running the farm while Burns's life was in turmoil, had matched that. Gavin Hamilton had found forty, James Smith forty-one, and the Ayr lawyer Aiken a resounding 145. Almost all the rest of the print run sold within a month.

Burns must have realised such success really was the start of the '*Fame*' mentioned on his subscription form, and marked his public recognition as the 'Bard' of his title page. But his book was as much an end as a beginning. It concluded his time in Lochlea and Mauchline, where so many of the poems had taken shape; it also signalled the end of his time in Scotland. The final poem, 'A Bard's Epitaph', asks anyone 'whim-inspir'd' and 'Owre fast for thought, owre hot for rule' to weep over the Bard's grave and learn '*self-controul*'.[180] The book was a monument to Burns's talent; in some moods he may also have seen it as testament to his own folly. Opening with 'The Twa Dogs', its forty-four poems range from 'Scotch Drink' to 'The Cotter's Saturday Night'. With highlights like 'To a Mouse', 'To a Louse' and 'The Holy Fair', it is magnificent for variety and energy, for exploration of daftness as well as piety, for sheer 'bardie' spirit. As for Burns's life, he saw that as a mess. His book was heavy with a past he sought to relinquish.

For 'The Farewell' he chose as epigraph a lengthy speech from James Thomson's emotive drama *Edward and Eleonora*: a man 'weeps his fortunes' when he sees the ruin of his intimate relationships, and exclaims he is 'undone!' Bidding Scotland 'Farewell', Burns's verses look forward with little enthusiasm to 'the torrid plains' that lie ahead, but lament 'A brother's sigh! a sister's tear!/ My Jean's heart-rending throe!' Exclamatory rather than emotionally achieved, this poem is revealing as it ranges round people Burns is leaving behind, including his daughter, his 'bosom frien'' Smith

(who he hopes will befriend Jean after his departure), plus friends 'Hamilton' and 'Aiken'. His life with them is ending – 'I'll never see thee more!'[181]

But he did not go. Ready to sail from Greenock with a Captain Smith whose vessel, the *Nancy*, was bound for Savanna la Mar in western Jamaica, Burns rode to Ayr on 13 August to make final arrangements with Dr Douglas, whose brother Burns now called 'my Master'.[182] There he met a Mr and Mrs White who 'derang'd my plans altogether'. Knowing the Jamaican terrain, the Whites pointed out to the poet that for him to travel from Savanna la Mar to Port Antonio would cost Charles Douglas £50; moreover, the journey would bring a high risk of fever 'in consequence of hard travelling in the sun'.[183] Douglas now vetoed Burns's travelling as planned; instead, he was to sail on 1 September, again from Greenock but with a different captain, a good friend of Gavin Hamilton.

This too was not to be. In late August Burns partied with his old friend Willie Niven, now a Maybole merchant, and a 'worthy knot of lads' – 'congenial souls'.[184] The bard spent time 'taking leave of my Carrick relations'. He also visited his old Kirkoswald sweetheart, Peggy Thomson, and her understanding husband, another old acquaintance. Robert gave Peggy a copy of his *Poems* in which he wrote an affectionate poem. It ends with his own fear he will soon be far away, feverish in 'torrid climes' or else drowned on his voyage. This upset Peggy and himself – surely the effect Burns was after. Parting, neither could speak a word. Her husband kept Burns company for three miles, 'and we both parted with tears'.[185]

By 30 August he was back at Mossgiel, claiming 'The Nancy, in which I was to have gone, did not give me warning enough. – Two days notice was too little for me to wind up my affairs and go for Greenock.'[186] He now planned to leave at the end of September aboard the *Bell*. Burns had not quite paid off Wilson's bill for printing his poems, but other factors may have tempted him to delay. Though James Armour still had his warrant against Burns, the *Poems* were winning admiration; as Robert noted with pride, 'some of the first Gentlemen in the county have offered to befriend me'.[187] In touch again with Jean, he knew she would give birth very soon. Writing to Richmond in Edinburgh on 1 September Burns suggested Jean might consider marrying him now, though that seemed unlikely. He reproached Richmond for having apparently abandoned Jenny Surgeoner. If this seems hypocritical, Burns surely expressed such

thoughts because he was wondering if he could really abandon Jean.

She gave birth to twins – a boy and a girl – in Mauchline on 3 September. Burns wrote excitedly to Richmond, celebrating the power of sexuality with a bawdy version of 'Green grow the rashes, O' and hoping God would bless the newly arrived 'poor little dears'.[188] He felt buoyant. Probably that morning he had made a satirical poem about a visiting preacher's sermon, taking it to Gavin Hamilton after church. He sent it to Mackenzie in Mauchline and Muir in Kilmarnock, aware this fresh experience of parenthood had brought him anxious pleasure. Three days after the twins were baptised Robert and Jean, he remarked to Muir on 8 September, 'I believe all hopes of staying at home will be abortive.'[189] This hints that, though he still intended to emigrate, Burns was also considering abandoning that plan.

By late September, due to voyage with Captain Cathcart on the *Bell*, Burns was still at Mossgiel. The *Bell* sailed without him. He had been reminiscing about his father, and wrote to his factor friend John Kennedy on the 26th about the strength of family feelings, mentioning not least 'The burning glow' a man feels 'when he clasps the Woman of his Soul to his bosom – the tender yearnings of heart for the little Angels to whom he has given existence – '.[190] He did not sound in a hurry to go.

Still, he identified 'after harvest' as his likely departure date.[191] Harvest was always a busy time. Extra hands were needed on the farm, but there were other reasons for Burns to wait. Locally his book had made a remarkable impression on all classes of people. Some fans were of 'high Ancestry' and 'exalted station' like Mrs Catherine Gordon Stewart of Stair whose appreciation 'the obscure Bard' acknowledged by sending her unpublished songs. Other admirers were less grand. Robert Heron, then living in Galloway, remembered how in 1786 'even plough-boys and maid-servants would have gladly bestowed the wages which they earned the most hardly, and which they wanted to purchase necessary clothing, if they might but procure the works of BURNS'. A friend of Heron's showed him a copy of this new work of 'extraordinary genius'. Heron was at first sceptical.

> It was on a Saturday evening. I opened the volume, by accident, while I was undressing, to go to bed. I closed it not, till a late hour on the rising Sunday morn, after I had read every syllable it contained.[192]

Heron was not alone. He claimed to have 'witnessed the passionate eagerness with which' Burns's *Poems* 'were received and read by all, from the parson to the plowman, – from the gentleman and lady in the parlour, to the cinder-wench, kneeling to read them before the kitchen-fire'.[193]

Faced with such eager responses, within eight weeks of publication Burns was already thinking 'perhaps to try a second edition of my book'.[194] A few copies started circulating in Edinburgh. An Ayrshire farmer called Cairns recited parts of 'To a Mouse' and other poems to polite Edinburgh journalist Robert Anderson, who made successful efforts to see (under the auspices of Edinburgh Ayrshireman Andrew Bruce) a copy of Burns's *Poems*, 'which I perused with wonder and delight, though its contents were, at times, offensive to taste'.[195] Even before the volume appeared, Professor Dugald Stewart (whose country home at Catrine was not far from Mauchline), had read three of Burns's poems to his poet friend, Edinburgh's Reverend Thomas Blacklock. Renowned for his 'Benevolence', blind and musical, Blacklock, who also possessed antiquarian tastes, was in some ways a modern bardic figure mediating between past poetic glories and a 'commercial and enlightened future' – but he lacked Burns's sheer talent.[196] Now when Blacklock obtained a copy of Burns's *Poems* from Ayrshire minister George Lawrie he found them 'astonishing', and told Lawrie so. Blacklock wanted to show the book to the Reverend Hugh Blair, the leading moderate Church of Scotland clergyman who was also Edinburgh University's Professor of Rhetoric and Belles Lettres. A quarter of a century earlier Blair had encouraged James Macpherson to collect the poems of the ancient bard Ossian. Sent on 4 September, Blacklock's letter was seen by Gavin Hamilton, who showed it to Burns. Blacklock 'wished, for the sake of the Young man [Burns], that a second edition, more numerous than the former, could immediately be printed, as it appears certain, that its intrinsic merit and the exertion of the Authors friends might give it a universal circulation, than any thing which has been published within my memory'.[197]

Around late September Burns sent his substantial poem 'The Brigs of Ayr' to its dedicatee John Ballantine. His 'friendly offices' had assisted Burns's 'Publication'. The poem is a debate between the old and the new, represented by the traditional bridge at Ayr (considered by some 'too ancient long to endure the violence of tide and rapid streams') and a brand-new bridge, emblem of Ayr's 'rising spirit',

whose principal backer was Ballantine.[198] Proclaiming itself by a 'simple Bard' bred to 'Independance', Burns's poem mentions several Ayr landmarks, including *Simpson's*, 'A noted tavern at the *Auld Brig* end' where he liked to drink. Though it articulates arguments for traditional mores, celebrating Scots life, the poem flatters the improver Ballantine and makes a case for modernisation; it also alludes to other supporters like Mrs Stewart of Stair and Professor Stewart of Catrine. With this poem of 'Minstrelsy' and 'Bards' Burns was cultivating the sort of allies who might help him with a second edition.[199]

He met John Wilson in early October and discussed the idea. Wilson wanted Burns to pay for the paper to print it on; Burns could not or would not pay. He may also have discussed his plans with a Glasgow printer, but nothing happened there either. He wrote a coat-trailing letter to Aiken in Ayr, saying how eager he was for a second edition that might include, for instance, 'The Brigs of Ayr' and 'shew my gratitude to Mr Ballantine'.[200] Aiken, lawyer and taxman, seems to have suggested to Burns that he stay in Scotland and even to have offered the poet help in trying to secure a post as an Excise officer. Though this career option stayed in his mind, Burns was unsure. He presented himself as 'pining under secret wretchedness'. As usual his literary skill intensified his sense of his own troubles, but he was clearly disturbed: 'Even in the hour of social mirth [i.e., companionable drinking], my gaiety is the madness of an intoxicated criminal under the hands of the executioner.'[201]

Part of what troubled Burns, he said, was that God might judge him harshly if he deserted his children. 'Though sceptical, in some points, of our current belief, yet, I think, I have every evidence for the reality of a life beyond the stinted bourne of our present existence.'[202] This accords with his earlier lines to Aiken's son, attacking 'preaching cant' but also saying that 'An *atheist-laugh*' is 'a poor exchange/ For *Deity offended*!'[203] Burns was no atheist but his 'Almighty God' was an 'unknown Power' of whom he might, at times, be afraid.[204] Probably he had other reasons to fear harsh judgement. He appears not to have seen 'Highland Mary' since May; though no letters survive, he had probably written to her, and must have remembered their parting and the understanding they had reached. Back then he had felt jilted, indignant, eager to publish and emigrate. Now, seeing Jean and his new twins in Mauchline, things seemed very different.

Isobel Burnes recalled how some time in later 1786 – perhaps early in November – a letter was delivered to Mossgiel one evening after harvesting. Burns 'went to the window to open and read it, and she was struck by the look of agony which was the consequence. He went out without uttering a word.'[205] 'Highland Mary' had died in Greenock. Thinking about the transience of human existence, Burns later wrote how 'a malignant fever . . . hurried my dear girl to the grave in a few days; before I could even hear of her illness', and elsewhere he speculated that 'If there is another life' then in it he would 'with speechless agony of rapture, again recognise my lost, my ever dear MARY, whose bosom was fraught with Truth, Honor, Constancy & Love.'[206] He then quoted from his song 'Thou lingering Star'. Exactly what he thought and felt about this woman in the summer and autumn of 1786 we will never know. However, although it is sometimes over-written and partial, a later interview given by Highland Mary's mother to a journalist writing for a 'Greenock paper' in 1823 gives us as reliable an account of Burns's relationship with 'Mary' and her family as we are likely to get. At the age of eighty, Mrs Campbell accurately described the two-volume bible Burns had given to Mary.

> She states that, when her daughter came from Ayrshire, she spoke often of the correspondence she had there maintained with Burns, and said that he repeatedly offered her his hand, and told her he would come to any part of the Highlands and marry her. He likewise mentioned that it was then his intention to go to the West Indies, but he said, in the event of this taking place, he would settle a yearly sum upon Mary until he returned. Burns's gallantry by this time formed a theme for gossips, and Mary almost dreaded a union with one whom her friends condemned as a rake. – Had she survived, however, these objections would doubtless have been surmounted, but alas! the resistless arm of death soon numbered Mary among his victims, and she was mingled with the clods of the valley, while the Bard, unconscious of his loss, was revelling in his visionary prospects of domestic bliss. Impatient at the delay and silence of his betrothed, Burns wrote repeatedly to the Highlands, but could obtain no information to quiet his doating and doubting soul. At length he addressed a letter of inquiry to her uncle at Greenock, and by him the striking and melancholy truth was unfolded. To one whose bosom was so tenderly alive to all the finer feelings and passions, this proved an overwhelming blow; his mental anguish was affecting in the extreme,

and his sorrows were vented in the well known, impassioned address 'To Mary in Heaven.' After Mary's death, several letters from Burns, breathing all the ardour and enthusiasm which characterized his amatory effusions, were discovered in her chest. – These, however, with a letter addressed to Mrs Campbell by her intended son-in-law, were committed to the flames by one of Mary's brothers.[207]

If remorse was among Burns's emotions when he learned what had happened to his Highland love, then her death and burial in Greenock also made it more likely that he would maintain his association with Jean and his growing family. More than that, he might remain in Scotland to see how a second edition of his poems would be received.

This impulse could only have been quickened by an invitation to dine with Dugald Stewart at Catrine. Also present at that meal on 23 October were Burns's friend Dr Mackenzie and Stewart's protégé Lord Daer. A fellow Freemason four years Burns's junior, Daer had just returned from France where he had met Condorcet and other republicans soon to be active in the French Revolution. Politically radical, Daer wrote on 'The Origin and Nature of Rights' for the *Proceedings of the Speculative Society of Edinburgh*.[208] Later he joined the democratic Scottish Association of the Friends of the People, before returning to France in 1792 and adopting the title 'Citizen Douglas'. Burns, 'Sir Bardie' as he called himself in 'Extempore Verses on Dining with Lord Daer', saw Daer as a true 'BROTHER'. Dugald Stewart was a 'plain, honest, worthy man' – among Burns's highest terms of praise and another signal that however taken he was to be dining with a lord, Burns reacted best to an egalitarian manner.[209]

The politics of republicanism might be a subject for discussion not only among diners at Catrine but also among Burns's close friends. This is apparent from topics debated at the Mauchline Conversation Society which met from 30 October 1786 in a local pub, numbering David Sillar and Gilbert Burns among its stalwarts. Eventually, in 1793, Gilbert, probably more conservative in inclination than his wilder elder brother, asked 'Whether it is probable, if a Republican form of Government were to take place, it would tend to more happiness for the present Generation?'[210]

Dugald Stewart clearly recalled Burns's conduct on 23 October 1786. The bard enjoyed talking shrewdly about people he had met,

'though frequently inclining too much to sarcasm'. As in letters, so in conversation Burns could be extravagant, with a degree of 'caprice and humour of the moment'. Speaking freely about his parents and upbringing, he had a remarkable memory for verse, readily reciting it at length. Stewart thought Burns's taste in English poetry excellent. Robert even wept when moved by a passage the professor quoted.

> His manners were then, as they continued ever afterwards, simple, manly, and independent; strongly expressive of conscious genius and worth; but without any thing that indicated forwardness, arrogance, or vanity. He took his share in conversation, but not more than belonged to him; and listened with apparent attention and deference, on subjects where his want of education deprived him of the means of information. If there had been a little more of gentleness and accommodation in his temper, he would, I think, have been still more interesting; but he had been accustomed to give law in the circle of his ordinary acquaintance, and his dread of any thing approaching to meanness or servility, rendered his manner somewhat decided and hard. – Nothing perhaps was more remarkable among his various attainments, than the fluency, and precision, and originality of his language, when he spoke in company; more particularly as he aimed at purity in his turn of expression, and avoided more successfully than most Scotchmen, the peculiarities of Scottish phraseology ... The idea which his conversation conveyed of the powers of his mind, exceeded, if possible, that which is suggested by his writings ... All the faculties of Burns' mind were, as far as I could judge, equally vigorous; and his predilection for poetry, was rather the result of his own enthusiastic and impassioned temper, than of a genius exclusively adapted to that species of composition ...[211]

For all its high tone, this description of Burns's gift of the gab and knowledge of literature accords well with the very differently expressed memories of Mauchline lass Nelly Miller, who went out for a time with Burns's younger brother, William. Long afterwards she recalled Robert 'in a licht blew-coat o' his mither's makin and dyeing; ay, and o' his mither's sewin', I'se warrand, in thae days; and his bonie black hair hingin down, and curlin' ower the neck o't; a buik in his han' – aye a buik in his han''. While she thought him 'an idler just, that did little but read', Nelly recalled Robert as 'unco, by-ordinar engagin in his talk ... He was na to ca' a bonie

man: dark and strong; but uncommon invitin in his speech –
uncommon! Ye could na hae cracket [chatted] wi' him for ae minute,
but ye wad hae studen four or five.'[212] Sensing this in his own way,
Professor Stewart in 1786 went on to lend him the 1772 *Essays on
Song-Writing* by John Aikin whom Burns in the following decade
called 'a great critic'.[213] Burns said he particularly liked Aikin's
encouragement to make use of natural history in poetry; but there
was little this polite critic could teach the poet of 'To a Mouse' or
'To a Louse'.

Without losing the admiration of local lasses like Nelly Miller,
Burns was acquiring a taste for genteel society. Visiting the Lawries
near Newmilns, he was captivated by their seventeen-year-old
daughter Louisa playing the spinet. Staying overnight at George
Lawrie's manse, he made a pious poem about the family, and soon
afterwards wrote to eighteen-year-old Edinburgh University Divinity
student Archibald Lawrie, commenting on the 'sweetest scenes of
domestic Peace and kindred Love' he had found in their home.[214]
This was very different from his own situation with Jean, but, for
all the class differences, not so far from his ideal in 'The Cotter's
Saturday Night'. Burns realised his reputation as 'a Poet' might act
as a passport, gaining him ready entry into polite society. He sent
Archibald Lawrie a book of songs and 'two Volumes of Ossian':
bardic gifts from the bard.[215]

Established now as a local celebrity, on 26 October Burns was
admitted an honorary member of Kilmarnock's Masonic lodge of
St John Kilwinning. He had become friendly with the lodge's Master,
Major William Parker, and Parker's brother Hugh, an influential
Kilmarnock banker. A lively Standard Habbie poem celebrates
another of their members, elderly Tam Samson who liked to shoot
birds on the local moors and play curling (a winter sport Burns
enjoyed) on nearby lochs. Representative of 'the muse', Burns was
honoured by Masons of the town where his *Poems* had been
published. He hymned their 'brotherly love'.[216]

Always sociable except when depressed, Burns found his poetry
made him welcomed by the whole spectrum of society: from
banker, grand lady, merchant, professor and peer to farm-worker,
housewife, servant-girl and local tradesman. As 'Sir Bard' he
wrote a warm Standard Habbie epistle to William Logan, a veteran
of the American War with a taste for fiddle music. Dated in manu-
script 'Oct: 30th, 1786', this poem shows Burns still regarded

his relationship with Jean as over and dreamed of a new life in 'the Indies'.[217] Now he was thinking of departing from the port of Leith in late December, shortly before his twenty-eighth birthday – but not before setting in motion a second edition of his poems.

To Mrs Frances Anna Wallace Dunlop, a spirited fifty-six-year-old local widow of aristocratic lineage who had written to Burns about her enthusiasm for his *Poems*, and requested further copies of his volume, he replied as 'the poor Bard' on 15 November: 'I am thinking to go to Edinburgh in a week or two at farthest, to throw off a second Impression of my book'. Burns was delighted by Mrs Dunlop's pleasure in her Wallace ancestry. He told her of his boyhood enthusiasm for 'your illustrious ancestor, the SAVIOUR OF HIS COUNTRY'.[218] This was to be the start of one of the most important correspondences of Burns's life.

Not all local ladies were won over, though. A few days after writing to Frances Dunlop, Burns sent off another extravagant letter, addressed to Miss Wilhelmina Alexander of Ballochmile, sister of a wealthy landowner. Barding away, he took the poetic licence he regarded as his right: 'Poets are such outré Beings, so much the children of wayward Fancy and capricious Whim, that I believe the world generally allows them a larger latitude in the rules of Propriety, than the sober Sons of Judgment and Prudence.' He enclosed a poem about 'The bony Lass o' Ballochmile', thirty-three-year-old Miss Alexander, whom he had seen while walking on her brother's land. Discoursing of 'visionary Bards', Burns's letter told Wilhelmina she was 'one of the finest pieces of Nature's workmanship'; if 'she were a country Maid,/ And I the happy country Swain!' then 'I would . . . nightly to my bosom strain/ The bony Lass o' Ballochmyle.' Miss Alexander kept the letter and poem all her life, but did not reply. Stung by what he perceived as upper-class disdain, Burns noted, 'Ye canna mak a silk-purse o' a sow's lug.'[219]

A second, Edinburgh edition of his poems was looking like a good idea. Now that well-connected men like Stewart and Blacklock were reading his work a review appeared in the October *Edinburgh Magazine* praising Burns as 'a striking example of native genius bursting through the obscurity of poverty and the obstructions of laborious life'.[220] Taking several cues from the *Poems*' 'Preface', it related his verse to that of Ramsay and Fergusson. Probably this

review was by the magazine's publisher, James Sibbald. His assist-
ant Robert Anderson inserted several Burns poems in the November
and December issues. Before long Anderson would meet the poet
at the house of David Ramsay, printer of the *Edinburgh Courant*
which on 13 and 15 November published a correspondence about
Burns's poems and the need to find patrons for him – 'to rescue
from penury a genius which, if unprotected, will probably sink into
obscurity'.

The first letter in this exchange accuses the county of Ayr of
failing to provide anyone who has 'stepped forth as a patron to
this man'. A reply, signed 'G.H.' and dated from Glasgow on
14 November, clearly comes from someone familiar with Ayrshire
and the exact size of Burns's Kilmarnock print run.[221] Probably this
was Gavin Hamilton. By 20 November Burns was concerned that,
though his other lawyer friend Aiken had been making inquiries in
Edinburgh about publishing the *Poems*, there was no news. In
Edinburgh Blacklock heard word that same week that a substantial
second edition was being planned 'at the expence of the gentlemen
of Ayrshire', piqued, perhaps, by the letter in the *Courant*. There
was talk of having Blacklock's letter praising Burns's poems published
as publicity. Burns wrote to Ballantine in Ayr on the 20th, sending
him a rather melodramatic, *King Lear*-derived poem about how the
rich must 'relieve' their 'brothers' – 'Affliction's sons' – and describing
Aiken as 'my first poetic patron'. Burns planned to visit Aiken in
Ayr on 24 November for advice, and to see Ballantine. 'I hear of
no returns from Edin[bu]r[gh] to Mr Aiken respecting my second
Edition business; so I am thinking to set out beginning of next week,
for the City myself. –'[222]

In late November this is what Burns did. Before leaving he excited
himself into the right frame of mind. On 20 November, the day he
wrote to Ballantine about going to Edinburgh, he sent what was
probably a bawdy poem to his friends Willie Niven and John McAdam,
the latter a wealthy Ayrshire landowner who, like Ballantine, had
interests in improvement. With the poem went an extravagant
proclamation mixing ambition and self-mockery. No longer in hiding
from James Armour's warrant but still with an aftertaste of sickness
at the Poet Laureate's royalist work, Burns now invoked a warrant
of his own. Usurping the place of the monarch, and invoking the nine
Muses, he dances forward gleefully to proclaim himself king of the
bards:

In the Name of the NINE. *Amen.*
We, ROBERT BURNS, by virtue of a Warrant from NATURE,
bearing date the Twenty-fifth day of January, Anno Domini one thou-
sand seven hundred and fifty-nine, POET-LAUREAT and BARD IN
CHIEF in and over the Districts and Countries of KYLE,
CUNNINGHAM, and CARRICK, of old extent . . .

Burns proceeds to describe himself as charged with 'care and
watchings over the Order and Police of all and sundry the MANU-
FACTURERS, RETAINERS, and VENDERS of POESY; Bards, Poets,
Poetasters, Rhymers, Songsters, Ballad-singers, &c. &c. &c. &c.
&c. male and female'. He signs off straightforwardly and decisively,

GIVEN at MAUCHLINE, this twentieth day of November, Anno
Domini one thousand seven hundred and eighty-six.
GOD SAVE THE BARD![223]

V

New World

On 28 November 1786, still with the option of sailing to the New World from Leith, Burns rode into Edinburgh on a borrowed pony. In Scotland's capital, he wrote, 'I was in a new world'.¹ Approaching from the west, he was presented with a scene recorded by another late eighteenth-century traveller and still recognisable from today's Princes Street. To his left, still under construction, was Edinburgh's neoclassical New Town, then a 'line of modern houses, built of white stone, upon an elegant and uniform plan'. To his right, 'The castle, on the naked rock, from its bold and exalted situation, its vastness, domineering aspect and pictur- esque irregularity of parts, its battlements and towers, &c. first seizes the traveller's sight, and, for some moments, rivets his attention. His eye next slides along the antique and lofty range of buildings, public and private, descending eastward from the castle, and impending over a deep valley, called the North-Loch.' Burns was seeing for the first time this city whose architecture so strikingly juxtaposed the ancient and the improved. Eighteenth-century eyes were trained to admire the elegant, but also wilder textures. 'The whole assemblage of objects toward the right exhibits, on the uneven site of this towering rock, an air of antiquity and uncouth grandeur.'²

Burns was ready to enjoy this new world. On his journey he had been fêted by Lowland farmers, carousing with them into the early hours of the morning – 'a most agreable little party'.³ Ayrshire contacts had helped him plan his journey, loaned him a 'pownie' to ride, and had briefed Edinburgh friends about the bard's imminent arrival.⁴ Immediately he was a celebrity. Within a week he met Dugald Stewart, the literary authority Hugh Blair, and Blair's younger assistant teacher of *belles-lettres*, the Reverend William Greenfield, whom Burns found warmer, more quick-witted. The Ayrshire poet

also met his favourite novelist, 'Author of The man of feeling', Henry Mackenzie, a lawyer in his early forties.[5] Mackenzie was impressed. Encouraged by Stewart, he began reviewing Burns for his genteel periodical, *The Lounger*: 'Mr Burns', a 'Heaven-taught ploughman', exemplified '*Original Genius*'. Mackenzie was well intentioned, but, Anglicised in his polite upper-class tastes, not quite on Burns's vernacular wavelength: 'Even in Scotland, the provincial dialect which Ramsay and he have used, is now read with a difficulty which greatly damps the pleasure of the reader.'

Ignoring the vernacular energy of his work, Mackenzie still admired this 'rustic bard' so perceptive about 'men and manners'. The lawyer-novelist had been talking to people who knew Burns's Ayrshire 'grief and misfortunes'. Pointing out that Burns 'has been obliged to form the resolution of leaving his native land, to seek under a West Indian clime that shelter and support which Scotland has denied him', Mackenzie hoped Burns would now find sustaining native 'patronage'.[6]

By the time Mackenzie's words appeared in the 9 December *Lounger*, Burns was well and truly patronised. 'An unknown hand,' he told Ballantine, 'left ten guineas for the Ayrshire Bard.'[7] The donor turned out to be Patrick Miller, brother of the Lord Justice Clerk whose house at Barskimming was close to Mauchline. Well off, inventive, and with an enthusiasm for improvement, Miller had a taste for artistic sponsorship; a few years earlier he had lent the Edinburgh artist Alexander Nasmyth £500 to travel to Italy and 'complete his artistic training'.[8] Miller now invited Burns for 'a glass of claret', the start of a lasting association.[9] Having shown Burns's poems to Robert Anderson, Edinburgh jeweller Andrew Bruce from James Boswell's estate at Auchinleck was only one among 'over a score of persons of Ayrshire origin' who befriended the bard in the capital.[10] Of the members of Edinburgh's nobility who first met the poet, several had Ayrshire connections. Some were carefully tipped off by Burns's supporters. Others were stung perhaps by that letter in 13 November's *Edinburgh Evening Courant* which sniped that though 'The county of Ayr is perhaps superior to any in Scotland in the number of its Peers, Nabobs, and wealthy Commoners, . . . not one of them has upon this occasion stepped forth as a patron to this man'. Now potential patrons with Ayrshire links were among those keenest to meet the bard in the capital.[11]

The spirited Duchess of Gordon, whose sister had married Sir

Thomas Wallace, estranged son of Burns's new admirer Mrs Dunlop, 'kindly and generously Patronized' the new arrival. Ayrshire laird James Dalrymple of Orangefield became 'what Solomon emphatically calls, "a Friend that sticketh closer than a Brother"'.[12] One of Ayr's extensive Dalrymple clan, James had helped Burns arrange his journey. On 7 December Dalrymple introduced Burns to the Masonic brothers of Edinburgh's Canongate Kilwinning Lodge No. 2; its members included Henry Erskine, who was Dean of the Faculty of Advocates, Patrick Miller, Classics teacher William Nicol, and an attorney called Alexander Cunningham. All would play significant parts in Burns's future.

Dalrymple had already introduced the poet to his brother-in-law, James Cunningham, fourteenth Earl of Glencairn. Among other things, the Earl was patron of Kilmarnock parish kirk. His West of Scotland factor, Alexander Dalzel, 'a poetical and convivial man', may have been a friend of Robert Fergusson, was 'Burns's most intimate friend', and seems to have got to know Burns in Kilmarnock; Dalzel is thought to have drawn his employer's attention to Burns's book, and possessed 'many of his poems and letters'.[13] The Dowager Countess of Glencairn, daughter of an Ayr carpenter and musician, was eager to meet Mr Burns. She introduced him to her daughter, Lady Betty. The Earl of Glencairn, until lately one of the Representative Scots Peers in the House of Lords, now became a principal patron.

Less than ten days after his arrival in Edinburgh Burns's Ayrshire-connected friends there, several with Masonic handshakes, had made such a fuss of him he could hardly take it in. He wrote to Gavin Hamilton,

I am in a fair way of becoming as eminent as Thomas a Kempis or John Bunyan; and you may expect henceforth to see my birthday inserted among the wonderful events, in the Poor Robin's and Aberdeen Almanacks, along with the black Monday, & the battle of Bothwel bridge. – My Lord Glencairn & the Dean of Faculty, Mr H. Erskine, have taken me under their wing; and by all probability I shall soon be the tenth Worthy, and the eighth Wise Man, of the world. Through my Lord's influence it is inserted in the records of the Caledonian Hunt, that they universally, one & all, subscribe for the 2d Edition. – My subscription bills come out tomorrow, and you shall [*sic*] some of them next Post. –[14]

Glencairn had suggested to the Caledonian Hunt, a club of rural gentry who organised sporting and social events, that they might support the Scottish bard by subscribing to his work. In this the Earl was seconded by fellow Hunt member, Burns's Ayrshire Freemason correspondent Sir John Whitefoord (after whose family Burns's favourite Mauchline inn was named). Like the musician the Honourable Andrew Erskine, Sir John seems to have been alerted to Burns's arrival in the capital by Mauchline's Dr Mackenzie, a mutual friend. Whitefoord was one of the first people to whom Burns had written on reaching Edinburgh.

This letter, mixing flattery with asserted independence, was typical of Burns's courting of patrons. He dealt with them on his own terms. Denying knowledge of etiquette, he writes in formal, high-register English, protesting his 'letter is not the manoeuvre of the needy, sharping author, fastening on those in upper life who honour him with a little notice'. Yet that is pretty much what it was. Burns was worried that in some circles at least gossip was circulating about his 'morals' and those recent 'unfortunate, unhappy' experiences Henry Mackenzie among others had got wind of. He thanks Whitefoord for defending him against hostile rumours, remarking on bards' need for protection, but also on his ability to stand up for himself.

> ... there must be, in the heart of every bard of Nature's making, a certain modest sensibility, mixed with a kind of pride, that will ever keep him out of the way of those windfalls of fortune, which frequently light on hardy impudence and foot-licking servility. It is not easy to imagine a more helpless state than his, whose poetic fancy unfits him for the world, and whose character as a scholar gives him some pretensions to the *politesse* of life – yet is as poor as I am.
>
> For my part, I thank Heaven, my star has been kinder; learning never elevated my ideas above the peasant's shed, and I have an independent fortune at the plough-tail.[15]

Pondering the situation of a 'bard . . . whose poetic fancy unfits him for the world', at the back of Burns's mind was his favourite and Edinburgh's laureate, Robert Fergusson. Thinking about how poets might find a place in society, and about patronage or lack of it, Burns in Edinburgh wrote several poems on Fergusson:

CURSE on ungrateful man, that can be pleas'd,
And yet can starve the author of the pleasure!

O thou, my elder brother in Misfortune,
By far my elder Brother in the muse,
With tears I pity thy unhappy fate!
Why is the Bard unfitted for the world,
Yet has so keen a relish of its Pleasures?[16]

Burns was now living in Fergusson's hard-drinking city of brothels, philosophical enlightenment, notorious sanitation and, in the Old Town, overcrowded, smelly tenements up to ten storeys high. He was invited to some of the elegant salons of Edinburgh's great and good, but returned each night to the cramped quarters of a legal clerk just like Fergusson. Before leaving Mossgiel Burns had arranged to share lodgings with his friend Richmond, who had come to clerk for Edinburgh lawyer William Wilson. A year after leaving Mauchline, Richmond was renting a room down Baxter's Close. This dark alley branched off the Royal Mile which, since medieval times, had been the Old Town's mile-long east–west axis. Downhill from what Burns called the 'rough, rude Fortress' of the Castle on its dark, precipitous crags of 'rugged rock', 'marked with many a seamy scar', the Royal Mile ran eastwards past what the poet, so recently admonished in Mauchline parish kirk, would have known as the Reverend Professor Hugh Blair's grand kirk of St Giles. Beside St Giles were the buildings of the old Scottish Parliament, abolished when 1707 brought political union with England and a new, British Parliament in London. At the Royal Mile's east end stood Holyrood Abbey, beside the ancient 'royal home', Holyrood Palace – empty in Burns's time, its Stuart 'royal Name low in the dust'.[17] Holyrood's royal court moved south to London when Scotland's Stuart King James VI, son of Mary, Queen of Scots, succeeded England's Queen Elizabeth in 1603. Enlightenment Edinburgh was a cultural hot spot, but, in terms of political power, it was an ex-capital.

You can still walk along the Royal Mile, seeing many sights Burns saw, including the Castle, St Giles and Holyrood. Now, though, the word 'Holyrood' tends to refer to Scotland's striking modern parliament building, opened in the twenty-first century. Edinburgh and a democratic Scotland have found fresh political confidence. Robert Fergusson gives the sharpest sense of the city

he and eighteenth-century cronies called 'Auld Reikie' – old smoky – the mêlée that was Burns's new world. From 'servant lasses' who at daybreak 'Early begin their lies and clashes', and 'barefoot house-maids' sniffing 'morning smells', to glowering traders, lawyers tossing their wigs in the air, and streetwise 'cadies' or errand-boys running past chair-men carrying better-off citizens in portable long-handled chairs, Fergusson in the decade before Burns arrived celebrated in the Scots tongue the traditional Old Town of 'damn'd whores and rogues'.

Eighteenth-century Edinburgh came to be celebrated throughout the Western world as a centre of philosophy, medicine, literature, history and learning. Even Voltaire presented one of his plays as if written by an enlightened Edinburgh minister. In Fergusson's poetry, though, men stagger from 'joyous tavern, reeling drunk', or lie 'In pools or gutters aftimes sunk'. With its 'stink, instead of perfumes', its 'gormandizing', 'Mirth, music' and port wine, through Fergusson's crowded cityscape 'debtors daily run' to seek sanctuary from jail and 'mony a hungry writer ... Dives down at night' along with 'naked poets' to buy 'thread-bare' second-hand clothes in dark alleys. This was still the Old Town Burns knew. Yet, begun in Fergusson's day, the regular, neoclassical, polite 'new city', the 'bonny' New Town down the hill north of what is now Princes Street Gardens, was growing rapidly by Burns's arrival. In 1786–7 the 'elegant buildings' of Charlotte Square were 'yet unfinished', as were the ballroom, tea-room and card room of the Assembly Halls in George Street – 'some of the completest rooms perhaps in Europe' – but thousands of workmen were constructing a 'spacious ... beautifully paved' new world. Fergusson's most substantial Edinburgh poem begins with the Scots words 'Auld Reikie'; its last line nods to more genteelly Latinate 'Edina'.[18]

Sharing digs with Richmond, Burns lived very much in Auld Reikie. Baxter's Close (near Lady Stair's Close which now houses Edinburgh's Writers' Museum) is long gone, but Mrs Carfrae, Burns's landlady, lives for ever in her lodger's description. 'A hale, well-kept Widow of forty five', she upped the rent soon after his arrival. 'A flesh-disciplining, godly Matron', her demeanour 'staid, sober, piously-disposed, sculduddery-abhoring', she told Burns she was sometimes dubious if he were even 'a rough an' roun' Christian'. Edinburgh's Old Town tenement-dwellers were socially stratified: the lower classes lived low down, middle classes above them, nobility on top. Deep

down this Old Town scale, Burns and Richmond in their wood-panelled first-floor room had a low, badly plastered ceiling. Immediately above it several rowdy young 'Daughters of Belial' – Mrs Carfrae's phrase – stayed up late, partying. Burns and Richmond heard everything: 'when they are eating, when they are drinking, when they are singing, when they are &c.' Mrs Carfrae lectured Burns: '"We should not be uneasy and envious because the Wicked enjoy the good things of this life; for these base jades who, in her own words, lie up gandygoing with their filfthy [*sic*] fellows, drinking the best of wines, and singing abominable songs, they shall one day lie in hell, weeping and wailing and gnashing their teeth over a cup of God's wrath!"'[19]

By the time he recorded her harangue, Burns had decided to remain under Mrs Carfrae's low ceiling, rather than heading for Jamaica. He was beginning to enjoy Edinburgh. Sometimes, though, it was a difficult place for strangers. Even a polished Cambridge graduate, three years younger than Burns when he arrived the following year, thought 'The deportment of the higher classes ... stiff and reserved ... they profess to keep up their dignity, by holding it necessary that strangers must be properly introduced to their families, particularly their daughters.' While this young man found 'The women ... in general handsome till they approach twenty, when much of their beauty vanishes, as they become large and masculine', Burns was prepared to take a more generous view of Edinburgh beauties.[20] At first, though, he was simply dazed by the flurry around him. It took him some time, for instance, to contact Dr Blacklock, though eventually he paid several visits. Keen to keep in touch with his Ayrshire supporters, he sent news to Hamilton and Mackenzie in Mauchline (enclosing *The Lounger*); to Ballantine and Aiken in Ayr; and to Robert Muir in Kilmarnock. Presumably he also wrote to his family, but these letters have not survived. Initially Burns felt ill, perhaps hungover 'with a miserable head-ach & stomach complaint'.[21] Excited, he was also nervous.

Edinburgh often accepted him on his own terms. In the second week of January 1787 the poet who had hoped in 'The Cotter's Saturday Night' that 'the *Patriot-Bard*' might be an ornament to Scotland found himself subject of a toast at a meeting of Edinburgh's Masonic lodges where recently elected Grand Master Francis Charteris invited the brethren to drink to 'Caledonia, & Caledonia's

Bard, brother B[urns]'. 'Repeated acclamations' ensued. Burns had not expected any of this. He felt 'downright thunderstruck'. 'Trembling in every nerve', he uttered a short speech of thanks.[22]

Already he was well advanced in preparing a much enlarged second edition of his poems. Within a fortnight of arriving he felt this was in the bag. Years earlier, the Earl of Glencairn had had as his travelling tutor former Edinburgh University medical student and printer William Creech. Freemason, minor poet and essayist, Creech was now an ambitious bookseller and printer, his shop a centre of Edinburgh literary life. Apparently Glencairn put Burns in touch with Creech, adding a publisher to that already impressive list of 'avowed Patrons & Patronesses'. On Wednesday, 13 December Burns wrote excitedly to Ballantine in Ayr, enclosing *The Lounger*: 'I am nearly agreed with Creech to print my book; and, I suppose, I will begin on monday. – I will send a subscription bill or two next post . . . If any of my friends write me, my direction is Care of Mr Creech Bookseller.'[23]

Glencairn was now Burns's 'guardian angel'. The Earl sent 'a parcel of subscription bills' to noble friends, soliciting interest 'in behalf of the Scotch Bard's Subscription'. He issued 'downright orders' to get these bills 'filled up with all the first Scottish names about Court'.[24] If Burns's strongest early supporters were almost all Ayrshire-connected, now the implication was that to subscribe to his new book would be a Scottish patriotic act. Burns could hardly believe his luck. 'Thy Sons, *Edina*, social, kind,/ With open arms the Stranger hail,' he wrote in his December 'Address to Edinburgh'.[25]

Edina's daughters caught his eye too. '"Fair B———"' in the 'Address to Edinburgh', he explained to William Chalmers back in Ayr, 'is the heavenly Miss Burnet, daughter to Lord Monboddo, at whose house I have had the honor to be more than once. – There has not been any thing nearly like her, in all the combinations of Beauty, Grace, and Goodness the great Creator has formed, since Milton's Eve on the first day of her existence. –'[26] A full-length portrait of the slim, elegant, dark-haired Elizabeth Burnet was painted by Alexander Nasmyth in the late 1780s; she poses a little languidly with a book in her hand.[27] In the metropolis, Burns was sometimes awe-struck. Edinburgh's 'honor'd shade' had 'Wealth . . . Trade . . . Architecture' and 'Learning'. Just weeks before he had been wandering 'on the banks of *Ayr*'. Now, trying his hardest to be

bardic about his nation's capital, he sent Glencairn's sister a formal English-language poem, exclaiming,

> EDINA! *Scotia's* darling seat!
> All hail thy palaces and tow'rs . . .[28]

This sounds unthinkingly high-falutin. One of Burns's Mauchline cronies might have joked that '*Scotia's* darling seat' meant the arse of Scotland. Burns struggled to connect his home world with this new world of Edinburgh, his celebrity status with his old self. On 20 December he sent a book from 'Robt Burns the Scotch Bard to his own friend & his Father's friend, John Tennant in Glenconner' back in Ayrshire.[29] Translated from French, *Letters concerning the Religion Essential to Man* expounded rather deistical arguments. Emphasising integrity and sincerity, it contended that some of Christ's 'maxims seem to be too rigorous . . . not only in forbidding men the sweetest satisfactions of life, but likewise in loading them with real punishments'.[30] However well meant, this was not exactly a book Burns's father would have smiled on.

To Willie Chalmers Burns tried to demonstrate he had not lost his sense of humour; Edinburgh was as full of 'wild beasts' as the Book of Revelation.[31] Trying to communicate to friends back home what life in Edinburgh was like for him, he also attempted to make new friends understand his Ayrshire background. He showed Greenfield, the belletrist, two Ayrshire songs, 'the works of Bards such as I lately was'. Burns wanted to preserve his integrity: 'I have long studied myself, and I think I know pretty exactly what ground I occcupy, both as a Man, & a Poet.' But at times, a ploughman who could quote *Hamlet*, he felt exhibited as a curiosity: 'to be dragged forth, with all my imperfections on my head, to the full glare of learned and polite observation, is what, I am afraid, I shall have bitter reason to repent. —'[32]

Eighteenth-century metropolitan taste liked to gawp at the exotic in its midst. In London fashionable folk had been captivated by the polite but primitive Tahitian, Omai; Robert Heron, who met Burns in Edinburgh, hinted the Ayrshire bard was similarly placed.[33] Thanking *Edinburgh Magazine* editor James Sibbald for his support, Burns quoted Othello when that tragic African explains his remote and supposedly 'primitive' background to the nobility and senators of Venice. In Edinburgh Burns viewed himself in Othello-like terms

more than once.[34] Fêted, patronised, encouraged, gawped at, for all he played up to titled backers, he was sure his new-found status was transitory, and said so to friends back in Ayrshire. To Greenfield (who led his own double life as a secretly homosexual kirk minister at a polite New Town church) he wrote 'in the Confessor style', quoting Shenstone and mixing ironic self-knowledge with melodrama:

'When proud Fortune's ebbing tide recedes' – you may bear me witness, when my buble [*sic*] of fame was at the highest, I stood, unintoxicated, with the inebriating cup in my hand, looking forward, with rueful resolve, to the hastening time when the stroke of envious Calumny, with all the eagerness of vengeful triumph, should dash it to the ground. –[35]

Meanwhile, he was checking how far political sentiments expressed in Ayrshire might be permissible in the capital. Stating he had 'a few first principles in Religion and Politics which, I believe, I would not easily part with', he sent his 'political ballad' on the American War and its consequences to the radical-minded lawyer Henry Erskine, and to Lord Glencairn, asking whether he should publish it in his second edition.[36] They were relaxed enough to let him go ahead. To his first edition's contents he added newer poems like 'The Brigs of Ayr' and 'Address to Edinburgh', but also older works like 'Address to the Unco Guid, or the Rigidly Righteous' which it might have been unwise to publish in Kilmarnock. In too went 'Epistle to Davie, a Brother Poet' and additional stanzas to 'The Vision' paying tribute to the Wallaces, the Lord Justice Clerk, and other figures and places associated with Ayrshire patrons. In all, where the Kilmarnock edition had run to 240 pages, this new edition filled nearly 350.

The best new poem Burns added was 'To a Haggis'. Perhaps composed in Mauchline for a 'Haggis Club' harvest supper in 1785 (as John Richmond claimed), the poem was certainly ready in time for 19 December's *Caledonian Mercury* – a 'taster' for his second edition, Burns had probably recited it at an Edinburgh feast.[37] A pudding of oatmeal, liver, beef, onions, and suet, all sewn inside a 'bag' made from a sheep's stomach and boiled for up to two hours, haggis was regarded as a rare treat in Scotland and parts of England. Along with 'A gude sheep's head', Fergusson had made it an emblem of Scottish cuisine. Listing foods appropriate

for Scots to feed to the often Scotophobic English man of letters Samuel Johnson, Fergusson had begun his menu, '*Imprimis*, then, a haggis fat'.[38] Burns, who uses the lawyerly phrase '*Imprimis*, then' in his 1786 verses for Robert Aiken, 'The Inventory', knew Fergusson's poem, but took his celebration of haggis to vertiginous new heights.

Burns's haggis is 'honest' and 'sonsie' (attractively good-natured), two of his highest terms of praise. It is too, in its odd way, a celebrity, but accorded a mock-heroic title: 'Great Chieftan o' the Puddin-race!' Presented as a '*grace*', a prayer of thanks before a meal, this poem celebrates the absurd strength both of the haggis – 'Your hurdies [buttocks] like a distant hill,/ Your *pin* [skewer] wad help to mend a mill' – and of the 'Rustic-labour', the strong Scottish countryman who slices its 'gushing entrails' to reveal 'a glorious sight,/ Warm-reekin, rich!' Mocking the sophisticated palate of the skinny 'Poor devil' whose genteel taste might prefer 'French *ragout*' and take a 'scornfu' view' of food like haggis, the poem praises manly strength not of metropolitan sophisticates but of the 'Rustic, *haggis-fed*,/ The trembling earth resounds his tread'. Praying to 'Ye Pow'rs wha mak mankind your care', this grace before meat ends with patriotic mention of 'Auld Scotland', suggesting 'if ye wish her gratefu' pray'r,/ Gie her a *Haggis*!'[39]

In giving sophisticates of polite Edinburgh the gushing entrails of his rustic haggis, Burns made fun of his celebrity among them. He also asserted in vernacular Standard Habbie the vigour of the rural Scots tradition he came from. His poem echoes Fergusson, Hamilton of Gilbertfield's *Wallace*, and other Scots works. It may sound bardic, but is also bardie. It skirls, but winks as well. Intricately mixed irony and vaunting hint how Burns the villager of genius dealt with the patronising adulation of 'The town . . . agog with the ploughman poet'. Observers thought he would be 'spoiled', but he was not, even if the *Evening Courant*'s editor worried that 'Burns assumes the great man'.[40] Keeping his 'rustic appearance', the poet coped with the metropolis, without becoming metropolitan.[41] At first sight he seems far removed from most English-speakers today, but he and his work are reminders that there is more life than the society of the city. From another angle, his strategies of coping and engaging with metropolitan culture as an incomer while asserting and in sophisticated ways maintaining the culture he came from make him a precursor not just of modern

writers from Seamus Heaney to Toni Morrison but of most people in today's world.

The man Edinburgh's polite classes were agog to see dressed plainly, like a farmer, but a farmer of note. Just under 'five feet ten inches in height', he was well built, swarthy, his 'well-raised forehead shaded with black curling hair'.[42] He wore 'a dark-coloured coat, light-figured waistcoat, shirt with ruffles at the breast, and boots, in which he constantly visited and walked about the Town'. In an age when urbane urban gentlemen customarily wore shoes to polite assemblies, Burns's countryman's boots made their own clear statement. He stood in them 'in no way disconcerted' in the drawing-room of David Ramsay, printer of the *Edinburgh Courant*, who held a dinner party for the bard where 'a large company of ladies and gentlemen assembled to see him'. Burns 'wore his hair, which was black and thin, in a queue, without powder,' and struck onlookers as having a 'person' which, 'though neither robust nor elegant, was manly and pleasing . . . his countenance, though dark and coarse, uncommonly expressive and interesting'. This was the bard on show. 'He recited his own beautiful Songs very readily, and with peculiar animation and feeling, though he affected to be ignorant of the principles of music.' Some thought his conversation 'even more fascinating than his poetry'. Speaking vehemently, he could sound 'powerful, ardent, and irritable'; polite ears were sometimes perturbed by his strong 'political, and religious' opinions. At times he might 'not condescend to practise the graces and respectful attentions required in the conversation of polite persons'. He could seem resentful, but also 'decent, dignified' and 'unassuming'.[43]

'Keep fast hold of your rural simplicity and purity,' wrote the Reverend Lawrie from Ayrshire in December 1786.[44] Sometimes Burns found it hard to strike the right balance. Proudly he wrote to his generous new patron Glencairn, 'I trust I have a heart as independant as your Lordship's, than which I can say nothing more; and I would not be beholden to favours that would crucify my feelings.' Yet at the same time he tells Glencairn he would like 'a Picture or Profile of your Lordship' and asks if he can publish a new poem praising the Earl: 'Bright as a cloudless Summer-sun,/ With stately port he moves'.[45] Sensibly, the Earl said no.

It was difficult for Burns to deal with the nobility other than with dismissive scorn or else what emerged as sycophancy. If this sounds

odd, it remains the case that many instinctively democratic Scottish people today feel and behave similarly towards titled people or royalty. Shrewdly, Glencairn was able to give Burns the kinds of help required, without clashing with the poet's determined need to preserve inner egalitarian independence. Burns was fed up with a society where titles and 'trappings' were taken as seriously as 'genius'. He struggled to understand how Glencairn could pay courteous attention to anyone, however titled, whom Burns regarded as a 'dunderpate'. Yet the bard knew he owed Glencairn a debt. He wrote in his private commonplace book, 'I shall love him untill my dying day!'[46]

Though he missed her sexually, and told Hamilton he felt 'a miserable blank in my heart, with want of her', Burns in Edinburgh felt independent of Jean Armour. While it has been speculated that the blank-hearted poet made a brief visit to Ayrshire at the very end of December 1786, it is clear that on 6 January 1787, drinking claret in Leith, he danced, and sang with several of the family of 'a very pretty girl, a Lothian farmer's daughter, whom I have almost persuaded to accompany me to the west country, should I ever decide to settle there'.[47] Keeping amorous and other options open, Burns had been discussing for some time with several supporters the possibility of joining the Excise service.

Captivating him with her piano-playing, his new love knew he had an unhappy romantic past; Burns told her he had felt 'widowed these many months', and had 'a kind of wayward wish' to spend ten minutes with her alone.[48] She may have been Margaret Chalmers, a 'lively', hazel-eyed farmer's daughter who later told poet Thomas Campbell that Burns had proposed to her some time before her marriage in 1788 and she turned him down.[49] Burns was also keen to take to the theatre piano-playing Christina Lawrie, daughter of his Ayrshire encourager the Reverend George. He told her father approvingly that Henry Mackenzie had spoken of Christina as having '"a great deal of the elegan[ce of a] well-bred Lady about her, with all the sw[eet simpli]city of a Country girl"'.[50] Burns would have found this combination appealing. Edinburgh ladies thought him 'strong and coarse' but with 'a most enthusiastic heart of love'; some men suspected, although he said no word 'offensive to decency in the company of ladies', 'His morality with regard to women was lax'.[51] Famous for partying (and, once in her youth, riding a pig along part of the Royal Mile), the Duchess of Gordon was a leading

socialite in her early forties. She 'kindly & generously Patronised' Burns.[52] He mentions in a February 1787 letter that cupid and he had been sadly at odds, though 'a certain Edin[bu]r[gh] Belle' had caught his eye.[53] His taste for flirtation flourished.

More lasting, though largely epistolary, was his regular contact with Frances Dunlop of Dunlop near Stewarton in Ayrshire. This spirited woman had recently lost her husband and ancestral estate; discovering Burns's poetry gave her a new interest, helping her overcome depression. She had generously sent his poems to 'one of the cleverest men in Britain', her London literary friend the Stirling-born, Glasgow-educated surgeon Dr John Moore, well-connected relation of novelist Tobias Smollett. Burns knew of and respected Moore as 'author of *The View of Society and Manners*'. He realised Mrs Dunlop, thirty years his senior, was no fool, and valued her as a patroness. She feared in Edinburgh 'will be lost the Rural Bard produced in Ayrshire'; he was determined this would not happen, telling her, 'I have studied myself, and know what ground I occupy'.[54] For all her aristocratic connections, she had a shrewd sense Burns's strength ran counter to the showiness of imperial wealth manifested by Ayrshire 'nabobs'. She worried 'Where Indian gold and English manners reign,/ Wallace might fight and Burns may write in vain.' He wanted to prove her wrong. Fussy, sometimes prissy, spirited, affectionate, and quick-witted, at the start of January 1787 Frances Dunlop was already suggesting to Burns how she might find him subscribers in India. By February she told him he was 'the best Bard ever adorned my country'.[55] She had never met him. She was old enough to be his mother; sometimes she wrote as if she *was* his mother. But her friendship was heartfelt. Proud to be from a Wallace family which had provided subject-matter 'for the bards and historians of Scotland', she sent him her poem 'To Robert Burns': 'To you, kind Bard, my warmest thanks I send,/ My country's poet and her saviour's friend.'[56] That comes as close as anything to what Burns wanted to be. 'By far my highest pride,' he replied, is 'the appelation of, a Scotch bard.'[57]

In Edinburgh Burns cultivated this appellation and image. There, as in Ayrshire, he saw and heard ambitious people in polite society attempting to adopt Anglicised tones. Trained by Murdoch, he could speak and write such language too, but valued native vernacular more than did men like Hugh Blair. Burns asserted to Dr Moore in London, 'my first ambition was, and still my strongest wish is, to

please my Compeers, the rustic Inmates of the Hamlet, while ever-changing language and manners will allow me to be relished and understood'.[58] Relishing work by Scottish poets in English like Thomson and James Beattie, in Edinburgh he upheld the vernacular tradition he valued – sometimes using formal English to do so.

Realising the remains of his favourite Scottish poet lay in an unmarked grave in Canongate Kirkyard off the Royal Mile, Burns wrote to local officials, paying tribute to Fergusson and asserting the importance of the figure of the Scottish bard. Fergusson was a 'justly celebrated Poet, a man whose talents for ages to come will do honor, to our Caledonian name'. Burns petitioned to erect a tombstone in Fergusson's memory so 'Lovers of Scottish Song' might come 'to shed a tear over the "Narrow house" of the Bard who is no more'.[59] Deploying Ossianic, bardic language, he offered to pay for a tombstone, and wrote formal verse for the inscription on it, quoting Gray's 'Elegy'. You can still see the inscribed tombstone on the left near the entry to the churchyard, outside which is a twenty-first-century bronze statue of Fergusson striding purposefully away from his grave. More revealing, though, is a poem Burns did not publish:

> ILL-FATED Genius! Heaven-taught Fergusson,
>   What heart that feels and will not yield a tear,
> To think Life's sun did set e'er well begun
>   To shed its influence on thy bright career.
>
> O why should truest Worth and Genius pine
>   Beneath the iron grasp of Want and Woe,
> While titled knaves and idiot-greatness shine
>   In all the splendour Fortune can bestow?[60]

These lines show some of Burns's frustration at the class system of 'titled knaves', but also how closely he saw Fergusson as his bardic precursor, 'POET' of 'SCOTIA'.[61] Mackenzie in his *Lounger* review had called Burns a 'Heaven-taught ploughman'; applying the same adjective to Fergusson, Burns expresses deep kinship.

Actually, Fergusson like many other Scottish poets had been taught at St Andrews University, but Burns means something else. He identified with 'heaven-taught' Fergusson's energetic, at times manic talent, with his humour, depression, sheer giftedness, and, not least,

his vernacular championing of Scottish values. Fergusson had died in Edinburgh aged twenty-four. In a poem of early 1787, 'Elegy on the Death of Robert Ruisseaux' (Ruisseaux is French for 'Burns' but also puns on Rousseau's surname), Burns imagines in Standard Habbie how he himself may be spoken of when he 'lies in his last lair'; he wants to be remembered as a poet of vernacular energy, 'bred to kintra wark [country work]', who could fight back 'wi' a rhyme or song' against poverty, hunger, fear and care.[62] Championing Fergusson, he defended the kind of poet he was and wanted to be. It was a sincere tribute to the earlier Robert, but also a manifesto-like commitment as the time approached for the Edinburgh publication of his own *Poems, Chiefly in the Scottish Dialect*. Burns's 'erecting a stone to the memory of Fergus[s]on' caught the imagination of Leith-born teenager John Armstrong whose poem about it regrets Fergusson's lack of prudence but sees Burns as Fergusson's honoured successor, hoping the Ayrshireman would be a 'more happy bard'.[63]

A friend of Fergusson who observed Burns closely at this time was sure 'He was not so much elated by the distinction he obtained in Edinburgh as might be expected. He knew that it would be transient, and he neglected not the means of turning it to his advantage.'[64] When this observer, man of letters Robert Anderson, privately pointed out to Burns that his poetry often imitated earlier verse, the poet readily agreed, saying it was 'part of the machinery, as he called it, of his poetical character to pass for an illiterate ploughman who wrote from pure inspiration'. So, though he might reply to a well-connected lady that he was a man from 'barn' and 'pleugh' who 'for poor auld Scotland's sake/ Some useful plan, or book could make,/ Or sing a sang at least', the Ayrshire bard could also reveal his more bookish side. Admiring him as extraordinary, Anderson realised that as literary artist and sometimes calculating projector of his bardic 'poetical character', Robert was cannily effective. He 'even admitted the advantages he enjoyed in poetical composition from the *copia verborum*, the command of phraseology, which the knowledge and use of the English and Scottish dialects afforded him; but in company he did not suffer his pretensions to pure inspiration to be challenged, and it was seldom done where it might be supposed to affect the success of the subscription for his *Poems* . . .'[65]

Burns wanted his second edition to succeed, but had no intention of staying in Edinburgh. He knew success might allow him to

return to his own countryside on a much surer footing. Just days after Burns's arrival, Sir John Whitefoord had suggested that instead of contemplating a career in the Excise, he should think about using money from subscriptions to stock a farm. By mid-January Burns was accepting Patrick Miller's offer of a farm to rent: 'now, when by the appearances of my second edition of my book, I may reckon on a middling farming capital, there is nothing I wish for more than to resume the Plough'. But he would go back as bard, not simply farmer. Wined and dined in Edinburgh, he knew he wanted a 'sequester'd romantic spot' for farming, with 'a spare hour now and then to write out an idle rhyme'.[66]

So when an eccentric patriot, the Earl of Buchan, sent a 'bombast epistle' with all sorts of high-toned 'advices', Burns replied on 7 February with a clear sense of plans both to enhance his position as Scotland's bard but also to take him back to the kind of community he came from: 'I wish for nothing more than to make a leisurely Pilgrimage through my native country; to sit and muse on those once hard-contended fields where Caledonia, rejoicing, saw her bloody lion borne through broken ranks to victory and fame; and catching the inspiration, to pour the deathless Names in Song . . .' But, he added equally fulsomely, 'I must return to my rustic station, and, in my wonted way, woo my rustic Muse at the Ploughtail.'[67] Lionised at Edinburgh literary parties, presenting himself as bard of 'old Scotia', and preparing his second edition, he took careful stock of his situation and knew he would soon be leaving.[68]

Meanwhile, repeatedly fêted, at the house of philosopher and historian Professor Adam Ferguson he met scientists James Hutton and William Black along with John Home, playwright of *Douglas*, and sixteen-year-old Walter Scott. Hutton had developed a view of the whole earth as a living organism. Years later Burns would make poetry from such geological speculations, fusing them with his own sense of human vulnerability and passion in one of his greatest love songs, 'A red red Rose', in which he imagines a time when 'seas gang dry' and 'rocks melt wi' the sun'.[69] During his first Edinburgh winter, though, when 'Every one was earnest to have the honour of subscribing for his book' and 'At every table his company was courted', Burns felt elated yet susceptible to disaster.[70] Not just Fergusson's fate might trigger his sense of ruin. The most 'remarkable' thing Scott recalled of his sole encounter with Burns was the poet in a crowded room weeping at a print by Henry William

Bunbury showing a soldier lying dead in the snow beside his widow, a child in her arms. Beneath this picture of ruin Burns read lines about 'the sad presage of his future years,/ The child of misery baptised in tears'.[71] Ruin-haunted, he still was, and wanted to be seen as, a 'man of feeling'; in April he wrote that Mackenzie's *Man of Feeling* 'rouses all the god in man'.[72] He shed, and treasured, public tears.

To Scott, a highly educated New Town lawyer's son, Burns's manners were 'rustic, not clownish'; he had the 'sort of dignified plainness and simplicity' of 'a very sagacious country farmer of the old Scotch school, *i.e.* none of your modern agriculturists, who keep labourers for their drudgery, but the *douce gudeman* who held his own plough'. Seeing in Burns another version of the 'Heaven-taught ploughman', Scott discerned more too. 'There was a strong expression of sense and shrewdness in all his lineaments; the eye alone, I think, indicated the poetical character and temperament. It was large, and of a dark cast, which glowed (I say literally *glowed*) when he spoke with feeling or interest.' Scott recalled that Burns, talking of Ramsay and Fergusson 'with too much humility as his models', was then 'much caressed in Edinburgh, but (considering what literary emoluments have been since his day) the efforts made for his relief were extremely trifling'.

For the young Scott, Burns's 'conversation expressed perfect self-confidence, without the slightest presumption. Among the men who were the most learned of their time and country, he expressed himself with perfect firmness, but without the least intrusive forwardness; and when he differed in opinion, he did not hesitate to express it firmly, yet at the same time with modesty . . . his dress corresponded with his manner. He was like a farmer dressed in his best to dine with the Laird . . . his address to females was extremely deferential, and always with a turn either to the pathetic or humorous, which engaged their attention particularly.'[73] Apparently deferential, even if he had to make occasional concessions or evasions Burns maintained the democratic stance of what he later called 'the man of independent mind'. Such an egalitarian style of address would characterise his best poetry and, becoming an international ideal, confirm him as that ideal's bard.

Excitement about Burns spread far and wide. On 2 March 1787 Matthew Campbell wrote from Wigtown in south-west Scotland to his merchant correspondent Robert Agnew at Bordeaux, mentioning

the plans of 'Burns, the Airshire poet' for publishing a second edition.[74] That same month one of Burns's most sophisticated correspondents regaled him with anecdotes of 'poor Fergusson', and, through knowing quotation, teasingly insinuated that Burns in Edinburgh was not just a literary but also a sexual star of the sort invoked in one of his favourite, laddishly bawdy poems, 'The Plenipotentiary', where exotic stranger becomes scandalous metropolitan celebrity:

> When his name was announc'd how the women all bounc'd,
>   And their blood hurried up in their faces;
> He made them all itch, from the nave to the breech,
>   And their bubbies burst out all their laces . . .[75]

Polite in public, privately Burns damned 'the pedant, frigid soul of Criticism' he found among some of Edinburgh's 'Literati'.[76] Professor William Robertson remarked 'he had never met with a man who discovered, in conversation greater energy of mind, than *Burns*', and elderly Professor Blair pronounced himself 'a great friend to Mr Burn's Poems'. But making suggestions about the second edition, Blair told the bard 'Love and Liberty' was 'too licentious' and 'altogether unfit' for publication.[77] Burns dropped that poem, but ignored several other counsels from Blair whom he thought prone to pomposity. For all the professor's championing of 'fine writing', to Burns he was 'meerly an astonishing proof what industry and application can do'.[78]

Meeting with Blair, but lodging with Mauchline's John Richmond, Burns wanted to keep in touch with people he had known before this 'new world' of Edinburgh. On 19 March 1787 he inscribed in a copy of Fergusson's poems lines about the fate of 'the Bard unfitted for the world', giving the book to Edinburgh's young poetess Rebekah Carmichael who had a liking for a 'lovely youthful bard', imitated Burns in her 'The Twa Dows', and is said to have asked the poet out.[79] Burns wrote warmly to his 'D[ea]r old friend' James Candlish on 21 March, assuring him that he still felt just the same as when they were boys together.[80] Next day he had almost finished correcting his new edition's proofs, and was already planning departure – not just on leisurely bardic 'pilgrimages through Caledonia', but also, he told Mrs Dunlop, 'to return to my old acquaintance, the plough . . . being bred to labor secures me independance'. He was proud

to be 'the Bard', he told her, but as for 'the trappings and luxuries of upper stations, I have seen a little of them in Edinburgh – I can live without them. –'[81]

Quoting Fergusson, Burns told Ballantine he would soon be appearing in Edinburgh '*in guid black prent*', and revealed he had sat for an engraving Edinburgh's John Beugo was preparing as frontispiece for the new edition: so 'I will appear in my book looking, like other fools, to my title page.'[82] Burns's exact contemporary, Beugo had a taste for older poetry in Scots, as well as for Ossian; a serious artist and poet who became Scotland's leading engraver, he and Burns eventually attended French lessons together. Enhanced by Burns's sittings, Beugo's engraving was done after a portrait by Edinburgh artist Alexander Nasmyth whose company Burns greatly enjoyed. It portrays the bard confidently relaxed at the centre of a breezy rural landscape, a hint of mountain and castle beyond. In its oval frame, this head-and-shoulders frontispiece has Robert wearing pale cravat and striped waistcoat under a dark topcoat. 'A head of a bard' Burns called it in a Jacobite-inclined poem that May.[83] The bard has long dark sideburns and a slightly receding hairline.

Born in 1758, Nasmyth, like Burns, was a Freemason interested in Ossian, landscape and people. Unlike Burns, Nasmyth came from a family of Edinburgh architects. Even though as a young artist he had been supported by the largesse of Patrick Miller, in Scotland's capital Nasmyth was an insider. His portrait is one of the most significant interpretations of Burns created during the poet's lifetime. From the older Edinburgh artist Allan Ramsay (son of the poet) Nasmyth took the classic device of framing his subject's head and shoulders within a dark-bordered oval painted on the rectangular canvas. As Ramsay and earlier painters had sometimes done, Nasmyth turned this oval into a window, with a discernible sill. Where conventionally portrait subjects were viewed through the window as if an outsider were looking at the head and shoulders of a person inside a room, unusually in his portrait of Burns (now in the Scottish National Portrait Gallery) Nasmyth reverses this convention. He presents the poet as if *outside* the imaginary room, at one with a picturesque landscape. This accords with Nasmyth's later description of Burns as 'The Much admired Poet of Nature and of Scotland'.[84] The 1787 portrait also situates Burns as an outsider viewed by a social insider: it is the viewer who stands inside the

room, and the brilliantly lit poet who is seen outside. This is how Edinburgh viewed Burns.

Nasmyth, whose son recalled him as a political radical who became inclined towards 'liberality in the system of government', developed a lifelong admiration for Burns and his verse. After the poet's death he made pictures of Alloway and other landscapes associated with Burns, and in 1827 he was 'commissioned by Robert Chambers' to paint a full-length portrait of Burns as a record of the poet's appearance.[85] Lockhart wrote in 1828 that

> Mr Nasmyth also prepared, for Constable's Miscellany, a sketch of the Poet at full-length, as he appeared in Edinburgh in the first hey-day of his reputation; dressed in tight jockey boots, and very tight buckskin breeches, according to the fashion of the day, and (Jacobite as he was) in what was considered as the Fox-livery, viz., a blue coat and buff waistcoat, with broad blue stripes. The surviving friends of Burns who have seen this vignette, are unanimous in pronouncing it to furnish a very lively representation of the bard as he first attracted public notice on the streets of Edinburgh.[86]

In Nasmyth's worked-up, full-length portrait (also now in the Scottish National Portrait Gallery) the poet in his prosperous farmer's hat (which looks to modern eyes very like a cowboy hat), riding boots and striped waistcoat, stands, arms crossed, in an outfit which proclaims his confidently non-metropolitan stance. Yet the coat is brown, not blue, and if the Tory Lockhart (who had never met Burns) saw it as 'Fox-livery' denoting sympathy with the liberal Whig statesman Charles James Fox, then Robert Anderson (who met Burns soon after the bard's arrival in Edinburgh) recalled him as 'a tory, an idolator of monarchy', adhering not to Fox but to the Tory William Pitt 'and the King'. If this sounds unlike the Burns of many of the poems, it suggests the poet was careful, even guileful, in how he presented himself to Edinburgh society. Still, like so many others, Anderson remembered Burns's Jacobitism and was aware of reports about the later 'progress of his sentiments from Jacobitism to Republicanism'. He also recalled how 'Such was his nationality that I could not shake his sentiments respecting the degradation of the imperial dignity of Scotland by the Union.'[87]

Excited about his forthcoming book, the stylishly dressed Burns longed for pleasures beyond those of the drawing-room. On 9 April

he found a new 'Confidante': a commonplace book in which he pledged among other things to record his 'amours'. He did not keep this pledge, but clearly was thinking about 'the sacred tie of Love', and feeling lonely. In the notebook (now sometimes called his Second Commonplace Book) he quotes from Pope's hothouse poem of doomed epistolary romance, 'Eloisa to Abelard'. The lines copied in on 9 April about 'the connection between two persons of different sex . . . "When thought meets thought ere from the lips it part,/ And each warm wish springs mutual from the heart"' suggest Burns was eager to find in Edinburgh an excited soul-mate.[88] It would be later in the year that he would conduct his own hothouse, largely epistolary Edinburgh romance. For the moment, he found another kind of sexual satisfaction.

Probably on 'April 14 or fifteen' he had sex with a young Highland servant, who later found herself 'in trouble' and lost her job. James Mackay identified her as twenty-year-old Margaret Cameron from Fortingall in Perthshire. She wrote to Burns that summer, by which time she was lodging with a shoemaker off Edinburgh's Canongate; the bard sent her money.[89] Sleeping with this servant even as he charmed genteel ladies, Burns reinforced a pattern which would continue throughout the rest of his life. His strong sexual appetite led him to exploit women of his own class; if he felt trapped by assumptions about sexuality and class boundaries, he was not just one of the exploited. Though occasional suspicions arose about his conduct – his first, unreliable biographer wrote of Burns spending time 'in the brothel, on the lap of the woman of pleasure' – polite encouragers such as Blair seem to have known nothing about this side of his behaviour in Edinburgh, for all they sometimes urged him to prune indecencies from his verse.[90]

On Monday, 16 April William Woods, an English actor who had been friendly with Fergusson and subscribed to the new bard's second edition, declaimed in an Edinburgh theatre lines by Burns praising Scotland as land of philosophers, historians, authors,

> . . . an ancient nation fam'd afar,
> For genius, learning high, as great in war –
> Hail, CALEDONIA, name for ever dear![91]

Next day, dedicated to the Caledonian Hunt, Burns's Edinburgh edition was published by subscription. 'A *Scottish Bard, proud of*

the name, and whose highest ambition is to sing in his Country's service', Burns added four fulsome pages fleshing out the dedication to the Hunt's '*NOBLEMEN AND GENTLEMEN*'. '*The Poetic Genius of my Country found me as the prophetic bard Elijah did Elisha – at the plough.*' This elegant Old Testament flourish about Burns's '*wild, artless notes*' and his singing of '*the loves, the joys, the rural scenes and rural pleasures of my natal Soil, in my native tongue*' was dated 4 April, and was part of his poetical 'machinery'. His muse, he said, '*whispered me to come to this ancient metropolis of Caledonia*', but characteristically he also stated, '*I was bred to the Plough, and am independent*' – which probably functioned as a reminder to leave the ancient metropolis once his book had appeared. His later lawyerly biographer Lockhart complains that Burns's constant assertion of independence was ungentlemanly. That was part of Burns's point. Not born a gentleman, he vaunted his independence as an act of assertiveness in a society ill at ease with democracy.

Burns's book was printed for 'The Author' by the distinguished, tight-fisted William Creech. In effect Burns's publisher, Creech, after months of delay, eventually paid his new poet 100 guineas for the copyright. 'The most prominent bookseller in late eighteenth-century Edinburgh', Creech was used to working with celebrated Edinburgh authors like Mackenzie, Blair and Stewart.[92] Burns thought him 'strange' and 'multiform', very vain, with a businessman's eye for his own interest.[93] Drawn up in the legal hand of Henry Mackenzie, Burns's memorandum of agreement with Creech is dated 17–23 April 1787.[94] Holding 'a *levée* in his house till twelve every day, attended by literary men and printers', Creech saw other clients at his shop in the afternoon.[95] Burns's typesetter was William Smellie, co-founder of the *Encyclopaedia Britannica*, yet another Freemason who became his close friend; throughout March Robert had spent long spells in Smellie's composing room, sitting on a favourite stool, checking his proofs page by page before the metal type was disassembled to print other sheets. Smellie's son Alexander read Burns's poems aloud while Burns in his farmer's boots and buckskin breeches listened and searched for errors. Sometimes, Smellie's son later recalled, Burns disconcerted the typesetters by walking up and down 'cracking a whip which he carried' – another of his farmer's accoutrements.[96] His subscription list had grown so long that halfway through typesetting it was decided not enough copies had been printed. The

printers, having disassembled their type, had to re-set the first part of the volume all over again. Hurry led to one famous error in the address 'To a Haggis': the word 'skinking' (watery), correct in the first batch of sheets, erroneously became 'stinking' in the second.

With 334 pages of poetry prefaced by its grand list of subscribers, the new edition ran to three thousand copies. Among poems Burns had added were the vigorous, slyly modulated vernacular 'Address to the Unco Guid' and 'Death and Dr Hornbook', as well as the formal 'Address to Edinburgh'. He kept his original title, its *Chiefly in the Scottish Dialect* allying him with Ramsay and Fergusson, rather than *'Belles Lettres'* culture. He had subscribers (mostly Scottish) from London to Madrid. Prominent were Edinburgh's great and good – from the Principal of the University to Lord Braxfield who had once ruled in favour of Burns's father. Adam Smith, who left Scotland to visit London two days before the edition appeared, subscribed for four copies; though Mrs Dunlop tried to bring them together, Smith and the poet seem never to have met. Copies of the *Poems* were ordered for Catholic Scots Colleges at Valladolid, Douay and Paris as well as the Scots Benedictine Monastery at Ratisbon. Subscribers ranged from an Oxford student ('Mr Simson, Gentleman Commoner, St John's') to the Mauchline draper Burns's old friend James Smith (two copies) and a Leith ship's carpenter, John Syme. The subscription list's composition confirms what was true of Burns in person and remains true of his work today: it will speak to anyone prepared to listen, regardless of class, culture or situation.

Not surprisingly, several subscribers were from the West of Scotland, but 'Mr P. Ballantyne, Jamaica' and 'John Erskine, Esq; Jamaica' ensured that even if Burns himself did not reach that new world, his poems did. If London's *Lyric Repository* thought the book showed that *'every poetical collection must, in a degree, be imperfect'*, reviews were generally laudatory.[97] On 5 July 1787 Cadell published a first London edition. Pirated editions in Belfast, Dublin, Philadelphia and New York followed soon afterwards, with individual poems immediately picked up for reprint in anthologies and magazines from London's *Cabinet of Genius* to Hamburg's *English Lyceum*. Often editors selected Burns's formal English works rather than more sparky vernacular poems, but one thing was certain: success.

Burns's poems have never been out of print. No English writers of note subscribed to the Edinburgh edition, but in England his

impact on the Romantic movement would be profound. In different ways as a vernacular bard he was an exemplar for Wordsworth (who read the *Poems* as a 1787 schoolboy), then for Keats, Clare and other English poets. Regarded as coarse by Oxonian Matthew Arnold, later the bard seemed peripheral to many elite twentieth-century modernists preoccupied with metropolitan culture. Still, even Ezra Pound and T. S. Eliot imitated him for fun, while in modernist Scotland Hugh MacDiarmid fused Burns's work with Nietzschean aesthetics. In our time ecological concerns make Burns the farmer poet, the villager able to find a global audience, much more culturally compelling. In his lifetime and long after, however, America made Burns its own. Soon after appearing, many of his poems were reprinted in American newspapers. In the later eighteenth and in the nineteenth century Burns became America's bard. Walt Whitman, setting himself up as a nineteenth-century democratic national poet, wrote with anxiety and perceptiveness about Burns's example. Burns mattered to farmer-poet Robert Frost, and you can still see statues of the Scottish poet in public parks from New York to California.

In 1787 Edinburgh and beyond, talk of Burns, Burns's poems, extracts, and reviews of his work were everywhere: 'The whole literary world was taken by surprise, and even the fashionable circles caught the contagion,' remembered one author, then in his twenties.[98] Stebbing Shaw, the first English writer to view Ayrshire in terms of Burns's 'genius of originality and fancy', explored 'many a wild, romantic grove' on the River Ayr that summer of 1787, quoting from Burns's new book, and sure 'the elegant little ode, on turning down a mountain daisy with his plough, may rival the most inspired bard'.[99] Even if that year some like Burns's future biographer James Currie thought 'Burns ought to have kept clear from politics, and we may add religion', the bard's admirers were everywhere.[100] Details of his life became public property, sometimes in distorted form. In London the *Catalogue of Five Hundred Celebrated Authors* proclaimed: 'Mr Burns was upon the point of embarking for America, when he was prevented from executing his intention by a letter, exciting him to the further pursuit of his literary career, by Dr Blacklock.'[101]

In Edinburgh Burns was sometimes taken aback by his celebrity status. A thief, he told a friend, even stole some of his correspondence, including a letter to Ayrshire in which he 'had taken to pieces r[igh]t Honorables, Honorables, and Reverends not a few'.[102] Occasionally

under pressure of adulation and advice he simply had to let off steam: 'I sometimes find it necessary to claim the priviledge of thinking for myself.'[103] Preparing to leave Edinburgh, he put it more strongly: 'I am determined to flatter no created being, either in prose or verse, so help me God. – I set as little by kings, lords, clergy, critics, &c. as all these respectable Gentry do by my Bardship.'[104] Though he had flattered many people, he liked thinking of himself as a rebel. Bishop John Geddes, who got on well with Burns when they twice met for supper at Lord Monboddo's, thought him 'a great Genius . . . but, I think, he will not be easily advised'.[105] To Mrs Dunlop Burns hinted he was 'resolved to study the sentiments of a very respectable Personage, Milton's Satan'.[106] Later Romantic poets, including Burns's admirer the Calvinist-educated libertine Byron, would take it for granted rebellion was bound up with art; with Burns this was more a private thought than part of his public image.

That image was in demand. Several portraits of the bard were painted during his first Edinburgh visit. The first, by coach-painter and sign-writer Peter Taylor, is now in Scotland's National Portrait Gallery; Taylor's widow remembered Burns 'attached himself' to Taylor in an Edinburgh gathering, both men being full of 'good heart' and 'good humour'. Taylor invited Burns to breakfast next day and began to paint him.[107] Burns readily befriended artists. Nasmyth, commissioned by Creech to paint the portrait Beugo engraved for the *Poems*, became a walking companion. The fêted darling of fashionable Edinburgh, Burns liked nothing better than strolling out of the city.

Early one spring morning he called on Dugald Stewart and they walked to what was then the village of Braid Hills. Burns enjoyed Stewart's egalitarianism. The philosopher valued someone not for their title but, Burns explained to Mrs Dunlop, 'merely as they *act their parts*'.[108] Stewart remembered his walk with the bard:

> he charmed me still more by his private conversation, than he had ever done in company. He was passionately fond of the beauties of nature; and I recollect once he told me, when I was admiring a distant prospect in one of our morning walks, that the sight of so many smoking cottages gave a pleasure to his mind, which none could understand who had not witnessed like himself, the happiness and the worth which they contained . . .[109]

Recalled in the early nineteenth century, this may sound pious, but it indicates how much Burns in Edinburgh still regarded himself as essentially a villager. He was given improving books by the metropolitan elite (Dr Gregory of the University presented him with *Cicero's Select Orations, translated into English* on 23 April), but he missed the vernacular life of the village.[110]

Over forty years later Alexander Nasmyth remembered with delight going for a walk with 'my Friend' Burns in late spring or early summer. In one version of Nasmyth's treasured story the walk started after an all-night session in a pub; in another it began with Burns making an early morning call at Nasmyth's house. In any event the two men set out around 5 a.m. on a beautiful day, heading south from Edinburgh to the 'Romantic Spot' of Roslin, a favourite landscape subject of the painter, but a new destination for the poet. They hiked 'down the Rocky and well-wooded banks of the Esk' which had inspired Allan Ramsay in his pastoral play *The Gentle Shepherd*, and took in dramatic views of Roslin Castle, whose 'romantic ruins' had given its name to a popular Scottish song of rural love published in the first volume of the *Scots Musical Museum,*

> From Roslin Castle's echoing walls
> Resound my shepherd's ardent calls;
> My Colin bids me come away,
> And love demands I should obey.[111]

Burns had written a song of farewell to Ayrshire to the tune 'Roslin Castle' when he thought he was off to Jamaica in 1786. For him as for others like Beugo and Nasmyth the site was rich in personal as well as historical associations.

Roslin's ancient chapel, today known to millions thanks to *The Da Vinci Code*, overlooks the wooded glen. It is a splendidly odd building, appearing, as modern Edinburgh-born novelist Candia McWilliam puts it, as if it has been 'cooked at different temperatures over much time'.[112] The chapel's remarkable stone carvings and architecture were bound up with traditions linking its foundation by the St Clair family to the history of Freemasonry. When Burns's antiquarian friend Francis Grose went there soon after Burns's visit he remarked that the chapel's roof had been repaired; vulnerable, Roslin Chapel was already renowned. Burns may or may not have

gained admission. He and Nasmyth spent several hours scrambling along the riverbanks, the poet sitting with a book in the sunshine, the artist sketching him in pencil. In the sketch it is Burns who looks like an artist – in tune with nature, if a little formally so; a bard with a notebook in the Scottish sunshine.[113] They dined at the local inn – tea, eggs and some whisky. Happily, quick-wittedly, Burns scribbled on the lower part of the bill verses he initialled for the landlady, Mrs Wilson:

> My blessings on ye, honest wife,
>   I ne'er was here before;
> Ye've wealth o' gear for spoon and knife –
>   Heart could not wish for more.

> Heav'n keep you clear o' sturt and strife,   *trouble*
>   Till far ayont fourscore,
> And by the Lord o' death and life,
>   I'll ne'er gae by your door![114]

From Roslin Burns and Nasmyth walked to Hawthornden, its castle once home and rural retreat to Renaissance poet William Drummond (Fergusson's 'wyliest an' best o' men'), then on to the villages of Lasswade and Dalkeith before returning to Edinburgh for supper at Nasmyth's house with his young wife and Creech.[115] This enjoyable day-trip is emblematic of four longer tours Burns made in 1787. They took him in congenial company through Scotland's countryside to see new vistas and people; visiting sites with literary and historical associations, they resulted in occasional poems, good food, and not infrequently (as in that dinner with Creech) meetings with literary or business contacts too. Burns's new world was not just Edinburgh; it also extended to parts of Scotland he had heard or read about but never before seen for himself.

In town, though, he often sought out pleasures he knew from Mauchline. His printer William Smellie, to whom a grateful bard presented a bound copy of his second edition, was a brilliant and unkempt forty-seven-year-old polymath whose hair Burns once described as 'thatch'd'.[116] Smellie enrolled his younger friend in the all-male club he had founded, the Crochallan Fencibles. Several members of this mock-regiment were fellow Masons. To 'Philosophic Smellie' Burns wrote letters so full of bawdiness they were later

destroyed by the printer's embarrassed family.[117] In an age of some-times rollicking, Fergussonian men's clubs, the Fencibles met in a pub not far from St Giles, down dark, narrow Anchor Close which still runs between tenements on the Old Town's High Street. The thin landlord, Daniel 'Dawney' Douglas, sang on occasion 'an old Gaelic song called Crochallan', or more properly '*Crodh Chailean*' (Colin's Cattle) in which a girl praises her hunter-lover's cattle, which turn out to be mountain deer – Burns would later write in a song how 'My heart's in the Highlands a chasing the deer.'[118]. Individual members of the Fencibles had military nicknames like '*depute-hangman* to the corps'. Their 'major and muster-master-general', in charge of initiating new recruits, was lawyer Charles Hay, a famous drinker in a hard-drinking age. The Fencibles liked clever 'rough banter' and mock-trials. The author of Mauchline's 'Court of Equity' felt at home among such 'harum-scarum Sons of Imagination and Whim' and collected for their entertainment verses as risqué as he could find or invent.[119]

The Fencibles' 'Colonel' was a lawyer and Freemason with literary tastes, William Dunbar. About to leave Edinburgh, Burns gave Dunbar some 'tatter'd rhymes' around the end of April. Admitting 'my numerous Edin[bu]r[gh] friendships are of so tender a construction that they will not bear carriage with me', Burns thought his alliance with Dunbar 'of a more robust constitution'.[120] Through Dunbar he met a poor, self-taught enthusiast for Scottish music. James Johnson was then about to publish the first volume of a projected anthology of the music and words of all the tradi-tional Scots songs: *The Scots Musical Museum*. As soon as he encountered Johnson, Burns liked him a lot: there were 'few whose sentiments are so congenial to my own'. He sent the anthologist a song the day before leaving 'this venerable, respectable, hospitable, social, convivial, imperial Queen of cities, AULD REEKIE'.[121] Burns also addressed formal farewells to Blair, Mackenzie, Glencairn and others. Next morning, a Saturday, he rose before six and was gone.

He now embarked on a very bardic activity. A generation earlier James Macpherson, 'discoverer' of Ossian, had been encouraged by Hugh Blair to travel round the Highlands collecting works by that ancient bard who had celebrated Scottish heroes. Portraying himself to Mrs Dunlop as proud to be 'a Scotch Bard', Burns told her he wished to make 'leisurely pilgrimages through Caledonia; to sit on

the fields of her battles; to wander on the romantic banks of her rivers; and to muse by the stately tower or venerable ruins, once the honored abodes of her heroes'.[122] This has a certain Ossianic dying fall to it. The ageing Blair, writing a little patronisingly to Burns just as Robert set out on his travels, implies this new bard is as important a 'discovery' as old Ossian:

> The Success you have met with I do not think was beyond your merits; and if I have had any small hand in contributing to it, it gives me great pleasure. I know no way in which literary persons who are advanced in years can do more service to the World than in forwarding the efforts of rising genius, or bringing forth unknown merit from obscurity. I was the first person who brought out to the Notice of the World the Poems of Ossian, first by the *Fragments of Antient Poetry* which I published, & afterwards by my setting on foot the undertaking for collecting and Publishing the Works of Ossian; and I have always considered this as a *meritorious* Action of my Life.[123]

Part of Burns's establishing himself as bard was bound up with an urge to be a poet of his whole country: to re-collect Scotland as a literary nation. His travels were at one with that aspiration. In summer and autumn 1787 he embarked on a series of tours in Scotland and (briefly) northern England. Scotland was his true focus – East and West, Highland and Lowland; where Ossian was associated with northern mountains, Burns as 'Caledonia's bard' wished to see and sing a variety of different Scotlands. In a crude sense he was simply putting himself about, meeting subscribers, Masonic contacts and other admirers; but he also wrote about some of what he saw – almost never the urban Scotland of Britain's growing industrial revolution but an independent-minded village-nation, a Scotland alive most in its songs. Flush with money from his second edition, he toured, observed, made poems, gathered material. It was a mixture of pilgrimage, publicity tour, and holiday. As spring came he wanted to escape Edinburgh for a while at least, spending time in the countryside in congenial company. This would also allow him to reconnoitre the Dumfriesshire farm Patrick Miller was offering to lease him.

He bought a new mare. On 'Jenny Geddes', named after a famously spirited Presbyterian Scotswoman said to have flung a stool at a cleric, he set out with a new pal. Laddish twenty-one-year-old Edinburgh law student and Freemason Robert Ainslie soon became

his close confidant. Though Ainslie later grew pious, he harboured substantial literary ambitions, would be remembered as 'imbued with great love for letters', and would be valued as 'particularly endeared to his friends by the benevolence of his heart, the easy frankness of his manners, the vivacity of his conversation, and his apparently exhaustless fund of anecdote'.[124] Ainslie and Burns got on well as the two headed for Ainslie's family home, Berrywell near Duns in Berwickshire, on 6 May. With Ainslie's father Burns talked farming, natural philosophy and politics, then went to church with the family in Duns. He kept a notebook of the whole trip, perhaps intending to write it up, but never did. This tour was the first of 'a few pilgrimages over some of the classic ground of Caledonia, *Cowden Knowes, Banks of Yarrow, Tweed*, &c.'; his journal reveals a taste for 'enchanting views and prospects', antiquities and ruins like Roxburgh Castle, Jedburgh and its Abbey, Dryburgh Abbey and Melrose.[125] For the first time ever, at Coldstream bridge, he 'went over to England'.[126] Scots people interested him most, not least young women eager to show him 'fairy scenes' like 'Love-lane' by the River Jed. There, strolling with a party including twenty-three-year-old Jedburgh doctor's daughter Isabella Lindsay ('engaging', but also engaged and about to emigrate to Russia), Burns 'somehow' managed to

> get hold of Miss Lindsay's arm – my heart thawed into melting pleasure after being so long frozen up in the Greenland bay of Indifference amid the noise and nonsense of Edinr. – Miss seems very well pleased with my Bardship's distinguishing her, and after some slight qualms which I could easily mark, she sets the titter round at defiance, and kindly allows me to keep my hold; and when parted by the ceremony of my introduction to Mr Somerville she met me half to resume my [hold (*deleted*)] situation –

Burns was 'afraid my bosom still nearly as much tinder as ever'.[127] He relished the fact. He encouraged it.

Burns toured, among other places, Innerleithen, Traquair, Berwick, and Eyemouth where he and Ainslie were received into the Masonic lodge and the bard took 'a sail after dinner'.[128] They visited sites famous from Border ballads and Scottish songs, including bawdy ones. Sometimes Robert was merry, sometimes grave and dispirited. After a day riding in rain he felt 'jaded to death' in Selkirk on

13 May, but wrote a lively Standard Habbie poem to Creech, then in London in connection with the edition of Burns's poems about to be published there.[129] Burns imagined sadness in Edinburgh when 'Willie's awa'', and sketched his own excursions: 'Up wimpling, stately Tweed I've sped,/ And Eden scenes on chrystal Jed.' Sometimes Burns and others grew high on his celebrity. After fantasising privately about Ainslie's nineteen-year-old sister ('I could grasp her with rapture on a bed of straw'), he was 'taken extremely ill with strong feverish symptoms' and recorded how 'embittering Remorse scares my fancy at the gloomy forebodings of death'.[130] This sudden bout passed, and the bard progressed south to Alnwick, arranging for his *Poems* to be sent to Rachel Ainslie. He next crossed northern England through Hexham to Carlisle.

There on 1 June 1787 Burns wrote his only surviving letter in Scots. It went to his friend William Nicol, an 'honest-hearted' working-class man from rural south-west Scotland who had become a sometimes angry Classics master at Edinburgh High School. Burns described riding Jenny Geddes, a mare 'as poor's a Sangmaker and as hard's a kirk', and apologised for not sending a longer letter, boasting he had got so drunk he could barely walk: 'sae notouriously bitchify'd ... I can hardly stoiter'.[131] Partly this was a rhetorical flourish; carefully transacting business by post throughout his trip, he soberly corresponded with booksellers about sales. Having separated from his 'cher Compagnon de voyage', Ainslie, who had to go back to his employer's law office in Edinburgh, Burns told him about escaping a young woman who had 'vexed, disgusted' and 'enraged' the bard by attempting to parade him as her sweetheart.[132]

In Dumfries, where Burns was awarded the freedom of the burgh, news reached him that the Highland servant he had slept with in Edinburgh, Margaret Cameron, was pregnant. Lodging with Edinburgh shoemaker James Hog, she had written asking for help, and Burns had become subject of a writ. At the back of his tour notebook, heading a list of addresses and things to do, Burns jotted Hog's name and address, then sent an embarrassed letter to Ainslie, begging his assistance:

> Please call at the Jas Hog mentioned, and send for the wench and give her ten or twelve shillings, but don't for Heaven's sake meddle with her as a *Piece*. – I insist on this, on your honor; and advise

her out to some country friends. – You may perhaps not like the business, but I tax your friendship thus far. – Call immediately, [for God (*deleted*)] or at least as soon as it is dark, for God sake, lest the poor soul be starving. – Ask her for a letter I wrote her just now, by way of token. – it is unsigned. – Write me after the meeting. –[133]

If James Shaw in the early nineteenth century and James Mackay in the late twentieth are right in their genealogical research, Margaret Cameron married a Highland cattle-drover about a year later, and there is no evidence she gave birth to a living child by Robert Burns.[134]

In early June Burns progressed to beautiful Dalswinton and looked over the farm Patrick Miller was offering him to rent. He liked the area and people, but thought farming prospects there 'slender'.[135] Back in Mauchline, he saw Elizabeth Paton and his daughter by her, visited the family of his friend James Smith, and caught up with Gavin Hamilton. Paton seems never to have tried to get Burns to marry her, but now he was famous and apparently well-off, Jean Armour's family were eager to know him; remembering their earlier attitude, he was disgusted by their total change of mind and 'servile compliance'.[136] Mauchline after his triumphs in Edinburgh was not what he had hoped. Success had to some extent alienated him from local people. Returned home, he was unsettled by the way his 'plebeian brethren' who 'perhaps formerly eyed me askance', now treated him as they might a visiting dignitary, with 'damn'd servility'.[137] Feeling isolated, he carried around a pocket edition of Milton, 'in order to study the sentiments – the dauntless magnanimity; the intrepid, unyielding, independance; the desperate daring, and noble defiance of hardship, in that great Personage, Satan'.[138] One other thing he did was make love to Jean Armour; though there is no evidence of this in his letters at the time, there would be evidence nine months later.

Though he soon treated his mother and sisters to silk for fine new clothes, it is not quite clear how his family received him; on his first night back in Mauchline he slept at the Whitefoord Arms, not at Mossgiel. His old friend Sillar later published a pastoral poem one of whose shepherds has taken 'a trip tae Enbrugh Town' and is now so successful a poet 'he forgets his frien's an' former state'.[139] Burns may have seemed a rich celebrity; privately he was unsure

where to settle. Bardic travels were an enjoyable way to procrastinate. From Mauchline he wrote to James Smith, now in Linlithgow,

> I cannot settle to my mind – Farming the only thing of which I know any thing, and Heaven above knows, but little do I understand even of that, I cannot, dare not risk on farms as they are. If I do not fix, I will go for Jamaica. Should I stay, in an unsettled state, at home, I would only dissipate my little fortune, and ruin what I intend shall compensate my little ones, for the stigma I have brought on their names.[140]

Later in June Burns set off on a West Highland tour taking in Argyll (where he complained about poor hospitality in Inveraray) and Loch Lomond; he adds a note of ironic realism to his evident enjoyment at being in Ossianically wild country 'where savage streams tumble over savage mountains, thinly overspread with savage flocks, which starvingly support as savage inhabitants'.[141] Thanks to contacts among subscribers and admirers, he found hospitality with the gentry. 'At a Highland gentleman's hospitable mansion' near Loch Lomond he danced to traditional Scots tunes, then drank until dawn when he bardically proposed a toast to the sunrise over Ben Lomond, repeating 'some rhyming nonsense, like Thomas a Rhymer's prophecies I suppose'.[142] Later, when he and two friends raced some Highlanders, Burns tumbled off his horse. He told a correspondent he had a new girlfriend – 'a fine figure, and elegant manners' – her identity a mystery.[143] On 29 June he was made an honorary burgess of the ancient settlement of Dumbarton on the Clyde's north bank, but by early July he was back at Mossgiel, still smarting from his riding accident, sore from 'bruises and wounds'.[144]

In Mauchline Burns wrote a lament for Ayrshire-born James Hunter Blair, who had become Edinburgh's Lord Provost but died in his mid-forties; the poem, he admitted, was 'mediocre', but well meant, striking several Ossianic notes.[145] The bard saw a good deal of Gavin Hamilton, but felt low, missing Edinburgh friends like Ainslie, the one person to whom he now felt able to 'talk nonsense'.[146] To Richmond (settled in Edinburgh for over eighteen months) he complained, 'Not one new thing under the sun has happened in Mauchline since you left it.'[147] Though in the new world of 'Edina' he had missed his village, coming home was not easy. He girned to Nicol about 'a lingering indisposition' and told Frances Dunlop he

was 'ailing'.[148] This sounds like a bout of his by now familiar occa-
sional depressive illness: 'lingering complaints originating as I take
it in the stomach' and a 'miserable fog of Ennui'.[149]

Burns took stock of his life by writing a long, autobiographical
letter to Mrs Dunlop's London Scottish friend Dr Moore with whom
he had been corresponding earlier in the year. Moore had sent Burns
his *View of Society and Manners in France, Switzerland and
Germany*; Robert had sent Moore and the doctor's poet friend Helen
Maria Williams copies of the Edinburgh edition of his *Poems*. Now,
writing to this sympathetic man of the world as 'the Scotch Bard',
he set out in extensive detail 'a history of MYSELF'. About six thou-
sand words long, Burns's letter reflected on his upbringing, and is
the fullest source of information about his childhood. Rich in humour,
it comes from a man who feels under an 'baneful Star'.[150] Saying
almost nothing of his time in Edinburgh, it presents all the forma-
tive experiences of his life as Ayrshire ones.

Switching at its conclusion from first to third person, this letter
shows Burns familiar with his own instability: 'That Fancy & Whim,
keen Sensibility and riotous Passions may still make him zig-zag in
his future path of life, is far from being improbable.'[151] Before he
had even posted the letter to Moore, Burns was off again – back to
Edinburgh, then away for a tour in the Highlands. At Mauchline
low spirits had been counterpointed by rushes of freewheeling
enthusiasm. He spoke eloquently at a Tarbolton Masonic meeting
on 25 July when Dugald Stewart and one of Burns's subscribers
from Glasgow, Dr George Grierson, were made honorary members
of his lodge. A few days later he wrote exultantly to Ainslie, whose
illegitimate child had just been born; Burns sent his friend poems
about sex, just before 'going to church'.[152]

Ayrshire was changing. Mining was on the increase, and that
August John Ballantine saw his dream of a new Ayr bridge advancing
towards fulfilment. An English visitor hailed this 'great instance of
public spirit', writing how 'The key-stone of the middle arch, on
which the whole depends, was just made secure as we arrived, which
occasioned an evening's jubilee of dancing, &c. amongst the artifi-
cers, as the undertaker was then relieved from the great anxiety,
occasioned the night before by the violence of rain and wind.' Later,
Burns's greatest long poem would feature a 'keystane' on a wild
night, but in 1787 the sort of progressive certainty exemplified by
the 'completely handsome' project of Ballantine's new bridge did

not correspond with Burns's state of mind. Like Ballantine he knew he was accomplishing the work he had dreamed of, but unlike his prosperous Ayr supporter, the bard, for all his love of home territory, avoided committing himself to a 'mercantile world' of improvement near Ayrshire's 'delightful capital'.[153]

Returning to Scotland's capital seemed more exciting, but once there Burns spent periods inside drinking alone, though there were also times when he socialised. Soon he was off in a chaise with his Latin-teaching literary drinking buddy Nicol on another Highland tour. Burns's own Latin hardly extended beyond a tag he relished – '*omnia vincit amor*' (love conquers all) – but he and Nicol shared other enthusiasms.[154] Departing on 25 August 1787, they first headed east. At Linlithgow Palace Burns, lover of the Stuarts, enjoyed seeing the room where 'beautiful injured Mary Queen of Scots was born'. Comparing 'the old Romish way' with the religious tradition he had been brought up in, he remarked in his journal,

> What a poor, pimping business is a Presbyterian place of worship, dirty, narrow and squalid, stuck in a corner of old Popish grandeur such as Linlithgow and, much more, Melrose! ceremony and show, if judiciously thrown in, absolutely necessary for the bulk of mankind, both in religious and civil matters.[155]

He crossed the 'grand canal' linking Clyde to Forth, one of Scotland's major industrial revolution projects, and wrote lines likening the Carron ironworks to 'hell', but historic sites and less 'improven' terrain stirred him more: he 'said a fervent prayer for old Caledonia over the hole in a blue whin-stone where Robert de Bruce fixed his royal Standard on the banks of Bannockburn'.[156] From Stirling Castle's ramparts he watched the sunset over the winding Forth. With a diamond stylus used for poetic graffiti he scratched on a Stirling inn window Jacobite verses bemoaning 'The injur'd STEWART-line' and calling Hanoverian royals 'An idiot race'.[157] Heading north, beyond Crieff he and Nicol passed sights like 'Ossian's grave' and, later, a 'hermitage', which exists to this day, 'on the Bran water, with a picture of Ossian'. This was bardic terrain, 'beautiful romantic' and with a 'wild grandeur'.[158] Burns was inspired to write a 'Lament' for a Highlander ruined by Culloden, and several poems about his 'savage journey' amid 'Th' incessant roar of headlong tumbling floods' where 'Poesy might wake her heaven taught

lyre'. 'Poet B**** . . . a Bard' with a capital 'B' ranged among 'heathy hills and ragged woods'.[159]

Such lines were received with immediate approval not just by Burns's hosts but also by tourists eager for bardic lore. On 29 August Burns left verses 'Written with a Pencil over the Chimney-piece, in the Parlour of the Inn at Kenmore, Taymouth'.[160] Days later, fresh from Ayrshire, English tourist Stebbing Shaw could hardly believe his luck,

> In the evening we rowed up the lake to see his lordship's romantic hermitage, and in our way called at the small Island, and saw the ruins of a once inhabited nunnery. Landed now on the opposite shore, we walked to the summit of this curious dell, where falls over a rocky precipice, amidst the hanging foliage, a considerable stream; descending towards the middle regions, we passed thro' an artificial cave to the supposed Hermits room, well feigned, and hung naturally with moss, roots, &c. From the window of this curious cell, another sweet fall of water is seen to dash over the opposite rock, near sixty feet, into a bason below, which adds greatly to the enchantment of this sequestered scene. But of this, and the whole landscape about Tamouth, I cannot give so good a description, as in a small poem found here two days before, written by R. Burns, the Ayrshire bard.[161]

Lightheaded with all this bardic excitement, Shaw quotes a text very close to the published version of Burns's poem beginning 'Admiring Nature in her wildest grace'. Elegant wildness appealed to eighteenth-century taste schooled on Ossian, but much better than Burns's formal landscape pieces were the songs he created, sometimes drawing on fragments of earlier material. At Aberfeldy he 'composed' on the spot 'The birks of Aberfeldey', taking a chorus from an older song about the birches of Aberdeenshire's Abergeldie.[162] The bard had an acquisitive ear.

At Inver inn in Perthshire Burns met the great local fiddler Neil Gow, 'a short, stout-built, honest highland figure, with his grayish hair shed on his honest social brow – an interesting face, marking strong sense, kind open-heartedness mixed with unmistrusting simplicity'.[163] The two men got on well. Burns made several songs to melodies by Gow, and wrote him a tribute, 'Amang the trees', celebrating Scottish music in 'Pibroch, Sang, Strathspey, or Reels'.[164] Hosts on this Highland tour ranged from relatives of Gavin Hamilton

to the Duchess of Atholl at Blair Atholl castle; but meeting artists in the folk tradition did most for Burns's work. As thanks for hospitality he liked to leave his aristocratic hosts verses: '[R]hyme is the coin with which a Poet pays his debts of honor or gratitude.' With people like Gow he was less 'musing bard' than respondent, sharing a practical, lively love of song.[165] He did, though, extend his influential contacts. At Blair Atholl he met Robert Graham of Fintry, recently appointed Commissioner of the Scottish Board of Excise, and later Burns's Excise patron.

Dining with novelist Henry Mackenzie's brother-in-law on the way, Burns and Nicol travelled on through Aviemore and Strathspey. Reaching Inverness on 4 September they viewed Loch Ness, the spectacular Falls of Foyers, and the disastrous Jacobite battle site at Culloden Moor, then headed for Gordon Castle at Fochabers, home of the Duke and Duchess of Gordon. Grand neoclassical wings added to the ancient tower of Gordon Castle had made it a great northern palace: with 'a front five hundred & fifty feet in length, of the finest polished stone work, and with battlements at the top of a lofty square tower in the center' it was a 'beautiful Edifice . . . in the middle of a fine lawn surrounded with wooded hills.'[166] Burns was welcomed warmly. It took some time for an invitation to be extended to Nicol, who had been left fulminating at the village inn and demanded they leave immediately. For Nicol, playing second fiddle to 'his Bardship' was becoming a strain; for Burns, who had originally looked forward to enjoying his 'good friend['s]' company, 'that obstinate Son of Latin Prose', disliked by many in Edinburgh as 'a most unprincipled savage' with a violent temper, was becoming a social liability.[167]

From Aberdeen where a phalanx of literary men had lined up to greet the bard, the two travellers headed south to Stonehaven and Montrose where Burns got on well with several of his paternal relations. Having let his cousin James know he was coming, he was struck not least by how 'John Caird', who had visited the family in Ayrshire after Burns's father's death, 'though born in the same year with our father, walks as vigourously as I can'; he enjoyed meeting a namesake in whom he probably saw something of himself: 'Robert Burnes, writer [i.e. lawyer] in Stonehaven, one of those who love fun, a gill, a punning joke, and have not a bad heart.' He liked the lawyer's wife too, 'a sweet hospitable body, without any affectation of what is called town breeding'.[168] Seeing this other Burnes family

made him reflect on his own circumstances; unusually, the day after returning to Edinburgh on 16 September, he sent a newsy letter to Gilbert. Burns said little of his journey through Perth and Fife: '[wa]rm as I was from Ossian's country where I had seen his very grave, what cared I for fisher-towns and fertile Carses?'[169] The bard was back from the mountains of the bard.

In Edinburgh he wrote to Patrick Miller, keeping his Dalswinton options open, that the 'journey through the Highlands was perfectly inspiring; and I hope I have laid in a good stock of new poetical ideas'.[170] He had been collecting songs and music too; in Inverness, for instance, he asked an old lady to write down 'a Gaelic song' tune he heard her singing – 'true old Highland'.[171] The poet had hoped to extract payments due from Creech; failing to do so, he set off on one further tour. His companion was twenty-two-year-old highly educated Edinburgh Ayrshireman James McKittrick Adair, a 'favourite' of Burns and a relation of Frances Dunlop.[172] They left on 4 October for Stirling, where Burns, worried his Jacobite lines on the inn window had attracted dangerous attention, smashed the glass. At Stirling they met Nicol who shared, Adair recalled, not just Burns's Jacobitism, wit and ready conversational ability but also his 'fondness for convivial society, and thoughtlessness of to-morrow'.[173] At Harvieston in Clackmannanshire Burns stayed again with Gavin Hamilton's relations. So did Adair, who fell in love with their daughter. Burns and Adair visited local beauty spots like precipitous Castle Campbell at the head of Dollar Glen. They also encountered an elderly Jacobite, Mrs Bruce. Claiming descent from the family of Robert the Bruce and possession of Bruce's helmet and two-handed sword, she graciously used the latter to confer knighthood on Burns and Adair.

It was probably during his stay for just over a week at Harvieston that Burns proposed to petite, hazel-eyed Margaret Chalmers. She turned him down. He wrote to her afterwards, 'My rhetoric seems quite to have lost its effect on the lovely half of mankind', but hoped her friendship would 'outlast the heavens and the earth'.[174] Almost a year later he assured her he had 'lived more of real life with you in eight days, than I can do with almost any body I meet with in eight years'; he 'could sit down and cry like a child' at the thought of never meeting her again.[175] Cultured, sophisticated, connected to Mauchline and to Edinburgh where she played and sang for blind Dr Blacklock, Margaret fascinated Burns, but knew her own mind.

Having resisted her bardic suitor, she married an Edinburgh banker the following year, and was concerned lest she be identifiable in 'poetic compliments' Burns paid her – probably in songs like 'My Peggy's Face'.[176] According to Robert Cromek, most of Burns's letters to Margaret were later burned.

Adair stayed on at Harvieston. Burns went to visit Sir William Murray and his wife Lady Augusta Mackenzie, a famous Jacobite's daughter, at Ochtertyre in Strathearn; then he called on John Ramsay, laird of another Ochtertyre in Menteith. John suggested the bard write a play to equal Ramsay's *Gentle Shepherd*, and perhaps also some 'Scottish Georgics'.[177] Burns usually resisted other people's suggestions about topics. He told Ramsay Edinburgh's learned men who had tried to get him to alter his work were like 'some spinsters in my country, who spin their thread so fine, that it is neither fit for weft nor woof'.[178] Yet he got on well enough with Ramsay, discussing plans to settle on a farm that would allow him time to write.

Returning to Edinburgh through Fife, Burns seemed cheerful. At Dunfermline he and Adair visited the ruined Abbey, now a Presbyterian place of worship. Ascending its pulpit, Burns directed at the supposed fornicator Adair (who had obligingly positioned himself on the stool of repentance) 'a ludicrous reproof and exhortation, parodied from that which had been delivered to himself in Ayrshire'. More solemnly, Burns 'knelt and kissed with sacred fervour' two broad flagstones reputedly marking the grave of Robert the Bruce, then cursed 'the worse than Gothic neglect of the first of Scottish heroes'.[179] A suitable gesture for a bard anxious about national resurgence.

Burns's excursions had a business angle: he visited subscribers. But more than that his 1787 travels furthered his interest in Lowland oral culture as well as Ossianically refracted Highland lore; the tours helped him assemble different Scotlands, nourishing him as 'Caledonia's bard'. Meeting sympathetic people, he made no secret that 'He was collecting on his tour the "auld Scots sangs," he had not before heard of, and likewise the tunes, that he may get them set to music.'[180] In Aberdeen he had been delighted to meet the son of the author of the song 'Tullochgorum', John Skinner. To Skinner as 'brother' in the quasi-Masonic 'craft of song-making' Burns wrote soon after, 'I have often wished, and will certainly endeavour, to form a kind of common acquaintance among all the genuine sons

of Caledonian song.'[181] Though he could not convene all the people involved, Burns tried the next-best thing, throwing his energies into making a great anthology of the poetry and song he had loved since childhood. Though the idea was not solely Burns's, he pursued it with passionate skill. This great literary project would dominate the rest of his life.

Before leaving Edinburgh in the summer he had realised it might be a possibility. Now, having collected and refashioned additional songs on his tours, he knew he could make it happen. He told Skinner about James Johnson:

> An Engraver in this town has set about collecting and publishing all the Scotch Songs, with the Music, that can be found. Songs in the English language, if by Scotchmen, are admitted; but the Music must all be Scotch. Drs Beattie and Blacklock are lending a hand, and the first musician in town presides over that department. I have been absolutely crazed about it, collecting old stanzas, and every information remaining, respecting their origin, authors, &c. This last is but a very fragmentary business . . .[182]

Where the Ossianic project had begun with *Fragments of Ancient Poetry*, then led to the internationally important literary task of collecting and reshaping supposedly ancient Highland Scottish bardic materials – and where Ramsay and others had collected largely Lowland Scots songs for smaller anthologies – here the new bard would follow. Collecting 'fragmentary' stanzas, bits of information and music, then bringing all together with a quickened sense of artistic purpose, Burns mixed delight with a sense of duty to his nation's vernacular culture. He would produce a bardic collection that would articulate and quicken the values of the Scottish people, pleasing future generations in Scotland and beyond. He did not immediately characterise the scheme in these terms, but that is what it became. The bard in his new world collected and made new the vernacular culture of his old. It was a cultural project with lasting political overtones. Though much of the verse was traditional, at the head of the second volume of Johnson's anthology appears Burns's modern song celebrating the victory of the American revolutionaries, 'When Guilford good': the power of Scots song could be harnessed in the present, and might even articulate the future.

Sympathetic to the 'honest Scotch enthusiasm' of Johnson who was collecting 'all our native Songs' for his large, six-volume anthology with music, Burns became an eager contributor. The first volume of Johnson's *Scots Musical Museum* had already appeared in May. The last would not be published until 1803. For the rest of his lifetime, though, Burns became *de facto* editor of this publication. He amassed a fine collection of song anthologies, referring familiarly in the closing months of 1787 to works like Daniel Dow's 1776 *Collection of Ancient Scots Music*. To Johnson's project he would contribute well over 150 of his own songs, while reworking others he collected. Mixing his voice with past and contemporary voices of Scottish popular poetry and song, Burns made some of his finest verse, by turns piercingly lyrical, challenging, playfully companionable.

Some songs Burns fashioned later achieved global circulation. The male-voiced 'O my Luve's like a red, red rose' or the female-voiced 'John Anderson, my jo' sound warmly direct, yet any autobiographical matter is subsumed into nurturing traditional form: the poet is at least as much transmitter, editor, bearer of tradition as he is a creator imposing his personality. In such songs, Burns established himself not only as one of the world's greatest love poets, but also as a superlative poet of friendship – his laddishness finding lasting apotheosis. Repeatedly, he intensified the emotional charge of work he collected and remade, but did so through instinctive and calculated artistry. To be a bard was not just a pose; it required artistic finesse.

By October 1787 he was renting a room at what was then 2 St James's Square, now part of Register House, overlooking St Andrew Square in Edinburgh's New Town. Ainslie, Nasmyth, Beugo, and Burns's new friend, law student Alexander Cunningham, were near neighbours. As winter advanced, the bard seems to have suffered some depression – 'bitter hours of blue-devilism' he called it, using Fergusson's phrase.[183] This may be connected with the death of his baby daughter, Jean, on 20 October. Miles away in Edinburgh, Burns mentions her passing in Ayrshire almost glancingly, saying in a letter to Richmond he is 'provoked' and 'vexed . . . a good deal' at being 'a girl out of pocket' through 'careless, murdering mischance'.[184] As often, it is hard to gauge Burns's innermost emotions; his correspondence not infrequently contains self-protective bravado. The infant Jean seems to have been living with her mother; it is not

known exactly how she died. Burns clearly knew Jean Armour was again pregnant. He asks Richmond on 25 October to let him know by return 'the news of Armour's family, if the world begin to talk of Jean's appearance any way'.[185]

November found Burns working on songs he had made or collected, and trying to negotiate with Creech, never a man to rush payment. Still experiencing 'melancholy reflections', Burns was registering 'the weary, thorny wilderness of this world'.[186] He planned leaving Edinburgh soon for 'my wonted leisure and rural occupation'; in town his mind sometimes turned to religion. He contrasted the apparently egalitarian warmth of his Catholic bishop friend John Geddes with Presbyterian 'gloomy Fury' and those 'beasts of prey', the Ayrshire 'Erebean Fanatics' conspiring to prosecute 'my learned and truly worthy friend, Dr M'Gill'. McGill's 1786 *Practical Essay on the Death of Jesus Christ* had been attacked by Kirk conservatives for its rational speculations about the 'secret torments' of Christ's soul.[187] Burns, no stranger to inner torment, was angered by the attacks on McGill by those 'savages', his detractors. He threatened to 'fly at them with the faulcons of Ridicule, or run them down with the bloodhounds of Satire'.[188]

The Sunday morning after writing these words he complained of 'vexatious soul concerns', telling Ainslie his friendship was 'almost necessary to my existence'.[189] Writing to Candlish about Johnson's projected Scots song collection, which 'you will easily guess, is an undertaking exactly to my taste', Burns asked his old friend for a song he remembered from boyhood, confessing he was preoccupied with Edinburgh 'hurry and dissipation'.[190] He sent Beugo a note one night saying 'a certain sour faced old acquaintance called Glauber's salts hinders me from my [French] lesson'.[191] He appears to have been taking a familiar purgative for his recurring combination of stomach trouble and depression. Apparently around this period of low spirits he paid a short visit to Dumfries in connection with his proposed move to a farm. He told Margaret Chalmers he felt 'rather hopeless' about his prospects; still, if those plans failed, he might begin a new partnership with Gilbert, a more 'prudent, sober man', and take 'another farm in the neighbourhood'.[192]

On 4 December 1787, still planning to leave soon for Ayrshire, Burns went to an Edinburgh tea party given by Miss Erskine Nimmo, a friend of Margaret Chalmers. There he met twenty-nine-year-old Mrs Agnes McLehose. This Glasgow surgeon's pretty daughter

had attended finishing school in Edinburgh, but was substantially self-educated. Some years earlier she had separated from her abusive lawyer husband. James McLehose had married Agnes when she was eighteen and fathered her four children; now he was in Jamaica. Living in polite Edinburgh on charity provided largely by her cousin William Craig, a successful lawyer and minor author, Agnes already knew Burns's poems. She had been eager to meet him. After the party, she invited him to tea two days later. He was unable to come, but accepted the alternative date of 8 December. He also sent verses he had written, since he gathered she was 'not only a Critic but a Poetess'.

His letter shows that he was attracted to Mrs McLehose: 'I leave this town this day se'ennight, and probably [I shall not return] for a couple of twelvemonth but must ever regret that I so lately gott [*sic*] an acquaintance I shall ever highly esteem, and in whose welfare I shall ever be warmly interested.' Just in case she might have thought that he was only being polite, he added that other than herself and Miss Nimmo 'there are scarcely two people on earth by whom it would mortify me more to be forgotten, tho, at the distance of nine-score miles'. Signing himself 'Madam, with the highest respect, your very humble serv[an]t', this was Rob Mossgiel at his most alluringly deadly. 'Saturday evening,' he wrote, 'I shall embrace the opportunity with the greatest pleasure.'[193]

A late eighteenth-century postal service allowed letters to be delivered every hour in central Edinburgh. Anachronistic though it may sound, this meant Robert and Agnes's relationship took on much of the immediacy, freedom and quickly reached intensity of a modern e-mail romance. Not long before Burns was due on Saturday Mrs McLehose sent a note of encouragement from her lodgings in a courtyard at the back of General's Entry off the Old Town's narrow Potterrow,

> Your lines were truly poetical; give me all you can spare. Not one living has a higher relish for poetry than I have; and my reading everything of the kind makes me a tolerable judge. Ten years ago such lines from such a hand would have half turned my head. Perhaps you thought it might have done so even *yet*, and wisely promised that 'fiction was the native region of poetry.' Read the enclosed, which I scrawled just after reading yours. Be sincere, and own that, whatever merit it has, it has not a line resembling poetry.[194]

Burns was raring to go to Potterrow and respond. That very day, though, he had an accident. Falling from a coach, he dislocated his kneecap on the cobbled street. The pain was intense. His friend Alexander Wood, the doctor who attended to him, told him he must rest, with the injured leg up on a cushion. All Burns could do was write to Mrs McLehose assuring her he had 'never met with a person in my life whom I more anxiously wished to meet again than yourself' and he had been 'intoxicated with the idea' of seeing her that night. He felt 'determined to cultivate your friendship with the enthusiasm of Religion':

> – I cannot bear the idea of leaving Edin[bu]r[gh] without seeing you
> – I know not how to account for it – I am strangely taken with some
> people; nor am I often mistaken. You are a stranger to me; but I am
> an odd being: some yet unnamed feelings; things not principles, but
> better than whims, carry me farther than boasted reason ever did a
> Philosopher. –[195]

With this exchange Robert and Agnes began a remarkable, intense and mannered epistolary affair. It grew all the more heated because for some of the time Burns was housebound, and suffered depressive episodes. With nothing else to do, he sat or lay in his room, reading his way through the Old Testament (by Wednesday he had reached the Book of Joshua), writing business and friendly letters as well as the occasional song or poem, and obsessing about Agnes McLehose. Hers, he told her, was 'Poetry; and good Poetry', while the verse he had sent was

> indeed partly fiction, and partly a friendship which had I been so
> blest as to have met with you *in time*, might have led me – God of
> love only knows where. – Time is too short for ceremonies – I swear
> solemnly (in all the tenor of my former oath) to remember you in
> all the pride and warmth of friendship until – I cease to be! –[196]

Less than a week later, Burns was able to hobble on crutches, 'with as much hilarity in my gait and countenance', he explained to Margaret Chalmers, 'as a May frog leaping across the newly harrowed ridge, enjoying the fragrance of the refreshed earth after the long-expected shower!' He was excited: mobility might let him visit Agnes. In fact, he was largely confined for another month. He knew his correspondence with Mrs McLehose risked both their

reputations, and that he was all too prone to 'imagination, whim, caprice, and passion'.[197] Nevertheless, he was fixated on her. She, meanwhile, sensed his feelings had 'a powerful effect', and worried their relationship might be condemned: 'If I was your *sister*, I would call and see you; but 'tis a censorious world this; and (in this sense) "you and I are not of this world".'[198] Typically, in her excited billet-doux, Agnes reshapes for Robert some words of Christ in St John's Gospel.[199] When she suggested to him there might be something dangerous in his seeming to pay 'addresses to a married woman', he hinted his heart might 'have gone astray a [little]'. He then defended himself with a rhetorical outpouring. She was 'perhaps one of the first of Lovely Forms and Noble Minds'. How could he be harshly judged for having met 'an unfortunate woman, amiable and young; deserted and widowed by those who were bound by every tie of Duty, Nature and Gratitude' and for wishing 'to protect, comfort and cherish her'?[200]

Some correspondence between Burns and McLehose has been lost or ignored by earlier biographers. By late December they were writing to each other under assumed names – perhaps in case their frequent letters miscarried. She had adopted the pseudonym 'Clarinda'. Common enough in eighteenth-century love songs and occurring in the *Spectator*, this was also the name of the tenement-lodging wife whose honour was suspected in a popular play by Benjamin Hoadly, *The Suspicious Husband*. The bard, in reply, signed himself (apparently at Clarinda's suggestion) 'Sylvander', meaning 'Man of the Woods'. Burns was mixing with 'The *bucks* of Edinburgh', and *The Entertaining Amour of Sylvander and Sylvia, A Fashionable Buck, and A Delicate Edinburgh Belle* was a steamy 1767 Edinburgh-published epistolary novel – just the sort of work Agnes (a fan of the 1787 epistolary novel *The Sorrows of the Heart*) enjoyed.[201] The *Amour's* Sylvander, exchanging verses and letters with his inamorata, asks passionately, 'WHEN, my Dear Madam, I revolve in my fond mind, the wonderful assemblage of divine perfections in you, how transported am I?' The fictional couple worry about 'loose passionate expressions . . . no way suitable to a female character'.[202]

Playing 'Sylvander' appealed to Burns's performative skills, though this time he performed in English prose rather than vernacular verse. He told Clarinda she had 'a heart form'd, gloriously form'd, for all the most refined luxuries of love', that his own 'great constituent elements are Pride and Passion', and that 'there is no holding converse

or carrying on correspondence, with an amiable woman, much less a *gloriously amiable, fine woman*, without some mixture of that delicious Passion, whose most devoted Slave I have more than once had the honour of being'.[203] Both correspondents counterpoised ardent moments with platonic pious speculations. Telling him 'My heart was formed for love' but that she desired 'to devote it to Him who is the source of love!' Clarinda protested alarm, urging her Sylvander 'not to mention our corresponding to one on earth. Though I've conscious innocence, my situation is a delicate one.'[204]

Through these epistles each titillated, then hushed, the other. Writing to his man-of-the-world sailor confidant Richard Brown on 30 December, Burns, while mentioning no names, could not keep to himself the 'mad tornadoes' he was experiencing. He quoted verses Clarinda had sent him which typified her way of exciting him. Self-protectively, perhaps self-deludingly, he quotes Milton on marriage and describes his new love not as a separated married woman but a widow:

Almighty Love still 'reigns and revels' in my bosom; and I am at this moment ready to hang myself for a young Edin[bu]r[gh] widow, who has wit and beauty more murderously fatal than the assassinating stiletto of the Sicilian Banditti, or the poisoned arrow of the savage African. My Highland durk, that used to hang beside my crutches, I have gravely removed into a neighbouring closet, the key of which I cannot command; in case of spring-tide paroxysms. – You may guess of her wit by the following verses which she sent me the other day –

> 'Talk not of Love, it gives me pain,
> 'For Love has been my foe;
> 'He bound me with an iron chain,
> 'And plung'd me deep in woe!
>
> 'But Friendship's pure and lasting joys
> 'My heart was form'd to prove:
> 'There welcome win and wear the prize,
> 'But never talk of Love.
>
> 'Your Friendship much can make me blest,
> 'O, why that bliss destroy!
> 'Why urge the odious, one request
> 'You know I must deny!'[205]

As Clarinda both enthused and withheld, Sylvander intensified his epistolary assault. At times each appears to have relished the relationship's ardently difficult nature, its need to develop through rapid correspondence: "Tis really curious – so much *fun* passing between two persons who saw each other only *once*!'[206] Clarinda tried interesting Sylvander in her younger unmarried friend Mary Peacock, who had 'a violent penchant for poetry', but Clarinda's description of Mary as 'comely, without being beautiful' was hardly designed to divert Burns absolutely.[207] In his lodgings, on crutches and mocked by visiting pals like Ainslie as '"a Poet on stilts"', Robert did not spend every moment obsessing about his nearby, unreachable love.[208] At the request of his Crochallan Fencibles friend, lawyer Charles Hay, he spent hours early one morning writing a jejune elegy for the Lord President of the Court of Session, one of the powerful Dundas dynasty whose authority permeated Scotland. Burns was piqued to receive no acknowledgement from the dead man's son Robert Dundas, Solicitor-General, to whom he had sent the poem.

More riskily, he also wrote verses for a Jacobite dinner to celebrate Prince Charles Edward Stuart's sixty-seventh birthday. Dugald Stewart recalled how 'In his political principles' Burns 'was then a Jacobite'.[209] New evidence shows the bard attended this dinner, finding it moving to meet two old Jacobite soldiers who had fought together at Culloden.[210] It is also probable that around this time Burns recast the older Jacobite fighting toast, 'Here is to the king, Sir', since this song exists in a manuscript in Burns's hand almost identical to the text that appeared in the second volume of the *Scots Musical Museum* (printed in spring 1788) but significantly different from the earlier, pre-1750 English-language transcription now in the National Library of Scotland. Burns's manuscript adds a verse to the older words, linking this song of Jacobite uprising to the tune 'Hey Tutti Taiti', traditionally held to have been played at the 1314 Battle of Bannockburn when Robert the Bruce's Scottish army defeated the English in the Wars of Independence. In Burns's manuscript there is a vigorous urging to rise and fight once more,

> When ye hear the trumpets sound
>   Tuti taity to the drum,
> Up your swords and down your gun
>   And to the louns again.[211]

This song appeared anonymously in the *Scots Musical Museum*, but some years after its linking of Jacobite uprising to the freedom-fighting Bruce of 'Hey Tutti Taiti', Burns would return to such a combination in one of his most famous and most politically radical songs, the one beginning, 'Scots, wha hae wi' WALLACE bled,/ Scots, wham BRUCE has aften led . . .'[212] Still, if at the close of 1787 he felt the excitements of Jacobitism, Clarinda consumed his principal imaginative energies. She wrote about how lonely she felt, lacking the 'dear charities of brother, sister, parent . . . I have none of these and belong to nobody.' As New Year 1788 began, 'when others are joyous, I am the reverse. I have no *near* relations; and while others are with theirs, I sit alone, musing upon several of mine, with whom I used to be – now gone to the land of forgetfulness.'[213]

Burns, enthusiast for the lonely survivors of Ossian, for the lost Jacobite cause, and for sentimental literature, emoted over Clarinda's situation: 'Did you, Madam, [know] what I feel when you talk of your sorrows! Good God! that one who has so much worth in the sight of Heaven, and is so amiable to her fellow-creatures should be so unhappy!'[214] She wrote of longing 'for a male friend' who might 'love me with tenderness – yet unmixed with selfishness; who could be my friend, companion, protector! and who would die sooner than injure me', and said she had 'sought, but . . . sought in vain', though now 'Heaven has, I hope, sent me this blessing in my Sylvander.'[215] She told him how, though in merry company she could seem 'only an enthusiast in *fun*', often afterwards 'My spirits are sunk for days'; Burns must have recognised in her something of the rushing highs and lows of what he called in a letter to her his own 'giddy inconsistencies'.[216] Matching her religious musings, he told her he was serious about 'real Religion', but wary of 'Presbyterean sourness'.[217]

On the evening of Friday 4 January 1788 Burns was well enough to visit her. Though still writing in terms of 'Friends', he was clear about the intensity of the connection. He saw the hours they spent together as enough to 'save the rest of the vapid, tiresome, miserable months and years of life'. He spoke to her of his continuing admiration for Milton's Satan, explaining in a note next day he meant no more than respect for 'his manly fortitude in supporting what cannot be remedied – in short, the wild broken fragments of a noble, exalted mind in ruins'.[218] Clearly at this meeting Burns

told McLehose much about his life, including his relationship with Jean Armour; next day he sent her a rather torn copy of the long autobiographical letter to Dr Moore, which he had mentioned when they met. Fascinated to hear and read about Sylvander's life before he came to the 'new world' of Edinburgh, Clarinda seems to have suggested his relationship with Jean might be nearing its conclusion.

Burns still thought about Jean, and Margaret Chalmers. However, Clarinda was now, he told her, 'in my heart's core'.[219] He was also transacting other business. Trying to secure a position with the Excise service, he had 'been examined', as required, 'by a Supervisor'.[220] Under thirty, and having been supplied by the Kirk with his necessary bachelor's certificate, Burns was eligible for consideration. He wrote to Robert Graham of Fintry to ask for his patronage. Burns worried that rumours of his Jacobite politics might tell against him; late in January he was 'question'd like a child about my matters, and blamed and schooled for my Inscription on Stirling window'. He despaired about 'the excise idea'.[221] Making money mattered, not least because Gilbert had confessed that Mossgiel was failing, and requested financial assistance. Burns had been sending home occasional small sums, and had tried without success to find a position for his younger brother William. Now, as soon as he could walk, he was determined to return to Ayrshire.

Thoughts of leaving further intensified his relationship with Clarinda. Several times she deliberately strolled in the courtyard below his window, failing to see him: 'you don't look to the proper story for a Poet's lodging – "Where Speculation roosted near the sky –"' he told her, quoting Edward Young's first epistle to Pope. Burns, looking down, was so frustrated he 'could almost have thrown myself over'.[222] As January advanced he paid at least six visits to her; they also exchanged many letters, his indicating intense imaginative agitation. As often, they also show calculated rhetoric. Racked with pain from his leg and feeling he had made a mess of his life, Burns may have felt suicidal. He told Mrs Dunlop on 21 January he had 'a hundred times wished that one could resign life as an officer resigns a commission'.[223]

Still, he neither threw himself over the sill into the courtyard outside nor did away with himself with his 'Highland durk'. His correspondence with Clarinda was suggestively allusive, quoting

from a play called *The Fatal Marriage* and from Henry Fielding's *Amelia,* a novel about a virtuous but persecuted woman: 'I like to have quotations ready for every occasion,' he told her teasingly. 'They give one's ideas so pat, and save one the trouble of finding expression adequate to one's feelings.'[224]

Express their feelings they did, repeatedly.

What luxury of bliss I was enjoying this time yesternight! My ever-dearest Clarinda, you have stolen away my soul: but you have refined, you have exalted it; you have given it a stronger sense of Virtue, and a stronger relish for Piety. – Clarinda, first of your Sex, if ever I am the veriest wretch on earth to forget you; if ever your lovely image is effaced from my soul,

'May I be lost, no eye to weep my end;
'And find no earth that's base enough to bury me!'[225]

Those lines of poetry are adapted from a speech in a Renaissance play (*Rule a Wife and Have a Wife*, attributed to Beaumont and Fletcher) about the cuckolding of a husband by a 'fair and young' wife – an act destroying 'at one instant . . . both name and honour'.[226] At one level Burns knew what he was involved in; at another, he was carried away by his new love's sheer excitement.

He asked her to let him have a silhouette of herself; she obliged. She advised him he should probably avoid marriage, 'for unless a woman were qualified for the companion, the friend, and the mistress, she would not do for you'.[227] But Burns had got into the habit of finding different women to fulfil these individual roles. He told Clarinda he believed 'The Supreme Being' had 'put the immediate administration' of salvation 'into the hands of Jesus Christ, a great Personage, whose relation to Him we cannot comprehend, but whose relation to us is a Guide and Saviour', assuring her religion was '*my* favorite topic' though he hated 'controversial divinity'; he trusted 'every honest, upright man, of whatever sect, will be accepted of the Deity'. Yet he also sat up late drinking port with 'silly or sordid souls' as depression alternated with ardour around his twenty-ninth birthday. He might protest, 'Clarinda, you have stolen away my soul', but seems to have failed to develop more physical love-making.[228] Now ambulant, and still in a state of sexual excitement, but realising that he was unlikely to possess Clarinda's body, he had sex with her maidservant instead.

Twenty-year-old Jenny Clow, like all the women Burns is known to have slept with, was a country girl from a working-class background. She had grown up in a large family in Newburgh, a Fife village in farmlands close to the River Tay reedbeds south-west of Dundee. Agnes McLehose regarded Clow as 'a good soul', using her at least once (on 25 January 1788) to deliver a message to Burns then call to see if there was any reply. So Jenny Clow must have had a good idea what was going on between her mistress and the celebrated bard who had just sent Mrs McLehose his new, 'slow and expressive' song, 'Clarinda, mistress of my soul', the night before Jenny visited his lodgings with another message.[229] When Burns's attentions turned to her, Clow may have found it hard to resist. When exactly Burns first slept with her is unknown, but she became pregnant by him in February. Their son was born in November.

In the early months of 1788 Agnes McLehose knew nothing of this. Much more concerned about her own reputation, she began to fear she could hear a voice telling her that as a married woman her behaviour 'approaches criminality'; even Burns, writing on his birthday and giving Jenny Clow the letter to convey, felt he might have 'seemingly half-transgressed the laws of Decorum'.[230] Mrs McLehose had worried earlier that the bard, despite his recent injury, should 'come a-foot, even though you take a chair home. A chair is so uncommon a thing in our neighbourhood, it is apt to raise speculation; but they are all asleep by ten.'[231] Now she felt shunned and gossiped about by acquaintances. Burns told her she had 'wounded my soul'; he called her repeatedly 'my Love', and 'my dearest Love', promising to do nothing to hurt her.[232] He was spurred to an extremity of protestation: 'I love to madness, and I feel to torture!'[233] He was editing her poetry. He was calling on her with his friend Ainslie. He was assuring her there was no 'criminality' in their relationship.[234] He was telling her 'never woman more intirely possessed my soul', and asking her for her silhouette so that it might become a brooch or 'a breast-pin, to wear next my heart'.[235]

Around mid-February Agnes McLehose received what Burns dismissed as a 'puritanic scrawl' reproaching her for her conduct and occasioning her to write saying he must cease to love her. He replied this was 'impossible': 'I love, and will love you, and will with joyous confidence approach the throne of the Almighty Judge of men, with your dear idea, and will despise the scum of sentiment

and the mist of sophistry.'[236] Feeling guilty because she was being reproached by people like her minister John Kemp and her cousin William Craig, Agnes tried to cool the relationship. Angry, Burns attacked whoever was 'haughtily and insultingly assuming, the dictatorial language of a Roman Pontiff' to try to 'dissolve a union like ours'. He argued that though legally she might be bound to a husband who had 'repeatedly, habitually and barbarously' mistreated her, in terms of 'the common feelings of humanity' and 'Common Sense' she might 'bestow that heart and those affections to another'.[237] She was obstinate, but he maintained 'I love you, as a friend', telling her he was hers 'for life'.[238] Meeting her on 16 February, he told her he was about to leave Edinburgh, but would go on writing: 'in a few weeks I shall be some where or other out of the possibility of seeing you'.[239]

For some time Burns had been making arrangements to go. He wrote to Glencairn at the start of February, telling him he planned to give more money to the struggling Gilbert; Robert would lodge the rest of his profits from his Edinburgh edition 'in a banking-house' to provide for his family.[240] In the same letter he asked Glencairn to help him secure a position with the Excise, sent him 'Holy Willie's Prayer' for entertainment, and expressed the hope they would meet soon. Though uncertain, Burns still hoped to sort out a Dumfriesshire farm. He told several Ayrshire friends he would soon be on his way. From Mauchline news had come that Jean Armour's parents, finding her again pregnant by Burns, had thrown her out.

Writing to John Richmond, who was now back in Mauchline, Burns called this 'an unlucky affair'. He made no mention of Clarinda or Jenny Clow. In Edinburgh, he said simply, 'every thing' was 'going on as usual – houses building, bucks strutting, ladies flaring, black-guards sculking, [*two words missing*], &c. in the old way'.[241] To Frances Dunlop he sent his lyric, 'Clarinda, mistress of my soul', hinting, 'there, the *bosom* was perhaps a little *interested*', but that was all.[242] Reactivating contacts in the west, he wrote also to Brown, hoping they might meet in Glasgow when Burns travelled there by coach. By 17 February, confident he had an Excise position in the bag, he had decided he would not also pursue a new farm; instead, he would stay three weeks in the west, then return to Edinburgh for a six-week course of Excise instruction. Actually, he ended up doing this training in Ayrshire. On Monday, 18 February Burns

VI

Rhinoceros

However much Burns reconnected with old friends, life had been complicated by his experiences in the new world of Edinburgh. Going to Glasgow in February 1788 reunited him with his brother William and his friend Richard Brown. He relished a convivial evening with both, but his thoughts soon turned to Clarinda; at nine o'clock he excused himself to write to her: 'How do you feel, my Love?' With characteristic over-emphasis, he quoted from the Book of Job he had so recently re-read, 'The hour that you are not in all my thoughts – "be that hour darkness! let the shadows of Death cover it! let it not be numbered in the hours of the day!"'[1] He was, he said, about to rejoin Brown and drink her health.

Returning to Mossgiel took several days. He met friends and patrons, sometimes seeing them with an Edinburgh eye. He told Clarinda how one well-off Paisley businessman complained that his daughter '"was a good spinner and sower [sic], till I was advised by her foes and mine to give her a year of Edin[bu]r[gh]!"'[2] To another Edinburgh correspondent Burns sniped at 'the savage hospitality of this Country'.[3] But he had not returned from Edinburgh to sneer at west-coast life. He knew he owed debts to Ayrshire. Spending two days with Mrs Dunlop, he talked about authors including Spenser, Gray, and the fashionable French novelist Marmontel. From Dunlop House he progressed to Kilmarnock; then to Mossgiel and Mauchline, visiting Gavin Hamilton. Though he did not write to her daily as he had promised, Burns kept up correspondence with Clarinda. She told him she had been warned again about her reputation. Manipulatively, 'Sylvander' sought to reassure her: though he had started seeing Jean Armour again, Jean could not compare with the sophistication of Clarinda in Edinburgh:

Now for a little news that will please you. – I, this morning [23 February] as I came home, called for a certain woman. – I am disgusted with her; I cannot endure her! I, while my heart smote me for the prophanity, tried to compare her with my Clarinda: 'twas setting the expiring glimmer of a farthing taper beside the cloudless glory of the meridian sun. – Here was tasteless insipidity, vulgarity of soul, and mercenary fawning; there, polished good sense, heaven-born genius, and the most generous, the most delicate, the most tender Passion. – I have done with her, and she with me. –⁴

A week later Burns was assuring Clarinda he was going to settle in Dumfriesshire, having looked over Ellisland farm. He would 'be in Edin[bu]r[gh] next week'; in any case Ellisland was just a day and a half's ride from the capital.⁵ After accompanying him to Dumfriesshire, his farming friend John Tennant advised renting Ellisland from Burns's Edinburgh supporter, Patrick Miller. Burns was distracted, though: relations with Jean were not quite as he portrayed them to Clarinda. Apparently thrown out by her parents, Jean was living in a room in John Mackenzie's Mauchline house. Burns and McLehose had agreed every Sunday 'at the sacred hour of eight' to focus their thoughts on each other. This, Burns assured his 'first of womankind' on Sunday, 2 March, he was just about to do.

Next day, though, still uncertain whether to become Ellisland's farmer or an Excise officer, he told a very different story to his Edinburgh friend Ainslie. He mentions Clarinda, but concentrates on his recent relations with Jean, soon to give birth to twins:

Jean I found banished, [like a martyr –] forlorn destitute and friendless: [All for the good old cause.] I have reconciled her to her fate, and I have reconciled her to her mother . . . [I have taken her a room. I have taken her to my arms. I have given her a mahogany bed. I have given her a guinea, and I have f——d her till she rejoiced with joy unspeakable and full of glory. But, as I always am on every occasion, I have been prudent and cautious to an astonishing degree. I swore her privately and solemnly never to attempt any claim on me as a husband, even though anybody should persuade her she had such a claim (which she had not), neither during my life nor after my death. She did all this like a good girl, and I took the opportunity of some dry horse litter, and gave her such a thundering scalade that electrified the very marrow of her bones. Oh, what a peacemaker is a guid weely-willy p——le! It is the mediator, the guarantee,

the umpire, the bond of union, the solemn league and covenant, the plenipotentiary, the Aaron's rod, the Jacob's staff, the prophet Elisha's pot of oil, the Ahasuerus' Sceptre, the sword of mercy, the philosopher's stone, the Horn of Plenty, and Tree of Life between Man and Woman.][6]

Though later Burnsians may have tried to destroy this letter, it remains remarkably revealing. To Ainslie, Burns uses the tone of a buck well schooled in the eighteenth-century pornographic poem, 'The Plenipotentiary'. Mixing protested sexual performance with pose-striking, he anticipates the cradle-Calvinist Byron in his determination to be libertine. Burns's written performance is charismatically compelling, linguistically inventive, carefully conceived. It is also shockingly self-serving. Saviour of 'martyr' Jean, the calculating bard gets her to swear she will never attempt to exercise a claim over him. So, as with Jenny Clow, he enjoys sex with Jean while his relationship with Clarinda continues. Unlike Clow, though, Armour was in the very advanced stages of pregnancy. What Burns presents as exclamations of pleasure may well have been cries of pain. Just days later she gave birth to twins.

Burns continued writing to Clarinda from Mossgiel. Hoping God would let him 'feel "another's woe"', he meant Clarinda's sufferings, not Jean's. He assures Mrs McLehose, 'The dignified and dignifying consciousness of an honest man, and the well-grounded trust in approving Heaven, are two most substantial [?foundations] of happiness.'[7] One twin born to Jean and Robert died a few days after Burns wrote these words; the other appears to have died about ten days later. Burns never mentions their deaths in surviving correspondence or poetry. However, a previously unidentified quotation in a letter to Clarinda written on 6 March 1788 comes from an often anthologised 'Poem Sacred to the Memory of a Dearly Beloved and Only Daughter, who Died in the Eleventh Year of her Age, Written by Her Mourning Father'. So when Burns quotes from memory,

'O what is life, that thoughtless wish of all!
'A drop of honey in a draught of gall' –

before going on to quote Job and remark, 'Nothing astonishes me more, when a little sickness clogs the wheels of life, than the thoughtless career we run, in the hour of health', parental anxiety surely

guides his thoughts.[8] The poem he quotes about a man who 'wip'd' his daughter's 'dying face/ And took the father's and the nurse's place' expresses intense parental grief.[9] Burns felt deeply for his children. Nevertheless his presentation of himself as 'honest man' could go hand in hand with deep duplicity and sometimes with disgraceful conduct.

His treatment of Jean Armour at this time is the sort of behaviour which led Robert Louis Stevenson in 1879 to term him a 'Don Juan' and to point out that 'It is the punishment of Don Juanism to create continually false positions – relations in life which are wrong in themselves, and which it is equally wrong to break or to perpetuate.'[10] Writing about Burns half a century later, Catherine Carswell maintained 'The love of women was necessary to him, but equally necessary his absolute domination as the male.'[11] In poetry, not least 'Tam o' Shanter', Burns could turn this male triumphalism to magnificent comic effect. He wrote also with sympathetic imagination about female suffering. Yet that same mobility of voice and viewpoint which gave him poetic range and depth let him live with clashing inconsistencies, not least in his treatment of women. 'Unkindness', he assured Clarinda around the time he pleasured himself with Jean just before the twins were born, is 'a sin so unlike me, a sin I detest.'[12] Like many imaginative people, Burns used his imagination to block off from himself aspects of his conduct. He deluded himself, two-timing others. The same Burns who boasted to Ainslie that he had 'electrified' Jean to 'the very marrow of her bones', protested to Clarinda how 'To be overtopped in anything else, I can bear; but in the lists of generous love, I defy all mankind! –'[13] Writing himself up as domineering lover with his Mauchline 'good girl', he simultaneously scripts his Sylvanderish role as 'man of keen sensibility' with his sophisticated Edinburgh lady.[14]

Financially matters were also complicated. His last surviving letter to Hamilton reads awkwardly. Burns refused to back Gilbert with the sort of money Hamilton argued was appropriate for the home-loving brother left looking after Mossgiel. Burns said on his return from Edinburgh he had already given Gilbert about £200. Gilbert farmed on, but Burns's attentions turned to Ellisland; disagreement with Hamilton seems to have led to a cooling of relations with him.[15] Still, Gilbert and Robert did not fall out. Advised by Tennant, Burns had written to Patrick Miller, hard-headedly indicating

Ellisland farm was 'worn out' and needed substantial improvement.[16] The poet argued that Miller should give him a better deal. Miller did.

Two years after publishing the Kilmarnock *Poems*, Burns was still chasing 'several small sums owing me for my first Edition, about Galston and Newmills'; he could have a long memory where debts were concerned, and used pursuing these as an excuse for not visiting his old supporter the Kilmarnock wine merchant Robert Muir, now seriously ill.[17] 'An honest man has nothing to fear,' Burns counselled Muir from Mossgiel on 7 March: if there was an afterlife then a man who dies 'goes to a great unknown Being who could have no other end in giving him existence but to make him happy; who gave him those passions and instincts, and well knows their force. –'[18] Muir, whom Gilbert recalled as 'very dear' to Burns's heart, died just weeks later, not long after the twins. Soon Burns headed to Edinburgh once more.

It was exciting to be back in the capital again, but the bard did not stay long. He was finalising with Miller details of Ellisland's lease, and arranging documentation to enter the Excise service. He met several Excisemen, and dined with one of the Commissioners. He also tried to extract a financial statement from the elusive Creech, and visited Lady Wallace, a kinswoman of Mrs Dunlop. More thrillingly he encountered Agnes McLehose. He hung about under her window at night: ''tis the star,' he told her, 'that guides me to paradise.'[19] Just as before, Burns in Edinburgh repeatedly sent Clarinda notes. She was his 'Queen of Poetesses', 'Empress of the Poet's soul'.[20] A week after the first of Jean's twins was buried in Mauchline, Burns presented Clarinda with two wineglasses: his toast, 'Long may we love!/ And long may we be happy!!!'[21] His relationship with her was as intense as ever, and developed, momentarily at least, a physical dimension. Ignored by previous biographers, a letter she sent him in Edinburgh, apparently on 18 March, tells how

> Last night I saw you low and Depress'd – my heart was bent upon soothing and raising your Spirits – the Intention was good – But it led me perhaps too far. To-day, I am quite sensible of it – even 'present in the very lap of Love.'[22]

Clarinda here quotes from a passage in Thomson's 'Spring' which cautions against sexual indulgence, warning that after 'wanton hours'

spent 'in the very lap of love/ Inglorious laid ... fierce repentance rears/ Her snaky crest'.[23] McLehose implies she and Burns have had sexual contact of some sort; 'chect at the Idea of impropriety ... I must forgive you'. She hopes 'almost ... that Heaven itself approves our union'. Her letter is alive with erotic excitement: 'Come to-morrow evening as soon as you can get off – You'll see no more *stars* – *without* at least; *within* you'll find the Star Venus which always attends the Sun you know.'[24] Her writing is interrupted, but evidently she and Burns are still involved in an intense affair, quick-ened by his feelings of desire and despondency. Days later, by the time his second twin was buried on 22 March, he was back in Mauchline.

Burns mentions 'a load of Care almost too heavy for my shoul-ders' in a letter to Brown dated '20th March'. Yet he focused on a fresh start in Dumfriesshire where he was, he confessed, 'an entire Strange[r]'.[25] Perhaps a new beginning made the move attractive, but he was unsure, complaining to an Edinburgh friend about 'melan-choly, joyless muirs' and feeling afflicted 'with Care and Anxiety about this farming project of mine'.[26] Having decided to become Ellisland's farmer and a Revenue officer as well, he might hope for a decent income. Yet, still in Mauchline in spring 1788, he repeat-edly sounds notes of anxiety. After some negotiation, an official letter of 31 March allowed Burns to undergo his six weeks' Excise training course in 'the art of gauging' supervised by Tarbolton Exciseman James Findlay, instead of in Edinburgh as stipulated earlier. Turning down invitations from local gentry, he concentrated on learning gauging and Excise book-keeping. This was a demanding process. The standard manual, John Dougharty's *The General Gauger*, is full of elaborate tables and advice about '*The Use of the Cube-Root*' and how '*To calculate any Diameter between the Bung and Head of a Spheroid, posited perpendicularly to the Horizon*'.[27] On 7 April he wrote to his fellow member of the Crochallan Fencibles, William Dunbar, hoping for news of Edinburgh's 'world of Wits, and Gens comme il faut which I lately left, and with whom I never again will intimately mix'.[28] Burns's decisiveness was no doubt strengthened by the alteration in his personal circumstances, his wistfulness by realising such a change might not sit well with Edinburgh's 'beaux Esprits'.[29]

As Excise training progressed, apparently concluding his affair with Clarinda had no future, he turned again to Jean. That April

he explained to James Smith, who had left Mauchline to work in a Linlithgow calico-printing business, 'there is, you must know, a certain clean-limb'd, handsome bewitching young Hussy of your acquaintance to whom I have lately and privately given a matrimonial title to my Corpus'.[30] Though no paperwork exists to prove it, Burns seems to have entered into some sort of civil marriage with Jean; they were living together in her room in Mackenzie's Mauchline house. Privately, though not yet publicly, Burns sometimes called her 'Mrs Burns'. As a token 'I have *irrevocably* called her mine', he ordered through Smith a printed shawl: 'The quality, let it be of the best.'[31]

Making no direct mention of the loss of their children, Burns told Smith, 'my girl ... has been *doubly* kinder to me than even the best of women usually are to their Partners of our Sex'.[32] Jean's pregnancies added to local gossip. Saunders Tait's poem 'B—rns's Hen' made fun of her bearing a 'double round' of babies, 'pull'd' out by Dr Mackenzie. Keen to 'see how Robin had her drest', Tait is the harshest of several commentators to hint that Burns was eager Jean looked good in public.[33] To the end of his life, a neighbour recalled, 'he was always anxious that his wife should be well and neatly dressed'.[34]

Perhaps proud of his local reputation as a rake, and having dallied so recently with more sophisticated Edinburgh ladies, Burns was awkward about revealing his new partnership to his various correspondents. Mrs Dunlop was struck by the roundabout way he let her know. To his uncle Samuel Brown of Kirkoswald, who was no stranger to smuggling and had himself done penance for fornication, trainee Exciseman Burns wrote jokily about his own sexual 'smuggling'; he was now 'thinking about takeing [*sic*] out a Licence and beginning in a Fair trade'.[35]

Apparently embarrassed about committing himself to Jean and the Excise, the bard generally aspired to reinvent himself. Reading Dryden's translation of Virgil's *Georgics*, lent him by Mrs Dunlop, he told her he was considering emulating them. Rob Mossgiel might become a literary gentleman farmer. Writing to James Johnson in late May, he complained Creech still owed him 100 guineas – urgently desired. Burns also informed Johnson of his marriage, bidding farewell to rakery, and making marrying Jean sound rather like an act of warm-hearted charity. On 26 May Burns wrote to Ainslie in Edinburgh, telling him 'Mrs Burns' was a 'title I now avow to the World'. Marriage

has indeed added to my anxieties for Futurity but it has given a
stability to my mind & resolutions, unknown before; and the poor
girl has the most sacred enthusiasm of attachment to me, and has
not a wish but to gratify my every idea of her deportment.[36]

It was hard for Burns to write of his new wife without making it
sound as if he thought her a little beneath him.

In mid-June he moved to his new, 170-acre farm six miles north
of Dumfries. Though the house is in a dell, Ellisland to this day
enjoys good views along the River Nith. Tradition has it Burns
was offered better land nearby, but Ellisland's fine vistas may have
appealed to a poet used to Mossgiel's panoramic outlooks. Still,
almost immediately he began having serious doubts about the
place. Suddenly he was cut off from familiar people and objects.
To Mrs Dunlop he complained about irritation and gloom; to
Ainslie, 'My Farm gives me a good many uncouth Cares & Anxi-
eties.'[37] His new situation and increased family responsibilities
disturbed Burns. Returning to his commonplace book, he even
hinted he felt ready to die. Yet he realised he owed it to Jean to
go on living.

Into that commonplace book Burns copied a 'favourite motto'
from Young's *Night Thoughts* – lines most recently quoted to
Clarinda. Now he rewrote them in the context of marriage to Jean:

> . . . On REASON build RESOLVE,
> That column of true majesty in man. –[38]

For the moment, marriage ended all contact with Agnes McLehose.
Taken aback, she seems to have entered into a relationship with
Robert Ainslie. It was Ainslie who told Burns around the start of
June that McLehose's servant, Jenny Clow, was pregnant. This
'affair', Burns confessed, 'vexed' him. It would soon grow more
vexatious when Clow took out a writ against him, but meanwhile
he stuck to his plan to 'build Resolve' around work and marriage.
'To the least temptation to Jealousy or Infidelity, I am an equal
stranger,' he told Mrs Dunlop that summer.[39] Perhaps she believed
him.

On 14 July 1788 Burns's Excise commission was issued. He spent
the summer moving between Mauchline and Ellisland. While he was
making preparations in Nithsdale, he told Mrs Dunlop, Jean in

Mauchline regularly served as 'apprentice to my Mother & Sisters in their dairy & other rural business', perfecting skills essential to a farmer's wife.[40] On 5 August, after apparently trying to get his friend James Smith to make a false statement about the legality of his 'Marriage affair', Burns admitted to the Reverend 'Daddy' Auld his irregular relationship with Jean.[41] The couple were rebuked by Mauchline Kirk Session, fined, then 'solemnly engaged to adhere faithfully to one another as husband and wife all the days of their Life'. Burns 'gave a guinea note for behoof [benefit] of the poor' and wished kirkmen would instead 'turn the[ir fie]ry Zeal' towards sexual enjoyment and the sort of bawdy songs he liked to circulate.[42] Pondering Jean's skills and attractions, he came close to the truth in telling Mrs Dunlop, 'I can easily *fancy* a more agreable [*sic*] companion for my journey of Life, but, upon my honor, I have never *seen* the individual Instance!'[43] Mrs McLehose may have looked the part, but it is hard to imagine her slogging away in a dairy. Jean might make a farmer's wife, yet retain wit and beauty. Burns ordered for her 'fifteen y[ar]ds [of] black lutestring silk' – first-rate, costly material for performing erotic allure.[44]

Preparing to move his new household, Burns also started building up his library, buying Smollett's novels and William Cowper's poems. After Edinburgh, he felt on his Dumfriesshire farm 'for all that most pleasurable part of Life called, Social Communication, I am here at the very elbow of Existence'. The locals exemplified 'Stupidity & Canting'; the only prose they knew came from prayers. As for poetry, 'they have as much idea of a Rhinoceros as of a Poet'.[45] Burns knew his own giftedness, and how, for all his often sociable bardic sense of fun, it sometimes set him apart. Conscious he could seem as alien as a rhinoceros, he struggled to come to terms with his Dumfriesshire habitat.

In 'this strange land, this uncouth clime', he began to worry he might have made 'a ruinous bargain'.[46] Since at Ellisland there were some old farm buildings but no proper farmhouse, he was getting a new house built, ready to receive Jean. Unusually, the local builder Alexander Crombie (who also worked for Patrick Miller) incorporated an upmarket parlour or 'spence' into the farmhouse and had the house windows 'orientated away from the yard' to make the most of the fine views.[47] Burns was eager to occupy his poet's farmhouse, and to keep up his contacts in Edinburgh. Through Ainslie he tried to find his brother William a job as a saddler's apprentice.

He also attempted to defuse a potential row with William Nicol who felt slandered by gossip Burns knew had been spread by Clarinda. Confident in the ongoing *Scots Musical Museum*, he was also collecting and sending songs to Johnson and others.

He made friends with some of his country gentlemen neighbours. One was local laird's son John Syme, Distributor of Stamps in Dumfries. In Syme's villa on the banks of the Nith Burns 'got almost tipsey'.[48] The poet's new landlord, Patrick Miller, friend and supporter of the artist Nasmyth, invited him to dinner on 15 August. Miller and his wife were painted by George Chalmers, probably around the time Burns moved to Ellisland. They look confidently prosperous, well-dressed; he sits holding a book, with another open beside him.[49] Now fifty-seven, the bibliophile Miller was a committed 'improver' and a director of the Carron ironworks. His work for Scottish agriculture included the introduction of swede turnips. At Dalswinton Miller went on to develop a 'mansion-house . . . with coach-houses, stable, and different Offices'. He had 'a Garden, Hot-houses, and a large Orchard, with about 200 acres of pasture grounds'.[50] Today from Burns's side of the Nith the imposing Dalswinton residence can be seen in the distance; from Dalswinton the small Ellisland farm looks nothing special.

The wealthy Miller had a pioneering scientific interest in paddle-ships, and the money to indulge it. At Miller's well-appointed house Burns enjoyed hearing one of his own songs played on the harpsi-chord, but felt acutely his relative poverty. Still, as poets often do, he tried to come to terms with his new environment by making it the subject of verse. As early as June 1788 he had visited the 'hermitage' – a stone hut or 'folly' recently erected at Friars' Carse, an ancient monastic foundation on the Nith's banks near Ellisland – and had adopted the chastening voice of a 'BEADSMAN OF NITH-SIDE' in a poem urging 'sober thought'.[51] A beadsman had originally been a Catholic man of prayer; in Scotland the word had come to denote a licensed beggar.

However he felt at times, Burns was neither poor as a beggar nor alien as a rhinoceros; his neighbours were characterised by more than stupidity and canting. On his 700-acre Nithside estate with 'charming holm . . . excellent Garden and Orchard' at Friars' Carse lived the talented amateur musician Robert Riddell of Glenriddell.[52] This local man had studied at St Andrews when Dr Johnson's visit there had been satirised by Robert Fergusson. As a student Riddell

had enjoyed travellers' tales, fiction, and Shenstone's works.[53] Following further study at Edinburgh he had joined the army. Retired from his captainship after the American War, Riddell inherited a substantial house at Friars' Carse. Burns's friend Alexander Nasmyth had visited Riddell in September 1787, drawing the house, Patrick Miller's estate and surrounding scenes.[54] On nearby land stood the 'hermitage' to which Riddell gave Burns a key. The poet savoured that sequestered spot.[55] A big, cultured man with a booming voice, Riddell did not mince his words; he wanted to improve the lot of his 'illiterate & superstitious neighbours'.[56] Attuned at times 'to black despairing thought', this antiquarian had a collection of such rarities as 'a Roman sandal' and 'a small gold coin . . . bearing the inscription AUGUSTUS'. He had recently read his 'Account of the ancient Lordship of Galloway' to the Society of Antiquaries, and liked the idea that he lived in the territory of an ancient beadsman.[57] To Riddell have been attributed the 'legendary fragments' of poetry in *The Bedesman on Nidsyde* (1790); in the second half of 1788 Burns worked carefully on his own beadsman poem celebrating Riddell's terrain.[58] He also wrote a song, 'The Banks of the Nith', later printed with music by Riddell and sung at the Dumfries theatre. On the song's manuscript Burns noted, 'My Landlord, Mr Miller, is building a house by the banks of the Nith.'[59]

The Nith remains a beautiful river, and of all the farms Burns worked, Ellisland, with its small replanted orchard where he and Jean gathered apples, and its simple farm buildings, is the best to visit. Set in its slight declivity at the end of a minor road, it is now a museum, relatively little changed since Burns's day. To sense why Burns chose it, stroll in summer beside the riverbanks, over Ellisland's fields into the bracken-covered wood edged by a drystane dyke, up the path to the hermitage. Restored in 1874, this is still a small, simple building, recognisable from early drawings. Its three windows look to yew, oak, beech, and sycamore trees. It remains, as it was for Burns, a calm retreat in the pastoral landscape of Dumfriesshire. From it you can walk through sun-dappled woods to Friars' Carse. Extensively rebuilt in Victorian times, Robert Riddell's former home has housed all sorts of visitors – from lady mental patients to wedding parties. Now an imposing hotel, with its grand piano, dark-beamed public area and corniced formal rooms, it still contrasts markedly with Burns's small plain interiors at Ellisland. Big, mature trees stand on the Carse's lawns where they slope towards the Nith; not

far beyond near the village of Auldgirth wild deer run in the woods.

Burns liked walking near Ellisland, but was set apart from his well-intentioned grander neighbours. Riddell and Miller, substantial local freeholders, had voting rights and voted for the Dumfries MP Sir Robert Laurie, a libertarian, anti-Tory Foxite.[60] Burns soon met and got on well with Lawrie too, but the poet, like almost everyone else in eighteenth-century Scotland, lacked voting rights. Without any direct electoral say in government and minus the social standing of his liberally minded neighbours, he had to live by his wits. Using his work to help develop friendships with sympathetic local landowners, he also deployed poetry for the practical purpose of obtaining advancement.

Concerned about his farm's viability, during harvest time in 1788 he composed a long poem 'To Robt Graham of Fintry Esqr., with a request for an Excise Division', the final version dated '*Ellisland – Sept. 8th 1788*'. This poem appealed to Mrs Dunlop and others, which encouraged Burns to explore formal English modes. Drawing on Pope's *Moral Epistles*, it is really an awkward begging letter. Qualified as an Exciseman, like others in that position Burns was expected to wait until a post became available through the Board of Excise; he could not assume that any job would be in his immediate vicinity, but wanted to secure an appointment close to his new family home. The bard, not the Board, took the initiative. Having once met Graham of Fintry, one of the Commissioners, Burns now sent him a long, wheedling poem with an accompanying letter mentioning his new farm ('in the last stage of worn-out poverty'), his 'aged mother', and his 'fireside family-circle' facing 'impending destruction'. In the poem he presented himself very much as 'A POET ... Prone to enjoy each pleasure riches give,/ Yet haply wanting wherewithall to live'. Eventually, he proposed 'a scheme'.[61]

Burns wanted Graham to arrange for Dumfries Excise Officer Leonard Smith to be stripped of his post, and the post given to Burns instead. The non-poet Smith, a near neighbour at Ellisland, was 'quite opulent', Burns argued, whereas the poet-farmer needed money. This was Burns at his most Machiavellian: 'When I think how and on what I have written to you, Sir, I shudder at my own Hardiesse.' With calculating piety he ended the letter by suggesting God was on his side in depriving Smith of his job: 'I am sure I go

on Scripture-grounds in this affair; for, I "ask in faith, nothing doubting;" and for the true Scripture-reason too – Because I have the fullest conviction that, "my Benefactor is good".'[62] Graham seems to have been flattered at being addressed by the bard. He replied in friendly fashion. It took a year for Burns's scheme to come to fruition, but in 1789 Smith was indeed removed from his post and replaced by Robert Burns.

In comparison with intrigues over positions in eighteenth-century politics or universities, Burns's machinations were minor. Well-off Smith may not have been the best of Excisemen. Still, Burns's calculating hard-headedness and readiness to curry favour with the powerful in order to secure his own ends are striking. The rather willed English-language verse accompanying his manoeuvres sounds unconvincing. As the scheming Burns asks, 'Why shrinks my soul, half-blushing, half-afraid [?]', we cringe.[63]

Lighter, more assured, and more lasting than this or other grandly planned 'pretty large Poetic works', are the songs the bard collected, made and remade in this period.[64] In Dumfriesshire his appetite for songs was undiminished. Decades later, Professor Thomas Gillespie of St Andrews recalled how

> when a schoolboy ... I saw Burns's horse tied by the bridle to the sneck of a cottage-door in the neighbourhood of Thornhill, and lingered for some time listening to the songs, which, seated in an iron chair by the fireside, Burns was listening to. Betty Flint was the name of the songstress. She was neither pretty nor witty, but she had a pipe of the most overwhelming pitch, and a taste for song. She was the very woman for Burns, when disposed to have 'song without supper;' in other words, to enjoy the sweet notes of music without the usual accompaniments. I remember that she sung, even to 'us laddies,' 'There's nae luck about the house,' and 'Braw, braw lads o' Gala water,' most inimitably ...[65]

In his earlier Dumfriesshire days, Burns was recalled as 'restless'.[66] Sometimes alone at Ellisland, sometimes with Jean in Mauchline ('just 46 miles' away as Burns calculated it), he sensed his love for her quicken.[67] When she knew he was coming back to Ayrshire she seems to have liked to travel towards him, 'to meet me on the road'.[68] Sometimes he rode through the night. The first of a very small number of surviving letters Burns sent his wife is dated 'Ellisland Friday 12th Sept. 1788'.

My dear Love,

I received your kind letter with a pleasure which no letter but one from you could have given me. – I dreamed of you the whole night last; but alas! I fear it will be three weeks yet, ere I can hope for the happiness of seeing you. – My harvest is going on. – I have some to cut down still, but I put in two stacks today, so I [am] as tired as a dog. –

[You migh]t get one of Gilbert's sweet milk cheeses, [*two or three words torn away*] & send it to [MS. *torn*]⁶⁹

Even though this letter is damaged, it rings true. Burns loves his wife, and asks her for cheese. He is not just thinking how they will set up home together at Ellisland ('I have just now consulted my old Landlady about table-linen'); he is also telling Jean about songs he is writing. One, published later in the *Scots Musical Museum*, was set to a variant of a traditional air, 'Alace I lie my alon'. Burns called his song simply, 'I love my Jean'. His title and first stanza say it all:

> Of a' the airts the wind can blaw,
>   I dearly like the West;
> For there the bony Lassie lives,
>   The Lassie I lo'e best:
> There's wild-woods grow, and rivers row,   *roll*
>   And mony a hill between;
> But day and night my fancy's flight
>   Is ever wi' my Jean. –⁷⁰

Songs like this and 'O, were I on Parnassus Hill' (which kicks loose from its Classical landscape and heads instead for the distinctive hill called Corsincon in Ayrshire, between Mauchline and Ellisland) are among the finest Burns wrote. If there were practical matters to be sorted, such as paying for new shoes and shoe repairs, and if anxieties about farming twined with financial ambitions to produce stiff, calculating productions like 'To Robt Graham of Fintry Esqr.', then Burns could also access a quite different part of his creative imagination, making vernacular songs of love, longing and delight.⁷¹ By the Nith he was pure songster as well as effective schemer; a complex, ambitious twenty-nine-year-old, he moved between different jobs, preoccupations and aspects of his personality in ways that, on occasion, released poetry of remarkable deftness and carrying power.

At Ellisland Burns hated the Isle, the damp, cold, smoky house

where he lodged with an older couple. September 1788 brought 'Hypochondria which I fear worse than the devil'; bad weather drove him indoors at harvest time; missing Jean, he thought too about Margaret Chalmers, writing her a long letter; towards the end of the month he suffered a bad bout of flu.[72] Then on 14 October he told Jean he had been offered another, furnished house nearby. Lawyer David Newall had vacated it to winter in Dumfries. Burns urged Jean to join him, bringing a maidservant, but it was late in the year before arrangements were completed. In Mauchline Burns's friends had included the lawyer Hamilton, but his closest companions were young lads; now at Ellisland his companions tended to be older, well-off neighbours. He is said to have witnessed Patrick Miller's small steam-powered vessel on Dalswinton Loch when it first sailed there on 14 October. Burns was not on board, however much later writers wished he had been. Instead, he farmed. He plotted. He read. He wrote.

A close sense of Burns the reader is apparent in his October 1788 letter to Creech's former clerk Peter Hill who had just set himself up as an Edinburgh bookseller. Hill had published James Cririe's *Address to Loch Lomond*. With landscape descriptions and mentions of Arran, Ailsa Craig and other places known to Burns, Cririe's *Address* owes much – Burns points out – to the landscape poetry of Thomson. Burns thought Cririe 'a true Poet of Nature's making', able to maintain and build lively momentum, so his 'progress . . . kindles in his course'. However, where for Cririe 'Truth' was 'The soul of ev'ry song that's nobly great', Burns points out that 'Fiction is the soul of many a Song that's nobly great'. For Burns poetry was imagination, not simply reportage. Thinking Cririe's Loch Lomond 'sublime', he warned against phrases like 'Great lake', 'vulgarised by every-day language'. A master of vernacular, Burns knew it must be used deftly in verse. While enthusiastic about Cririe's occasionally proto-Wordsworthian work, Burns admired most the passages about wild birds and a sportsman hunting them. He responded not least to the concluding lines where, after invoking Scottish writers such as Smollett and George Buchanan, Cririe calls on the spirit of ancient British Ossianic heroes to inspire 'the independent soul' so

> in the songs of future bards, our names
> May still, in every distant clime, well-known,
> For virtuous deeds and useful arts renown'd,
> Descend respected to the end of time.

Burns pronounced this conclusion 'admirably fine, & truly Ossianic'. As a bard, he too might use words like 'Briton' and 'British' when what he really celebrated was the culture of Scotland.[73] He scorned Scots who tried to act or speak as if English: 'Thou Englishman who never was south the Tweed' was an insult he relished.[74]

Burns's sense of Scottishness should be borne in mind in considering his letter to the *Edinburgh Evening Courant* of 8 November. Signing himself 'A BRITON', he addresses 'every Briton, and particularly every Scotsman'. He had been stung by an anti-Jacobite sermon preached in 'my parish church' to celebrate the centenary of the 1688 'Glorious Revolution' which had brought the royal House of Hanover to power in Britain.[75] The preacher was the Reverend Joseph Kirkpatrick. Burns later described him privately as 'one vast constellation of dullness' and 'stupidity'.[76] Publicly Burns protests loyalty to Hanoverianism, describing himself as 'Bred and educated in revolution principles'. However, annoyed at descriptions of the Stuarts as '"bloody and tyrannical"', he asks, 'Were the royal contemporaries of the Stuarts more mildly attentive to the rights of man?'[77] This last phrase was soon to become the title of a famous 1791 pamphlet by republican Thomas Paine; in books published in the 1780s it was often used of supposedly inalienable liberties in arguments about Ireland, France, the slave trade, and the American Revolution. Burns would have encountered it in Cowper's poetry and Smollett's 'Ode to Independence' where it was used of Swiss republicanism in a passage quoted by John Moore in Britain and John Adams in America. Most recently, in 1788 Burns had read the phrase in French novelist Marmontel's *Belisarius*, 'one of the most glorious mental entertainments I ever enjoyed'.[78] It occurs in Belisarius's account of the relations between people and monarch,

> And indeed, till fatal experience opened the eyes of men, who could foresee that kings would ever sink to such a degree of infatuation, as to divorce themselves from their people, and combine with the avowed enemies of all the rights of man? ... It was not in the simplicity of ancient manners to expect so shocking a revolution.[79]

Burns's letter ostensibly supports the 'Glorious Revolution' and Hanoverian monarchy, yet mounts a public defence of the Stuarts

to whose Jacobite cause we know he was sympathetic. Towards its end it moves in a different direction:

> Who would believe, Sir, that in this our Augustan age of liberality and refinement, while we seem so justly sensible and jealous of our rights and liberties, and animated with such indignation against the very memory of those who would have subverted them, who would suppose that a certain people, under our national protection, should complain, not against a Monarch and a few favourite advisers, but against our whole legislative body, of the very same imposition and oppression, the Romish religion not excepted, and almost in the very same terms as our forefathers did against the family of Stuart! I will not, I cannot, enter into the merits of the cause; but I dare say, the American Congress, in 1776, will be allowed to have been as able and enlightened, and, a whole empire will say, as honest, as the English Convention in 1688; and that the fourth of July will be as sacred to their posterity as the fifth of November is to us.[80]

Here, under the guise of celebrating an 'English Convention' and protesting himself 'A BRITON', Burns displays sympathy with American revolutionary republicanism. As in his much earlier fragment on the American War, he seems on the surface a patriotic Brit but slyly reveals that underneath all is not as it seems.

The ambitious aspiring Exciseman did not put his name to this letter; its recipient, Edinburgh editor David Ramsay, who not long before had hosted a dinner party for the bard, would have identified its author. On one level, Burns was making use of his Edinburgh acquaintance to get the better of a local preacher who had annoyed him. Yet this letter also hints at private political sympathies. If Kinsley is correct in dating to 1788 the verse 'To the beautiful Miss Eliza J——n, on her principles of Liberty and Equality', that poem, for all it flirtatiously celebrates Miss Eliza as 'a proud DESPOT' who 'enchainest' mankind, is another signal that 'principles of Liberty and Equality' were interesting Burns in the run-up to the French Revolution.[81]

Though arguably of a piece with it, such hints are more telling than the light, mid-1788 verse of 'The Fête Champêtre'. Deploying again the Jacobite tune 'Gilliecrankie' he had used for his earlier American War fragment, Burns suggests contemporary politics is inherently corrupt. If he harboured radical political views, he was usually careful how he coded or expressed them. His 'Elegy on Capt

M[atthew] H[enderson]' memorialises a convivial Edinburgh gentleman Burns admired not least for his 'generous contempt of the adventitious distinctions of Men'.[82] Egalitarianism could lead the bard towards politically dangerous territory in his undemocratic, inegalitarian nation. 'For Lords or kings I dinna mourn' begins 'Elegy on the Year 1788'.[83] The safest channels for such sentiments lay in songs which might be accepted simply as variations on or additions to a traditional Scots repertoire.

Among several songs he seems to have worked on at Ellisland as Jean prepared to join him there in late 1788, one sums this up. Its tune ironically close to 'The British Grenadiers', this fragment is at once acceptably private and heartily erotic. It is also revolutionary in the American rather than the Hanoverian sense, thumbing its nose at French and British monarchs, then skipping off to bed:

> LOUIS, what reck I by thee,
>   Or Geordie on his ocean: *King George*
> Dyvor, beggar louns to me,   *Bankrupt*
>   I reign in Jeanie's bosom.
>
> Let her crown my love her law,
>   And in her breast enthrone me:
> Kings and nations, swith awa!   *quickly*
> Reif randies I disown ye! –[84]   *thieving louts*

Burns did his best work at Ellisland in song, not in grand poetic projects. Describing himself privately to Mrs Dunlop on 7 December as 'Revolution-mad', he calls attention to his letter to the *Courant*, explaining 'mine is the madness of an enraged Scorpion shut up in a thumb-phial; the indignant groans and bloodshot glances of ruined Right, gagged on the pillory of Derision to gratify the idiot insolence of ———— [surpation (*deleted*)] – '.[85] Burns breaks off an apparent Jacobite outburst, suppressing his dangerous anger. Instead, he turns to 'an old song and tune which has often thrilled thro' my soul' – an early version of 'Auld Lang Syne' – adding, 'Light be the turf on the breast of the heaven-inspired Poet who composed this glorious Fragment! There is more of the fire of native genius in it, than in half a dozen of modern English Bacchanalians. –'[86]

Setting what he presents here as an older Scots drinking song against 'modern English', Burns hints at a political edge in one of his most famous poems. Even the Unionist Kinsley points out, 'Editors have turned up a number of political songs, against the Union and the Hanoverians, which make use of the sentiments of "auld lang syne".'[87] For Burns the ancient Scottish nation was 'bold, independant, unconquered and free'; bardically, he regarded 'Caledonia' as 'immortal'.[88] Produced when he felt political anger, 'Auld Lang Syne' may subtly encode a harking back to older times before the Union of Parliaments and the Glorious Revolution, covertly celebrating an older, politically independent Stuart Scotland.

If it hints at this, though, much more obviously it is about unspecified 'auld acquaintance' – old friendship – which Burns's letter also discusses. Brilliant use of a refrain toasting 'auld lang syne' means even as the song's verses stress distance from the past, that refrain constantly asserts and pledges fidelity to it. Politics may play a part, but other aspects of Burns's biography – his removal from Ayrshire and childhood friends, relationships with Clarinda and 'Highland Mary', recent reading about Mrs Dunlop's meeting with an 'old Schoolfellow & friend' – may also have conditioned it.[89] Elements can be traced to broadside ballads and other popular sources. Burns has recast these. As in many of the best poems of his later years, he fuses his own work with popular tradition, making himself absolutely a bard of the popular voice. Political, personal and emotional tones, even when discernible, are attributable to the Scottish people as much as to the bard himself. There was safety *and* poetic power – an unusual combination of advantages – in this way of writing. As in his childhood, Burns made and was made by songs. Two men who drank with Burns at an inn in Hamilton when he was at the height of his fame recalled how he 'requested a song' from each of them, then sang one of his own: 'He was rather harsh in the voice, but gave it with much feeling.'[90]

Gathering and reshaping songs – 'wanton' ones like 'Come rede me, dame' as well as pure ones like the 'slow and tender' elegy to a dead Mary that begins 'Flow gently, sweet Afton' – made Burns all the more the bard of his people – 'the most rascally' as well as the genteel.[91] Yet his health wavered. 'My knee, I believe, never will be entirely well,' he complained to his Classics teacher friend, William

Cruikshank, with whom he had lodged in Edinburgh's St James's Square the previous winter.[92] The end of 1788 saw him uneasy, discontented.

Gilbert wrote piously but warmly to his 'dear brother' on New Year's Day, sending 'the compliments of the season to you and Mrs Burns'.[93] As 1789 got under way, Burns grew increasingly impatient to move into his new farmhouse. He wrote to Dr Moore about hopes for a secure livelihood which would let him focus on poetry. From Mauchline merchants he and Jean ordered new clothes, and household materials: a copper kettle, tables, chairs, a mahogany-cased clock.[94] Jean had taken on a relation, seventeen-year-old Elizabeth Smith, as a maid. Jean's surviving child, 'Robert the second' as Gilbert called him, was to be looked after at Mossgiel for much of 1789 before eventually joining his parents.[95] Burns's father's brother, Robert Burnes, died on 3 January at Stewarton in Ayrshire; Burnes's son William had been staying at Ellisland and it was arranged he would be apprenticed to Jean's father as a stonemason. Now William's sister Fanny was moving to Ellisland long-term also, to be followed by another brother, John, who helped Burns on the farm and was later said to have remembered his poet-cousin as 'a good master, but absent-minded . . . very ready to go from one thing to another in the most unexpected fashion'.[96] Burns soon wondered if he should concentrate on writing and the Excise, handing Ellisland over to the committed farmer Gilbert, whose lease at Mossgiel was 'near expiring'.[97] Immediately, Burns needed to go to Edinburgh to sort matters with pregnant Jenny Clow; he asked Ainslie for her current address. It is unclear if Jean knew about Clow's pregnancy, but she must have shared Burns's impatience to move into the new Ellisland house.

Conscious of his growing number of dependants, Burns was full of plans for poetry and career. He suggested to several correspondents that with his Excise prospects 'squalid Poverty' would transform to 'comfortable Independance'; he had 'a hundred different Poetic plans, pastoral, georgic, dramatic, &c. floating in the regions of fancy, somewhere between Purpose and resolve'.[98] He composed poems on horseback. He enjoyed himself at a Dumfries curling competition with Syme and others in clear, calm winter weather, consuming 'Beef & Kail & Tody' with the curlers until morning broke.[99] Making poetry on New Year's Day, he wrote to Mrs Dunlop

about the need to take time out from routine work, simply to laugh or cry, to worship and relish holidays as holy days: the morning of New Year's Day, the first Sunday in May, and good days at the start and end of autumn were for him such times. He also listed his favourite spring flowers, including mountain-daisy, harebell and hawthorn.[100]

Yet if Burns sounded at ease with himself, there were also indications of how insecure he still felt in the social hierarchy. In verse and prose the 'poor Bard' snapped at a deceased Mrs Oswald – a 'Keeper of Mammon's iron chest' – for whose grand funeral procession he had been asked to vacate an inn.[101] He remained very aware of 'the different situations of a Great and a Little man'; circulating to many correspondents his sycophantic poem to Graham of Fintry, he continued intriguing over his Excise prospects.[102]

In early February he told several Edinburgh friends he was coming to town. He published under the pen-name 'John Barleycorn' a letter in the 9 February *Edinburgh Evening Courant*, arguing Scottish Distillers were being taxed unfairly by the London Parliament which favoured 'a few opulent English Distillers . . . of vast Electioneering consequence'.[103] As King George III lapsed in and out of insanity and politicians argued over how to cope, Burns like many others followed national events, sometimes with anger. Writing how Scotland as 'An ancient nation that for many ages had gallantly maintained [its independance (*deleted*)] the unequal struggle for independance with her much more powerful neighbour, at last agrees to a union which should ever after make them one people', he implies this is not how things have worked out. He hopes William Pitt will act 'like a healing angel' and treat Scottish Distillers justly.[104]

This letter was part of Burns's campaign to advance himself in Excise circles. It hints too at underlying political thoughts. These relate to his love of an independent Scotland but also, for all his cap-doffing to Pitt, to a sense of the political absurdity of an inegalitarian Britain where 'The little Great-man' and 'the very Great-man' buy and sell votes.[105] Back in Edinburgh for ten days in late February, Burns renewed several old contacts, was 'impressed into the service of Bacchus', and protested he missed his home where Jean was in an advanced state of pregnancy.[106] In Edinburgh he seems to have settled up with Jenny Clow, who had given birth to his son – yet another Robert Burns – in November. Whatever settlement Burns

reached, he returned to Ellisland apparently free of further responsibilities. He even obtained from Creech a satisfactory statement of accounts.

Back home, the new house was still not ready. Burns chivvied the builders. He also set up with Riddell a community 'circulating library', the Monkland Friendly Society. Later, as 'A PEASANT', he wrote an account of its principles, stressing 'improvement' among 'the lower classes', and suggesting this was a model 'every country gentleman' might follow. Members subscribed five shillings, then sixpence a month, deciding by majority which books to buy; after three years the books were auctioned among subscribers.[107] Burns closely influenced the purchases, which included Enlightenment standard works as well as imaginative writings like *Don Quixote* and *The Man of Feeling*.

Encouraging readers, he was wary of would-be writers, complaining to Mrs Dunlop, 'my success has encouraged such a shoal of ill-spawned monsters to crawl into public notice under the title of Scots Poets, that the very term, Scots Poetry, borders on the burlesque'.[108] Things would only get worse: the devil in *Poems, Chiefly in the Scottish Dialect* by David Morison (1790) hailed Burns as 'Bardie'; Scottish gardener-poet John Learmont, invoking 'Robby Burns' in Standard Habbie, addressed *'the PLEBEIANS'* in 1791, maintaining 'MAN *was not made to MOURN*'; even a presumed distant relative, baker-poet John Burness of Bogjordam in his 1791 *Poems, Chiefly in the Scottish Dialect* turned *'the Ayreshire Bard*, Renowned BURNS' into an awkward acrostic.[109] Just weeks after Burns in 1788 had complained about this emerging 'shoal', London's *Star* and *Gazetteer* newspapers published in late March Scots poetry ridiculing the Duchess of Gordon. This was attributed to Burns. Annoyed – the Duchess was among his patrons – Burns wrote to complain, having asked Hill for the address of the *Star*'s editor, London Scot Peter Stuart, whose brother had known Robert Fergusson. Praising Burns in his paper, Stuart achieved a *rapprochement* with the bard who had sent him for publication his lines for Fergusson's tombstone. Publishing the occasional anonymous 'political Squib' in 'some London Newspaper' appealed to Burns. He gave Stuart an 'Ode to the departed Regency Bill'. Presenting 'the roaring Civil Storm' of 'A Nation's commotion', the ode hinted at government corruption, and 'ruin' exemplified by Scotland's supremo Henry Dundas.[110] In London

Stuart censored the poem ('mangled' was Burns's word). The bard knew 'Politics is dangerous ground for me', but could not resist. He may have recommended to his younger brother, William, 'that invaluable apothegm, Learn taciturnity'; he did not always follow it himself.[111]

Peter Stuart seems twice to have offered him a salary to write exclusively for the *Star*. Burns declined, just as he sidestepped Mrs Dunlop's April 1789 suggestion that he apply for Edinburgh University's chair of agriculture. Still, thanks to Stuart's generosity, he found himself for several months in receipt of London's first daily evening paper. He enjoyed boasting that 'the Publisher of one of the most blasphemous party London Newspapers is an acquaintance of mine'.[112] Sadly, delivery of the paper was erratic: 'Dear Peter, dear Peter/ ... Tho' glad I'm to see 't ... / I get it no ae [one] day in ten.'[113] We know Burns enjoyed newspapers, but it is usually impossible to know exactly which ones he read. Still, the four-page *Dumfries Weekly Journal*, crammed with overseas – especially French – reports, indicates how much news was readily available and discussed in the local community. Throughout the months leading up to the French Revolution, newspaper-reading Burns at Ellisland would have had a surprisingly detailed knowledge of the wider world.

None of Burns's correspondence with 'brother Poet' Kilmarnock's Gavin Turnbull survives, but they shared enthusiasms.[114] Turnbull, like Burns, loved Shenstone, Thomson, Fergusson, Ramsay and Robert Blair, but the English verse of this singer of 'Arran' and 'Fair Irvine' is bland. Turnbull's few 'Poetical Essays, in the Scottish Dialect' pall beside Fergusson or Burns. A friend of David Sillar, Turnbull apostrophised Burns in 'The Bard', dedicated to 'Mr R***** B*****'. Turnbull asks 'COILA'S BARD' to pay heed to the bard-protagonist in this poem whose 'name ... through all Caledonia rung' since 'ne'er did Scottish Bard so much enchant the ear' but who, for all his 'wooden shelves' of 'fav'rite authors' and his 'fragments' of planned poems, ends up debt-ridden, homeless, dead in a farmer's field.[115] Burns paid for half a dozen copies of Turnbull's book in April, complaining about a plethora of 'Subscription bills for Scots Poems'.[116] 'The Bard', suggesting that the fate of Scottish peasant bards, however famous, led to ruin, could not have comforted Robert. At the end of February his Edinburgh friend Cunningham had presented him with Johnson's *Lives of the Poets*,

wishing him 'prosperity and happiness' but mentioning that these had 'not always been the concomitant, or realized in the lives of those who have written'.[117] The bard was only too aware of such daunting, haunting examples.

Often he was being asked for advice about the work of poet-asters. One was the late farmer James Mylne whose 'To Mr Burns, on his Poems' praised the bard but warned that the 'Muse' was a 'jilt' who tended to 'misuse/ The best o' poets'. Left 'spoilt for ilka ither game', they paid too little attention to 'affairs, and hame', letting themselves slide into ruin.[118] If Burns seems calculating, even careerist, planning his farm and Excise business he was swimming against a tide of cultural assumptions about poets, especially peasant bards. His mapping himself on to Fergusson – in his thoughts again when he wrote to Stuart in spring 1789 – indicates how far he too had internalised such values. Haunted by fears of ruin that came from his father's fate and conventional wisdom about poets, not least Scottish lower-class ones, Burns sought determinedly to succeed. That spring, voicing his independent-mindedness, he showed himself 'not devoutly attached to a certain monarch' in poems satirising political affairs and church politics; elsewhere, as in senti-mental lines 'On Seeing a Wounded Hare limp by me' or the later sycophantic sonnet 'To Mr Graham of Fintry, On being appointed to my Excise Division' he reveals fears and vulnerabilities as well as ambitions.

Spring 1789 saw him out sowing grass seeds in the early mornings. Following his father's methods of improvement, during his tenancy he had stones cleared, and lime added to Ellisland's soil. Innova-tively, he began importing dairy cows from Ayrshire. At last, after tensions with builders (whose bill Burns delayed paying for two years), he and Jean moved into the completed farmhouse. Jean's maid recalled Burns insisting she carry salt and a family bible over the threshold, according to traditional custom, before Burns followed, 'his wife on his arm'.[119] He seems to have begun passing to Jean responsibility for many arrangements on what was becoming a small dairy farm, while he concentrated on developing his Excise career. Ellisland's single-storey, five-apartment thatched building had loft-space for farm servants and other help. Usually there were two male and two female servants. Jean was well organised, and popular with her servants, whom she fed well. Robert was regarded as kind, knowledgeable, but sometimes quick-tempered. One servant recalled

that at home Burns 'usually wore a broad blue bonnet, a blue or drab long-tailed coat, corduroy breeches, dark-blue stockings and *cootikens* [gaiters], and in cold weather a black-and-white-checked plaid wrapped round his shoulders'.[120]

Ambitious and affable, Burns continued sending handwritten copies of new work to correspondents. In mid-May he told Graham of Fintry he intended 'making a little manuscript book of my un-published Poems for Mrs Graham'; more laboriously he began to transcribe a selection of his poems and letters (of which he frequently kept fair copies) into two volumes Riddell had given him for this specific purpose.[121] It took two years to complete volume one; Burns spent a further two years or so on the second. Both are among the treasures of the National Library of Scotland.

As spring advanced towards summer Burns portrayed himself working on the farm, sometimes 'sauntering by the delightful wanderings of the Nith ... praying for seasonable weather, or holding an intrigue with the muses'. But to another correspondent he complained on 8 June of being 'condemned to drudgery beyond sufferance', caught up in 'incessant toil'. Jean was far advanced in pregnancy, and Burns wrote preachily to the unmarried Ainslie, 'The welfare of those who are very dear to us, whose only support, hope and stay we are – this, to a generous mind, is another sort of more important object of care than any concerns whatever which center [*sic*] merely in the individual.'[122] Actually the bard was dividing his time among many matters: 'frequent meetings' with musician Stephen Clarke about Scots songs for Johnson's *Musical Museum*; farming; dealing with builders; increasing his dairy herd of about ten cows. He was also studying for the Excise, perusing new, unappetising-sounding works like William Marshall's *The Rural Economy of Yorkshire* but also 'that extraordinary man, Smith, in his Wealth of Nations'. Burns and Smith never met; Burns wished they might: 'I would covet much to have his ideas respecting the present state of some quarters of the world that are or have been the scenes of considerable revolutions since his book was written.'[123] This is clearly a reference to the American Revolution – Smith, like Burns, having expressed revolutionary sympathies. It is also in all likelihood one of several signs that Burns was following newspaper reports from France prior to the fall of the Bastille. By early July the *Dumfries Weekly Journal* was declaring, 'the revolution in France is the most extraordinary in the annals of history'.

French political discontents were reported alongside campaigns for 'Reform' at home.[124]

Burns was thinking of writing a long poem, 'The Poet's Progress', but did not persist with it. At Riddell's he met and greatly liked the obese English antiquary, ex-soldier and lover of slang and drinking, Captain Francis Grose. In his late fifties, Grose – 'a chearful-looking grig of an old, fat fellow' – was following up his six-volume *Antiquities of England and Wales* (1773–87) with two projected volumes on the antiquities of Scotland. He spent at least two months at Riddell's, growing 'intimately acquainted' with the bard, who suggested that Grose include Kirk Alloway.[125] Riddell, who had 'in 12 Vol[umes] of M[anu]s[cript]s: a great variety of materialls for Galwegian history', gave Grose 'a full account of Lincluden' Abbey near Dumfries, which Grose soon published.[126] Perhaps in a spirit of emulation, Burns supplied 'an Itinerary thro' Ayr-shire'.[127] Out of the friendship between Burns and Grose 'Tam o' Shanter' emerged the following year.

Meanwhile, Burns followed with interest the collapse of the case against Ayr's Reverend Dr John McGill at the Church of Scotland's General Assembly. The *Dumfries Weekly Journal* recorded how 'Dr McGill of Ayr' had been 'accused of having published heretical doctrines' in a case which involved 'Mr Auld at Mauchline'.[128] McGill had partly recanted. His crime, Burns thought, was simply 'To join FAITH and SENSE'. The bard's 'new song' entitled 'The Kirk of Scotland's Garland' ridiculed conflict over McGill's 'heretic blast'.[129] To Mrs Dunlop Burns wrote that he believed in 'an incomprehensibly Great Being, to whom I owe my existence', in an afterlife, and that 'Jesus Christ was from God'.[130] Yet his beliefs were slippery, his expression not always straightforward: to the same correspondent he protested he had 'no romantic notions of independancy of spirit'.[131]

Complaining of 'low spirits' and that 'for some time my soul has been beclouded with a thickening atmosphere of evil imaginations and gloomy presages', Burns savoured Captain Grose's company, worked, marked up a copy of his fulsome English admirer Helen Maria Williams's 1788 *Poem on the Bill Lately Passed for Regulating the Slave Trade* (commending its treatment of 'Oppression' and 'this infernal traffic'), and waited for Jean to give birth.[132] More and more a cultural landmark, he was quoted in William Gilpin's influential 1789 *Observations, relative chiefly to Picturesque Beauty*,

and held up as 'a bard as he calls himself, from the plough'.[133] But writing to Sillar, for whose collection of poems he had gathered subscriptions, the celebrated bard wished they could be like 'Robin' and 'Davie' of old, rather than simply exchanging business letters; he worried that married life was reducing his poetic output.[134] Sillar's book, with its suggestion Burns had grown 'secure/ Against the wretched thought o' being poor' and forgotten his old friends, could not have cheered a bard unable to escape fears of poverty and ruin, and who had no wish to be perceived as having become a remote exotic, a rhinoceros.[135]

In early August, just as Peter Stuart was calling him 'successor in national simplicity and genius' of 'my late inestimable friend, Bob Fergusson', Burns got word he was to be given an Excise appointment in the local First Dumfriesshire Division covering the 'fine romantic Country' of Upper Nithsdale.[136] The Dumfries Collector of Excise, Gilbert Gordon, 'a gentleman much and justly esteemed', had died in late July, and Burns had succeeded in getting Leonard Smith removed, creating a vacancy 'in the [Excise] Division in which I live'.[137] The 18th of August saw the birth of Francis Wallace Burns – 'your little Godson', Burns cooed to Mrs Dunlop.[138] The bard's mother and sisters came to assist in the household, bringing with them Burns's son Robert. Harvest time approached; Burns felt 'the hurry of a farmer' as well as the start in September of his new Excise duties. Although they paid £50 a year, these were demanding: 'Five days in the week, or four at least, I must be on horseback, and very frequently ride thirty or forty miles ere I return; besides four different kinds of book-keeping to post every day.'[139] Excise record-keeping was elaborate and regularly inspected. The work was exhausting.

On 18 August 1789 one of Burns's poems – his epitaph on Fergusson – appeared in the *Dumfries Weekly Journal*, but the paper called Burns, 'the Ayrshire Bard', giving no indication he lived in the vicinity.[140] The bard, though, played his part in Dumfriesshire affairs. He wrote a mocking ballad on 'Election-mad' antics of local politicians, including his landlord Patrick Miller's son, then standing for Parliament.[141] The subtlest point of Burns's poem may be that it offers support to no particular candidate. Soon the voteless poet wrote he was 'too little a man to have any political attachments', but also added, 'a man who has it in his power to be the Father of a Country, and who is only known to that Country by the mischiefs he does in it, is a character of which one cannot speak with

patience'.[142] The ending of his election ballad, 'The Five Carlins', reads, 'God grant the king, and ilka man,/ May look weel to themsel.'[143] Since the King was celebrated for lunacy and Burns seems to have scorned the candidates' manoeuvrings, these lines offer a subversive nudge. The local paper was reporting the French National Assembly's Declaration of Rights: 'All men are born equal and free.'[144] Of his new son, Wallace, Burns hoped simply 'he will one day stand on the legs of INDEPENDANCE and hold up the face of AN HONEST MAN'.[145]

With men like Grose and Riddell, Burns enjoyed male-bonding. This is exemplified in a drinking contest over an antique ebony whistle said to have been brought to Scotland in the time of 'James the sixth of Scotland's Queen' and competed for by 'Bacchanalians of the Scotish Court'.[146] Associated with an older, independent Scotland's male drinking contests, with music, and now with Friars' Carse, this whistle was competed for there by Riddell and two cousins on 16 October 1789. The winner was Alexander Fergusson of Craigdarroch, who downed eight bottles of claret before blowing the whistle. 'A bard ... selected to witness the fray', Burns wrote it up with heroic Ossianic allusions in 'The Whistle'. 'Our Bard' calls Craigdarroch a hero from a 'line, that have struggled for freedom with Bruce', and suggests 'one bottle more'.[147]

This sort of thing went down well with Riddell, but a fuller picture of his own life was sent by Burns in a Standard Habbie verse letter to the blind minister Dr Blacklock dated 'Ellisland 21st Oct. 1789'. In August Blacklock, who was probably a Freemason, had addressed a poem to 'Burns, thou brother of my heart', asking after Robert's wife, family and poetry. Burns seems to have given his reply to Robert Heron, Hugh Blair's bibulous assistant, who lost it. To Blacklock Burns complains he may write less poetry now he has 'turn'd a Gauger', but he needs the money to support his growing family. The poem is often quoted for its assertion that

> To make a happy fireside clime
> To weans and wife,
> That's the true *Pathos* and *Sublime*
> Of Human life. –

However, Burns also sounds a note of exhausted resentment. His use of the word 'brithers' may relate to Masonic brotherhood. After

a summer full of the 'TUMULT or rather REVOLUTION in PARIS' and French debates on 'the rights of man', Burns's 'brithers' may also resonate with that egalitarian *fraternité* so recently and forcefully articulated by France's revolutionaries.

> Lord help me thro' this world o' care!
> I'm weary sick o't late and air!
> Not but I hae a richer share
>   Than mony ithers;
> But why should ae man better fare,
>   And a' Men brithers![148]

As often, Burns wished to speak up for egalitarianism and fraternity even as he worked to maximise household income. If this is thought inconsistent or even hypocritical, would it have been better if he had not dreamed of a more desirable way of living, or had sacrificed the well-being of his family in order to try to advance dangerously egalitarian sentiments? On paper around this time he simply mentioned concern with 'what French mischief was brewin' as chief among his interests in foreign and domestic news.[149] His sense of brotherhood was expansive and politically idealistic, but also practical. Robert Chambers and John Wilson recorded how, 'According to a recollection of his son Robert, the poet gave shelter and succour at Ellisland for about six weeks to a poor broken down sailor, who had come begging in the extremity of want and wretchedness. The man lay in an out-house until he recovered some degree of health and strength, when, being able once more to take to the road, he departed, leaving as a token of his gratitude a little model of a ship for the amusement of the poet's children.'[150]

Thanks to campaigns waged by Burns and his supporters he had strings pulled for him in the Excise. It was unusual for an officer to be appointed to a Division immediately beside his home. More than that, he did not serve as 'an Expectant, as they call their Journeymen Excisemen', but was appointed to a full fixed post.[151] He was pleased, but there are signs of stress: by early November he was complaining his Excise Division had 'no less than ten parishes to ride over, & besides abounds with so much business, that I can scarce steal a spare moment'.[152] Soon he had 'a most violent cold' and a lasting headache. He tried to impress his Excise patron Graham of Fintry, telling him 'hurried life' was not 'greatly

inimical to my correspondence with the Muses', but by mid-December he was suffering what may well have been a depressive episode.[153] Certainly Gilbert, who knew his brother's health better than anyone, found it *'alarming'*.[154] For at least three weeks Burns had a persistent 'nervous head-ach'; he was, he protested to Mrs Dunlop, 'groaning under the miseries of a diseased nervous System'.[155] He brooded on death, on his father's ruin, and on Robert Muir, his friend and encourager who had died the previous year at the age of thirty, the age Burns was now. Not least he wrote to Mrs Dunlop of 'my lost, my ever dear MARY, whose bosom was fraught with Truth, Honor, Constancy & Love'; he had written a song set to the tune 'Capt[ai]n Cook's Death' about how 'My Mary from my Soul was torn'.[156]

What Jean (not mentioned at all in this letter of 13 December) made of all this is hard to say. She coped. The baby was howling with a sore mouth; Jean suffered from sore nipples as she breast-fed him.[157] For a time at least Burns never left the house; generally, however, he continued to ride extensively. Writing down woes and fears, he may have indulged in rhetorical effect to impress corres-pondents with his sensitivity, but there are recurrences of a familiar pattern. 'I am a good deal inclined to think with those who main-tain that what are called nervous affections are in fact diseases of the mind.'[158] In mid-December he sent Jacobite verses to Lady Winifred Maxwell Constable, who was descended from an old Nithsdale Jacobite family; he pondered how, having 'left their humble cottages', his ancestors 'shook hands with Ruin'. A week later he was still complaining of the 'chearless gloom and sinking despondency of December weather and diseased nerves'.[159]

Reading Shakespeare, wondering if he might write a Scottish drama, Burns sent a prologue to the Shakespeare-loving manager of an actors' company in Dumfries. He attended several perform-ances, but his illness malingered into the new year. Trying to cheer himself up by writing a bawdy poem each of whose last lines contained the rhyme-word 'cunt', he sent this to a whisky-drinking friend and minor poet, Provost Maxwell of Lochmaben. He also wrote a Standard Habbie poem about Grose, warning Scots, 'A chield's amang you, taking notes,/ And, faith, he'll prent [print] it'.[160] But, despite cheerful intervals, the bard remained downcast. Ellisland, he told Gilbert on 11 January 1790, was 'a ruinous affair on all hands'. 'My nerves are in a damnable State. – I feel that

horrid hypochondria pervading every atom of both body & Soul.'[161]

By his thirty-first birthday he was beginning to feel better, but worried the new baby might fall victim to a smallpox outbreak. In February he wrote energetically to Hill about literary business, and denounced people attempting to banish from Edinburgh a celebrated prostitute known as 'Miss Burns': 'May Woman damn them! May her lovely hand inexorably shut the Portal of Rapture to their most earnest Prayers & fondest essays for entrance!' The bard who eight days later warned his younger brother William against 'Bad Women' sounds a different man.[162] He was corresponding with Clarinda again, stung by her telling him she looked on his letters 'with a smile of contempt'. Particularly after the birth of Burns's son to Jenny Clow, Agnes McLehose thought the poet had wronged her. In a surviving fragment of correspondence he maintains he could not and would not 'enter into extenuatory circumstances'; he sought, not without calculation, to rekindle something of the old ardour of their relationship by sending her a recent song 'because it pleases myself':

> Thine am I, my faithful fair,
> Thine, my lovely Nancy;
> Ev'ry pulse along my veins,
> Ev'ry roving fancy.[163]

Dating this fragment is difficult. Assuming reference to Burns's 'incessant headache' and 'depression of spirits' lasting 'this whole winter' indicates early 1790, the song can be read as trying to suggest Burns's 'roving fancy' was at root an expression of his love for the married, apparently unattainable Nancy. The song is a song, not a straightforward piece of autobiography, but neither Mrs McLehose nor Burns was likely to regard the choice of the name 'Nancy' as accidental. Burns later published the song with 'Chloris' substituted for 'Nancy', but his sending it to McLehose signals a continuing wish to uphold erotic power over her, asserting that in some way their relationship continued.

As Burns's health began to improve the third volume of Johnson's *Scots Musical Museum* appeared. It included such famous compositions as the jaunty 'My love she's but a lassie yet', Jacobite songs like 'Johnie Cope', and the tender lyric of a long-married couple,

'John Anderson, my jo'. In manuscript many of these songs are listed as 'Mr Burns's old words'. This phrasing is felicitous. Repeatedly Burns takes fragments or versions of older songs and recasts them, drawing on both written and oral traditions. Often it is hard to be sure just what is Burns and what is 'old words'. Sometimes, though, his alterations are striking. 'John Anderson, my jo', for instance, is very much a purification of a bawdy song Burns had probably known since youth. He transcribed a bawdy version into the collection known as the *Merry Muses of Caledonia*. Turning an old wife's complaints about her husband's loss of potency into a celebration of love and fidelity, he recast the second verse's sexual 'gae-ups' and 'gae down' as a much more decorous ascent and descent; also a more moving one:

> John Anderson my jo, John,
>   We clamb the hill the gither;
> And mony a canty day, John,
>   We've had wi' ane anither:
> Now we maun totter down, John,
>   And hand in hand we'll go;
> And sleep the gither at the foot,
>   John Anderson my Jo.[164]

Burns made direct references to his own biography in songs, but adapting traditional material also encouraged investigation of a wide spectrum of emotions, attitudes and political standpoints. Tendencies such as Jacobite sympathies could be indicated, but consistency was not required. Collecting songs, Burns explored aspects of Scotland's cultural inheritance, but also the extent of his own feelings. Sides of his personality he may have found hard to reconcile might here function simply as assets, widening his range. The work of collection, creation and re-creation he saw as patriotic and artistically enriching. If English and Scots were the languages used, music was also vital. Songs like 'The Battle of Sherra-moor' with its 'Clans frae woods, in tartan duds' reminded readers and listeners the Highlands too were part of the distinctive, sometimes combative mix of Scottish culture.[165] Having toured his nation, Burns now presented a rich national assembly, singing certainly as Lowland bard, but also as Ossian-loving collector and celebrator of Highland songs:

My heart's in the Highlands, my heart is not here;
My heart's in the Highlands a chasing the deer;
Chasing the wild deer, and following the roe;
My heart's in the Highlands, wherever I go. –[166]

Wherever Burns's heart was, it was not in farming Ellisland. Now on the Excise promotion list, he planned to give up the farm in 1791 when his rent was due to rise. For the moment, having advised his friend Nicol on the purchase and liming of a nearby farm, Burns had to pay attention to his own – but not so much that it stopped him reading and writing. He ordered books of English and French drama that spring, apparently still hoping he might write a Scottish-themed play. This did not materialise, but he scripted a prologue for Mrs Sutherland, an actress whose husband was the manager involved in rebuilding Dumfries's playhouse. Burns made a show of sending his prologue to the influential Provost, magistrate David Staig, for approval, since 'there is a dark stroke of Politics in the belly of the Piece'.[167] It praises Scotland's proud independent history and struggle ''Gainst mighty England'. Mention of 'mad Rebellion's arms' refers to the Scots' own hostility to Mary, Queen of Scots – also subject of Burns's 'Lament' that spring which both denounces 'mony a traitor' in Scotland, and promises 'Grim vengeance' on England's Queen.[168]

Such poems were safely, distantly historicised, far from the actual rebellion which convulsed France and ended a modern monarchy. Burns, however, expressed to Mrs Dunlop what we would now call his nationalist feelings: 'You know my National Prejudices . . . Alas! have I often said to myself, what are all the boasted advantages which my Country reaps from a certain Union, that can counter-balance the annihilation of her Independance, & even her very Name!' He complained about being fed up with the use of 'English' to mean British. He felt strongly attached to Scotland's independ-ence and honour, but 'I believe these, among your *Men of the world*, men who in fact guide [& (*deleted*)] govern our world, *they* look on such ways of thinking as just so many modifications of wrong-headedness.'[169] Such sentiments were scarcely treasonable; Burns must have been confident Mrs Dunlop, with her passion for Wallace, would accept them. Nonetheless they were risky for a government Exciseman. Deflecting them on to historical personages was a canny course of action.

Even when Burns confined political views to local events, self-censorship might play a part. Writing a Standard Habbie 'Epistle' to Graham of Fintry about 'the Election for the Dumfries string of Boroughs' in summer 1790, Burns suppressed vitriolic stanzas on the 'Follies and Crimes' of the elegant, sophisticated, corrupt William Douglas, fourth Duke of Queensberry, who lived at nearby Drumlanrig. Burns thought Queensberry 'bent on buying Borough-towns', having 'left the all-important cares/ Of fiddles, wh—res and hunters' to shake hands with local weavers and kiss their hangers-on.[170] The poem pokes fun at Burns's Whig friends such as 'Glen-riddel, skill'd in rusty coins' as well as their Tory opponents. Burns presents himself as 'the Bard, afar', keeping his distance from the squabbling. He damns all who 'wad Scotland buy, or sell'.[171] That July Burns saw local election candidates rouse an army of 'upwards of two hundred Colliers from Sanquhar Coal-works & Miners from Wanlock-head' who were eventually routed by an opposing 'superiour host of Annandale warriors'.[172] This did not lead Burns to take an optimistic view of the Scottish politicians, who included his Ellisland landlord's family. Such poems on local elections align Burns less with a particular party than with the contemporary Scottish burgh reform movement. Since the 1780s one of its aims had been to reform local government, and election processes for burgh MPs. Along with England's Association Movement these reformers campaigned at Westminster in the late 1780s and early 1790s, their attempts widely reported.[173]

Burns remained controversial for his political and religious views. William Nicol hinted to Ainslie in a letter of 13 August 1790 that Burns, allied with 'Beelzebub', might be linked with 'government ... *enemies*'.[174] In 1788 Paisley poet James Maxwell had reprinted Burns's lines '*said to be written on a Window in Stirling*' denouncing the Hanoverian monarchy as 'An ideot Race'. Burns – 'a drunkard, a rake and a sot' – was reviled for flinging such 'rebellious jav'lins' at his 'lawful King', and even told, 'For this thy life in danger stands.'[175] In 1790 Maxwell renewed his assault: not only did Burns's 'pretended paraphrase on the xcth Psalm' show he 'despise[d]' 'all reveal'd religion', he was also to be classed with 'Ayrshire ... Poet-asters' who had 'sprung up quick, like mushrooms in a night ... Some of them smutty; some of them far worse/ ... Making a mock of ev'ry sacred thing,/ And rankest treason too against the king'.[176] In 1790 to be accused of treason, even in verse, was dangerous. This

year also saw the reprinting of 1789 verses by Thomas Walker of Hill of Ochiltree in Ayrshire attacking 'Robin' Burns and bewailing how

> Saints now a-days may weep and mourn,
> To think how ages yet unborn,
> Will see religion turn'd to scorn
> By Robin's books ...

These lines were reprinted by Robert Jackson in Dumfries as part of the Ochiltree royalist James Fisher's *Poems on Various Subjects*, which also cocks a snook at rebellious Burns, imaging him as 'this Burn' which

> nearly did the kirk o'erturn,
> An' a' the clergymen swoop doun;
> The kintry a' did hear its soun';
> Its waters raise sae high an' keen,
> They very near had wet the king.[177]

Again, in this year following the French Revolution, the strong implication is not just that Burns is a religious rebel; he is also opposed to his monarch. It was as well for Burns he was at times a skilled intriguer, able to retain powerful supporters inclined to advance his career.

In July 1790 he was promoted to the Dumfries Third Foot-walk Division – salary £70 per annum, duties largely confined to Dumfries itself. Having grown up familiar with smuggling, and with several smugglers in his family, it sometimes embarrassed him that he was an Exciseman, but he did his job thoroughly as well as sympathetically. A Dumfriesshire inn worker told Ramsay of Ochtertyre that when Burns 'met with anything seizable, he was no better than any other gauger; in every thing else, he was perfectly a gentleman'.[178] Generally he commuted on horseback between Ellisland and Dumfries for the next eighteen months; sometimes he stayed overnight at the Globe Inn in Dumfries High Street. He liked this pub whose origins went back to the early 1600s, and soon began an affair with the barmaid, Ann Park, just out of her teens. At Ellisland he went on sleeping with Jean. Both women became pregnant that summer. In due course, having moved to the east coast, Park gave birth to a daughter, Elizabeth, on 31 March 1791, nine days before Burns's

wife bore William Nicol Burns. Ann later married a carpenter in Edinburgh.[179] Eventually Jean went on to raise both children as part of Burns's household, though a neighbour recalled that when little Elizabeth joined the Burns family about 1794, 'it was upon the understanding', Jean made clear, 'that she was not to associate with her children, which she never did, but was confined to the kitchen'. Still, the girl was treated 'kindly' and was looked after by Jean until she married.[180]

Around the time he embarked on his adultery with Ann, Burns was writing to his old teacher Murdoch, now in London, putting him in touch with the poet's brother William, who had found work as a London saddler. Burns also introduced Grose by letter to Dugald Stewart. His letter shows him unsure, like many Scots, whether to write 'I shall' or 'I will'.[181] Small-scale uncertainties were matched by larger ones. Burns still thought he might become a playwright and told Ramsay of Ochtertyre, who visited him in the autumn, he intended writing a drama involving 'Robert Bruce'.[182] No play appeared. Still enthusiastic for independence (usually his own), Burns was once again linking himself to 'that poor, blackguard Miscreant, Satan'.[183] His reading of John Moore's novel *Zeluco* (1786) with its villainous hero may have encouraged him. Yet even as he conducted his adulterous affair and wondered if he might become a playwright, he experienced – almost treasured – familiar anxieties, musing that 'Bewitching Poesy is like bewitching WOMAN', leading man towards 'the vortex of Ruin'. He penned these thoughts for Helen Craik, a local sentimental poet. As often, Burns got carried away with his own rhetoric, restating in fanciful language thoughts he had first entertained about Fergusson and bards unpitied by the world yet with so keen a relish of its pleasures.

> Take a being of our kind; give him a stronger imagination and more delicate sensibility, which will ever between them engender a more ungovernable set of Passions, than the usual lot of man; implant in him an irresistible impulse to some idle vagary, such as, arranging wild-flowers in fantastical nosegays, tracing the grashopper [*sic*] to his haunt by his chirping song, watching the frisks of the little minnows in the sunny pool, or hunting after the intrigues of wanton butterflies – in short, send him adrift after some wayward pursuit which shall eternally mislead him from the paths of Lucre; yet, curse him

with a keener relish than any man living for the pleasures that only Lucre can bestow; lastly, fill up the measure of his woes, by bestowing on him a spurning sense of his own dignity; and you have created a wight nearly as miserable as a Poet. –[184]

There is self-pity here: Burns is rather relishing Being a Poet. As often happens in such circumstances, he was writing little verse. His focus on how poetry like woman can lead the sensitive poet towards ruin may have been underpinned by his betrayal of Jean with Ann Park, as well as by his wish for career success when Ellisland was dragging him down financially. Whatever was going on in Burns's mind, it found more splendid expression in the poem he was about to write.

During the summer he had sent Grose summaries of three traditional stories about Alloway's old ruined church. One concerned a local boy flying away on a horse made of ragwort. The other two were to underpin 'Tam o' Shanter'. They show that Burns already had the basic shape and even some phrasing for his poem which, like so many of his songs, grew from a mixture of older material he reshaped and from fresh composition. A dramatic narrative, it also drew on his impulse for play-writing. Much later Jean apparently told Robert Cromek that while Burns was composing the poem she saw him gesticulating wildly, '*croonin to himsel*', weeping tears of delight beside the Nith.[185]

Certainly Burns was enjoying convivial evenings: some with local worthies like Riddell, Grose, and the laird's son with an eye for the ladies, John Syme. Syme breakfasted with Burns at Ellisland in early September, a little disappointed with '"Bonny Jean"'.[186] Riding backwards and forwards to Dumfries and further afield, Burns relied absolutely on his mount; he would often pass the ecclesiastical ruins still visible at Lincluden about whose 'roofless tower' Burns made a 'midnight' song; galloping along at one point in 1790 his 'poor jackass skeleton of a horse' became so exhausted Burns 'almost broke' his neck.[187] Whatever the perils, though, that summer he was also enjoying his affair with Ann Park. He celebrated in song the 'dying raptures in her arms/ I give and take with Anna!!!'[188] Exclamatory and sexually explicit, 'Tam o' Shanter' is a frolicsome poem about a farmer who, drinking in town away from home, realises he must ride back to his wife; passing an old ruined kirk, he is almost undone by a sexual experience with an

erotically exciting younger woman, but in the end he and his horse gallop home, just skirting death. Our hero, menaced by bewitching female sexuality, hellish hordes, and his sulking wife, gets off free in the end. The poem celebrates male-bonding, drinking, a brush with death and the devil, sexual adventuring, galloping home on horseback, and (though it also mocks this) the triumph of male over female.

In terms of Burns's biography, it is not hard to think why this poem's narrator seems so engaged with such subject-matter. 'Tam o' Shanter' is a poem of haunting, ruin, and dark fears. From one angle its treatment of a man enjoying extra-marital sexual excitement may be a masculinist celebration of adultery – probably the greatest oblique celebration of adultery in any variety of English. Yet with its spooks and storminess it is so witty, teasing, energetic and well paced that it has become universally enjoyable. The poem is no direct transcription of Burns's experiences, but can be seen as transmuting his emotional excitements and anxieties. Not least, its sense of life-threatening danger may relate to the fact that around the time of its composition he had a bout of serious illness, 'seized' in late September and early October 'with a slow, illformed Fever' followed by 'a most malignant Squinancy [tonsillitis] which had me very near the precincts of the Grave'.[189] Biographers have expended so much energy following up assertions that the poem's hero was Douglas Graham of Shanter farm near Kirkoswald, supposedly married to a shrewish wife Helen, that they have missed the deeper connections with Burns's own situation.

'Tam o' Shanter. A Tale' begins with Tam (minus wife) and his male 'drouthy' cronies in an Ayr pub. It then sends its drunken protagonist on a storm-swept night-ride past Kirk Alloway where Tam sees 'Warlocks and witches in a dance'; excited by a 'winsome', 'souple', sexy witch in a short shirt ('Cutty-sark'), Tam cries out and is chased by the 'hellish legion'. Eventually his 'gray mare, *Meg*' rescues him, but loses her own tail to a pursuing witch in an apparent parody of castration; the poem ends with a po-faced mock-moral, urging men to 'Remember Tam o' Shanter's mare' whenever they are inclined to drink or lewdness. Varying pace and diction, and characterised by power surges of reeling humour, this poem in Hudibrastic couplets is one of Burns's greatest achievements. A great carnival of verse, it is all the more thrilling because permeated by dark threats at once potentially fatal yet able to be laughed off –

as in those supernatural stories Burns had known from childhood. Set in the haunted places of his boyhood, it *is* in all probability a tale he had known since childhood, but quickened by adult fears and excitation.

> The wind blew as 'twad blawn its last;
> The rattling showers rose on the blast;
> The speedy gleams the darkness swallow'd;
> Loud, deep, and lang, the thunder bellow'd:
> That night, a child might understand,
> The Deil had business on his hand.[190]

In a country lacking a strong theatrical heritage, 'Tam o' Shanter' is verse drama in monologue form. The poem enjoys its own internal audience, and its spiritedness attracts an audience round it. It is a social poem about isolation: for all his drinking buddies, Tam is ultimately alone with just his horse to save him. He is a man of the people, yet, galloping along at the poem's crisis, he is dangerously isolated. Burnished to perfection, varying in tone and pace, the poem is the triumph of a performative bard. Burns wondered if he might write other narrative poems. Almost as soon as 'Tam o' Shanter' was completed, he realised he might never match it.

In October he recited a version of 'Tam' to Ainslie who was visiting and depressed. Burns tried to cheer him up with jokes. The two got very drunk together. Another evening the Burnses held a dance, but Ainslie found the company (which included a Dumfries innkeeper, Patrick Miller's gardener, a former clerk and their respective wives) vulgar. Mrs Burns, he told Clarinda, though kind enough, did not clean her house properly. No doubt Clarinda savoured such news, and enjoyed being informed that Jean was sidelined by local gentry. Ainslie found Burns's life an odd mixture of poetry and constant petty business. Burns told Ainslie what he had told Syme the previous month: he would soon 'give . . . up' farming.[191] He had expressed a wish to Graham of Fintry to work eventually as an Excise Supervisor in northern Scotland; more immediately he would settle for Port Glasgow, Greenock, 'or Dumfries'.[192]

Shortly after visiting Burns Ainslie seems to have passed an advance draft of 'Tam o' Shanter' to Mrs Dunlop. She told Burns the following month she found its imagery 'beyond praise or comparison', but when in 1791 she saw the published text she thought some of it 'a

little too strong for me'.[193] Generally, though, the strength of 'Tam o' Shanter' made it an immediate hit, and rendered Burns's birth-place famous. As early as 1791 a Renfrewshire traveller riding near Ayr experienced the thrill of recognition which tourists still sense today:

> At the third mile I passéd a little ruinous church or chapple from which the road winds down a hill & then crosses the water of Downe. The scene resembled one drawn by Robert Burns, and I found on enquiry that the Ruin was Alloa-kirk where OShanter saw the initiation of a Witch, and that the hill was the very hill down which the beldams pursuéd the Drunkard to avenge their disturbed rites![194]

Though we get occasional glimpses of Burns's private life from visitors, inevitably most evidence comes from letters where more often than not he constructs suitable versions of himself as The Bard. So, for instance, he penned a grand missive of encouragement to agricultural improver and literary patriot Dr James Anderson who was starting a magazine, *The Bee*. Soon in its pages Burns's work was found bardically 'Sweet as the song of Ossian'; his voice was 'The Song of the Lark'. Hailing him in terms of the Gaelic 'Oran Ussaig', one writer explained 'The adjective or synonyme' was appropriately that of a 'bard or poet in the Scots, Celtic or Gaelic language'.[195] Though he sent no poetry, Burns collected several local subscriptions, hoping *The Bee* might gather Scottish honey 'for delicacy of flavor' equal to 'the flowery luxuriance of the plains of Kent'. This, for Bard Burns, who had never seen the plains of Kent, was appropriately flowery; but a manuscript now in the Central Library, Liverpool reveals how in a draft cancelled passage of the letter Burns complained he had no new work to offer because the demands of his Excise labours made him feel like Satan in *Paradise Lost* who was, as Milton put it, compelled 'To do what yet tho' damn'd I would abhor'.[196]

Sensibly, Burns decided not to reveal he felt such resentments even as he courted Graham of Fintry about Excise promotion, and aimed to give up farming. The Dumfries Excise Examiner Alexander Findlater wrote to 'William Corbet, General Supervisor of Excise' on 20 December, recommending Burns for promotion.[197] Sending 'Tam o' Shanter' to Grose that December, the bard took pleasure

in recent editions of Blind Hary's medieval Scots *Wallace* and John Barbour's *Bruce*. He was at once true to old passions and eager to find a new way of life.

First, though, he fell off his horse. Ranting against poverty which condemned 'the Man of Sentiment whose heart glows with Independance' to pine and writhe 'under the contumely, of arrogant, unfeeling Wealth', he sent a rhetorical January letter to Hill, with part-payment of his book bill. Burns also ordered further books, including fiction, and the 'damned trash' of a theological nature which Monkland Friendly Society members insisted on.[198] Several times when Burns was late paying a bill or answering a letter he liked to joke or bardically manoeuvre his way out of trouble. He was not dead, he told fellow Crochallan Fencible, William Dunbar in Edinburgh, to whom he had long owed a letter; he had simply been 'serving my God by propagating his image, and honoring my king by begetting him loyal subjects'.[199]

Soon, though, at the time when evidence of Burns's propagation became public, he found himself in considerable pain. He had fallen 'not from my horse but with my horse', and become 'a cripple'.[200] It turned out he had broken his arm – just as one of his admirers, Mrs Dunlop's protégé milkmaid-poet Janet Little (whose work Burns disliked), arrived at Ellisland to see her hero, 'the bard', and found 'His lovely wife . . . drown'd in tears'.[201] Recuperating, Burns went on writing letters (sometimes late at night), and re-read Moore's *Zeluco* with gusto, but 1791 would be a year when he produced relatively little new poetry, and suffered several blows.

One was the death of the nobleman who had done so much for him in Edinburgh. Only ten years Burns's senior, Lord Glencairn died in late January. In a 'Lament' the 'Bard', 'Laden with years and meikle [great] pain', bewails his lord:

> 'The mother may forget the child
> 'That smiles sae sweetly on her knee;
> 'But I'll remember thee, Glencairn,
> 'And a' that thou hast done for me!'[202]

Voicing this poem through a supposedly elderly Ossianic Bard, Burns produced a speaker self-consciously lonely, sounding 'a stranger grown'. This was not a description of his Ellisland situation, but undeniably he was struck by several losses: of his own health, of

Glencairn, and of Lord Monboddo's beautiful daughter, Elizabeth, whom he recalled from his Edinburgh days and who had died of consumption in 1790. From among his 'dreary glens' Burns had spent months trying to elegise her; he couldn't get the poem right, abandoning it as 'A Fragment'.²⁰³

Such losses and his own injury overshadowed news that he had been placed on the Excise promotions list and might now expect to become a Supervisor. Still, he must have been pleased to see 'Tam o' Shanter' appear in print in March in the *Edinburgh Magazine* prior to April publication in the second volume of Grose's *Antiquities of Scotland*. Late March brought the birth of Ann Park's baby; exactly when Burns heard this news is unclear, but arrangements seem to have been made for his new daughter Elizabeth to be conveyed to his mother at Mossgiel before, later, Jean agreed to look after her.

On the morning of Saturday, 9 April Jean gave birth to William Nicol Burns, named after Burns's difficult schoolteacher friend. Two days afterwards, a pleased bard reported to Mrs Dunlop that Jean, regaining her strength, 'laid as lustily about her today at breakfast as a Reaper from the corn-ridge'. Making his wife sound like a farm servant, it is hard not to sense that for all his pride in her as mother of another new 'fine boy', Burns was conscious how people of rank were said to look down on Mrs Burns.²⁰⁴ Sometimes he could share their patronising attitude.

His 1791 attentions to the 'young Lady' of 'charms, wit & sentiment', Deborah Duff Davies, whom he hymned as 'Lovely Davies', is yet another example of how he looked continually beyond Jean.²⁰⁵ Throughout adult life Burns enjoyed relationships, epistolary and otherwise, with cultured literary women, while enjoying extra-marital sex with servants and barmaids. Jean remained at best a loved compromise. Two days after she had given birth, Burns, perhaps while he and she were in the same room, remarked in a letter how often honeymoons turned to disappointment; that same day he confided to Mrs Dunlop about 'hale, sprightly damsels' like Jean 'that are bred among the hay & heather',

We cannot hope for that highly polished mind, that charming delicacy of soul, which is found among the Female world in the most elevated stations of life, which is certainly by far the most bewitching charm in that famous cestus [bridal girdle] of Venus . . . But as this

angelic creature is I am afraid extremely rare in any station & rank of life, & totally denied to such a humble one as mine; We meaner mortals must put up with the next rank of female excellence . . .[206]

He goes on to list 'the charms of lovely woman' in his own 'humble walk of life'. These include 'Nature's mother-wit, & the rudiments of Taste' plus 'a sound, vigorous constitution' and 'as fine a figure & face' as met with in 'any rank'. It is hard not to feel Burns experienced some discontent. Yet the same man who sometimes looked down on his wife was the poet who wrote that spring the 'slow and tender' song, eventually set to the tune 'The Caledonian Hunt's Delight', where a woman 'weary, fu' o' care' sings beautifully to 'Ye banks and braes o' bonie Doon' about how 'my fause Luver staw [stole] my rose,/ But, ah! he left the thorn wi' me. –'[207] In his imaginative work Burns achieved a sympathetic sense of femininity beyond anything he expressed in prose and, perhaps, beyond what he felt in daily life. His songs understand women like Jean at least as much as women like Mrs Dunlop or Clarinda. His own sense of sorrow or weariness, love or loneliness, could assume a girl's Scots voice. That too was part of his bardic gift.

As spring passed into summer Burns completed the first volume of his letters and poems he had been transcribing as a private gift for Riddell, and began work on the second. Less formally in late April, as 'a Fiddler & a Poet' signing himself 'Johnie Faa' (after an Ayrshire ballad), he sent poems to local writer and musician, Charles Sharpe. As travelling barefoot balladeer Faa, Burns reiterated the problem of the poet lacking wealth and status, yet proclaimed himself 'as independant, & much more happy, than a monarch of the world'.[208] As if to remind him not all monarchs were happy, he received through Patrick Miller a snuffbox with an image of Mary, Queen of Scots – the gift of Burns's Jacobite correspondent Lady Winifred Maxwell Constable. Burns probably knew 'the song *Queen Mary's Lamentation*' sung by Fergusson's friend Tenducci, and had written his own 'Lament of Mary Queen of Scots' in 1790.[209] Burns's attraction to Mary and Jacobitism, like his fondness for Fergusson, involved seeing them as examples of victimhood and injustice. 'Johnson's Lives of the Poets', he had remarked the previous year, were the most rueful of 'Martyrologies'.[210] Feeling at times a martyr to circumstance, he struggled all the harder for independence. He also stood up for others facing ruin – not just

for a mouse, a Scottish Queen or a wounded hare, but also for local people. As Exciseman he could be resolute, as in June 1791 against 'the dark maneouvres [*sic*] of a Smuggler'.[211] But he could also campaign for those he viewed as victims. That same month he began an extended effort to help defend his friend James Clarke of Moffat, reputedly a brutal schoolteacher but seen by Burns as one of the poor 'children of Dependance ... Hated & persecuted by their enemies'.[212]

Later that summer, turning down the Earl of Buchan's pompous invitation to a 'coronation' of a bust of the poet Thomson, Burns sent a formal public tribute. More privately he wrote verses imaging Thomson as another martyred bard, 'Helpless, alane'. Burns cursed great folks who were happy to celebrate a dead poet but scorned to help a living one.

> To whom hae much, shall yet be given,
>   Is every Great man's faith;
> But he, the helpless, needful wretch,
>   Shall lose the mite he hath. –[213]

Burns was not alone in such resentment. In his verses 'On Burns', written around this time, the young Scottish poet-lawyer James Grahame (enthusiastic translator of 'To a Mouse' into Latin) reproached an 'Ungrateful country' for celebrating the dead Thomson while failing to support 'neglected Burns', with the result that 'The bard whose song each lovely tongue recites,/ Is left to moil like men of common mould.'[214]

Several years later, others would echo such reproaches, but in the meantime Burns simply got on with his life. He attended Gilbert's wedding in Kilmarnock in June, then in July was transferred to Dumfries's Third Excise Division, but his main concern was divesting himself of Ellisland. In August he sold his crops for a good price in a 'roup' (auction), accompanied, he told a friend, by a near-riot:

> ... such a scene of drunkenness was hardly ever seen in this country. – After the roup was over, about thirty people engaged in a battle ... & fought it out for three hours. – Nor was the scene much better in the house. – No fighting, indeed, but folks lieing drunk on the floor, & decanting, untill both my dogs got so drunk by attending them, that they could not stand. – You will easily guess how I enjoyed the scene as I was no farther over than you used to see me. –[215]

Jean and the family seem to have been spending time in Ayrshire, leaving Burns to relish this wild behaviour. Merry spectator rather than participant, he savours the anarchy. Though he could get 'Exceedingly drunk' on occasion, there is no evidence Burns had the sort of serious alcohol problem detractors attributed to him.[216] To Syme and others he appeared confident his Excise career would take him far from Dumfriesshire when he renounced Ellisland's lease. Patrick Miller bought it back from him on 10 September.

The Earl of Buchan might be convinced that prudent bard Burns had avoided 'the shipwreck of the sons of Apollo, by continuing his profession of a farmer', but Burns thought differently.[217] Ellisland having proved a bad bargain, he felt resentment towards Miller, whom he thought vain. The poet's temper was not improved by a leg injury. Confined indoors 'in my elbow chair', resting his bruised limb on a stool in front of him, he wrote to friends and patrons, sending them poems.[218] To Mrs Catherine Gordon Stewart in Ayrshire he posted a small collection, with the dedication to 'The first person of her sex & rank that patronised his his [*sic*] humble lays'.[219] Preparing to leave Ellisland, he remembered former generosities, but was careful also to cultivate people who might support him in the present and future. To Graham of Fintry went a long verse epistle, beginning with a complaint about being 'Late crippled of an arm, and now a leg', and feeling 'Dull, listless, teased, dejected, and deprest'. Into this he incorporated what seem fragments of longer, unfinished works, and a poem he had been developing for some time, 'The Poet's Progress'. Popeian in tone, its couplets reiterate Burns's sense of 'the Bard' as victim. Oppressors range from 'Vampyre booksellers' (Burns was sore about Creech's terms for a third edition of the *Poems*) to general 'blockheads' and 'miscreants' annoying 'The hapless Poet' as he 'flounders on thro' life'.[220]

Though this poem embodies self-pity, it also articulates genuine worry. About to leave Ellisland, Burns realises that with Glencairn dead he will have to depend for his livelihood entirely on the Excise, whose most sympathetic representative is Graham. Praying for '*bliss domestic*', the poem's Bard also exclaims, 'I dread thee, Fate, relentless and severe,/ With all a poet's, husband's, father's fear!' These rhetorical lines may be designed to 'milk' his patron; they also accurately represent Burns's deepest anxieties. Hoping Graham may find eventual comfort on his 'bed of death', Burns reveals fears of his own on which, especially in depressive moods, he tended to

VII

Staunch Republicans

In November 1791, after selling off horses, cows and farm equipment, Burns moved with his family to first-floor rooms in a tenement in the Wee Vennel (now 11 Bank Street), Dumfries.[1] Today Dumfries is an attractive small town with a university campus, but unevenly distributed prosperity and social problems. When I walked past the privately owned 11 Bank Street on a summer evening in 2007 young men were roaring their hot hatchbacks along the riverside street at the alley's end while a youth staggered by, shouting 'Ah'll kill 'em! Ah'll fuckin stab 'em!' In Burns's day many Dumfries civic leaders were Tories, and there was a considerable divide between rich and poor. The year 1792 saw 'a great number of poor people' in the area during a period when rising food prices, the presence of many soldiers, and a growing number of local unmarried mothers were all causing concern.[2]

Dumfries is the only substantial urban settlement in which Burns lived for a really extended period of time, and the nature of its society conditioned his life and work there, so it makes sense to pay sustained attention to the place. Admiring its 'brick and red free-stone' houses on the banks of the Nith, the local minister Dr Burnside may have regarded 'the situation of the town, rising gradually from the river', as 'beautiful and advantageous'. For some, though, the water-side location had drawbacks. An open sewer ran down the middle of the Wee Vennel, also known as the Stinking Vennel, which led downhill from High Street to the river and was subject to flooding in a town where 'Consumptions and rheumatisms' were 'frequent'.[3] There was a brothel near the river end of the Wee Vennel, not far from the Burnses' house. Moving to this three-room apartment whose middle chamber was not much bigger than a cupboard must have felt like failure after the brand-new Ellisland farmhouse. Yet

337

the Excise held good prospects, while much of Dumfries was and is beautiful: swans glide on the river at the fourteenth-century, multiple-arched Devorguilla's Bridge, and a diagonal weir, the Caul, marks what was in Burns's day the furthest point vessels could sail in from the sea.

Dumfries, an English traveller noted in the late 1780s, was 'a well built town at the mouth of the river Nith, whose full-flowing tide admitting ships of burden, gives it the advantage of commerce superior to most places'.[4] A windmill (today a museum) was built in 1796 on a riverside hill. A local poetaster who knew Burns in the 1790s later enthused,

> The prospect is pleasing, seen from the wind-mill –
>   But no walk like the Dock of Dumfries; –
>   You see the fish flounce in the net –
>   The corn spring up – potatoes set –
> Ships sailing – herds grazing – along the Nith banks,
> Where the local militia are marching in ranks . . .[5]

On the Nith's east bank, Dumfries was a successful port, not unlike Ayr. When Burns moved in, there was an almost entirely white population of around seven thousand: 'We have only one Negroe in Town, no Jews Gipseys or Foreigners residing. There is one Nobleman.'[6] Dumfries was the most important town in south-west Scotland. In an age when 'Excise' denoted a tax paid on all sorts of goods – from alcohol to candles – at their point of manufacture or importation, Excise work here was no sinecure. Still, as at Ellisland there was scope for recreation in countryside that was, as Burns put it, 'charmingly romantic & picturesque'.[7]

Though they were cold and wet in November, beautiful walks ran along the Nith's grassy banks; at the head of the docks were avenues of lime trees. Today's Nith is silted, the docks gone, but Dock Park is still attractive. Burns's friend Riddell painted a charming watercolour (after Paul Sandby) of the spires and handsome, generally slate-roofed houses of Dumfries on a calm, sunny day, blue hills rising in the background, hatted men and women strolling along the riverbank past fishermen, orderly rows of trees, a few grazing cattle.[8] Comfortably off citizens in the early 1790s liked being seen to 'delight in fine and fashionable clothes'.[9] Their ancient royal burgh regarded itself as a cut above the tougher, west-bank burgh of

Bridgend (later called Maxwelltown) just across the Nith. 'Bridgend' was outside Dumfries magistrates' jurisdiction and, though some local worthies were beginning to develop properties nearby, Burns knew it as a place of 'rascally creatures'.[10] It had a reputation for crime.

The most celebrated crime in Dumfries was proudly historical. In 1306 Robert the Bruce had murdered his rival the Red Comyn in a local church – Comyn was 'stabbed . . . to the heart', as Burns, who relished these local Bruce connections, put it bloodthirstily in 1795.[11] Associated with Bruce, and several times burned by English invaders, Dumfries was and is a spirited survivor. The Renaissance Scottish Latin poet Arthur Johnston hymns its durable elegance; Robert Fergusson, a visitor in 1773, had admired the 'beauties' and the pubs of the town by the 'bonny Nith', suggesting it might have suited the Latin poet Horace.[12] Burns, when enthusiastic, called Dumfries 'the third town for importance & elegance in Scotland'.[13] Like Ayr, Dumfries had benefited from the slavery-driven tobacco trade in the earlier eighteenth century and, perhaps in emulation of Ayr, it was busy adding a new bridge to complement its old. This new crossing suitable for carriages was being constructed between 1791 and 1794, closely monitored by town councillors. Shortly after its completion one of Burns's 1790s visitors approached Dumfries from the south:

The appearance of the Country from Annan to Dumfries, is very rude & uncultivated. As one approaches the latter town however the Country changes much for the better, & a vast plain surrounded by Mountains on every side, excepting to the south where the Solway firth appears, with the neat romantic Town of Dumfries with its three elegant steeples and two Bridges, present to the eye of a Stranger a very admirable landscape. On my riding thro' the Town I was much pleased with the neatness & cleanliness of every house and shop and person I saw. The streets are broad, well aired, and remarkably clean from every spicies [*sic*] of Nuisance. The people also dress neatly, speak with ease & correctness; and have something very agreeable in their faces. I think the Inhabitants of this Town and of the neighbouring parts of Galloway are uncommonly lean, with expressive eyes, high cheek bones, fair or red hair, and legs and thighs remarkably long in proportion to the size of their bodies. The black bonnet of the women of the borders has disappeared, and I am pleased with seeing the Mutch or Cap re-assume their places. The river Nith is a

beautiful and large stream at this place; and admits boats of consider-
able burden up to the bridge of the Town. There is no manufacture
of any sort carried on here; the place being supported by the Courts
of law, the Markets for Corn and Cattle held in it, and its being the
direct road to England for the Cattle carried thither from Galloway
and the north of Ireland. There are excellent flour Mills standing on
the Galloway or West side of the Nith; I visited them with pleasure,
as they display much ingenuity and even taste. A Wind Mill is just
erecting . . .'[14]

This was the landscape and townscape familiar to Burns throughout
his thirties. Recovered from rough treatment by Bonnie Prince
Charlie's Jacobite army in 1746, Burns's Dumfries was prosperous,
with several schools, churches and inns, imposing merchants' houses,
three banks, library facilities, a recently built hospital, a jail, a news-
paper, and impressive public buildings such as the steepled early
eighteenth-century red sandstone town-house, the Midsteeple, used
as the burgh's court-house and today impressively restored. Each
labouring day was punctuated by the Midsteeple bells, rung at 6
a.m., then six and ten at night. A fine public space, Queensberry
Square, had been set out just off the High Street in 1770, adorned
with a monument designed by Robert Adam. 'The streets are well
lighted,' wrote Burns's acquaintance the politically conservative
Robert Heron, who visited in the autumn of 1792; the 'principal
street extends full three-fourths of a mile in length: In the middle,
it may be nearly an hundred feet wide.'[15]

Dumfries's burgh charter allowed for two weekly markets and
three annual fairs to which cattle from the surrounding area were
brought for sale. Dumfries tradesmen worked leather (there were
110 shoemakers in 1791), wove cloth, manufactured hats and stock-
ings, milled crops. Shops sold, among other things, 'from fifteen
hundred to two thousand dozens of hare-skins . . . annually'.[16] It
was a compact, busy place where at least seventy people in 1791
held 'Licences . . . for retailing Exciseable Liquors'.[17] 'The propor-
tion of the inhabitants, who are descended of respectable families,
and have received a liberal education, is greater here,' Heron was
convinced, 'than in any other town in this part of the island.'[18] Polite-
ness was cherished and sometimes self-consciously displayed.

Balls, exhibitions and other gatherings for the well-off were held
in the eighteenth-century Assembly Rooms. Eager for elegant

improvement, the town was proud of its new Theatre Royal in Shakespeare Street. Still functioning in the twenty-first century, that theatre's praises were sung by the *Dumfries Weekly Journal* after the opening on 29 September 1792. Its founding was overseen by Robert Riddell. Burns loved it.

The social highlight of the year was in autumn when gentry of the Dumfries and Galloway Hunt met for a week to 'rouse the town to festivity'. In autumn 1792 Robert Heron found the Caledonian Hunt also resident, and Dumfries at its liveliest:

> Every inn and ale-house was crowded with guests. Many, even of the more respectable citizens had been persuaded by the tempting offers of very high rent, to let their best rooms for a few days. In the mornings, the streets presented one busy scene of hair-dressers, milliner's apprentices, grooms, and valets, carriages, driving and bustling backwards and forwards. In the forenoon, almost every soul, old and young, high and low, master and servant hastened out to follow the hounds, or view the races. At the return of the crowd, they were all equally intent, with the same bustle, and the same ardent animation, on the important concerns of appetite. The bottle, the song, the dance, and the card-table endeared the evening, and gave social converse power to detain and to charm till the return of morn.[19]

Though not of the gentry, and hardly an admirer of hereditary wealth and privilege, Exciseman Burns was well connected in Dumfries. Among his friends John Syme, appointed Distributor of Stamps in Dumfries in 1791, had his office right underneath the Burnses' apartment. Burns's employment afforded access to men like the influential, improving Tory Provost David Staig, and local Tory newspaper editor Baillie Robert Jackson; internationally minded though conservative in politics, Jackson had published Fergusson's poem 'Dumfries' within a day of its being composed, though, for all he was a Scottish celebrity, Burns featured little in Jackson's columns.[20] Still, with a good job, money from selling off the stock at Ellisland, and fine prospects, the bard looked set to become a man of substance.

Yet no sooner had he and his family moved in than life was in turmoil. Agnes McLehose wrote urging Burns to help Jenny Clow. Clow was dying in Edinburgh with no one to look after her. Burns wrote on 23 November, asking McLehose to send her 'five shillings

in my name'. He promised to set off for the capital: 'I shall see the poor girl, and try what is to be done for her relief. I would have taken my boy from her long ago, but she would never consent.'[21] Burns visited Clow, but was unable to save her. She died two months later of tuberculosis. As James Mackay discovered, her son Robert Burns survived, though there is no extant evidence the poet played any part in his support, or even that they ever spoke to each other. The boy grew up to become a successful merchant.[22]

In Edinburgh Burns met McLehose again. By 1791 Agnes was sending rhymed invitations to gentlemen other than Burns.[23] Yet if in November they had written to each other as 'Sir' and 'Madam', by December, returned from Edinburgh, Burns was calling her 'My dearest Nancy', posting her letter after letter, and having a lock of hair she had given him made into a ring by a Princes Street jeweller.[24] He sent her in early December the 'Lament of Mary Queen of Scots' (composed the previous year), now linking Agnes and 'unfortunate Mary' as sharers of 'Misfortune', the word he had also used to bond himself to Fergusson. Burns felt low. Signing off, he told McLehose he was 'literally drunk'.[25] Knowing she had been summoned to Jamaica by her estranged husband, the bard expected never to see her again.

What Jean made of all this we cannot tell – she did not speak of it later – but it could not have improved their relationship and may have led to a strained domestic atmosphere. A 1790s neighbour recalled Jean's 'very strong regard to decorum and propriety of conduct'.[26] Depressed that winter, Burns wrote to Ainslie, who knew both McLehose and Clow. Quoting *Macbeth* with a familiarly self-dramatising flourish, and complaining of 'hell within, and all around me', the bard set out his woes,

Can you minister to a mind diseased? Can you, amid the horrors of penitence, regret, remorse, head-ache, nausea, and all the rest of the d——d hounds of hell, that beset a poor wretch, who has been guilty of the sin of drunkenness – can you speak peace to a troubled soul?

Miserable perdu that I am! I have tried every thing that used to amuse me, but in vain: here must I sit, a monument of the vengeance laid up in store for the wicked, slowly counting every chick [sic] of the clock as it slowly – slowly, numbers over these lazy scoundrels of hours, who, d——n them, are ranked up before me, every one at his

neighbour's backside, and every one with a burden of anguish on his back, to pour on my devoted head – and there is none to pity me. My wife scolds me! my business torments me, and my sins come staring me in the face, every one telling a more bitter tale than his fellow. –[27]

In this depressed mood Burns was also making songs. One of these, 'Gloomy December', sighs over 'Parting wi' Nancy, Oh, ne'er to meet mair!'[28] On 27 December, just minutes before the post was due to go, he rushed to send 'ever dearest Nancy' this and two other songs, one naming 'my Nancy' as 'darling of my heart'; set to a Gaelic lament that haunted Burns, it bemoans her imminent voyage.[29] The other poem he enclosed is set to a 'slow and tender' tune attributed to blind Lewis-born harper Roderick Morison (*c.* 1656–*c.* 1714), known to Burns as 'Rory Dall'. Burns's friend Ramsay of Ochtertyre had written about Morison in a book Burns mentions that month, Patrick McDonald's *Collection of Highland Vocal Airs*, where harper Rory is 'the last performer on that instrument in the Hebrides', linked to 'one of the last chieftains that had in his retinue' such figures as 'bard' and 'harper'.[30] All this melancholy lastness is appropriate to Burns's mood and song. His words adapt a conventional English lyric from Robert Dodsley's collection *Colin's Kisses* (1742), 'The Parting Kiss':

> One kind Kiss before we part,
>   Drop a Tear, and bid Adieu;
> Tho' we sever, my fond Heart
>   Till we meet shall pant for you.
>
> Yet, yet weep not so, my Love,
>   Let me Kiss that falling Tear;
> Tho' my Body must remove,
>   All my Soul will still be here.
>
> All my Soul, and all my Heart,
>   And every Wish shall pant for you;
> One kind Kiss then e'er we part,
>   Drop a Tear, and bid Adieu.[31]

Burns metamorphoses this poem: not just by setting it to a powerful tune of sadness and giving it greater vernacular urgency but also by heightening its language, lingering over obsessively repeated

words and phrases, and sharpening its emotion. He promotes, for instance, the word 'sever' in the third line to become a crucial end-rhyme with 'for ever' in a lyric at one with Burns's state of depressive agitation. Artistry here is as important as emotion. A sentimental, yet genuine man of feeling, the bard takes leave of his Nancy in a song whose publication he already anticipates, allowing him to perform his intense, private erotic sadness before a public audience.

> AE fond kiss, and then we sever;
> Ae fareweel, and then for ever!
> Deep in heart-wrung tears I'll pledge thee,
> Warring sighs and groans I'll wage thee. –
>
> Who shall say that Fortune grieves him,
> While the star of hope she leaves him:
> Me, nae chearful twinkle lights me;
> Dark despair around benights me. –
>
> I'll ne'er blame my partial fancy,
> Naething could resist my Nancy:
> But to see her, was to love her;
> Love but her, and love for ever. –
>
> Had we never lov'd sae kindly,
> Had we never lov'd sae blindly!
> Never met – or never parted,
> We had ne'er been broken-hearted. –
>
> Fare-thee-weel, thou first and fairest!
> Fare-thee-weel, thou best and dearest!
> Thine be ilka joy and treasure,
> Peace, Enjoyment, Love and Pleasure! –
>
> Ae fond kiss, and then we sever!
> Ae fareweel, Alas, for ever!
> Deep in heart-wrung tears I'll pledge thee,
> Warring sighs and groans I'll wage thee. –[32]

Late in January 1792 McLehose wrote to Burns, saying she 'could have lived or died with' him, bidding farewell, hoping that they might meet again in heaven 'in perfect and never-ending bliss'.[33] She

sailed to Jamaica on 29 January. Though some correspondence passed between them, they never met again.

Burns could not stop thinking about her. Since 1788 he had returned obsessively to a poem in English Augustan couplets, attempting to articulate the doomed intensity of their affair. Originally carrying an epigraph beginning 'I burn, I burn' (from Pope's Ovidian 'Sappho to Phaon'), this work both cursed and blessed 'that fatal night' Burns had met 'Clarinda'.[34] Over the years he several times reworked the piece, which a later editor called 'Passion's Cry'. In 1789, drawing on a recent law case, Burns had tried deflecting his passion by presenting the poem as a Popeian verse epistle from a married Ayrshirewoman to her lover, but five years later, sending some of its lines to Agnes McLehose, he would address it explicitly to 'Clarinda' despite what he awkwardly but defiantly called 'Prudence' direst bodements'.[35] Rhetorically projecting his own exclamatory passion while simultaneously defending it, the poem, as grandiose as 'Ae Fond Kiss' is heartbreaking, is not a success. Yet, especially in its fullest articulation, its couplets indicate how Burns's recurring taste for self-dramatisation and his determined treasuring of his 'erring' passion for Clarinda must have continued to complicate his own psychology, his family life, and the life of Agnes McLehose. Though Kinsley and other scholars have been unable to locate it, the manuscript containing the most extended version is now in the Robert Burns Birthplace Museum collection, and is published here for the first time. Not mentioning Clarinda, but annotated in another hand as 'Noble verses by the Bard to Clarinda – on an occasion when she had said that "they must part"', the poem is suspended between externalised rhetorical flourish and covert emotional autobiography:

> My steps Fate on a mad conjuncture thrust,
> 'Twas grav'd in ir'n, the stern decree, 'You Must!' –
> Ah, No! the plume pluck'd from the am'rous dove,
> The Sentence flam'd in golden lines of love. –
> Wild erring from the path by Virtue shown,
> I snatch'd a flower in Virtue's ways unknown;
> With charms methought to raptur'd sense more sweet
> Than aught in Virtue's walks I e'er could meet: –
> The lovely Flower fond in my bosom worn,
> I knew, or heeded not, its poison'd thorn. –

O, why is bitter mem'ry so alive,
When Pleasures, Friendships, Loves, nor Hopes survive!
O'er joys no more, fond recollection burns;
Thy image haunts & blesses me by turns. –
The desp'rate barbs are flesh'd deep in my heart,
Death, & Death only, can extract the dart: –
His bowl alone can drug my soul to rest:
But be thou happy! be thou ever blest!
Mild zephyrs waft thee to life's farthest shore,
Nor think of me, or my distresses more! –
Falsehood accursed! – No! still I beg a place,
Still near thy heart some little, little trace,
For that dear trace, the world I would resign,
Oh, let me live – and die – & think it mine!

Thou despot, Love, whom all my powers obey,
Why lord it thus with such tyrannic sway! –
In vain the Laws his feeble force oppose;
Chain'd at his feet, they groan Love's vanquish'd foes:
In vain Religion meets my shrinking eye;
I dare not combat – but I turn & fly:
Conscience in vain upbraids th' unhallow'd fire;
Love grasps her scorpions, stifled they expire:
Reason drops headlong from his sacred throne,
Thy dear idea reigns & reigns alone: *image*
Each thought intoxicated homage yields,
And riots, wanton, in forbidden fields. –

By all on high, adoring mortals know!
By all the conscious Villain fears below!
By, what, Alas! much more my soul alarms,
My doubtful hopes once more to fill thy arms!
E'en should'st thou, false, forswear the guilty tie,
Thine, & thine only, I must live & die!!![36]

'Flesh'd deep' in Burns's drama-prone heart, the 'barbs' of his feelings for Clarinda do seem to have been inescapable. Part of the poet treasured this. Another part was conscious, albeit falteringly, how much he owed to Jean Armour. But he found it hard not to let his attention, and particularly his exclamatory, imaginative erotic attentions, wander again and again.

Burns worked on. Once or twice a week, he told Mrs Dunlop,

he hunted smugglers, but he supplied few details. He also crafted further songs, while subscribing to and promising to gather subscriptions for 'The Scotch Milkmaid' Janet Little's *Poetical Works*. The bard, though, was fascinated by another, more local woman writer. The remarkable Maria Riddell, nineteen-year-old English wife of the younger brother of Robert Riddell, had moved to the 'genteel family' mansion and estate of Woodley Park (three miles from Dumfries) with her husband Walter and their baby daughter around the end of 1791.[37] By late January 1792 Maria travelled from Friars' Carse with 'our Caledonian bard, the celebrated Burns' and others as part of a group who set out before dawn to visit the Wanlockhead lead mines.

There, in the bleak Leadhills fifteen hundred people were said to live, sustained by lead mining and maintaining 'To compensate for their exclusion from society ... a circulating library, established in the bosom of these hills, at their village, near the mine'. The library and lead mines are now a museum; in the 1790s the mines were an exotic spectacle in the midst of 'nakedness and sterility above ground'.[38] Having breakfasted at nearby Sanquhar, Burns, Mrs Riddell and their party set off in a post-chaise along a sometimes precipitous road, Burns fascinating Maria Riddell with his conversation. At Wanlockhead a miner took them through a tunnel cut into solid rock. Robert, Maria and the others held tapers to guide them through the darkness. They had to bend almost double under the low roof, 'wading up to the mid leg in clay and water' as Maria boasted to her mother. 'The stalactical fluid continually dropping from the rock upon our heads, contributed to wet us completely thro'.' Cutting her gloves on rocks and slimy from soaking timber beams supporting the tunnel roof, Maria pressed on, exploring a mineshaft. Burns, though, could stand no more of 'the damp and confined air'.[39] The party agreed to turn back.

Though this subterranean excursion was too much for a Burns who knew that his Nancy was about to sail for Jamaica, it was just another escapade for the teenage Maria. She had been climbing West Indian mountains, dealing with deadly insects and singing to lizards not long before moving to the tamer surroundings of Dumfries. Impressed with his new young woman friend, Burns wrote her a hearty introduction to his pal Smellie, to whom she presented it on her first visit to Edinburgh. Within a year Maria published with Peter Hill her *Voyages to the Madeira and Leeward Caribbee Islands*.

Though no Clarinda, this intelligent, outspoken, cosmopolitan 'young lady . . . in the first ranks of fashion' would become one of Burns's favourites. His letter to her in February 1792 begins warmly, 'My Dearest Friend'.[40]

Maria Riddell got to know Burns very well. A minor poet herself, she rated his 'brilliant repartee' even above his poetry. He seemed to her always 'manly', someone who excelled in 'refined' society even though he was what his physique suggested: a man who had grown up on a farm. Like so many who met him, she was struck by Burns's charismatic animation, his bright eyes the arresting counterparts to his depressive temperament. Written shortly after Burns's death, her shrewd, highly coloured portrait confirms what others felt when they encountered the bard's gaze and voice:

> I believe no man ever was gifted with a larger portion of the *vivida vis animi* [vivid power of soul]. The animated expressions of his Countenance were almost peculiar to himself. The rapid lightnings of his eye were always the harbingers of some flash of genius, whether they darted the fiery glances of insulted and indignant superiority, or beamed with the impassioned sentiment of fervent and impetuous affections. His Voice alone could improve upon the magic of his eye; sonorous, replete with the finest modulations, it alternately captivated the ear with the melody of poetic numbers, the perspicuity of nervous reasoning, or the ardent sallies of enthusiastic patriotism.[41]

Although the sophisticated young mother Maria Riddell could be teasingly, excitedly in awe of him, most of Burns's local friends were men. Later to become its senior warden, he joined Dumfries's St Andrew's Masonic Lodge on 27 December 1791. Furthering local contacts and ambitions, he intrigued with his Excise Supervisor, Alexander Findlater, and others over a move to a local 'Port Division' worth an additional £20 to his salary, plus 'as much rum & brandy as will easily supply an ordinary family'.[42] Burns corresponded with the Supervisor-General, William Corbet in Edinburgh, while Mrs Dunlop used her friendship with Corbet's wife to enhance Burns's chances. If he anticipated money and drink, Burns paid his debts too, albeit with poetic justice. To Robert Burn, who had taken two years to erect the headstone over Fergusson's grave, he sent payment, two further years after receiving Burn's account. 'He had the hardiesse to ask me interest on the sum; but considering that the money was due by one Poet, for putting a tomb-stone over another, he may,

with grateful surprise, thank Heaven that ever he saw a farthing of it.'[43] Whilst the bard felt depressed at losing Clarinda, he could also laugh at himself, circulate his manuscript collection of bawdy poems among male friends, and, privately at least, give vent to radical complaints about a society where the 'high & mighty will' of a titled 'Great Man' was always scandalised by any opposition from a 'Plebeian & the Son of a Plebeian'.[44]

Such talk in 1792 was increasingly dangerous. Revolutionary France was viewed as threatening the British state, and home-grown democrats were suppressed. Fortunately for his credentials as a servant of His Majesty's Excise, Burns on 29 February 1792 played his part in apprehending a smuggling schooner at Sarkfoot, south-east of Dumfries, near Gretna on the Solway Firth. With friend and fellow Excise officer John Lewars and a recently appointed colleague William Crawford, who took the leading role with a party of dragoons, Burns helped capture the *Rosamond* of Plymouth. Nearby residents aided the smugglers by sabotaging local boats so the dragoons could not make use of them. From the *Rosamond* the smugglers shot at their attackers. Eventually the troops were reconfigured as three assault formations, the third under Burns's command. These moved on foot across the quicksands, the water sometimes as high as their chests. The smugglers kept firing, but as government forces neared the vessel, its crew could not direct their large guns down on to the attackers. Realising this, they fled across the side of the ship, heading south over dry sand towards the English shore, abandoning a rich prize to Burns and his colleagues.

Writing up expenses incurred during this adventure, Burns recorded the smugglers had attempted to render the *Rosamond* unseaworthy by firing a 'carronade down through her broadside'.[45] Finally the officers and dragoons managed to get the vessel pumped out and repaired. Apparently unending March rains and 'very considerable quantities of snow' made this work exhausting.[46] Two carpenters and four professional seamen were employed for eleven days. Refloated on the spring tide, the vessel was then guided into dock at Kelton near Dumfries for unloading. The *Rosamond*, most of her cargo and fittings were sold at Dumfries in April at a profit of over £120. Some of this went to the Excise officers as a reward for their exertions.

In 'his glee' Burns was said by his 1828 biographer J. G. Lockhart to have purchased the ship's four carronades and sent these guns

via Dover to the revolutionaries in France. Britain and France were not yet at war, so this was not an illegal action, but Lockhart, a staunch Tory, presents it as 'a most absurd and presumptuous breach of decorum'.[47] This story is disputed, but it is clear Lockhart was drawing on papers subsequently lost; only some have been rediscovered. Walter Scott, Lockhart's father-in-law, was told by contacts in London's Customs House headquarters that the guns had been stopped at Dover. No official records of this survive. Robert Chambers in the nineteenth century said he had seen proof that Burns purchased the carronades. While the exact truth may never be known, there were efforts in the west of Scotland to send practical support to the French revolutionaries, and at the very least this story's existence and uncontradicted circulation in a widely read 1820s book suggests Burns was regarded by local people and early researchers as markedly sympathetic to French revolutionary ideals. This is supported by passages in poems and letters, though often Burns's expression is sly and glancing. He knew such sentiments expressed by a servant of the Crown could get him into serious trouble. They did.

Meantime, though, he was safe enough, and wanted to be seen as loyal and upstanding. April 1792 brought him the more lucrative Excise position he had hoped for, the Dumfries First Foot-walk; on 10 April he received his diploma as a member of the Royal Archers of Scotland, the monarch's ceremonial bodyguard. Nevertheless, around this time he was also making songs whose tone suggests much less of an allegiance to the establishment.

One of these is 'The De'il's awa wi' th' Exciseman'. As often, having written a poem with a wink in it, Burns cleverly sent it to a figure in authority, as if to make sure it might escape censure. He posted 'The De'il's awa' to an Excise Supervisor in Edinburgh, telling him he had already sung it at one of the Dumfries 'Excise-court dinners'.[48] 'The De'il's awa' presents an orthodox moral: when the regulatory figure of the Exciseman is absent the people 'brew . . . laugh, sing, and rejoice'; yet drinking, laughing, singing and rejoicing were among the things Burns most valued in life, and he had a deep suspicion of regulatory figures. 'The De'il's awa' sings in public what Burns had hinted at in that rejected draft letter of November 1790 where he likened himself to Milton's Satan, compelled 'To do what yet tho' damn'd I would abhor'.[49] Probably this sentiment was common among Excisemen, obliged

to do jobs they must sometimes have disliked. Still, the song's unforgettable jaunty devilry goes beyond that, so it reads like – and more importantly sounds like – a carnivalesque subversion of authority. Its author was not so much Exciseman Burns as the Burns who admired Milton's Devil as the ultimate independent-minded rebel.

> There's threesome reels, there's foursome reels,
>   There's hornpipes and strathspeys, man,
> But the ae best dance e'er cam to the Land
>   Was, the deil's awa wi' th' Exciseman.[50]

Ever since his youthful attendance at dancing-classes against his father's wishes, dancing had been for Burns an expression of independent-mindedness. In 'Tam o' Shanter' 'mirth and dancing' are literally expressions of devilry. 'The De'il's awa', for all he sang it as an Exciseman to Excisemen, is a lyrical expression of rebellion. The more the bard positioned himself as a figure of regulatory authority, the more rebellious he became.

'I am just now devilish drunk' begins a letter written to his Edinburgh friend Alexander Cunningham at 3 o'clock one spring morning. On occasion Burns liked to proclaim his drunkenness, 'criminal indolence', 'deafened conscience', and sense of a 'life of Reproach'.[51] Like many passages in his correspondence, these phrases are as much gestural as anything else. He worked hard, read intensively (Jean remembered him reading all through meals); he wrote. Though he was with his fellow Exciseman, Lewars, in May 1792 when Lewars drunkenly attacked a local girl, it was Burns, drunk or not, who pulled Lewars off.[52] The bard's conduct was orderly, not disorderly, his drinking usually contained. Still, apparently throwaway references in correspondence do reveal a sense that he was troubled, not least by inner conflicts which, however productive in poetry, might be hard to manage in life.

Revealingly, in several letters Burns tells the recipient he is drunk. This does not mean he became an alcoholic; it does signal that protesting his own drinking grew significant to him. Sometimes (as when he tells Ainslie or Clarinda he is drunk) these protestations are presented as explanations of strong emotions, even despair. If Burns was drinking too much, this would only have intensified his depressive tendencies. 'Occasional hard drinking is the devil to

me,' he told Mrs Dunlop at the start of 1793, alluding also to 'my complaint', which probably means that 'hypochondria' we might now term depression.[53] Excise work giving him access to confiscated booze also meant the 'wild' Burns who had always enjoyed sociable drinking, who associated drink with imaginative freedom, and who had strong family links to smugglers, now found himself in the awkward position of being a repressive authority figure in a community where availability of illicit alcohol was regarded by many as a right. Those circumstances, too, made for internal conflict – resolved in art in 'The De'il's awa wi' th' Exciseman'. In life he went on, as he put it in September 1792, 'grinding the faces of the Publican & the Sinner on the merciless wheels of the Excise'; but also 'making ballads, & then drinking, & singing them'.[54]

Trying to manage conflicting loyalties in his own position, and sometimes conferring with musician friend Stephen Clarke, Exciseman Burns produced an increasing body of songs which, even as he filled out official government paperwork, let him sing from the point of view of people that governments oppressed. 'The Slave's Lament' of 1792, giving voice to a Senegalese slave in Virginia, seems an odd poem from a white poet who might well have gone to help manage a Jamaican plantation, but it was in tune with growing and widespread unease. That spring many local people were concerned about 'petitioning Parliament for an abolition of the slave trade'. The *Dumfries Weekly Journal* reported in detail a House of Commons debate that included William Wilberforce's arguments against slavery.[55] Admired today by Maya Angelou as 'a perfect example of the ways in which a poet transcends race, time, and place', Burns's poem also accords with Dumfries Kirk Presbytery's 'unanimously' resolving to petition Parliament via 'Patrick Miller, jun. Esq.' in March 1792 for the 'abolition of the African slave trade'.[56]

Burns's Senegalese slave poem is among several which can be related to the abolitionist movement with its use of Josiah Wedgwood's slogan 'Am I not a Man and a Brother?' 'The Slave's Lament' gives voice to the downtrodden, as does the Jacobite song, 'Bonnie laddie, Highland laddie', which, around the same time, presents the oppressive victor of Culloden, the Duke of Cumberland, as getting his devilish comeuppance:

Satan sits in his black neuk,
  My bonie laddie, Highland laddie,
Breaking sticks to roast the Duke,
  My bonie laddie, Highland laddie,
The bloody monster gae a yell,
  My bonie laddie, Highland laddie,
And loud the laugh gaed round a' hell!
  My bonie laddie, Highland laddie. —57

Again, set to the tune 'The old Highland laddie', this is based on older material; Burns is the perfecter, not the originator. He reworked many Scots songs throughout 1792, some bawdy, some tenderly erotic, drawing on airs associated with both Highland and Lowland popular culture.

Not all of Burns's work in this area has been recognised. So, for instance, though it is not credited to him, the version of the song 'Logie o' Buchan' published in the 1792 fourth volume of the *Scots Musical Museum* exists in an identical wording in Burns's hand, complete with his manuscript footnote. The manuscript now in the Robert Burns Birthplace Museum collection differs from other known versions of the same song. Sung in a woman's voice, while its chorus presents the words of her lover, this lyric was probably collected by Burns on his tour of north-east Scotland. It is impossible to say how much, if at all, he has reworked it, but it contains just the sort of defiant kick that often appealed to him. This song celebrates a couple whose relationship has met with parental disapproval like that which Jean Armour had known. As one verse in Burns's manuscript puts it,

My daddie was sulkie, my minnie was sour,
They gloom'd on my Jamie because he was poor;
But daddie & minnie altho' that they be,
There's nane o' them a' like my Jamie to me. —
  O think na lang, lassie, tho' I be awa,
  An' think na lang, lassie, tho' I be awa,
  The simmer is come & the winter's awa,
  And I'll come & see thee in spite o' them a'. —58

Burns used his British government salary to collect and perfect songs of and for the Scottish people. In so doing he gave those songs to the world, often for the sheer joy of it, but not infrequently with

a bolshie political edge, whether giving expression to a slave, a defeated Jacobite, a poor Scots peasant, or rebel brothers of some other sort. The independent-minded man whose sympathies were with the folk he came from, but whose job often distanced him from those very people, was now an employee of Crown and government at a slave-owning time when democracy was a dangerous word, notes of dissent increasingly suspect, and Scottish independent-mindedness perhaps lost for ever. Burns took the money and sang.

> Fareweel to a' our Scotish fame,
>   Fareweel our ancient glory;
> Fareweel even to the Scotish name,
>   Sae fam'd in martial story!
> Now Sark rins o'er the Solway sands,
>   And Tweed rins to the ocean,
> To mark whare England's province stands,
>   Such a parcel of rogues in a nation!
>
> What force or guile could not subdue,
>   Thro' many warlike ages,
> Is wrought now by a coward few,
>   For hireling traitors' wages.
> The English steel we could disdain,
>   Secure in valor's station;
> But English gold has been our bane,
>   Such a parcel of rogues in a nation!
>
> O would, or I had seen the day
>   That treason thus could sell us,
> My auld grey head had lien in clay,
>   Wi' BRUCE and loyal WALLACE!
> But pith and power, till my last hour,
>   I'll mak this declaration;
> We're bought and sold for English gold,
>   Such a parcel of rogues in a nation![59]

This song draws on several older Scottish denunciations of those who agreed to 1707 parliamentary Union with England creating the British Parliament in London and the modern British state. The Burns who in helping capture the *Rosamond* had bravely done the British government's work for the Excise precisely where 'Sark rins o'er the Solway sands', sent this song to Johnson; when it appeared

in the *Scots Musical Museum* in August 1792, Burns's name was not attached to it. Events that summer made it dangerous to be associated with anything seditious-sounding. The British government was hunting its own 'traitors' in the 'nation', not least in a Scotland excited by news that the auld ally France had become a republic in August.

Earlier that summer Edinburgh experienced riots on the King's Birthday, traditionally a time for unruly behaviour in the Scottish capital. On 4–6 June 1792 grievances over failure to achieve electoral reform combined with heightened concern about liberty and equality to produce substantial disturbances. These were directed against establishment figures like the General Supervisor of the Excise.[60] Anticipating trouble, the authorities drafted in four companies of dragoons and put on alert soldiers quartered in Edinburgh Castle. Troops were brought on to the streets. Protests ensued, including the burning in effigy of the city's MP, Henry Dundas (seen as absentee ruler of Scotland from the Westminster Parliament) and an attack on the house of Robert Dundas, Lord Advocate. The Riot Act was read. Troops several times fired on the crowds. Additional marines were drafted in and arrests made. Many of the rioters were working-class men. Some were defended in court by radical advocate Thomas Muir, soon to be among several Scots transported by the British government to Botany Bay for republican sympathies. These events were widely reported in the press, not least in the recently founded reformist periodical the *Edinburgh Monthly Intelligencer*. Later in 1792 the radical *Edinburgh Gazetteer* began to appear, making the establishment deeply suspicious.

Among those arrested for 'seditious, and disorderly behaviour' in the King's Birthday riots was one John Taylor, accused by Robert Dundas of being 'ringleader' of a 'mob' which had ranged through Edinburgh in a 'riotous and tumultuous manner'. Taylor was brought before Burns's publisher, William Creech, in Creech's capacity as an Edinburgh magistrate, and one of the witnesses against him was Burns's principal Excise patron Robert Graham of Fintry. A member of the Edinburgh assize or jury listed on the indictment was Burns's friend 'Alexander Naesmith painter'.[61] In a small country like Scotland where news spread not just through newspapers – in which Burns always took a keen interest – but also by word of mouth, Burns would have known a good deal about what was happening. Nasmyth, sympathetic to reform and even to the French Revolution, must have

been in touch with Burns that summer when designing scenery 'at the desire of Robert Burns' for the new, 'very elegant' Dumfries theatre, which could 'contain about 600 people' and opened in September.[62] So when Burns, preparing a new, slightly expanded edition of his *Poems* for Creech in autumn 1792 while the Caledonian Hunt with assembled 'gentry' and 'handsome carriages' filled Dumfries, signed off his letter to that publisher and magistrate by quoting four lines of 'The De'il's awa' and using the French Revolutionary salutation 'Ça ira', the bard knew he was indulging in a wild, risky, flourish.[63]

Burns loved such flourishes. On 10 September, first with 'a nipperkin of TODDY by me', then later mentioning 'this Rum is damn'd generous Antigua', he wrote in full flow to Cunningham a letter full of 'Nonsense!' In it, among other things, he mocked 'Lordlings' for 'conceited dignity' whenever 'they accidentally mix among the many-aproned Sons of Mechanical life'.[64] Full of fun, and with a characteristically sly egalitarian wink, this letter was written not long before Burns composed a prologue to be spoken at Dumfries's theatre. Entitled 'The Rights of Woman', his prologue again included the expression 'ça ira!'[65] Praised as 'immortal' in the 1792 French National Assembly, Tom Paine's pro-democratic *The Rights of Man* had been circulating throughout Scotland but would soon be outlawed.[66] Paine's works were denounced as 'insidious and malevolent' by a correspondent in the 1792 *Dumfries Weekly Journal*, which reported his trial for sedition; Ayr Library Society officially minuted the burning of their copies in early 1793.[67] Reputedly a worried Burns offloaded his copies of Paine on his blacksmith neighbour, George Haugh, fearing to be caught with seditious books.[68]

Careful to keep on good terms with the influential General Supervisor of Excise, William Corbet, Burns facetiously complained his own predicament was worse than that of 'A negro wench under the rod of a West-Indian Mistress'; but Burns was certainly interested in struggles for equality.[69] To Mrs Dunlop, who was anxious about a young woman stranded in Revolutionary France, he wrote about 'that Land convulsed with every horror that can harrow the human feelings'; but he also wrote enthusiastically to the half-pay Captain William Johnston who had chaired a meeting to form an Edinburgh Society of the Friends of the People, and who had recently founded the *Edinburgh Gazetteer*:

I have just read your Prospectus of the Edinr Gazetteer. – If you go on in your Paper with the same spirit, it will, beyond all comparison, be the first Composition of the kind in Europe ... Go on, Sir! Lay bare, with undaunted heart & steady hand, that horrid mass of corruption called Politics & State-Craft! Dare to draw in their native colors these

'Calm, thinking VILLAINS whom no faith can fix' –
whatever be the shiboleth [*sic*] of their pretended Party. –[70]

Burns's admired Lord Daer, 'as "Citizen President", conducted at Edinburgh a meeting of the Scottish reform societies'.[71] The London government introduced a state of emergency on 15 December, then martial law three days later. Six days after Burns wrote to William Johnston, Dumfriesshire laird Sir William Maxwell contacted the Duke of Buccleuch, telling him that 'emissaries of sedition' were agitating among working people in the county sympathetic to getting rid of the monarchy. Maxwell feared 'the consequences that may arise from the present discontents, the absurd doctrine of equality, and the spirit of licentiousness, which seems everywhere to prevail in these kingdoms, amongst the lowest classes of the people'.[72]

In this tense atmosphere Burns wrote for declamation in Dumfries's theatre on 26 November 1792 'The Rights of Woman'. Later published in the radical *Edinburgh Gazetteer*, this poem was sent with an admiring letter to actress Louisa Fontenelle, for her benefit performance. She later emigrated to democratic America. Essentially a comic actress who had performed in London and Edinburgh, Fontenelle was petite enough to play child parts, though in Dumfries she also essayed Desdemona ('her first appearance in that Character'), and Lady Teazle in Sheridan's *School for Scandal*.[73] Burns's opening stanza tunes in to political concerns of the hour:

> WHILE Europe's eye is fixed on mighty things,
> The fate of Empires, and the fall of Kings;
> While quacks of State must each produce his plan,
> And even children lisp The Rights of Man;
> Amid this mighty fuss, just let me mention,
> The Rights of Woman merit some attention. –[74]

Being an 'advocate for the *rights of women*' had been regarded as a little ridiculous by the *Dumfries Weekly Journal* a few months

earlier.[75] Burns's prologue's tone here is light, playful, but there is no suggestion its audience should condemn 'the fall of kings' or 'The Rights of Man'; he rather enjoys both before moving on to 'The Rights of Woman'. Though actresses were sometimes subject to abuse, few feminists (including Mary Wollstonecraft whose *Vindication of the Rights of Woman* was being advertised by Creech in summer 1792) would have been wildly enthused by Burns's suggestion that woman's rights were 'Protection . . . Decorum' and 'Admiration'. However, his assertion that in olden days men 'Would swagger, swear, get drunk, kick up a riot' whereas now they were all polite sounds ironic in a Scotland where the Riot Act had recently been read. Characteristically, Burns's prologue for Fontenelle manages to be at once flirtatiously decorous and subversively knowing in its conclusion,

> But truce with kings, and truth with Constitutions,
> With bloody armaments, and Revolutions;
> Let MAJESTY your first attention summon,
> Ah, ça ira! THE MAJESTY OF WOMAN!!!

Feminine grace and power are more important than politics, this seems to argue, but the final 'ça ira' hints, however ironically, at a fondness for the rhetoric of egalitarian politics after all. At a time when, as the *Dumfries Weekly Journal* put it on 20 November, 'the eyes of all Europe' were 'fixed' on the 'approaching' French 'trial of Louis XVI', Burns (then very closely involved with Dumfries theatre), would have known that such 'ça ira'-ing on 26 November would clash with the pre-announced singing of 'RULE BRITANNIA IN FULL CHORUS'.[76] His subversive hint would be bound to be picked up in the playhouse. Soon he had to confess to Graham of Fintry there had been 'a Riot' in Dumfries theatre when Louisa Fontenelle had been performing and playgoers in the pit sang the French revolutionary song,

> Ça ira
> La liberté s'établira,
> Malgré les tyrans tout réussira . . .[77]

> It shall be so,
> Liberty will be established
> Despite the tyrants everyone will rise up . . .

Reports later asserted Burns had either joined in this singing, or kept his hat on through the National Anthem, a mark of disrespect to the King. Whatever the particulars, in this period when, as the local newspaper put it, 'There are some iniquitous spirits at work, to *raise* a spirit of sedition and alarm', he did nothing to discourage disloyalty.[78] Instead he went on reshaping traditional Scots songs like the rebel Jacobite 'Here's a Health to them that's awa', voicing in the guise of an older folk acoustic, very contemporary concerns,

> May Liberty meet wi' success!
> May Prudence protect her frae evil!
> May Tyrants and Tyranny tine i' the mist,   *get lost*
> And wander their way to the devil![79]

Into this poem Burns wove allusions to Tom Paine's lawyer, Thomas Erskine, as well as men like James Maitland, a Scottish founder of the Friends of the People. Maitland had travelled to revolutionary France that August with Burns's admired Dr Moore. Burns's publishing this poem in the *Edinburgh Gazetteer* in 1792 was as clear a gesture as sending guns to revolutionary France.

On 20 September the French revolutionary General Dumourier – whose activities were written up in detail in the *Dumfries Weekly Journal* – had defeated an army led by the British King's brother-in-law, the Duke of Brunswick. In late 1792 Burns made a song suggesting that instead of trying 'Republican billies to cowe', the King's kinsman should stay 'At hame with his Princess to mowe [have sex]'. Celebrating sexual energy, 'Why should na poor folk mowe' presents the royal family as just like everyone else. Attuned more to *égalité* than courtly protocol, its conclusion seems a loyal toast but suggests with egalitarian disrespect that 'George our gude king and Charlotte his queen' should simply 'tak a gude mowe'.[80] In a Scotland where men like Burns's establishment contact Heron supported government efforts to 'suppress seditious writings' Burns was taking big risks.[81] On the surface his early 1793 'Address to General Dumourier' appeared to support that general's recent defection from the revolutionary cause, but its enthusiastic protestation, 'Then let us fight about,/ 'Till freedom's spark is out,/ Then we'll be d——mned no doubt – Dumourier' shows the freedom-loving Burns being bitterly ironic.[82] Again he *seems* loyal to the British government, while slyly making clear where his true sympathies lie.

Heron, editing Dumourier's letters, stated that French *'Republi-canism'* was *'a wicked and treacherous stratagem'*; Burns, ironically supporting the turncoat Dumourier, and invoking his own country's royals only to suggest they should make love not war, rather enjoys wicked and treacherous poetic stratagems.[83]

It was an appropriate time to celebrate the power of lovemaking. Jean had given birth to a daughter, Elizabeth Riddell Burns, on 21 November. Burns felt 'not equal to the task of raising girls'. 'Besides,' he had written to Mrs Dunlop, 'I am too poor: a girl should always have a fortune.'[84] For all he became better off, like many people born poor he continued to worry about increasing his income. This feeling intensified as his family grew. He never achieved financial contentment. A tender, discontented song completed by early 1793 complains about 'Wealth and State'; in its treatment of 'poortith' (poverty) it apparently hints at Burns's sense of family responsibility:

> O POORTITH cauld, and restless love,   *poverty*
>   Ye wrack my peace between ye;
> Yet poortith a' I could forgive
>   An 'twere na for my Jeanie.[85]

Burns sent this song to George Thomson, an Edinburgh lawyer and amateur musician who had written to the bard in 1792, inviting him to improve or compose 'our national melodies' for a *Select Collection of Original Scotish Airs*, to be arranged by celebrated composers including Haydn's pupil Joseph Pleyel.[86] Eventually Burns contributed over a hundred songs to Thomson's *Select Collection*, which appeared in six volumes between 1793 and 1841 and for which settings were written by Haydn, Beethoven, Weber and Hummel.

At first Burns was keen, but wary of Thomson's polite tastes. The bard wanted to supply not bland *'English* verses' but vernacular songs with 'a sprinkling of our native tongue'. Enthusiastic and proud, he told this Edinburgh lawyer payment would be 'downright Sodomy of Soul'. Going on to discuss songs with Thomson at great length, Burns, for all his eagerness to increase his Excise salary, did this work for nothing. Psychologically, that probably helped him separate it from his official career. He later told Thomson many of his finest songs were written for a 'lovely Friend' for whom he had a 'Platonic love'.[87] This seems to have been Jean Lorimer (aged seventeen in 1792) who had eloped but been deserted by her husband.

So, while a song about 'Jeanie' might be heard as referring to Jean Armour Burns, it might also have quite another reference.

Even as his wife nursed their newborn daughter, Burns's attentions strayed. He had been corresponding with Agnes McLehose's friend Mary Peacock, seeking information about Clarinda, who had asked Burns not to write to her in Jamaica lest her husband found out. Frustrated at hearing nothing from Peacock, on 6 December 1792, the fifth anniversary of his meeting with Mrs McLehose, Burns wrote pleading for news. Peacock's reply arrived, but Burns was away in Ayrshire and Jean may not have gone to great pains to make sure he received the letter. He discovered it much later when moving furniture, and was taken aback to discover McLehose was once again in Edinburgh, her attempt at reconciliation with her husband having failed.

It is not surprising letters went missing in the Burns household: there were unignorable anxieties. At the very end of 1792 Burns was seriously alarmed when John Mitchell, his Dumfries Excise boss, informed him instructions had come from the Board of Excise to inquire into Burns's 'political conduct'. Burns had been accused of being 'a person disaffected to Government'.[88] This was very dangerous. The country was on the brink of conflict with France. A frightened Burns wrote immediately to Graham of Fintry a letter full of fear of 'Ruin'. He begged Graham as 'a Husband – & a father' to think how he would feel 'to see the much-loved wife of your bosom, & your helpless, prattling little ones, turned adrift into the world, degraded & disgraced from a situation in which they had been respectable & respected, & left [without (*deleted*)] almost without the necessary support of a miserable existence'. Faced with losing his job, and potentially with imprisonment or transportation, Burns protested the charge against him was 'a LIE! To the British Constitution, on Revolution principles, next after my God, I am most devoutly attached! – '[89] Use of that phrase 'on Revolution principles', alluding to the Hanoverian 'Glorious Revolution' of 1688, would have signalled to Graham that Burns was not a Jacobite; significantly Burns, aware he could be attacked for French republican Jacobinism and for Jacobitism, felt obliged to include it.

He wrote anxiously to Mrs Dunlop on 2 January 1793 about fears of 'Beggary & Ruin' for his family. While protesting to Corbet that the charge against him was 'a LIE', with Mrs Dunlop he took a different line, saying simply, 'I have set, henceforth a seal on my

lips, as to these unlucky politics.' Even then he continues, 'to you, I must breathe my sentiments . . . War I deprecate: misery & ruin to thousands, are in the blast that announces the destructive Demon. – But. . .' Just after this 'But' in the manuscript large sections have been cut away, presumably by someone fearful for Burns's political reputation. Even in what remains, it is noticeable that he lapses into French at one point, and calls the French 'that gallant people'.[90]

Within a few days of his anxiety-ridden plea, while in times of 'the greatest convulsions' London's House of Commons debated its 'Alien bill' and pondered 'Scots Borough Reform', Burns was setting out to Graham of Fintry what he presented as full details of his political position: he knew of no organisations geared to Reform or Republicanism, 'except an old party of Borough-Reform; with which I never had any thing to do'. He had been in the Dumfries theatre one night 'when Ça ira was called for', and knew a few people involved, but took no part. He felt 'the soundest loyalty' towards King and Constitution, and had pledged this in public, though he hoped for some measure of parliamentary reform. While he had sent some poems to the *Edinburgh Gazetteer* 'they have nothing whatever to do with Politics'. He even mailed 'The Rights of Woman' to Mrs Corbet as 'a sincere Compliment to that Sex'. Burns assured his superior that having been France's 'enthusiastic votary in the beginning of the business', he had now 'altered my sentiments' because of French belligerence.[91] At a time when loyal Dumfries worthies including Robert Riddell and Patrick Miller were pledging 'to check and suppress all seditious, unconstitutional, and levelling publications' and the Town Council urged that 'the present alarming state of the Country requires the hearty assistance and exertions of every body', Burns was putting the best possible gloss on things, and sometimes bending the truth.[92] It just about worked. He received an informal dressing-down rather than a formal reproach.

Confident he had got himself off the hook, the bard was soon inviting the Provost of Dumfries to the theatre and offering him thoughts on 'your good town's revenue'.[93] Sending detailed advice about Scots songs to his new Edinburgh correspondent Thomson, Burns asked carefully whether Jacobite ones might not give offence. That spring he published under his own name in the *Edinburgh Advertiser* a song toasting King and Constitution. He presented this to the local loyal Dumfriesshire Volunteers, then celebrating the tenth anniversary of Admiral Rodney's British naval victory over

the French.[94] This was Burns on his best behaviour. Dumfries was well aware that in the name of *'liberty* and *equality'* the French King had just been executed with cries of *'Behold the blood of a tyrant!'*[95] The bard was watching his step.

That February the Dumfries kirk minister Dr Burnside preached against French 'phrenzies in politics' and hymned Britain's 'Constitution'.[96] To old friends Burns wrote in very different terms. On 20 February, by which time France and Britain were officially at war, he sent a political catechism to Alexander Cunningham with questions such as

> Quere, What is a Minister?
> Answer, A Minister is an unprincipled fellow, who by the influence of hereditary, or acquired wealth; by superiour abilities; or by a lucky conjuncture of circumstances, obtains a principal place in the administration of the affairs of government. –

'Politics,' he maintained, 'is a science wherewith, by means of nefarious cunning, & hypocritical pretence, we govern civil Polities for the emolument of ourselves & our adherents.'[97] A spiritedly mocking letter to William Nicol refers to Burns's own 'Political heresies' for which Nicol had upbraided 'Christless Bobbie', recommending that Burns ignore questions of '"Ça Ira"' or '"God save the King"' and simply follow the chameleon-like example of the turncoat 'Vicar of Bray'.[98] Having just escaped an inquiry into his political conduct, Burns was very unwise to circulate such opinions, especially in a Dumfries where 'French Liberty' was equated with 'riot' and it was regarded as absurd to say, 'Let all be equal, ev'ry man's my brother'.[99] More prudently, he made a point of protesting to the sympathetic Earl of Mar that 'whatever might be my sentiments of Republics, ancient or modern, as to Britain, I abjured the idea', and he penned and published in the *Edinburgh Advertiser* a poem toasting 'the King' while denouncing traitors.[100] This was his official public position. Yet, though he suppressed the accusations of disloyalty made against him to the Excise at this point, some in early nineteenth-century Dumfries still recalled 'Burns had been a Jacobin, or tinged with Jacobinism.'[101]

In public he had to seem respectable; he wanted the benefits of his status. March 1793 saw him asking Dumfries Council if, already an honorary burgess, he could be treated as a full Freeman of the

Town and granted reduced school fees for his children. The Council agreed. The local library also granted him free privileges. Burns cared about his children's education. James Gray, a Dumfries school-teacher who admired Burns and was later called 'a violent demo-crate', recalled seeing the bard teaching his nine-year-old eldest son about 'the English poets from Shakespeare to Gray'.[102] Burns himself was acquiring classic status; Heron had noted how in Burns's native Ayrshire some months earlier his work was 'in every person's hands'.[103] From admirers in America to Scots poet Samuel Thomson in Belfast, many praised 'his BARDSHIP'S POETICAL TALENTS', eager to meet the 'sweet bard'.[104] Confident his verse was likely to 'be read when the hand that now writes it, is mouldering in the dust', Burns sent out that spring to patrons like Patrick Miller and Mrs Graham of Fintry inscribed copies of the third edition of his *Poems*. A book went also to Clarinda, now he had an address for her, with an agitated letter calling her 'MY Angel!' Mentioning 'paths that lead to madness', Burns maintained, 'I despise Advice, & scorn Controul'; if she replied with 'sanctimonious Prudence', he would 'tear' her reply 'into atoms!'[105]

Exciting himself and trying to excite Mrs McLehose, Burns was also spending time with Maria Riddell, a woman who later in the 1790s signed off a letter to James Currie with the words 'Salut à fraternité!' and dated it using the French Revolutionary calendar.[106] Signing himself simply 'THE BARD', Burns sent her a flirtatious missive with a present of confiscated contraband French gloves 'from the LAND OF LIBERTY & EQUALITY'.[107] To another 'Friend I love', Deborah Duff Davies, he expressed admiration, exclaiming, 'They talk of REFORM – My God! what a reform would *I* make among the Sons, and even the Daughters of men!'[108] While conducting such correspondence, Burns was thinking about moving house with Jean. If in politics he led something of a double life, then in his addresses to women and his daily relationship with the woman who shared what he called, somewhat jadedly in 1793, his 'conjugal yoke', life was as complex as ever.[109]

The Burns family moved in May to a much larger, handsome two-storey red sandstone house at 24 Mill Hole Brae (now Burns Street), close to St Michael's Kirk. Wary of its minister, Burns attended that substantial, galleried kirk occasionally; towards the back of the sanctuary, under the gallery an inscription indicates his family pew. Its line of sight means that, depending on how far along he sat, he

could see and be seen by the minister from the elevated, elaborately canopied pulpit, or else could place a stone pillar between himself and the preacher. This choice of pew sums up his attitude towards conventional religion.

Now a museum, his Mill Hole Brae house has good-sized downstairs rooms and stone stairs leading to two bedrooms on either side of a very small, snug, windowed room Burns used as a study. The house was rented by a bard confident that income from seized goods in the Dumfries Port Division would boost his finances. When war with revolutionary France meant that imports slumped, Burns had problems paying his rent and bills. With the move, though, came new society. He became friends with an oboe player, Thomas Fraser. Fraser instructed a military band quartered in the area and went on to give a concert at Dumfries's New Assembly Room. He could play songs Burns had known from childhood; the two worked together on several compositions. Burns enjoyed speculating about 'Gaelic Songs' and an old heritage of tunes shared by 'Minstrels, Harpers, or Pipers' in 'Scotland & Ireland'.[110] Now the first volume of Thomson's *Select Collection of Original Scotish Airs* had appeared, Burns devoted himself more than ever to song-collecting. He told Thomson in July that as a 'Bard of Nature' his second sight assured him the anthology would be treasured in future ages.[111] Such thoughts did not make him forget past kindnesses. When the widow of his old friend and his father's old friend William Muir of Tarbolton Mill was having legal problems, Burns helped get them settled.

Anti-democratic demonstrations were held in Dumfries on the King's Birthday, 4 June 1793. People in nearby Ruthwell parish had burned Tom Paine in effigy on New Year's Day, and by June the *Dumfries Weekly Journal* reported with staunch approval that local young men 'having procured two effigies of Tom Paine, paraded with them through the different streets of this Burgh; and at six o'clock in the evening consigned them to the bonfires, amid the patriotic applause of the surrounding crowd'. Prominent among denouncers of democracy and praisers of 'the best of sovereigns on this joyous day' were the 'Loyal Natives' Burns so loved to mock.[112] In July 'many constitutional toasts' were drunk in Dumfries, with such sentiments as 'May the convulsed soul of France shew Democracy in its proper colours.'[113]

Burns got out of town. Since 1791 his friend Syme, a keen collector of poems, had been trying to persuade the bard to accompany him

on a tour of Galloway. Burns and Syme saw much of each other and in summer 1793 they at last set out on their tour. Burns had been showing Syme songs he was writing 'on the Beauties of Dumfries', and epigrams on its '*Boars*'.[114] Sometimes, like Syme, he seemed fed up with the place. Setting out at the end of July, they visited the 'classical ground' of Scots song, seeing sights like the 'terribly romantic' castle of Kenmore where Burns relished an old Jacobite family's hospitality. He enjoyed less a downpour in 'savage and desolate regions' around Gatehouse of Fleet, and got 'utterly drunk' there. Later he tore his good, waterlogged boots, trying to pull them on. 'Mercy on me how he did fume & rage,' wrote Syme on 3 August. Burns vented his spleen by composing a squib against a local 'aristocratic elf', the High Tory Lord Galloway: 'I have about half a dozen of capital extempores which I dare not write,' Syme told Alexander Cunningham.[115] Syme strove to cope with 'Burns's obstreperous independence'; the bard insisted on staying at an inn rather than a private house: he 'would not dine but where he should as he said, eat like a Turk, drink like a fish & swear like the Devil'.[116]

Still, Burns was keen to visit another local laird, since 'it occurred once or twice to him that the Isle was the seat of a Lord yet that Lord was not an *aristocrate*'.[117] '*Aristocrate*' here gestures towards the French 'Royalists (called by the people *Aristocrates*)', detested by revolutionary 'Republicans' and 'Democrats', as reported in detail in the 1790s Dumfries newspaper.[118] The lord who was 'not an *aristocrate*' was the radical Lord Selkirk, father of Burns's admired old acquaintance, Lord Daer, now associated with the Friends of the People. Syme had been reading recent works like the *Patriot* – possibly a radical publication, but more probably Edinburgh Professor Thomas Hardy's establishment reflections on French and American republicanism, Paine, and the British constitution. For all, like Burns, he was a government employee, Syme's own sympathies were hardly unthinkingly loyalist. Aware of the sensitivity of 'the subject in these times', his 3 August 1793 account of touring with Burns quotes with approval a 1791 poem published anonymously by William Roscoe. Celebrating 'equal rights', it begins,

O'er the vine-cover'd mountains and vallies of France
See the day-star of Liberty rise,
Tho' clouds of detraction unwearied advance
And hold a new course thro' the skies.[119]

This is the very same poem Burns attributes to 'my friend Roscoe in Liverpool', quoting it the following year when he attacks the French King and Queen as a lying fool and a prostitute.[120] A copy of Roscoe's poem transcribed by Burns is said to have been found among his papers on his death.[121] Burns's Galloway tour was not simply a bardic excursion; he met with several radically minded allies in dangerous circumstances.

Just how strong and close were the dangers is emphasised by the fact that on 30 July the radical lawyer Thomas Muir, 'being accused of seditious practises', was arrested at Portpatrick, 'carried to Stranraer jail', then on Sunday, 4 August taken through Dumfries *en route* to Edinburgh for trial.[122] Another of Burns's supporters, Henry Erskine, offered to defend Muir, but in a trial widely reported not just in the *Dumfries Weekly Journal* and the Scottish press but also in London papers like the *Morning Chronicle* Muir conducted his own defence, lost, and was sentenced to transportation. Among Muir's political sins were his 'spirit of disloyalty and disaffection to the King', his 'desire' for the playing of the 'ÇA IRA', and his 'exhorting persons to purchase and peruse seditious and wicked publications and writings (viz. Paine's works . . .)'.[123] Burns was probably vulnerable on each of these counts. Muir's conviction was followed by other trials and convictions of Scottish radicals. These included democrat William Skirving who had tried 'to obtain a *proper constitution* for the country', and Burns's remarkable friend James Tytler, poet and pioneering balloonist.[124] At Muir's trial a former servant accused him of encouraging a public performance of the 'Ça ira'.[125]

When exactly Burns learned of Muir's arrest or what his immediate reaction was we cannot tell. From evidence like the shared enthusiasm Burns and Syme felt for Roscoe's 'day-Star of liberty' and Burns's eagerness to denounce Lord Galloway but visit Daer's father Lord Selkirk we know that the bard's political antennae remained acute. Several poems are linked to his stay at St Mary's Isle. One is known as 'The Selkirk Grace', which Burns is said to have recited at dinner and which was probably an older folk-poem. Almost in English, it is conventionally spoken as Scots – 'cannae' for cannot; its plainness seems almost brusquely democratic:

Some have meat and cannot eat,
     Some can not eat that want it:
But we have meat and we can eat,
     Sae let the Lord be thankit.[126]

The other poem associated with this period is riskier, and more famous. At St Mary's Isle Burns met the fashionable composer Pietro Urbani. Soon afterwards Urbani spent several days in Dumfries having 'a great deal of converse' with Burns about Scots songs.[127] Burns discussed the tune 'Hey Tutti Taiti' traditionally regarded as 'Robert Bruce's March at the battle of Bannock-burn'. According to a disputed account given by James Currie, Syme recalled the bard 'rapt in meditation' on the ride to and from Lord Selkirk's house, and later claimed Burns immediately afterwards presented him with the song beginning, 'Scots, wha hae'.[128] Burns wrote to Thomson saying it was Urbani's suggestion he put words to the tune, after Burns showed it to the composer.

Whatever the exact circumstances, Burns makes clear 'Scots, wha hae' is not only about the historical Scottish struggle for 'Liberty & Independance' but also 'associated with the glowing ideas of some other struggles of the same nature, *not quite so ancient*'.[129] The italics are Burns's own, and may serve as a reminder that his manuscript of the Jacobite song 'Here is to the king, Sir' links a Jacobite uprising to the music of 'Tuti taity to the drum', but Burns's italicised phrasing also alludes to the French 'day-star of Liberty'.[130] The goriness of 'Scots, wha hae' conjures up Bannockburn but also recent events such as the execution of the French King many viewed as a tyrant. Drawing on Hamilton of Gilbertfield's *Wallace*, Burns taps into boyhood enthusiasm for Scottish freedom-fighting and winning independence from 'proud EDWARD's' English 'power' – but also into his feelings about the French Revolution:

By Oppression's woes & pains!
By your Sons in servile chains!
We will drain our dearest veins,
     But they *shall* be free!

Lay the proud Usurpers low!
Tyrants fall in every foe!
LIBERTY's in every blow!
     Let us DO – or DIE!!![131]

Sending the poem to the Earl of Buchan in 1794 Burns uses the word
'Europe' in connection with it, saying it involved 'the desperate relics
of a gallant Nation, devoting themselves to rescue their bleeding
Country'.[132] Ostensibly this meant Wallace's and Bruce's Scots strug-
gling against the English; but 'a gallant Nation' recalls Burns's earlier
description of 'that gallant people', the modern-day French. Its histor-
ical guise let Burns send the song to Scotland's great and good; the
biographical context of its composition shows it has a dangerous
edge.

Most songs Burns discussed with Thomson that summer are
politically unexceptionable. Many – like 'Auld Lang Syne' and 'John
Anderson, my jo' – are deft, warm and resolute. To collect songs
while political radicalism was crushed might seem frivolous. Yet,
though it was only occasionally Burns struck a strong political note,
his collecting asserted and glorified the voice of the people. Songs
of love and sex had their own power – at once levelling and exalting.
Erotic impulses represent what can never be repressed, even if

> IN Edinburgh town they've made a law,
>   In Edinburgh at the Court o' Session,
> That standing pr——cks are fauteors a',   *wrong-doers*
>   And guilty of a high transgression. –[133]

That song he did not send to Thomson. Instead, as trials of radicals
continued in Edinburgh and elsewhere, he posted it on 25 October
to his farmer friend Robert Cleghorn at Saughton-mills near
Edinburgh with the cryptic comment, 'Well! the Law is good for
something, since we can make a B——dy-song out of it. –'[134] In an
age when it was dangerous to speak out, the bard knew the answer
was to sing.

In September he presented several books to Dumfries library. One
was Jean Louis De Lolme's paean, *The British Constitution*. Osten-
sibly, this gift signalled that Exciseman Burns was a thoroughly loyal
chap. Yet even Thomas Muir at his trial that month had quoted
Montesquieu's 'spirited eulogium on the British constitution', and
Burns could not resist writing on the flyleaf, 'Mr Burns presents this
book to the Library & begs they will take it as a Creed of British
Liberty – untill they find a better. –'[135] Soon afterwards, realising
this was too risky an equivocation, he went back and glued the
flyleaf shut.

Though there are stories that he toasted George Washington rather than the British Prime Minister, it was sex, not politics, that got Burns into real trouble. He and Maria Riddell were 'constantly together'. They shared a liking for music, for theatre and animated conversation, for William Roscoe's work.[136] Though the bard and this young mother flirted, they were not lovers. Like Louisa Fontenelle, for whose Dumfries benefit night on 4 December 1793 Burns wrote a 'NEW OCCASIONAL ADDRESS' and as librettist teamed up with Robert Riddell on 'a new Scots Air called THE BANKS OF NITH', Maria was a 'Fair Friend' attached to another man.[137] However, one evening at Friars' Carse late in 1793 Burns seems to have taken part in a drunken romp which led to his assaulting Maria's sister-in-law, Elizabeth Riddell, wife of Robert. Tradition has it that Burns was helping re-enact the Roman Rape of the Sabine Women. Certainly he was 'in the heat of a fever of intoxication'; he tried to atone in a letter (later censored) written next morning 'from the regions of Hell', but a split ensued between the bard and the Riddells.[138]

Burns was saddened and made bitter by this. He had already portrayed himself as 'gloomy' in his prologue for Louisa Fontenelle, and had complained to Mrs Dunlop he was 'in a compleat Decemberish humour, gloomy, sullen, stupid'.[139] As their only breadwinner – 'all their stay' – he worried about his family's health, imagining what would happen if he died suddenly.[140] Such depressive musings were not new for Burns, especially in the dark of winter, but his break with the Riddells made things worse. When he met Maria one day, her reception 'froze the very life-blood of my heart'.[141] He sent her Goethe's *The Sorrows of Young Werther*, a novel about a suicidal artist, telling her he adored her as 'the first of Friends'. Nothing worked, but 'a stubborn something' led to several hostile poems in the succeeding months.[142]

Early in 1794 Burns again suffered 'low spirits & blue devils' in 'this accursed time'.[143] Still, while war was reducing Excise seizures and hence his own income, he managed to propose a somewhat self-interested reorganisation of Dumfries's Excise divisions (the plan was not adopted), and to send James Johnson forty-one songs he had collected or composed. He also boasted to Johnson he had got hold of 'an old Highland durk' that had once belonged to the Jacobite Lord Balmerino; it was now one of his cherished possessions. An Exciseman with a rebel's knife, Burns felt 'like Judas

Iscariot preaching the gospel'.[144] He went on worrying about his job, and enjoying alcohol. Protesting he was 'an honest fellow', he fretted lest the Excise Office in Edinburgh 'have conceived a prejudice against me as being a drunken dissipated character'.[145] Brooding once more on God and the next world, he complained in late February to Cunningham of having been from earliest childhood 'blasted with a deep incurable taint of hypochondria, which poisons my existence'. Interestingly, in the same letter he links a sense of religion to 'a musical ear', a means of sensing the deep harmony of God in nature, and hopes his baby son, 'this sweet little fellow, who is just now running about my desk', will come to sense such things.[146]

There seem to have been moments for Burns, as for most poets, when the harmony of lyric spoke of a wider sense of attunement. Usually, though, he avoided transcendental expressions, preferring excited earthiness. That March he recalled how 'Charlie Caldwell, a drunken Carrier in Ayr' would get thoroughly intoxicated with his lover, then, in 'the region of rapture', hug her tightly, exclaiming '"MARGET! YE'RE A GLORY TO GOD, & THE DELIGHT O' MY SOUL!!"'[147]

In early 1794 Burns designed himself a coat of arms to be engraved on a Highland pebble as his letter-seal. It featured a shepherd's pipe and crook, with 'a woodlark perching on a sprig of bay-tree'. He chose for it two mottoes: 'Wood-notes wild' at the top; underneath, the proverbial 'Better a wee bush than nae bield [shelter]'. Carefully he explained he wanted the shepherd's gear not to look like 'the nonsense of Painters of Arcadia' but like actual stuff imaged in his favourite edition of Ramsay's Scots pastoral *The Gentle Shepherd*. In this heraldic way Burns, the 'wild' singer imaging himself as poor yet independent, might assert the bard was as great as any 'Nabob' or nobleman.[148] Whereas Poet Laureate Henry James Pye's 'Ode for the New Year' – syndicated in the *Dumfries Weekly Journal* and elsewhere – had championed the British 'Monarch's throne' against 'Anarchy's infuriate brood', 'The Bard', Syme recorded on 1 February 1794, had been working on 'a grand elevated & sublime Pindaric ode to Liberty'. Writing to Cunningham, Syme, who was then seeing a lot of Burns and Burns's work in progress, added that the Liberty was 'not of the Gallic species'.[149]

In mid-January at Edinburgh's High Court the trial of William Skirving who had advocated *'Universal Suffrage'* was widely reported, making the news in Dumfries and elsewhere. Skirving was

found guilty. In London his associate Maurice Margarot was convicted, among other things, of having walked on Edinburgh's North Bridge under 'a wreath, or arch, with the words *Liberty, Justice*, inscribed upon it.'[150] Burns's 'ode to Liberty' that February may not have openly supported 'the Gallic species', but in its outspoken praise of America, this 'Ode [For General Washington's Birthday]' celebrates Liberty as republican rebellion – 'a People freed' from 'a Despot's nod'.[151] At the end of 1792 Dumfries's theatre had hosted a performance with Louisa Fontenelle and a comic opera, *The American Slaves; or Love and Liberty*, which included a view of 'an American camp' with 'General Washington', and was followed by a 'Grand Martial Entertainment, called THE SIEGE OF PERTH; OR, SIR WILLIAM WALLACE the Scots Champion'.[152] Just over a year later, Burns's ode also juxtaposes Washington and Wallace. While 'Caledonia', land of 'heaven-taught song', is seen as needing Wallace's inspiration, England is reproached for repression of republican rebellion: 'England in thunder calls – "The Tyrant's cause is mine!"'[153] This was as close as Burns could get to 'the Gallic species' of liberty without losing everything. Addressing Washington here, like addressing Wallace in the less high-toned, more powerful 'Scots, wha hae', is a way of presenting dangerously contemporary sentiments in protectively historical guise. Open support for Washington in Burns's youth would have branded him a traitor to the Crown. In 1794, though he does not use the words 'The Rights of Man', in his ode to liberty Burns's striking phrase 'The Royalty of Man' elevates the people, questioning the monarch's special status.[154]

The same year also saw re-publication of his poem of the American Revolution, 'When Guilford good', in an anthology of *Scotish Songs*, with the editorial comment, 'The events and allusions which form the subject of this song, are too recent and familiar to need a comment.'[155] However, just how dangerously unorthodox was expression of revolutionary sentiments in Dumfries is emphasised by the public observance there of the fast held throughout Scotland on 27 February 1794 'on account of the War' with France. At St Michael's Church, which the Burns family sometimes attended (and where Burns is buried), a topical sermon considered 'The Miseries of France, A Warning to Britain'. The preacher was a visitor, David Trail, and his sermon made such an impact it was soon printed by Robert Jackson, editor of the *Dumfries Weekly Journal*.[156] Trail fulminated against the way in France 'The ignorant and unsuspecting

multitude' had been 'seduced by the specious artifices of discontented and designing men, and made converts to the novel and ensnaring system of *Equality*'. Rebels against 'every law, usage, and authority', the French revolutionaries were destroying 'the entire fabric of civilized society'. He and his congregation joined to 'grieve for the righteous blood that has been shed, especially for that of an innocent and virtuous King, and his ill fated Consort', but were consoled that those responsible for executing the monarch were now 'in their turn become the victims of triumphant villany'. For Trail, his local hearers and readers, the horrors of revolutionary France were not distant but an immediate danger to be fought on all fronts, including in their own community:

> The period is still recent, and our recollection of it must be strong, when all the evils which afflict France seemed to be impending over ourselves. – The blood-stained rulers of that wicked land, not satisfied with the multitude of their domestic sins and sufferings, and envious of our happiness, sent hither wicked emissaries to sow sedition among our people, and, if possible, to seduce them from their loyalty, and excite them to rebellion. Unhappily, too many were deceived by their artifices, and blindly adopted doctrines; – plausible indeed in theory, – but in practice calamitous, iniquitous and fatal. The pretence of these sowers of sedition, and their associates, was fair – They were to obtain *Liberty*, and establish *Equality*: but their liberty was licentiousness, and a mere cloak for rebellion; while their equality, as in France, would have produced nothing but anarchy, desolation and woe.

Trail argued that these seditious reformers 'who have been, and still continue to be, the cool and deliberate instigators of a conduct, pregnant with so much mischief, and who wish to introduce confusion, massacre and devastation, into their native land, under the specious pretence of reformation, are monsters, whose characters we must regard with abhorrence and detestation'. Whether or not he was in the congregation when this 'Kirk and King' sermon was preached, Burns, living just along the road, must have been well aware of the impact of such sentiments on this national day of fasting. The culmination of Trail's sermon celebrated the existing British constitution and vehemently denounced the tree of liberty, that emblem of republican democrats hymned by Thomas Paine, erected by French revolutionaries, and on occasion (as in Dundee in 1792) relished by radical democratic and republican Scots.

The tree is known by its fruits: and what are the fruits which this boasted tree of liberty has produced? Calamities, greater perhaps than have ever before existed upon the earth, – oppressions more grievous than have heretofore been the lot of any people – Crimes so enormous and atrocious, that the bare recital of them fills the mind with horror ... Such is the frightful catalogue of the fruits, with which this fatal tree has overwhelmed that most wretched country. Like the apple that tempted our first parents to transgress, its fruit appeared at first to be fair, and sweet, and pleasant: but alas! like that of the forbidden tree, it has been pregnant with mischief, misery and death.[157]

In the 1790s when the French Terror brought the word 'terrorist' into the English language, and pro-government voices denounced the sort of radicalism associated with democracy, republicanism and the tree of liberty, to be associated with such ideas was like being suspected of terrorism today. It is in this incendiary local, national and international context that we should view 'The Tree of Liberty', the radical poem Robert Chambers in 1838 printed 'from a M[anu]S[cript]' then owned by 'James Duncan' of 'Mosesfield, near Glasgow'. Even Kinsley, most careful and conservative of Burns's editors, finds 'a Burnsian quality' in at least parts of the poem, and thinks it unlikely Chambers would have been duped by a forgery.[158] 'The Tree of Liberty' celebrates how a branch of the tree was brought from America beyond 'the western waves' to France and grew there. It alludes to royal opposition and the January 1793 execution of the French monarch,

> King Loui' thought to cut it down,
>   When it was unco sma', man;
> For this the watchman cracked his crown,
>   Cut aff his head and a', man.[159]

These sentiments accord closely with Burns's later (January 1795) comments about the French King and Queen, in total opposition to the orthodox view preached by Trail. Burns thought, in comparison with larger issues at stake, there was nothing to 'arrest for a moment, attention' in 'the delivering over a perjured Blockhead & an unprincipled Prostitute into the hands of the hangman'.[160] Such comments, which led Mrs Dunlop to break off all contact with the bard, are more outspoken even than 'The Tree of Liberty' with its praise of 'equal rights and equal laws', and its hope that 'auld England' will

join France, America and the Scottish voice of the poem in welcoming 'this far-fam'd tree'. Outspokenly political, the poem can also be nimbly, jauntily Burnsian:

> HEARD ye o' the tree o' France,
>   I watna what's the name o't;
> Around it a' the patriots dance,
>   Weel Europe kens the fame o't.
> It stands where ance the Bastile stood,
>   A prison built by kings, man,
> When Superstition's hellish brood
>   Kept France in leading strings, man.[161]

Though it cannot be dated precisely, this poem most probably was written in 1794. A spiritedly radical counterblast to the sentiments of Trail's Dumfries sermon, it sounds the most convincing of all the disputed 'radical' poems attached to Burns's name. Even Kinsley is open-minded about its attribution, while Chambers, Noble and Hogg argue vigorously for Burns's authorship.[162] I think the attribution is strong and, like the new evidence about Burns's continuing republican sympathies adduced later in this chapter, the poem demonstrates how vigorously he continued both to hint at and to articulate directly a republican position in his last years – for all his public swearing of loyalty to his employer the Crown, and his maintaining in the face of Excise 'accusations' that he 'abjured the idea' of a British republic.[163]

Around the time Burns's republican sympathies put him in a dangerous position in Dumfries, he was tempted by an offer of work from London's politically reformist *Morning Chronicle* which would have paid him a guinea a week. Yet Burns resolved to stay with the Excise. 'You well know my Political sentiments,' he wrote to a friend of the *Chronicle*'s editor in March 1794, saying he would have taken the job and 'despised all consequences that might have ensued' if he had not needed to think of his wife and family; apparently worried about deteriorating health, he was comforted by the thought that in the event of his death the Excise would pay a pension to his dependants.[164] Still, he did consider writing 'little Prose Essays' and sent several pieces to the *Morning Chronicle*, including 'Scots, wha hae', asking it be inserted by the journalists 'as a thing they have met with by accident, & unknown to me'. Burns knew government

'spies' and informers monitored the activities and even corres-
pondence of those associated with sedition.[165] On 8 May the *Morning
Chronicle* published his poem, with a strong hint about Scottish
bards which, without naming him, implied Burns was the author.
Noble and Hogg identify the poem's last line as 'the tennis court
oath of the French revolutionaries'.[166] Had such a point been made
in 1794, or had Burns's name been linked to the poetry of 'The Tree
of Liberty', it could have had serious consequences.

His fellow poet Gavin Turnbull, living in Dumfries and writing
for its Theatre Royal while working as an actor, published his *Poems*
locally in 1794; as well as plangently elegising Robert Fergusson,
Turnbull called on soldiers 'To plunge in Gallic blood th' avenging
blade', and hoped 'Justice shall avenge a Monarch's wrongs,/ And
teach the duty that to Kings belongs!'[167] Burns evidently felt other-
wise, and in spring 1794 continued taking risks. Politics, though,
was hardly his sole preoccupation. Alongside Excise tasks he went
on working on a range of songs, plus squibs against Maria and
Walter Riddell. Then, on 21 April, at the age of thirty-eight, his
former staunch supporter Robert Riddell died. Burns was shocked.
For all their estrangement, Riddell had beeen a *'man I loved'* – the
emphatic italics are Burns's own.[168] With bardic, Ossianic phrasing,
he publicly memorialised this *'Man of Worth'* – again the italics are
Burns's – in the *Dumfries Weekly Journal*.[169] Privately he wrote an
anguished letter to the Riddell family, stung there was now no earthly
opportunity to be reconciled to 'the friend of my soul'.[170] He begged
the Riddells to return or destroy the collection of manuscripts he
had given Riddell, lest they fell into the hands of Burns's enemies
and were used against him. He got them back, but Riddell's death
led to the sale of Friars' Carse, and Burns remained estranged from
Maria.

Meanwhile, Burns's wife was keeping in intermittent contact with
her family in Mauchline. She wrote to them on 4 June 1794 and
eleven days later her father replied, saying there was 'a great Death
of Children hear with the Smal pox and a fever'. He also informed
Jean, as if it was news, 'Mr Burns at Mosgill has got a Son the first
of April.' This suggests Robert and Jean were in less than constant
touch with Gilbert, but evidently James Armour had paid a visit to
Dumfries and Jean's family worried at times lest she 'had forgot us
Alltoghether.' Her father, whatever his earlier view of her relation-
ship with Burns, was keen to send affectionate good wishes, and to

stay in touch: 'NB we expect to hear from you on the rec[eip]t of this.'[171]

While Jean was sometimes too busy to write to Mauchline, Robert had found new friends among local radicals. When in May word reached Dumfries that in Edinburgh 'some young fellows have perambulated the streets, carrying green branches, which they call the *Tree of Liberty*, and to which they compel passengers to make obedience,' the official reaction was to denounce such 'offenders'.[172] Burns, though, associated with friends unlikely to denounce them. His fellow Mason, David McCulloch of Ardwall in Dumfriesshire, had recently returned to be with his dying father. McCulloch had a fine voice and shared Burns's passion for Scots songs. He had been living happily in revolutionary France for several years. Another recent arrival was Dr William Maxwell of Kirkconnell near Dumfries, a French-educated contemporary of Burns from an old Dumfriesshire Jacobite family. A staunch republican, Maxwell had been denounced by England's *Sun* newspaper for being involved in purchasing daggers for the revolutionaries, and had been a member of the revolutionary National Guard at the execution of the French King. As Burns was well aware, Edmund Burke, brandishing a dagger, had denounced Maxwell, an acquaintance of Thomas Paine, in the House of Commons. 'Maxwell,' Burns wrote to Mrs Dunlop in 1794, 'is my most intimate friend, & [is (*deleted*)] one of the first characters I ever met with; but on account of his Politics is rather shunned by some high Aristocrates.'[173] Burns was also in touch with David Blair from Dumfries, a Birmingham gunsmith and 'violent Leveler' who in 1789 had presented Burns with pistols and who in 1793 was linked like Maxwell to the affair of the daggers.[174]

Burns too was being 'rather shunned' by some people. Around this time he wrote a squib 'On an old acquaintance who seemed to pass the Bard without notice'. He also linked Burke to a 'poisonous Reptile'.[175] Syme gleefully recorded such rhymes, and he, Maxwell and Burns were listed as 'sons of sedition' by a local group calling themselves the Loyal Natives. These 'Natives' were 'particularly anxious to shew their attachment to the best of Sovereigns', as the *Dumfries Weekly Journal* put it.[176] James Muirhead, a nearby minister, distributed rhymes against Burns; in one (based on Martial) he is called 'a traitor'.[177] Burns in turn hurled '*darts of contempt*' at the Loyal Natives – not that he dared turn his darts into print.[178] When Syme wrote to Cunningham on 15 June 1794 about Burns's

attitude towards the Loyal Natives, he carefully made it sound as if Burns was not being disloyal to the Crown, but the weight of evidence points the other way. Syme's letter gives a good sense of 'Robin' Burns's situation:

> . . . the wild Bard has just now popped in while I was writing this and no less than a very elegant female figure of good rank reading a book aside me (She is the wife of an intimate acquaintance of mine – a Writer in Kirkcudb[righ]t – a very clever respectable woman whom I much esteem & so does Robin) Her husband was out – & Robins confounding wit began to play – He remained all day – and was according to use & wont charming company. The wicked fellow had read a vehemently loyal advertisement by a Club of bucks here who call themselves the loyal Native Club – The individuals who compose it are neither Robins favourites nor mine, but we are far from differing from them on sentiments of loyalty – we differ on sentiment abstractedly considered – They know scarcely the meaning of the word Sentiment & their Society consists in roaring & drinking – Robin spouts the following – on the advertisement of the loyal Natives
>
> Pray who are these Natives the rabble so ven'rate?
> They're our true ancient natives, and the breed undegen'rate:
> The ignorant savage that weather'd the storm,
> When the *Man* and the Brute differ'd but in the form
>
> Don't let any Dumfries person see this for one of the Savages, if he heard it, might cut Robins pipe –[179]

Robin's pipe remained uncut, and he and 'Collector Syme' made another 'long projected' tour of Galloway in late June.[180] Again their route may have had political overtones. They visited the Francophile McCulloch to whom Burns complained about being 'indeed ill at ease whenever I approach your Honorables & Right Honorables'. The bard was feeling ill; prison was on his mind: he made an uneasy joke about 'Solitary confinement' in the same letter to Mrs Dunlop as communicated to her part of the 'Ode for Gen[era]l Washington's birth-day'. Even if it did not chime with her own political views, Burns was confident she would like his lines about 'the hallowed turf where WALLACE lies!'[181] On tour he toasted Clarinda – 'Mrs Mack' he called her in front of fellow drinkers – and wrote to tell her so. She had urged him to write only 'In Friendship'. 'It will not

do,' he retorted. "'Tis like Jove grasping a pop-gun, after having wielded his thunder. –'[182] And, returning to those Augustan couplets on their relationship which he had been revising for six years, he sent his 'lovely Clarinda' eight lines of them, then drank her health again.[183]

Travelling with Syme, he was feeling 'in poor health'. Having discussed his condition with medical friends who diagnosed 'a flying gout', he feared he might be 'about to suffer for the follies of my youth'.[184] Back in Dumfries, where Jean was expecting yet another child, Burns was still being 'the wild bard'. Worried what he might have said when 'drunk last night' at a public gathering, he wrote anxiously that the toast, '"May our success in the present war be equal to the justice of our cause"' was 'A toast that the most outrageous frenzy of loyalty cannot object to'. But he feared it might be objected to: 'the report of certain Political opinions being mine, has already once before brought me to the brink of destruction. – I dread lest last night's business may be misrepresented in the same way –.'[185]

Nevertheless, Burns could not resist poking fun at the war effort of 'glorious Crusaders' fighting against 'the savage thraldom of Democratic Discords', and, in a letter which refers to his libertarian '"Bannockburn"' poem 'Scots, wha hae', he unwisely mocked the idea of allied victory over the French as a predicted 'golden age, spotless with Monarchical innocence & Despotic purity – That Millenium [*sic*], of which the earliest dawn will enlighten even Republican turbulence, & shew the swinish multitude that they are but beasts, & like beasts must be led by the nose & goaded in the backside.'[186] Burns was better known for sympathies with an oppressed populace than for polite prostration before any supposed 'Monarchical innocence'. 'Man is a soger [soldier], and Life is a faught [fight],' maintained one of the songs he worked on in 1794; this song, which he regarded as 'the picture of my mind', continued, 'my FREEDOM's my Lairdship nae monarch dare touch'.[187] Syme recorded another coarser impromptu performance by the bard:

> No more of your titled acquaintances boast,
>   Nor of the gay groups you have seen;
> A crab louse is but a crab louse at last,
>   Tho' stack to the [Cunt] of a Queen.[188]

Just like Burns, Dr Maxwell had a respectable as well as a wild side. When Maxwell saved the daughter of Dumfries's Provost Staig from illness Burns celebrated his action. Maxwell, for a moment, could be seen as a local hero. Burns too wanted to be well regarded. He sent poems to Alexander Findlater, the Dumfries Supervisor of Excise, and wrote successive songs about the beautiful blonde 'Chloris' (Jean Lorimer), on whom another former Dumfries Excise colleague, 'a particular friend of mine', was sweet.[189] Burns was sweet on her too. They may well have become lovers, though in 1795 he mentioned merely 'fictitious reveries of Passion'.[190] 'I put myself in a regimen of admiring a fine woman,' he explained to Thomson, '& in proportion to the adorability of her charms, in proportion you are delighted with my verses.'[191] Around the time he was in this 'regimen' the other Jean, his wife, gave birth to James Glencairn Burns on 12 August: one more loved mouth to feed. Burns could be characteristically generous, sending a splendid kippered salmon to Peter Hill – but he still philandered. He worried too about his 'little flock', his Excise income, and people he described to Mrs Dunlop as 'My Enemies'.[192]

No doubt he was concerned about his 'Enemies' in a year Gilbert recalled as initiating a period of 'public alarm and apprehension of intestine commotion'.[193] Dumfries Kirk Session minutes show an ongoing scandal occasioned by the reporting in August 1794 that one of the elders, Robert Halliday, after reading Tom Paine, had drunkenly protested that 'he had no business with kings'; scared, a sober Halliday apologised for his 'unguarded expression'.[194] In November the radical Lord Daer died. The *Dumfries Weekly Journal* wanted to 'throw a veil' over his politics, and busily reported the London trial of the radical John Horne Tooke for High Treason.[195] One of the clearest signs of Burns's political anxiety occurs in a formal English poem, 'From Esopus to Maria'. Maria Riddell had returned to Dumfriesshire after an absence in England following her brother's death; she and Burns appear to have had something of a *rapprochement* in late 1794. Addressing Maria in the voice of the Roman actor Esopus, Burns images himself among the prison ships at Woolwich where arrested radicals such as Thomas Muir and Dundee's Unitarian minister Thomas Fyshe Palmer were held before being transported for their supposed crimes.

The shrinking Bard adown an alley sculks,
And dreads a meeting worse than Woolwich hulks –
Tho' there his heresies in Church and State
Might well award him Muir and Palmer's fate . . .[196]

In the same poem he mocks the 'veni, vidi, vici' attitude of local military officers who paid court to Maria Riddell, and refers in passing to French revolutionary 'Sans Culotes'. Dumfries was now awash with drilling and strutting wartime soldiery. For a Crown official like Burns to be seen distancing himself from them was a dangerous course of action; he could only hope no such reports again reached the Excise in Edinburgh.

The Caledonian Hunt, Burns's old sponsors, were in Dumfries too that October. He sniped in verse at an 'Hon[oura]ble' absurdly proud of 'his high Phaeton', and found himself thinking longingly of Ayr races rather than the 'roar of Folly & Dissipation' of 'fashionable young men' in Dumfries.[197] He was also pondering old loves and new, none, apparently, his wife. 'Conjugal-love is a Passion which I deeply feel, & highly venerate; but somehow it does not make such a figure in Poesy as that other species of the Passion – "Where Love is liberty & Nature law –",' he wrote to Thomson, alluding to Chloris and quoting Pope on the illicit love of Abelard and Eloisa.[198] His long letters to the sometimes inept lawyer Thomson reveal a connoisseur of song; he was building a library of anthologies. Working thoroughly and intensively, Burns was now the leading player in the *Select Collection*.

At home he experimented with a 'stock & horn'. He had long wanted to lay hands on this sort of shepherd's flute – a sheep's thigh bone pushed inside a cow's horn. Blowing into a reed loose inside the stock, he couldn't produce the exact sound he wanted: was he not blowing properly? or were the holes in the instrument bored wrongly? His listening family may have breathed a sigh of relief when in December 1794, despite fears of being denounced as a radical, Burns was promoted Acting Supervisor of Excise and 'the load of business' reduced his time for such musical efforts.[199] Duties could be arduous. December brought several lengthy inspection tours beginning before dawn, ending after nightfall – with official paperwork to match. 'My Political sins seem to be forgiven me,' he told Mrs Dunlop. Then, as if to celebrate he was getting away with those sins, he added remarks about Dr Moore 'whining over the deserved

fate' of the executed French monarchs. 'These London trials have given us a little more breath,' he opined in January 1795, hoping a time was soon coming when one could complain about the government without being called an enemy of the country.

Burns's letter to Mrs Dunlop seems to have crossed in the post with a letter she had sent him on 12 January while visiting London when fears of French invasion were growing. After a slighting mention of '*sans-culottes*' (who had been defeating the British and their allies in Europe), she complained Dr Moore seemed 'a sad democrat'; she feared Moore's fondness for 'independence' would tell against his writings.[200] Receiving from Burns soon afterwards a letter in which he expressed so forthrightly his views on the execution of the French monarchs was too much for the sixty-five-year-old widow. Though the bard sent her several further letters, she never wrote to him again.

Early 1795 was a winter of intense blizzards. In February Burns found himself stranded in Ecclefechan, the roads blocked by 'snows of ten feet deep'.[201] Uncharacteristically, he joked about feeling suicidal; he got drunk instead. Appalled by his political outspokenness, Mrs Dunlop probably paid little attention to thirty-five-year-old Burns's complaints about 'the rigid fibre & stiffening joints of Old Age coming fast o'er my frame'. On New Year's Day he had reflected, 'Very lately I was a boy; but t'other day I was a young man'. Now, though, for all he was only halfway through the biblical span of threescore years and ten, he felt not middle-aged but 'Old'.[202] Not just the weather but also familial, financial and political pressures intensified this feeling. Now he had a 'large Family' to provide for, Burns found war so reducing his income that he was 'in serious distress', unable to pay bills or rent. Humiliatingly, in 'these accursed times' he had to borrow money.[203] He tried cheering himself up with bawdy verse on the 'early f——s' of spring, but pressures continued to increase.[204] His frustration can be sensed in a letter apparently drafted for a friend; it scorns those 'to whom *Situation of Life alone* is the criterion of Man', and quotes Thomson's *Seasons* on efforts '"to save a Rotten State"'.[205]

With fears of invasion rife, a home-guard-style regiment, the Royal Dumfries Volunteers, was being formed. Led by a local retired colonel, its founders included Burns's landlord John Hamilton, and other respectable citizens from Provost Staig and Robert Jackson, editor of the *Dumfries Weekly Journal*, to Excise colleagues. Dr

Burnside, minister of St Michael's Church where David Trail had declaimed against the tree of liberty, became the Volunteers' chaplain; many 'Loyal Natives' Burns had denounced were now Volunteers. Among his circle only Maxwell seems to have avoided membership. For Acting Supervisor of Excise Burns to have refused to participate would have sent a ruinous public signal. In January 1795 he applied to join along with friends like Syme. February's local paper announced another national day of fasting ordered by the King.[206] By 28 March Private Burns was swearing his Oath of Allegiance. Soon afterwards, kitted out in military uniform (blue coat, red cape, white vest and trousers, cockaded hat), he was marching and drilling with his firelock among the lime trees of Dumfries dock park.

While making such public gestures he was also circulating what is now his best-known poem of egalitarian *fraternité*, the 'Song – For a' that and a' that –'. That he had both *égalité* and *fraternité* in mind is indicated by his use of the word 'equals' in the last line of an early version sent to Thomson in mid-January (when Burns made his outspoken comments on the French revolutionaries to Mrs Dunlop), and his later replacement of 'equals' by 'brothers'. Arguing shrewdly the song 'represents the transformation of the Masonic concept of Brotherhood into the French revolutionary ideal of Fraternity', Thomas Crawford, following John Maccunn, has called attention to similarities in thought and phrasing between Burns's song and Paine's *Rights of Man*. Paine praises the French constitution for asserting '*There shall be no titles*', so that 'the *peer* is exalted into MAN', rather than fussing about an aristocratic 'fine *blue ribbon*' or '*garter*'. The republican Paine also praises 'The patriots of France' for realising social 'rank and dignity' need a new foundation, based not on titles but on 'the NOBLE of Nature', and Paine looks forward to a more universal republicanism: 'For what we can foresee, all Europe may form but one great Republic, and man be free of the whole.'[207] Marilyn Butler calls Burns's poem's concluding lines 'probably the closest rendering in English of the letter and spirit of the notorious Jacobin "Ça ira"'.[208] It takes a tin ear and narrow mind to miss the sense of conviction and protested radical idealism in the poem which draws on a Jacobite song directed against 'bra' militia lads', recently collected by Joseph Ritson in his 1794 *Scotish Songs*.[209] Beginning 'Is there, for honest Poverty', Burns's lines to the same tune assert 'The rank is but the guinea's stamp,/ The Man's the gowd [gold] for a' that.' Denouncing aristocratic

the corps who had a loyal dinner in April 1795. Burns's song takes the phrase 'haughty Gaul' from Addison's 'The Campaign' (familiar from Burns's boyhood Masson anthology). Its first stanza makes no bones about matters:

> DOES haughty Gaul invasion threat,
>   Then let the louns bewaure, Sir,
> There's WOODEN WALLS upon our seas,
>   And VOLUNTEERS on shore, Sir:
> The *Nith* shall run to *Corsincon**   **A high hill at the source*
>   And *Criffell*† sink in *Solway*,   *of the Nith* [Burns's note]
> E'er we permit a Foreign Foe   †*A high hill at the confluence of*
>   On British ground to rally.   *the Nith with Solway Frith* [RB]

Its second stanza uses the words 'Britain' or 'British' four times; surely there can be no mistaking the loyal protestations of this song that concludes,

> Who will not sing, GOD SAVE THE KING,
>   Shall hang as high's the steeple;
> But while we sing, GOD SAVE THE KING,
>   We'll ne'er forget THE PEOPLE!
> Fal de ral &c.[212]

In wartime this may have made a Royal Dumfries Volunteer sound utterly committed. However, those last lines sound uncannily like the widely reported rhetoric of Thomas Muir who had told a London audience in 1793 before his arrest, 'He loved his sovereign but could not on that account forget the people.'[213] A sceptical ear listening to the conclusion of Burns's song might suspect it advocates paying lip-service to royalty while maintaining a deeper loyalty to the cause of the people. His song is far more ambiguous than the satirical poem 'The Clubs' which Gavin Turnbull had published in Dumfries in 1794, presenting a group 'planning a reform', who meet in a pub to discuss political ideas such as a 'resolution . . . to o'erturn the constitution'. Burns, Syme and Maxwell belonged to such a coterie in the Globe Inn. Where Turnbull protests himself 'sworn a foe to the Convention' and ends, 'while I've breath I'll gladly sing/ That loyal song, "GOD SAVE THE KING!"', Burns's concluding 'But while we sing, GOD SAVE THE KING,/ We'll ne'er forget THE PEOPLE!' sounds like a sly retort.[214]

Publishing 'The Dumfries Volunteers' while circulating his song of universal brotherhood and equality, Burns was struggling to satisfy his employers in other ways. His local supervisor, Findlater, was off ill for several months in early 1795, greatly increasing Burns's workload and the distances he had to cover on horseback and on foot in appalling weather. As snowfall succeeded snowfall, drifts tens of feet deep were reported across Scotland. Even if in Dumfries the snow was lighter, there was, Syme grumbled on 22 January, 'as intense a frost as well can be in Galloway'. Burns's duties frequently took him into the deep drifts of nearby areas. Syme complained Burns's work was now so 'laborious' that for six weeks at the start of the year he hardly saw 'the *Bard*'.[215] This sheer slog was one thing making Burns feel suddenly old, but he was concerned also to be seen by his employers as doing his job well. Even by April, when the weather was improving and Findlater had returned to work, Burns felt nervous he might 'incur censure' over a minor piece of paperwork, and wrote to the Excise Office in Edinburgh, 'I hope it will be considered, that this Officiating Job being my first, I cannot be supposed to be completely master of all the etiquette of the business.'[216]

Trying to stay true to his own political ideals while apparently protesting loyalty and keeping up the 'incessant drudgery' needed to keep his job and provide for his family; juggling Excise form-filling with work on song anthologies; living with one Jean and his family, while making song after song about another Jean; riding out each day feeling he must measure up not just to local critics and 'Enemies' but also to the inquisitorial gaze of the Excise Board: all these strains – physical as well as psychological – were beginning to tell on Burns. Though still hoping to work his way towards achieving a Collector's comparatively wealthy 'life of compleat leisure', he suffered from spring 1795 onwards increasingly severe bouts of illness.[217]

Meantime, though, continuing his interest in local politics, in early 1795 he wrote, had printed and circulated a series of poems supporting the successful Whig candidate for the Stewartry of Kircudbright by-election, Patrick Heron. Burns viewed Heron as a sympathetic patron. Writing the first election ballad he drew on phrases from his recent 'Song – For a' that and a' that'. Sometimes toning down his radicalism, he lets it sound through in lines like 'A lord may be a lousy loun,/ Wi' ribband, star and a' that. –'[218] He had visited Heron the

year before and clearly got on well with this man who, in his thirties, had stared ruin in the face when the bank he had helped found, the so-called 'Ayr Bank' of Douglas, Heron & Company, failed. Despite having been among the many who felt the impact of that failure, Burns inclined far more to support the Whig Heron than his Tory opponent young Thomas Gordon of Balmaghie, bankrolled by a famously wealthy uncle and backed by the Earl of Galloway.

The bard satirised Heron's Tory opponents, including the titled, singularly rich Douglas family; Sir William Douglas had a reputation for sucking up to the Earl of Galloway, and had grandly obtained a royal warrant so the Scots village of Carlinwark could '*be called, in all time coming* . . . CASTLE-DOUGLAS' – which got up Burns's nose:

> And there will be [*Douglas*]es doughty,
>   New-christening towns far and near;
> Abjuring their democrat doings
>   By kissing the a[rse] of a *Peer*.[219]

This is the only time in his poetry Burns uses any form of the word 'democracy'. The strong implication is the poem's maker is much more attracted to 'democrat doings' than to the Douglases. That March Burns had keenly perused the *Travels of Anacharsis the Younger in Greece* where 'democracy' was not a bad word. In these electioneering poems he positioned himself as one of Heron's supporters, but also more generally as radical Whig 'poet-laureate to a highly respectable political party', as he put it in late April. Heron, sung by Burns as an 'independant Patriot' and 'Honest Man', won the election, but the Whigs remained in opposition so Heron's patronage pulled no Excise strings for their would-be Whig laureate.[220]

Burns was in a similar position to Syme, another Heron supporter, who confessed he had become 'involved in politics, a business I had determined to keep clear of, as my situation precludes [me] from political existence'; now Syme had 'become a partizan at the hazard of all consequences'.[221] Burns, like Syme, was a dependent servant of the Crown at a time of Tory government; his public intervention on the Whig side was risky. Local elections were notoriously corrupt and volatile. Observing drunken gentry in Dumfries after a 1796 election dinner, a young man who visited Burns complained,

These Elections are the bane of Morality. There is nothing which more clearly proves the deplorable degeneracy and corruption of our manners and Government than the practises there exhibited. The source of legislation being filthy and abominable, how can we expect any thing good from the streams that flow from it?[222]

Daring even to ridicule the Sheriff Clerk of the county, Burns in 1795 at least managed to back the winning side while mocking anti-democratic impulses; at the same time he protested his apparent loyalty by supporting the Royal Dumfries Volunteers.

In May when Thomson gifted to his greatest contributor David Allan's painting of a scene from 'Tam o' Shanter', Burns gleefully recorded how 'the very joiner's apprentice' who helped Mrs Burns open the crate immediately recognised one of the figures in the picture as representing Burns himself. The bard liked the picture – 'My phiz is *sae kenspeckle*' – and was struck that 'Several people think that Allan's likeness of me is more striking than Nasemith's [*sic*], for which I sat to him half a dozen times.'[223] In spring 1795 Burns was also enjoying having his portrait painted 'at Reid's painting-room' in Dumfries. As it progressed, local artist Alexander Reid's miniature (now in the Scottish National Portrait Gallery) struck Burns as 'by far the best likeness of me ever was taken', though later he felt the artist had 'spoilt' it.[224] He was pleased enough to show it to Maria Riddell, with whom he was again on good terms. Glad to be recognised by a joiner's apprentice, he was not averse to being esteemed by 'Great Folks', and rejoiced in Maria's renewed friendship.

They teased each other. '*You* a Republican!' he exclaimed, claiming she exercised 'despotic . . . sway' over men.[225] This is one of several hints that although she might the following year invite the bard to a party she was holding on the King's Birthday, her politics, like his, were other than those of the establishment. If Burns was a regular attender at Volunteers' parades in summer 1795, there is no record of his private reaction to the denunciation of French liberty and equality delivered to the assembled men on 4 June (the King's Birthday) by Dr Burnside, now minister of St Michael's Church. After the Volunteers' commander, 'tall, soldier-like', poetry-loving Colonel de Peyster, who thought Burns 'sometimes wrong', expressed the hope his men would 'trample on all who . . . dare to raise their heads against the King and Constitution', Dr Burnside denounced French

'pretended zeal for liberty' and 'pursuit of an equality, which no political establishment upon earth will ever be able to realise'. He hymned 'the British Constitution' as 'the best, perhaps, which human wisdom and experience have ever been able to devise'.[226] Burnside's address is as hostile to radical ideas as the sermon given at St Michael's by Trail the year before. It may have been around this time that, as a Dumfries correspondent recalled in the 1820s, Burns stood up in a gathering of 'civic soldiers and local townsmen ... and slowly lifting his glass, he said, with an arch, indescribable smile, "Gentlemen, may we never see the French, or the French see us!"'[227]

Among songs he sent to Thomson that wartime spring was one that exalted female beauty but mocked 'The world's imperial crown'. Burns told Thomson it was written for and should be set to the 'Tune, Deil tak the wars'.[228] As he put it in a bawdy ballad matching many others he collected in the gathering of often pornographic songs he circulated among his male companions and which was published posthumously as *The Merry Muses of Caledonia*,

> Some cry, Constitution!
>   Some cry, Revolution!
> And Politicks kick up a rowe;
>   But Prince and Republic,
>   Agree on the Subject,
> No treason is in a good [mowe].[229]   *fuck*

Despite his show of cheerfulness that spring, Burns was feeling ill. Privately he teased Maria Riddell about what appears to have been her protested republicanism; more openly he helped draft an official letter to the Volunteers' commanding officer, arguing the men should not have to advertise or 'go a begging' for the cost of their maintenence.[230] Yet he also told Maria he felt 'so ill as to be scarce able to hold this miserable pen'; by early summer he was worried that health was 'flown from me for ever'.[231]

One affliction was toothache:

> MY curse on your envenom'd stang,
> That shoots my tortur'd gums alang,
> An' thro' my lugs gies mony a bang
>   Wi' gnawin vengeance;
> Tearing my nerves wi' bitter twang,
>   Like racking engines.[232]

If we take his clearly autobiographical 'Address to the Tooth-Ache' literally, Burns found it too painful to shave, and grew a temporary beard. To Peter Hill on 30 May he described his toothache as 'omnipotent'; he was still complaining about it in July.[233] Toothache was just one sign that after his exertions in the excessively hard winter his health had broken. He might try to sound jaunty, but some days was in a state of near-collapse, staying in bed much of the time. He still worked energetically at songs, though in one, sent to Maria Riddell around July, a lover complains of a 'withering blast' which consumes 'youth and joy', leading to absolute 'Despair'.[234]

He was writing yet more songs for twenty-year-old Jeany Lorimer ('Chloris'), and seeing her from time to time. The formal phrasing of a surviving note to Jeany's father sounds awkward, mentioning that 'Mrs Burns desired me yesternight to beg the favor of Jeany to come and partake with her, and she was so obliging as to promise that she would.'[235] Jean stood by her husband. Maria Riddell, who may not have been a dispassionate observer, recalled in a 1799 letter,

> Burns said little or nothing ab[ou]t his Wife to me latterly; but as I believe her conduct, *subsequent to their union by marriage*, was exemplary towards him, so it is just to add that he always spoke of her with a high tribute of respect & esteem. he did not love her, but he was far from insensible to the indulgence & patience, the meekness with which she bore her faculties on many occasions very trying to the tempers of most individuals of our sex. an illegitimate child of his, born after wedlock, who had lost her mother, was I know adopted by Mrs Burns, & is I believe still an inmate of her house, & no distinction shewn between that & the rest of their children. this trait she told me of with much sensibility.[236]

Though Maria's observations may be inaccurate, they add to a sense that there were strains in Burns's marriage. With all his charisma – which a visitor around August 1795 recalled strongly, hearing him recite unpublished poems, 'chiefly political' – Burns could be demandingly difficult to live with.[237] Jean, running the household through her series of pregnancies, was remarkably loyal – not just as her husband wrote song after song to his other Jean, and returned again to musing on Clarinda, but also as his health collapsed, with consequent fears about the family's income. Burns remained close to male

friends like Maxwell, and William Hyslop, landlord of what he called 'my HOWFF [favourite pub]', the Globe Inn, but the bard's relationship with his wife is difficult to trace. Certainly she must have provided support during the summer when Burns seems to have suffered depression as well as physical illness.

Robert and Jean had another source of anxiety. Their daughter, Elizabeth Riddell Burns, had been seriously ill and was being looked after in Mauchline during a long, painful sickness whose exact nature remains unclear. 'My only daughter & darling child', Burns once called her, in one of the most tender (albeit inaccurate) allusions to any of his children by a man recalled in Dumfries as a loving, attentive father.[238] The little girl died in September, aged four. 'My friend,' Burns wrote to the young mother Maria Riddell, 'may [you] never experience such a loss as mine.'[239] Too ill to attend her funeral, he seems to have been plunged into psychological and physical collapse. Few letters survive from winter 1795, probably because Burns wrote hardly any. His child's death and associated anxieties 'put all literary business out of my head', he told Maria.[240] He had drunk 'deep of the cup of affliction'; by January 1796, sending a letter to Robert Cleghorn '*Per favor of Mr Mundell, Surgeon*' (one of Burns's medical friends and advisors), he wrote he had 'indeed been much the child of disaster'. After the shock of his daughter's death he had fallen 'the victim of a rheumatic fever, which brought me to the borders of the grave'.[241]

Burns in the 1790s was able to muse on consolations which a virtuous old age might hold in store. A manuscript fragment written on the back of a poem dating from the period sounds a philosophic note:

> Tho' life's gay scenes delight no more,
>   Still much is left behind,
> Still rich art thou in nobler store,
>   *The comforts of the Mind.* –
>
> Thine is the self-approving glow,
>   On conscious Honor's part [. . .][242]

Yet if he could envisage what a virtuous old age might be like, Burns expected less and less to experience one. He was living too dangerously, too feverishly, for it to appear likely.

Poleaxed by the death of his daughter, he spent 'many weeks' in his 'sick-bed' in December 1795 and January 1796, when he was 'just beginning to crawl about'. Josiah Walker remembered visiting in November, walking with Burns by the Nith, and hearing the bard recite 'fragments of an *Ode to Liberty*, with marked and peculiar energy'. Suppressing the details, Walker recalled this led to a riskily radical outburst: after hymning Liberty, Burns 'shewed a disposition which, however, was easily repressed, to throw out political remarks, of the same nature with those for which he had been reprehended'. Having repressed this tendency in Burns, Walker then went with him to the pub, the bard drinking 'freely without being intoxicated'.[243] In mid-December, unable to come to dinner with Syme, Burns sent a witty quatrain. On Hogmanay he sent a short Standard Habbie epistle to his Dumfries Excise superior, Collector Alexander Mitchell, wishing him well and asking for a guinea advanced against the next year's salary, adding in postscript, 'Ye've heard this while how I've been licket,/ And by fell Death 'maist nearly nicket.'[244] Now, he hoped, 'by good luck' he had managed to give death the slip.

Wartime conditions were hard. As early as November 1795 a correspondent in the local paper complained about 'the exorbitant and rising prices of grain, and all sorts of provisions'; that same month in England an attempt had been made on the King's life.[245] Dumfries Town Council sent 'An Address . . . to His Majesty congratulating him on his escape from the hands of hired assassins' in this 'traitorous and wicked attempt'; locally they reacted to 'some disturbances about shipping of grain' by authorising the Provost to purchase additional supplies for the town, then 'very scantily supplied'.[246] Like the King, Burns felt he had had a narrow escape. By the end of January, having celebrated his thirty-seventh birthday, he attended his first Masons' meeting for some time, and sent a salmon to Peter Hill – 'your *annual* KIPPER'.[247] He also told Syme of a plan to send their mutual friend Cunningham verse and prose reflections. Syme informed Cunningham,

He is to sit down as the spirit moves him and write you prose & poetry on every subject which strikes him – to form a sort of Journal business of it – and when it grows thro' two or three sheets to send the foliage – This will surely be a very valuable and entertaining farrago of Burnsana (is this a right term?). I have prompted him to execute the design & shall not miss giving him the spur.[248]

Enthusiastic again, Burns risked thinking about a future of writing and friendship. He wrote once more to Mrs Dunlop: why had she ceased to correspond? The question may have been disingenuous; Burns probably had a very good idea his pro-republican remarks on the French monarchs' execution had alienated her: as if to atone, he had already sent her a specially transcribed copy of 'Does Haughty Gaul invasion threat'. Now he invited sympathy, detailing the death of his daughter, his illness, and current anxieties. He even used the expression *'Swinish Multitude'* of restless elements among the Dumfries common folk.[249] Italicised here by Burns, this phrase was much bandied about in the 1790s, having been used in his *Reflections on the Revolution in France* by the Edmund Burke who feared civilisation might be 'trodden down under the hoofs of a swinish multitude'.[250] There was a radical song, 'Burke's Address to The "Swinish Multitude"'. In 1794, writing to Thomson, Burns had deployed the phrase ironically.[251] His use of it in an effort to placate Mrs Dunlop does not indicate he now sided with the Burke he had linked to a 'poisonous Reptile' two years earlier. Mrs Dunlop received Burns's letter but did not respond.

Burns's fears for himself and Dumfries were real. After 1795's bad harvest and unusually stormy weather in early 1796 food supplies were running low. 'We have actual famine,' he wrote at the end of January. 'Many days my family, & hundreds of other families, are absolutely without one grain of meal; as money cannot purchase it.'[252] Rightly, he anticipated civil unrest. Returned to Excise work in February after his illness, he was alert to disquiet which led to troops being placed on the streets of Dumfries in early March when food rioting broke out. People knew meal was available in the surrounding area but farmers were holding it back. When supplies were re-established the 'tumult' subsided.[253] Though rumours filled Dumfries and the authorities were on edge, the worst that happened was that a mob seized several meal carts and broke into the town's main granary.

Burns responded to another note of 'discord' early that year. His old supporter Henry Erskine, Whig Dean of Edinburgh's Faculty of Advocates who had volunteered to defend Thomas Muir at his 1793 sedition trial, had been protesting against government attempts to curb wartime freedom of speech and public assembly. Following the passing of 1795's Sedition Bill many Tory advocates wished to replace Erskine with the fiercely orthodox Robert Dundas who had brought

charges against suspected radicals. When in January Erskine failed to retain his position, Burns hit back in 'The Dean of Faculty – A New Ballad –'. Politically heretical as ever, he satirised the Tory Dundas's 'purblind, mental vision' as opposed to the 'Merit' of Erskine. Burns sides with Erskine's 'heretic Eight and thirty' supporters against Dundas and 'a certain King'.[254] Though he refrained from publishing this song, its very existence shows the bard was down, but not out. In February he took out a subscription to a newspaper, supporting its line of 'honest independence'.[255]

To some extent Burns's health rallied in early spring 1796. Late in February he was dining with Syme. 'Quite sober – only one bottle port betwixt us –' Syme assured Cunningham: 'I like this better than a debauch.'[256] Burns attended a Masons' meeting on 14 April. He, Syme and Maxwell were enjoying each other's conversation. Then illness returned. Burns was unable to shoulder a full Excise workload, so, in line with regulations, his pay was reduced. He grew increasingly dependent on family and neighbours. Through the wife of his close friend the Globe innkeeper William Hyslop he sent a letter to Thomson (to whom that spring he signed away some rights over his songs), complaining of 'the heavy hand of SICKNESS'. He 'counted Time by the repercussions of PAIN!' With a self-dramatising, depressive flourish he wrote, 'Rheumatism, Cold & Fever, have formed, to me, a terrible Trinity in Unity, which makes me close my eyes in misery, & open them without hope.' He was once more mapping his own situation on to that of Robert Fergusson, and quoted to Thomson from one of Fergusson's terrifying last poems, an Old Testament paraphrase where the afflicted Job cries in agony to God. Burns saw 'health & enjoyment' now as a '*damning* subject'. He signed off simply, 'FAREWEL!!!'[257]

But he still had spirit. On 2 June he was paid in full for the previous six weeks' Excise work; James Currie pointed out that this was due to 'the kindness of Mr Stobbie, a young expectant in the Excise, who performed the duties of his office without fee or reward'.[258] What no previous biographer has realised is that on 1 June Burns had a visitor. The Gaelic-speaking Reverend James Macdonald, recently licensed as a Kirk minister, was a well-travelled twenty-four-year-old Hebridean-born admirer of Ossian with an interest in the Jacobites. Knowledgeable about farming, and a great lover of poetry, Macdonald was also devoted to the example of William Wallace. Later (in 1798) aware of being called by 'the hard

names of Jacobin, democrat, etc.', Macdonald in 1796 was no fan of 'aristocratical arrogance'. He came to meet Burns just after making a pilgrimage to the birthplace of his 'favourite Bard', Thomson.[259] Macdonald and Burns were made for each other. They hit it off from the start on 1 June.

Macdonald's journal, written up in Sanquhar next evening and here quoted from manuscript, is a key document not only for its perception of Burns's politics but also because it is the last extended account of his conversation written during the bard's lifetime.

Yesterday Burns the Ayrshire Poet dined with me; and few evenings of my life passed away more to my satisfaction. He looks consumptive, but was in excellent spirits, and displayed as much wit and humour in 3 hours time as any man I ever knew. He told me that being once in Stirling when he was a young lad, & heated with drink, he had nigh got himself into a dreadful scrape by writing the following lines on the pane of a glass window in an Inn

> Here Stewarts once in triumph reign'd,
> And laws for Scotland's weal ordain'd;
> But now unroof'd their Palace stands,
> Their Sceptre's fall'n to other hands;
> Fall'n indeed unto the Earth
> Whence grovelling reptiles take their birth;
> And since great Stewarts' line is gone,
> A race outlandish fills their throne;
> An idiot race to honour lost,
> Who know them best dispise them most.

These lines are a proof of Burn's rashness & folly. He promised to send me an ode he composed when chosen poet Laureat to a Meeting of Jacobite Gentlemen once in Edin[burgh], when old Farquharson of Monalterie happened to meet with a poor Man who had fought by his side at the Battle of Culloden, which circumstance when he mentioned it brought the tears into the Poets Eyes. He told many anecdotes of himself and others in the very best & most genuine spirit of pleasantry. The landlord of our Inn commonly known by the name of the Marquiss Johnstone, is also a good humoured fellow, and served as a whetstone for Burn's Wit. They are both staunch republicans. Burns repeated an ode he composed on the Pretender's birth day, replete with grand imagery & brilliant expression. I am sorry I do not remember the words of the ode, one simile which

referred to the Swiss Avalanche was sublime. He promised to send me a copy of it. At parting the poor Poet with tears in his Eyes took an affectionate leave of me. He has vast pathos in his voice, and as he himself says in his Vision, 'His eye e'en turn'd on empty space, beams keen wi' honour.' I am happy to have seen, and enjoyed the company of this true heaven born Genius, whose conversation is at least correspondent to his published thoughts, and whose personal appearance and address, partake more than is generally allowed of, those of the Gentleman & of the scholar.[260]

Although Macdonald thought he looked 'consumptive', clearly Burns, while more than usually close to tears, momentarily forgot his illness. He evidently enjoyed the company of his radically minded visitor and of the publican Johnstone whom he called 'a mock Marquis' and whose pub was in a Dumfries alley called 'The Marquis's Close'.[261] Relishing a sense of his rebellious past, Burns's conversation moved readily from Jacobite convictions to Jacobin, republican ones – a movement often perceptible in his work: that is one reason for the significant number of Jacobite songs among the last ones he contributed to the *Scots Musical Museum*. This evident republicanism maintained in private right to the end of his life accords fully with a letter written to Maria Riddell and assigned by editors to around 1 June: Robert tells Maria he is 'rackt . . . with rheumatisms', but may see her that Saturday at a gathering she is holding to mark the King's Birthday.[262] Dumfries was so full of dragoons at the time there were even complaints from locals about the amount 'of the Dung made from the horses billeted on them'.[263] Still ready to lash out in what must have sometimes seemed like a garrisoned town, Burns adds spiritedly,

> . . . if I must write, let it be Sedition, or Blasphemy, or something else that begins with a B, so that I may grin with the grin of iniquity, & rejoice with the rejoicing of an apostate Angel.
>
> – 'All good to me is lost;
> 'Evil, be thou my good!' –[264]

This is Burns the spirited rebel, Bard of Sedition, even Blasphemy. For all he might have to sing 'God save the King', he would never forget 'the People'; for all he might occupy a pew in St Michael's Kirk, he stayed true to his own resolutely unorthodox, strongly

maintained faith. It would be as naïve to conclude that the Scottish republican Burns craved an immediate French invasion as that he was a Dumfries Devil-worshipper. But heresies in politics and religion that set him on the side of 'staunch republicans' and agin the 'unco guid' were vital to his life and poetry.

So when, probably in May, he sent more songs to Thomson via his young Edinburgh-bound Excise colleague John Lewars, describing Lewars as 'a young fellow of uncommon merit – indeed, by far the cleverest fellow I have met with in this part of the world. – His only fault is – D—m—cratic heresy', the heretical bard identifies Lewars as yet another clever radical he liked to mix with.[265] The extent of such networks will never be known fully. Intriguingly, for instance, in the context of 'great friends of Burns', Syme mentioned on 26 July 1796 Burns's letters to 'Mrs Imley (formerly Woolstoncroft) a particular correspondent &c of Burns & Dr Maxwells'.[266] Scholars of Mary Wollstonecraft seem unaware of this link; Burns is mentioned neither in editions of the feminist radical's correspondence nor in biographies of her. Travelling in France and Scandinavia in the 1790s and moving house repeatedly, Wollstonecraft may have lost or destroyed her letters from the bard. None of hers to him seems to have survived either. But Syme knew Burns intimately, and records here another radical connection: between the poet of 'The Rights of Woman' and the author of *A Vindication of the Rights of Woman*.

Around the time he described young John Lewars as subject to democratic heresy, Burns seems to have believed his own illness was 'a flying gout', but by early June, even if he could captivate his visitor Macdonald and write spiritedly to Maria Riddell, he felt terminally sick with a 'protracting, slow, consuming illness'.[267] Outside his immediate circle few knew he was seriously ill. Poems to the 'happy Bard' came from Scotland, England, Ireland and America.[268] In late June Robert Anderson of Carlisle, one of his many northern English admirers, sent Burns a Standard Habbie epistle:

> Now tint me, Rab, I'm thinkin soon   *heed*
> To gi'e a ca' in DUMFRIES town:
> Aiblins some bonie afternoon   *Perhaps*
>   We twa may meet;
> If sae, we'se spen' a white half-crown –
>   Wow, 'twill be sweet![269]

For Burns it was too late for such pleasures. Taken in her carriage to dine with Maria Riddell on 5 July, he struck her as 'already touching the brink of eternity'.[270] Maria too was unwell; the friends conducted a flirtatious exchange on the topic of mortality. Soon afterwards, she recalled Burns's greeting to her, '"Well, madam, have you any commands for the other world?"' to which she replied, 'it seemed a doubtful case which of us should be there soonest', and hoped he would yet live to write her epitaph. 'He looked in my face with an air of great kindness, and expressed his concern at seeing me look so ill, with his accustomed sensibility.'[271] On neither side was this a pretence: suffering recurrent illnesses, Maria would die in her mid-forties. Burns poured out his worries about his family's future, his pregnant wife, the state of his own papers and poems. It was, as each was certain, their last meeting.

Trying to say appropriate farewells, Burns had already written to Johnson, the 'honest Scotch enthusiast' with whom he had been working for a decade collecting Scots songs. He told the Edinburgh engraver he expected to die soon, but wanted his 'ever dear Friend' to know that he realised the importance of the *Scots Musical Museum* Johnson had initiated:

> Your Work is a great one; & though, now that it is near finished, I see if we were to begin again, two or three things that might be mended, yet I will venture to prophesy, that to future ages your Publication will be the text book & standard of Scotish Song & Music.[272]

On 26 June, when he described himself as 'emaciated', he presented to his democratic friend John Lewars's sister, Jessy, who was helping to nurse him, a copy of volumes of the *Scots Musical Museum*. Signing them, he inscribed a specially composed poem, ending,

> These be thy GUARDIAN & REWARD!
> So prays thy faithful friend, THE BARD.[273]

To his schoolteacher friend Clarke, whose career he had saved, he confessed that thinking about Jean as a widow and his children faced with destitution made him 'weak as a woman's tear'. 'Enough of this!' Burns added, ''tis half my disease! –'[274] His medical advisors, including Mundell, Maxwell and a Dr Brown, seem to have told him his illness was not just the 'excruciating rheumatism' of which

he complained repeatedly but also what we would now call depression: 'my Physician assures me that melancholy & low spirits are half my disease'.[275] Burns knew this, but sank deeper. 'Adieu dear Clarke! That I shall ever see you again, is, I am afraid, highly improbable. –'[276] In an ordered, heartbroken way he was saying goodbye to his friends.

He also did his best to say farewell to his family. Five-year-old Betty, his illegitimate daughter by Ann Park, was by this time living in the Dumfries household. When an old woman, she recalled how she had regarded Jean as her 'mither' – 'an unco gude body'. Betty also remembered her last conversation with her father: 'He had on carpet shoes . . . and a fur hunting cap drawn down about his ears, and he was pallid and thin. He took me on his knee and clappit me on the head, and tauld me to be a gude girl.'[277]

The ailing poet sent his last Standard Habbie epistle to Colonel de Peyster, who had been asking after Private Burns. This 'Poem on Life' with its image of 'A gibbet's tassle' is really a poem on death by a bard 'Surrounded thus by bolus pill,/ And potion glasses'.[278] At the start of July, under medical advice from Dr Maxwell as a last-ditch effort to find a cure, Burns went ten miles south-east of Dumfries to Brow in Ruthwell parish on the Solway Firth. Ruthwell is now famous for its eighth-century Cross on which are carved in runic inscriptions passages from the great Anglo-Saxon poem about Christ's crucifixion, *The Dream of the Rood*. In Burns's day, though, the Cross was just beginning to be investigated. Brow had an ancient well, which can still be seen, albeit with a modern surround, near the shore. The sick could drink its reputedly curative chalybeate waters from an iron cup. Maxwell had told Burns to wade out daily (at set times as the spring tides allowed) into the cold waters of the Firth and stand there. If, as modern medical opinion has opined, one of the afflictions of the bard who complained of a 'palpitating heart' and 'inveterate rheumatism' was either rheumatic fever leading to 'an infection of the lining, or the body, or the containing sac of the heart', or else heart-weakening 'bacterial endocarditis', he had been given very bad advice.[279]

Nevertheless, he followed it. Physically, he felt unrecognisable. To Cunningham he wrote from 'Brow-Sea-bathing quarters' on 7 July, 'You actually would not know if you saw me. – Pale, emaciated, & so feeble as occasionally to need help from my chair – my spirits fled! fled! – but I can no more on the subject – only

the Medical folks tell me that my last & only chance is bathing & country quarters & riding.'[280] On the last page of the letter Burns transcribed his melancholy 'Lord Gregory'. This song about a 'waefu' wanderer' begins, 'O mirk, mirk is this midnight hour,/ And loud the tempest's roar.'[281] He grew anguished, convinced that his salary, when reduced to sick pay, would not let him follow such medical advice and keep his family provided for. Jean, expecting another baby any day, was trying to keep things going at the family home in Dumfries. 'For Heaven's sake & as you value the wefare [sic] of your daughter, & my wife,' Burns wrote to her father, 'do, my dearest Sir, write to Fife [where Jean's mother was visiting relatives] to Mrs Armour to come if possible.' Knowing Jean was being left to cope, Burns tried to get assistance for her. He told his father-in-law that, though he was taking a bathing cure, he had 'secret fears' he would die.[282] He wrote to Mrs Dunlop, thanking her for her long 'friendship dearest to my soul', and telling her how her letters had sustained him '– With what pleasure did I use to break up the seal!' This was clearly an appeal for last-minute help. None came. Her last word from him was 'Farewell!!!'[283]

'Dear Brother . . .' His last letter to Gilbert signals he was 'not likely to get better', mentioning his debts and fears for his family: 'I leave them in your hands. – Remember me to my Mother. –'[284] When a local 'rascal of a Haberdasher' got wind the bard was dying and demanded payment of an outstanding bill, this almost tipped Burns over the edge. He wrote desperately to James Burnes, his Montrose cousin, for £10 (largely to pay for Burns's Royal Dumfries Volunteers uniform). Haunted as ever by the threat of financial ruin that had faced his dying father, he was almost hysterical, convinced his creditor 'will infallibly put my emaciated body into jail'.[285] He wrote similarly to Thomson in Edinburgh: 'the horrors of a jail have made me half distracted'.[286] Burnes and Thomson arranged for payment to be sent. Both moneys arrived too late for the bard to arrange settlement with his creditors.

Though clearly indicating to friends he expected to die soon, Burns at Brow tried to keep this from Jean in Dumfries. His note to her, written on 14 July, signals that, whatever strains their relationship had undergone, Burns wished to tell his pregnant wife he loved her and, without lying about his condition, to sound as positive as he could. Loving and direct, it is a good letter.

Brow, Thursday

My dearest Love,

I delayed writing until I could tell you what effect sea-bathing was likely to produce. It would be injustice to deny that it has eased my pains, and, I think, has strengthened me; but my appetite is still extremely bad. No flesh nor fish can I swallow; porridge and milk are the only thing I can taste. I am very happy to hear, by Miss Jess Lewars, that you are all well. My very best and kindest compliments to her, and to all the children. I will see you on Sunday.

Your affectionate husband,
R.B.[287]

Two days later, saying a change in spring tides had put an end to his bathing regime and that, not having had news of Jean for two days, he anxiously wished to return to Dumfries, Burns wrote to local laird John Clark, to borrow a gig. He feared that if he rode his own horse, and it rained, getting wet would finish him. Back home, frightened for his wife, he sent word again to her father,

My dear Sir,

Do, for heaven's sake, send Mrs Armour here immediately. My wife is hourly expecting to be put to bed. Good God! what a situation for her to be in, poor girl, without a friend! I returned from sea-bathing quarters to-day, and my medical friends would almost persuade me that I am better, but I think and feel that my strength is so gone that the disorder will prove fatal to me.

Your son-in-law,
R.B.[288]

Not only Burns was shocked and fearful. Syme, who just three years before had described the wild bard as 'brawny', wrote to Cunningham on 17 July about Burns's 'cadaverous aspect and shaken frame'. 'Extremely alarmed', Syme still hoped that with Dr Maxwell's help the poet might live.[289] Two days later Maxwell told Syme Burns would die. Syme visited regularly, and had seen for himself that day 'the hand of Death is visibly fixed upon him'. Too upset to go into details, Syme wrote to Cunningham telling him they had to think what they might do for Burns's family after the bard's death. Later they would help provide for Jean; at the time Syme recorded simply a sense of being overcome by sadness when he spoke to Burns.

He had life enough to acknowledge me – and Mrs Burns said he had been calling on you & me continually – He made a wonderful exertion when I took him by the hand – with a strong voice he said, 'I am much better today, – I shall be soon well again, for I command my spirits & my mind But yesterday I resigned myself to death' –[290]

This is the last speech of Burns recorded during his life. Later there were various claims about his dying words. '"John, don't let the aukward squad fire over me,"' he is reported to have said to 'one of his fellow volunteers . . . by the bed side'.[291] Many people wanted to claim a share in his final days. The Victorians, loving deathbed scenes, craved elaborate accounts. 'Dumfries', as he lay dying, was said to have been 'like a besieged place'.[292] It is more dignified, and probably more accurate, to state that over several days as he grew weaker Burns was visited by his friends – both radical pals and orthodox work colleagues like Alexander Findlater. Eventually slipping into delirium, the bard cried out about fear of being cast into jail: though he had been anxious at Brow lest some poems might endanger his reputation or family, this horror of jail was surely not fear of a charge of sedition but of ruin that might confine him to a debtors' prison. At home, visited by friends, his family around him, sometimes Burns seemed able to focus, other times not. He died, aged thirty-seven, at 5 a.m. on 21 July 1796.

Nearly three decades later material from the *London Magazine* that seems to draw on an eyewitness account was reprinted in the *Caledonian Mercury*. Its author was Allan Cunningham, twelve years old in Dumfries when the poet died:

His last moments have never been described; he had laid his head quietly on the pillow, awaiting dissolution, when his attendant reminded him of his medicine, and held the cup to his lip. He started suddenly up, drained the cup at a gulp, threw his hands before him like a man about to swim, and sprung from head to foot of the bed – fell with his face down, and expired with a groan.

The same writer described Burns shortly afterwards, 'laid out for the grave':

He lay in a plain unadorned coffin, with a linen sheet drawn over his face, and on the bed, and around his body, herbs and flowers were thickly strewn, according to the usage of the country. He was

wasted somewhat by long illness; but death had not increased the swarthy hue of his face, which was uncommonly dark and deeply marked – the dying pang was visible in the lower part, but his broad and open brow was pale and serene, and around it his sable hair lay in masses, slightly touched with grey, and inclining more to a wave than a curl.[293]

Its striking details soon contested, Allan Cunningham's account, lifting for one last time the linen sheet from Burns's face, anticipates later generations of admirers, journalists, souvenir-hunters and biographers, all eager to discover or construct their own specially salvaged treasured mementoes of the poet, however intrusive or grotesque.

A rather pompous, albeit well-intended funeral was arranged. Burns's body was taken from his home to the courthouse in the Midsteeple on the night of 24 July. Next day at noon uniformed soldiers lined the streets to St Michael's Church. The town's bells tolled. A Cavalry band played the Dead March from Handel's *Saul* as the bard was carried to the kirkyard. Once the procession reached St Michael's, Royal Dumfries Volunteers wearing black armbands fired three volleys over the coffin after it had been lowered into the grave. Gilbert was there, but Jean was not. She had gone into labour and gave birth that morning to a boy, Maxwell, who died before his third birthday. Years later, the bard's body was exhumed for reburial in a grander mausoleum still in St Michael's kirkyard. Within days of Burns's death elegies were being rushed out – Scotland paying tribute to 'Scotia's darlin' . . . her bard!'[294] South of the border Burns's death became something of 'a political matter' in the press, being presented as 'a tragedy for the Opposition cause', but admirers like William Roscoe confirmed in English Standard Habbie Burns's status as 'Immortal bard'.[295] On the continent James Macdonald was behind the 1796 obituary in *Neuer Teutscher Merkur* which drew on his meeting with Burns just months before, stressing his value as a Scottish political poet and an example of 'Bardengeist'.[296] Macdonald would continue to champion 'my friend Burns', regretting the lack of an edition containing 'the finest pieces, namely his little political couplets', and seeing Burns as 'a mind of gigantic mould' representing 'the heavenly flame of liberty'.[297] Thanks to Macdonald, the friend of Herder, Goethe, and so many other German writers, Burns began to be transmuted into the heroic Highland figure of Emilie von Berlepsch's *Caledonia* (1802–4) – one of the most striking among many, many

afterlives given to the bard.[298] In Scotland the first biography of Burns, by his establishment acquaintance Robert Heron, was published hurriedly in 1797, something of a hatchet job. Many other accounts of the 'heaven-taught ploughman' followed. Before long, Robert Burns junior, nine years old when his father died, had to point out that the man he liked to refer to as 'The Bard' was no uneducated ploughman but a person whose 'Library ... contained ... Chaucer, Spencer, Milton, Dryden, Pope, Goldsmith, Tasso, Voltaire, Moliere, Boileau, Rousseau, and the Immortal Shakespeare' as well as 'these Scotch Poets, who had a more immediate influence on the direction which his poetical talents took'.[299] After his death Burns was endlessly reviewed and revisited. There were eventually national exhibitions. Poets like Keats made pilgrimages to Burns sites, and were sometimes disappointed. People recorded distorted memories. Souvenirs, organised tours, celebrations of all sorts proliferated. Sailing-ships, steamships, racehorses and coaches all bore Burns's name. Statues were erected from New York to New Zealand; no other poet since the Renaissance boasts so many likenesses in bronze, marble and varieties of stone. All this bardolatry – some noble, some jejune or tacky – is a legitimate subject for study and amazement, but is not what this biography is about.

It seems truest to Burns to end with songs, the first poetry he ever knew, and among the finest he made. Contained in the mass of his papers were many songs and song-fragments. Some, like this cancelled fragment written on the back of one of his last songs for the *Scots Musical Museum*, have appeared in no book until now, but show his characteristic spirit:

> I courted a lassie, I courted her lang,
>   The lassie she did comply;
> But she has prov'd fickle & broken her vow,
>   And e'en let her gang, say I!
> Chorus
>   And e'en let her gang – & e'en let her gang,
>   And e'en let her gang – say I –[300]

Other surviving songs are sadder and subtler. Several of Burns's manuscripts were treated carelessly or destroyed, but many were lovingly cared for. After the bard died his young friend Jessy Lewars lived for over half a century, treasuring memories of a number of poems. There

were verses scribbled by the dying Burns on the back of an advertising flyer for an exhibition of twenty wild animals – a 'Royal Bengal striped Tiger', a 'MALE PANTHER', a 'LARGE POLAR MONSTER' – which one of Burns's doctors had gone to see in Dumfries. 'Talk not to me of savages,' Burns scrawled in red crayon on the back of the flyer, going on to praise instead 'Jessy's lovely hand in mine'.[301] Blue-eyed Jessy was eighteen then, Burns in no condition to make physical love to her; he was being characteristically, recklessly affectionate. She was proud to have a manuscript copy of his song 'The blue-eyed Lassie' (written years earlier at Ellisland), which Jean too liked to sing.[302] Having lived for some time as Burns's next-door neighbour, Jessy told Robert Chambers years afterwards how the bard teased her about her admirers: one, he said, had 'not as much brains as a midge could lean its elbow on'; claiming bardic second sight, Burns had predicted correctly the man she would eventually marry.[303] For Jessy, Burns wrote his last great song. Plunging him from extremes of cold to burning hot fevers, illness made this independent-minded eighteenth-century man dependent on the help of a teenage girl. His song's proud, generous, erotically tender chivalry might seem almost comical given his feverish, emaciated condition. But it sings in a way that is not comical. Written from a male perspective, it was made in tribute to a young woman who sang to the dying bard and was, he noted with pleasure, 'a young lady who sings well'.[304]

> OH wert thou in the cauld blast,
> On yonder lea, on yonder lea;
> My plaidie to the angry airt,
> I'd shelter thee, I'd shelter thee:
> Or did misfortune's bitter storms
> Around thee blaw, around thee blaw,
> Thy bield should be my bosom,
> To share it a', to share it a'.
>
> Or were I in the wildest waste,
> Sae black and bare, sae black and bare,
> The desart were a paradise,
> If thou wert there, if thou wert there.
> Or were I monarch o' the globe,
> Wi' thee to reign, wi' thee to reign;
> The brightest jewel in my crown,
> Wad be my queen, wad be my queen.[305]

Here, characteristically, as one of those 'staunch republicans', Burns does not hesitate to take to himself what he had called in his paean to George Washington and to Wallace's ideal of liberty 'The Royalty of Man'; he kings it over earthly monarchs. Equally characteristically he commandingly yet tenderly and lovingly has at his side a queenly girl from Dumfries who did housework and amateur nursing.

There is a danger that in the twenty-first century we will forget that Scotland's greatest poet belongs to the art form of poetry, not as an adjunct to or excuse for tourism, 'creative industries', rock concerts or marketeers' gigs. Nonetheless, he excelled nowhere more than in popular song. During his lifetime readers like Hugh Blair, James Macdonald or Mrs Dunlop often valued him at his most decorously Anglicised, finding the soaring bardic sublime farthest from the mucky surface of Scots earth. Those Freemasons who hailed him as 'Caledonia's bard, brother Burns' and Ayrshire contemporaries who laughed with, read aloud and sang his work were more accurate in their judgement. Even they knew only some of his work. Many of his most radical political poems and finest lyrics were published years after his death. Some seem lost for ever. His is a body of verse whose full shape became apparent gradually and confirmed him as not just Scotland's but the world's bard.

Burns's glory as a political poet lies in a democratic impulse subtly inflected in ways that are republican and Scottish nationalist. This makes him awkward for a British establishment which has constantly tried to tame him. But alongside and bound up with the radicalism is something akin to it, perceptible even by those whose politics are much more conservative. That quality is at its best in what is now regarded as one of his greatest songs, known to few people in Burns's lifetime, and only published in the *Scots Musical Museum* the year he died.

> O my Luve's like a red, red rose,
>   That's newly sprung in June;
> O my Luve's like the melodie
>   That's sweetly play'd in tune. –
>
> As fair art thou, my bonie lass,
>   So deep in luve am I;
> And I will love thee still, my Dear,
>   Till a' the seas gang dry. –

Till a' the seas gang dry, my Dear,
   And the rocks melt wi' the sun:
I will love thee still, my Dear,
   While the sands o' life shall run. –

And fare thee weel, my only Luve!
   And fare thee weel, a while!
And I will come again, my Luve,
   Tho' it were ten thousand mile! –[306]

Perceptively, if insufficiently, some scholars may discuss this song in terms of cutting-edge Scottish Enlightenment geological theory. In a poem that uses the word love seven times most people can trace a confident, subtle acoustic of intensification through echo, present right from the first line's alliterative 'red, red rose'. Readers may relate this poem of imagined separation and reunion to Burns's obsession with Clarinda, though the vernacular tenderness of 'Luve' might go at least as well with Jean Armour.

Yet what is unquenchable here is something most striking throughout Burns's life and so much of his best poetry – whether tender, hilarious or stinging. That quality is why people repeatedly want to regard him as belonging to all humanity. After his death in 1796, his poetry was left to go on without him, but remarkably, with all its technical deftness, its mixture of *furor poeticus* and sheer craftsmanship, Burns's poetry carries so much of its maker with it that it seems to extend a hand to invite, grasp and caress our own. In an era when the death of the author is often seen as essential to a work of art, Burns's verse in its vernacular address, its slyness, solidarity and style still seems vital with warmth, humour, political longings, irony, pace and love. This provocative, winning combination predates and crosses all sorts of mental and physical borders, inviting us to acknowledge that the intelligent, skilful, radically minded Robert Burns may still be for readers and listeners around the world so winningly and nimbly The Bard.

Abbreviations

The following abbreviations have been used in the notes to this book:

BC	*The Burns Chronicle.*
Cooksey	J. C. B. Cooksey, *Alexander Nasmyth HRSA, 1758–1840.* Whittingehame House, Scotland: Paul Harris, 1991.
CPB1	*Robert Burns's Commonplace Book 1783–1785*, ed. James Cameron Ewing and Davidson Cook, with an introduction by David Daiches. Fontwell, Sussex: Centaur Press, 1965.
CPB2	'Burns's Unpublished Common-place Book', ed. William Jack. *Macmillan's Magazine*, March 1879, 448–60. This is often called Burns's 'Second Common-place Book', to distinguish it from the 'First Commonplace Book' listed above.
Crawford	*Robert Burns and Cultural Authority*, ed. Robert Crawford. Edinburgh: Edinburgh University Press, 1997.
Crawford and MacLachlan	*The Best Laid Schemes: Selected Poetry and Prose of Robert Burns*, ed. Robert Crawford and Christopher MacLachlan. Edinburgh: Polygon, 2009.
Currie	*The Works of Robert Burns, with an Account of his Life and a Criticism on his Writings*, ed. James Currie. 4 vols. London: T. Cadell and W. Davies, 1800. Reference is also made to later editions, indicated by date.
CW	*The Life and Works of Robert Burns*, ed. Robert

	Chambers. Revised by William Wallace. 4 vols. Edinburgh: W. & R. Chambers, 1896.
DWJ	*The Dumfries Weekly Journal.*
Gilbert	Gilbert Burns's account of his brother as given in Currie (1800), I, 57–84.
L1, L2	*The Letters of Robert Burns*, ed. J. De Lancey Ferguson. 2nd edn, ed. G. Ross Roy. 2 vols. Oxford: Clarendon Press, 1985.
Macdonald	Journal of the Reverend James Macdonald, 1796. Manuscript in St Andrews University Library Special Collections, MS Deposit 14 box 6 (Playfair Papers).
Mackay	James Mackay, *Burns, A Biography of Robert Burns.* Edinburgh: Mainstream, 1992.
McLehose	*The Correspondence between Burns and Clarinda*, ed. W. C. McLehose. Edinburgh: William Tait, 1843.
Memoirs	'Memoirs Wrote in August 1785' by Gilbert Burns (RBBM), W, 4102–25.
NBC	The National Burns Collection. A collection of over 40,000 objects in 38 venues across Scotland. See www.burnsscotland.com
NLS	The National Library of Scotland.
P1, P2, P3	*The Poems and Songs of Robert Burns*, ed. James Kinsley, 3 vols. Oxford: Clarendon Press, 1968.
RBBM	Robert Burns Birthplace and Museum, Alloway, Ayrshire.
Shaw	[Stebbing Shaw,] *A Tour in 1787 from London to the Western Highlands of Scotland*. London: L. Davis et al. [1788?].
Statistical Account	*The Statistical Account of Scotland*, ed. Sir John Sinclair. 29 vols. Edinburgh: William Creech, 1791–9.
Tait	*Poems and Songs* by Alexander Tait. n.p.: The Author, 1790.
Views	*Views in North Britain Illustrative of the Works of Robert Burns* by James Storer and John Greig. London: Vernor and Hood, 1805.
W	*The Definitive Illustrated Companion to Robert Burns*, ed. Peter J. Westwood. 7 vols. 'A Private Publication for Reference Libraries, Museums, Universities and Researchers'. n.p., 2004. Since some volumes of this collection of reproductions of Burns

	manuscripts are bound in several parts, references are to the continuous pagination throughout.
Walker	[Josiah Walker, ed.,] *Poems of Robert Burns*. 2 vols. Edinburgh: Trustees of the late James Morison, 1811.

Notes

I have given a note reference for the source of all quotations in the main text. Manuscripts in the notes are usually identified by their library and, if published in W, their page number in that work; if not published in W, they are identified by an individual library call number or by their database number in NBC.

Introduction

1 See Robert Crawford, 'The Bard: Ossian, Burns, and the Shaping of Shakespeare', in Willy Maley and Andrew Murphy, eds, *Shakespeare and Scotland* (Manchester: Manchester University Press, 2004), 124–40.

2 Hugh MacDiarmid, '[Robert Burns:] His Influence', *Scottish Field*, January 1959, 22.

3 *P1*, 127.

4 Don Paterson, 'Introduction' to his edition of *Robert Burns* (London: Faber and Faber, 2001); Don Paterson, private communication, 2005.

5 Paterson, 'Introduction', vii and x–xi.

6 See Thomas Keith, 'Burns Statues in North America, A Survey', *BC*, 2001, 71–83.

7 Maya Angelou, 'Angelou on Burns', 1996 BBC TV documentary directed by Elly M. Taylor.

8 Yuan Kejia, inscription in my presentation copy of his Chinese translation of *Poems of Robert Burns*; Chiang Yee, *The Silent Traveller in Edinburgh* (1948; repr. Edinburgh: Mercat Press, 2007), 155.

9 Norman MacCaig, '[Robert Burns:] The Man', *Scottish Field*, January 1959, 25.

10 Robert Heron, *A Memoir of the Life of the Late Robert Burns* (Edinburgh: T. Brown, 1797), 51.

11 James Kinsley, 'Introduction' to J. G. Lockhart, *Life of Robert Burns* (1828; repr. London: Dent, 1976), v.

12 Thomas Carlyle, *On Heroes and Hero-Worship* (1841; repr. London: Oxford University Press, 1963), 250.

13 See Thomas Crawford, 'Introduction' to Catherine Carswell, *The Life of Robert Burns* (1930; repr. Edinburgh: Canongate Classics, 1990), ix.

14 Franklyn Bliss Snyder, *The Life of Robert Burns* (New York: Macmillan, 1932), 396.

15 Nigel Hamilton, *Biography: A Brief History* (Cambridge, Mass.: Harvard University Press, 2007), 118.

16 Murray G. H. Pittock, 'Robert Burns and British Poetry', *Proceedings of the British Academy*, 121 (2003), 191–212.

17 *P1*, 87.

18 Their essays are collected with those of other writers and critics in Crawford; the Kennedy quotation is from p. 34.

19 Stephen Breen and Catherine Lockerbie, 'Writer in Disgrace as Book Halted by Publisher', *Scotsman*, 5 March 1999, available online at http://web.bham.ac.uk/forensic/news/99_00/scotsman.html

20 Carol McGuirk, ed., *Critical Essays on Robert Burns* (New York: G. K. Hall, 1998), 299.

21 See, e.g., Lucyle Werkmeister, 'Robert Burns and the London Daily Press', *Modern Philology*, May 1966, 322–35; Patrick Scott Hogg, *Robert Burns: The Lost Poems* (Glasgow: Clydeside Press, 1997).

22 Marilyn Butler, 'Burns and Politics', in Crawford, 86–112; W. J. Murray, 'Poetry and Politics: Burns and Revolution', *BC*, 1990, 52–66; Norman R. Paton, *Song o' Liberty: The Politics of Robert Burns* (Fareham: Sea Green Publications, 1994); Liam McIlvanney, *Burns the Radical: Poetry and Politics in Late Eighteenth-Century Scotland* (East Linton: Tuckwell Press, 2002).

23 Gerard Carruthers, 'The Canongate Burns', *Review of Scottish Culture* (2006), 42, 48, 47; Robert Crawford, 'A Bard of Friendly Fire', *London Review of Books*, 25 July 2002, 16–18.

24 James A. Mackay, *Burns-Lore of Dumfries and Galloway* (Ayr: Alloway Publishing, 1988), 5.

25 *CPB2*, 453.

26 James Glencairn Burns, letter to Jean Armour Burns, 22 February 1813, RBBM (NBC 1559).

27 Michael Alexander, *Medievalism* (New Haven and London: Yale University Press, 2007).

28 Robert Crawford, *The Modern Poet* (Oxford: Oxford University Press, 2001).

29 As well as Crawford, Crawford and MacLachlan, and *The Modern Poet* see Robert Crawford, *Devolving English Literature*, 2nd edn (Edinburgh: Edinburgh University Press, 2000); Robert Crawford, *Scotland's Books* (London: Penguin, 2007); on Burns and Shakespeare see note 1 above.

30 Tim Cornwell, 'Is this Burns?', *Scotsman*, 24 May 2007, 18.

Chapter I: First an' Foremost

1 *P2*, 766.

2 See the remark of Buchanan and the Latin poem of John Johnston in William Keith Leask, ed., *Musa Latina Aberdonensis*, Vol. III (Aberdeen: New Spalding Club, 1910), 150.

3 *P2*, 557.

4 Macdonald, 43.

5 Shaw, 114.

6 William McGill, 'Parish of Ayr' in *Statistical Account*, XXI, 36.

7 *Views*, 25.

8 William Guthrie, *A New Geographical, Historical, and Commercial Grammar; and Present State of the Several Kingdoms of the World* (London: J. Knox, 1770), 65, 67, 76.

9 Isabella Begg, recalling her grandmother in a letter to Robert Chambers, 27 August 1850 (Rosenbach Museum and Library, Philadelphia), W, 718.

10 Ibid.

11 *L2*, 204.

12 *L1*, 191.

13 *L2*, 74.

14 I am grateful to Dr Lorn Macintyre and to Professor Donald Meek for their advice about the Gaelic.

15 *L2*, 317; RBBM, NBC 962.

16 *L1*, 94–5.

17 *L1*, 306–7.

18 Dugald Stewart, quoted in *P3*, 1535.

19 *L2*, 218.

20 *P2*, 690, 716; *L2*, 256.

21 *L2*, 212.

22 *L2*, 213.

23 *P1*, 157, 169, 171.

24 *L1*, 135.

25 *L1*, 93.

26 *L2*, 52.

27 *L1*, 119.

28 *L2*, 145–6. The second sentence refers to the dreary glen through which the herd boy must move quickly on his evening route from the outlying field.

29 Guthrie, *A New . . . Grammar*, 72.

30 Burns's annotated copy of James Johnson's *Scots Musical Museum* (RBBM), W, 2734.

31 Burns, 'Fareweel, fareweel, my bony lass', RBBM, NBC 1209.

32 Burns's annotated *Scots Musical Museum*, W, 2767–8; *P2*, 601–3.

33 *L2*, 88.

34 Burns's annotated *Scots Musical Museum*, W, 2753.

35 *P1*, 152.

36 Shaw, 118.

37 *P1*, 153.

38 John Strawhorn, *The History of Ayr* (Edinburgh: John Donald, 1989), 122.

39 CW, I, 42.

40 Ibid.

41 'Death of the Sister of Burns', *Glasgow Herald*, 15 December 1858.

42 John Murdoch, letter to Joseph Cooper Walker, dated London, 22 February 1799, in appendix to William Will, 'John Murdoch, Tutor of Robert Burns', BC, 1929, 83–4.

43 *L1*, 7; *L2*, 387.

44 *L1*, 134.

45 *L1*, 461.

46 Burns's annotated *Scots Musical Museum*, W, 2729.

47 *L1*, 134.

48 Gilbert, 58–9.

49 Certificate of character for William Burnes, 1748 (RBBM), W, 186.

50 Simpson and Brown Architects, *Conservation Plan: Burns Birthplace, An International Museum* (Edinburgh: National Trust for Scotland, 2006), 42, 46, 48. I am grateful to David Hopes, Project Curator, RBBM, for making this available.

51 Certificate of Good Conduct for William Burnes, 27 November 1754 (RBBM), W, 2300.

52 *P1*, 153.

53 *L1*, 295.

54 Memoirs, W, 4103.

55 Guthrie, *A New ... Grammar*, 66.

56 Sir James Justice, *The British Gardener's New Director, Chiefly Adapted to the Climate of the Northern Countries*, 4th edn (Dublin: John Exshaw, 1765), Preface. The italics are in the original.

57 L1, 247.

58 Gilbert Burns in Currie (1801), I, 373.

59 Memoirs, W, 4103.

60 See Richard Sher, *Church and University in the Scottish Enlightenment: The Moderate Literati of Edinburgh* (Princeton: Princeton University Press, 1985).

61 William Dalrymple, *Christian Unity Illustrated and Recommended, from the Example of the Primitive Church* (Glasgow: R. and A. Foulis, 1766), 5, 6, 10–11, 12, 13, 15–16, 27, 35.

62 Gilbert, 70.

63 John Ramsay of Ochtertyre, *Scotland and Scotsmen in the Eighteenth Century*, ed. Alexander Allardyce, 2 vols (Edinburgh: Blackwood, 1888), II, 554–5.

64 L1, 144; P1, 471.

65 William Dalrymple, *A History of Christ for the Use of the Unlearned* (Edinburgh: Balfour, 1787), title page, dedication, epigraphs.

66 William Dalrymple, *A Sequel to the Life of Christ* (Air: John Wilson, 1791), v, vi, 1.

67 William Dalrymple, *A Legacy of Dying Thoughts from an Affectionate Old Pastor to his Flock* (Air: J. and P. Wilson, 1796), title page, i, 82, 87, 107, 139.

68 L1, 454.

69 William McGill, *A Practical Essay on the Death of Jesus Christ* (Edinburgh: Mundell and Wilson, 1786), 234, 237, 238.

70 William McGill, *The Prayer of Our Saviour for the Union of his Followers Considered: A Sermon* (Glasgow: Robert and Andrew Foulis, 1758), 35.

71 James Currie, letter to Maxwell Gartshore, 1 January 1801 (RBBM), W, 4216.

72 L1, 135.

73 A. Fisher, *The New English Tutor ... also, A Practical Abstract of English Grammar* (London: J. Richardson, 1762), 142, 143; Arthur Masson, *A Collection of English Prose and Verse, for the Use of Schools*, 4th edn (Edinburgh: Masson et al., 1764), 122; P3, 1013; P1, 20.

74 L1, 134–5.

75 [William Burnes,] A Manual of Religious Belief (RBBM), W, 182.

76 CW, I, 457–8.

77 L1 135.

78 L1, 145; Richard Daniel, *A Paraphrase of Some Select Psalms* (London: Lintot, 1722), 15.

79 Murdoch, letter to Joseph Cooper Walker, 22 February 1799, repr. in appendix to William Will, 'John Murdoch, Tutor of Robert Burns', *BC*, 1929, 80, 84, 85.

80 Murdoch, letter to Robert Burns, 28 October 1787, *BC*, 1929, 75.

81 Currie (1801), I, 381.

82 See John Robotham, 'The Reading of Robert Burns', *Bulletin of the New York Public Library*, November 1970, 561–76.

83 Murdoch, letter to Walker, *BC*, 1929, 81.

84 L1, 135.

85 Gilbert, 60–61.

86 John Murdoch, *The Pronunciation and Orthography of the French Language*, 2nd edn (London: The Author, 1795), Preface.

87 Ibid., 139.

88 Ibid., 5.
89 Murdoch, *BC*, 1929, 81.
90 *P*1, 86.
91 *L*2, 242.
92 *L*1, 135.
93 Masson, *Collection*, 80, 92, 94, 96, 114, 149.
94 *L*2, 64; Masson, *Collection*, 132, 127.
95 *L*1, 348; *Spectator*, Vol. II (London: Tonson and Draper, 1766), RBBM, NBC 69.
96 *L*2, 33.
97 Masson, *Collection*, 72.
98 Ibid., 3, 20–21.
99 Ibid., 28, 61, 153.
100 Ibid., 168.
101 Ibid., 232, 220, 188, 198.
102 Ibid., 136, 133.
103 *L*1, 350; *P*1, 54.
104 Gilbert, 61.
105 *The Life of Hannibal*, translated from the French of Mr Dacier (London: John Gray, 1737), 4, 6, 31, 32, 50, 157, 156, 147.
106 *P*2, 708.
107 *P*1, 472.
108 *L*1, 136.
109 Gilbert, 61; *L*1, 136.
110 *L*1, 151.
111 *L*1, 62.
112 *L*2, 78.
113 *L*1, 99–100.
114 Murdoch to Walker, 22 February 1799, in appendix to Will, 'John Murdoch', *BC*, 1929, 81.
115 Murdoch to Burns, 28 October 1787, in appendix to Will, 'John Murdoch', 75.
116 William Hamilton of Gilbertfield, *Blind Harry's Wallace* (Edinburgh: Luath Press, 1998), 1, 55, 14.
117 Guthrie, *A New ... Grammar*, 77, 97, 100.
118 Hamilton, *Wallace*, 80, 112.
119 *P*1, 105, 106.
120 *L*2, 238; *P*2, 708.
121 Gilbert, 64, 70.
122 Letter from William Fergusson to William Burnes, 6 April 1767, RBBM, NBC 79 (W, 1532).
123 Gilbert, 62.
124 *L*1, 53.
125 Gilbert, 64.
126 *L*1, 137, 135.
127 Gilbert, 62; *L*1, 139.
128 Gilbert, 63.
129 William Whitehead, *The School for Lovers* (London: R. and J. Dodsley, 1762), title page, 4, 64, 66, 84, 22, 86.
130 Memoirs, W, 4104–5.
131 Ibid., W, 4105.
132 Gilbert, 64–5.
133 Thomas Stackhouse, *A New History of the Holy Bible*, 2nd edn, Vol. I (London, 1742), 477.

134 William Derham, *Physico-Theology*, The Third Scots Edition (Glasgow: Robert Urie, 1758), 250; John Ray, *The Wisdom of God Manifested in the Works of the Creation*, 13th edn (Glasgow: J. Bryce and D. Paterson, 1756), xvi.

135 Ray, *The Wisdom of God*, 252.

136 Memoirs, W, 4106.

137 Precept on decreet of forthcoming, William Burnes against Robert Kennedy and William Campbell, 1771, RBBM, NBC 81.

138 *L2*, 75.

139 *L2*, 333.

140 Gilbert, 66.

141 *L2*, 74.

142 Tobias Smollett, *The Adventures of Ferdinand Count Fathom*, ed. Paul Gabriel Boucé (London: Penguin Classics, 1990), 341.

143 See, e.g., the entry on Murdoch in the 2004 *Oxford Dictionary of National Biography* and the full citations of the works by Murdoch listed on the *Eighteenth Century Collections Online* database, which rely on the *Eighteenth-Century Short-Title Catalogue*.

144 Carlo Denina, *An Essay on the Revolutions of Literature*, trans. John Murdoch (London: T. Cadell et al., 1771), 277, 281, 283.

145 See Will, 'John Murdoch', *BC*, 1929, 70, note 3.

146 Robert and Andrew Foulis published an Italian 'edizione seconda' of Denina's *Discorso* in 1763; in the same year 'Scotus' was responsible for the publication of a substantial parallel-text *Extract* of Scottish-related material from Denina's *Essay*.

147 Denina, *An Essay*, 247, 250.

148 Gilbert, 67.

149 The book was published in London by Cadell. See also Josephine Grieder, 'The Prose Fiction of Baculard D'Arnaud in Late Eighteenth-Century England', *French Studies* XXIV.2 (1970), 113–26.

150 Murdoch to Walker, 22 February 1799, in appendix to Will, 'John Murdoch', *BC*, 1929, 82.

151 See Robert Crawford, *Scotland's Books* (London: Penguin, 2007), 250–52.

152 Gilbert, 68.

153 Ibid., 69; *L2*, 75–6.

154 Memoirs, W, 4107.

155 See Strawhorn, *History of Ayr*, 128.

156 Currie (1801), I, 68.

157 *L1*, 137.

158 W, 252.

159 Gilbert, 71.

160 *L1*, 140.

161 Gilbert, 71.

162 Ibid., 71–2.

163 Ibid., 67.

164 Burns's annotated *Scots Musical Museum*, W, 2737.

165 *L1*, 147.

166 *L1*, 138–9.

167 Hans Hecht, *Robert Burns* (1936; repr. Ayr: Alloway Publishing, 1991), 196.

168 *The Goldfinch* (London: R. Baldwin, jun., 1748), 276, 3, 95.

169 'John Anderson, my jo', *The Masque* 2nd edn (London: Richardson and Urquhart, 1768), 309.

170 Burns's annotated *Scots Musical Museum*, W, 2729.

171 Burns, note in Glenriddell Manuscripts (NLS), W, 256.
172 Thomson in Masson's *Collection*, 126 and 128.
173 *L*1, 137–8.
174 *P*1, 3.
175 *CPB*1, cited in *P*3, 1003–4.
176 *P*1, 4.

Chapter II: Wits

1 Gilbert, 65.
2 *L*1, 204–5, 212; cp. John Newbery, *Letters on the Most Common, as well as Important Occasions in Life,* 5th edn (London: J. Newbery, 1760), 209, 77.
3 *L*1, 141.
4 Newbery, *Letters*, i, xi, iii.
5 *L*1, 138.
6 *Spectator*, Vol. III (1776, No. 223), East Ayrshire Council Collection, NBC 2295.
7 *L*1, 254; Gilbert, 73.
8 Newbery, *Letters*, iv–v; cp. *Spectator*, Vol. II (1766), RBBM, NBC 69.
9 *L*1, 136.
10 *L*2, 203.
11 *L*2, 147.
12 *L*1, 140.
13 Ibid.
14 Ibid.
15 Niven cited in Michael Moss, *The 'Magnificent Castle' of Culzean* (Edinburgh: Edinburgh University Press, 2002), 103.
16 *L*1, 140–41.
17 *P*1, 5.
18 *P*1, 4–6, 127; see also *P*3, 1006.
19 *P*1, 290; *L*1, 24.
20 *P*1, 290.
21 *L*1, 140.
22 Burns, Notes on Songs, Edinburgh University Library, Laing MSS. III. 586 (W, 2863–4).
23 William Shenstone, *Works*, 2 vols (Edinburgh: Donaldson, 1768), I, 13, 240, 17.
24 *L*1, 59.
25 *L*1, 141.
26 Newbery, *Letters*, 213–14.
27 Ibid., 209; *L*1, 204–5, 291.
28 Newbery, *Letters*, 208.
29 Ibid., 237, 102 and 108.
30 Ibid., 102–3, 165.
31 Ibid., 168, 169.
32 Shenstone, *Works*, II, 158; *L*1, 319.
33 Instrument of Seisin, 1776, RBBM, NBC 82.
34 *L*1, 137.
35 Shenstone, *Works*, I, 33, 233, 254, 273.
36 *L*1, 136.
37 *P*1, 139–41; Shenstone, *Works*, I, 240.
38 David Hume in E. C. Mossner and I. S. Ross, eds, *The Correspondence of Adam Smith* (Oxford: Clarendon Press, 1977), 161.
39 Tait, 32, 49.

40 See Richard Saville, *Bank of Scotland: A History, 1695–1995* (Edinburgh: Edinburgh University Press, 1996), 156–64; also John Strawhorn, *The History of Ayr* (Edinburgh: John Donald, 1989), 100; L1, 19.
41 P1, 49.
42 See Strawhorn, *History of Ayr*, 119.
43 L1, 138.
44 P1, 10.
45 L1, 139.
46 Gilbert, 80–81.
47 P1, 13, 14.
48 L1, 238.
49 Gilbert, 73–4.
50 L1, 139, 141.
51 L1, 17.
52 Scott in J. G. Lockhart, *Life of Robert Burns* (1828; repr. London: Dent, 1976), 81.
53 L1, 141.
54 L1, 17.
55 David Sillar to Robert Aiken in Walker, II, 259.
56 L1, 18.
57 Shenstone, *Works*, I, 234.
58 Ibid., 34.
59 P3, 1007.
60 Ibid., 1006.
61 P1, 12.
62 P3, 1009.
63 P1, 39.
64 *Statistical Account*, XIX, 457, 455, 454, 456.
65 Tait, 41, 175, 15, 107–8.
66 David Sillar, *Poems* (Kilmarnock: John Wilson, 1789), v, 14.
67 Ibid., 143.
68 Ibid., 31.
69 Ibid., 56.
70 Ibid., 140, 143.
71 Ibid., 101.
72 P1, 68.
73 Sillar, *Poems*, 162.
74 P1, 9.
75 Sillar, *Poems*, 213.
76 Ibid., vi.
77 Ibid., 97; cp Burns's 'kick the ba'' reference in 'Epistle to Davie', P1, 66.
78 P1, 66.
79 Robert Burns, *Poems, Chiefly in the Scottish Dialect* (Edinburgh: The Author, 1787), 363.
80 Sillar, *Poems*, 78, 77.
81 Ibid., 56.
82 Ibid., 114.
83 Sillar to Aiken in Walker, II, 257–60.
84 P3, 1042; L1, 140.
85 P1, 107.
86 L2, 118.
87 Tait, 127.
88 P1, 107, 187.

89 Ibid., 107.
90 Arthur Masson, ed., *A Collection of English Prose and Verse* (Edinburgh: Masson et al., 1764), 82.
91 Sillar, *Poems*, 183.
92 *P1*, 233.
93 *P1*, 107.
94 *P3*, 1080.
95 Shaw, 121.
96 John Mackenzie, letter of 21 April 1810 to Josiah Walker, in Walker, II, 264.
97 *P1*, 108.
98 *P3*, 1535.
99 *P1*, 106–8.
100 Sillar, *Poems*, 170, 59.
101 *P1*, 471; *P3*, 1047.
102 *P3*, 1066.
103 *Letters Concerning the Religion Essential to Man* (Glasgow: Urie, 1761), 3, 10.
104 William Preston, *Illustrations of Masonry*, 9th edn (London: G. and T. Wilkie, 1796), vi.
105 Ibid., 1.
106 Ibid., 4, 5–6, 7–8.
107 Ibid., 8.
108 Ibid., 409.
109 Memoirs, W, 4108–9.
110 Ibid., W, 4110.
111 *P3*, 1115.
112 *P1*, 14.
113 *P3*, 1012.
114 *P1*, 19.
115 James Candlish to Robert Burns, 13 February 1779 (RBBM), W, 893–4.
116 Alexander Pope, *The Poems*, ed. John Butt (London: Methuen, 1965), 516.
117 Candlish to Burns, 13 February 1779, W, 894; Pope, *Poems*, 517–18.
118 *L1*, 7; *L1*, 99; Pope, *Poetical Works*, 4 vols (Edinburgh: Apollo Press, 1776), II, 25, 30.
119 Pope, *Poems*, 531.
120 Ibid., 536, 537.
121 Ibid., 544.
122 *P1*, 12.
123 Pope, *Poems*, 546.
124 Ibid., 547.
125 Candlish to Burns, 13 February 1779, W, 894; see also David Daiches, 'Burns and Pope', *Scottish Literary Journal*, May 1989, 5–20.
126 *L1*, 3.
127 Ibid.
128 Pope, *Poems*, 521; *L1*, 4.
129 *L1*, 6.
130 Ibid., 14.
131 Pope, *Poems*, 80.
132 *L1*, 17.
133 Ibid., 18.
134 Burns, inscription on Vol. I of Sterne's 1779 *Works* (RBBM),W, 1851.
135 Pope, *Poems*, 155.
136 *L1*, 59.

137 Matthew 20: 3 (Authorized Version).

138 Currie (1801), I, 96.

139 L1, 4, 5.

140 Tait, 135.

141 Gilbert, 74.

142 Tait, 133.

143 'Premiums for Flax-Raising', *Glasgow Mercury*, VI.164 (16–23 January 1783), 25.

144 David McClure, ed., *Ayrshire in the Age of Improvement* (Ayr: Ayrshire Archaeological and Natural History Society, 2002), 106, 112, 71.

145 P1, 27.

146 L1, 140.

147 Ibid.

148 L1, 8.

149 See 'The Poet Burns', *Liverpool Mercury*, 1 June 1847, which claims to draw on an 1818 interview with John Blane; but see also 'Literature: The Heroines of Burns' Songs', *Glasgow Herald*, 2 October 1848, and Mackay, 83–90.

150 Mackay, 83–90; Mackay also attacked theories about a supposed 'Alison Begbie'.

151 L1, 11; Pope, *Poems*, 252, 254.

152 L1, 9.

153 L1, 10, 13.

154 L1, 12.

155 L1, 13.

156 Ibid.

157 Mackay, 88.

158 Currie (1801), I, 104.

159 Hans Hecht, *Robert Burns*, trans. Jane Lymburn (1936; repr. Ayr: Alloway Publishing, 1991), 22.

160 L1, 138.

161 Currie (1800), I, 109.

162 Ibid., 117.

163 L1, 9.

164 Currie (1800), I, 121.

165 Ibid., 369.

166 Ibid., 365, 367.

167 *The Freemason's Pocket Companion* (Edinburgh: Ruddiman, Auld, and Company, 1761), 112.

168 Tait, 8.

169 Minutes of Tarbolton Kilwinning St James No. 135 Masonic Lodge, as set out on their website.

170 L1, 16.

171 P1, 39, 38.

172 P1, 270.

173 P1, 270–71.

174 P2, 763.

175 L1, 3.

176 William Burnes to James Burnes, 14 April 1781 (The Writers' Museum, Edinburgh), W, 224.

177 L1, 6.

178 L1, 12.

179 Andrew Wight, *Present State of Husbandry in Scotland*, 2 vols (London: Strahan and Cadell, 1778), I, 389.

180 Gilbert, 74.

181 *L*1, 142.
182 Quoted in John Strawhorn, *The History of Irvine* (Edinburgh: John Donald, 1985), 86.
183 Ibid., 87.
184 Hugh White, *The Divine Dictionary* (Dumfries: Robert Jackson, 1785), v, 13, 23; *Number Second, of The Divine Dictionary* [Edinburgh: Brown, 1786], 70.
185 *L*1, 22.
186 Mackay, 103.
187 *L*1, 142–3.
188 See Strawhorn, *History of Irvine*, 41 and 77.
189 *L*1, 192.
190 *L*1, 193.
191 *L*1, 142.
192 Ibid.
193 Kames in Wight, *Present State of Husbandry*, I, 389.
194 *L*1, 142.
195 Ibid.
196 James Rymer, *A Treatise upon Indigestion, and the Hypochondriac Disease*, 5th edn (London: G. Kennedy et al., 1789), 5–6.
197 R. D. Thornton, *James Currie: The Entire Stranger and Robert Burns* (Edinburgh: Oliver and Boyd, 1963), 158.
198 Rymer, *A Treatise*, 7.
199 Mackay, 99.
200 John Elliot, *The Medical Pocket-book* (London: J. Johnson, 1794), 155.
201 Thomas Skeete, *Experiments and Observations on Quilled and Red Peruvian Bark* (London: John Murray, 1786), 274, 280.
202 *Encyclopaedia Britannica*, 3 vols (Edinburgh: Bell and Macfarquhar, 1771), II, 199–200.
203 Currie (1801), I, 213–14.
204 William Cullen, *First Lines of the Practice of Physic*, new edn, 4 vols (Edinburgh: C. Elliot, 1788), III, 257, 259–60, 258.
205 *L*1, 142.
206 Matthew, 25: 41 and 46 (Authorized Version).
207 *L*1, 6–7.
208 Pope, *Poems*, 508.
209 See Kay Redfield Jamison, *Touched with Fire: Manic Depression and the Artistic Temperament* (New York: Free Press, 1993).
210 *P*1, 19–22.
211 *P*3, 1014.
212 'The Paraphrases, Supplementary Note', *Free Church Magazine*, May 1847, 160–62.
213 *P*1, 24–5.
214 *CPB*1, 18.
215 *CPB*1, 8.
216 *P*1, 26–7.

Chapter III: Belles

1 John Lapraik, *Poems on Several Occasions* (Kilmarnock: John Wilson, 1788), 51.
2 See Sir John Sinclair, *Analysis of the Statistical Account of Scotland* (Edinburgh: William Tait, 1831), Appendix, 40, 41. For more on Burns and farming conditions

see Gavin Sprott, *Robert Burns, Farmer* (Edinburgh: National Museums of
Scotland, 1990).
3 *L*1, 14–15.
4 *P*2, 707 and 762–3.
5 *L*1, 14.
6 CW, I, 42.
7 *P*1, 24 and *P*3, 1015.
8 *P*1, 23.
9 *P*1, 39.
10 *L*1, 143, 138.
11 Tait, 151.
12 See John McVie, 'The Lochlie Litigation', *BC*, 1935, 69–87; also 'The Lochlea
Sequestration', *BC*, 1910, 149–52.
13 *L*1, 18.
14 *L*1, 18–19.
15 Walker, I, xxv–xxvi.
16 *L*1, 17.
17 *P*1, 55.
18 *L*1, 17–18.
19 John Mackenzie to Josiah Walker, 21 April 1810, in Walker, II, 261–3.
20 Ibid., 263.
21 Tait, 49.
22 *P*1, 145.
23 *L*1, 20.
24 Gilbert, 75–6.
25 William Shenstone, *Works*, 2 vols (Edinburgh: Donaldson, 1768), II, 187 and I,
300.
26 *CPB*1, 1.
27 Ibid., 3.
28 Ibid.
29 Ibid., 3, 4, 5.
30 Ibid., 5, 6.
31 Gilbert Burns in Currie (1801), III, 380.
32 *P*1, 33.
33 See 'Marriage of Robin Redbreast and Jenny Wren' in [R. Burns Begg], *Isobel
Burns (Mrs Begg), A Memoir* (n.p., privately printed, 1891), 61–2.
34 *P*1, 29, 30.
35 Memoirs, W, 4113.
36 *L*1, 138.
37 Tait, 152.
38 *P*3, 1104.
39 CW, I, 109–10.
40 *Views*, 30.
41 CW, I, 109.
42 Currie (1801), I, 144, 145.
43 *CPB*1, 14–15.
44 *P*1, 27.
45 *The Poems of Gray, Collins, and Goldsmith*, ed. Roger Lonsdale (London:
Longmans, Green & Co., 1969), 678, 679, 680, 683.
46 *L*1, 21.
47 Memoirs, W, 4113–14.
48 William Wordsworth, 'Sonnets Composed or Suggested During a Tour in

Scotland in the Summer of 1833, XXXV', in *Poetical Works* (London: Warne, n.d.), 539.

49 Gilbert, 76.

50 *L1*, 143.

51 Small, *Treatise* (East Ayrshire Museums Collection), W, 1847.

52 *L1*, 19.

53 Ecclesiastes 7: 23 (Authorized Version).

54 2 Peter 2: 20–22 (Authorized Version).

55 Tait, 153.

56 *CPB1*, 6–7.

57 *P1*, 9–10; *CPB1*, 7–8.

58 Tait, 147.

59 *P3*, 1025; *P1*, 47.

60 *CPB1*, 14; *P1*, 47.

61 *P3*, 1024–5 and *P1*, 47.

62 *CPB1*, 15–16.

63 *P1*, 53 and 58.

64 See *P3*, 1026.

65 Robert Bisset, *Sketch of Democracy* (London: Matthews, Dilly, White, 1796), 254, 323.

66 See David Allan, 'The Age of Pericles in the Modern Athens: Greek History, Scottish Politics, and the Fading of Enlightenment', *Historical Journal*, XLIV.2 (2001), 401, 396.

67 See *Oxford Dictionary of National Biography* entry for Millar; also Christina Bewley, *Muir of Huntershill* (Oxford: Oxford University Press, 1981), 5.

68 J. Knox, *A View of the Empire* (1785) cited in Eric J. Graham, *A Maritime History of Scotland 1650–1790* (East Linton: Tuckwell Press, 2002), 250. Other information here about naval matters and sea trade is taken from this volume.

69 Anon., *Paul Jones* (Edinburgh, 1779), 2.

70 Graham, *A Maritime History*, 264.

71 *L1*, 142.

72 *L1*, 19.

73 *L1*, 136.

74 John Galt, *The Provost*, ed. Ian A. Gordon (Oxford: Oxford University Press, 1982), 43.

75 *P1*, 196.

76 *P1*, 198.

77 *P1*, 62.

78 *P2*, 822.

79 *P1*, 49.

80 Ibid.

81 *L1*, 143.

82 *P3*, 1014.

83 *P1*, 323 and *P3*, 971.

84 Shenstone, *Works*, II, 188 and I, 30.

85 *P1*, 323.

86 Robert Fergusson, *Selected Poems*, ed. James Robertson (Edinburgh: Birlinn, 2000), 164 and 185.

87 See Robert Crawford, ed., *'Heaven-Taught Fergusson', Robert Burns's Favourite Scottish Poet* (East Linton: Tuckwell Press, 2003) and Crawford.

88 Fergusson, *Selected Poems*, 47.

89 *P1*, 34.

90 See Douglas Dunn, 'Burns's Native Metric' in Crawford, 61–2.
91 James Macpherson, *Fingal* (London: T. Becket and P. A. De Hondt, 1762), 13.
92 *L*1, 61, 265.
93 *Scottish National Dictionary*; David McCordick, ed., *Scottish Literature: An Anthology*, Vol. I (New York: Peter Lang, 1996), 853.
94 Alexander Pope, *The Poems*, ed. John Butt, (London: Methuen, 1965) 646; *P*3, 1035.
95 *CPB*1, 21; *P*1, 61.
96 *P*1, 58.
97 CW, I, 119.
98 *P*1, 58.
99 *P*1, 56.
100 Tait, 174, 153, 147.
101 'The Poet Burns', *Liverpool Mercury*, 1 June 1847, quoting an 1818 interview with Blane; see also 'Literature: The Heroines of Burns' Songs', *Glasgow Herald*, 2 October 1848.
102 *P*1, 55–6.
103 Shenstone, *Works*, II, 44.
104 *P*1, 57.
105 *P*1, 58.
106 *L*2, 198; *CPB*1, 16.
107 Dylan Thomas, *The Poems*, ed. Daniel Jones (London: Dent, 1974), 77.
108 *CPB*1, 17.
109 *The Confession of Faith, the Longer and Shorter Catechism* (Glasgow: John Robertson, 1756), 359.
110 *CPB*1, 17–18.
111 Ibid., 18, 19.
112 *L*1, 22.
113 *CPB*1, 7.
114 Ibid.
115 *P*1, 52.
116 Matthew 16: 6 and 8 (Authorized Version).
117 *P*1, 52–4.
118 Henry Mackenzie, *The Man of the World* (London: Strahan and Cadell, 1773), I, 21; *P*1, 42.
119 *L*1, 139.
120 CW, I, 115.
121 *L*1, 23.
122 Ibid.
123 Memoirs, W, 4124–5.
124 *L*1, 308.
125 *P*3, 1033, 1137; *L*1, 275.
126 *L*1, 24.
127 Kirk Session Certificate, Tarbolton Church, 4 August 1784 (RBBM), W, 621.
128 Fergusson, *Selected Poems*, 71–2.
129 Tait, 96.
130 *P*1, 61.
131 *P*1, 61; *P*3, 1037; Numbers, 16: 33 (Authorized Version).
132 *P*1, 62, 61.
133 *P*1, 62–3.
134 *P*1, 101.
135 *L*1, 24.

136 *P*1, 64.
137 CW, I, 119.
138 Mackay, 139.
139 *P*1, 101, 102.
140 CW, I, 119.
141 Andrew Noble, quoted in Mackay, 140.
142 *P*1, 70, 71, 72, 73.
143 *L*1, 144.
144 *P*1, 73; on McGill see J. Walter McGinty, *Robert Burns and Religion* (Aldershot: Ashgate, 2003), 239–40.
145 For a more detailed account of the Session minutes see Mackay, 162–5, on which the present summary depends.
146 *L*1, 144.
147 Shenstone, *Works*, II, 57.
148 *P*1, 74–5.
149 *P*1, 74.
150 John Lapraik, *Poems on Several Occasions* (Kilmarnock: John Wilson, 1788), 51 and 54.
151 *P*1, 76.
152 *P*1, 76, 77, 78.
153 *P*1, 79.
154 *P*1, 80; *P*3, 1053.
155 Gilbert Burns in Currie (1801), III, 382.
156 *L*1, 31.
157 *P*1, 79.
158 *P*1, 83.
159 *P*1, 81.
160 Memoirs, W, 4114.
161 'Memoranda: by Mr McDiarmid, from Mrs Burns's Dictation', in P. Hately Waddell, ed., *Life and Works of Robert Burns* (Glasgow: David Wilson, 1867), Appendix, xxv.
162 *CPB*1, [facsimile 37].

Chapter IV: Bard

1 John McDiarmid, 'Death and Character of Mrs Burns' (1834), repr. BC, 1934, 39, 35.
2 '[Notes by Mrs Burns]' in P. Hately Waddell, ed., *Life and Works of Robert Burns* (Glasgow: David Wilson, 1867), Appendix, xxv.
3 *L*1, 318.
4 McDiarmid, 'Death and Character', 39.
5 *L*1, 318.
6 McDiarmid, 'Death and Character', 39.
7 *L*1, 316.
8 Nelly Millar, quoted in 'Mauchline – Death of a Contemporary of Burns', *Glasgow Herald*, 31 December 1858.
9 McDiarmid, 'Death and Character', 40.
10 William Jolly, *Robert Burns at Mossgiel, with Reminiscences of the Poet by his Herd-Boy* (Paisley: Alexander Gardner, 1881), 34, 35.
11 Hans Hecht, *Robert Burns* (1936; repr. Ayr: Alloway Publishing, 1991) 45.
12 Macdonald, 43.
13 William Auld, 'Parish of Machlin', *Statistical Account*, II, 114.

14 Ibid., 113.
15 Jolly, *Robert Burns at Mossgiel*, 35.
16 Auld, 'Parish of Machlin', 109.
17 *P1*, 163–4; *L1*, 308.
18 *P1*, 69, 65; 'An Epistle to Davy' (East Ayrshire Museums Collection), W, 1409, 1408.
19 Gilbert Burns quoted in CW, I, 144; *P1*, 65.
20 Mackay, 154; *P1*, 69, 65.
21 *CPB1*, 12, 11, 39.
22 Tait, 174, 147.
23 Hately Waddell, *Life and Works*, Appendix, xxxvi; *P1*, 54.
24 Memoirs, W, 4115 and 4117–18.
25 *P1*, 65; *CPB1*, 7.
26 *P1*, 65–9.
27 *P1*, 65, 68, 69.
28 Christopher MacLachlan, 'Burns and Ramsay', *Scottish Studies Review*, Autumn 2006, 10.
29 *P1*, 66–9.
30 *CPB1*, 39.
31 CW, I, 144.
32 *CPB1*, 26.
33 Currie (1801), III, 383.
34 John Lapraik, *Poems, on Several Occasions* (Kilmarnock: John Wilson, 1788), 178.
35 CW, I, 157.
36 *P1*, 87.
37 *P3*, 1059.
38 *P1*, 91–2.
39 John Lapraik to John Richmond, ?30 October 1787, Edinburgh University Library, La. II. 210/18 (NBC, 1027).
40 *P3*, 1060.
41 *P1*, 96, 98.
42 *P1*, 99.
43 CW, I, 382–3.
44 Declaration by Elizabeth Paton, 1 December 1786, NLS Dep. 308 (NBC 2873).
45 *P3*, 1067; *P1*, 99.
46 *P3*, 1072.
47 *L1*, 312; Burns's annotated *Scots Musical Museum* (RBBM), W, 2762–3.
48 *CPB1*, 36.
49 *P1*, 103.
50 *P1*, 109, 110.
51 CW, I, 144.
52 *P1*, 108, 107, 111.
53 Ibid., 108.
54 CW, I, 216.
55 *P1*, 117.
56 *P1*, 118; *P3*, 1089.
57 W, 3137; *P1*, 137–45.
58 *P1*, 118.
59 See Crawford.
60 'The Holy Fair – composed in Autumn 1785' (East Ayrshire Museums Collection), W, 3121.

61 Eric Schmidt, *Holy Fairs* (Princeton: Princeton University Press, 1989), 35.
62 Anon., *A Letter from a Blacksmith, to the Ministers and Elders of the Church of Scotland* (London: J. Coote, 1759), 10.
63 *P*3, 1094.
64 *P*1, 131, 132, 133.
65 John Russel, *The Reasons of our Lord's Agony in the Garden* (Kilmarnock: John Wilson, 1787), 24.
66 *P*1, 135, 134, 137.
67 *P*1, 114.
68 *P*1, 124–6.
69 *P*1, 122, 123.
70 *CPB*1, 37, 38, 38–9.
71 Ibid., 39.
72 *L*1, 26–7; see also *Robert Burns 1759–1796, A Collection of Original Manuscripts* (Philadelphia and New York: The Rosenbach Company, 1948), 10.
73 *P*1, 123; Francis Sempill of Beltrees, 'Maggie Lauder', in Robert Crawford and Mick Imlah, eds, *The New Penguin Book of Scottish Verse* (London: Penguin, 2000), 207.
74 *P*1, 195.
75 *P*1, 204.
76 *P*3, 1149.
77 *P*1, 198, 206, 208–9.
78 Franklyn Bliss Snyder, *The Life of Robert Burns* (New York: Macmillan, 1932), 165.
79 John Keats, *The Complete Poems*, ed. John Barnard, 2nd edn (Harmondsworth: Penguin, 1977), 309.
80 Shenstone, *Works*, I, 92.
81 Nigel Leask, '"The Cottage Leaves the Palace Far Behind": Pastoral Idealism and Social Change in *The Cotter's Saturday Night*', *BC*, Winter 2006, 26–31.
82 William Shenstone, *Works*, 2 vols (Edinburgh: Donaldson, 1768), I, 198.
83 *P*1, 128.
84 In Burns's Ayrshire 'the 11th of November' was 'commonly called Hallowe'en' – Currie (1800), I, 108.
85 *The Poems of Gray, Collins and Goldsmith*, ed. Roger Lonsdale (Harlow: Longmans, 1969), 686.
86 *P*1, 152.
87 *P*3, 1111.
88 *L*1, 27, 28.
89 *P*1, 145, 148, 151, 150.
90 *L*2, 294; *P*3, 1111.
91 *P*3, 1111; *P*1, 149.
92 *P*1, 151, 152.
93 *L*1, 33.
94 *P*1, 191, 192.
95 *P*1, 178, 179.
96 Robert Fergusson, *Selected Poems*, ed. James Robertson (Edinburgh: Birlinn, 2000), 71.
97 *P*1, 183, 179.
98 *P*1, 185, 189.
99 *P*1, 176.
100 *P*1, 191.
101 *L*2, 396.

102 Trevor Burnard, *Mastery, Tyranny, & Desire: Thomas Thistlewood and his Slaves in the Anglo-Jamaican World* (Chapel Hill: University of North Carolina Press, 2004), 74, 89, 75.

103 *L1*, 27, 28.

104 *P1*, 172.

105 *L1*, 28.

106 William Patrick in Jolly, *Robert Burns at Mossgiel*, 60.

107 Currie (1801), I, 75.

108 *L1*, 28; *P1*, 178.

109 *P1*, 184.

110 *P1*, 193, 194.

111 Adam Smith, *The Theory of Moral Sentiments*, 4th edn (London: W. Strahan et al., 1774), 222.

112 *P1*, 213.

113 *P1*, 215.

114 Anon ['a resident in Inchinnan parish'], *Tour through Scotland and the Borders of England made in the Years 1791 & 1792* (St Andrews University Library manuscript DA 855 A9 T7), 241.

115 *P1*, 217, 219.

116 *P1*, 220.

117 CW, I, 247.

118 *P1*, 222.

119 *P1*, 221.

120 *P1*, 227.

121 *L1*, 30.

122 *L1*, 30–31.

123 *L1*, 32.

124 Subscriber's form for the Kilmarnock Edition (RBBM), W, 1928.

125 *L1*, 30.

126 *L1*, 32.

127 *P1*, 229.

128 *L1*, 32.

129 *P1*, 230, 231, 232; *L1*, 144.

130 *L1*, 33.

131 *L1*, 34.

132 *P1*, 234; Fergusson, *Selected Poems*, 197.

133 *L1*, 36.

134 *L1*, 37.

135 *P1*, 233.

136 *L1*, 37.

137 *L1*, 39.

138 CW, I, 336.

139 Nelly Millar, Mrs Martin, in 'Mauchline – Death of a Contemporary of Burns', *Glasgow Herald*, 31 December 1858.

140 Joseph Train in Robert T. Fitzhugh, ed., *Robert Burns, his Associates and Contemporaries* (Chapel Hill, NC: University of North Carolina Press, 1943), 54.

141 Mackay, 212–13.

142 *L1*, 37.

143 *P1*, 253.

144 *P2*, 657; *P3*, 1409.

145 See Robert H. Cromek, ed., *Reliques of Robert Burns* (London: Cadell and

Davies, 1808), 237; the text quoted in the present book is from Burns's manuscript (RBBM) available digitally as BMT192A on the SCRAN database at www.scran.ac.uk

146 *P*1, 242.
147 *P*1, 248, 249.
148 W, 713 (RBBM); *BC*, 1998, 9.
149 *P*1, 237.
150 *P*1, 235.
151 *L*1, 38.
152 *P*1, 238–9.
153 *P*1, 256, 257, 258.
154 *P*1, 254.
155 *P*1, 243, 246.
156 *P*1, 265 and 269.
157 *P*1, 189.
158 *L*1, 36.
159 *L*1, 39.
160 Ibid.
161 *P*1, 271.
162 *P*3, 971.
163 *L*1, 41.
164 *L*1, 42.
165 *L*1, 44.
166 *L*1, 43.
167 *L*1, 44.
168 Charles Douglas to Patrick Douglas, 19 June 1786 (RBBM, NBC 247).
169 Currie (1801), I, 76.
170 Edward Long, *The History of Jamaica*, 3 vols (London: T. Lowndes, 1774), II, 405.
171 S. R. G., 'Burns and Jamaica', *BC*, 1911, 80–81.
172 J. R. Ward, *British West Indian Slavery, 1750–1834* (Oxford: Clarendon Press, 1988), 201.
173 Ibid., 80.
174 Currie (1801), I, 76.
175 William Guthrie, *A New Geographical, Historical, and Commercial Grammar* (London: J. Knox, 1770), 673, 674, 675, 676, 680.
176 *P*2, 657.
177 *P*1, 239.
178 *L*1, 45.
179 Ibid.
180 *P*1, 247.
181 *P*1, 272.
182 *L*1, 47.
183 Ibid.
184 *L*1, 49.
185 *P*1, 290.
186 *L*1, 49.
187 Ibid.
188 *L*1, 51.
189 *L*1, 52.
190 *L*1, 54.
191 Ibid.

192 Robert Heron, *A Memoir of the late Robert Burns* (Edinburgh: T. Brown, 1797), 17.
193 Robert Heron, *Observations*, 2nd edn, 2 vols (Perth: W. Morison, 1799), II, 347.
194 *L*1, 54.
195 Robert Anderson to James Currie, 27 October 1799, *BC*, 1925, 13.
196 See Edward Larrissy, *The Blind and Blindness in Literature of the Romantic Period* (Edinburgh: Edinburgh University Press, 2007), 16, 60.
197 Thomas Blacklock to George Lawrie, 4 September 1786 (National Archives of Scotland), W, 4187–8.
198 Shaw, 115, 114.
199 *P*1, 280–89.
200 *L*1, 58.
201 Ibid.
202 Ibid.
203 *P*1, 250.
204 *L*1, 59.
205 CW, I, 431–2.
206 Burns's manuscript note (BMT192A in RBBM), available digitally on the SCRAN database; *L*1, 457–8.
207 'Burns's Highland Mary', *Caledonian Mercury*, 31 March 1823.
208 CW, I, 435.
209 *P*1, 298, 299; *L*1, 60.
210 CW, I, 441.
211 *P*3, 1534.
212 Nelly Miller in Hately Waddell, *Life and Works*, Appendix, xxvi–xxvii.
213 *L*2, 336.
214 *L*1, 61.
215 Ibid.
216 *P*1, 299, 300.
217 *P*1, 300, 302.
218 *L*1, 62.
219 *L*1, 63–4; *P*1, 224; *P*3, 1170.
220 See Donald A. Low, ed., *Robert Burns, The Critical Heritage* (London: Routledge and Kegan Paul, 1974), 64.
221 Ibid., 65, 66.
222 Thomas Blacklock to George Lawrie, 27 November 1786 (National Archives of Scotland), W, 4189; *P*1, 305; *L*1, 66.
223 *L*1, 65, 66.

Chapter V: New World

1 *L*1, 145.
2 John Lettice, *Letters on a Tour through Various Parts of Scotland* (London: T. Cadell, 1794), 511, 510.
3 *L*1, 67.
4 Archibald Prentice, 'The First Visit of Robert Burns to Edinburgh', *Manchester Times*, 27 March 1841.
5 *L*1, 69.
6 Mackenzie, unsigned essay in *The Lounger*, repr. in Donald A. Low, ed., *Robert Burns, The Critical Heritage* (London: Routledge & Kegan Paul, 1974), 67–70.

7 *L*1, 71.

8 Cooksey, I, 2.

9 *L*1, 71.

10 John Strawhorn, 'Who was Andrew Bruce?', *BC*, 1996, 169.

11 'Allan Ramsay' in Low, ed., *Robert Burns, The Critical Heritage*, 65.

12 *L*1, 70.

13 Robert Anderson to James Currie, 19 September 1799, *BC*, 1925, 10; see also Maurice Lindsay, *The Burns Encyclopedia*, 2nd edn (London: Hale, 1980), 99.

14 *L*1, 70.

15 *L*1, 68.

16 *P*1, 323.

17 *P*1, 309, 310.

18 Fergusson, 'Auld Reikie' in *Selected Poems*, ed. James Robertson (Edinburgh: Birlinn, 2000), 100–113; Shaw, *Tour*, 185, 192.

19 *L*1, 83–4.

20 Shaw, 205–6.

21 *L*1, 70–71.

22 *L*1, 83.

23 *L*1, 71.

24 *L*1, 73.

25 *P*1, 309.

26 *L*1, 76.

27 Cooksey, II, 62, plate N15.

28 *P*1, 308.

29 *L*1, 75.

30 [Marie Huber], *Letters concerning the Religion Essential to Man* (Glasgow: R. Urie, 1761), 10–11.

31 *L*1, 76.

32 *L*1, 74; see *Hamlet*, I, v, 79.

33 Robert Heron, *A Memoir of the Life of the Late Robert Burns* (Edinburgh: T. Brown, 1797), 23.

34 *L*1, 78 and 105.

35 *L*1, 74; on Greenfield see Martin Moonie, 'William Greenfield: Gender and the Transmission of Literary Culture', in Robert Crawford, ed., *The Scottish Invention of English Literature* (Cambridge: Cambridge University Press, 1998), 103–15.

36 *L*1, 77.

37 John Richmond to James Grierson of Dalgoner, 17 December 1817, in Robert T. Fitzhugh, *Robert Burns, his Associates and Contemporaries* (Chapel Hill, NC: University of North Carolina Press, 1943), 37.

38 Fergusson, *Selected Poems*, 164.

39 *P*1, 311–12.

40 Alicia Cockburn in Sarah Tytler and J. L. Watson, eds, *The Songstresses of Scotland*, 2 vols (Edinburgh: Strahan, 1871), I, 180; David Ramsay, undated letter to Robert Anderson (NLS), W, 2656.

41 John Moir, printer, in CW, II, 29.

42 Currie (1801), I, 226.

43 Robert Anderson in *P*3, 1536–7.

44 Currie (1801), II, 33.

45 *L*1, 80; *P*1, 312.

46 *CPB*2, 455.

47 Craig Sharp, 'The Mystery of Burns' Hogmanay, 1786', *BC*, Autumn 2006, 39–46; *L*1, 79.

48 *L*1, 81.

49 CW, II, 207.

50 *L*1, 89.

51 Alicia Cockburn in Tytler and Watson, eds, *The Songstresses*, I, 180; Robert Anderson in *P*3, 1537.

52 *L*1, 69.

53 *L*1, 94.

54 William Wallace, ed., *Robert Burns and Mrs. Dunlop* (London: Hodder and Stoughton, 1898), 6, 5; *L*1, 85.

55 Wallace, *Robert Burns and Mrs. Dunlop*, 5, 12.

56 Ibid., 14.

57 *L*1, 101.

58 *L*1, 88.

59 *L*1, 90.

60 *P*1, 323.

61 *P*1, 322.

62 *P*1, 321–2.

63 John Armstrong, *Juvenile Poems* (Edinburgh: Peter Hill, 1789), 227.

64 Robert Anderson in *P*3, 1537.

65 Anderson, *P*3, 1538; *P*1, 325–6.

66 *L*1, 86–7.

67 *L*1, 91–2.

68 *L*1, 97.

69 *P*2, 735.

70 Robert Heron, *Observations*, 2nd edn, 2 vols (Perth: W. Morison, 1799), II, 348.

71 CW, II, 80.

72 *P*1, 331.

73 Walter Scott in J. G. Lockhart, *Life of Robert Burns* (1828; repr. London: Dent, 1976), 81–2.

74 National Archives of Scotland (NBC 2225).

75 Currie (1801), II, 62; 'The Plenipotentiary' in *The Festival of Anacreon* (London: George Peacock, n.d.), 22.

76 *L*1, 98.

77 Heron, *Observations*, 348; Blair in Low, ed., *Robert Burns, The Critical Heritage*, 82.

78 CPB2, 455.

79 Miss Carmichael, *Poems* (Edinburgh: The Author, 1790), 82, 4; Anderson to Currie, 27 October 1799, BC, 1925, 17.

80 *L*1, 100.

81 *L*1, 101–2.

82 *L*1, 96.

83 *P*1, 332.

84 Alexander Nasmyth to William Cribb, 23 August 1829, in Cooksey, I, 128.

85 James Nasmyth to Alexander Fraser, 15 December 1871, in Cooksey, I, 133; see also Cooksey, I, 48 and II, 63.

86 Lockhart, *Life of Burns*, 102.

87 Anderson to Currie, 27 October 1799, BC, 1925, 16.

88 CPB2, 454.

89 See *L*1, 124 and 284 in conjunction with CW, II, 121–2 and Mackay, 316–18.

90 Heron, *Memoir*, 27.

91 *P*1, 331.

92 Richard B. Sher, *The Enlightenment and the Book* (Chicago: University of Chicago Press, 2006), 401.
93 *CPB2*, 456.
94 RBBM, NBC 224.
95 CW, II, 266
96 CW, II, 52.
97 *Lyric Repository* (London: J. French, 1787), Advertisement.
98 Alexander Campbell, *An Introduction to the History of Poetry in Scotland* (Edinburgh: Andrew Foulis, 1798), 306.
99 Shaw, 123, 122, 124–5.
100 James Currie to Graham Moore, 11 June 1787, in Rhona Brown, 'Making Robert Burns: The Correspondence of James Currie', *BC*, Winter 2005, 5.
101 [Marshall], *Catalogue of Five Hundred Celebrated Authors* (London: R. Faulder et al., 1788), entry for Burns.
102 *L1*, 106.
103 *L1*, 100.
104 *L1*, 108.
105 Letter of Dr John Geddes (Scottish Catholic Archive), W, 4247–8.
106 *L1*, 108.
107 Robert Carruthers, 'More Information Concerning Robert Burns – The New Portrait, &c.', *Edinburgh Literary Journal*, November 1829, 385.
108 *L1*, 175.
109 Dugald Stewart in Currie (1800), I, 143.
110 East Ayrshire Museums Collection, W, 4280.
111 Nasmyth to William Cribb, 23 August 1829, in Cooksey, I, 128; see also Helen Rosslyn, 'Rosslyn: "That Romantic Spot"' in Helen Rosslyn and Angelo Maggi, *Rosslyn, Country of Painter and Poet* (Edinburgh: National Gallery of Scotland, 2002), 38; Shaw, 204; James Johnson, ed., *The Scots Musical Museum* (Edinburgh: James Johnson, 1787), I, 9.
112 Candia McWilliam, *Debatable Land* (London: Picador, 1994), 77.
113 Nasmyth's sketch is now owned by the National Galleries of Scotland.
114 *P1*, 339.
115 Fergusson, *Selected Poems*, 165; Nasmyth to Cribb, 23 August 1829, in Cooksey, I, 128.
116 *P2*, 588.
117 *P1*, 437.
118 See Robert Chambers cited in William Chambers, *Memoir of Robert Chambers* (Edinburgh: W. & R. Chambers, 1872), 198; *P2*, 528.
119 *P3*, 1271–2; Robert Chambers, *Traditions of Edinburgh*, revised edn (1868; repr. Edinburgh: Chambers, 1912), 164; *L2*, 458; *L1*, 109.
120 *L1*, 109.
121 *L1*, 114.
122 *L1*, 101.
123 Hugh Blair to Robert Burns, 4 May 1787 (NLS), W, 708.
124 'Death of Robert Ainslie, Esq. W. S.', *Caledonian Mercury*, 16 April 1838.
125 *L1*, 107.
126 *Robert Burns's Tour of the Borders*, ed. Raymond Lamont Brown (Ipswich: Boydell Press, 1972), 17.
127 Ibid., 18–19.
128 Ibid., 23.
129 *L1*, 115.
130 *P1*, 335; *Burns's Tour of the Borders*, 25.

131 *L*1, 120.
132 *L*1, 118.
133 *L*1, 284 (for the redating of this letter, see Mackay, 316).
134 See Mackay, 318–19.
135 *L*1, 122.
136 *L*1, 121.
137 *L*1, 122.
138 *L*1, 123.
139 David Sillar, *Poems* (Kilmarnock: John Wilson, 1789), 161, 162.
140 *L*1, 121.
141 *L*1, 124.
142 *L*1, 125.
143 *L*1, 126.
144 *L*1, 128.
145 *P*3, 1239.
146 *L*1, 129.
147 *L*1, 128.
148 *L*1, 132.
149 *L*1, 133.
150 *L*1, 134, 133, 145.
151 *L*1, 146.
152 *L*1, 131.
153 Shaw, 115, 114.
154 Currie (1801), I, 145.
155 Burns's journal in Raymond Lamont Brown, *Robert Burns's Tours of the Highlands and Stirlingshire 1787* (Ipswich: Boydell Press, 1973), 17.
156 Ibid., 18, 16; *P*1, 348; *L*1, 151.
157 *P*1, 348.
158 Burns's journal in Brown, *Burns's Tours of the Highlands*, 19.
159 *P*1, 349, 351, 352, 355, 358.
160 *P*1, 351.
161 Shaw, 166–7.
162 *P*1, 352; *P*3, 1244.
163 Burns's journal in Brown, *Burns's Tours of the Highlands*, 19.
164 *P*1, 354.
165 *L*1, 155; *P*1, 357.
166 Anon., *Tour through Scotland 1791 & 1792*, MS. DA855 A9 T7 (St Andrews University Library), 114, 113.
167 *L*1, 160; Burns's journal in Brown, *Burns's Tours of the Highlands*, 16; *L*1, 163; Charles Hope quoted in Robert T. Fitzhugh, *Robert Burns, The Man and the Poet* (London: W. H. Allen, 1971), 160.
168 *L*1, 156; *Burns's Tours*, 23.
169 *L*1, 157.
170 *L*1, 158.
171 *L*1, 179.
172 Mrs Dunlop in *Robert Burns and Mrs. Dunlop*, 138.
173 Adair in Brown, *Burns's Tours of the Highlands*, 52.
174 *L*1, 165, 166.
175 *L*1, 317.
176 *L*1, 171; *P*1, 366.
177 CW, II, 194.
178 Ibid.

179 Adair in Brown, *Burns's Tours of the Highlands*, 53–4.
180 John Skinner, *A Miscellaneous Collection of Fugitive Pieces of Poetry* (Edinburgh: John Muir, 1809), 107.
181 *L*1, 167.
182 *L*1, 168.
183 *L*1, 176.
184 *L*1, 166.
185 *L*1, 167.
186 *L*1, 174.
187 *L*1, 175; see J. Walter McGinty, *Robert Burns and Religion* (Aldershot: Ashgate, 2003), 240.
188 *L*1, 175.
189 *L*1, 176.
190 *L*1, 176 and 177.
191 *L*1, 179.
192 *L*1, 178, 179.
193 *L*1, 181.
194 Agnes McLehose, letter to Burns of 8 December 1787 in John D. Ross, ed., *Burns' Clarinda* (Edinburgh: John Grant, 1897), 134.
195 *L*1, 182.
196 *L*1, 184.
197 *L*1, 184–5.
198 CW, II, 219.
199 John, 8: 23.
200 *L*1, 185.
201 Heron, *A Memoir*, 27.
202 Anon., *The Entertaining Amour of Sylvander and Sylvia* (Edinburgh: n.p., 1767), 10, 80.
203 *L*1, 189–90.
204 McLehose, 104, 98.
205 *L*1, 193.
206 McLehose, 107.
207 Ibid., 100.
208 *L*1, 200.
209 Currie (1801), I, 139.
210 See chapter 7 below.
211 James Johnson, ed., *The Scots Musical Museum*, Vol. II (Edinburgh: James Johnson, 1788), 178; NLS Adv. MS. 19.3.44, pp. 168–9; Burns's manuscript is RBBM 309.08; for full discussion see note on 'The Rediscovered Poems in this Book' in Crawford and MacLachlan.
212 *P*2, 707.
213 McLehose, 106.
214 *L*1, 194.
215 McLehose, 61.
216 Ibid., 62; *L*1, 195.
217 *L*1, 195.
218 *L*1, 198.
219 Ibid.
220 *L*1, 199.
221 *L*1, 220.
222 *L*1, 203.
223 *L*1, 215.

224 *L*1, 207.
225 *L*1, 210–11.
226 Francis Beaumont and John Fletcher, *The Dramatick Works of Beaumont and Fletcher*, 10 vols (London: T. Evans et al., 1778), III, 466.
227 McLehose, 121.
228 *L*1, 201, 204, 202, 210.
229 *P*1, 408; *L*1, 218.
230 McLehose, 69; *L*1, 219.
231 McLehose, 64.
232 *L*1, 218, 220, 221.
233 *L*1, 219.
234 *L*1, 226.
235 *L*1, 227.
236 *L*1, 231.
237 *L*1, 232–3.
238 *L*1, 234, 236.
239 *L*1, 236.
240 *L*1, 224.
241 *L*1, 228.
242 *L*1, 229.

Chapter VI: Rhinoceros

1 *L*1, 241.
2 *L*1, 243.
3 *L*1, 248.
4 *L*1, 244.
5 *L*1, 247.
6 *L*1, 251.
7 *L*1, 253.
8 *L*1, 252.
9 William Giles, ed., *A Collection of Poems* (London: Buckland et al., 1775), 82, 85.
10 Robert Louis Stevenson, 'Some Aspects of Robert Burns', *in Familiar Studies of Men and Books*, Skerryvore Edition, Vol. XXIII (London: Heinemann, 1925), 58, 40.
11 Catherine Carswell, *The Life of Robert Burns* (1930; repr. Edinburgh: Canongate, 1990), 312.
12 *L*1, 253.
13 *L*1, 254.
14 Ibid.
15 *L*1, 351 and 388.
16 *L*1, 249.
17 *L*1, 258.
18 Ibid.
19 *L*1, 263.
20 *P*1, 410.
21 Ibid.
22 'Letters of Robert Burns, IX', *BC*, 1929, 14.
23 James Thomson, *Poetical Works*, 2 vols (Glasgow, 1784), I, 46.
24 'Letters', *BC*, 1929, 14, 15.
25 *L*1, 266.

26 *L*1, 269, 270.
27 A. Pearson, letter of 31 March 1788, Edinburgh University Library La. II. 210/12 (NBC 1020); John Dougharty, *The General Gauger*, 6th edn (London: John and Paul Knapton, 1750), 36, 184. See also NBC 8501.
28 *L*1, 273.
29 Ibid.
30 *L*1, 274.
31 *L*1, 275.
32 *L*1, 274.
33 Tait, 155, 154.
34 Jessy Lewars, CW, IV, 119.
35 *L*1, 278.
36 *L*1, 281.
37 *L*1, 287.
38 CPB2, 458; *L*1, 236.
39 *L*1, 293.
40 Ibid.
41 *L*1, 289.
42 Mauchline Kirk Session minute of 5 August 1788, reproduced in John Strawhorn, 'The Wedding of the Year', *BC*, 1999, 172; *L*1, 292.
43 *L*1, 293.
44 *L*1, 304.
45 *L*1, 311–12.
46 *P*1, 412; *L*1, 294.
47 James Mackay, 'Ellisland Today', *BC*, August 1993, 44.
48 John Syme to Alexander Cunningham, 5 January 1789 (RBBM), W, 2886.
49 Sold in 2007, the portraits by Chalmers are reproduced in the *Scotsman*, 11 October 2007, 7.
50 *DWJ*, 28 March 1797, 4.
51 *P*1, 417, 416.
52 *DWJ*, 24 June 1794, 4.
53 See Riddell's entry in the Library Receipt Book for Students, 1772–7 (St Andrews University Library LY 207 2).
54 Cooksey, I, 115 and II, 9.
55 *L*1, 361.
56 See *L*2, 406.
57 'Despair: A Poem' in Robert Riddell's Commonplace Book (Dumfries County Archives); Dr Burnside, *Statistical Account*, V, 142.
58 [Robert Riddell], *The Bedesman on Nidsyde* (London: S. Hooper, 1790), 2; *P*3, 1274–5.
59 *P*1, 424.
60 [Anon.], *A View of the Political State of Scotland at the Late General Election* (Edinburgh: Ainslie et al., 1790), 82.
61 *L*1, 314, 315; *P*1, 426.
62 *L*1, 314, 315.
63 *P*1, 427.
64 *L*1, 319.
65 'A Letter from Dr Gillespie Concerning Robert Burns,' *Edinburgh Weekly Journal*, December 1829, 401.
66 CW, III, 41.
67 *L*1, 324.
68 *L*1, 328.

69 *L*1, 315.
70 *P*3, 1277; *P*1, 421–2.
71 Account, Robert Burns to John Weir for shoes and shoe repairs, June to September 1788, Edinburgh University Library La. II. 210/11 (NBC 1019).
72 *L*1, 311, 320.
73 [James Cririe], *Address to Loch Lomond* (London and Edinburgh: Dilly and Hill, [1788]), 19; *L*1, 326–7.
74 *L*2, 93.
75 *L*1, 335, 333.
76 *L*2, 82.
77 *L*1, 333.
78 *L*1, 246.
79 Marmontel, *Belisarius* (London: Nourse, 1783), 74.
80 *L*1, 335.
81 *P*1, 436.
82 *P*3, 1286.
83 *P*1, 454.
84 *P*1, 450.
85 *L*1, 341–2.
86 *L*1, 345.
87 *P*3, 1289.
88 *P*1, 459.
89 *L*1, 342.
90 'Burns', *The Morning Chronicle*, 10 April 1830.
91 *P*1, 457 and 461.
92 *L*1, 346.
93 Currie (1801), II, 190.
94 Archibald Mickle, Account to Robert Burns, 6 January 1789 (Rosenbach Museum and Library, Philadelphia),W, 2115; see also W, 2318.
95 CW, III, 17.
96 *L*1, 377; CW, III, 41.
97 *L*1, 389.
98 *L*1, 356, 357.
99 Syme to Cunningham, 5 January 1789 (RBBM), W, 2886.
100 *L*1, 348.
101 *L*1, 363; *P*1, 446.
102 *L*1, 358.
103 *L*1, 371.
104 *L*1, 373, 375.
105 *L*1, 372.
106 *L*1, 379.
107 *L*2, 108, 107.
108 *L*1, 382.
109 David Morison, *Poems, Chiefly in the Scottish Dialect* (Montrose: David Buchanan, 1790), 35; John Learmont, *Poems* (Edinburgh: The Author, 1791), 217, 1, 88; John Burness, *Poems, Chiefly in the Scottish Dialect* (Dundee: The Author, 1791), 87.
110 *L*1, 392; *P*1, 462, 463, 464.
111 *L*1, 392, 384.
112 *L*1, 403.
113 *P*1, 469.
114 *L*1, 399.

115 Gavin Turnbull, *Poetical Essays* (Glasgow: David Niven, 1788), 135, 138, 142, 145, 146.
116 L1, 400.
117 Cunningham's inscription, quoted in CW, III, 42.
118 James Mylne, *Poems* (Edinburgh: Creech, 1790), 40.
119 Elizabeth Smith in CW, III, 98.
120 William Clark in CW, III, 198.
121 L1, 410.
122 L1, 415, 416.
123 L1, 410.
124 *DWJ*, 7 July 1789, 3, and 14 July 1789, 3.
125 L1, 423.
126 Riddell, Commonplace Book, 'An Account of the ancient Lordship of Galloway', 11 (Dumfries County Archives).
127 L1, 423.
128 *DWJ*, 28 July 1789, 3.
129 P1, 470.
130 L1, 419.
131 L1, 421.
132 L1, 418 and 430.
133 William Gilpin, *Observations, relative chiefly to Picturesque Beauty*, 2 vols (London: Blamire, 1789), I, 215.
134 L1, 432.
135 David Sillar, *Poems* (Kilmarnock: John Wilson, 1789), 161.
136 Stuart in Currie (1801), II, 245; L1, 435.
137 *DWJ*, 21 July 1789, 3; L1, 435.
138 Ibid.
139 L1, 437 and 440.
140 *DWJ*, 18 August 1789, 4.
141 L1, 440.
142 L1, 454–5.
143 P1, 481.
144 *DWJ*, 1 September 1789, 1.
145 L1, 441.
146 P1, 484.
147 P1, 487, 488.
148 P1, 489, 491.
149 P2, 505.
150 John Wilson and Robert Chambers, *The Land of Burns*, 2 vols (Edinburgh: Blackie, 1840), II, 10–11.
151 L1, 446.
152 L1, 448.
153 L1, 453.
154 L2, 412.
155 L1, 456.
156 L1, 457–8; P1, 492.
157 L2, 5.
158 L1, 458.
159 L1, 461, 463.
160 P1, 496–8 and 494.
161 L2, 3.
162 L2, 9 and 14.

163 *L2*, 10, 11.

164 *P3*, 1335 and *P2*, 529.

165 *P2*, 535.

166 *P2*, 527.

167 *L2*, 18.

168 *P2*, 544, 546.

169 *L2*, 23–4.

170 *P2*, 550.

171 *P2*, 551, 554.

172 *L2*, 35.

173 See, e.g., Bob Harris, ed., *Scotland in the Age of the French Revolution* (Edinburgh: John Donald, 2005), 59, 86, 108.

174 CW, III, 200.

175 James Maxwell, *Animadversions on Some Poets and Poetasters of the Present Age, Especially R——t B——s and J——n L——k* (Paisley: J. Neilson, 1788), 8, 5, 9–10.

176 James Maxwell, *The Divine Origin of Poetry* (Paisley: Neilson, 1790), 6, 9.

177 James Fisher, *Poems on Various Subjects* (Dumfries: Robert Jackson, 1790), 91, 157.

178 Currie (1801), I, 195.

179 Mackay, 458.

180 J. Thomson [i.e. Jessy Lewars], letter of 21 September 1844, printed in 'The Daughter of Robert Burns', *Northern Star and Leeds General Advertizer*, 5 October 1844.

181 Burns to Stewart, July 1790 (NLS), W, 2809.

182 CW, III, 200.

183 *L2*, 44.

184 *L2*, 46–7.

185 *P3*, 1348.

186 Syme to Cunningham, 11 September 1790 (RBBM), W, 2889.

187 *P2*, 832; *L2*, 49.

188 *P2*, 556.

189 *L2*, 55.

190 *P2*, 557–64.

191 CW, III, 210.

192 *L2*, 53.

193 *Robert Burns and Mrs. Dunlop, Correspondence*, ed. William Wallace (London: Hodder and Stoughton, 1898), 289, 325.

194 [Anon.,] 'Tour through Scotland ... 1791 & 1792', St Andrews University Library Special Collections MS. DA855 A9 T7, 35.

195 'K', 'To Robert Burns', *The Bee*, 23 March 1791, 120; 'Oran Ussaig – To R. Burns', *The Bee*, 27 April 1791, 317.

196 Burns, draft of letter to James Anderson, 1 November 1790 (Liverpool Central Library), W, 59.

197 RBBM, NBC 216.

198 *L2*, 65, 66.

199 *L2*, 67.

200 *L2*, 69.

201 Janet Little, *Poetical Works* (Ayr: John and Peter Wilson, 1792), 112.

202 *P2*, 582, 584.

203 *P2*, 569.

204 *L2*, 83.

205 *L2*, 112; *P2*, 580.
206 *L2*, 83–4.
207 *P2*, 575–6.
208 *L2*, 86, 87.
209 See Robert Cleghorn's letter in Currie (1801), II, 130–31.
210 *L2*, 46.
211 *L2*, 98.
212 *L2*, 94–5.
213 *P2*, 579.
214 [James Grahame], *Poems, in English, Scotch, and Latin* (Paisley: J. Neilson, 1794), 45, 43.
215 *L2*, 104.
216 Robert Ainslie to Agnes McLehose, 18 October 1790, W, 4017.
217 D[avid] S[tewart] Earl of Buchan, *Essays on the Lives and Writings of Fletcher of Saltoun and the Poet Thomson* (London: J. Debrett, 1792), 244.
218 *L2*, 117.
219 *L2*, 118.
220 *P2*, 585, 587.
221 *P2*, 589, 586.

Chapter VII: Staunch Republicans

1 See James Urquhart, 'The Songhouse of Scotland: Robert Burns's First Home in Dumfries, 1791–1793', *BC*, 1983, 43–50.
2 John Jameson to Dumfries Council, 21 August 1792, in Marion Stewart, 'Authentic Voices: Burns's Neighbours in Dumfries', *BC*, December 1995, 15.
3 Dr Burnside, 'Town and Parish of Dumfries', *Statistical Account*, V, 123, 138.
4 Shaw, 103.
5 Arent Schuyler de Peyster, *Miscellanies* (1813), ed. J. Watts de Peyster (n.p., 1888), 74.
6 List of the different craftsmen working in Dumfries Burgh, 1791 (Dumfries Museum).
7 *L2*, 296.
8 Robert Riddell's watercolour, owned by the Library of the Society of Antiquaries of Scotland, is reproduced as the colour plate opposite p. 285 of Robert Donald Thornton, *James Currie the Entire Stranger & Robert Burns* (Edinburgh: Oliver and Boyd, 1963).
9 Robert Heron, *Observations Made in a Journey through the Western Counties of Scotland* (Perth: R. Morison Junior, 1793), 2 vols, II, 77.
10 *L2*, 274.
11 See the 'hitherto unpublished' letter in Andrew Noble and Patrick Scott Hogg, eds, *The Canongate Burns* (Edinburgh: Canongate, 2001), 473.
12 Robert Fergusson, *The Poems*, ed. Matthew P. McDiarmid, 2 vols (Edinburgh: Blackwood for the Scottish Text Society, 1954–6), II, 195.
13 *L2*, 296.
14 Macdonald, 23–4.
15 Robert Heron, *Observations*, 2nd edn, 2 vols (Perth: W. Morison, 1799), II, 72.
16 Ibid., 74.
17 List of craftsmen, 1791 (Dumfries Museum).
18 Heron, *Observations*, II, 77.
19 Ibid., 78.

20 G. W. Shirley, *Dumfries Printers in the Eighteenth Century* (Dumfries: Thos. Hunter, Watson & Co., 1934), 18–19, 21.

21 *L2*, 122.

22 Mackay, 425.

23 Agnes McLehose, rhymed invitation to Archibald Menzies, 1791, RBBM, NBC 1293.

24 *L2*, 123.

25 *L2*, 123, 124.

26 J. Thomson [Jessy Lewars], letter of 21 September 1844, *Northern Star and Leeds General Advertizer*, 5 October 1844.

27 *L2*, 121.

28 *P2*, 590.

29 *L2*, 125; *P2*, 714; *P3*, 1445.

30 *P2*, 591; *L2*, 125; see William Matheson, ed., *The Blind Harper* (Edinburgh: Scottish Gaelic Texts Society, 1970), xxxi.

31 [Robert Dodsley], *Colin's Kisses* (London: Dodsley, 1742), 9.

32 *P2*, 591–2.

33 McLehose, 276.

34 *P3*, 1441; *P2*, 710.

35 *P2*, 710.

36 RBBM 465 (NBC 1294); Kinsley (*P2*, 710) mentions a '42-line MS which 'has not been traced'. I believe this is it.

37 *DWJ*, 1 April 1794, 2.

38 John Lettice, *Letters on a Tour through Various Parts of Scotland* (London: T. Cadell, 1794), 44.

39 Maria Riddell, letter of 30 January 1792, quoted in Angus Macnaghten, *Burns' Mrs Riddell* (Peterhead: Volturna Press, 1975), 31, 32.

40 *L2*, 130, 135.

41 *P3*, 1545; see also photostat of proof of 'Robert Burns by Maria Riddell' (Ewart Library, Dumfries Db151 (821) P BUR).

42 *L2*, 131.

43 *L2*, 133.

44 *L2*, 134.

45 Robert Burns, statement regarding the 'Rosamond' seizure (NLS), W, 2604.

46 *DWJ*, 13 March 1792, 3.

47 J.G. Lockhart, *Life of Robert Burns* (1828; repr. London: Dent, 1976), 164, 165.

48 *L2*, 139.

49 Robert Burns, draft of letter to James Anderson, 1 November 1790 (Liverpool Central Library), W, 59.

50 *P1*, 656.

51 *L2*, 140, 139.

52 See Mackay, 529–30.

53 *L2*, 170.

54 *L2*, 145.

55 *DWJ*, 27 March 1792, 3; see also 10 April 1792, 1–3.

56 Maya Angelou, 'Angelou on Burns', 1996 BBC documentary directed by Elly M. Taylor; *DWJ*, 27 March 1792, 3.

57 *P2*, 613.

58 RBBM 356; in Burns's manuscript the chorus is written out in full after verse one.

59 *P2*, 643–4.

60 See Bob Harris, 'Political Protests in the Year of Liberty, 1792' in Harris, ed.,

Scotland in the Age of the French Revolution (Edinburgh: John Donald, 2005), 51. I am indebted to Harris's article for other background material in this chapter.

61 Indictment of 1792 beginning 'John Taylor present prisoner in the tolbooth of Edinburgh' (Eighteenth-Century Short Title Catalogue No. T213804), 1, 2, 4, 7.

62 Cooksey, I, 62 and II, 44; *DWJ*, 11 September 1792, 3.

63 Heron, *Observations*, 78, 79; James Mackay, ed., *The Complete Letters of Robert Burns* (Ayr: Alloway Publishing, 1987), 307.

64 *L*2, 145, 147, 146.

65 *P*2, 662.

66 *DWJ*, 4 September 1792, 2.

67 *DWJ*, 10 December 1792, 3 and 25 December 1792, 2; Ayr Library Society Committee minutes of 6 February 1793, reproduced in John Strawhorn, *The History of Ayr* (Edinburgh: John Donald, 1989), 89.

68 CW, IV, 55.

69 *L*2, 150–51.

70 *L*2, 158.

71 Robert Donald Thornton, *William Maxwell to Robert Burns* (Edinburgh: John Donald, 1979), 63.

72 Maxwell quoted in David J. Brown, 'The Government Response to Scottish Radicalism, 1792–1802' in Harris, ed., *Scotland in the Age of the French Revolution*, 102–3.

73 *DWJ*, 13 November 1792, 3 and 16 October 1792, 3.

74 *P*2, 661.

75 *DWJ*, 13 March 1792, 1.

76 *DWJ*, 20 November 1792, 3.

77 *L*2, 173.

78 *DWJ*, 4 December 1792, 3.

79 *P*2, 663.

80 *P*2, 668–9.

81 [Robert Heron], *Facts, Reflections, and Queries, submitted to the Consideration of the Associated Friends of the People* (Edinburgh: n.p., 1792), 33.

82 *P*2, 680.

83 Robert Heron, trans., *Letters which Passed between General Dumourier, and Pache* (Perth: R. Morison Jr., 1794), 'Advertisement'.

84 *L*2, 152.

85 *P*2, 677, 676.

86 Thomson to Burns, September 1792, in CW, III, 330.

87 *L*2, 149 and 315; see also *P*3, 1383–4.

88 *L*2, 168.

89 *L*2, 168–9.

90 *L*2, 170, 171, 172.

91 *DWJ*, 8 January 1793, 1; *L*2, 173–6.

92 *DWJ*, 8 January 1793, 4; Council Book, 18 February 1793 (Dumfries County Archives).

93 *L*2, 179.

94 *P*2, 681; *P*3, 1425.

95 *DWJ*, 29 January 1793, 2 and 3.

96 *DWJ*, 5 February 1793, 3.

97 *L*2, 182.

98 *L*2, 184; CW, III, 394, 395.

99 *DWJ*, 26 February 1793, 3.
100 *L2*, 208; *P2*, 681.
101 John McDiarmid, *Sketches from Nature* (Edinburgh: Oliver and Boyd, 1830), 373.
102 James Hogg and William Motherwell, eds, *The Works of Robert Burns*, 5 vols (Glasgow: A. Fullarton, 1834–6), V, 152; James Gray in William McDowall, *History of Dumfries* (Edinburgh: Adam and Charles Black, 1867), 713.
103 Heron, *Observations*, II, 346.
104 Samuel Thomson, *Poems* (Belfast: The Author, 1793), dedication and 88.
105 *L2*, 189–90.
106 Maria Riddell to James Currie, ?1797 (RBBM), W, 4374.
107 *L2*, 199.
108 *L2*, 202.
109 *L2*, 223.
110 *L2*, 229.
111 *L2*, 222.
112 Stewart, 'Authentic Voices', 22; *DWJ*, quoted in McDowall, *History of Dumfries*, 706.
113 *DWJ*, 8 July 1793, 3.
114 John Syme to Alexander Cunningham, 8 May 1793 (RBBM), W, 2902.
115 Syme to Cunningham, 3 August 1793 (RBBM), W, 2906–9.
116 Ibid., W, 2910.
117 Ibid.
118 *DWJ*, 11 September 1792, 1.
119 Syme to Cunningham, 3 August 1793, W, 2909.
120 *L2*, 334.
121 Noble and Hogg, eds, *Canongate Burns*, 460.
122 *DWJ*, 6 August 1793, 3.
123 *DWJ*, 3 September 1793, 3 and 4.
124 *DWJ*, 20 August 1793, 4.
125 See Christina Bewley, *Muir of Huntershill* (Oxford: Oxford University Press, 1981), 74.
126 *P2*, 820.
127 *L2*, 258.
128 Syme in Currie (1800), I, 213; cp. *P3*, 1439.
129 *L2*, 235, 236.
130 See chapter 5 above, and Crawford and MacLachlan.
131 *L2*, 236.
132 *L2*, 276.
133 *P2*, 718.
134 *L2*, 255.
135 *DWJ*, 3 September 1793, 4; *L2*, 253.
136 Maria Riddell to James Currie, 16 November 1797 (RBBM), W, 4363.
137 *DWJ*, 3 December 1793, 3; *P2*, 721; *L2*, 263.
138 *L2*, 271.
139 *P2*, 721; *L2*, 267.
140 *L2*, 268.
141 *L2*, 272.
142 *L2*, 272, 275, 276.
143 *L2*, 280, 278.
144 *L2*, 280, 282.
145 *L2*, 282.

146 Ibid.
147 *L2*, 285.
148 *L2*, 285–6.
149 *DWJ*, 7 January 1794, 3; Syme to Cunningham, 1 February 1794 (RBBM), W, 2915.
150 *DWJ*, 14 January 1794, 3, and 21 January 1794, 4.
151 *P2*, 732.
152 *DWJ*, 25 December 1792, 3.
153 *P2*, 733.
154 Ibid.
155 [Joseph Ritson, ed.,] *Scotish Songs*, 2 vols (London: J. Johnson, 1794), II, 123.
156 See *DWJ*, 22 April 1794, 3.
157 David Trail, *The Miseries of France, A Warning to Britain* (Dumfries: Robert Jackson, 1794), 8, 11, 14, 15–16, 17, 20.
158 *P2*, 910; *P3*, 1528.
159 *P2*, 911.
160 *L2*, 334.
161 *P2*, 910–11.
162 *P3*, 1528; Noble and Hogg, eds, *Canongate Burns*, 847–51.
163 *L2*, 208.
164 *L2*, 288.
165 *L2*, 288–9.
166 Noble and Hogg, eds, *Canongate Burns*, 467.
167 Gavin Turnbull, *Poems* (Dumfries: The Author, 1794), 8, 10.
168 *L2*, 291.
169 *P2*, 730.
170 *L2*, 292.
171 James Armour, letter to Jean Armour Burns, 15 June 1794 (Ellisland Farm Collection), NBC 2977.
172 *DWJ*, 20 May 1794, 3.
173 *L2*, 311.
174 Thornton, *William Maxwell to Robert Burns*, 67.
175 *P2*, 757.
176 *DWJ*, 10 June 1794, 3.
177 *P3*, 1477; see the full text in James A. Mackay, *Burns-Lore of Dumfries and Galloway* (Ayr: Alloway Publishing, 1988), 130.
178 *P2*, 732.
179 Syme to Cunningham, 15 June 1794 (RBBM), W, 2919.
180 *L2*, 296, 297.
181 *L2*, 297.
182 *L2*, 299, 298.
183 *L2*, 299.
184 *L2*, 297.
185 *L2*, 301.
186 *L2*, 302; on the phrase 'swinish multitude' see later in the present chapter.
187 *P2*, 755; *P3*, 1463.
188 *P2*, 827.
189 *P3*, 1383.
190 *P2*, 798.
191 *L2*, 316.
192 *L2*, 310, 321.
193 Gilbert Burns, 'Additional Remarks' (RBBM), W, 4075.

194 Robert Halliday in Stewart, 'Authentic Voices', 21, 22.
195 *DWJ*, 18 November 1794, 3; *DWJ*, 2 December 1794, 1.
196 *P2*, 770.
197 *P2*, 747; *L2*, 321.
198 *L2*, 323.
199 *L2*, 333.
200 *Robert Burns and Mrs. Dunlop: Correspondence*, ed. William Wallace (London: Hodder and Stoughton, 1898), 415.
201 *L2*, 341.
202 *L2*, 333.
203 *L2*, 337.
204 *P2*, 761.
205 *L2*, 339.
206 *DWJ*, 20 January 1795, 3.
207 See CW, IV, 186; Thomas Crawford, *Burns: A Study of the Poems and Songs* (1960; repr. Edinburgh: James Thin, The Mercat Press, 1978), 365.
208 Marilyn Butler, 'Burns and Politics', in Crawford, 102.
209 [Joseph Ritson, ed.,] *Scotish Songs*, II, 105.
210 *P2*, 762-3.
211 See Noble and Hogg, eds, *Canongate Burns*, 515-16.
212 *P2*, 765-6.
213 1793 *Morning Post* account of Muir's speech quoted in Bewley, *Muir of Huntershill*, 53.
214 Turnbull, *Poems*, 31, 32.
215 Syme to Cunningham, 22 January 1795 (RBBM), W, 2928.
216 *L2*, 349.
217 *L2*, 346.
218 *P2*, 776.
219 *DWJ*, 28 August 1792, 4; *P2*, 778; *P3*, 1477.
220 *L2*, 348; *P2*, 775.
221 Syme to Cunningham, 22 January 1795 (RBBM), W, 2928.
222 Macdonald, 27.
223 *L2*, 355-6.
224 *L2*, 343, 354.
225 *L2*, 361.
226 De Peyster, *Miscellanies*, 60; *DWJ*, 9 June 1795, 3.
227 *DWJ*, 16 October 1827, 1.
228 *P2*, 790; *L2*, 351.
229 *P2*, 897.
230 *L2*, 351.
231 *L2*, 354, 361.
232 *P2*, 791.
233 *L2*, 358, 361.
234 *P2*, 794.
235 *L2*, 365.
236 Maria Riddell to James Currie, 7 July [1798] (RBBM), W, 4397.
237 John Pattison (*Glasgow Courier*, January 1848), quoted in Mackay, 610.
238 *L2*, 374.
239 *L2*, 371.
240 Ibid.
241 *L2*, 373-4.
242 RBBM 480.

243 Walker, I, cxiii, cxv.

244 *P2*, 803, 805.

245 *DWJ*, 10 November 1795, 3.

246 Dumfries Council Book, minutes of 5 November 1795 and 26 December 1795 (Dumfries County Archives); *DWJ*, 22 December 1795, 3.

247 *L2*, 373.

248 Syme to Cunningham, 24 February 1796 (RBBM), W, 2931.

249 *L2*, 375.

250 Edmund Burke, *Reflections on the Revolution in France* (London: Dodsley, 1790), 117.

251 *L2*, 302.

252 *L2*, 375.

253 Dumfries Council Book, minute of 14 March 1796 (Dumfries County Archives).

254 *P2*, 807.

255 *L2*, 377.

256 Syme to Cunningham, 24 February 1796 (RBBM), W, 2931.

257 *L2*, 378–9.

258 Currie (1801), I, 224.

259 Macdonald, 45, 11, 15, 29; Hew Scott, *Fasti Ecclesiae Scoticanae*, new edn, Vol. V (Edinburgh: Oliver and Boyd, 1925), 184; Macdonald to Karl August Böttiger, 4 March 1798, in Alexander Gillies, *A Hebridean in Goethe's Weimar: The Reverend James Macdonald and Cultural Relations between Scotland and Germany* (Oxford: Blackwell, 1969), 45.

260 Macdonald, 24–6; see also Donald A. Low, 'A Last Supper with Scotland's Bard', *BC*, 1996, 188–91, which provides a slightly edited version of this passage from Macdonald's journal.

261 *P2*, 824; *P3*, 1495.

262 *L2*, 382.

263 Dumfries Burgh Letter Book, 1787–1810, letter of 4 June 1796 (Dumfries County Archives).

264 *L2*, 382.

265 *L2*, 379.

266 Syme to Cunningham, 26 July 1796 (RBBM), W, 2942.

267 *L2*, 380, 381.

268 Currie (1801), I, 361, 363.

269 R[obert] Anderson, *Poems on Various Subjects* (Carlisle: J. Mitchell, 1798), 75.

270 *P3*, 1546.

271 Ibid.

272 *L2*, 381–2.

273 *L2*, 383, 384.

274 *L2*, 383.

275 *L2*, 385, 388.

276 *L2*, 383.

277 'The Daughter of Robert Burns', [from the *Glasgow Morning Journal*], *Freeman's Journal and Daily Commercial Advertiser* (Dublin), 8 January 1859.

278 *P2*, 810, 809.

279 *L2*, 387; Dr Stanley Bardwell, 'Appendix B' in Robert T. Fitzhugh, *Robert Burns the Man and the Poet, A Round, Unvarnished Account* (London: W. H. Allen, 1971), 415.

280 *L2*, 385.

281 *P2*, 678.

282 *L2*, 386.

283 *L2*, 387.
284 Ibid.
285 *L2*, 388.
286 *L2*, 389.
287 *L2*, 390.
288 *L2*, 391.
289 Syme to Cunningham, 3 August 1793 and 17 July 1796 (RBBM), W, 2908, 2932.
290 Syme to Cunningham, 19 July 1796 (RBBM), W, 2935.
291 [Allan Cunningham], 'Robert Burns and Lord Byron', *Caledonian Mercury*, 16 August 1824.
292 Ibid.
293 'Robert Burns and Lord Byron', *Caledonian Mercury*, 16 August 1824, later reprinted as 'By Allan Cunningham' in the *Caledonian Mercury*, 22 August 1827.
294 Robert Lochore, *Patie and Ralph: An Elegiac Pastoral on the Death of Robert Burns* (Glasgow: Brash and Reid, [1796]), 3.
295 Lucyle Werkmeister, 'Robert Burns and the London Daily Press', *Modern Philology*, May 1966, 332; William Roscoe, 'Stanzas to the Memory of Robert Burns', in Anon., ed., *Flowers of Poesy* (Carlisle: J. Mitchell, 1798), 41.
296 [James Macdonald,] 'Edinburg', *Der Neuer Teutscher Merkur*, 3 Bd., 1796, 392.
297 Macdonald quoted in Gillies, *A Hebridean in Goethe's Weimar*, 57–8.
298 See Alexander Gillies, 'Emilie von Berlepsch and Burns', *Modern Language Review*, 1960, 584–7.
299 'Robert Burns, The Eldest Son of the Poet', *Derby Mercury*, 16 October 1850; 'Robert Burns', *Morning Chronicle*, 7 June 1819.
300 RBBM 326.
301 Advertising flyer, 'Wild Beasts Alive' (RBBM), W, 4153; *P2*, 811.
302 'Death of Burns's Jessy Lewars', *Glasgow Herald*, 1 June 1855; 'Death and Character of Mrs Burns', *Manchester Times and Gazette*, 5 April 1834.
303 CW, IV, 272.
304 *L2*, 382.
305 *P2*, 813.
306 *P2*, 735.

Index

Burnside, Dr William, 337, 363, 383, 388–9
Butler, Marilyn, 10, 383
Byron, George Gordon, Lord, 262

'Ça ira' (song), 356, 358, 362, 367, 383
Cabinet of Genius, 260
Caird, John, 274
Cairnhill, 104, 105
Caldwell, Charlie, 371
Caledonian Hunt, 239–40, 258–9, 356, 381
'Caledonian Hunt's Delight, The' (tune), 333
Caledonian Mercury, 246, 402
Calvinism, 32, 35, 42, 44, 53, 116, 167, 170, 171, 173, 179, 262
Cambridge University, 91, 243
Cameron, Margaret (Peggy), 258, 268–9
Campbell, Margaret 'Mary' (*see* Highland Mary)
Campbell, Matthew, 254
Campbell, Mrs (Highland Mary's mother), 13, 230–31
Campbell, Thomas, 249
Campbell, William, 37, 53
Canada, 219
Candlish, James (*see* McCandlish, James)
Canongate Burns, 9–10
Canute, King, 42
'Captain Cook's Death' (tune), 320
Carfrae, Mrs, 242–3
Caribbean (*see also* West Indies), 15, 114
Carleton, General, 150
Carlinwark, 387
Carlisle, 268, 397
Carlyle, Thomas, 7, 159
  On Heroes and Hero-Worship, 7
Carmichael, Rebekah, 255
  'The Twa Dows', 255
Carnell, 105
Carrick, 16, 48, 139, 226, 236
Carron ironworks, 272, 300
Carruthers, Gerry, 10
Carswell, Catherine, 7, 294
Cassilis, 23, 54
Castle Campbell, 275
Castle Douglas, 387
Catalogue of Five Hundred Celebrated Authors, 261
Catechism (*see also* Shorter Catechism), 17
Cathcart, Captain, 227
Cathcart, David, 113
Catholicism, 102, 115, 260, 272, 279, 289, 300
Catrine, 92, 228, 229, 231
Cervantes, Miguel de, 312
  Don Quixote, 312
Cessnock Castle, 105
Cessnock, River (*see following entry*)
Cessnock Water, 97, 105
Chalmers, George, 300
Chalmers, Margaret, 107, 249, 275–6, 279, 281, 286, 305
Chalmers, William, 244, 245
Chambers, Robert, 7, 13, 214, 257, 319, 350, 374, 375, 405
Charles I, King, 54
Charlotte, Queen, 359

Charteris, Francis, 243
Chaucer, Geoffrey, 101, 404
  'The Merchant's Tale', 101
Cherokees, 90
China, 6, 15
Chippendale, Thomas, 208
'Chloris' (*see* Lorimer, Jean)
Christ, Jesus, 282, 287, 316
Church of Scotland, 16, 22, 24, 30, 31, 54, 84, 89, 93, 102, 112, 113, 142, 145, 150, 159, 161, 162, 167, 169–70, 185, 228, 272, 279, 285, 316
Cicero, 263
Cinchona, 119
Clackmannanshire, 275
Clare, John, 261
Clarinda (use of the name), 61, 282 (*see also* McLehose, Agnes)
Clark, John, 401
Clarke, James, 334, 398–9
Clarke, Stephen, 315, 352
Cleghorn, Robert, 369, 391
Clow, Jenny, 288, 289, 298, 310, 311–12, 321, 341, 342
Clyde, 146, 147, 214, 270, 272
Coila, 191–2
Coilsfield, 90, 92, 95, 150, 184, 214
Coilus, 48, 90
Coldcothill, 83
Coldstream, 267
Commissioners and Trustees for Fisheries, Manufactures and Improvements in Scotland, 104
Common Sense philosophy, 33, 34, 170, 207 (*see also* Reid, Thomas)
Complete Letter-Writer, The, 66
Comyn, John ('The Red Comyn'), 339
Condorcet, Nicolas de Caritat, Marquis de, 231
Connaught, 147
Constable, Lady Winifred Maxwell, 333
Constable's Miscellany, 257
Constitutional Reform, 145, 316, 324, 357, 362
Corbet, William, 330, 348, 356, 361–2
Corbet, Mrs William, 362
Corsincon, 304, 385
Court of Session, 91, 113, 126, 137, 284
Covenanters, 17, 72, 84, 93, 150
Cowper, William, 299, 306
Craig, William, 280, 289
Craigie, 48, 95
Craik, Helen, 326
Crambo-jingle, 39–40, 64, 187
Crawford, John, 28
Crawford, Thomas, 8, 383
Crawford, William, 349
Creech, William, 56, 141, 244, 259, 264, 268, 275, 279, 295, 297, 305, 312, 335, 355, 356
Crieff, 272
Cririe, James, 305
  Address to Loch Lomond, 305–6
Crochallan Fencibles, 264–5, 284, 296, 331
'Crodh Chailean' (song), 265
Crombie, Alexander, 299

Index

Index

Index